Vocabulary

approp (appropriateness), pp. 396–418, 456, 510–11 (**Diction**)

Words and phrases must be appropriate in context: *Professor Smith did his best work when he was a very old geezer/ Professor Smith did his best work when he was a very old man*.

cliché

A cliché is a hackneyed idea or expression which implies that the writer does not think, but merely responds: *The dog is man's best friend.*

colloq (colloquialism), pp. 510–11 (**Diction**)

A colloquialism is an expression from informal language that may be out of place in formal writing: *My better half makes magnificent stew/My wife makes magnificent stew.*

D (diction in general), pp. 396–418, 456, 510–11

The diction in an essay should be consistent with the purpose and the audience.

id (idiom)

Idiomatic expressions should not be garbled: *He was up to his head in work/ He was up to his ears in work OR He was over his head in work.*

WW (wrong word), pp. 516–17 (**Malapropism**)

Word choice should be accurate: *The study of the history of words is entomology/The study of the history of words is etymology.*

Punctuation (**Pn**)

In Edited Standard English, the system of punctuation is fairly regular and rigid. See **Apostrophe**, pp. 496–97; **Colon**, p. 505; **Comma**, pp. 505–06; **Dash**, pp. 509–10; **Hyphen**, pp. 515–16; **Parentheses**, p. 520; **Quotation Marks**, pp. 526–27; **Semicolon**, p. 528.

Substance and Structure

cl (clarity)

Lack of clarity puts readers off.

coh (coherence), pp. 226–29, 265–66

Essays should be coherent; readers should be able to follow the development of ideas and to perceive connections.

emph (emphasis)

More important points should have greater emphasis than less important.

fig (figurative language), pp. 419–36

Figures used should be consistent and appropriate.

log (logic), pp. 255–63, 280–87

The essay should be logical.

¶ (paragraph), pp. 110–35

Paragraphing should aid the reader in perceiving the logic and organization of the essay.

Minor Editing

cap (capitalization), p. 501

Capitalization must conform to standard usage.

ital (italics), p. 516

Conventionally, certain words and phrases are *italicized* (like this) in printing and underlined (like this) in printing and handwriting.

lc (lower case)

Certain words and phrases are not capitalized.

sp (spelling), pp. 529–30

Most readers of Edited Standard English demand conventional spelling.

The Contemporary Writer

The Contemporary Writer

W. Ross Winterowd
University of Southern California

 HARCOURT BRACE JOVANOVICH, INC.
New York   Chicago   San Francisco   Atlanta

ISBN: 0-15-513724-7

Library of Congress Catalog Card Number: 74-33750

Printed in the United States of America

Preface

Most of the textbooks that an average student goes through in his or her freshman year—economics, biology, psychology, and so on—are in a sense *real* books; that is, they are interesting because they are conceptually rich. The one freshman textbook that few people read for or with pleasure is the rhetoric-handbook that most students use (or at least carry about) for one or two semesters.

Now, most rhetoric-handbooks are undoubtedly more or less useful, for they cover such matters as punctuation and verb agreement, and, the world being what it is, most freshmen need that kind of information. But rhetoric-handbooks can be, even though they seldom are, useful *books.* When you read a real book, you carry on an intellectual dialogue with it; you are engaged. To be frank and brief: I view *The Contemporary Writer* as a real book. Its conceptual basis is rich and unified; it is not, I feel certain, overly difficult, but I have tried to give it the intellectual depth and unity that will allow students to become engaged with it.

Conceptual substance is a great virtue in any book, but a rhetoric-handbook needs other important virtues as well: completeness, reliability, modernity, practical usefulness. *The Contemporary Writer* has these.

A glance at the Table of Contents and the Index will give some idea of the completeness of the book: all modes of writing are dealt with, and the major concepts in regard to writing and language are covered in detail. Furthermore, the scholarly background that informs the book makes for high reliability of both general concepts and specific information.

The book is modern—both in tone and in theory. Again, a survey of the Index will demonstrate that important contemporary thought and thinkers are amply represented.

And the book is useful, in that it is carefully designed to be practical for students at all levels of ability. No theory is presented merely for the sake of theory: all aspects of the book contribute to the goal of helping students express themselves to an audience in writing.

I would like to say something graceful and witty by way of thanking three scholars whose help with this book has been invaluable, but grace and wit, it occurs to me, always seem tortuous in a preface. So unadorned but sincere thanks to Richard Young of the University of Michigan, Robert Gorrell of the University of Nevada, and Edward P. J. Corbett of Ohio State University.

An old American folk song tells of simple pleasures; among my simple pleasures are bagels with chopped liver, sherry at three in the afternoon, and good company. Often my friend Rose Kreitzberg supplies the bagels with chopped liver and the good company, while I supply the sherry. Rose was much more than the patient and meticulous worker who typed my rough draft; indeed, her comments and suggestions were very useful. She has had an influence on every chapter of this book. My thanks to her.

My editors at Harcourt Brace Jovanovich have been more than kind and helpful: they have been magnificent. Gordon R. Fairburn has, with unfailing common sense and good humor, shepherded the project since it was little more than an idea and a stack of scratchy pages making less than a fragment of a manuscript.

Cecilia Gardner has been nothing short of phenomenal in her work with the manuscript. With intelligence and tact she showed me where I went astray and invariably made just the right strokes to put me on the track again. I particularly admire Cele's work because she is a real prose craftswoman, with tremendous sensitivity to the nuances of words and the movement of sentences. I am not exaggerating when I say that working with her edited copy— which might have been an odious task—was always a pleasure and at times fascinating. My very special thanks to her for the care she has taken.

My thanks also to Tina Norum, whose careful work in styling the manuscript and handling the proof has made this a better book.

And I am grateful to Pat Smythe for her handsome design and to Alice Sánchez for her attentive supervision of the production of the book.

My sons, Jeff and Tony; my mother, who provides the ballast for our family; and Norma, my wife and best pal—these four make my circle just, and make me end where I begun.

W. Ross Winterowd

Contents

Part Two   Style   289

10   *The Writer's Language*   291

11   *The Sentence*   340

12   *Words*   396

13   *Figurative Language*   419

PART ONE

The Uses of Writing

The Uses of
Writing: Self-Expression

Part One of *The Contemporary Writer* will discuss, in detail, four kinds of writing: self-expressive, expository, persuasive, and imaginative. Each type of writing will be discussed from two viewpoints: the writer's problems and the reader's interest. (Of course, this separation is artificial; the reader's interests and the writer's problems are really one and the same. But the division allows us to discover some basic principles and gives us a convenient way to approach the subject.)

The problems of the writer and the concerns of the reader will be classed under five headings: the *writer,* the *context* in which the writing is done (including external reality as well as internal, mental reality), the *structure* of the piece, the *style,* and the *audience* for whom the piece seems to be intended.

Summary of the Chapter

It may be unusual to find a summary at the beginning of the chapter, but actually it makes very good sense to begin this way. The most efficient way to approach a reading task is to attempt to gain an overview of what is to come. The more "clues" you bring with you to the text, the easier it will be for you to understand and master what you read. The chapter summary gives you an overview, an idea of what is to come, and therefore should help you with the detailed and sometimes thorny material in the chapter.

The summary is also a good device for putting it all together after you have read the chapter. Therefore, I suggest that you come back to the summary after you have finished the chapter. That way you will begin and end by taking a broad general view of the materials.

In this chapter, four types of self-expressive writing will be considered: the interior monologue, the personal letter, the journal, and the autobiography.

The Interior Monologue. The best way to characterize this sort of writing is to say that it is you, as the writer, talking to yourself. Since your purpose in the "pure" interior monologue—if there is any such thing as a pure use of language—is to talk to yourself, to attempt to find yourself through your writing, you do not need to be concerned with structure, style, or audience.

The Personal Letter. While the interior monologuist does not care about audience, the writer of a personal letter cares very much, for there is a very definite audience, someone who will read the letter. And usually the letter contains news—that is, it deals with exterior context. The writer's adjustment to the audience for a personal letter is usually automatic, causing no problems.

The Journal. The journal is usually a record of the writer's impressions of internal and external reality—that is, of the world and the writer's reactions to it. The writer probably does not have a given audience in mind, but does intend the journal to be read by someone or some group. The basic structure is chronological, and the style cannot be "private," for it must be understandable to a reader.

The Autobiography. The autobiography is normally the most "public" kind of self-expressive writing. Therefore, it is more formal in organization, tone, and style than the other kinds. The audience for the autobiography is usually an unspecified group that might be called "the reading public."

What Is Useful?

A hammer and a screwdriver are useful, but what about a painting or a piece of sculpture? A recipe in *The New York Times Cook Book* is useful, but what about a lyric poem? The instructions for using a pay telephone are useful, but what about the "Damn it!" that I uttered last night when I stubbed my toe in the dark?

What I'm suggesting is that we shouldn't interpret usefulness too narrowly. The abstract painting in my parlor and the piece of "junk" sculpture that sits before it, the lyric poetry that I constantly read—these are as useful to me in their way as screwdrivers, hammers, recipes, and pay phone instructions are in theirs.

Frankly, it is hard for me to argue that learning to write well is "useful" in the narrow sense, to argue that you won't be able to get along in life without learning to accomplish the sorts of writing that this book teaches. Most people in the real world outside of school do not need to write very much. I think, for instance, of a friend who works for the Navy: his professional writing consists of filling in forms. Another friend is a physician, and the important writing that he does, of course, is cryptic scribbling on small pieces of paper that his patients carry to the drugstore. A petroleum engineer friend must write a great deal in his profession, but since he composes technical reports according to a rigidly prescribed format, he almost never does the kind of "free" writing that this book will concentrate on.

Your own experience also tells you that very few people in the real world "out there" need to write in order to be successful. It was ever thus. During the Middle Ages, members of the ruling class felt that a skill such as writing was beneath them, so they hired scribes, to compose as well as to copy. In the *Phaedrus,* Plato even said that the invention of the alphabet was a curse, for when ideas were written down, they were no longer growing, organic things, but rather became fixed, like butterflies pinned in an exhibit case; furthermore, contended Plato, writing had the effect of ruining people's memory.

What about the world "in here," the world of higher education? You will probably do more writing per week during your years in college than you will ever do again in your life, and yet I suspect that most students could get through their four undergraduate years perfectly well without ever taking a composition course.

So I would argue that for most people the ability to write with grace, clarity, and conviction is not essential, is not even useful in the narrow sense.

But there is a broader and more important sense of usefulness, and when viewed from this perspective, learning to write well becomes terribly important.

The real usefulness of writing can be equated with the usefulness of dreaming. The great Swiss psychiatrist Carl Gustav Jung wrote, "The general function of dreams is to try to restore our psychological balance by producing dream material that re-establishes, in a subtle way, the total psychic equilibrium."[1] I like to view all writing as one way in which we can express ourselves and thus find ourselves. All writing is the kind of psychic outlet for the conscious mind that dreaming is for the unconscious. This is just the point, for instance, that Eldridge Cleaver discovered when he began to write *Soul on Ice:*

1   After I returned to prison, I took a long look at myself and, for the first time in my life, admitted that I was wrong, that I had gone astray—astray not so much from the white man's laws as from being human, civilized—for I could not approve the act of rape. Even though I had some insight into my own motivations, I did not feel justified. I lost my self-respect. My pride as a man dissolved and my whole fragile moral structure seemed to collapse, completely shattered.

   I realized that no one could save me but myself. I had to seek out the truth and unravel the snarled web of my motivations. I had to find out who I am and what I want to be, what type of man I should be, and what I could do to become the best of which I was capable.

All of which is *not* to say that writing doesn't have many practical uses for everyone. The ability to write well can help you get through school with

[1] Carl G. Jung, "Approaching the Unconscious," *Man and His Symbols* (Garden City, N.Y.: Doubleday, 1964), p. 50.

greater ease and better grades and might even put money in your pocket in the world "out there."

I am stressing usefulness so strongly only because I don't want the discussion that follows to be viewed merely as a guide for accomplishing a practical task that must be gotten through if one wants the bachelor's degree. In a very real sense, you can't write about anything but yourself. Therefore, learning to write is a way to achieve personal growth. That mystic substance, that island called *you,* must find ways out of itself. One of the best ways out is through writing.

Elements of Writing

To think profitably about so large a subject as writing, one needs some way of organizing the topic, of taking it apart so that its constituents can be viewed systematically. This is an important concept, one that we will return to in great detail.

The next few paragraphs will present a "way into" the generality called writing, a way of seeing its parts and their purpose. The concepts that will be outlined also serve as the organizational framework for this book; therefore, what is about to be discussed is a kind of map of *The Contemporary Writer.*

A linguist named Roman Jakobson devised the following diagram of the elements of discourse:[2]

```
2                              CONTEXT
                               MESSAGE
    ADDRESSER . . . . . . . . . . . . . . . . . . . . . . . . . . . . . . . . . . . . . . . . . . . . ADDRESSEE
                               CONTACT
                               CODE
```

The diagram simply means that any time speech or writing takes place, there is

> *an addresser,* someone who does the speaking or writing;
> *a context,* a time and place in which the discourse occurs;
> *a message,* something that the discourse says;
> *contact,* something to convey the message;
> *a code,* a language of some kind;
> *an addressee,* someone or some group for whom the message is intended.

It is well to remember that *every* language act involves all six elements. And, as will become apparent, all this is not just theoretical fluff, but, rather, it all boils down to some very practical considerations for the writer. Just one example: If you are writing for young children, you will need to approach your subject in a different way than if you were writing for college students; that is, you need to keep the concept of addressee, or audience, firmly in mind.

[2]From Thomas A. Sebeok, ed., *Style in Language* (Cambridge, Mass.: M.I.T. Press, 1960), p. 353.

Controlling Purpose of Each Element

A *controlling purpose* can be associated with every element in the diagram.

Addresser. Closely associated with the speaker or writer—the address-er—is the purpose of *self-expression.* Everyone uses language purely for self-expression at times, as in the example I gave earlier of a vehement "Damn it!" when I stubbed my toe in the dark.

Context. Everyone uses language to deal with the abstract and with physical reality: to explain democracy or socialism, to give instructions for putting together a new barbecue or for getting to Chicago, to report on an experiment or to describe a landscape. Jakobson calls this use of language *referential.* We will call it *expository* and talk about *expository writing,* the sort of writing that is intended primarily to convey information.

Message. If the controlling purpose of discourse is the message conveyed, that discourse is *imaginative* or *poetic.* In this book, we will opt for the term *imaginative.*

Contact. Only limited sorts of discourse have contact as their purpose. An example: You are talking on the telephone. You ask a question, and get no answer. You say, "Are you there?" You have used language just to maintain contact. Most discussions of the weather take place to establish contact, not because the participants are really interested in the weather. Some language, then, is used just to establish and maintain contact. Jakobson calls this purpose of language the *phatic.* We will not deal with it any further in this book.

Code. Sometimes language is used to discuss language (the code). This is the *metalinguistic* purpose for language use, and Chapter 10, "The Writer's Language," is a good example of it. Much of any book concerning writing must be metalinguistic.

Addressee. The purpose related to the addressee is *persuasive.* (Jakobson calls it *conative.*) That is, if your main purpose is to influence or convince an audience, you are using language persuasively. An example of pure persuasion is the sales appeal: "Use Blog and look younger."

Thus, we can modify the diagram to show the purpose that is associated with each element.

3

```
                              CONTEXT
                              (EXPOSITORY)


                              MESSAGE
ADDRESSER                     (IMAGINATIVE)                    ADDRESSEE
(SELF-EXPRESSIVE). . . . . . . . . . . . . . . . . . . . . . . . . .(PERSUASIVE)
                              CONTACT
                              (PHATIC)


                              CODE
                              (METALINGUAL)
```

Now then, all this is very tidy: six purposes, six pigeonholes—and we ought to be able to stick any piece of discourse that we encounter into one of those pigeonholes. But think, for instance, of the material in this chapter so far. From one point of view, you can say that it is *metalinguistic,* because it is language about language; but since its purpose is to inform you, the reader, about language, you can also say that it is *expository.* At the beginning of the chapter, I tried to convince you that writing is useful, so the material was also *persuasive.* I enjoyed writing it, and put my own ideas and observations into it, so it was also *self-expressive.*

Note how Jakobson's schema gives you not only a way to classify uses of language according to purpose, but also a way to sort out the various purposes in a given piece of discourse, to view it from different angles. I can hardly put too much stress on the usefulness of devices such as this one. They enable us to open a subject up and think about it productively. I call devices such as this *discovery procedures,* and we will deal with a variety of them in Chapter 3.

Expository writing, persuasive writing, and imaginative writing will be discussed in later chapters. In this chapter, we will discuss self-expressive writing.

There's a very good chance that learning to do self-expressive writing will constitute the greatest benefit that you gain from *The Contemporary Writer.* The discussion of the other types of writing will largely concern tactics that you can adopt to accomplish your various purposes, but there is no set of *external* tactics for accomplishing genuinely self-expressive writing. The reason is apparent: When you write self-expressively, all you have to build with is your own honesty.

And yet, though exposition, persuasion, and imaginative composition are in some ways easier than self-expression, self-expression might well be more useful to you in the long run than the other types. To paraphrase the earlier quote from Jung: The general function of self-expressive writing is to try to restore our psychological balance by producing written material that re-establishes, in a subtle way, the total psychic equilibrium.

The best way to learn to write is to pay close attention to successful examples of the kind of writing that you want to do; so now that these important general remarks have been made, we will take a close look at four kinds of self-expressive writing: the interior monologue, the journal, the personal letter, and the autobiography.

The Interior Monologue

When you write an interior monologue, you attempt to record your thoughts just as they come. The best interior monologue will give you a sense that your writing has made an almost photographic record of what you were thinking. Sounds easy, doesn't it? Just turn on the thoughts and let the writing flow. But thoughts come rapidly, and they are often vivid with images; writing is a slow process, even if one is a good typist, and images are difficult to capture.

The nearest thing to pure self-expression and the best example of interior monologue that I can think of is an entry from Allen Ginsberg's *Indian Journals:*

4   *Friday 13 July 1962*
Top floor Hotel Amjadia Chandy Chowk & Princep St. Calcutta: looking out the barred window at sunset & the clouds like a movie film over the sky with cheap red paper kites fluttering over the 4 story roofs against the mottled green & orange mists of maya—down for a cup of tea, the sloppy Moslem waiters barefoot & bearded in black-edged white uniforms—the clang of rickshaw handbells against wooden pull staves—bells under hand cars—slept all afternoon after the M last nite and visit to doctor this morning—worm pills—& read Time & Newsweek & Thubten Jigme Norbu's autobiography—constantly the unnoticed details of the going universe outside the room where in heat & sickness & lethargy Peter & I drowse & read & browse & sleep—Now it's dark evening time and the reality of the thousand barefoot street vendors & car honkers outside visible from both windows downstairs as I sit leg folded under me in bed—Peter wakes half asleep—"my arm's falling apart" I massage it it's asleep & feels dead & sweaty—neon lights in the porcelain & dish store downstairs—half a dozen streetlights dot-burning the picture—looks like Lima Chinatown 2 years ago—most cars speeding by have red tail lights—nasal beggar or vendor voices—the fan whirling overhead for the last 12 hours—Everything random still, as any cut up. Burroughs it's already a year still haunting me. I slept all afternoon & when I woke up I thought it was morning, I didn't know where I was. I had no name for India.[3]

Learning Through Analysis

Because the best way to learn to write is to look closely at what other writers have done, we shall dissect the Ginsberg example. Much of *The Contemporary Writer* will consist of just such close analysis of pieces of writing from various points of view. All analyses will be based on five questions, which in turn are based on Jakobson's diagram of the elements of discourse (though not all the questions will be applied in each case):

1. What "picture" of the *writer* emerges from the writing? (That is, on the basis of the writing, what sort of person does the writer seem to be?)
2. How does the writing relate to its *context,* or the world "out there"? (With self-expressive writing this question is not very important, but it is tremendously important in the case of expository writing.)
3. What is the *structure* of the message? (This question brings up the whole matter of *organization.*)
4. How can the *style* of the writing be characterized? (Under "style," we can include such microscopic considerations as punctuation and move from there to word choice to sentence structure to general tone.)
5. How does the writing relate to its *audience?*

[3]Allen Ginsberg, *Indian Journals* (San Francisco: Dave Haselwood Books and City Lights Books, 1970), pp. 42–43. Copyright © 1970 by Allen Ginsberg. Reprinted by permission of City Lights Books.

Analysis of Ginsberg

On to Ginsberg's piece, then.

Authors in writing can assume one of their own various roles: father, friend, teacher, pleader. An author can also assume a fictitious personality and create an imaginary teller of a story; but since this device is most common in imaginative writing, we will deal with it in the appropriate chapter. However, if you think about it, you will realize that you can sense a personality, or a stance, behind most of the writing that you read.

The Writer

The sense that we get of Ginsberg the author in his journals is that Ginsberg the author and Ginsberg the private person are one and the same.

We get this sense as much from what Ginsberg leaves out of his monologue as from what he puts into it. Note this:

> 5 [I am on the] Top floor [of the] Hotel Amjadia[,] Chandy Chowk & Princep St.[,] Calcutta.

The feeling of the whole piece is that the author is recording fragments of thought, raw, as they occur to him.

Even more important, notice that he seems to choose details because they are important to him, not because a reader might be interested in the details as such:

> 6 slept all afternoon after the M last nite and visit to doctor this morning—worm pills—& read Time & Newsweek & Thubten Jigme Norbu's autobiography—

In fact, it is legitimate to ask, "Why might readers be interested in a selection such as the Ginsberg excerpt?" And the answer is, not because of any intrinsic interest that the selection holds, but because some people are interested in Ginsberg the man and in the way his mind works.

If readers are interested in an interior monologue that you write—and there is no reason why you should write one to interest a reader—it will be because of their sense that they are getting an honest and candid look at your mind as it roams the fields of your conscious and unconscious. It is the sense of honesty that the reader gets from the Ginsberg selection that makes it valuable.

The best way for a writer to convey a sense of honesty and candor to the reader is simply to be honest and candid. This advice is not as simple-minded as it sounds, for in order to record the flow of thought, the writer of self-expressive monologues must *want* to capture it.

The Context

In relation to the interior monologue, of course, context, the world "out there," is not important at all. What is important is the inner reality in the writer's mind. Ginsberg tells us where he is; he gives us the date before the entry; and we can follow the time sequence in the piece. That is, we feel that the selection does relate to its context, but, in fact, we don't really care, for we are not interested in what it tells us about the Hotel Amjadia or Calcutta; we are interested in what it tells us about Allen Ginsberg.

In this connection, it is interesting to think about the most self-expressive of all self-expressive language—that produced by schizophrenics. There is no real context for their writing because it is the nature of their disease that they have withdrawn from reality, from the world "out there." Here are two examples of schizophrenic writing. As you read them, I think you will be interested not in whether they make sense or whether they tell you anything about the world, but in the strange nature of the minds that produced them.

> 7 The subterfuge and the mistaken planned substitutions for that demanded American action can produce nothing but the general results of negative contention and the impractical results of careless applications, the natural results of misplacement, or mistaken purpose and unrighteous position, the impractical serviceabilities of unnecessary contradictions. For answers to this dilemma, consult Webster.

> 8 Now to eat if one cannot the other can—and if we cant the girseau Q. C. Washpots prizebloom capacities—turning out—replaced by the head patterns my own capacities—I was not very kind to them. Q. C. Washpots under-patterned against—bred to pattern. Animal sequestration capacities under leash—and animal secretions.[4]

This is not the place to play amateur psychoanalyst, but notice the questions that **7** and **8** arouse: What were the authors trying to say? What sorts of minds produced these?

In a way, the interior monologue—the most self-expressive kind of writing—is schizoid too, but in a healthy sense. It frees the writer from the obligation of context—of making one's writing square with reality—and allows one to use as material that reality which exists only inside the mind.

The Structure

The structure of the interior monologue is merely the structure of the thoughts as they arise; in that sense, the interior monologue has no structure. Organization is no problem. One senses this structural flow in the Ginsberg piece. Notice how it ends:

> 9 Everything random still, as any cut up. Burroughs it's already a year still haunting me. I slept all afternoon & when I woke up I thought it was morning, I didn't know where I was. I had no name for India.

The first sentence in this passage more or less sums up what has gone before; Ginsberg tells us that he can see no pattern to his thoughts. The second sentence refers to William Burroughs, friend of Ginsberg and author of *Naked Lunch.* The third sentence jumps back in time to the morning. The fourth sentence is a metaphorical way of restating the third.

In other kinds of writing, this randomness generally would not work; in the interior monologue, it is a positive virtue. If Ginsberg had revised, had

---

[4]Quoted by Brendan A. Maher in "The Shattered Language of Schizophrenia," *Psychology Today,* Nov. 1968, p. 30.

grouped his ideas according to time or subject, and had put together a well-organized piece, he would have lost his credibility as an interior monologuist. And his piece would have been much less interesting than it is.

The Style

As the writer of an interior monologue, you have total freedom of style. You can use whatever forms of language you feel most nearly approximate your thoughts. You can forget about conventional punctuation—as Ginsberg does—and about spelling. If you are writing simply for yourself and do not expect anyone else to read your piece, you need not even be intelligible to anyone but yourself.

Notice the magic quality of Ginsberg's monologue:

> 10   looking out the barred window at sunset & the clouds like a movie film over the sky with cheap red paper kites fluttering over the 4 story roofs against the mottled green & orange mists of maya [a Hindu word meaning "the illusory appearance of the world"]—

One sees the barred window, the clouds, the colors—red, green, orange. The piece is full of sounds and sights. This magic quality is especially important to the sort of thing that Ginsberg is doing; it creates *for the reader* the context in which the mind of the author is working, and the reader sees reality as filtered through the mind of the musing Ginsberg. Remove the images, and interest in the piece would simply evaporate.

Not that images are all that difficult to create in writing. They merely demand that you look either at the world your senses can apprehend or within, at the scene your mind has constructed, and then, with concrete accuracy and in some detail, record what you see.

The Audience

Ideal, pure self-expression does not involve an audience, but realistically speaking, if one goes to the trouble of writing something, one usually has an audience in mind. In expository and persuasive writing, as we shall see, the audience is a controlling factor in how the composition is planned and presented, but with the interior monologue, the audience—if there is one—is a minor consideration. The writer says, in effect, "Look, I'm writing this primarily for me. If you want to read it, OK, but you'll have to take it on my terms."

Some Advice for Writers

A summary of advice for writers of interior monologues might go like this:

1. You should be totally honest and candid.
2. You can forget about all reality except that in your own mind. Your mind is the source of your material. Get your material from introspection—

from thinking about your thinking. You might even take notes and then reconstruct the whole thought sequence from memory later on.

3. For the most part you can disregard structure. The thoughts as they occur provide their own structure, their own organization, and if you tamper with that, you are falsifying.

4. You can use whatever language you think best suits your purpose. The only restraint is that if you want someone to read your monologue, you must at least be intelligible.

5. Since the primary audience of your interior monologue is you yourself, you can forget about making adjustments so that your readers will like or understand what you say; they must take you on your own terms.

The Personal Letter

When one writes a personal letter, the audience is sharply defined, for the letter is addressed to someone whom the writer knows more or less intimately. It might be said that in the personal letter there is a writer-audience ratio and that this ratio controls the message.

When Nathaniel Hawthorne had just begun to establish his reputation as a writer, he met Sophia Peabody, an invalid. He fell desperately in love with her and resolved to marry her, but that event did not take place for two years. In the meantime, he worked as a weigher and gauger in the Boston customhouse and wrote passionate letters to Sophia, addressing her as his wife even though they were not yet married.

11   *Salem, October 4th, 1840.—1/2 past 10 A.M.*

Mine Ownest,

Here sits thy husband in his old accustomed chamber, where he used to sit in years gone by, before his soul became acquainted with thine. Here I have written many tales—many that have been burned to ashes—many that doubtless deserve the same fate. This deserves to be called a haunted chamber; for thousands upon thousands of visions have appeared to me in it; and some few of them have become visible to the world. If ever I should have a biographer, he ought to make great mention of this chamber in my memoirs, because so much of my lonely youth was wasted here, and here my mind and character were formed; and here I have been glad and hopeful, and here I have been despondent; and here I sat a long, long time, waiting patiently for the world to know me, and sometimes wondering why it did not know me sooner, or whether it would ever know me at all—at least, till I were in my grave. And sometimes (for I had no wife then to keep my heart warm) it seemed as if I were already in the grave, with only life enough to be chilled and benumbed. But oftener I was happy—at least, as happy as I then knew how to be, or was aware of the possibility of being. By and by, the world found me out in my lonely chamber, and called me forth—not, indeed, with a loud roar of acclamation, but rather with a still, small voice; and forth I went, but found nothing in the world that I thought preferable to my old solitude, till at length a certain Dove was revealed to me, in the shadow of a seclusion as deep as my own had been. And I drew nearer and nearer to the Dove, and opened my bosom to her, and she flitted into it, and closed her wings there—and there she nestles now and forever, keeping my heart warm, and renewing my life with her own. So now I begin to understand why I was imprisoned so many

years in this lonely chamber, and why I could never break through the
viewless bolts and bars; for if I had sooner made my escape into the world, I
should have grown hard and rough, and been covered with earthly dust, and
my heart would have become callous by encounters with the multitude; so
that I should have been all unfit to shelter a heavenly Dove in my arms. But
living in solitude till the fullness of time was come, I still kept the dew of my
youth and the freshness of my heart, and had these to offer to my Dove.

Well, dearest, I had no notion what I was going to write, when I began; and
indeed I doubted whether I should write anything at all; for after such
intimate communion as that of our last blissful evening, it seems as if a sheet
of paper could only be a veil betwixt us. . . .[5]

Analysis of Hawthorne

The Writer

In this letter, Hawthorne reveals himself with a passionate intensity that
would be quite out of place if the audience were anyone but his own
beloved. Compare the tone of the letter to Sophia Peabody with the tone of
this passage from a letter that Hawthorne wrote to Henry Wadsworth
Longfellow:

12   Dear Sir,
      Not to burthen you with my correspondence, I have delayed a rejoinder to
      your very kind and cordial letter, until now. It gratifies me to find that you
      have occasionally felt an interest in my situation; but your quotation from
      Jean Paul about the "lark's nest" makes me smile. You would have been
      nearer the truth if you had pictured me as dwelling in an owl's nest; for mine
      is about as dismal; and, like the owl I seldom venture abroad till after dark.[6]

In the letter to Longfellow, we sense that Hawthorne is formal, reserved.

The Context

Notice that Nathaniel's letter conveys almost no news to Sophia. She
undoubtedly knows the biographical details of Nathaniel's past and does
not need to be informed again. Insofar as the letter conveys information,
that information concerns the writer's attitude toward his past and, in
particular, his attitude toward Sophia. In short, the letter is a classic love
letter.

Of course, some personal letters are written to convey news to the
recipient—but not this one. Notice that Hawthorne says, "Well, dearest, I
had no notion what I was going to write, when I began . . . ."

The Structure

The structure of the personal letter can be almost as loose as that of the
interior monologue, because the letter and the monologue are usually
generated in the same way: as the thoughts arise, they are expressed, with

[5]Malcolm Cowley, ed., *The Portable Hawthorne* (New York: Viking Press, 1948), pp. 611–12.
[6]*Ibid.*, pp. 607–08.

no advance planning. The long paragraph from Hawthorne's letter sounds almost as if it proceeded by free association, like the interior monologue.

The Style

It is primarily through style that a writer's personality can be expressed, and in the personal letter one has great leeway to be idiosyncratic, zany, or whatever mood fits the purpose.

Hawthorne's use of **Mine Ownest,** an unusual construction, sets the tone of the whole letter. This use of **mine** was archaic even in Hawthorne's time, and one does not usually put nominals, as **own** is here used, into the superlative degree. In other words, Hawthorne twists language for his own purposes, but such twisting would not have worked in the letter to Longfellow.

There are also many emotionally charged words in the letter: **soul, haunted, visions, lonely, glad, hopeful, despondent,** and so on. Hawthorne's mere choice of words gives the passage much of its intensity.

The letter is also highly metaphorical. (We will discuss metaphor in Chapter 13.) Sophia is a dove, and Nathaniel's heart is a nest for the dove. He characterizes the literary reputation that he has gained in the following way: "By and by, the world found me out in my lonely chamber, and called me forth—not, indeed, with a loud roar of acclamation, but rather with a still, small voice . . . ."

As to Hawthorne's sentences: In Chapter 11, we will have a good deal to say about sentence structure and will carry out a good deal of analysis. For the time being, it will suffice if you take a look at the way Hawthorne puts ideas into structures, doing whatever analysis you are able to. Becoming aware of the way sentences work is a method that you can use profitably to develop your own ability to write mature, graceful, successful sentences.

The Audience

As has been said, the audience for a personal letter is one of the main factors controlling its development. When we discuss expository and persuasive writing, you will find that defining the audience is a crucial step. But that problem does not arise in the case of the personal letter; you are writing to someone you know—your girlfriend, your parents, your Aunt Emma—so you can automatically adopt the correct stance. Hawthorne's letter is very intimate; that intimacy was determined by the fact that he was writing to his fiancée.

Some Advice for Writers

A brief "cookbook" formula for writers of personal letters might go like this:

1. You should keep your relationship with the addressee in mind. The stance of a letter to your mother will be different from that of a letter to your former high school chum.

2. The addressee probably wants news about you. Therefore, context—the news that the letter transmits—should be complete enough and lucid enough to satisfy your reader.
3. Structure is relatively unimportant. The letter can ramble, developing itself on the basis of free association, much like the interior monologue.
4. You can use whatever language best suits your purpose. Usually you do not need to worry about the niceties of formal English.
5. Since the audience consists of one member (or a very few members), the interests of that person (or those persons) are foremost, and you should keep a mental picture of your audience before you at all times.

The Journal

Another common type of self-expressive writing is the diary, though I sense that this type of writing is not as popular as it was some years ago. Perhaps if we use the more acceptable term *journal,* we will find a form of writing that will be both useful and pleasurable to most people.

The journal is simply a record of the events, people, ideas, sensations, and emotions that one finds significant. It has the advantage that a single entry can be of any length, from a couple of words to a couple of thousand words, and there is no necessity to bring continuity or organization into it. You simply write about the things that impress you.

With the journal, however, there is a slight shift of focus. The interior monologue is concerned only with the writer; the writer makes no attempt to persuade or convince or please an audience. Ideally, there is no audience in mind. But what happens with the journal, usually, is that you have a reader in mind and are thinking, perhaps, about making your experience meaningful to others, so you can't be totally private. In the interior monologue, you have no responsibility to explain obscure references, to ascertain that all your sentences make sense, to be sure that there is some sort of connection between the sentences—if, indeed, you have written your monologue in sentences. In the journal, though, you are usually thinking of a reader, so you bring more orderliness and less of yourself into the writing.

One of the most sensible and readable books on educational theory is *How Children Learn,* by John Holt, and it is in the form of a journal, written over the years as Holt watched children learn. Thus, the first entry from John Holt's journal:

13

August 9, 1960

I am sitting on a friend's terrace. Close by is Lisa, 16-month-old, a bright and bold child. She has invented a very varied pseudo-speech which she uses all the time. Some sounds she says over and over again, as if she meant something by them. She likes to touch and handle things, and is surprisingly dexterous; she can fit screws and similar small objects into the holes meant for them. Can it be that little children are less clumsy than we have always supposed?

One of Lisa's favorite games is to take my ball point pen out of my pocket, take the top off, and then put it on again. This takes some skill. She never tires of the game; if she sees me with the pen in my hand, she lets me know right away that she wants it. There is no putting her off. She is stubborn, and if I pretend—which is a lie—not to know what she wants, she makes a scene. The trick, when I know I will need to use my pen, is to have an extra one hidden in a pocket.

The other day she was playing on the piano, hitting more or less at random with both hands, pleased to be working the machine and making such an interesting noise. Curious to see whether she would imitate me, I bounced up and down the keyboard with my index finger. She watched, then did the same.[7]

Analysis of Holt

Writer

The most important factor in the interior monologue is the writer. In the personal letter, the relationship between the writer and the reader, between the addresser and the addressee, controls. In the journal, one can say that the controlling factor is the relationship of the addresser (writer) to context (subject matter). A journal records the sensations, events, and impressions that the writer encounters and thinks are meaningful enough *to him or her* to set down. The selection by John Holt is a good example of this.

The addresser in the journal appears to the reader as an observer and recorder of *outward* events, people, and so on, and of *inward* thoughts and impressions. Look at Holt's first paragraph:

14   I am sitting on a friend's terrace [event]. Close by [event] is Lisa [person], 16-month-old, a bright and bold child [impression]. . . . Some sounds she says over and over again [event], as if she meant something by them [impression]. She likes to touch and handle things, and is surprisingly dexterous [impression]; she can fit screws and similar small objects into the holes meant for them [observation]. Can it be that little children are less clumsy than we have always supposed [speculation]?

The journal writer is a camera, recording what he or she sees, thinks, and feels.

The Context

As the writer of a journal, you have a personal, intimate relationship with context—the data that the writing reports—for you are saying, in effect, "In this journal, I want to record my own impressions of the world around me and of my interior world." You do not need to be objective, to see all sides of a question, for that is not your purpose. You want to give a running account of how the world appears to you. And you do not argue in favor of your viewpoints or support your opinions; they are yours, and that is enough. The journal is simply a report of context as the writer sees it.

[7]John Holt, *How Children Learn* (New York: Pitman Publishing, 1967), p. 2. Copyright ©, 1967, 1969 by Pitman Publishing Corp. Reprinted by permission of Pitman Publishing Corp.

The Structure

The structure of the journal is open and fluid. Its overall structure is chronological, for the writer makes entries day by day. The structure of the individual entries will vary, however, according to the subject matter. The three paragraphs in the selection from Holt *almost* constitute a little expository essay, but not quite, because the reader of an expository essay would want a conclusion, perhaps a paragraph that summed up and stated what the writer was getting at. Notice how inconclusive the three paragraphs do seem. The reader asks, "And so?" But the writer of the journal is not obliged to draw conclusions or to round out the entries.

The Style

The style of the journal, too, can be anything the writer wants it to be. Like the interior monologue and the personal letter, the journal is not "public" writing; though it may have thousands of readers—as does Holt's journal—its first purpose is to give the writer the opportunity to record the world as he or she sees it.

Holt's style is lucid and conventional—and low-keyed. (Compare it with the style in Hawthorne's personal letter or Ginsberg's interior monologue.) His word choice is straightforward; there are no puns, no plays on words, no prominent figures of speech.

We will take only a quick look at Holt's sentence structure. Consider the first sentence in the last paragraph. It might have been written like this:

15   The other day she was playing on the piano. She was hitting more or less at random with both hands. She was pleased to be working the machine and making such an interesting noise.

Instead—and fortunately—Holt wrote it as he did. The following schematization should help you discover his technique:

16   The other day she was playing on the piano,
          hitting more or less at random with both hands,
          pleased to be working the machine and making such an interesting noise.

This technique is called *embedding*, and in Chapter 11, on the sentence, we'll discuss it in detail.

The Audience

The audience for the journal varies. Some journals are written just for the writer and are therefore much like, if not the same as, interior monologues. Others are written with a generalized audience in mind. Surely Holt was not writing only for himself, but just as surely he did not have a particular person or group of persons in mind. His audience, if he thought about it, was probably a vaguely defined group that might be called "the reading public."

Some Advice for Writers

Here is a summary formula for writing journals:

1. You need to be a close observer, both of outward reality and the inward experiences of thought, impression, and so on. You are a camera, recording in detail.
2. The context that provides the subject matter for journal writing is reality as subjectively interpreted by the writer. In some kinds of writing, you must defend and justify, develop and explain; such is not the case with the journal, for you are saying to the reader, "Here's the way I see the world. You can take it or leave it." The reader will come to the journal precisely because he or she is interested in your view of context. The reader's interest is divided between the subject matter and the personality and intellect that developed that subject matter. In the journal, you do not disappear behind your words; you remain very much in evidence.
3. The basic structure of the journal is chronological, but individual entries or parts of entries may demand various kinds of organization.
4. The style of the journal, like the style of the interior monologue, can be pretty much anything the writer wants it to be. Holt's style is very conventional; he punctuates according to accepted usage, his vocabulary is straightforward, his sentences are conservative and tightly constructed. But there is no reason for the journal writer to worry about style. You might choose to approximate your spoken idiom and to forget about conventional punctuation; on the other hand, you might choose to adopt a fussy, conservative style.
5. As a journal writer, you need not attempt to adjust your writing to a given audience; rather, you can assume that if what you say interests you, it will also interest some other people.

The Autobiography

The least personal kind of self-expressive writing, strangely, is autobiography. The autobiographer turns his or her eyes inward, to be sure, but is also keenly aware of a possible audience. One writes an autobiography not just to express oneself but also to capture readers.

Let's take a look at an example of autobiographical writing, a selection from *The Autobiography of Malcolm X:*

17   One afternoon in 1931 when Wilfred, Hilda, Philbert, and I came home, my mother and father were having one of their arguments. There had lately been a lot of tension around the house because of Black Legion threats. Anyway, my father had taken one of the rabbits which we were raising, and ordered my mother to cook it. We raised rabbits, but sold them to whites. My father had taken a rabbit from the rabbit pen. He had pulled off the rabbit's head. He was so strong, he needed no knife to behead chickens or rabbits. With one twist of

his big black hands he simply twisted off the head and threw the bleeding-necked thing back at my mother's feet.

My mother was crying. She started to skin the rabbit, preparatory to cooking it. But my father was so angry he slammed on out of the front door and started walking up the road toward town.

It was then that my mother had this vision. She had always been a strange woman in this sense, and had always had a strong intuition of things about to happen. And most of her children are the same way, I think. When something is about to happen, I can feel something, sense something. I never have known something to happen that has caught me completely off guard—except once. And that was when, years later, I discovered facts I couldn't believe about a man who, up until that discovery, I would have given my life for.

My father was well up the road when my mother ran screaming out onto the porch. *"Early! Early!"* She screamed his name. She clutched up her apron in one hand, and ran down across the yard and into the road. My father turned around. He saw her. For some reason, considering how angry he had been when he left, he waved at her. But he kept going on.

She told me later, my mother did, that she had a vision of my father's end. All the rest of the afternoon, she was not herself, crying and nervous and upset. She finished cooking the rabbit and put the whole thing in the warmer part of the black stove. When my father was not back home by our bedtime, my mother hugged and clutched us, and we felt strange, not knowing what to do, because she had never acted like that.

I remember waking up at the sound of my mother's screaming again. When I scrambled out, I saw the police in the living room; they were trying to calm her down. She had snatched on her clothes to go with them. And all of us children who were staring knew without anyone having to say it that something terrible had happened to our father.

My mother was taken by the police to the hospital, and to a room where a sheet was over my father in a bed, and she wouldn't look, she was afraid to look. Probably it was wise that she didn't. My father's skull, on one side, was crushed in. I was told later. Negroes in Lansing have always whispered that he was attacked, and then laid across some tracks for a streetcar to run over him. His body was cut almost in half.[8]

Analysis of Malcolm X

The Writer

Writers of autobiography are, needless to say, not impersonal; they do not allow themselves to disappear behind their ideas or their narrative. The selection from *The Autobiography of Malcolm X* is primarily an account of the death of the author's father, but consider what happens in the third paragraph. He tells about his mother's vision and her intuition, but then he slows the narrative down long enough to tell about himself: "When something is about to happen, I can feel something, sense something." Then, in the fifth paragraph: "She told *me* later, *my* mother did, that she had a vision of *my* father's end." Everything is seen through the eyes of the writer and is filtered through his personality: "*I* remember waking up at the

[8]*The Autobiography of Malcolm X* (New York: Grove Press, 1966), pp. 9–10. Reprinted by permission of Grove Press, Inc. Copyright © 1964 by Alex Haley and Malcolm X.

sound of ***my*** mother's screaming again. When ***I*** scrambled out, ***I*** saw the police in the living room . . . ."

In writing an autobiography you are attempting to interpret yourself for an audience. In order to do this, you must be extremely selective, choosing only those details of your life that are significant. Of course, an autobiography can be an account of your whole life seen in retrospect, of a period in your life (say, high school days), or of a week or a day.

Suppose that you decide to write an autobiography about one day in your life. You cannot, and would not want to, record everything that happened during that day: "At seven o'clock, the alarm rang, and after yawning, I scratched my left ear. After seven seconds I sprang out of bed with a bound and went to the bathroom, where I opened a tube of Crest and applied a dab to the toothbrush. . . ." And so on.

The selection by Malcolm X tells of perhaps eight or ten hours in his life, very important hours. To tell of these important hours, the author uses only 550 words.

The Context

To achieve effectiveness—and the selection is, I think you'll agree, extremely moving—Malcolm X chooses carefully among the details of the total context. In the first paragraph, the details about the rabbit are startling, even shocking. The last sentence couldn't be more vivid: "With one twist of his big black hands he simply twisted off the head and threw the bleeding-necked thing back at my mother's feet."

And look at the fourth paragraph. It too is vivid, not because it contains a great deal of detail, but because it contains just the right detail: "She clutched up her apron in one hand . . . ."

In autobiography, there is a strong writer-context ratio. The writer is attempting to sort out the facts of his or her existence and present them so that a clearly drawn portrait emerges.

Structure

The structure of autobiography is basically chronological, for the autobiography is a narrative: first this happened and then that and then that, and so on. Since an autobiography is not only a record of outward events, but also of the inner life of the writer, within the narrative framework there will be patches of exposition that explain ideas, and of musings that are very similar to interior monologues. To refer back to context, the successful autobiography is that which gives readers a sense that they really know the writer; therefore the writer must sort out the meaningful data—events and thoughts—and present them to readers vividly. And vividness always implies detail. To illustrate the necessity of carefully chosen detail, I will rewrite Malcolm X's first paragraph, omitting most of the detail. The paragraph thus loses its ability to grip the reader:

18 One afternoon my mother and father were having an argument. There had lately been tension around the house. We raised rabbits, and my father killed one and told my mother to cook it.

Style

Style in autobiography, as in all other kinds of self-expressive writing, depends entirely upon the personality that the author is trying to convey. To state the point another way: self-expressive writing confers greater freedom of style than do other types of writing, because the writer's concern about audience expectations is not as great. In expository and persuasive writing, as we shall see, this freedom is appreciably diminished in most cases, and the style must be adjusted not according to the writer's own sense of personality, but according to the demands of subject matter and audience.

The question of style in Malcolm X's autobiography is complicated by the fact that the book was written "with the assistance of Alex Haley." Did Haley do the actual writing? Did he revise a rough manuscript that Malcolm X submitted to him? I don't know. I can only deal with the book as it was published. And, it seems to me, from the standpoint of a reader, that the weakest aspect of this basically interesting, moving book is its style. I can only criticize on the basis of my own tastes, and your tastes may be different from mine. However, when I read a long stretch of writing, I tend to be bothered if there is not a good deal of variety in sentence structure.

As an illustration of what I mean, look at the end of the first paragraph. The sentences are blunt and simply patterned.

19   My father had taken a rabbit from the rabbit pen. [Subject, Verb, Object, Adverbial]

20   He had pulled off the rabbit's head. [Subject, Verb, Object]

21   He was so strong, he needed no knife to behead chickens or rabbits. [Adverb Clause, Subject, Verb, Object, Adverbial]

This simplicity and rigidity of sentence pattern is typical of the whole book, and I think that most readers subconsciously react against the monotony. In other words, the writer has not used the devices of syntax to bring variety to his language. You can best demonstrate this to yourself by reading the passage aloud and letting your ears react.

So we discover here another principle that is worth noting and thinking about: variety in sentence structures, like variety in words and variety in ideas, is *generally* a positive virtue. After a while, the reader tends to tire of any kind of repetitiveness. Therefore, learning to handle sentences gives you the syntactic devices that are necessary to handle complex ideas, but syntactic versatility also gives you the ability to make your writing more interesting.

The Audience

The audience for autobiography can be highly specialized or very general. My father-in-law wrote an account of his life, but he intended that autobiography only for his own children. On the other hand, Malcolm X apparently had in mind a much wider audience that might be termed "the reading public." Might one not say that Malcolm X's intended audience was about the same as John Holt's?

It might be worthwhile to characterize briefly some of the expectations of the reading public. The reading public normally expects that the writer will use standard English, will spell accurately, and will punctuate in a way that approximates the usage of, say, national magazines such as *Time* and *Harper's*. The reading public does not have specialized knowledge and expects the writer to explain fully. For instance, Malcolm X mentions the Black Legion, and the audience has the right to expect him to explain what that group is (in the book, Malcolm X does explain). For better or for worse, the reading public has certain prejudices and certain tabus, both philosophical and sexual. One becomes explicit only at the risk of alienating great numbers of readers.

But it must be stressed that any generalization about writing is dangerous, for any given piece of writing has its own dynamics. What works in one instance will not work in others. Learning to write is largely the process of mastering as many as possible of the countless techniques that are at the disposal of a good writer to make *this* piece of writing work for *this* audience at *this* time. Nonetheless, it is a good idea to realize that there is something called a *reading public* and that much writing is aimed at that audience.

Some Advice for Writers

1. When you are writing an autobiographical narrative, you must assume that your readers will be interested in what you say primarily because the narrative does concern you; the readers want the details about you that will help you to emerge from the pages of your autobiography as a living, breathing person. In other words, you must supply the details, as did Malcolm X.
2. In an autobiography, you have a responsibility to convey information clearly and accurately, unless, of course, you want your narrative to be viewed as fiction. In other words, the context of autobiography is the events of your own life.
3. As has been pointed out, the structure of autobiography is basically chronological. Your responsibility is to keep the reader oriented.
4. Since by its very nature autobiography is not private, but is intended for an audience, you must write in a style that meets the expectations of the audience that you are addressing. If your audience is simply the reading public, you will probably be reluctant to violate the niceties of mechanics—spelling, punctuation, verb agreement, and so on—that the reading public has come to expect.

Finally

We have been talking about self-expressive writing, one of the four loose classifications into which *The Contemporary Writer* divides the field of writing for convenience of discussion: self-expressive, expository, persuasive, and imaginative. You should not expect these categories to be airtight, for the kinds of writing tend to overlap, and distinctions blur. A given piece might be self-expressive when viewed from one angle and imaginative when viewed from another, persuasive for one reader and expository for another.

We have also said that we can view the writer's task and the reader's response on the basis of five factors: addresser (writer), context (the data that the writing contains), structure, style, and addressee (intended audience). Again, these are artificial categories, adopted simply because they give us a systematic way to view writing.

The following two charts represent graphically what has been said about self-expressive writing in this chapter.

21   The concerns of the *writer* of self-expressive writing.

	Writer	Context	Structure	Style	Audience
Interior Monologue	Maximum				
Personal Letter	Maximum	Intermediate			Maximum
Journal	Maximum	Intermediate			
Autobiography	Maximum	Maximum			Intermediate

Legend:
- ■ Maximum Concern
- ▨ Intermediate Concern
- □ Minimum Concern

22   The concerns of the *reader* of self-expressive writing.

	Writer	Context	Structure	Style	Audience
Interior Monologue	Intermediate				
Personal Letter	Intermediate		Intermediate		
Journal	Intermediate	Intermediate			
Autobiography	Intermediate	Intermediate	Intermediate		

These charts are an attempt to give a graphic summary of this chapter. A verbal summary has already been made at the beginning of the chapter, and you should reread that summary now.

Discussion and Activities

Classifying Kinds of Writing

What seems to be the purpose of the following four selections (all by Joseph Conrad concerning his experiences in the Congo)? Remember, the purpose associated with the author is *self-expressive;* the purpose associated with context is *expository;* the purpose associated with the message itself is *imaginative*; the purpose associated with the audience is *persuasive.*   That is, according to purpose, we can classify writing as self-expressive, expository, imaginative, or persuasive. But remember also that one seldom finds a "pure" piece of writing. As you think about the following examples, you will be asking yourself about the author's purpose; you should also be able to give your reasons for attributing a purpose to the author. That is, what do you find in each selection that leads you to make your classification? (There are no "right" or "wrong" answers in this exercise.)

a   *Friday, 1st of August, 1890*

Left at 6:30 A.M. after a very indifferently passed night. Cold, heavy mists. Road in long ascents and sharp dips all the way to Mfumu Mbe. After leaving there, a long and painful climb up a very steep hill; then a long descent to Mfumu Kono, where a long halt was made. Left at 12:30 P.M. towards Nselemba. Many ascents. The aspect of the country entirely changed. Wooded hills with openings. Path almost all the afternoon thro' a forest of light trees with dense undergrowth.

After a halt on a wooded hillside, reached Nselemba at 4:10 P.M. Put up at Govt. shanty. Row between carriers and a man, stating himself in Govt. employ, about a mat. Blows with sticks raining hard. Stopped it.

Chief came with a youth about 13 suffering from gunshot wound in the head. Bullet entered about an inch above the right eyebrow, and came out a little inside the roots of the hair, fairly in the middle of the brow in a line with the bridge of the nose. Bone not damaged apparently. Gave him a little glycerine to put on the wound made by the bullet coming out.

Harou not very well. Mosquitos—frogs—beastly! Glad to see the end of this stupid tramp. Feel rather seedy. Sun rose red. Very hot day. Wind Sth.

General direction of march N.E. by N. Distance about 17 miles.[9]

b   *Kinshasa, 26 September 1890*

Dearest and best of Aunts!

I received your three letters all at once on my return from Stanley Falls, where I went . . . in the vessel *Roi des Belges* to learn the river. . . . My days here are dreary. Make no mistake about that! I am truly sorry to have come here. Indeed, I regret it bitterly. . . .

Everything is repellent to me here. Men and things, but especially men. And I am repellent to them, too. From the manager in Africa—who has taken the trouble of telling a good many people that I displease him intensely—down to the lowest mechanic, all have a gift for getting on my nerves; and conse-

---

[9]Joseph Conrad, *Heart of Darkness,* ed. Robert Kimbrough (New York: W. W. Norton, 1963), pp. 116–17.

quently I am perhaps not as pleasant to them as I might be. The manager is a common ivory-dealer with sordid instincts who considers himself a merchant though he is only a kind of African shopkeeper. His name is Delcommune. He hates the English, and I am of course regarded as an Englishman here. Moreover, he has said that he is but little bound here by promises made in Europe, so long as they are not in the contract. Those made me by M. Wauters are not. Likewise I can look forward to nothing, as I have no vessel to command. The new boat will be finished in June of next year, perhaps. In the meanwhile my status here is vague, and I have been having trouble because of this. So there you are![10]

c   It was in 1868, when nine years old or thereabouts, that while looking at a map of Africa of the time and putting my finger on the blank space then representing the unsolved mystery of that continent, I said to myself with absolute assurance and an amazing audacity which are no longer in my character now:

"When I grow up I shall go *there*."

And of course I thought no more about it till after a quarter of a century or so an opportunity offered to go there—as if the sin of childish audacity was to be visited on my mature head. Yes. I did go there: *there* being the region of Stanley Falls which in '68 was the blankest of blank spaces on the earth's figured surface.[11]

d   Black shapes crouched, lay, sat between the trees, leaning against the trunks, clinging to the earth, half coming out, half effaced within the dim light, in all the attitudes of pain, abandonment, and despair. . . .

They were dying slowly—it was very clear. They were not enemies, they were not criminals, they were nothing earthly now—nothing but black shadows of disease and starvation, lying confusedly in the greenish gloom. Brought from all the recesses of the coast in all the legality of time contracts, lost in uncongenial surroundings, fed on unfamiliar food, they sickened, became inefficient, and were then allowed to crawl away and rest. These moribund shapes were free as air—and nearly as thin. I began to distinguish the gleam of the eyes under the trees. Then, glancing down, I saw a face near my hand. The black bones reclined at full length with one shoulder against the tree, and slowly the eyelids rose and the sunken eyes looked up at me, enormous and vacant, a kind of blind, white flicker in the depths of the orbs, which died out slowly. The man seemed young—almost a boy. . . . I found nothing else to do but to offer him one of my good Swede's ship's biscuits I had in my pocket. The fingers closed slowly on it and held—there was no other movement and no other glance. . . .[12]

The Interior Monologue

Writing interior monologues is an excellent way to begin to become fluent in the "scribal mode." The interior monologue is a "photographic" representation of your thoughts as they flow. In writing the interior monologue, you can forget about punctuation, spelling, sentence structure,

[10]*Ibid.*, p. 119.
[11]*Ibid.*, p. 104.
[12]*Ibid.*, pp. 17–18.

and the other "mechanics" of writing. What you are attempting is fidelity to your stream of consciousness. Write down the ideas that come, the visions you "see," the sensations you have in a ten- or fifteen-minute period of relaxed meditation.

The Personal Letter

Think of an interesting event that has happened to you recently, something that you can relate in fifty or a hundred words. In three brief personal letters, tell that event to (a) your parents, (b) your girlfriend or boyfriend, (c) your English instructor. In these writings, do you consciously or subconsciously adjust to the different audiences? How?

The Journal

In Chapter 3, we will discuss journal-keeping in some detail. But you should begin now. Each day, enter a brief account of the events that are meaningful to you. Capture enough detail so that you can use your entries as the basis for future writing and so that your instructor (if you choose to let him or her read the journal) can understand the significance of what you have recorded.

The Autobiography

Write an autobiographical sketch of a short period in your life—an interesting day or, at most, week. Your audience is a generalized "reading public"; therefore, you must choose details that will allow the audience to know you and to understand the importance of what you are saying.

Survey of the Composing Process 2

> Consider that a good half of writing consists of being sufficiently sensitive to the moment to reach for the next promise which is usually hidden in some word or phrase just a shift to the side of one's conscious intent.
>
> —Norman Mailer, *The Armies of the Night*

Summary of the Chapter

There are two kinds of knowledge: *knowing-that* and *knowing-how*. This survey of the composing process will keep knowing-that in mind—for the process itself is an endlessly fascinating subject for thought and theorizing—but the focus will be on knowing-how. The purpose of this chapter is to give you a schematic overview of the important activities that take place as one writes.

Situation. All writing takes place in a situation, either in the classroom or in the real world, and all writing has some kind of *purpose* that involves a *subject* and an *audience*. In the composition class, subjects are usually assigned or prescribed in some way, and one often does not have a real audience; therefore, classroom writing is often more difficult than writing in the real world, where there is a real purpose. However, classroom writing has the same end as scrimmages in football: to prepare one for the real thing—whatever that may be.

Writing takes place under the various *constraints* of the situation. The *place* in which a piece is written influences that piece, as does the *time* of composition. The *publishing agency* (if a piece is published in any way) also imposes constraints on the writing.

Prewriting. Much of the composing process takes place either before writing begins or, at least, before the writer has any idea of what the end result of the composing process will be. The writer must find a subject. Some subjects are assigned, some are based on reading, and some arise from the writer's interests and experiences.

Prewriting: Focusing the Subject. The composing process, then, involves finding a subject, but it also involves determining just what to say about that subject. A subject such as democracy is too large to be workable for most kinds of writing; therefore, the writer must focus on some relatively small aspect of democracy. But it is a mistake to think that one must have a well-defined, clearly focused subject before beginning to write. In fact, sometimes we write to find out what we think about a subject; that is, the focusing takes place during the writing.

Prewriting: Gathering Material. To find subject matter, we can search *our own experiences;* we can do *research* or make *observations* of the world "out there" (context). Any piece of *reading* provides its own subject matter for writing, for the reader can become an analytical writer, interpreting and evaluating the reading. The *code* of a piece of writing can provide subject matter for a stylistic analysis. Furthermore, one can view the intended *audience* of a piece of writing as a source of subject matter.

Planning: Sense and Nonsense About Outlines. Very few writers prepare elaborate, formal outlines before they begin to compose, but most writers use informal, scratch outlines, which they change and add to as the piece of writing grows. Used this way, outlines can stimulate thought and serve as guides toward goals.

A detailed formal outline—such as those explained in the chapter—should be completed after the writing is finished to serve as a guide and overview for the reader.

Formal outlines are of two types: *sentence* and *topic.* In a formal outline, sentences and topics (phrases) should not be mixed.

Starting: Overcoming Inertia. Finally getting under way is frequently a problem. But there are ways to make starting easier. One of these is to use a tape recorder to go through a *talk-retalk-write-rewrite* process as outlined in the chapter. Another technique is simply to begin writing, almost anything, merely to get under way. Often, direction emerges after one has begun to write almost at random.

The first paragraph should somehow arouse the reader's interest. It can be almost a summary of your essay. It can take the form of an analogy, a definition, an anecdote, a narrative, and so on.

Revising. Revision is usually an ongoing process. It takes place at every stage of composing, not just at the end. A writer can revise words, sentences, and larger chunks such as paragraphs. The kinds of revisions are *deletions, reorderings, substitutions,* and *embeddings.*

Stopping. The completed piece of writing should not be inconclusive; it should not raise questions that it does not answer. You should continually make quick checks to see that your writings are complete.

To Begin With

In Chapter 1 we discussed one kind of writing: self-expressive writing. Before we turn to expository, persuasive, and imaginative writing, some detours are necessary.

There are two kinds of knowledge: *knowing-that* and *knowing-how*. I know *that* electricity provides energy, but I don't know *how*.

Chapters 2 and 3 will deal with knowing-that to some extent, but they will concentrate more heavily on knowing-how—knowing how to write expository and persuasive essays. All the practical advice that will come is embedded in a rich conceptual framework. We will be using modern theory concerning the way in which the composing process transpires in order to develop some practical notions of how to compose. Therefore, I hope that you will not lose sight of this theoretical, conceptual background, for it is a rich source of ideas and speculation about an intricate process: that of composing. In other words, we will be talking about a quite miraculous phenomenon. Somehow, the skilled writer is able to start from zero and work through to a completed piece of writing that is meaningful to the reader. This creative process is at least as complicated and interesting as any of the processes that scientists investigate in the natural world.

Situation

It is truistic to state that writing does not take place in a vacuum. One writes at a given time, in a given place, for a certain reason, and for some kind of audience. As we have seen, in the case of purely self-expressive writing, writer and audience are the same; you are writing for yourself. Your purpose is to express yourself, to explain yourself to yourself, to use writing in the same way the subconscious uses dreams: as a method of restoring psychic balance. In expository and persuasive writing, however, the situation is more complicated, for you are doing more than merely expressing yourself, and you are trying to reach an audience.

The situation in which writing takes place is, of course, the universe, with all the complexity that that implies; but it is possible to classify and examine some of the important factors that influence composition. We will talk first about *purpose* and then about *constraints*.

Purpose

Purpose in writing can be diagramed like this:

1

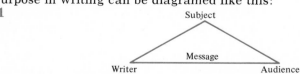

The writer finds a subject—or, ideally, the subject finds the writer. You encounter a situation in which, for some reason, something needs to be written: a letter home to ask for more money; a set of directions to inform a friend of the route to your house; a letter to a newspaper to make public your attitude toward taxation. In writing about the subject, you keep the audience in mind, and the message results from your desire to communicate the subject to that audience. In other words, there must be a desire to write something for some audience.

Consider the variety of purposes that can be detected in the following short passages:

2   Three passions, simple but overwhelmingly strong, have governed my life: the longing for love, the search for knowledge, and the unbearable pity for the suffering of mankind. These passions, like great winds, have blown me hither and thither, in a wayward course, over a deep ocean of anguish, reaching to the very verge of despair.

When one realizes that this paragraph is the first in Bertrand Russell's *Autobiography,* the purpose seems almost too apparent. Russell (the writer) wants to explain his life (the subject) to the world and posterity (the audience). It is worth stressing that we cannot talk about purpose without considering writer, subject, and audience.

3   We are as gods and might as well get good at it. So far remotely done power and glory—as via government, big business, formal education, church—has succeeded to point [*sic*] where gross defects obscure actual gains. In response to this dilemma and to these gains a realm of intimate personal power is developing—power of the individual to conduct his own education, find his own inspiration, shape his own environment, and share his adventure with whoever is interested. Tools that aid this process are sought and promoted by THE WHOLE EARTH CATALOG.   —*The Last Whole Earth Catalog*

Here the writer is anonymous; the subject is clearly defined as tools that will help people develop their intimate, personal power as against remote, institutionalized power; the audience is clearly defined as people who are fed up with institutional anonymity.

The specific kind of purpose in writing that interests us here is purpose in relation to the composition class in college. Unfortunately, the very nature of the composition class can deter the writer from achieving maximum success. In order to explain, I will talk about writing in the real world as opposed to writing for the classroom, even though I realize that this distinction may be more than a little unfair, since classroom writing can have real purpose.

In the real world, the writer encounters subjects through work (for example, professional reports), through hobbies (for example, accounts of fishing trips in personal letters), through passions (for example, letters to the editor prompted by strong political opinions), through idle curiosity (for example, an Elizabethan sonnet written just to see if one could do it)—in short, through the countless situations of life.

In the real world, one writes about subjects that engage one for some reason; there is a real need to write. One is aiming at a given audience. The writer usually has a great deal of freedom. In the classroom, however, the subject usually results from a more or less narrow assignment, the audience is generally the instructor, and the writer is forced to work on a fairly rigid timetable. The result is inevitably a certain artificiality of purpose. Writings for composition classes frequently are—and must be—dry runs.

As this chapter progresses, we will be talking about ways to make writing for composition classes a more "real" experience. Choosing subjects that engage your interest, or cultivating an interest in subjects that are assigned, is an important consideration, and aiming your writings at real or imagined audiences is another.

And, after all, the football player is quite willing to go through hundreds of dry runs (scrimmages) so that he'll be ready for the real thing—and this is exactly the case with the violinist, the ballet dancer, the painter. If dry runs in a composition class seem to have no real purpose, try thinking of them as scrimmages that will ultimately pay off with tactical and strategic skills that you can use when "the real thing" comes along.

Constraints

All writers work under a great variety of constraints that influence what they write about and how. It is worthwhile to become aware of some of the constraints that influence composition.

Place

First is place, broadly interpreted. We have discussed how the classroom, as a place, influences writing. Whether or not one must deal with assigned topics and regardless of how free the classroom appears, the fact that one is writing in a classroom has a great effect on the process and the product. For instance, if the composition class is restricted to expository writing, as many are, then the student will be discouraged from writing interior monologues or poems. The influence of place on a student in a report-writing class at Georgia Tech is quite different from that on a student in a creative writing class at the University of Iowa.

But place need not be interpreted so narrowly. Undoubtedly, William Faulkner was a product of place—the American South—just as every writer must be a product of his or her own place in the world.

Time

Next is the influence of time. At the moment that these words are being written, the Watergate affair is at the center of national attention; by the time these words are read, Watergate will probably be history, and its cast of characters and scenario may already be unfamiliar. If I intended what I write about Watergate at this moment to be read in the next few days or weeks or even months, then there would be no need for me to outline the background of the case; almost everyone knows it. But if you were to read my words in 1990, what would they mean to you? Would you be able to identify G. Gordon Liddy and John Dean III, or even Maurice Stans and John Mitchell?

Publication

If writing is to be published, one encounters a major constraint: the editorial policy of the agency of publication. The laws against libel impose certain constraints, of course, but here we are referring to the limitations imposed by the publication medium itself.

One way in which writing gets "published" is by television; that is, writers produce scripts that are then made into television shows. In a book called *Only You, Dick Daring!* Merle Miller and Evan Rhodes tell of the frustrations that they encountered in doing the script for a TV pilot film, to be called *Calhoun.* In the introduction, Miller gives a hilarious synopsis of their experience:

4   The script for *Calhoun* was totally rewritten at least nineteen times by me; it was partially rewritten by me and Evan 782,946.17 times. It was tampered with unnumbered times by people I have never seen and by people I have seen.

   As anyone who has the good sense to buy this book will discover, at one point it was reported that the president of a television network (Princeton, 1941, *cum laude,* English literature) was said to have thought *he* had written the script.

   In all fairness—and if this book is anything it is fair—it should be admitted that while the mob writing of *Calhoun* took five months and eight days (a total of 3792.8 hours), longer than Shakespeare took to turn out *Macbeth, Hamlet,* and *Titus Andronicus,* it was never even as good as *Titus.* Although there were many times when I sympathized with, even envied the heroine of *Titus.* All that happened to her was they raped her, lopped off her limbs, and tore out her tongue to keep her from telling the truth.

   She couldn't type or anything.

The causes for all the rewriting and frustration are apparent to anyone who watches TV. Advertisers exert considerable influence, and TV executives attempt to reach the widest possible audience with their shows, for TV is a commercial medium that becomes more profitable as more viewers watch. Furthermore, constraints of propriety are more rigorous in TV than in other media such as books, cinema, and the theater. Whereas complete nudity is common in films and on the stage, TV bans bare flesh.

I am not implying that there is anything sinister in all of this—only that the constraints imposed by the TV medium are real.

If you glance through any national magazine, you will see immediately that editorial policy determines the sort of material published. You will not find articles on home decoration in *The Western Outdoorsman,* nor articles on fly fishing in *Better Homes and Gardens.*

Publication and Tone

Less obvious than the previously mentioned constraints, but more interesting, are the influences that the agency of publication has on the tone, the style, of what is written. It is instructive—and sometimes amusing—to consider the attitudes magazines adopt in addressing their readers. Here's a sampling.

The following piece from *McCall's* ("First Magazine for Women/Circulation Over 7,500,000") makes one speculate: (1) How dumb do the editors really think their readers are? (2) Are the readers actually as dumb as the editors imply?

> 5   Spring-cleaning doesn't have to be the major upheaval it once was—it can be done without destroying your sanity. The secret: planning, organization, a calm approach, an open mind about new ways of doing things and about new products, full utilization of modern cleaning aids and equipment and simplified methods. [Thus the first paragraph sets up the woman of the house for the ads that make up the bulk of the magazine. The hundred hints that follow the first paragraph are stunning in their simple-mindedness. I give only one example.]
>
>   Use a step stool, ladder or a long-handled cleaning tool for reaching high places. It's safer and easier.[1]

The best way to characterize *Oui* is to remind you that it's the companion publication of Hugh Hefner's *Playboy;* that is, it's a magazine that presents a highly marketable blend of naked female flesh and pseudosophistication. The following appeals to me because of its slightly off-color nature and its pointlessness:

> 6   It was a foggy day in London town, and two British movie producers were chewing the fat. [Note how, right away, the editors show their attitude toward the readers by talking about "London ***town***" and using the figure "chewing the fat." We're clever, cynical dogs, aren't we?] How about, says one to the other, we make a movie called *Sinderella* in which our voluptuous heroine loses her bra (instead of that tacky glass slipper) and, as a graphic climax, balls Prince Charming. Right, says the other chap, and we'll do it all as a six-minute animated short. So they did. It was a smash at the Cannes Film Festival. Some 92 countries picked it up for distribution. The United States Customs Department, however, pronounced itself unamused and confiscated the cans of film as they sailed into New York harbor. But the English producers remained undaunted: They announced plans to start production on a new porno cartoon, to be called: *Snow White and the Seven Perverts.*[2]

One of the most sophisticated magazines in the United States is *The New Yorker.* You may or may not be comfortable with the tone of *The New Yorker,* but there is little doubt about the sort of audience the magazine is addressing—for instance, in the following:

> 7   Alexander (Sandy) Calder, who now spends most of the year in France, came here for a show of his oil paintings at the Perls Galleries, where we joined him and his wife, Louisa, the other afternoon. They had just driven in from their place in Roxbury, Connecticut, where we had last seen them several years ago, and which they now occupy for a month or so in the spring and fall. The rest of the time, they live in a house on the Indre River at Saché, in Touraine. We settled down with them in an upstairs gallery full of Picassos, Braques,

---

[1]"If You Hate Spring Cleaning," *McCall's,* May 1973, p. 16.
[2]"Dirty Shorts," *Oui,* Oct. 1972, p. 5. Originally appeared in *Oui* Magazine; copyright © 1972 by Playboy Publications, Inc. Used with permission.

Mirós, and Calder mobiles, and Klaus Perls offered drinks from the adjacent bar. The Calders asked for mild Scotch-and-Sodas.[3]

These three selections were chosen to illustrate, as briefly as possible, how agencies of publication can differ in tone—and thus, because of their different purposes, can put very real constraints upon their authors. From the simple-mindedness of *McCall's* through the hip prurience of *Oui* to the ultrasophistication of *The New Yorker*—that's quite a range. And, of course, we could go on looking at example after example.

The principle to be noted here is one that cannot be stressed too much: writers must learn to sense the constraints they are working under and to adjust. Again and again, we will return to the notion of adjustment to the intended audience. Indeed, learning to write might be characterized as the process of learning various ways to adjust subjects to audiences, within a variety of constraints.

Competence

Another constraint that the writer works under—perhaps the most obvious one—is the limitations of his or her own abilities and knowledge. In Chapter 10 we will discuss writing competence and writing performance. You should emerge from that discussion convinced that you can increase your ability as a writer and thus minimize constraints from that quarter.

Situation: An Example

It might be interesting and instructive to consider the situation in which the present chapter is being composed. I choose to use as an example what you are reading now because (a) you presumably are familiar with what has been written and (b) I have an intimate knowledge of what is going on, since I'm the writer. What I am about to say will be totally candid; that is, I want you to know as much as I can tell you. (I can't tell you everything because I don't know everything about what's going on right at this moment—not consciously, at least. I am fascinated by the very mystery of what is happening right now. Somehow I am generating ideas, and I am giving them expression in the forms allowed me by the language. Like the two-faced Roman god Janus, I am looking backward at the pages already typed and forward at what is to come, but I can't predict exactly what is to come; the writing develops itself as it moves forward, and I am continually amazed at where my own thought and my own language have taken me—and even more amazed that what gets written is apparently coherent. Of course, I backtrack and cross out a good deal; some starts lead me to dead ends, others open up new possibilities and then I race onward, elated.)

The subject? Well, the subject is here, in these pages, isn't it? As a matter of fact, the subject found me; I didn't find it. For two or three years now, I have been engrossed by the question, "What goes on when people write?" I know as little about the answer as anyone else, but I find that the concept

[3]"Calders Revisited," *The New Yorker,* 28 Oct. 1972, p. 30.

preoccupies me; therefore, it really isn't work for me to think and write about the composing process. Nor is it difficult for me to find things to say. I have a head full of ideas and a file box crammed with notes; I have read dozens of articles and books relating to the subject. In short, both my conscious and my subconscious minds are permeated with the subject.

The audience? You are the audience. I have a fairly clear picture of you. You're an undergraduate in a college or university, and you're intelligent and motivated. During your education, you are interested in acquiring skills that will make you useful and will enable you to earn a living, but you also have an active curiosity that makes you want to know *why* as well as *how.* If this book were not intellectually challenging, you would be turned off; but the concepts that are being developed are new to you, so I must always try to explain clearly and try even harder not to fly off into discussions that will leave you behind. Therefore, I'm doing a delicate balancing act. I want the book to challenge you intellectually, but not to be too difficult. I would guess that your composition class is not your favorite. You probably view it as a necessary evil. And I would also guess that you would not be reading *The Contemporary Writer* if it were not required. Therefore, I'm very cautious with you. I keep wondering if the discussion is getting too dry or detailed. I take great care in choosing examples that I think you will find interesting.

Time and place? Right now it's 3:40 on the afternoon of May 19, 1973, and I'm working on my patio. I have serious doubts about traditional writing courses; I even have serious doubts about the academic world's insistence that everyone learn to write. Is it possible that the ability to compose in writing is becoming unnecessary, what with electronic devices and so forth? So you see, I'm very insecure. That's why I talked at such great length about the *uses* of writing for self-expression. I keep thinking of all the cultured, happy, productive people I know who would have a miserable time in a composition course. They don't need to write in order to be happy and moderately prosperous. But I really believe that they would live better lives if they were writers. (I sincerely wish that I had learned—or would learn—to play the violin, and not because I want to earn my living by giving concerts.)

Publication agency? Enter audience again. This book will be published by a large corporation, and it must appeal to enough people to make its publication worthwhile. Therefore, my editor is looking over my shoulder as I write.

I'll end this discussion of my situation by telling you a true story. Just a couple of hours ago, I was thumbing through a stack of magazines to choose examples of the influence of publication agency. (The ones that I finally chose appear above.) In one magazine, I found a discussion of masturbation—an absolutely simple-minded chat obviously aimed at parents who are still living in the Dark Ages. The little piece was so funny and did such a nice job of revealing how the editors of the magazine viewed their readers that I decided to use it. I typed it into my manuscript. But then I began to think: How would my publisher react? How would you react? Would you feel that the piece was gratuitous prurience, included just for its shock value? I finally decided to omit the piece. Cowardice? No, I think not. Just a realistic assessment of the constraints I'm working under.

A Final Word About Situation

I could say a great deal more about situation, but there is a good deal that I cannot say. No one can begin to understand at the conscious level the infinite number of factors that influence writing. Learning to write is largely the business of developing one's intuition. The writer is a computer with a soul, infinitely more complex than any that IBM will ever develop— working just as rapidly, making instantaneous choices, running well ahead of conscious knowledge of what is happening, drawing on a data bank that includes everything ever known or experienced or dreamed. The only service that a book about writing can perform is to help the writer put more options into the mental program. Once you become consciously aware of some principles, you can internalize them so that eventually you will use them automatically.

By way of epilogue, consider the following:

8

The Thought-Fox[4]
Ted Hughes

I imagine this midnight moment's forest:
Something else is alive
Besides the clock's loneliness
And this blank page where my fingers move,

Through the window I see no star:
Something more near
Though deeper within darkness
Is entering the loneliness:

Cold, delicately as the dark snow,
A fox's nose touches twig, leaf;
Two eyes serve a movement, that now
And again now, and now, and now

Sets neat prints into the snow
Between trees, and warily a lame
Shadow lags by stump and in hollow
Of a body that is bold to come

Across the clearings, an eye,
A widening deepening greenness,
Brilliantly, concentratedly,
Coming about its own business

Till, with a sudden sharp hot stink of fox
It enters the dark hold of the head.
The window is starless still; the clock ticks,
The page is printed.

[4]Ted Hughes, "The Thought-Fox," *The Hawk in the Rain* (New York: Harper & Row, 1957). Copyright © 1957 by Ted Hughes. Originally appeared in *The New Yorker* and reprinted by permission of Harper & Row, Publishers, Inc.

Prewriting

The writing process usually begins long before you ever sit down to start scribbling or typing. It would be a happy situation if the following were an accurate model of the composing process:

9   Choose a subject.
      Outline.
      Write.

In fact, if the composing process were that simple, we would be amazed to find writing difficult for anyone. We have already explored the complexities of the situation in which writing takes place, and now we will investigate the activities and processes that occur before writing can begin.

However, writing is not a linear process that proceeds systematically, step by step; it is, rather, a web of activities, and individual strands are difficult to isolate. The writer may sit down with a perfectly blank mind and generate a first paragraph concerning something; this first paragraph may trigger a whole planning process. In such a case, writing prepares one to plan. In other instances, planning prepares one to write. Often a given piece of writing gets developed by fits and starts. A section is written, and then a good deal of planning is done in preparation for writing another section. And there is no reason why one can't start by writing the middle or the end.

In any case, you must have a subject. Choosing one ought to be easy. You are an infinitely small dot in an infinitely large universe; out there around you are more things and concepts and sensations and feelings, paradoxically, than there are under the sun; you should be able to reach out mentally and grasp some subject, quite at random, and begin to write about it. For the sake of convenience, we will break down this universe of subject matter into three categories: subjects that are assigned, subjects that develop from reading, and subjects that find the writer.

You and Your Subject

Regarding the kinds of subjects that you can write about, there is another paradox: regardless of what you choose, you are, from one point of view, the world's greatest expert on that subject. Open-heart surgery, the War of 1812, John Berryman's poetry, fishing for albacore—whatever—you know more about how much you know, and how you feel, about these subjects than anyone else in the world. No one can take that from you. You also, of course, know your own limitations.

Let me give a specific example of what I mean. Though I'm interested in computers, I know very little about them. Nothing that I could say about the technology or the programing of computers would be of much interest to anyone, least of all an expert in the field. And yet I think I could write an essay on computers that *would* interest both the layman and the expert, for my experiences with the machines are unique, and I think that a discussion of how I began to react emotionally to the computer that I worked with might be of interest to most readers. In other words, I could give expert testimony regarding computers, provided I limited myself to my own particular realm of expertness.

Another example: You are probably not an expert on the intricacies of financing higher education, but you are an expert concerning the impact that rising costs of higher education are having on you.

Subjects That Are Assigned

There is little to say about choosing a subject from a group that are assigned. You have some latitude, but not very much, and you must work as best you can within the strictures of the assignment. It is important to remember, though, that an essay results from the writer's encounter with the subject; if the subject does not come to you, you must bring yourself to the subject. Therefore, you ask yourself, "What do I know about this subject? What can I find out about it? How do I feel about it?" And so on. More about this later.

Subjects That Develop from Reading

Much of your writing in college will—and probably should—be based on what you read. Almost everything that you read can be a source of ideas for writing, and you should use your readings as productively and efficiently as possible.

Reading should not be passive, but rather should consist of your intense interaction with the text. As we will see in Chapter 10, meaning does not hide down there in the text, nor does it arise up there in your head, independent of text; meaning results from the interaction of your mind with the text. In one sense, the text gives the possibility of meaning, and in another sense, you construct the meaning that is possible in the text. As you read, you are guessing, predicting, confirming. You are reacting for or against. You are stimulated to go beyond the text in your speculations. In short, the reading generates ideas that could be subjects for writing.

A Brief Essay

To see how this works, we will take as an example one paragraph from *Understanding Media,* by Marshall McLuhan.

10   There is a basic principle that distinguishes a hot medium like radio from a cool one like the telephone, or a hot medium like the movie from a cool one like TV. A hot medium is one that extends one single sense in "high definition." High definition is the state of being well filled with data. A photograph is, visually, "high definition." A cartoon is "low definition," simply because very little visual

Definition of **hot** and **cool.**

What does he mean by **data?**

information is provided. Telephone is a cool medium, or one of low definition, because the ear is given a meager amount of information. And speech is a cool medium of low definition, because so little is given and so much has to be filled in by the listener. On the other hand, hot media do not leave so much to be filled in or completed by the audience. Hot media are, therefore, low in participation, and cool media are high in participation or completion by the audience. Naturally, therefore, a hot medium like radio has very different effects on the user from a cool medium like the telephone.

Does this observation square with my own experience?

As I read this passage—and it could be viewed as a one-paragraph essay—certain thought processes start. I want to know what McLuhan means by **hot** and **cool**, and ultimately I satisfy myself that I do know. I also want to know what he means by **data**, but to find that out, I must go beyond the passage quoted. It turns out that **data** means the impressions conveyed to the senses, not the idea content. So the data of this page concern black marks against a white background; the data in a conversation concern sounds, not their meaning.

By the time I have finished the paragraph, I know what McLuhan is saying. His point is that cool media engage the audience more than hot media. Thus, one is more engaged by the telephone than by the radio, because the auditory data conveyed by the telephone are much sparser than the auditory data conveyed by the radio. A simple, and not inaccurate, way of stating this point is to say that listeners must concentrate their aural capacities more during a telephone conversation than when listening to the radio, for the telephone leaves more to fill in. As for visual media, TV is cooler than the movies, because the TV screen, with its several thousand dots, conveys less data than the hot movie screen with its plethora of visual data.

So, yes, I think I understand what McLuhan is getting at, and I begin to react. Each of my reactions might well serve as the topic for a piece of writing. In particular, I ask myself, "Does this observation square with my own experience?"

Some Topics

Within a minute or two after having read the piece by McLuhan, I have a list of possible topics for essays. Some of these topics are directly related to the piece, and some are tangentially related, having been suggested by the reading. Now I have something to start working with, thus:

11   My involvement with media. (Do McLuhan's theories square with my own experience? Do I become more engaged with cool media such as TV than with hot media such as movies? Might I not do a survey of the influence of media

on my life? How much time do I spend with each medium? Which ones are most meaningful to me? Why?)

12 Media and teen-agers. (Living with two teen-agers, I am fascinated by their absorption with various media, particularly with the radio. One son is passionate about movies, and the other is equally passionate about TV. I might write an essay based on my observations of my sons. If I decide to write about teen-agers in general, I will probably need to do a great deal of research.)

13 Data and content of media. (I would like to explore the relationship of the data that media convey with the content or message that the data convey. I will file this idea away and let it germinate, for it will take a good deal of thought and probably some reading. Even though the concept intrigues me, I know that I don't have enough ideas to begin to write.)

14 The poem as a medium. (For some time, I have been thinking about form in poetry. Modern poetry has moved away from rigid forms toward what might be called free verse, and I have read a great many statements concerning this new mode. It would be relatively easy for me to write about free verse. As a matter of fact, this subject is so interesting to me that I might well choose it.)

15 Commercial TV. (This is an interesting subject—and all of the material is readily at hand, both on the tube and in the *TV Guide.* Since I feel strongly about commercial TV—have already formed an attitude—I might write a critical essay on the subject.)

16 Marshall McLuhan. (The man interests me. I'd like to find out more about him. I've read all his books and many of his articles. Maybe I could do a critical review of McLuhan's theories and methods.)

So reading one paragraph stimulated all these ideas for writing. Let it be said that I immediately wrote all my ideas down so that they wouldn't escape me and so that I could think all of them over before committing myself to one or another. In regard to **11**, I even came up with a possible title that I like: "Me and Media."

Finding Topics

There are ways of surveying things that you read in order to discover topics for writing. In fact, the most useful survey that I can think of goes right back to the model used again and again in this book: writer, context, structure, style, audience. You can ask given questions, and the answers to these questions might well be essays. Thus, in regard to the McLuhan piece, you can systematically ask:

17 What sort of a person is the author? (This brings up the whole idea of biography and biographical sketches and would involve research.)

18 What is the truth value of the piece? (That is, how does the material in the piece square with reality as I know it? The answer to this question will involve arguing for or against the piece.)

19 How is the piece structured? (Here you are focusing on the message itself, the way it is put together. This is a particularly interesting question in regard to

McLuhan because he has broken free of the logical, sequential, linear organization that is typical of Western writing and uses, instead, what he terms a mosaic organization in which the individual bits and pieces go to make up a whole; if you read one of McLuhan's books, you will find that this method is quite different from that of most authors that you are familiar with. Therefore, an essay dealing with McLuhanesque structure could be interesting for you and illuminating for your reader.)

20   What sort of style does McLuhan use? (In this instance, you would be doing a stylistic analysis, and you would be looking at his word choice, at his use of figures of speech, and at his sentence structure, among other considerations.)

21   What is my impression of the piece? (In answering that question you would be explaining your personal reaction to what you had read.)

In other words, when your essay is based on a piece of reading, it can be a *biographical* treatment of the author; a *critical review;* a *structural analysis; a stylistic analysis;* or an *impressionistic* response. Obviously, too, the reading that you do can suggest topics that do not relate directly to the reading.

Sources of Subjects That Find the Writer

Carl Gustav Jung was a psychiatrist. (He was quoted in Chapter 1.) Ted Hughes is a poet. (He wrote "The Thought-Fox.") Both of them have a good deal to say about getting subjects. So far, in this discussion, we have been schematizing and therefore falsifying to a certain extent. Now, let's take a more organic look at this discovery procedure; we will find that what goes on is infinitely complex and only partially explainable. Here is part of a discussion of dreams and the unconscious by Jung.

22   Freud made the simple but penetrating observation that if a dreamer is   1
encouraged to go on talking about his dream images and the thoughts   2
that these prompt in his mind, he will give himself away and reveal the   3
unconscious background of his ailments, in both what he says and what   4
he deliberately omits saying. His ideas may seem irrational and irrele-   5
vant, but after a time it becomes relatively easy to see what it is that he is   6
trying to avoid, what unpleasant thought or experience he is suppressing.   7
No matter how he tries to camouflage it, everything he says points to the   8
core of his predicament. A doctor sees so many things from the seamy   9
side of life that he is seldom far from the truth when he interprets the   10
hints that his patient produces as signs of an uneasy conscience. What he   11
eventually discovers, unfortunately, confirms his expectations. Thus far,   12
nobody can say anything against Freud's theory of repression and wish   13
fulfillment as apparent causes of dream symbolism.   14
   Freud attached particular importance to dreams as the point of depar-   15
ture for a process of "free association." But after a time I began to feel   16
that this was a misleading and inadequate use of the rich fantasies that   17
the unconscious produces in sleep. My doubts really began when a   18
colleague told me of an experience he had during the course of a long   19
train journey in Russia. Though he did not know the language and could   20

not even decipher the Cyrillic script, he found himself musing over the ²¹
strange letters in which the railway notices were written, and he fell into ²²
a reverie in which he imagined all sorts of meanings for them. ²³

One idea led to another, and in his relaxed mood he found that this ²⁴
"free association" had stirred up many old memories. Among them he ²⁵
was annoyed to find some long-buried disagreeable topics—things he had ²⁶
wished to forget and had forgotten *consciously*. He had in fact arrived at ²⁷
what psychologists would call his "complexes"—that is, repressed emo- ²⁸
tional themes that can cause constant psychological disturbances or ²⁹
even, in many cases, the symptoms of a neurosis. ³⁰

This episode opened my eyes to the fact that it was not necessary to use ³¹
a dream as the point of departure for the process of "free association" if ³²
one wished to discover the complexes of a patient. It showed me that one ³³
can reach the center directly from any point of the compass. One could ³⁴
begin from Cyrillic letters, from meditations upon a crystal ball, a prayer ³⁵
wheel, or a modern painting, or even from casual conversation about ³⁶
some quite trivial event. The dream was no more and no less useful in ³⁷
this respect than any other possible starting point. Nevertheless, dreams ³⁸
have a particular significance, even though they often arise from an ³⁹
emotional upset in which the habitual complexes are also involved. (The ⁴⁰
habitual complexes are the tender spots of the psyche, which react most ⁴¹
quickly to an external stimulus or disturbance.) That is why free associa- ⁴²
tion can lead one from any dream to the critical secret thoughts. ⁴³

At this point, however, it occurred to me that (if I was right so far) it ⁴⁴
might reasonably follow that dreams have some special and more signifi- ⁴⁵
cant function of their own. Very often dreams have a definite, evidently ⁴⁶
purposeful structure, indicating an underlying idea or intention—though, ⁴⁷
as a rule, the latter is not immediately comprehensible. I therefore began ⁴⁸
to consider whether one should pay more attention to the actual form and ⁴⁹
content of a dream, rather than allowing "free" association to lead one off ⁵⁰
through a train of ideas to complexes that could as easily be reached by ⁵¹
other means. ⁵²

This new thought was a turning-point in the development of my ⁵³
psychology. It meant that I gradually gave up following associations that ⁵⁴
led far away from the text of a dream. I chose to concentrate rather on the ⁵⁵
associations to the dream itself, believing that the latter expressed ⁵⁶
something specific that the unconscious was trying to say. ⁵⁷

The change in my attitude toward dreams involved a change of ⁵⁸
method; the new technique was one that could take account of all the ⁵⁹
various wider aspects of a dream. A story told by the conscious mind has a ⁶⁰
beginning, a development, and an end, but the same is not true of a ⁶¹
dream. Its dimensions in time and space are quite different; to under- ⁶²
stand it you must examine it from every aspect—just as you may take an ⁶³
unknown object in your hand and turn it over and over until you are ⁶⁴
familiar with every detail of its shape.⁵ ⁶⁵

It seems to me that this narrative is inherently interesting, but particularly so to anyone who is speculating about where ideas (including subjects
for essays) come from.

⁵Carl G. Jung, "Approaching the Unconscious," *Man and His Symbols* (Garden City, N.Y.:
Doubleday, 1964), pp. 27–28. Copyright © 1964 by Carl G. Jung. Copyright © 1964 by Doubleday
& Company, Inc. Reprinted by permission of Doubleday & Company, Inc., and the Jung Estate.

Background of Knowledge and Experience

If an idea is a plant that grows according to its own dynamics, then certainly the intellectual background of the author of the idea is the soil in which the plant grows. As Jung tells us in his first paragraph, the rich and exciting field of the new Freudian psychology was the soil in which his own ideas could blossom.

Needless to say, Freudian theory is one of humanity's great intellectual constructs. However, Jung has a hunch, a feeling, that all is not right or complete: "But after a time I began to *feel* that this was a misleading and inadequate use of the rich fantasies that the unconscious produces in sleep" (lines 16–18; emphasis added). Jung is uneasy; he feels that something is wrong, but doesn't know what.

The Crystallizing Experience

And then comes the crystallizing experience: his friend's tale about the train ride in Russia. "My doubts really began . . ." (line 18).

Notice how important this one experience was for Jung. It was the insight, the breakthrough that he needed. In his own narrative, he dwells on it in some detail.

Insight

The result was great insight (lines 31–43): "This episode opened my eyes to the fact that it was not necessary to use a dream as the point of departure for the process of 'free association' if one wished to discover the complexes of a patient."

One idea leads to another (lines 44–52), and this chain of thought and experience eventually leads to the great breakthrough that is outlined in the last two paragraphs.

To summarize: Jung didn't start from scratch; he had his own immersion in Freudian theory to begin with. He relied on hunches and feelings, on his own intuition and subconscious. He was ready to see the meaning in the experience that triggered his new insight. Once he had achieved the insight, he followed up its implications, and this following-up led to a dramatic breakthrough in his theory. Once the breakthrough had been achieved, he worked on the implications of his new theories. And we can boil all this down into a series of sentences that serve as advice for writers:

1. In searching for subjects, stay in areas that you know a good deal about.
2. Use your subconscious; don't imagine that all your ideas will result from conscious, systematic thinking. Play your hunches.
3. Be ready for the insight that will set you off.
4. Work on the insight until you know what its implications are, and then state those implications.

Materials at Hand

Ted Hughes provides another discussion of subjects that find the writer:

23   Are your relatives a nuisance? Perhaps you are like a person I know, whose
life is absolutely swamped by brothers, sisters, uncles, aunts and cousins. The
trouble with relatives is, you did not choose them and now you cannot change
them: you are stuck with them whether you like them or not. And they seem to
think they own you as if you were their pet cat or something of that sort. They
feel they have a right to know all about what you are doing, and if they do not
like it they say, "You'll have to stop that," and they begin to give you advice.
They can be a nuisance.

On the other hand, they can be endlessly interesting, and to a writer nothing
is quite so interesting or important as his relatives. Now why should this be
so?

All writers agree, you cannot write about something for which you have no
feeling. Unless something interests or excites you or belongs to your life in a
deep way, then you just cannot think of anything to say about it. The words
will not come. Now, unless you are an unusual person, you will never in this
world get to know anybody quite as well as you know your relatives, and your
feeling will never be tied up with anybody or with anything quite so deeply as
it is with them. Accordingly, most writers find they have plenty to say about
their relatives. And these feelings we have for our relatives are not unshakeably fixed to those particular people. This is one of the curious facts
about feelings. If we get on well with our brother, we tend to be attracted to
make friends with boys or men who remind us of our brother, and begin to feel
that this new friendship is somehow using the feeling we originally had for
our brother alone. In the same way, if you are a writer, and you invent a
character who reminds you in some way of your brother, then all your old
feelings about your brother flow into this invented character and help to bring
it to life. Some very great writers have written their best books in this way,
rearranging their relatives in imagination, under different names and appearances of course.[6]

As Hughes says, everyone—or almost everyone—is surrounded by relatives, and they're all subjects that find the writer. By extension, all of us are
surrounded by the details of our own lives: relationships with people, tastes
in food, passions for certain ideas, habits and ambitions, embarrassing
failures and satisfying successes. You have your own mind—as another
poet put it, your dreams, lies, and wishes.

But, says Hughes, "All writers agree, you cannot write about something
for which you have no feeling. Unless something interests or excites you or
belongs to your life in a deep way, then you just cannot think of anything to
say about it."

Finally, Hughes makes a point that is worth taking seriously: "these
feelings we have for our relatives are not unshakeably fixed to those
particular people." What he is saying is that we can extend our own
immediate perceptions beyond ourselves. Interest in a little brother can be
projected onto little boys in general. Involvement with a hobby—say coin
collecting—can result in an extended interest in, for instance, national

[6]Ted Hughes, *Poetry Is* (Garden City, N.Y.: Doubleday, 1970), pp. 82–83. Copyright © 1967 by Ted
Hughes. Reprinted by permission of Doubleday & Company, Inc.

money systems, great collectors, the economics of coin collecting, acquisitiveness . . . .

And now a statement that will appear contradictory: All subjects must find you, for you can never find a subject. As Ted Hughes has implied, the concrete and abstract things out there in the universe—all of which *might* be subjects for writing—have no meaning until they become a part of you emotionally or intellectually. Therefore, the subjects will find you, will come from you and nowhere else.

Focusing the Subject

My younger son has an admirable goal in life: he wants to start a business and make, as he says, scads of money. Needless to say, I wish him well and am glad that he has an ambition to carry him into the future. However, his general goal is not enough. You can't merely be in business; you must be in a given business. At the moment, my son finds the motel business to be attractive. Therefore, he has made an important strategic move: he has narrowed his general goal of becoming a millionaire to the specific goal of making money through innkeeping. If, indeed, he keeps this goal, he and I can begin to plan his tactics for accomplishing it; we can look toward a degree in business administration for him, with specialized postgraduate work in hotel-motel management. Ultimately, he can try to get into the business and finally come up with the financing to start his own chain.

Subject and Topic

And this is pretty nearly the situation in writing. With general goals (such as the desire to make a million dollars) we can equate subject, a broad area of interest; with specific goals (such as innkeeping), we can equate topic, the relatively narrow part of the subject that will be dealt with. (Notice the specialized use of **subject** and **topic.** These are handy terms that will simplify the discussion that is to follow.)

In discussing subject and topic, I would like first to simplify—and therefore falsify—the process whereby a writer comes to the realization that *this* is the topic he or she wants to deal with. After the simplification, I'll turn back and trace the development of topic in the whole composing process.

Briefly, then, let's establish a simple but crucial point.

A subject, such as commercial TV, for instance, is far too broad to serve as a topic for an essay. A topic such as situation comedies is perhaps manageable. You could survey the situation comedies currently playing on TV and write about them. But the topic "situation comedies" has no direction: what *about* situation comedies?

Getting a topic that you want to write about, then, involves narrowing a subject and finding out what you want to say about that narrowed subject, or topic. The following statements could work as topics that would yield interesting essays:

1. TV situation comedies falsify the nature of American life.

2. TV situation comedies reveal much about the tastes and aspirations of the American people.
3. The humor in situation comedy X is built around certain themes and devices.
4. TV situation comedies insult my intelligence.

Finding a Topic: A Case History

An instructive description of how a writer finds a topic is Tom Wolfe's introduction to his book *The Kandy-Kolored Tangerine-Flake Streamline Baby:*

24   I don't mean for this to sound like "I had a vision" or anything, but there was a specific starting point for practically all of these stories. I wrote them in a fifteen-month period, and the whole thing started with the afternoon I went to a Hot Rod & Custom Car show at the Coliseum in New York. Strange afternoon! I was sent up there to cover the Hot Rod & Custom Car show by the New York *Herald Tribune*, and I brought back exactly the kind of story any of the somnambulistic totem newspapers in America would have come up with. A totem newspaper is the kind people don't really buy to read but just to *have*, physically, because they know it supports their own outlook on life. They're just like the buffalo tongues the Omaha Indians used to carry around or the dog ears the Mahili clan carried around in Bengal. There are two kinds of totem newspapers in the country. One is the symbol of the frightened chair-arm-doilie Vicks Vapo-Rub *Weltanschauung* that lies there in the solar plexus of all good gray burghers. All those nice stories on the first page of the second section about eighty-seven-year-old ladies on Gramercy Park who have one-hundred-and-two-year-old turtles or about the colorful street vendors of Havana. Mommy! This fellow Castro is in there, and revolutions may come and go, but the picturesque poor will endure, padding around in the streets selling their chestnuts and salt pretzels the world over, even in Havana, Cuba, assuring a paradise, after all, full of respect and obei-sance, for all us Vicks Vapo-Rub chair-arm-doilie burghers. After all. Or another totem group buys the kind of paper they can put under their arms and have the totem for the tough-but-wholesome outlook, the Mom's Pie view of life. Everybody can go off to the bar and drink a few "brews" and retail some cynical remarks about Zora Folley and how the fight game is these days and round it off, though, with how George Chuvalo has "a lot of heart," which he got, one understands, by eating mom's pie. Anyway, I went to the Hot Rod & Custom Car show and wrote a story that would have suited any of the totem newspapers. All the totem newspapers would regard one of these shows as a sideshow, a panopticon, for creeps and kooks; not even wealthy, eccentric creeps and kooks, which would be all right, but lower class creeps and nutballs with dermatitic skin and ratty hair. The totem story usually makes what is known as "gentle fun" of this, which is a way of saying, don't worry, these people are nothing.

So I wrote a story about a kid who had built a golden motorcycle, which he called "The Golden Alligator." The seat was made of some kind of gold-painted leather that kept going back, on and on, as long as an alligator's tail, and had scales embossed on it, like an alligator's. The kid had made a whole golden suit for himself, like a space suit, that also looked as if it were covered with scales and he would lie down on his

stomach on this long seat, stretched out full length, so that he appeared 42
to be made into the motorcycle or something, and roar around Greenwich 43
Village on Saturday nights, down Macdougal Street, down there in Nuts 44
Heaven, looking like a golden alligator on wheels. Nutty! He seemed like 45
a Gentle Nut when I got through. It was a shame I wrote that sort of 46
story, the usual totem story, because I was working for the *Herald* 47
Tribune, and the *Herald Tribune* was the only experimental paper in 48
town, breaking out of the totem formula. The thing was, I knew I had 49
another story all the time, a bona fide story, the real story of the Hot Rod 50
& Custom Car show, but I didn't know what to do with it. It was outside 51
the system of ideas I was used to working with, even though I had been 52
through the whole Ph.D. route at Yale, in American Studies and every- 53
thing. 54

Here were all these . . . *weird* . . . nutty-looking, crazy baroque custom 55
cars, sitting in little nests of pink angora angel's hair for the purpose of 56
"glamorous" display—but then I got to talking to one of the men who 57
make them, a fellow named Dale Alexander. He was a very serious and 58
soft-spoken man, about thirty, completely serious about the whole thing, 59
in fact, and pretty soon it became clear, as I talked to this man for a 60
while, that he had been living like the *complete artist* for years. He had 61
starved, suffered—the whole thing—so he could sit inside a garage and 62
create these cars which more than 99 per cent of the American people 63
would consider ridiculous, vulgar and lower-class-awful beyond com- 64
ment almost. He had started off with a garage that fixed banged-up cars 65
and everything, to pay the rent, but gradually he couldn't stand it 66
anymore. Creativity—his own custom car art—became an obsession with 67
him. So he became the complete custom car artist. And he said he wasn't 68
the only one. All the great custom car designers had gone through it. It 69
was the *only way. Holy beasts!* Starving artists! Inspiration! Only 70
instead of garrets, they had these garages. 71

So I went over to *Esquire* magazine after a while and talked to them 72
about this phenomenon, and they sent me out to California to take a look 73
at the custom car world. Dale Alexander was from Detroit or some place, 74
but the real center of the thing was in California, around Los Angeles. I 75
started talking to a lot of these people, like George Barris and Ed Roth, 76
and seeing what they were doing, and—well, eventually it became the 77
story from which the title of this book was taken, "The Kandy-Kolored 78
Tangerine-Flake Streamline Baby." But at first I couldn't even write the 79
story. I came back to New York and just sat around worrying over the 80
thing. I had a lot of trouble analyzing exactly what I had on my hands. By 81
this time *Esquire* practically had a gun at my head because they had a 82
two-page-wide color picture for the story locked into the printing presses 83
and no story. Finally, I told Byron Dobell, the managing editor at 84
Esquire, that I couldn't pull the thing together. O.K., he tells me, just 85
type out my notes and send them over and he will get somebody else to 86
write it. So about 8 o'clock that night I started typing the notes out in the 87
form of a memorandum that began, "Dear Byron." I started typing away, 88
starting right with the first time I saw any custom cars in California. I 89
just started recording it all, and inside of a couple of hours, typing along 90
like a madman, I could tell that something was beginning to happen. By 91
midnight this memorandum to Byron was twenty pages long and I was 92
still typing like a maniac. About 2 A.M. or something like that I turned on 93
WABC, a radio station that plays rock and roll music all night long, and 94

got a little more manic. I wrapped up the memorandum about 6:15 A.M., 95
and by this time it was 49 pages long. I took it over to *Esquire* as soon as 96
they opened up, about 9:30 A.M. About 4 P.M. I got a call from Byron 97
Dobell. He told me they were striking out the "Dear Byron" at the top of 98
the memorandum and running the rest of it in the magazine. That was 99
the story, "The Kandy-Kolored Tangerine-Flake Streamline Baby." 100
  What had happened was that I started writing down everything I had 101
seen the first place I went in California, this incredible event, a "Teen 102
Fair." The details themselves, when I wrote them down, suddenly made 103
me see what was happening. Here was this incredible combination of 104
form plus money in a place nobody ever thought about finding it, namely, 105
among teen-agers. Practically every style recorded in art history is the 106
result of the same thing—a lot of attention to form, plus the money to 107
make monuments to it. The "classic" English style of Inigo Jones, for 108
example, places like the Covent Garden and the royal banquet hall at 109
Whitehall, were the result of a worship of Italian Palladian grandeur . . . 110
plus the money that began pouring in under James I and Charles I from 111
colonial possessions. These were the kind of forms, styles, symbols . . . 112
Palladian classicism . . . that influence a whole society. But throughout 113
history, everywhere this kind of thing took place. China, Egypt, France 114
under the Bourbons, every place, it has been something the aristocracy 115
has been responsible for. What has happened in the United States since 116
World War II, however, has broken that pattern. The war created money. 117
It made massive infusions of money into every level of society. Suddenly 118
classes of people whose styles of life had been practically invisible had 119
the money to build monuments to their own styles.[7] 120

  This piece tells us more about the emergence of a topic from a general
subject than anything else I can think of.

Analysis of Wolfe

  Wolfe's discovery of a topic, one that resulted first in the title essay of his
book and finally in the whole book, did not come about through a simple
cookbook procedure. That is, he did not follow a set of directions: first do
this and then do this and then do this. And I think that one learns more
about writing from examining writing and how people do it than from sets
of instructions—though, heaven knows, this book contains enough sets of
instructions.
  Anyway, Wolfe first encounters a subject. He encounters it in much the
same way that most writing students encounter theirs: he is given an
assignment. A newspaper editor tells him to visit a hot rod and custom car
show and write about it.
  Being a good newspaperman, Wolfe has a formula for writing stories, and
he turns out the usual stuff, "exactly the kind of story any of the somnambulistic totem newspapers in America would have come up with" (lines
7–8); that is, he had mastered a formula and could use it almost automatically.

[7]Tom Wolfe, *The Kandy-Kolored Tangerine-Flake Streamline Baby* (New York: Farrar, Straus
& Giroux, 1965). Reprinted with permission of Farrar, Straus & Giroux, Inc. Copyright © 1965
by Tom Wolfe.

Then Wolfe tells us that he became interested in the kid who had built the golden motorcycle, and Wolfe is sorry to have written about him in the usual condescending, totem way. And Wolfe is also trapped by his own preconceptions and writing habits: "The thing was, I knew I had another story all the time, a bona fide story, the real story of the Hot Rod & Custom Car Show, but I didn't know what to do with it. It was outside the system of ideas I was used to working with . . ." (lines 49–52).

Suddenly Wolfe has a breakthrough that allows him to escape the system of ideas that had confined him. He draws an analogy between the car customizers and artists. The analogy works. "*Holy beasts!* Starving artists! Inspiration! Only instead of garrets, they had these garages" (lines 70–71).

A topic is beginning to form, and Wolfe proposes to do an article for *Esquire.* It is important to note that he does not yet have a topic—only a deadline. So in desperation, he begins to type; he must turn something out. "I started typing away, starting right with the first time I saw any custom cars in California. I just started recording it all, and inside of a couple of hours, typing along like a madman, I could tell that something was beginning to happen" (lines 88–91).

He has a topic for a thesis: "The war created money. It made massive infusions of money into every level of society. Suddenly classes of people whose styles of life had been practically invisible had the money to build monuments to their own styles" (lines 117–20).

At what point did Wolfe's topic emerge? The answer, I think, is that it grew as the composing process went along. Only after a good deal of writing was done did the author himself know exactly what his topic was. He narrowed and focused as he worked.

It should be said, however, that it is not uncommon for a writer to have the topic ready-made before beginning the actual writing.

Generalizing is difficult and risky. Sometimes we write *in order to find out what we think.* At other times, we know quite precisely what we want to say, and the big question becomes *how.* Nonetheless, writing is an organic process, and the individual piece develops itself as much as the writer develops it. The minute you put down your first sentence, you have opened some possibilities and closed others. If, as my first sentence, I write, "Situation comedies interest me," I have begun to set up a causative network that will become more complex as I proceed. From all the possible subjects in the universe, I have chosen situation comedies, and I have injected my own opinion into the essay. If readers are interested at all in the subject, I will have set up expectations in them. They are going to want to know what it is about situation comedies that interests me. Therefore, my working out of the essay involves not only the subject that I have chosen, but also the promises that I make to readers with every word I write.

Because the composing process is so infinitely complex, I am reluctant to give you pat models that will falsify that complexity. I would much prefer to assume that in ways no one understands, the learner internalizes tactics and strategies; the best that a textbook about writing can do is to bring to the level of consciousness *some* of the possible ways in which composition can be accomplished.

Examples of Focusing

It might be well to conclude this discussion of focusing with some examples and comments.

25   *Subject:* Sex
      Narrowing: Homosexuality
      Narrowing: The Gay Liberation Front
      Topic: The Gay Liberation Front at my college

Sex is so large a subject that it overwhelms. It's a mountainous concept, and you must blast away a small chunk on which you can begin sculpting. (Seldom is a sculptor as ambitious as Gutzon Borglum, the man who planned and executed the portraits at Mount Rushmore. Normally the sculptor, like Michelangelo, knows that the subject is hiding in a relatively small piece of marble that has been taken from the quarry.) Even the Gay Liberation Front is such a big chunk that you probably can't get it into your studio to begin work with hammer and chisel. But once you get down to "The Gay Liberation Front at my college," you have materials that are workable for a relatively brief essay.

To carry on the sculpting metaphor: "The Gay Liberation Front at my college" is a workable chunk of marble, but hiding within that chunk are countless possibilities. After all, a sculptor can make a man or a woman, a mythical beast or a bear, emerge from a block of marble. You can give your topic focus by formulating a sentence concerning it. Notice how this works:

26   What are the objectives of the Gay Liberation Front at my college?

27   The Gay Liberation Front at my college should be given official status as a student organization.

Suddenly, once you put your topic into a sentence, it assumes a direction, a purpose. Writing on the basis of sentence **26**, the student would systematically outline and explain the objectives of the Gay Liberation Front, and writing on the basis of sentence **27**, the student would argue in behalf of a proposition.

At this point, it is well to remember that Tom Wolfe did not develop a thesis until after he began to write. It is an oversimplification and a falsification to say that one must have a clear-cut purpose or a thesis before one begins to put sentences and paragraphs down on paper. It is even a falsification to say that every essay, after it is written, will have a clear-cut purpose that can be summarized in one sentence, though most do.

Another example:

28   *Subject:* Writing
      Narrowing: Expository writing
      Narrowing: Expository writing in freshman English
      Topic: My problems with expository writing in freshman English

The topic "My problems with expository writing in freshman English" can yield a variety of focuses, thus:

29   My high school English classes did not prepare me for college writing.

30   I find the writing instruction in my freshman English class irrelevant to my educational goals.

31   It is difficult for me to write on assigned topics and according to the timetable established in the class.

32   The emphasis in my freshman English class should be on practical kinds of writing such as library papers, technical reports, and business letters.

Sentence **29** requires the writer to do a complete survey of the kinds of instruction received in high school and to show its inadequacies in the light of college writing. Sentence **30** implies that the writer should outline his or her educational goals and then demonstrate why his or her college writing class is irrelevant to those goals. Sentence **31** gives the writer a chance to write about his or her methods of composing and would demand a great deal of self-scrutiny. And sentence **32** demands an argument in behalf of a viewpoint.

The important point about narrowing and focusing, in short, is that the writer needs to determine, at some point in the composing process, where the writing is going.

Gathering Material

The methods whereby the writer can gather materials for composition will be discussed in detail in the next chapter. At this point, only a brief survey of the subject will be presented. Once again, the *writer-context-structure-style-audience* schema will be used as our principle of organization.

The Writer as a Resource

As the writer, you have your own resources, your past experiences, your perceptions, your dreams, your feelings; you can draw upon your own inner life for material.

33   *Social* also means *economic,* as any reader of nineteenth-century European philosophy will understand. The economic is part of the social—and in our time much more so than what we have known as the spiritual or metaphysical, because the most valuable canons of power have either been reduced or traduced into stricter economic terms. That is, there has been a shift in the actual meaning of the world since Dante lived. As if Brooks Adams were right. Money does not mean the same thing to me it must mean to a rich man. I cannot, right now, think of one meaning to name. This is not so simple to understand. Even as a simple term of the English language, money does not possess the same meanings for the rich man as it does for me, a lower-middle-class American, albeit of laughably "aristocratic" pretensions. What possibly can "money" mean to a poor man? And I am not talking now about those courageous products of our permissive society who walk knowledgeably into "poverty" as they would into a public toilet. I mean, The Poor.

   I look in my pocket; I have seventy cents. Possibly I can buy a beer. A quart of ale, specifically. Then I will have twenty cents with which to annoy and seduce my fingers when they wearily search for gainful employment. I have no idea at this moment what that seventy cents will mean to my neighbor around the corner, a poor Puerto Rican man I have seen hopefully watching my plastic garbage can. But I am certain it cannot mean the same thing. Say to David Rockefeller, "I have money," and he will think you mean something entirely different. That is, if you also dress the part. He would not for a moment think, "Seventy cents." But then neither would many New York painters.[8]

In his first paragraph, LeRoi Jones develops his thesis that "*Social* also means *economic.*" In the second paragraph he illustrates and supports his argument on the basis of his own personal experience. The whole passage is developed on the basis of Jones's own attitudes and ideas. He needs no research to present his ideas.

One of the handful of books that are at the very fiber of America is Henry David Thoreau's *Walden.* Toward the middle of the nineteenth century, Thoreau built his cabin on the shore of Walden Pond in Massachusetts and set out to live a kind of life that has become an American archetype, existing simply and relying on his daily experiences as well as introspection to provide the materials for his magnificent book. The following profound and timely passage is a glorious illustration of how the writer can be his own best resource.

34   I went to the woods because I wished to live deliberately, to front only the essential facts of life, and see if I could not learn what it had to teach, and not, when I came to die, discover that I had not lived. I did not wish to live what was not life, living is so dear; nor did I wish to practice resignation, unless it was quite necessary. I wanted to live deep and suck out all the marrow of life, to live so sturdily and Spartan-like as to put to rout all that was not life, to cut a broad swath and shave close, to drive life into a corner, and reduce it to its lowest terms, and, if it proved to be mean, why then to get the whole and genuine meanness of it, and publish its meanness to the world; or if it were sublime, to know it by experience, and be able to give a true account of it in my next excursion. For most men, it appears to me, are in a strange uncertainty about it, whether it is of the devil or of God, and have *somewhat hastily* concluded that it is the chief end of man here to "glorify God and enjoy him forever."

Still we live meanly, like ants; though the fable tell us that we were long ago changed into men; like pygmies we fight with cranes; it is error upon error, and clout upon clout, and our best virtue has for its occasion a superfluous and evitable wretchedness. Our life is frittered away by detail. An honest man has hardly need to count more than his ten fingers, or in extreme cases he may add his ten toes, and lump the rest. Simplicity, simplicity, simplicity! I say, let your affairs be as two or three, and not a hundred or a thousand; instead of a million count half a dozen, and keep your accounts on your thumb nail. In the midst of this chopping sea of civilized life, such are the clouds and storms and quicksands and thousand-and-one items to be allowed for, that a man has to live, if he would not founder and go to the bottom and not make his port at all, by dead reckoning, and he must be a great calculator indeed who succeeds. Simplify, simplify. Instead of three meals a

[8]LeRoi Jones, "Expressive Language," *Home: Social Essays* (New York: William Morrow, 1966), pp. 167–68. Reprinted by permission of William Morrow & Co., Inc. Copyright © 1963, 1966 by LeRoi Jones.

day, if it be necessary eat but one; instead of a hundred dishes, five; and reduce other things in proportion. Our life is like a German Confederacy, made up of petty states, with its boundary forever fluctuating, so that even a German cannot tell you how it is bounded at any moment. The nation itself, with all its so called internal improvements, which, by the way, are all external and superficial, is just such an unwieldy and overgrown establishment, cluttered with furniture and tripped up by its own traps, ruined by luxury and heedless expense, by want of calculation and a worthy aim, as the million households in the land; and the only cure for it as for them is in a rigid economy, a stern and more than Spartan simplicity of life and elevation of purpose. It lives too fast. Men think that it is essential that the *Nation* have commerce, and export ice, and talk through a telegraph, and ride thirty miles an hour, without a doubt, whether *they* do or not; but whether we should live like baboons or like men, is a little uncertain. If we do not get out sleepers, and forge rails, and devote days and nights to the work, but go to tinkering upon our *lives* to improve *them*, who will build railroads? And if railroads are not built, how shall we get to heaven in season? But if we stay at home and mind our business, who will want railroads? We do not ride on the railroad; it rides upon us. Did you ever think what those sleepers are that underlie the railroad? Each one is a man, an Irishman, or a Yankee man. The rails are laid on them, and they are covered with sand, and the cars run smoothly over them. They are sound sleepers, I assure you. And every few years a new lot is laid down and run over; so that, if some have the pleasure of riding on a rail, others have the misfortune to be ridden upon. And when they run over a man that is walking in his sleep, a supernumerary sleeper in the wrong position, and wake him up, they suddenly stop the cars, and make a hue and cry about it, as if this were an exception. I am glad to know that it takes a gang of men for every five miles to keep the sleepers down and level in their beds as it is, for this is a sign that they may sometime get up again.

Why should we live with such hurry and waste of life? We are determined to be starved before we are hungry. Men say that a stitch in time saves nine, and so they take a thousand stitches today to save nine to-morrow. As for work, we haven't any of any consequence. We have the Saint Vitus' dance, and cannot possibly keep our heads still. If I should only give a few pulls at the parish bell-rope, as for a fire, that is, without setting the bell, there is hardly a man on his farm in the outskirts of Concord, notwithstanding that press of engagements which was his excuse so many times this morning, nor a boy, nor a woman, I might almost say, but would forsake all and follow that sound, not mainly to save property from the flames, but, if we will confess the truth, much more to see it burn, since burn it must, and we, be it known, did not set it on fire,—or to see it put out, and have a hand in it, if that is done as handsomely; yes, even if it were the parish church itself. Hardly a man takes a half hour's nap after dinner, but when he wakes he holds up his head and asks, "What's the news?" as if the rest of mankind had stood his sentinels. Some give directions to be waked every half hour, doubtless for no other purpose; and then, to pay for it, they tell what they have dreamed. After a night's sleep the news is as indispensable as the breakfast. "Pray tell me any thing new that has happened to a man any where on this globe,"—and he reads it over his coffee and rolls, that a man has had his eyes gouged out this morning on the Wachito River; never dreaming the while that he lives in the dark unfathomed mammoth cave of this world, and has but the rudiment of an eye himself.

For my part, I could easily do without the post-office. I think that there are very few important communications made through it. To speak critically, I never received more than one or two letters in my life—I wrote this some years ago—that were worth the postage. The penny-post is, commonly, an institution through which you seriously offer a man that penny for his thoughts which is so often safely offered in jest. And I am sure that I never read any memorable news in a newspaper. If we read of one man robbed, or murdered, or killed by accident, or one house burned, or one vessel wrecked, or one steamboat blown up, or one cow run over on the Western Railroad, or one mad dog killed, or one lot of grasshoppers in the winter,—we never need read of another. One is enough. If you are acquainted with the principle, what do you care for a myriad instances and applications? To a philosopher all news, as it is called, is gossip, and they who edit and read it are old women over their tea. Yet not a few are greedy after this gossip. There was such a rush, as I hear, the other day at one of the offices to learn the foreign news by the last arrival, that several large squares of plate glass belonging to the establishment were broken by the pressure,—news which I seriously think a ready wit might write a twelvemonth or twelve years beforehand with sufficient accuracy. As for Spain, for instance, if you know how to throw in Don Carlos and the Infanta, and Don Pedro and Seville and Granada, from time to time in the right proportions,—they may have changed the names a little since I saw the papers,—and serve up a bull-fight when other entertainments fail, it will be true to the letter, and give us as good an idea of the exact state or ruin of things in Spain as the most succinct and lucid reports under this head in the newspapers: and as for England, almost the last significant scrap of news from that quarter was the revolution of 1649; and if you have learned the history of her crops for an average year, you never need attend to that thing again, unless your speculations are of a merely pecuniary character. If one may judge who rarely looks into the newspapers, nothing new does ever happen in foreign parts, a French revolution not excepted.

What news! how much more important to know what that is which was never old! "Kieou-he-yu (great dignitary of the state of Wei) sent a man to Khoung-tseu to know his news. Khoung-tseu caused the messenger to be seated near him, and questioned him in these terms: What is your master doing? The messenger answered with respect: My master desires to diminish the number of his faults, but he cannot accomplish it. The messenger being gone, the philosopher remarked: What a worthy messenger! What a worthy messenger!" The preacher, instead of vexing the ears of drowsy farmers on their day of rest at the end of the week,—for Sunday is the fit conclusion of an ill-spent week, and not the fresh and brave beginning of a new one,—with this one other draggletail of a sermon, should shout with thundering voice,— "Pause! Avast! Why so seeming fast, but deadly slow?"

Shams and delusions are esteemed for soundest truths, while reality is fabulous. If men would steadily observe realities only, and not allow themselves to be deluded, life, to compare it with such things as we know, would be like a fairy tale and the Arabian Nights' Entertainments. If we respected only what is inevitable and has a right to be, music and poetry would resound along the streets. When we are unhurried and wise, we perceive that only great and worthy things have any permanent and absolute existence—that petty fears and petty pleasures are but the shadow of the reality. This is always exhilarating and sublime. By closing the eyes and slumbering, and consenting to be deceived by shows, men establish and confirm their daily life of routine and habit every where, which still is built on purely illusory foundations. Children, who play life, discern its true law and relations more clearly than men, who fail to live it worthily, but who think that they are wiser by experience, that is, by failure. I have read in a Hindoo book, that "there was a king's son, who, being expelled in infancy from his native city, was brought up by a forester, and, growing up to maturity in that state, imagined himself to belong to the barbarous race with which he lived. One of his father's ministers having discovered him, revealed to him what he was, and the misconception of his character was removed, and he knew himself to be a prince. So soul," continues the Hindoo philosopher, "from the circumstances in which it is placed, mistakes its own character, until the truth is revealed to it by some holy teacher, and then it knows itself to be *Brahme*." I perceive that we inhabitants of New England live this mean life that we do because our vision does not penetrate the surface of things. We think that *is* which *appears* to be. If a man should walk through this town and see only the reality, where, think you, would the "Mill-dam" go to? If he should give us an account of the realities he beheld there, we should not recognize the place in his description. Look at a meeting-house, or a court-house, or a jail, or a shop, or a dwelling-house, and say what that thing really is before a true gaze, and they would all go to pieces in your account of them. Men esteem truth remote, in the outskirts of the system, behind the farthest star, before Adam and after the last man. In eternity there is indeed something true and sublime. But all these times and places and occasions are now and here. God himself culminates in the present moment, and will never be more divine in the lapse of all the ages. And we are enabled to apprehend at all what is sublime and noble only by the perpetual instilling and drenching of the reality that surrounds us. The universe constantly and obediently answers to our conceptions; whether we travel fast or slow, the track is laid for us. Let us spend our lives in conceiving then. The poet or the artist never yet had so fair and noble a design but some of his posterity at least could accomplish it.

Let us spend one day as deliberately as Nature, and not be thrown off the track by every nutshell and mosquito's wing that falls on the rails. Let us rise early and fast, or break fast, gently and without perturbation; let company come and let company go, let the bells ring and the children cry,—determined to make a day of it. Why should we knock under and go with the stream? Let us not be upset and overwhelmed in that terrible rapid and whirlpool called a dinner, situated in the meridian shallows. Weather this danger and you are safe, for the rest of the way is down hill. With unrelaxed nerves, with morning vigor, sail by it, looking another way, tied to the mast like Ulysses. If the engine whistles, let it whistle till it is hoarse for its pains. If the bell rings, why should we run? We will consider what kind of music they are like. Let us settle ourselves, and work and wedge our feet downward through the mud and slush of opinion, and prejudice, and tradition, and delusion, and appearance, that alluvion which covers the globe, through Paris and London, through New York and Boston and Concord, through church and state, through poetry and philosophy and religion, till we come to a hard bottom and rocks in place, which we can call *reality*, and say, This is, and no mistake; and then begin, having a *point d'appui*, below freshet and frost and fire, a place where you might found a wall or a state, or set a lamp-post safely, or perhaps a gauge, not a Nilometer, but a Realometer, that future ages might know how deep a freshet of shams and appearances had gathered from time to time. If you stand right fronting and face to face to a fact, you will see the sun glimmer on both its surfaces, as if it were a cimeter, and feel its sweet edge dividing you through the heart and marrow, and so you will happily conclude your mortal career. Be it life or death, we crave only reality. If we are really dying, let us hear the rattle in our throats and feel cold in the extremities; if we are alive, let us go about our business.

Time is but the stream I go a-fishing in. I drink at it; but while I drink I see the sandy bottom and detect how shallow it is. Its thin current slides away, but eternity remains. I would drink deeper; fish in the sky, whose bottom is pebbly with stars. I cannot count one. I know not the first letter of the alphabet. I have always been regretting that I was not as wise as the day I was born. The intellect is a cleaver; it discerns and rifts its way into the secret of things. I do not wish to be any more busy with my hands than is necessary. My head is hands and feet. I feel all my best faculties concentrated in it. My instinct tells me that my head is an organ for burrowing, as some creatures use their snout and fore-paws, and with it I would mine and burrow my way through these hills. I think that the richest vein is somewhere hereabouts; so by the divining rod and thin rising vapors I judge; and here I will begin to mine.

Context as a Resource

"The world out there," the context, is obviously the main source of materials for many writing tasks. We can get data about the world out there from observation, experimentation, reading. Every time a chemist writes up an experiment, he or she is recording the precise observation of a segment of context. A historian goes through stacks of musty documents, a student in a sociology class searches through the card catalogue and bibliographies in the library, a reporter follows up leads—and all these activities result in writing. The gathering and use of data are neatly summed up in a paragraph about dictionary making by Albert H. Marckwardt:

35   The making of a dictionary is both a science and an art. The painstaking accumulation of reliable data, consisting of thousands upon thousands of individual facts of the language; the proper classification of this data; and finally the formulation of sound conclusions from this mass of material—all illustrate the inductive process that is basic to every science. At the same time, the presentation of information about the language, the phrasing of definitions, and the ordering of word treatments demand of the lexicographer the ability to manipulate the language with economy and precision. The science without the art is likely to be ineffective; the art without the science is certain to be inaccurate.[9]

In expository writing, one goes to various sources to assemble data, one classifies these data, and finally one draws conclusions from them or interprets them.

Message as a Resource

It is perhaps not so obvious that the message, when we read, is a source of subject matter for writing. We can paraphrase its ideas; we can summarize; we can react pro or con. To give you an idea of how this works, read

[9]Albert H. Marckwardt, "Preface," *Funk & Wagnalls Standard College Dictionary* (New York: Harcourt Brace Jovanovich, 1963), p. vii.

the following poem and then look carefully at how Cleanth Brooks uses it as the basis for an essay:

36   *After Apple-Picking*[10]
                                  Robert Frost

My two-pointed ladder's sticking through a tree
Toward heaven still,
And there's a barrel that I didn't fill
Beside it, and there may be two or three
Apples I didn't pick upon some bough.
But I am done with apple-picking now.
Essence of winter sleep is on the night,
The scent of apples: I am drowsing off.
I cannot rub the strangeness from my sight
I got from looking through a pane of glass
I skimmed this morning from the drinking trough
And held against the world of hoary grass.
It melted, and I let it fall and break.
But I was well
Upon my way to sleep before it fell,
And I could tell
What form my dreaming was about to take.
Magnified apples appear and disappear,
Stem end and blossom end,
And every fleck of russet showing clear.
My instep arch not only keeps the ache,
It keeps the pressure of the ladder-round.
I feel the ladder sway as the boughs bend.
And I keep hearing from the cellar bin
The rumbling sound
Of load on load of apples coming in.
For I have had too much
Of apple-picking: I am overtired
Of the great harvest I myself desired.
There were ten thousand thousand fruit to touch,
Cherish in hand, lift down, and not let fall.
For all
That struck the earth,
No matter if not bruised or spiked with stubble,
Went surely to the cider-apple heap
As of no worth.
One can see what will trouble
This sleep of mine, whatever sleep it is.
Were he not gone,
The woodchuck could say whether it's like his
Long sleep, as I describe its coming on,
Or just some human sleep.

[10]Robert Frost, "After Apple-Picking," *The Poetry of Robert Frost,* ed. Edward Connery Lathem (New York: Holt, Rinehart and Winston, 1971). Copyright 1930, 1939, © 1969 by Holt, Rinehart and Winston, Inc. Copyright © 1958 by Robert Frost. Copyright © 1967 by Lesley Frost Ballantine. Reprinted by permission of Holt, Rinehart and Winston, Inc.

And here is what Cleanth Brooks says about Frost's poem.

37   In the more ambitious poems Frost's central problem is to develop depth of feeling without seeming to violate the realistic and matter of fact elements of the situation with which the poem deals.

His successful poems are thus successes in the handling of tone. Some of Frost's admirers, in insisting on the poet as a sort of kindly homespun philosopher, neglect the far more important matter: that popular poetry of this sort usually becomes pretentious or sentimental, and have thus failed to see that Frost's really remarkable pitch is considerably lower, the problem simpler, but the method is essentially that of the poets earlier discussed.

One of the best examples of management of tone occurs in "After Apple-Picking," a poem in which he extends his symbolism further, and achieves more intensity, than is usual for him. But to demonstrate this is to indicate that the poem is in reality a symbolist poem.

The concrete experience of apple-picking is communicated firmly and realistically; but the poem invites a metaphorical extension. The task of apple-picking, it is suggested, is any task; it is life.

The drowsiness which the speaker feels after the completion of the task is associated with the cycle of the seasons. Its special character is emphasized by a bit of magic, even though the magic is whimsical:

> Essence of winter sleep is on the night,
> The scent of apples: I am drowsing off.
> I cannot rub the strangeness from my sight
> I got from looking through a pane of glass
> I skimmed this morning from the drinking trough
> And held against the world of hoary grass.
> It melted, and I let it fall and break.

The speaker goes on to speculate playfully on the form that his dreaming will take. It will surely be about apples, for his instep arch still feels the pressures of the ladder rung, and his ears are still full of the rumble of apples rolling into the cellar bin. But he returns to the subject of his drowsiness, and the phrase, "whatever sleep it is," renews the suggestion that his sleepiness may not be merely ordinary human sleepiness:

> Were he not gone,
> The woodchuck could say whether it's like his
> Long sleep, as I describe its coming on,
> Or just some human sleep.

The end of the labor leaves the speaker with a sense of completion and fulfillment—in short, with a sense of ripeness which savors the fruit with which he has been working and of the season in which the work has been done. The ice sheet through which he has looked signals the termination of the harvest and the summons to the winter sleep of nature. The woodchuck has already begun his hibernation. The speaker does not over-emphasize his own connection with nature—the reference to the woodchuck is merely one more piece of whimsy—but the connection is felt.

The poem even suggests that the sleep is like the sleep of death. We are not to feel that the speaker is necessarily conscious of this. But perhaps we are to feel that, were the analogy to present itself to him, he would accept it. In the context defined in the poem, death might be considered as something eminently natural, as a sense of fulfillment mixed with a great deal of honest weariness and a sense of something well done—though with too much drowsiness for one to bother that every one of the apples had not been picked. The theme thus turns out to be a sort of rustic New England version of "Ripeness is all," though the theme is arrived at casually—stumbled over, almost—and with no effect of literary pretentiousness.[11]

Brooks's interpretation of the Frost poem is an excellent example of a principle: writing is meaningful to a reader. The data are the words, sentences, and so forth in the piece of writing, all of which must be interpreted by a reader before meaning comes into existence. Therefore you, as a reader, create meaning. The meaning that you create can be of great interest to another reader, if you work scrupulously and have a basis for your interpretation. That is how the message itself—the text that you read—is a source of material for writing.

Style as a Source

The style (code) of a piece is also a source of material for essays. As we have seen, you can talk about the message—what the piece says—but you can also talk about the way in which the message or meaning is conveyed; that is, you can do a stylistic analysis.

One easy system for approaching stylistic analysis will be discussed in Chapter 14. Briefly, it involves examination and analysis of word choice, figurative language, and sentence structure. The following is a good example of what can be done with the analysis of word choice. The paragraph concerns J. D. Salinger's popular novel *The Catcher in the Rye.*

38   Holden's informal, schoolboy vernacular is particularly typical in its "vulgarity" and "obscenity." No one familiar with prep-school speech could seriously contend that Salinger overplayed his hand in this respect. On the contrary, Holden's restraints help to characterize him as a sensitive youth who avoids the most strongly forbidden terms, and who never uses vulgarity in a self-conscious or phony way to help him be "one of the boys." Fuck, for example, is never used as a part of Holden's speech. The word appears in the novel four times, but only when Holden disapprovingly discusses its wide appearance on walls. The Divine name is used habitually by Holden only in the comparatively weak for God's sake, God, and goddam. The stronger and usually more offensive for Chrissake or Jesus or Jesus Christ are used habitually by Ackley and Stradlater; but Holden uses them only when he feels the need for a strong expression. He almost never uses for Chrissake in an unemotional situation. Goddam is Holden's favorite adjective. This word is used with no relationship to its original meaning, or to Holden's attitude toward the word to which it is attached. It simply expresses an emotional feeling toward the object: either favorable, as in "goddam hunting cap"; or unfavorable, as in "ya goddam moron"; or indifferent, as in "coming in the goddam windows." Damn is used interchangeably with goddam; no differentiation in its meaning is detectable.[12]

---

[11]Cleanth Brooks, *Modern Poetry and the Tradition* (Chapel Hill, N.C.: University of North Carolina Press, 1939), pp. 114–16. Reprinted by permission of the publisher.

[12]Donald P. Costello, "The Language of *The Catcher in the Rye,*" *American Speech,* 34 (Oct. 1959), 172–81.

Audience as a Resource

Finally, the *audience* that writing is intended for is a source of material for essays. The analysis of advertisements focuses our attention quickly on the possible audiences for which the ads are intended. This amusing paragraph from Vance Packard's *The Hidden Persuaders* is based on the concept of audience:

39 A motivationally minded executive of a Chicago ad agency claims his researchers have concluded that people who have body odors secretly don't want to give them up. He told me, "B. O. is a hostile act. A person with B. O. is like a skunk and uses his B.O. as a defense mechanism." His investigators reached this fascinating conclusion as a result of making a depth study for a soap firm that had tried to modify the odor of a pungent-smelling soap it had long marketed. When it brought the soap out with a pleasanter, milder odor, it received many vigorous complaints. The complaining customers apparently felt a strong subconscious attraction to the disagreeable odor. This man added, as if it were a most obvious fact: "People with extreme B. O. are extremely angry or hostile people. Their B. O. is a defense mechanism. They fear attack."

The paragraph is perhaps more amusing than informative or convincing, but it does illustrate how audience can be a source of material for writing.

Summary: Gathering Material

1. You can draw on your own experience.
2. You can observe and do research.
3. You can write about the ideas in the material that you read.
4. You can write about the style in which those ideas are expressed.

Planning: Sense and Nonsense About Outlines

Some writers prepare detailed outlines before they begin to write, but most don't. Most writers use some kind of brief outline or notes, but some writers don't. You just can't generalize. However, outlines can be useful. They act both as guides and as stimulants to thought—but they should never become straightjackets. To illustrate how outlines can be useful, we will discuss my planning of this chapter. I began with a fairly sketchy outline that looked like this:

40

Chapter 2
Survey of the Composing Process

Context
Prewriting
　Finding a subject
　Focusing the subject
　Gathering material
Planning
　The uses and misuses of outlines

> *The use of notes, journals, and so on*
> *A useful model of the creative process*
> Starting
> *Overcoming inertia*
> *The first paragraph*
> Revising
> *Deletion*
> *Reordering*
> *Substitution*
> *Embedding*
> Stopping
> *A quick check for completeness*
> *Some practical advice about conclusions*

Now this was a *working outline,* intended merely to give me some notion of where I was going—to keep me oriented during a rather lengthy job of composition.

As I typed the individual sections, I wrote further and more detailed outlines. These outlines and notes helped me form each section. The ideas for them were generated concurrently with the writing; I used these scribbled outlines to let myself know the way in which the section (and my thought) was developing.

Topic Outline

A detailed outline of this chapter's introduction and discussion of situation will serve two purposes: it will give you an idea of what my sketchy original outline actually generated, and it will serve as an example of outline form.

41

Chapter 2
Survey of the Composing Process

I. Introduction
  A. Knowing-that and knowing-how
  B. Interest in the conceptual background of the chapter
II. Situation
  A. Purpose
    1. In the real world
    2. In the composition class
  B. Constraints
    1. Place
    2. Time
      a. Example: Watergate
    3. Publication
      a. On television
      b. In national magazines
        I. Example from *McCall's*
        II. Example from *Oui*
        III. Example from *The New Yorker*
    4. Learning to adjust to constraints

This outline could have contained more detail, of course. What it illustrates quite vividly is the difference between my sketchy original plans and the manuscript that I actually produced.

Sentence Outline

The outline in **41** is a *topic outline.* It contains only phrases, no sentences. It could have been done as a *sentence outline:*

42

Chapter 2
Survey of the Composing Process

I. The chapter will explore the process of writing.
  A. In regard to any subject, there are two kinds of knowledge—knowing-that and knowing-how—and the chapter will deal with both kinds, emphasizing knowing-how.
  B. Though some of the details of the chapter may seem dry and obvious, the student should remember that the conceptual background on which the details are based (the way the mind generates language) is a rich and fascinating subject.
II. Writing always takes place in a situation.
  A. The purpose for writing comes from the writer's attempt to convey subject matter to an audience.
    1. In the real world, one has an actual purpose for writing.
    2. In the classroom, purpose is at least somewhat artificial.
  B. A variety of constraints influence what can be written.
    1. The place in which writing takes place is one such constraint.
    2. The time of the writing is another constraint.
      a. Years from now, readers will not remember the details of the Watergate affair.
    3. If writing is to be published in any form, the agency of publication is another important constraint.
      a. A good example is television, which forces writers to make a great many adjustments.
      b. National magazines demand a certain tone.
        I.   An example from *McCall's* illustrates a condescending, simple-minded tone.
        II. An example from *Oui* illustrates a pseudosophisticated prurience.
        III. An example from *The New Yorker* illustrates an almost rarefied sophistication.
    4. The writer must learn to recognize and adjust to constraints.

The Mechanics of Outlining

Now for some nuts-and-bolts advice about outline form. The numbering system used in the examples is standard and is generally accepted. Sentences and topics should not be mixed, as they are in the following example:

43 II. Situation
  A. The purpose of writing comes from the writer's attempt to convey subject matter to an audience.

    1. The real world
    2. The classroom
  B. A variety of constraints influence what can be said and how it can be said.

A telegraphic sentence is not a phrase. Thus, "Time of writing another constraint" is just another way of saying "Time of writing *is* another constraint." To put that in a phrase, you would need to say something like "The constraint of time."

Do not use single subtopics, except to indicate examples. A subject cannot be broken into one part. If you have I, you must have II; if you have A, you must have B. Thus, the following is inaccurate:

44
    I.
        A.
    II.
        A.
        B.
            1.
        C.

Summary: Outlining

The principle to understand about outlining is that you should use outlines to help your essays grow organically. Most writers do not simply make detailed outlines and then follow them to the letter as they compose. Your initial outline, if you use one, will give you a general idea of the shape of your subject. Your working outlines will help you develop your thoughts. Your final detailed outline—either sentence or topic—is made after the piece is completed and serves at least two purposes: it allows you to take a bird's-eye view of what you've written so that you can judge whether you have really accomplished your purpose, and it makes your reader's task easier by providing an overview of what is to come.

Starting: Overcoming Inertia

Getting the first sentence down on paper is often an agonizing process. The following discussion will outline some ways in which you can get the writing process under way.

Talk-Retalk-Write-Rewrite

Wilson Currin Snipes suggests a *talk-retalk-write-rewrite* strategy. Using a tape recorder, you merely talk: "talking includes what you normally call 'talking to yourself,' conversing, discussing, during which 'you talk off the top of your head,' associate ideas and attitudes freely, make tentative choices among possible points of view, ideas, attitudes, values."[13] That is, in the *talking* stage, you attempt to discover what you think.

Then you listen to what you have recorded, selecting the ideas that you want to preserve. You choose a tentative order for those ideas and then talk your way through them again; that is, you *retalk,* recording what you say.

In the *writing* stage, you listen to what you have said, make an informal outline, and write a first draft of your essay.

During the *rewriting* stage,

45 (1) You will refine this content, incorporating into what you say more carefully selected details, clearer examples and illustrations, statements from authorities and articles you have read, facts and statistics if these are available and appropriate, concrete experiences of things that have happened to you; (2) you will keep your audience in mind at all times, recognizing continuously that your object is to communicate your purpose, both your thoughts and feelings to this audience; and (3) you will make an effort to present a written composition that your audience can read and understand easily.[14]

The value of this plan is that it enables you to move from random talking into controlled writing. Speech, an activity that is natural to everyone, precipitates writing, an activity that, it seems to me, is natural to no one.

Another technique for getting under way, this one extremely simple: just begin writing; don't wait for the "right" idea or the "right" opening sentence. Remember that you can always throw away or revise the first page or so. Once the sentences begin to appear on the page, the essay stands a chance of finding its own direction.

The First Paragraph

Ultimately, for better or for worse, you must concoct an opening paragraph for your essay. Sometimes the opening paragraph of the final version is the first one that is written in the rough draft and stands without change. Other times the opening paragraph is the last one to be written.

Here are some opening paragraphs from essays, intended to make you aware of some of the opening gambits that experienced writers use.

A Summary Paragraph

46 American colleges and universities are wondering whether they are entering an era of basic change in the relations between students and their professors. The rules of student life are probably going to be liberalized; militant undergraduates, viewing themselves not without reason as an "exploited class," will ask for more than an advisory role in the formation of courses and curriculums. A new mode of student self-government, which extends both the duties and the rights of self-discipline, is long overdue. At the same time there

[13]Wilson Currin Snipes, "Oral Composing as an Approach to Writing," *College Composition and Communication.* 24 (May 1973), 200–05.
[14]*Ibid.*, p. 204.

is a growing concern that the demands for students' "rights" may take on the character of ideological pressures on the university and pose a threat to its fundamental work as the bearer and transmitter of the heritage of science and learning. An "ideological university" has ceased to be a community of free-minded scholars.[15]

This opening paragraph is a summary of the essay that follows. In fact, one could make a pretty good outline of the entire essay just by looking at the ideas in the opening paragraph. If you can write such a paragraph *before* you produce the rest of the first draft, then you will have made a great leap forward in your composing task, for it is clear that you have the body of your essay firmly in mind, and your job is to deal with each of the ideas fully enough to satisfy the reader. Of course, we can't say whether this author wrote his opening paragraph before or after he had completed the rest of his essay.

An Unexpected Twist

47   The wife of a new neighbor from up on the corner came down and walked up to my wife and started acting nice, which must have exhausted her.[16]

This short first paragraph does not indicate what is to come in the essay, but it is vivid and arresting; it catches the reader's interest with its unexpected twist.

A Question

48   Why were so few voices raised in the ancient world in protest against the ruthlessness of man? Why are human beings so obsequious, ready to kill and ready to die at the call of kings and chieftains?[17]

An essay can begin with a general question that the body of the essay answers.

"Once Upon a Time"

49   There was once a town in the heart of America where all life seemed in harmony with its surroundings. The town lay in the midst of a checkerboard of prosperous farms, with fields of grain and hillsides of orchards where, in spring, white clouds of bloom drifted above the green fields. In autumn, oak and maple and birch set up a blaze of color that flamed and flickered across a backdrop of pines. Then foxes barked in the hills and deer silently crossed the fields, half hidden in the mists of the fall mornings.

—Rachel Carson, *Silent Spring*

This descriptive-narrative paragraph is a variation of the "once-upon-a-time" beginning.

---

[15]Lewis S. Feuer, "The Risk Is Juvenocracy," *New York Times Magazine*, 18 Sept. 1966, p. 56.

[16]Jimmy Breslin, "The Sign in Jimmy Breslin's Front Yard," in *The World of Jimmy Breslin* (New York: Viking Press, 1967), p. 11.

[17]Abraham J. Heschel, "History," in *The Prophets* (New York: Harper & Row, 1969), p. 159.

A Statement of Purpose

50   You know you have to read "between the lines" to get the most out of anything. I want to persuade you to do something equally important in the course of your reading. I want to persuade you to "write between the lines." Unless you do, you are not likely to do the most efficient kind of reading.[18]

This is a clear, blunt statement of purpose, and it was a very effective way to start this particular essay.

An Analogy

51   Drawing a daily comic strip is not unlike having an English theme hanging over your head every day for the rest of your life. I was never very good at writing those English themes in high school, and I usually put them off until the last minute. The only thing that saves me in trying to keep up with a comic strip schedule is the fact that it is quite a bit more enjoyable.[19]

Schulz starts his essay by making an analogy between drawing a daily comic strip and writing English themes.

An Anecdote

52   Recently I have had occasion to live again near my old college campus. I went into a hole-in-the-wall bakery where the proprietor recognized me after ten years. "You haven't changed a bit, son," he said, "but can you still digest my pumpernickel? The stomach gets older, no? Maybe you want something softer now—a nice little loaf I got here."

—Herbert Gold, *The Age of Happy Problems*

You can start an essay with an anecdote from personal experience—one that is relevant to the topic of the essay.

Using Ingenuity

53   August Bank Holiday [in Britain]—a tune on an ice-cream cornet. A slap of sea and a tickle of sand. A fanfare of sunshades opening. A wince and whinny of bathers dancing into deceptive water. A tuck of dresses. A rolling of trousers. A compromise of paddlers. A sunburn of girls and a lark of boys. A silent hullabaloo of balloons.[20]

I don't know what *general* principle this example illustrates—or even if it should illustrate a general principle—but it's delightful, and it shows that verbal wit and ingenuity can invent novel beginnings that engage the reader.

   And that's the point that we're getting at here: there is no reason for every essay to begin with a simple announcement of the subject ("In the following paragraphs I intend to discuss . . ."), even though that bare,

---

[18]Mortimer J. Adler, "How to Mark a Book," *Saturday Review of Literature*, 6 July 1940, p. 11.
[19]Charles M. Schulz, "But a Comic Strip Has to Grow," *Saturday Review*, 12 April 1969, p. 73.
[20]Dylan Thomas, "Holiday Memory," in *Quite Early One Morning* (New York: New Directions Publishing, 1960), p. 33.

direct kind of opening is just right for some pieces. You should use your imagination to invent openings that fit your purpose and tone and that will engage the reader.

Revising

In the composing process, revision is an ongoing activity. Every time you change your mind about a word or a phrase, you are revising. Furthermore, most writers do a more or less thorough final revision once they have completed their manuscripts. Every revision comes from a tactical decision made by the author, either consciously or unconsciously. The following discussion will be aimed at exploring the realm of revision and at making tactical decisions easier.

Revisions can take place at the level of the word, and in Chapter 12, on words, a great deal will be said about this. Revisions can also be made at the level of the sentence, and much of Chapter 11, on the sentence, will deal with revision. Finally, writers revise larger chunks of their writing—paragraphs and sections—and we will talk about that sort of revision in Chapter 4, on the paragraph. For now, the sentence will serve as a good model for the general classes of revisions that a writer can make.

Ways of Revising

Deleting

You can delete elements from a sentence:

54   The fisherman ~~who was~~ at the front of the boat tied into a huge yellowtail.

Reordering

You can reorder elements in a sentence:

55   The councilman decided to run for mayor *at the very last minute.*
At the very last minute, the councilman decided to run for mayor.

Substituting

You can substitute elements in a sentence:

56   *Knowing that the class would wait patiently,* the professor dawdled.
Because he knew that the class would wait patiently, the professor dawdled.

Embedding

You can embed elements in a sentence:

57   The race will be terrifying. The race will be run on Memorial Day.
The race, *to be run on Memorial Day,* will be terrifying.

Deleting, reordering, substituting, embedding—these are the possible operations of revision at the sentence level and beyond. You should be aware of the nature of revision; frequently it's a simple matter, as a very bright senior girl in one of my classes explained: "When I discovered that I could use scissors and paste to rearrange the rough drafts of my essays, I'd solved one of my greatest writing problems."

Revising: An Example

In my own manuscript for this chapter, I have made all of the varieties of revisions at every level, from word to sentence to paragraph to section. For instance, a sentence on one page (page 51 in the book) looks like this:

58 You can give your topic focus by formulating a ~~thesis~~ sentence concerning it.

My reasons for crossing out ***thesis*** and substituting ***sentence*** are fairly complex, but show the kind of tactical decisions that a writer makes continually. In the first place, if I used ***thesis*** I felt that I would need to define it, and I didn't want to sidetrack the discussion for the definition of a technical term. Furthermore, a thesis is a proposition to be proved or disproved, supported or argued against, and I did not want to imply that all writing takes a definite stand and then follows inexorably through. Finally, I didn't want to give the impression that the main thrust of a piece of writing can always be summarized in one declarative sentence. Therefore, my substitution.

The following appears on another page of my manuscript for this chapter (page 62 of the book):

59 A detailed outline of ~~the~~ *this* chapter ~~so far~~ *'s introduction and discussion of situation* will ~~give you an idea~~ serve ~~a variety of~~ *two* : purposes. *I*t will give you an idea of what my sketchy original outline actually generated *, and*. *I*t will serve as an example of outline form. ~~And it will constitute a handy review of the chapter so far.~~

The final version of the passage, then, came out like this:

60 A detailed outline of this chapter's introduction and discussion of situation will serve two purposes: it will give you an idea of what my sketchy original outline actually generated, and it will serve as an example of outline form.

Here are the reasons for the revision:

After I had gotten well into the complete outline, I realized that I could make my point without doing as much as I had intended. The outlining was boring me, the writer, and I felt that reading the outline would bore you, the reader. Therefore, I decided not to do the total outline. This decision necessitated the changes that are indicated in **59**. Thus, you can see that a tactical decision to delete a large chunk of the planned discussion brought about revisions at the word and sentence level—revisions that deleted and substituted.

Much more about revising will come in later chapters. For the present, it is enough to realize the sorts of operations that revision involves and to know that it is an ongoing process, not reserved for "cleaning up" the penultimate manuscript.

The writing process is a complex of operations, all taking place simultaneously, at a rate so fast that the writer cannot possibly hope to understand every decision at the conscious level. A discussion of writing must stress the fearful complexity of what is going on and must not give the impression that writing is ever cut and dried.

Stopping

Finally, at some point, the composing process must end. You must make a final revision and type the final draft.

At the basis of stopping is a profound question: How do I know that I'm finished? That question can be translated, Is my essay conclusive? Will the reader think that I have adequately covered all the points that I raised in my essay? Will the reader be satisfied that I have delivered on my promises? Kenneth Burke says that form in writing "is an arousing and fulfillment of desires. A work has form in so far as one part of it leads a reader to anticipate another part, to be gratified by the sequence."[21] As soon as your essay leaves nothing more to be anticipated, it is concluded.

You should make a quick check of everything you write in order to ensure that you have completed every idea. The way to do this is to ask yourself if you have said enough about each point you raise so that the reader will know exactly what you're talking about. Have you left any questions unanswered? Have you left any ideas undeveloped?

And, of course, answering these questions is a difficult process that involves both your *knowledge of the subject* and your *awareness of the audience* that you are writing for. An example will illustrate the principle in action.

61
                          A Surfeit of Subcults[22]
                              Alvin Toffler

1   Thirty miles north of New York City, within easy reach of its towers, its traffic and its urban temptations, lives a young taxicab driver, a former soldier, who boasts 700 surgical stitches in his body. These stitches are not the result of combat wounds, nor of an accident involving his taxi. Instead, they are the result of his chief recreation: rodeo riding.

2   On a cab driver's modest salary, this man spends more than $1200 a year to own a horse, stable it, and keep it in perfect trim. Periodically hitching a horse-trailer to his auto, he drives a little over one hundred

[21]Kenneth Burke, *Counter-Statement* (Los Altos, Calif.: Hermes Publications, 1953), p. 124.
[22]Alvin Toffler, *Future Shock* (New York: Random House, 1970). Copyright © 1970 by Alvin Toffler. Reprinted by permission of Random House, Inc.

miles to a place outside Philadelphia called "Cow Town." There, with others like himself, he participates in roping, steer wrestling, bronco busting, and other strenuous contests, the chief prizes of which have been repeated visits to a hospital emergency ward.

3   Despite its proximity, New York holds no fascination for this fellow. When I met him he was twenty-three, and he had visited it only once or twice in his life. His entire interest is focused on the cow ring, and he is a member of a tiny group of rodeo fanatics who form a little-known underground in the United States. They are not professionals who earn a living from this atavistic sport. Nor are they simply people who affect Western-style boots, hats, denim jackets and leather belts. They are a tiny, but authentic subcult lost within the vastness and complexity of the most highly technological civilization in the world.

4   This odd group not only engages the cab driver's passion, it consumes his time and money. It affects his family, his friends, his ideas. It provides a set of standards against which he measures himself. In short, it rewards him with something that many of us have difficulty finding: an identity.

5   The techno-societies, far from being drab and homogenized, are honeycombed with just such colorful groupings—hippies and hot rodders, theosophists and flying saucer fans, skin-divers and sky-divers, homosexuals, computerniks, vegetarians, body-builders and Black Muslims.

6   Today the hammerblows of the super-industrial revolution are literally splintering the society. We are multiplying these social enclaves, tribes and mini-cults among us almost as fast as we are multiplying automotive options. The same destandardizing forces that make for greater individual choice with respect to products and cultural wares, are also destandardizing our social structures. This is why, seemingly overnight, new subcults like the hippies burst into being. We are, in fact, living through a "subcult explosion."

7   The importance of this cannot be overstated. For we are all deeply influenced, our identities are shaped, by the subcults with which we choose, unconsciously or not, to identify ourselves. It is easy to ridicule a hippie or an uneducated young man who is willing to suffer 700 stitches in an effort to test and "find" himself. Yet we are all rodeo riders or hippies in one sense: we, too, search for identity by attaching ourselves to informal cults, tribes or groups of various kinds. And the more numerous the choices, the more difficult the quest.

The first paragraph arouses a number of questions in the reader. Why does Toffler stress that the cab driver lives near the urban temptations of New York City? Why would a cab driver in New York State be interested in rodeo riding?

The second paragraph further arouses our interest, but it does not answer any questions. We learn how much the cowboy-cabbie spends to pursue his hobby, and we learn about "Cow Town."

The third paragraph begins to "pay off," in that it starts to satisfy our curiosity: apparently the cowboy-cabbie finds nothing in New York City that interests him; therefore, he has joined a subcult that is antiurban and that harks back to the preindustrial era in American history.

The fourth paragraph finally lays it on the line. The cabbie finds an *identity* in the rodeo subcult; that is why he joined it.

The fifth paragraph, you will note, generalizes, but it also raises more questions. We want to learn more about the colorful groupings that honeycomb our techno-society.

The sixth paragraph elaborates the idea introduced in the fifth and further arouses our curiosity concerning these subcults that apparently interest the author so much.

The seventh paragraph further arouses our curiosity; we definitely want an adequate discussion of the kinds of subcults that attract people; we sense that the author knows a good deal he's not telling us, and we want him to fulfill his promises by letting us in on his detailed knowledge. In short, we finish the reading with a sense of dissatisfaction. We feel that the piece is incomplete.

If the selection had been an essay, our feelings would have been justified, but, in fact, the seven paragraphs are only the introductory section of a long chapter on subcults. Once one has read the chapter, one has the feeling that the discussion is indeed complete.

Finally

In conclusion, I would like to say that . . . .

No. That sort of trite, hackneyed statement will never serve to end this chapter—or anything else. A conclusion such as the one that I just started is enough to make any reader yawn, and who wants the last response of the reader to a piece of writing to be a yawn (or a groan)? Instead, I'll end this chapter by purposely making it seem incomplete, by injecting, right here at the end, a note of inconclusiveness.

This chapter has covered much territory, but has left much territory uncovered. Do you have any questions concerning the composing process that the chapter has aroused but not answered?

Discussion and Activities

Situation

1. Examine the purposes for which you write. Do you ever write for impractical purposes, just to express yourself? Why or why not?
2. Be prepared to discuss your reactions to and problems with writing assignments that you receive in all your classes, not just English. Would you work better if you were allowed to choose your own subject and if you were not forced to meet deadlines?
3. Suppose that you know the details concerning a particularly grisly rape-murder and you intend to write an account of it. What will be the constraints if
   a. you are doing a report for a daily newspaper?
   b. you decide to write it up for an underground newspaper?

c. you have a contract to dramatize the event for television?

d. you use the subject for an English theme?

4. The following selection talks about some powerful constraints that are imposed on users of language, either written or spoken. Read it carefully, and be prepared to discuss its ideas concerning constraints.

Why Do Some Dialects Have More Prestige Than Others?[23]

In a specific setting, because of historical and other factors, certain dialects may be endowed with more prestige than others. Such dialects are sometimes called "standard" or "consensus" dialects. These designations of prestige are not inherent in the dialect itself, but are *externally imposed,* and the prestige of a dialect shifts as the power relationships of the speakers shift.

The English language at the beginning of its recorded history was already divided into distinct regional dialects. These enjoyed fairly equal prestige for centuries. However, the centralization of English political and commercial life at London gradually gave the dialect spoken there a preeminence over other dialects. This process was far advanced when printing was invented; consequently, the London dialect became the dialect of the printing press, and the dialect of the printing press became the so-called "standard" even though a number of oral readings of one text would reveal different pronunciations and rhythmic patterns across dialects. When the early American settlers arrived on this continent, they brought their British dialects with them. Those dialects were altered both by regional separation from England and concentration into sub-groups within this country as well as by contact with the various languages spoken by the Indians they found here and with the various languages spoken by the immigrants who followed.

At the same time, social and political attitudes formed in the old world followed to the new, so Americans sought to achieve linguistic marks of success as exemplified in what they regarded as proper, cultivated usage. Thus the dialect used by prestigious New England speakers early became the "standard" the schools attempted to teach. It remains, during our own time, the dialect that style books encourage us to represent in writing. The diversity of our cultural heritage, however, has created a corresponding language diversity and, in the 20th century, most linguists agree that there is no single, homogeneous American "standard." They also agree that, although the amount of prestige and power possessed by a group can be recognized through its dialect, no dialect is inherently good or bad.

The need for a written dialect to serve the larger, public community has resulted in a general commitment to what may be called "edited American English," that prose which is meant to carry information about our representative problems and interests. To carry such information through aural-oral media, "broadcast English" or "network standard" has been developed and given precedence. Yet these dialects are subject to change, too. Even now habit patterns from other types of dialects are being incorporated into them. Our pluralistic society requires many varieties of language to meet our multiplicity of needs.

[23]*Students' Right to Their Own Language* (Urbana, Ill.: National Council of Teachers of English, 1974), p. 5. Copyright © 1974 by the National Council of Teachers of English. Reprinted by permission of the publisher.

5. Go back to "The Thought-Fox," by Ted Hughes, on page 37. Read the poem carefully, and explain in one paragraph the point that Hughes seems to be making.

Prewriting

1. Reread the passage from *Understanding Media*, by Marshall McLuhan, on pages 39–40. List five theme topics that the passage suggests to you, and explain why you might like to write on each of them.
2. Formulate each of the five topics into a sentence that you think would serve as a good starting point for a relatively brief essay.
3. Use "The Uses of Writing: Self-Expression," the first chapter of this book, as a test case for discovering ideas to write about. Jot your ideas down in complete sentences. Use the following questions to generate your ideas:
   a. What sort of person does the author seem to be? How do I know? What elements in the chapter can I cite or quote in order to verify my impression?
   b. What is the structure of the chapter? Does it hang together? What is the logic of its development?
   c. What do I learn from the chapter? What do I disagree with? Why?
   d. What sort of language does the chapter use? Are there any prominent features of style that I can point to? What are they?
   e. What is my reaction to the chapter? Do I like it? Why? Do I find it uninteresting? Why?
4. Everyone has sudden breakthroughs in knowledge, moments when, almost in a flash, something becomes clear—the motives behind some action of a friend, the solution to a mathematical problem, the understanding of a riddle. Think of an instance in which you have had such a breakthrough and be prepared to discuss it, either orally or in writing. What was the nature of the problem? What seems to have been the crystallizing experience? What was the nature of the insight?
5. At random, without any attempt to organize, write down all the details that you can think of concerning your favorite relative. Think of looks, speech, actions, mannerisms. Be specific; give concrete details. Don't merely say, "My Uncle Clayton has gray hair," but characterize that hair; for example, "My Uncle Clayton has silvery gray hair, combed straight back in a pompadour and cascading down the back of his neck over his collar."
6. In a paragraph or two, summarize what you learned about the composing process from reading the selection by Tom Wolfe on pages 47–49.
7. For each of these subjects, state five items of information or specific ideas that you have concerning them: (a) United States foreign policy; (b) Montana; (c) roses; (d) mental illness; (e) elementary education. Do not consult any sources.
8. Without trying to put your ideas into any sort of logical order, discuss the selection from Thoreau on pages 53–57.

a. What sort of person does Thoreau seem to be? How do you know?
b. What is he trying to say? Can you state his thesis in one sentence?
c. Can you point to any interesting features of his style?
d. What is your personal reaction to the piece? Did it move or interest you? Why or why not?

9. In your own words, paraphrase Robert Frost's "After Apple-Picking" on page 58.

Planning

1. Discuss your use of outlines. Do you prepare a detailed outline before you begin to write? Do outlines help or hinder you in composing? What did you learn about outlining in your high school English courses?

2. Recently, I heard a panel discussion by four talented young screen-writers, Gloria Katz and Willard Huyck *(American Graffiti),* David Ward *(The Sting),* and John Milius *(Jeremiah Johnson).* Here, briefly, is what they said about their methods of composing. Katz and Huyck outline scenes on three-by-five cards, and then they arrange these cards into meaningful sequences. The cards serve as the "map" to guide the writers through their first draft of the script. After they have produced a first draft, they revise, often doing five or six complete versions. David Ward thinks his whole story through, working out every detail, before he sets pen to paper. Once he has the total story in mind, he writes the script, and his revisions are minor. John Milius thinks of a character or a situation and begins to write. He says that the ending of his script is as much a surprise to him as he hopes it will be to the audience.

   In your own words, summarize what the above paragraph tells you about planning a composition.

Starting

1. If you have a tape recorder, experiment with the talk-retalk-write-rewrite strategy (see pages 64–65). As an assignment, use this strategy to compose a paragraph or two in which you explain your reaction to the following passage from *The Secret Agent,* by Joseph Conrad:

   > Her hands shook so that she failed twice in the task of refastening her veil. Mrs. Verloc was no longer a person of leisure and irresponsibility. She was afraid. The stabbing of Mr. Verloc had been only a blow. It had relieved the pent-up agony of shrieks strangled in her throat, of tears dried up in her hot eyes, of the maddening and indignant rage at the atrocious part played by that man, who was less than nothing now, in robbing her of the boy. It had been an obscurely prompted blow. The blood trickling on the floor off the handle of the knife had turned it into an extremely plain case of murder. Mrs. Verloc, who always refrained from looking deep into things, was compelled to look into the very bottom of this thing. She saw there no haunting face, no reproachful shade, no vision of remorse, no sort of ideal conception. She saw there an object. That object was the gallows. Mrs. Verloc was afraid of the gallows.

She was terrified of them ideally. Having never set eyes on that last argument of men's justice except in illustrative woodcuts to a certain type of tales, she first saw them erect against a black and stormy background, festooned with chains and human bones, circled about by birds that peck at dead men's eyes. This was frightful enough, but Mrs. Verloc, though not a well-informed woman, had a sufficient knowledge of her country to know that gallows are no longer erected romantically on the banks of dismal rivers or on windswept headlands, but in the yards of jails. There within four high walls, as if into a pit, at dawn of day, the murderer was brought out to be executed, with a horrible quietness and, as the reports in the newspapers always said, "in the presence of the authorities." With her eyes staring on the floor, her nostrils quivering with anguish and shame, she imagined herself all alone amongst a lot of strange gentlemen in silk hats who were calmly proceeding about the business of hanging her by the neck. That—never! Never! And how was it done? The impossibility of imagining the details of such quiet execution added something maddening to her abstract terror. The newspapers never gave any details except one, but that one with some affectation was always there at the end of a meagre report. Mrs. Verloc remembered its nature. It came with a cruel burning pain into her head, as if the words "The drop given was fourteen feet" had been scratched on her brain with a hot needle. "The drop given was fourteen feet."

2. If your class is using a collection of essays—a reader—go through it and make a survey of the kinds of beginning paragraphs used in the essays. Discuss what you learn from professional writers regarding first paragraphs.

Prewriting: Generating Subject Matter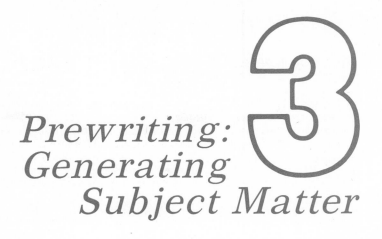

Summary of the Chapter

Once you find a subject, you must develop ideas about that subject, ideas that will result in a complete statement (essay, report, or whatever).

The *journal* is a significant aid to invention (developing ideas), primarily because it acts as a stimulus to the subconscious, a major factor in the development of ideas for writing.

Another way of inventing subject matter is unsystematic but effective: *brainstorming.* You ask as many questions as you can think of concerning your subject. In answering those questions, you develop subject matter.

Heuristics—procedures for developing ideas, for discovering subject matter—are more or less systematic devices that aid the writer.

The *Pentad* is one heuristic for analyzing—and thus developing ideas about—either spoken or written discourse. It is based on analysis of the message itself, the author, the source of publication, the time and place of publication, and the purpose.

A second procedure involves stating the topic as a problem; this heuristic then develops ideas for analyzing and solving the problem, and hence generates material for an essay.

The third heuristic consists of a series of questions that can be asked about any subject (whether a concrete thing or an abstraction): What features characterize it? How does it fit into larger systems of which it is a part? How is it changing? What are the parts, and how do they work together?

The chapter ends with a series of questions that can be used to develop subject matter about a variety of kinds of topics.

Chapter 2 outlined some of the problems that the writer encounters *before actually beginning to write.* This chapter will offer some detailed, systematic solutions to those problems. "Once I have chosen my subject, how can I discover things to say about it?" That is the question to be answered in this chapter.

From Self-Expression to Exposition: The Journal

The more you write, the better and more easily you'll write. Here is advice from one successful writer, Donald Hall: "While you are learning to write, it is a good idea to write something every day. Continual application of pen to paper will ease the work of writing, and will give you a collection of words and sentences in which to look for ideas and for work to revise."[1]

The journal, as noted in Chapter 1 on self-expressive writing, is the ideal mode for daily writing. Its usefulness cannot be overestimated.

The Journal: An Example

Let me start out by citing a dramatic example. In Chapter 2, a long passage from Thoreau's *Walden* was cited. If you do not remember that passage, go back and renew your acquaintance with it, and then read the following from Thoreau's journal entry for July 6, 1846:

1   I wish to meet the facts of life—the vital facts, which are the phenomena or actuality the gods meant to show us—face to face, and so I came down here. Life! who knows what it is, what it does? If I am not quite right here, I am less wrong than before; and now let us see what they will have. The preacher, instead of vexing the ears of drowsy farmers on their day of rest at the end of the week,—for Sunday always seemed to me like a fit conclusion of an ill-spent week and not the fresh and brave beginning of a new one,—with this one other draggletail and postponed affair of a sermon, from thirdly to fifteenthly, should teach them with a thundering voice pause and simplicity. "Stop! Avast! Why so fast?" In all studies we go not forward but rather backward with redoubled pauses. We always study *antiques* with silence and reflection. Even time has a depth, and below its surface the waves do not lapse and roar. I wonder men can be so frivolous almost as to attend to the gross form of negro slavery, there are so many keen and subtle masters who subject us both. Self-emancipation in the West Indies of a man's thinking and imagining provinces, which should be more than his island territory,—one emancipated heart and intellect! It would knock off the fetters from a million slaves.

You see, this journal entry of some 240 words served as the basis—the germinating seed—for a long passage in Thoreau's classic book. Just one example of how he transformed the journal into the finished manuscript

[1]Donald Hall, *Writing Well* (Boston: Little, Brown, 1973), p. 19.

will emphasize both the usefulness of a journal and the generative process of composition. In the journal, Thoreau says,

2   Even time has a depth, and below its surface the waves do not lapse and roar.

In *Walden,* Thoreau uses this somewhat bare metaphoric idea thus:

3   Time is but the stream I go a-fishing in. I drink at it; but while I drink I see the sandy bottom and detect how shallow it is. Its thin current slides away, but eternity remains. I would drink deeper; fish in the sky, whose bottom is pebbly with stars.

The first entry is saying something like this: below the surface of time in which we live, with its momentary tempestuousnesses, lies the endless calm of eternity. The passage in *Walden* tells us that time is shallow and passing, like the brook that one fishes in. When one looks at the sky, "whose bottom is pebbly with stars," one senses eternity.

From germ to germination to flower.

The Journal and the Subconscious

In the journal, Thoreau caught the shadow of an idea, *and he recorded it so that it wouldn't get lost*—that is the real function of the journal. But what happened between the journal and the final version?

That question cannot be answered positively, but it is safe to speculate that Thoreau planted the seed of the idea in his subconscious and that the final version was as much the product of the subconscious as of the conscious mind. That is, I believe that Thoreau let his subconscious work for him. The idea incubated in Thoreau's subconscious after he had prepared by entering it in his journal.

Richard E. Young, Alton L. Becker, and Kenneth Pike explain this process:

4   The preparation stage [such as a journal entry] is followed by a period of subconscious activity that is somewhat mysterious and hard to discuss explicitly. People tend to ignore its importance, placing undue emphasis on the conscious analytical procedures as if these alone were sufficient for solving problems. But each of us has a subconscious intelligence, a strong and vital force in our mental life that seems to have a greater capacity than reason for dealing with the complex and the unfamiliar. Poets have called it their muse; others, their imagination or creative ability. In the incubation period this subconscious intelligence is brought to bear on the problem.

If it has been adequately instructed, a person's subconscious mind continues to work even after that person has shifted his attention to other matters. For example, each of us has had the experience of not being able to recall a familiar name and then having it come to mind after our attention has moved on to something else. This is a simple illustration of continuing subconscious activity that leads to the sudden appearance of an idea in the conscious mind. The alternation of conscious and subconscious activity is as natural and necessary in our mental life as breathing in and out or waking and sleeping are in our physical life.[2]

²Richard E. Young, Alton L. Becker, and Kenneth Pike, *Rhetoric: Discovery and Change* (New York: Harcourt Brace Jovanovich, 1970), pp. 73–74.

The journal, then, is a means of preserving ideas—of aiding one's memory—but also of enlisting the aid of the subconscious.

The Journal and the Subconscious: An Example

In order to illustrate the interplay of subconscious and conscious mind, and the use of a journal, I would like to recount an experience of mine. One night, I had an extremely vivid dream—so vivid that I arose immediately (about 3:00 A.M.) and made the following journal entry:

> 5   A farm in a valley. It is the greenest of green May evenings, a pre-dark quiet. A gigantic whiteface bull dumbly chews his cud in the pasture. A man comes from the farmhouse and pulls the head off a chicken. [This image was probably triggered by the passage from Malcolm X's autobiography reprinted on pages 19–20.] Later. In the dark, the farm family climbs the hill out of the valley and attends a movie in a white church-like building that stands in a clearing.

I had no idea what I would do with this entry, but I did know something of its significance to me. I had been arguing against people who escape from life into art, people who feel that art is an escape from—or even preferable to—life.

In any case, for a couple of days I didn't think much about my journal entry. Then, one afternoon the lines that I had scribbled popped into my mind, and I began to write in my journal a little prose narrative, which came out like this:

> 6   It is a May dusk. A farmyard surrounded by meadow sits in a lush green valley. The air has a characteristic pre-dark stillness, but there is vivid activity in the farmyard. A gigantic whiteface bull mounts a Holstein heifer, and the father of the farm family catches a chicken and pulls its head off. It must be Saturday night, and the chicken is intended for Sunday dinner. The headless corpse of the chicken flops around the yard, spraying vivid blood. The "dance" that the chicken does reminds me of Russians that I have seen dancing, gyrating, kicking out their legs, standing on their hands. Later, after dark, the family climbs a hill out of the valley and attends a movie in a building that looks much like a white rural church.

The next day, I sat down to turn this into a poem. From here on, the activity was mostly conscious, and the poem went through five or six versions before I finally arrived at this:

7   *Cinema*

> In that May dusk, the whiteface bull
> climbed the heifer's rump,
> his ballocks, pink as peaches, swinging.
> When Papa pulled the head off a hen,
> that chicken did a bloody dance,
> wilder than any Russian kid,
> around the yard in the valley.
>
> That night in May, we climbed the hill

> to see a Chaplin movie—
> in black and white, we lived our lives
> in a Charlie Chaplin movie.

The poem is not great literature, but it pleased me to write it, and that's what is important.

The history that I have given you is, of course, an oversimplification; nor could I tell all, even if I wanted to, for the processes whereby I went from stimulus to dream to journal entry to second journal entry to first, second, third, fourth, and fifth drafts to final version is largely hidden from me. But this little history is typical of what can take place on the basis of a journal entry.

The journal can stimulate ideas. And it can be a "file" wherein you store the ideas that you have generated.

Making the Most of Journal Entries

A journal entry such as the following will not be of much use:

8 Yesterday was the hottest Memorial Day in Los Angeles history. The Indianapolis 500 was postponed because of rain and because of an eight-car crackup at the beginning of the race.

But the following entry might well stimulate some more extensive writing:

9 Yesterday was the hottest Memorial Day in Los Angeles history, but it was raining in Indianapolis, where the 500 was to be run. A slight paradox, yes. The newspaper had been full of advice to drivers: don't go anywhere over the holiday, and if you do go, make sure that you have a full tank, because there will be a gasoline shortage in the Los Angeles basin. At last, our gas-guzzling monsters are beginning to die for lack of food. Just at the beginning of the Indianapolis 500, eight cars—great roaring masses of power—were involved in a spectacular smashup, and the race was *postponed for one day*. A great paradox? Yes!

It is obvious, I trust, that a purpose hides somewhere in the second entry, the germ of an idea that might be developed. The first journal entry is directionless.

Once you get a subject, use your journal to record and develop your ideas concerning it.

Brainstorming

Suppose—God forbid!—that for some reason I were required to write a 10,000-word essay on the ballpoint pen that now lies on the desk in front of me. My subject is predetermined: the pen. But a major problem arises: What should I say about it? I am confronted with the necessity of coming up with a great number of ideas concerning that pen.

In an effort to develop ideas, I might sit numbly and stare at the pen, waiting for inspiration to strike. I might pace the floor and gnaw my fingernails, hoping that brilliant ideas will emerge.

Or I might examine the pen carefully and begin asking questions about it: What color is it? What is it made of? How large is it? How well does it write? What might it be used for other than writing? How much did it cost? What are its bad features? How might it be improved? Into what general class of objects in the world does it fit? How is it like other objects in its class? How does it differ from others? How does it taste? How does it feel? Is the ink poison? Might it be possible to write a murder mystery about a poison pen? What possibilities are there in the pun "poison pen"? Who invented ballpoint pens? How many ballpoint pens are sold in the United States each year? What is ballpoint ink made of? How many fountain pens are still manufactured and sold?

And my list of questions could go on and on. The point is, however, that asking questions will generate subject matter. Complete answers to all the questions asked in the above paragraph would generate enough information to write several 10,000-word papers.

You can do this same kind of brainstorming with abstract concepts such as democracy or education. Figuratively speaking, you can pick an idea up and begin to examine it from various angles, asking all the questions that occur to you.

This kind of unsystematic inquiry is productive, but even more productive and interesting are methods of systematic inquiry concerning subjects. The discussion from here on will deal with *heuristics*—that is, systematic procedures that are used for discovery of ideas or to stimulate investigation.

The Pentad

The first heuristic that we will deal with is adapted from Kenneth Burke's Pentad. If you are interested in the Pentad, you can read Burke's explanation of it in his "Introduction" to *A Grammar of Motives.*

Needless to say, it is frequently necessary in college to analyze, understand, and write about various kinds of writing—from editorials to textbooks to political speeches to detergent ads. In the attempts to analyze and understand, there are certain questions that one can systematically ask and attempt to answer.

The Five Questions of the Pentad

What does it say? The best way to answer this question is to summarize or paraphrase the piece. Of course, summarizing is not always easy, depending on the complexity of the writing. As will be seen immediately, summarizing an article from *Time* is very easy, but doing a summary of one of John Donne's sonnets can be an extremely difficult task. (Think of Cleanth Brooks' essay on Robert Frost's "After Apple-Picking"—both reprinted in Chapter 2—and you will see not only how difficult summary can be but also how summary can contribute to an interpretive essay.)

Who wrote it? As will be demonstrated, this question can be extremely important. For example, an article about DDT by the president of Montrose Chemical Co., a firm that makes the pesticide (which has been banned for most uses in the United States), might be expected to contain certain biases, as would an article on the same subject by a member of the conservationist Sierra Club.

In what source was it published? Some publications are generally more reliable than others. An obvious example: one would put more faith in a story that appeared in the *Los Angeles Times* than in one that appeared in the *National Enquirer.* A house organ might well be biased in favor of its company's products. And so on.

Where and when was it published? It goes without saying that the date and geographical location of the publication are important. A 1939 article on photochemical smog will have mainly historical interest, and an article on birth control published in the Vatican can be expected to reflect certain viewpoints.

What is its purpose? Ostensible purpose is not always real purpose. The real purpose of a patent-medicine ad is not to promote the cure of illness, but to sell patent medicine.

These five simple questions, applied systematically to a piece of writing and answered conscientiously, will generate understanding of what is going on in the piece and hence will generate ideas that can be set forth in an essay.

Applying the Pentad: First Example

In order to demonstrate how this simple inquiry procedure works, let's turn to an article from the June 12, 1972, issue of *Time:*

10   *College, Who Needs It?*

It is clear from their cries of gloom and doom that a number of colleges and universities are endangered by falling enrollments. In fact, according to a study by the Carnegie Commission on Higher Education published this week, 110,000 freshman places in four-year institutions went unfilled last fall, 24% more than the year before. Are economic circumstances the major reason for those empty seats? Not according to the author of the report, Richard Peterson, a research psychologist for the Educational Testing Service.

Far more important, Peterson argues, is a fundamental change in the attitude toward college of white, middle-class youngsters. He sees signs that "a college education is not needed for what they consider the good life. More and more, they feel that they can live satisfactorily without a college degree." While some may simply be dropping out, or not going in the first place, Peterson believes that even more have a new-found desire for "no-nonsense" job training offered at vocational schools.

Shifts. Actually, in spite of the missing freshmen, the total enrollment figure is still growing, owing to the new popularity of two-year public colleges and graduate schools. There is also a marked increase in the number of part-time students. While middle-class students are dropping out, or "stopping out," of college, blue-collar and minority students, who see education as their best means of access to the middle class, are taking their places. The number of Chicanos attending college increased by 19.1% last year, and blacks by 17.2% (although enrollment in black-studies courses fell by 8%). Women's enrollment rose too, by 5.1%.

The shifting student population is a costly matter to many institutions. California's huge, 19-campus state college and university system lost not only $1,000,000 in tuition when its full-time enrollment declined by 4,530 this year, but another $2.9 million in state support, which fluctuates according to the number of students enrolled. To recruit new students, some colleges have resorted to colorful brochures, radio commercials and high-pressure salesmanship. At the University of Southern California, professors themselves are making follow-up phone calls to prospective students, and the appeals to ordinary high school graduates have been compared to the recruiting of athletes in previous years.

Innovations. Enrollment figures seem to indicate that to attract students, colleges should consider ways to accommodate stop-outs, special programs for minority students, more vocational training and new interdisciplinary curriculums. Largely because they lack the money, few schools have made such changes. Some that have, however, are flourishing. Three examples:

• In 1968 the University of Wisconsin focused the entire academic program at its Green Bay campus on environmental problems and saw enrollment there more than double to 3,450 this year. Students major in such broad topics as Ecosystems Analysis, for example, in which traditional subjects like biology and chemistry are related to the problems of controlling pollution.

• Ferris State College in Big Rapids, Mich., which offers associate degrees in automobile repair and body mechanics, has so many applicants that it cannot admit new students to such programs until September 1973. Its enrollment has grown by 25% in two years.

• Evergreen State College in Olympia, Wash., which opened with about 1,000 students last year, encourages students to contract with faculty members on what to study. For example, one group agreed to design a municipal park for the city of Lacey. The college has no grades, no departmental requirements and expects to almost double its enrollment by next fall.

Some of these innovations may turn out to be only passing fads, but for the moment they seem to serve a need. Insofar as the drop in enrollments will force schools to reconsider their goals, Peterson believes "the fact that students are not accepting a college education and a degree uncritically any more will have salutary effects on higher education." Thus, after flexing their muscles in campus demonstrations for several years, students may find that their real power lies not on the picket line but in the registrars' offices.

• • •

Another critic of the educational Establishment is Oscar Handlin, professor of history at Harvard. At Brooklyn College's commencement exercises last week, he commiserated with the graduates, saying that 16 years in a classroom is simply too long. Noting that their ancestors were considered men and women at age 13 or 14 and "had tested their powers well before they were out of their teens," Handlin said: "Nothing real happens to those lapped in comfortable dependence and shielded by beneficent institutions against exposure to the elements." Colleges, Handlin concluded, are actually killing education. "In the 1970s we sentence more of our youth to more years in school than ever before in history, so that never before have Americans been as poorly educated as now."[3]

What Does It Say?

Answering this question involves briefly summarizing the piece in your own words. In my own words, this article can be summarized as follows: Enrollments are falling in colleges and universities through the nation. But according to Richard Peterson, a research psychologist for Educational Testing Service, the reason for the apparent decrease in enrollments is not the faltering economy, but a change in the attitudes of the group from which most enrollees traditionally come, namely middle-class youths. While blue-collar, minority, and female enrollment is rising, it seems that fewer middle-class teen-agers look toward college as the means to achieve their goals in life. However, enrollment at two-year colleges is continuing to rise, and there is some evidence that to attract students, colleges and universities will have to offer vocational training and new interdisciplinary curricula. Peterson feels that the new student attitudes toward a college education may in the long run be healthy.

This brief summary pretty much reiterates the main points of the article, without going into any of the details. (The point of the summary is to make sure that the article is understood. One should not do formal summaries just for the sake of doing them, and, needless to say, many analyses of writing do not contain summaries, though in some instances summaries are essential. In any case, it isn't a bad idea to develop the ability to do accurate summaries.)

Who Wrote It?

In the case of the present article, that question is easily answered: someone in the employ of *Time* magazine. Since articles in *Time* are unsigned, we cannot determine just who did write "College, Who Needs It?" But we can notice that the magazine has a style, which all its writers follow. And we know that *Time* has certain policies that its writers must adhere to. (We will speak more about this matter in a moment.)

In What Source Was It Published?

This turns out to be the most important question concerning the piece that we are analyzing. The answer seems easy enough: *Time* magazine. But the next question, of course, is What sort of publication is *Time* magazine? Well, it is the enormously successful news magazine that Briton Hadden and Henry R. Luce established in 1923. Its circulation in 1973 was about four and a quarter million.

As we glance through *Time,* we become aware that it attempts to give some kind of overview of what's going on in the world, for we find sections on art, behavior, books, cinema, the economy and business, education, environment, law, medicine, modern living, music, the nation, people, religion, science, the sexes, show business and television, sports, and the world. Since all these topics are covered in less than 100 pages, we can conclude that the magazine is not very probing. If we wanted an in-depth report on college enrollment at present, we would go to a source other than

Time. In fact, it is inevitable that *Time* must popularize its material, must make it readable at all costs, must choose the items that are most likely to appeal to a mass audience. (And, by the way, I am not criticizing *Time;* I read it almost every week and enjoy much of it.) The fact that *Time* is *Time,* then, dictates the sort of items that will be found in the magazine, as well as the way in which those items are treated by the anonymous author. One has the feeling after reading several issues of *Time* that a general policy regarding political stands is enunciated by the editors, and every writer is expected to adhere to that policy, though it would be hard to demonstrate that such is the case.

Where and When Was It Published?

The answer is the United States of America in June of 1972. Without belaboring the point, it is easy to see that at times, in the analysis of various pieces of writing, this information could be crucial. In the case of "College, Who Needs It?" we need only be aware of the date of the magazine in which the piece appeared.

What Is Its Purpose?

This is frequently the most difficult but most telling question. Do you think that the sole purpose of "College, Who Needs It?" was simply to inform readers, or is there some kind of missionary purpose for college reform behind the article? Though we can't answer that question definitely, we should be aware of it. Furthermore, we should realize that articles in *Time* are carefully chosen to boost circulation; that is, the magazine is carefully designed to appeal to its readers, not necessarily to present a balanced view of what's going on in the world.

So much for the first brief demonstration of how a heuristic works. Now I would like to apply the same procedure to a more complicated piece of writing.

Applying the Pentad: Second Example[4]

Here is a short passage from Samuel Taylor Coleridge's *Anima Poetae:*

11   The love of Nature is ever returned double to us, not only the delighter in our delight, but by linking our sweetest, but of themselves perishable feelings to distinct and vivid images, which we ourselves, at times, and which a thousand casual recollections recall to our memory. She is the preserver, the treasurer of our joys. Even in sickness and nervous diseases, she has peopled our imagination with lovely forms which have sometimes overpowered the inward pain and brought with them their old sensations. And even when all men have seemed to desert us and the friend of our heart has passed on, with one glance from his "cold disliking eye"—yet even then the blue heaven spreads it out and bends over us, and the little tree still shelters us with its

---

[4]The analysis of Coleridge is an adaptation of an essay by this author in *The Relevance of Rhetoric,* ed. E. V. Stackpoole and W. Ross Winterowd (Boston: Allyn & Bacon, 1966), pp. 36–39. Copyright © 1966 by Allyn and Bacon, Inc. Used with permission.

plumage as a second cope, a domestic firmament, and a low creeping gale will sigh in the heath-plant and soothe us by sound of sympathy till the lulled grief lose itself in fixed gaze on the purple heath-bloom, till the present beauty becomes a vision of memory.

The Author

In applying our heuristic to this passage, we can begin from whatever vantage point we choose. For instance, since we know a good deal about the author, Samuel Taylor Coleridge, we might ask what our knowledge of him will add to our understanding of what he has to say. From one point of view, we can regard Coleridge's writing in this passage as self-expressive, and self-expressive writing can be viewed as an attempt to adjust to or reconcile oneself to some situation. But what was the situation of the writer when he set down the passage in question? A complete answer would take us more deeply into Coleridge's biography than the purposes of the present discussion warrant, but certain well-known facts about Coleridge's life help us to understand what situations the passage in question might help him to adjust to. First, we know that bad health and perhaps hypochondria led Coleridge to an opium addiction that lasted from 1803 to 1816, and perhaps longer. This slavery to narcotics was a central fact of the poet's existence, one that inflicted on him terrific pangs of guilt and moments of euphoric escape. As important as the destructiveness of his addiction was Coleridge's life-long friendship with the poet Wordsworth; and it was Wordsworth who said in "Tintern Abbey,"

> These beauteous forms
> Through a long absence, have not been to me
> As is a landscape to a blind man's eye:
> But oft, in lonely rooms, and 'mid the din
> Of towns and cities, I have owed to them
> In hours of weariness, sensations sweet,
> Felt in the blood, and felt along the heart.

Without carrying biography any further, one sees resonances of Coleridge's life in the passage from *Anima Poetae*. Nature (or the particular view of nature that Coleridge and Wordsworth shared) sustains and heals: "Even in sickness and nervous diseases, she has peopled our imagination with lovely forms which have sometimes overpowered the inward pain and brought with them their old sensations." One can, with justification, go deeper and surmise that for Coleridge, Nature provided a substitute home, an emotional escape from the shambles of his domestic life: the little tree becomes "a domestic firmament."

The Place

In the discussion of the article from *Time* we used the term **place** to indicate place of publication, but in regard to the Coleridge piece, the place of composition is the important factor, not the place of publication. And it is important to realize that heuristics are not straightjackets, not a set of rules that you must follow, but rather are devices for generating subject matter.

Thus, you can stretch or reinterpret the terms in any way you see fit, just as *place* referred to place of publication in one instance, but will refer to place of composition here. Anticipating a bit, I might also point out that the publishing agency is unimportant as regards the Coleridge piece; thus it is not discussed here.

The place in which Coleridge wrote this passage was the house of Dr. James Gillman, with whom he lived from the age of forty-three. At Gillman's, Coleridge managed to control his drug addiction, but he was isolated from the places and people that had made his earlier years meaningful. Though Coleridge remained the center of an impressive circle of admirers and friends, we can assume that he felt immured, "city pent," in the Gillman home at Highgate, London. The place of composition, then, was away from Nature, but Nature had peopled the poet's imagination. Coleridge's situation in London, we can speculate, made him long for the countryside, as, perhaps, an extended visit to the country might bring on a longing for the bustle of London. (Note that even though we are talking about Coleridge, a nineteenth-century writer, the concept of place is a universal factor in evaluating and interpreting both written and spoken discourse, and particularly so in the case of modern mass media. Political climate, laws, economic conditions, public opinion—all these pressures from the place of composition influence the mass media.)

The Purpose

As we said earlier, the purpose of a piece of writing may be apparent or hidden. Without reservations, we can conclude that Coleridge's purpose in the passage from *Anima Poetae* was to adjust to a situation, perhaps to reassure himself of the values to which he ascribed. Ostensibly, he was setting forth his philosophy of life for a reader, and that ostensible purpose is part of the whole purpose. But what Coleridge said is obviously too much a cry from his own depths for us to write off the utterance as mere exposition. We should remember that the ostensible purpose in discourse is not always the whole purpose or even the real purpose.

The Text Itself

Finally, there is the text itself, what has been written (or spoken, for it is apparent that this inquiry procedure applies as well to spoken discourse as to written). Paradoxically, the text might be its own motive, as when we talk or write self-expressively, just for the sake of talking or writing. But the utterance—either written or spoken—is an act with its own internal logic, a piece of experience that we can turn to and conscientiously attempt to understand.

One thing we might do is look carefully at the language that the writer uses, for it represents his or her choices, conscious and unconscious. A hint may illustrate how analysis of language can bring insights. Note that Coleridge is writing at a time "when all men have seemed to desert us." The feeling of the passage is desolate, lonely. But note what the poet does with the language in order to bring about a poetic corrective of this situation. "The love of Nature" becomes reflexive in meaning; it symbolizes the poet's love for Nature (the capital letter is important), but also, because of the personification (in which Nature becomes a person), Nature's love for the poet. Furthermore, Nature "has peopled our imagination with lovely forms." The little tree itself and the heath-plant are personified. Hence, the poetic devices of the language provide symbolic companions for the desolate poet; imaginatively, he is not alone at all.

Analysis of the language of a piece of writing need not stop at the level at which we leave it here. Obviously, there is layer upon layer of suggestion, and each exfoliation that analysis brings about takes one nearer the central meaning of the passage. (It is interesting to note that the source of publication can have a great influence on the language that the piece contains. This idea was hinted at in the discussion of the piece from *Time* magazine. The policy of a newspaper or magazine may preclude the writer's use of certain kinds of language; the dictates of taste subscribed to by a television network might rule out discussion of certain issues in either dramatic or news programs. The possibilities here are endless, but an understanding of the limitations imposed on language can lead one to a more certain appraisal of the utterances being investigated.)

Ratios in the Pentad

The five factors that we have discussed (meaning, author, source of publication, place and time of publication, and purpose) influence one another, of course, in ways that result in what might be called ratios. For instance, when an editor of a newspaper assigns a reporter to do a story, we have a case of a ratio between the source of publication and the writer; that is, the source imposes its needs on the writer. Proletarian literature of the 1930s can be viewed as an example of a ratio between place and time and writer, since the economic conditions in America during the 1930s impelled various writers to turn out novels and short stories of social protest.

An Interim Summary

At this point, let's stop and summarize what we have been doing, and why.

1. We are exploring the idea of generating subject matter about a topic, that is, of finding things to say, of discovering ideas. Another way to put the idea is this: We are investigating ways of solving the problem of understanding subjects. When we are confronted with a topic that we must write or speak about, we must somehow discover or generate subject matter for our essay or speech. That is what we are getting at here, the generation of subject matter.

2. A personal journal can be a rich source of material. Brainstorming, though unsystematic, can also be effective. The most efficient way of generating subject matter is to use a systematic inquiry procedure, a

heuristic that will develop productive questions about the topic. The answers to these questions constitute the subject matter that is being sought.

3. To illustrate how heuristics work, we took the Pentad, a very simple five-item list of questions that will generate subject matter concerning written discourse of any kind (and, in fact, spoken discourse). We applied this inquiry procedure to a piece from *Time* magazine, in which we asked more questions than we answered; then we applied the same procedure to a piece of writing by Samuel Taylor Coleridge and, in effect, developed a short analytical essay concerning that passage.

If you understand what has happened here, you will have grasped the basic nature of heuristics—and you will, furthermore, have made a large step forward in your ability to solve problems of all sorts.

Practice

I suggest that at this point you stop reading and begin to practice using the heuristic that has been outlined. Get a piece of writing—an essay, a newspaper article, or whatever—and view it from the five perspectives of meaning, author, source of publication, time and place of publication, and purpose.

Remember that the importance of the various questions changes with the piece being analyzed. For instance, in the case of the Coleridge piece, the source of publication was so unimportant that the analysis ignored it, but if we were looking at an article in *The Daily Worker,* a communist newspaper, we would want to consider the source very carefully.

Devising Heuristics

In the following pages, we will be discussing and trying out a variety of heuristics; but before we go on, I'd like to make an important remark. Even though we will be taking a rather close look at a variety of heuristics that are "ready made," it is perfectly feasible, and often necessary, for you to devise your own. The way to do this is simple enough: define the topic, and then determine what the important questions concerning that topic are. In answering the questions, you generate subject matter.

A brief example concerning a topic that means a great deal to me: fishing the waters of Mexico's Todos Santos Bay. Suppose I want to write an essay on that topic. Here are the questions that I would ask:

12   Where is Todos Santos Bay?
       How does one arrange to fish there?
       What are the best seasons for fishing there?
       What kinds of fish does one catch there?

What sort of equipment does one need?

How does one fish for the varieties of fish that are caught in Todos Santos Bay?

What do people that I know say about fishing there?

In answering these questions, I would develop an essay that would interest someone who plans to fish in Todos Santos Bay or who is interested in fishing in general.

For instance, in answering the first question (Where is Todos Santos Bay?), I would talk about the drive from my home in Huntington Beach through San Diego and Tijuana, along the coast of Baja California to Ensenada, and then I would describe Ensenada and undoubtedly tell about some of the interesting and frustrating experiences that I have had there. And so on.

Notice that once I have developed the questions that I want to answer, I can arrange them any way that I want. For example, in the case of the essay that is under discussion, I would certainly want to explain how one arranges to fish Todos Santos Bay (in answer to the second question) before I went on at length about the trip to Ensenada. The point is that *a set of questions developed by the writer can serve as an inquiry procedure that will generate subject matter concerning a topic.*

Problem Solving

Often the reason for writing—the purpose—involves an ill-defined problem and feasible solutions to that problem. The following heuristic for problem solving was outlined by Richard L. Larson.[5]

1. Define the Problem

This involves the formulation of a sentence that precisely states the problem that is to be investigated. The sentence may be declarative (in the form of a statement) or interrogative (in the form of a question).

13   a. *Topic:* My college education

Problem: If I major in music, the field in which I am interested, will I be able to obtain a job and make a decent living in the field after I graduate?

b. *Topic:* Drug use among undergraduates at my college

Problem: What are the reasons for the use of drugs among undergraduates at my college?

c. *Topic:* Buying a new automobile

Problem: A number of factors (initial cost, accommodations for passengers, gas mileage, frequency of repair records) will influence my choice of a new car.

d. *Topic:* The Sanpete dialect of central Utah

Problem: The Sanpete dialect of central Utah is characterized by differences in vocabulary, idioms, and pronunciation from standard English.

[5]Richard L. Larson, "Problem-Solving, Composing, and Liberal Education," *College English,* 33 (March 1972), 628–35.

We could, of course, easily list five or five hundred more topics entailing problems that can be precisely stated. What is interesting to note, however, is the transformation that topics undergo the minute a problem is stated. This is basically an extremely simple point (and one I have made earlier), but it is so important that I would like to deal with it in some detail.

In a real sense, it is impossible to write about "My College Education," "Drug Use Among Undergraduates at My College," "Buying a New Automobile," or "The Sanpete Dialect of Central Utah." Before one can write about these topics, they must be changed into something that is usable. But why is a topic such as "My College Education" unusable? For this reason: it has no shape and no direction. What is one to say about it? What kind of college education? At what college? In other words, the "raw" topic simply doesn't contain enough hints about where the writing should go. So the first job is to narrow the topic down, to focus it, to make it so that it points toward something. One way of doing this is to turn the topic into a problem.

In other words, if you try to write about

My College Education

you don't know where to begin or where you might end, but if you try to answer the question

> If I major in music, the field in which I am interested, will I be able to obtain a job and make a decent living in the field after I graduate?

you have something to work on, for you can investigate the job opportunities for musicians, you can inquire about the possibility of majoring in a marketable subject and taking elective classes in music, and so on. In short, you have a point of departure, something to get going on, and a good deal of direction concerning the way in which your essay will develop.

The point is that when the topic is formulated as a problem, there is something to solve. Analogously, a number is not a problem. What can you say about 1,589,731? Not much. But once that number gets into a problem, you can say things; thus, What is 1,589,731 divided by 9.8? The result of that problem will be a mathematical calculation that will end in an answer. Such is precisely the nature of the essay topic when it is put in the form of a problem.

Of course, the topic might be stated as a problem to begin with. For instance: What would be the results of nationalization of the steel industry in the United States?

2. Determine Why the Problem Is Indeed a Problem

From this point on, we will be using the following problem as our example: What is the impact on education of dialect differences in the United States? We will use this problem because it is timely, it is interesting, and you already know something about dialect (and you will know more if you skip ahead to Chapter 10).

William Labov gives an excellent statement of reasons why dialect is a problem in American education:

14   When we compare American schools to their French, German, Spanish, or Russian counterparts, we find that we are relatively free in our approach to language. Proposals for an Academy to legislate correct English have been made over and over again and defeated every time. Yet we have not lacked for authority in the classroom. The dictionary, the spelling book, and the school grammar have traditionally been regarded as absolute authorities, far outweighing the teacher himself. The authoritarian position of the spelling book reflects, as we shall see, a real uniformity in American attitudes towards language. Almost all Americans recognize an external standard of correct English—that is, a standard which is something other than the way they speak themselves. The "doctrine of correctness" first began to dominate English speakers in the seventeenth and eighteenth centuries, when large numbers of middle class people rose into the high positions previously dominated by the landed aristocracy; this doctrine has remained strongly entrenched ever since. The uniformity of American attitudes towards English is also reflected in our attitudes towards the native languages of immigrant groups. The language of the immigrant generation has been allowed to disappear with remarkable regularity in the second and third generation with very few expressions of regret, as part of the general pattern of assimilation of these ethnic groups into American society.

To most Americans, it does not seem unusual that English should replace the native language of immigrants in the first few years of school, since it has been assumed that everyone learns the English language in school. Whatever equipment the child brings to school has been considered not the language itself but rather a very imperfect approximation to it. As a result, those who have not had much schooling (and many who have had) form a very low opinion of their own linguistic competence. To the question, "What do you think of your own speech?" we often obtain answers such as "Terrible," "Horrible," "Awfully sloppy," or "Not too good." Some rural idioms and a few urban dialects have retained a certain amount of prestige, but most "dialect" speakers are made to feel painfully aware of their inadequacy in school. Such urban dialects as the everyday vernacular of New York, Philadelphia, Pittsburgh, or Chicago are ranked very low in the social scale, and speakers quickly learn to prefer (consciously) the more standard forms which teachers hold up as a model.

This modeling is in fact all of the teaching method and philosophy that has been required in the school. It is assumed that the teacher speaks the standard English of the textbook, that the students should all acquire this standard, and that it is sufficient for the teacher to correct any departures from the model as they occur. "Do it as I do it" is the basic instruction. Little attention is given to the question of *why* the student makes a particular departure from standard English, any more than one asks why a student makes a mistake in addition—it is assumed that he has not learned the right answer yet. Whether or not this method of modeling has in general succeeded is not the issue here. In cold fact, the number of differences between most nonstandard dialects (especially those of the middle class speakers) and standard English are relatively few. In one way or another, most students have gradually learned to approximate the teacher's style, more or less. More important, their dialects have not obviously interfered with the learning of reading and writing to any serious degree.

Now, however, two major problems for American education have appeared in the urban ghettos. First there is the group plainly labeled by the color bar—the black students—who now form the majority in many northern schools. Their nonstandard vernacular seems to be far more different from standard English than that of most white nonstandard dialects. Furthermore, the overall educational achievement of black children is well below that of white working class groups. It is quite difficult for the teacher to assume that this language is simply an imperfect copy of his own. The total numbers of "errors" and "deviations" mount alarmingly until it becomes apparent to most observers that there are some fundamental differences in the rules. Teachers are faced with so many problems that they simply "do not know where to begin," and many now feel the need for some understanding of the language they are dealing with, if only to economize and concentrate their efforts.

The second major problem is that of the Spanish-speaking groups in the United States, who are not losing their native language as rapidly as other groups have done. Here it is immediately evident that a knowledge of the Spanish vernacular, whether it is Puerto Rican or Mexican Spanish, will be helpful in understanding students' performance in class. It is true that "English as a second language" is often taught without reference to the language of origin, but no one would defend this as the best approach. In our Spanish-speaking urban ghetto areas, the most immediate source of interference with standard English is not Puerto Rican or Mexican Spanish but rather the Spanish-influenced English spoken every day on the streets. This dialect plays the same role for the teacher of Spanish-American children that nonstandard Negro English does for the teacher of black children: it is the source of interference and difficulty, but it is also the best means of direct communication between him and the child. An understanding of this nonstandard language is a necessary first step in understanding one's students and achieving the basic goals of education.[6]

That is a full answer to the question of why the problem is indeed a problem. On the basis of that answer, we are ready to take the third step in problem solving.

3. Enumerate the Goals That Must Be Served by Whatever Action Is Taken

Not all problems require action for their solution, but if the solution does involve action, then step 3 is applicable, as certainly it is to the problem of the effects of dialect on education. As Larson says,

15   Problem-solving behavior is behavior that seeks means for achieving ends: before the means can be sought, the precise goals (things to achieve and things to avoid) must be known. Sometimes the determination of precise goals itself is a problem requiring solution.[7]

[6]William Labov, *The Study of Nonstandard English* (Urbana, Ill.: National Council of Teachers of English, 1969), pp. 3–5. Copyright © 1969 by the National Council of Teachers of English. Reprinted by permission of the publisher and the author.
[7]Larson, "Problem-Solving, Composing, and Liberal Education," p. 629.

Now that the nature of the problem has been explored, definite goals can be enumerated. These are:

a. Educating teachers concerning the facts about dialect. Teachers need to know the dynamics whereby dialects develop and are maintained and the specific differences between standard and the various nonstandard dialects.

b. Finding dialect options for students. Classes must be conducted so that children can function in their native dialects without incurring the severe penalties that are now common.

c. Developing new textbooks. Handbooks and grammars must get away from the prescriptive attitudes that they have traditionally conveyed and must recognize the richness of dialect diversity in American English. Collections of literature used in the schools must also reflect this diversity.

d. Developing new standardized tests. Speakers of nonstandard English are frequently at a disadvantage when they take tests that are written in standard English. If the purpose of a test is to find out what a child knows about a subject, the language of the test should not serve as a block to its purpose.

e. Educating the general public. The public at large must begin to tolerate—even appreciate—dialect diversity. This education can best begin in the schools.

Summary

Notice that an extremely interesting thing has happened.

We have chosen a topic: Dialects in the United States.

We have defined a problem in connection with the topic: What is the impact on education of dialect differences in the United States?

We have determined why the problem is indeed a problem: See Labov's discussion.

And we have enumerated the goals that must be served by whatever action is taken: See above.

And for each of the goals, we can develop a variety of subtopics:

> Goal: Educating teachers concerning the facts about dialect
> > Subtopic: What are the best means of providing teachers with the training that they need?
> Goal: Finding dialect options for students
> > Subtopic: How would a multidialect class in English, for example, be conducted?

And so on. Each of these subproblems can be solved by the procedure that we are outlining, and explanation of the problems and the proposed solutions are a legitimate, even necessary, part of the full discussion of our topic as defined by the problem.

In effect, our stock of ideas concerning the topic grows more and more rich. We are "inventing" a great deal of subject matter.

4. Where Possible, Determine Which Goals Have the Highest Priority

In problem solving, you will want to put the most effort into the most important goals, and in answering the questions Which goal is the most important? and Why? you will have generated still more subject matter. Furthermore—and this is important—in ranking the goals from the most important to the least important, you will have revealed something about the organization that your essay should take as it discusses the goals: namely, they should probably be discussed in order of importance, with the most important saved for last. Though we will be talking about organization in some detail later, it stands to reason that you will not want to have your essay, as it progresses, become less and less important, but rather you will want it to increase in significance as it goes along. That is why, as a general rule, the most important points are saved for last. (Like other rules of thumb about writing, this one is not sacred and can often be violated to good purpose if there is adequate reason.)

5. Find the Procedure That Might Attain the Stated Goals

This process might be carried out through research, technology, brainstorming, or the use of a heuristic. (It should be apparent by now that we use heuristics to solve problems raised by heuristics—and in the process we discover ideas; that is, we invent subject matter. If you do not thoroughly understand the process as described in this discussion so far, then go back and reread this section and rethink the problems and principles that it introduces.)

Finding the procedure that we think *will* attain the stated goals often involves eliminating procedures that will *not* attain them. Here is a wonderful comment that bears on three of our goals: educating teachers, finding dialect options for students, and educating the general public:

> **16**   As long as most people agreed that up is toward Schlitz and another TV set, and as long as they could pretend that every American eaglet can soar to those great heights, Fidditch McFidditch the dialectologist could enforce the speech-taboos of the great white middle class without complaint: either the child learned the taboos and observed them, or he was systematically penalized. But the damage done to the Wasps' nest by World War II made difficulties. People who talked all wrong, and especially black people, began to ask for their share of the loot in a world that had given them an argument by calling itself free, while a minority of the people who talked right began to bad-mouth respectability and joined the blacks in arguing that it was time for a real change. Some black people burned up the black parts of town, and some students made study impossible at the universities, and in general there was a Crisis. Optimists even talked of a revolution.
>
> The predictable response of the frightened white businessman's society was to go right on doing what it had done before—which had caused the crisis—but to do it harder and to spend more money at it. Education was no exception. Government and the foundations began to spray money over the academic landscape like liquid fertilizer, and the professional societies began to bray and paw at the rich new grass. In that proud hour, any teacher who could

dream up an expensive scheme for keeping things as they were while pretending to make a change was sure of becoming the director of a project or a center and of flying first-class to Washington twice a month. The white businessman strengthened his control of the educational system while giving the impression of vast humanitarian activity.

Black English provided the most lucrative new industry for white linguists, who found the mother lode when they discovered the interesting locutions which the less protected employ to the detriment of their chances for upward mobility. In the annals of free enterprise, the early sixties will be memorable for the invention of functional bi-dialectalism, a scheme best described by an elderly and unregenerate Southern dame as "turning black trash into white trash." Despite some signs of wear, this cloak for white supremacy has kept its shape for almost a decade now, and it is best described in the inimitable words of those who made it. Otherwise the description might be dismissed as a malicious caricature.[8]

6. Predict the Consequences of Each Possible Action

Once the procedures for attaining the goals have been found, one must evaluate the possible consequences of taking those actions, and this could be the most difficult of all the steps. As an example of predicting consequences, suppose we recommend that every speaker of nonstandard English be forced to become bidialectal, using either native nonstandard or acquired standard according to the circumstances. Here is what Sledd predicts as the consequence of that course of action:

17   The present argument against biloquialism [the ability to speak two languages or dialects] is not a militant argument (though biloquialists have called it one in the attempt to discredit it with a label they think is frightening), and it is not primarily a humanitarian argument (though biloquialists have called it inhumane). . . . The argument here is the argument of an unashamed conservative individualist. With his own eyes the arguer has seen British working people, and Chicanos, and black Americans humiliated by contempt for their language and twisted by their own unhappy efforts to talk like their exploiters. An expert is no more needed to prove that such humiliation is damaging or such efforts an expense of spirit than a meteorologist is needed to warn of the dangers of urinating against the wind: but the weight of the argument rests mainly on the fact that if any man can be so shamed and bullied for so intimate a part of his own being as his language, then every man is fully subject to the unhampered tyrants of the materialist majority. To resist the biloquialist is to resist Big Brother, and to resist him for oneself as well as others. Big Brother is not always white.[9]

7. Choose the Best Course of Action

This step often involves weighing consequences against one another. For instance, what are the consequences of allowing students to function in

---

[8]James Sledd, "Bi-Dialectalism: The Linguistics of White Supremacy," *English Journal*, 58 (Dec. 1969), 1308. Copyright © 1969 by the National Council of Teachers of English. Reprinted with permission.
[9]James Sledd, "Doublespeak: Dialectology in the Service of Big Brother," *College English*, 33 (Jan. 1972), 451.

their own dialects as opposed to the consequences of insisting on bidialectalism?

And that ends our rather lengthy outline of the second heuristic. While the first one, the Pentad, was aimed at understanding pieces of writing (or speaking), the one that we have just discussed concerned solving problems, particularly where the solution would involve recommending a course of action. It could well be applied to such problems as the following:

18   What should I major in?
     How might local taxes be more equitably assessed?
     How could departments in a university be realigned so that they would be more productive?
     Should American medicine be socialized?
     What kind of automobile should I buy?
     Where should I spend my summer vacation?
     What recommendations might be made concerning prison reform?

This heuristic will generate detailed solutions to problems that range from the personal and essentially trivial to the general and universally important. In generating solutions, of course, one generates subject matter. Therefore, if the essay topic is a problem or can be formulated as a problem, the heuristic becomes applicable.

Before we go on with the discussion, a couple of points need to be made. First, there is no reason to memorize any heuristic; if you need to use it, you can look it up. Second, it is important that you understand the principles behind heuristics—that you have a firm grasp of what is going on. If you do not, review this chapter and consult with your instructor.

Varying Perspectives

In *Rhetoric: Discovery and Change,* Richard E. Young, Alton L. Becker, and Kenneth L. Pike develop an extremely elaborate—and extremely interesting—heuristic. It would be well worth your time to read Chapters 4, 5, 6, and 7 of that book.

Young, Becker, and Pike point out that any thing or concept can be viewed, mentally, from different perspectives. For instance, I can view my Mirandy rosebush

19   as an isolated, static entity, as if it were not changing moment by moment and as if it were not part of a whole garden;
     as an entity that is undergoing change—that is, as a process;
     as a system, with roots that nourish, leaves that breathe, flowers that reproduce.

Furthermore, I can ask three questions about any thing or concept:

1. What are its distinctive features, or how does it differ from similar things?
2. How much can it change without either becoming something else or losing its identity?
3. How or where does it fit into larger categories to which it belongs?

Drawing heavily on Young, Becker, and Pike, I have developed the following simple and productive heuristic.

If we think of anything—a ballpoint pen, the Los Angeles freeway system, the concept of democracy—we realize that it can be examined from a number of viewpoints.

Ways of Viewing a Subject

The Los Angeles freeway system, for instance, can be viewed

1. As an Isolated, Static Entity

We ask, What features characterize it? We can draw a map of it; we can measure its total length; we can count the number of overpasses and underpasses. We can describe it in great detail. In fact, such a description could well demand a number of thick volumes. But the point is that we can view anything as an isolated, static entity and begin to find those features that characterize it.

2. As One Among Many of a Class

We ask, How does it differ from others in its class? From this point of view, we would compare the Los Angeles freeway system with others like it. I, for instance, immediately think of the differences between the L.A. freeway system and the turnpikes of the East and Midwest, as well as the German Autobahnen.

3. As Part of a Larger System

We ask, How does it fit into larger systems of which it is a part? The L.A. freeway system would be worthless if it did not integrate with national, state, and county highway systems; therefore, its place in these larger systems is crucial.

4. As a Process, Rather Than as a Static Entity

We ask, How is it changing? In regard to the L.A. freeway system, this question brings up the whole problem of planning for the future, which implies the problem of history, or how the system got to be the way it currently is.

5. As a System, Rather Than as an Entity

We ask, What are the parts, and how do they work together? Now we are focusing on the L.A. freeways as a transportation system, each part of which must integrate and function with the whole.

Such is the inquiry procedure. Needless to say, the questions can be asked in any order, but sometimes the nature of the subject itself will indicate to the writer which questions will be most important and which should come first.

Experimenting with a Heuristic

In order to experiment with heuristics, it might be interesting to see how many ideas the one outlined above will generate concerning so mundane an item as a ballpoint pen.

1. *Viewing the subject as an isolated, static entity.* (What features characterize it?) The pen is a cylinder exactly five inches long. The upper two inches consist of a silverish metal, slightly under one-half inch in diameter, and tapering slightly toward the top, which consists of a button that is depressed to retract or push out the ballpoint. Also on the metal part of the pen is a pocket clip, in the shape of an arrow, which is one and one-half inches long. The bottom three inches of the pen consist of a black plastic shaft, tipped with metal and tapering markedly from the middle of the pen to the tip. The top of the pen unscrews from the bottom, and inside is the ink cartridge, which could also be described in detail. (The features that characterize the pen—or anything else—can be described in meticulous detail or simply in general, depending on the writer-investigator's purpose. Since the point about describing the features of an object has probably been made, I will not go on with my description. But, for certain purposes, I would want much more, including micrometer measurements and diagrams.)

2. *Viewing the subject as one among many of a class.* (How does it differ from others of its class?) Some ballpoints do not have retractable tips, but rather have plastic caps that must be put on and removed. Most ballpoints tend to accumulate ink around the writing tip, so that periodically they leave on the paper a smear or a blob of ink; the ballpoint being discussed does not do that. This ballpoint is somewhat more expensive than others, costing ninety-eight cents. And, undoubtedly, if I took the time to do research, I would find a long list of further differences between my ballpoint and others.

3. *Viewing the subject as part of a larger system.* (How does it fit into larger systems of which it is a part?) If by **larger system** we mean "writing instruments," we can relate the ballpoint to the typewriter, chalk, fountain pens, and so on. However, the notion that interests me here is the real difference I experience in writing with a pen and with a typewriter. That is, I find it almost impossible to compose coherently if I use a pen, and I think the reason is that writing by hand slows me down so drastically that I lose my train of thought. This is not to say that my experience is universal, for many writers cannot compose on a typewriter. In any case, what I am trying to illustrate here is that the imaginative use of an inquiry system will open up areas of thought that one would not have discovered otherwise.

4. *Viewing the subject as a process, rather than as a static entity.* (How is it changing?) In the case of my ballpoint, two questions immediately

arise: How long does the ink supply last? How fast does the pen wear out? I have no definite answers to those questions, but could easily get tentative answers.

5. *Viewing the subject as a system, rather than as an entity.* (What are the parts, and how do they work together?) Now we are asking, How does it work? Briefly, the plunger at the top of the pen forces the point out the metal-reinforced tip. The point is, in fact, an extremely small ball bearing at the end of a metal tube, and the tube is filled with a thick ink, about the consistency of printer's ink. As the ball moves over the paper, it turns; as it turns, it picks up ink from the tube and deposits that ink on the paper, thus making the continuous trail demanded for writing.

What I have attempted to do in this example is to illustrate that the inquiry procedure can be used to generate raw material for an essay on even so uninteresting a subject as my ballpoint pen. In fact, if you think about it, the material that this discussion has generated could, with very little reworking, be turned into an essay entitled, perhaps,

The Ontology and Teleology of the Parker Ballpoint Pen

(Even though we haven't said much that's very important, if we choose a title that sounds fancy enough, maybe our readers will think that the essay contains profundities that they have just never discovered.)

Questions for a Variety of Subjects

The following categories of questions—which are self-explanatory—were developed by Richard L. Larson.[10] The chart should be useful to writers who are groping for ideas concerning almost any subject. Take a careful look at the chart, and make use of it.

I. Topics That Invite Comment

A. Writing About Single Items (in present existence)

What are its precise physical characteristics (shape, dimensions, composition, etc.)?
How does it differ from things that resemble it?
What is its "range of variation" (how much can we change it and still identify it as the thing we started with)?
Does it call to mind other objects we have observed earlier in our lives? Why? In what respects?
From what points of view can it be examined?
What sort of structure does it have?
How do the parts of it work together?
How are the parts proportioned in relation to each other?

---

[10]Richard L. Larson, "Discovery Through Questioning: A Plan for Teaching Rhetorical Invention," *College English*, 30 (Nov. 1968), 126–34. Copyright © 1968 by the National Council of Teachers of English. Reprinted by permission of the publisher and the author.

To what structure (class or sequence of items) does it belong?
Who or what produced it in this form? Why?
Who needs it?
Who uses it? For what?
What purposes might it serve?
How can it be evaluated for these purposes?

B. Writing About Single Completed Events, or Parts of an Ongoing Process

(These questions can apply to scenes and pictures, as well as to works of fiction and drama.)
Exactly what happened? (Tell the precise sequence: Who? What? When? How? Why? Who did what to whom? Why? What did what to what? How?)
What were the circumstances in which the event occurred? What did they contribute to its happening?
How was the event like or unlike similar events?
What were its causes?
What were its consequences?
What does its occurrence imply? What action (if any) is called for?
What was affected (indirectly) by it?
What, if anything, does it reveal or emphasize about some general condition?
To what group or class might it be assigned?
Is it (in general) good or bad? by what standard? How do we arrive at the standard?
How do we know about it? What is the authority for our information? How reliable is the authority? How do we know it to be reliable (or unreliable)?
How might the event have been changed or avoided?
To what other events was it connected? How?
To what kinds of structures (if any) can it be assigned?

C. Writing About Abstract Concepts (e.g., "religion," "socialism")

To what specific items, groups of items, events, or groups of events, does the word or words connect, in your experience or imagination?
What characteristics must an item or event have before the name of the concept can apply to it?
How do the referents of that concept differ from the things we name with similar concepts (e.g., "democracy" and "socialism")?
How has the term been used by writers whom you have read? How have they implicitly defined it?
Does the word have persuasive value? Does the use of it in connection with another concept seem to praise or condemn the other concept?
Are you favorably disposed to all things included in the concept? Why or why not?

D. Writing About Collections of Items (in present existence)

(These questions are in addition to the questions about single items, which can presumably be asked of each item in the group.)
What, exactly, do the items have in common?

If they have features in common, how do they differ?
How are the items related to each other, if not by common characteristics?
What is revealed about them in this way?
How may the group be divided?
What bases for division can be found?
What correlations, if any, may be found among the various possible subgroups? Is anything disclosed by the study of these correlations?
Into what class, if any, can the group as a whole be put?

E. Writing About Groups of Completed Events, Including Processes

(These questions are in addition to questions about single completed events; such questions are applicable to each event in the group. These questions also apply to literary works, principally fiction and drama.)
What have the events in common?
If they have features in common, how do they differ?
How are the events related to each other (if they are not part of a chronological sequence)?
What is revealed by the events when taken as a group?
How can the group be divided? On what bases?
What possible correlations can be found among the several subgroups?
Into what class, if any, can the events taken as a group fit?
Does the group belong to any other structures than simply a larger group of similar events? (Is it part of a more inclusive chronological sequence? One more piece of evidence that may point toward a conclusion about history? And so on.)
To what antecedents does the group of events look back? Where can they be found?
What implications, if any, does the group of events have? Does the group point to a need for some sort of action?

II. "Topics" with "Comments" Already Attached

A. Writing About Propositions (statements set forth to be proved or disproved)

What must be established for readers before they will believe it?
Into what subpropositions, if any, can it be broken down? (What smaller assertions does it contain?)
What are the meanings of key words in it?
To what line of reasoning is it apparently a conclusion?
How can we contrast it with other, similar, propositions? (How can we change it, if at all, and still have roughly the same proposition?)
To what class (or classes) of propositions does it belong?
How inclusive (or how limited) is it?
What is at issue, if one tries to prove the proposition?
How can it be illustrated?
How can it be proven (by what kinds of evidence)?
What will or can be said in opposition to it?
Is it true or false? How do we know (direct observation, authority, deduction, statistics, other sources)?
Why might someone disbelieve it?

What does it assume? (What other propositions does it take for granted?)
What does it imply? (What follows from it?) Does it follow from the proposition
that action of some sort must be taken?
What does it reveal (signify) if true?
If it is a prediction, how probable is it? On what observations of past
experience is it based?
If it is a call to action, what are the possibilities that action can be taken? (Is
what is called for feasible?) What are the probabilities that the action, if
taken, will do what it is supposed to do? (Will the action called for work?)

B. Writing About Questions (interrogative sentences)

Does the question refer to past, present, or future time?
What does the question assume (take for granted)?
In what data might answers be sought?
Why does the question arise?
What, fundamentally, is in doubt?
How can it be tested? Evaluated?
What propositions might be advanced in answer to it?
Is each proposition true?
If it is true:
   What will happen in the future?
   What follows from it?
Which of these predictions are possible? Probable?
What action should be taken (avoided) in consequence?
[Most of the other questions listed under "Propositions" also apply.]

Finally

As a final gambit, let me remind you of a heuristic that you have seen in
action already. I refer to the Jakobson diagram of the act of speech or
writing that was discussed in such detail in Chapter 1. Here it is again:

CONTEXT

MESSAGE

ADDRESSER . . . . ADDRESSEE(S)

CONTACT

CODE

It was used so extensively and in so many forms in Chapter 1 that I hesitate
to illustrate its use again. But perhaps if the elements are now listed
according to the main questions that they generate, the usefulness of the
schema will become even more apparent. If you are analyzing (and writing about) any piece of writing (or spoken discourse), you can ask

1. *Addresser?* What can I learn about the speaker or writer? How does
   what I know about the addresser influence my interpretation of the
   message?
2. *Context?* Is the message true or false? That is, does the message square
   with what I know about the context, the reality "out there"? What do I
   learn from the piece?

3. *Message?* Do I understand what the message is saying? Can I paraphrase it? How is the message structured? What influence does that structure have on my reception and interpretation of it?
4. *Code?* What are the stylistic features of the message? Word choice? Figures of speech? Sentence structure?
5. *Addressee(s)?* What about the apparent audience? Does the intended audience have an influence on the message? Is the manner of presentation appropriate for the intended audience?

(The sixth element, contact, does not generate useful questions because it merely refers to the use of language to establish or maintain contact.)

The whole purpose of this chapter has been to demonstrate that there are ways of coming up with ideas—insights—concerning subjects for writing. There is no reason why you can't develop your own heuristics, and in fact, if you use the basic principle, you will improvise every time you encounter a subject. You will learn to turn it over in your mind and view it from different angles. You will learn to ask questions about it, to probe, to take it apart and put it together again, to see it from perspectives that no one else has thought of.

Discussion and Activities
Brainstorming

Choose a mundane topic—paper clips, toenails, light bulbs, typewriter paper, or something of the kind—and brainstorm it. That is, for ten or fifteen minutes, write down every idea concerning your subject that pops into your head.

An interesting way to do this is the following: Cut notebook or typing paper into slips, and enter each idea on a separate slip. After you have completed your short period of brainstorming, you can see if any pattern has emerged in your ideas. Arrange the slips so that ideas that are related are in the same pile.

It is also possible, of course, to brainstorm with a group of three or four people.

The Pentad

Kenneth Burke explains the Pentad as follows:

> In a rounded statement about motives, you must have some word that names the *act* (names what took place, in thought or deed), and another that names the *scene* (the background of the act, the situation in which it occurred); also, you must indicate what person or kind of person *(agent)* performed the act, what means or instruments he used *(agency)*, and the *purpose*. Men may violently disagree about the purposes behind a given act, or about the character of the person who did it, or how he did it, or in what kind of situation

he acted; or they may even insist upon totally different words to name the act itself. But be that as it may, any complete statement about motives will offer *some kind* of answers to these five questions: what was done (act), when or where it was done (scene), who did it (agent), how he did it (agency), and why (purpose).[11]

Below is a story in the form of a poem, "Barbara Allan." It must be appealing, for it has been widely known for hundreds of years, and yet it's enigmatic. In order to make sense of it, we answer a series of questions: What sort of person was Barbara Allan (agent)? What exactly had she done (act)? What did she do it with (agent)? Why is it significant that the action takes place in the West Country "in and about the Martinmas time,/When the green leaves were a-falling" (scene)? Why did Barbara do what she did (purpose)? If you will conscientiously answer these questions, you will probably understand the poem as fully as it can be understood.

Barbara Allan[12]

It was in and about the Martinmas time,
   When the green leaves were a-falling,
That Sir John Graeme, in the West Country,
   Fell in love with Barbara Allan.

He sent his men down through the town,
   To the place where she was dwelling:
"O haste and come to my master dear,
   If ye be Barbara Allan."

O slowly, slowly rose she up,
   To the place where he was lying,
And when she drew the curtain by,
   "Young man, I think you're dying."

"O it's I'm sick, and very very sick,
   And 'tis all for Barbara Allan."
"O the better for me you'll never be,
   Though your heart's blood were a-spilling.

"O dinna ye mind, young man," said she,
   "When ye was in the tavern a-drinking,
That ye made the healths go round and round,
   And slighted Barbara Allan?"

And slowly, slowly rose she up,
   And slowly, slowly left him,
And sighing said, she could not stay,
   Since death of life had reft him.

She had not gone a mile but two,
   When she heard the dead-bell ringing,
And every stroke that the dead-bell gave,
   It cried, Woe to Barbara Allan!

[11]Kenneth Burke, *A Grammar of Motives and a Rhetoric of Motives* (Cleveland: World Publishing 1962), p. xvii.
[12]The text has been slightly "regularized" to eliminate the need for glosses.

"O mother, mother, make my bed!
O make it soft and narrow!
Since my love died for me today,
I'll die for him tomorrow."

Problem Solving

Make a one-sentence formulation of an actual problem that you are currently having—for instance, a financial problem. Use the problem solving device outlined in the book to arrive at a tentative solution.

Varying Perspectives

1. The heuristic explained on pages 98–101 is based on the notion that we can take a variety of perspectives when we think about any subject. The heuristic was applied to the Los Angeles freeway system and to a ballpoint pen. It is also valuable in helping us to understand and develop ideas concerning what we read. We can use this selection as a test case:

In Praise of BIC Pens[13]

David Hilton

Others always skip over the word
That will bring the belligerents of the world
To the negotiating table, if only

I can get it written, or will
Teach thin kids in Woetown, West Virginia,
To rebound tough and read Ted Roethke—

I'm writing along in a conspiracy
Of birds and sun and pom-pom girls
Lines to cheer old ladies with shopping bags

Waiting by their busstops at 5PM
Or lines to get the 12-year-olds off cigarettes
Or save the suicides in gay-bar mensrooms

Or save the fat man from his refrigerator
Or the brilliant boy from color TV
Or the RA private from re-upping for six

Or the whole Midwest from wanting to conquer Asia and
the Moon
Or the current president from his place in history—
Oh, if only I can get it written

No one will burn kittens or slap little boys or make
little girls cry
Or cower at cancer or coronaries or plain palsied
old age
Or get goofy from radiation in his cornflake milk—

[13]David Hilton, "In Praise of BIC Pens," *Chicago Review,* 20 and 21 (1969), 212–13. Copyright © 1969 by *Chicago Review.* Reprinted by permission.

If only I can get it written. But always
When I get close to the word and the crowd begins to
    roar
The common pen skips. Leaves the page blank—

But you, BIC pen, at nineteen cents, could trace
    truce terms on tank treads,
Could ratify in the most flourishing script
The amnesty of love for our most dreaded enemies:

The ugly, the poor, the stupid, the sexually screwed-up—
Etching their releases across the slippery communiqués of
    generals and governors,
For Behold you can write upon butter, Yea inscribe
    even through slime!

But at nineteen cents no one pays attention
To the deadwood you shatter or the manifestoes you
    slice in the ice—
For who would believe the Truth at *that* price.

View the poem as an isolated, static entity. What can you say about its form? Can you state its meaning in a sentence or two or three?

View the poem as one among many of its class. How does it differ from other poems that you have read? Think in terms of both form and subject matter.

View the poem as part of a larger system. Think of the poem as a statement, and relate it to other kinds of statements, for example, essays, political speeches, sermons.

View the poem as a process, rather than as a static entity. This may seem strange at first; however, you must realize that *you* made the poem, for in itself it is nothing more than black squiggles against a white background. These squiggles allowed you to construct a meaning. How did that meaning develop as you read and thought about the poem?

View the poem as a system, rather than as an entity. If the poem is coherent and meaningful, its parts work together to make up the whole, but what are the parts? Most obviously, there are eleven stanzas. If you'll think about it, though, there are parts in another sense: ideas, metaphors, symbols, style. For example, the BIC pen is the main symbol. Of what?

2. In the chapter, we pointed out that you can view anything as an isolated, static entity (in the terms of modern physics, as a *particle*), as a process of change (a *wave*), or as a system with parts (a *field*). For instance, physicists view atoms sometimes as *particles*—"stop" them and describe them as if they were unchanging, diagram them, and so on. But an atom or anything else can be viewed as a process, a *wave* of change. Even an object as seemingly permanent as the great pyramid of Cheops was built, was used as a burial place, was explored by archeologists, is gradually decaying, and so on. And anything can be viewed as *field,* a group of parts functioning together to make up a whole.

  Furthermore, it was stated that to know anything, we must understand how it differs from everything else in its class, for if we could not

see differences—in location, in time, in physical makeup, and so forth—
a thing would have no identity. (For example, the only way that we can
differentiate identical twins is to know that one is "here" and the other
"there." If that were not the case, we would not realize they were twins,
but would consider them the same person.) In other words, we must
understand *contrast.* We must also know how much a thing can change
and still be itself. Here is a farfetched example. If Tom's brain is
transplanted into Bill's body, is the result Bill or Tom or neither? And
distribution. In order to know anything, we must understand how it fits
into a larger system. If we were archeologists digging in Africa and we
found a strange object, we could not begin to understand what it was
until we determined that it was a weapon or a cooking utensil or a
primitive calendar.

Particle. Wave. Field.

Contrast. Variation. Distribution.

Here is a somewhat difficult, but interesting and rewarding exercise. I
am going to put these six concepts into a framework. You will write
down the questions that this framework generates. The framework will
suggest that you can view any particle on the basis of contrast, variation, and distribution and any wave or any field on the same bases. The
framework follows. (Once you have generated your questions, you might
want to check them against the questions that are included in the
framework presented by Young, Becker, and Pike in *Rhetoric: Discovery and Change.*)

	Contrast	Variation	Distribution
Particle			
Wave			
Field			

Developing Ideas: The Paragraph

(or, Science Fiction, Ecology, Women's Liberation, Religion, Politics, Drugs, and Other Topics of Great Interest)

Summary of the Chapter

This chapter extends the discussions of the composing process and of invention. But it deals with those processes in terms of a major definable unit of written discourse: the paragraph.

The chapter stresses some concepts of structure and subject matter, with the intent of making them accessible to you in your own writing. This method is based on the assumption that one learns to write through unconscious and conscious imitation of techniques that one encounters in reading.

It can be demonstrated that the sentence is a convention, for literate people can identify sentence boundaries in stretches of writing from which clues such as capitals and end punctuation have been removed. In like manner, readers can agree with high consistency on how long stretches of discourse should be divided into paragraphs.

Paragraphs gain coherence because of transitional markers (such as **however** and **therefore**), because of chains of words and phrases that have the same reference, and because of certain structural features. The level of generality, higher or lower, among the sentences in a paragraph is one such structural feature, and another is the tendency for paragraphs to have certain forms, such as a topic statement followed by a restriction of that topic statement and then one or more illustrations of the topic.

A variety of methods are used to develop paragraphs: examples, extended illustrations, images, facts, analogy, definition, and so on. Of the methods, analogy and definition are perhaps the most interesting to speculate about, though not necessarily the most useful.

It is a truism that the paragraph is an essay in miniature. Whether or not that statement is valid, the paragraph is a sufficiently limited chunk of writing to allow examination of such matters as the distance of the author from the writing, or the vividness with which the personality of the author appears in the writing. Various writings can be placed on a spectrum from the intensely personal to the impersonal. This range is examined in a series of example paragraphs.

Furthermore, every writer has a background of experience, opinions, and feelings concerning almost every subject under the sun. The writer can call on this reservoir in attempting to deal with subject matter.

The Concept of Paragraphs

The concept of paragraphs is interesting for a variety of reasons. By the time you finish reading this chapter, you just might be interested in that concept, and, of course, you might find that your ability to write effective prose increases with your awareness of how paragraphs work.

A Note on Method

If your brain were no more than a computer, a teacher of writing could program it. And if the techniques of successful writing constituted a finite list, we could list the techniques and program you to use them. But your brain is more complex than a computer. And the techniques of effective writing cannot be stated precisely, and they are too numerous to list.

Probably what happens when you learn to write is that you encounter a device or technique that for some reason is meaningful to *you,* and without even thinking—unconsciously, intuitively—you make that technique part of your own repertory. The more you read, the more kinds of techniques you will encounter; the more you write, the more versatile you will become in using the techniques that you have learned.

What a writing teacher or a textbook about writing can do to facilitate the learning process is this: isolate, emphasize, and analyze certain techniques to make learners consciously aware of them.

That is what this chapter is going to do concerning paragraphs. But the paragraphs used in this chapter were chosen because they are inherently interesting, not merely because they illustrate principles of writing (though they do in fact serve that purpose). The chapter might well be called "An Anthology of Paragraphs," and it is intended to be read as a collection of interesting one-paragraph essays on a variety of topics.

Some Theory, High and Low Level

It is easy to demonstrate that the sentence is a convention that native speakers recognize (even if they cannot define **sentence**). To show that the sentence is a convention with recognizable boundaries, I will continue this discussion in the next paragraph without giving you, the reader, the normal punctuational clues; but in spite of the lack of punctuation, you will know, almost without fail, where my sentences begin.

in fact you can make a little test put a check mark or an X before every word that you think begins a sentence ask your classmates to do the same thing in their books my guess is this you'll find that you get *almost* total agreement even though there will be just a little bit of disagreement since I have constructed this passage in such a way that there is more than one choice at some points however if you do indeed gain substantial agreement as I'm sure you will then you can conclude that the sentence is somehow a unit that your brain has defined even though you can't I would contend that such is exactly the case with paragraphs in other words I will take a passage of coherent prose and reproduce it here without the paragraph indentations but even though they are absent you and your classmates will pretty much agree where they ought to go in order to test that contention put a check mark or an X in the following selection wherever you think a paragraph begins and compare your results with those of your classmates.

An Experiment in Paragraphing

1   A few years ago, Steven F. Maier, J. Bruce Overmier and I stumbled onto the behavioral phenomenon of learned helplessness while we were using dogs and traumatic shock to test a particular learning theory. We had strapped dogs into a Pavlovian harness and given them electric shock—traumatic, but not physically damaging. Later the dogs were put into a two-compartment shuttlebox where they were supposed to learn to escape shock by jumping across the barrier separating the compartments. A nonshocked, experimentally naive dog, when placed in a shuttlebox, typically behaves in the following way: at the onset of the first electric shock, the dog defecates, urinates, howls, and runs around frantically until it accidentally scrambles over the barrier and escapes the shock. On the next trial, the dog, running and howling, crosses the barrier more quickly. This pattern continues until the dog learns to avoid shock altogether. But our dogs were not naive. While in a harness from which they could not escape, they had already experienced shock over which they had no control. That is, nothing they did or did not do affected their receipt of shock. When placed in the shuttlebox, these dogs reacted at first in much the same manner as a naive dog, but not for long. The dogs soon stopped running and howling, settled down and took the shock, whining quietly. Typically, the dog did not cross the barrier and escape. Instead, it seemed to give up. On succeeding trials, the dog made virtually no attempts to get away. It passively took as much shock as was given. After testing alternative hypotheses, we developed the theory that it was not trauma per se (electric shock) that interfered with the dog's adaptive responding. Rather, it was the experience of having *no control* over the trauma. We have found that if animals can control shock by any response—be it an active or a passive one—they do not later become helpless. Only those animals who

receive uncontrollable shock will later give up. The experience in the harness had taught the dog that its responses did not pay, that its actions did not matter. We concluded that the dogs in our experiments had learned that they were helpless. Our learned-helplessness hypothesis has been tested and confirmed in many ways with both animal and human subjects. Tests with human beings revealed dramatic parallels between the behavior of subjects who have learned helplessness and the major symptoms exhibited by depressed individuals.[1]

The content and the moral ramifications of this hideously interesting excerpt are not our concern here. Rather, our purpose is to concentrate on its form. Our question, then, is this: Did all members of the class agree pretty much on where the paragraphs should begin? I suspect that the answer is yes. And if so, we can conclude that the paragraph is a convention in much the same way that the sentence is, and just as we talk about something called sentence sense, so there must be a corresponding paragraph sense.

Paragraph Coherence

The following somehow just does not seem like a paragraph:

2   The albacore are beginning to run. In Montana, it often snows in August. Freud created a revolution in the way we view the human mind. Grammar seems to be a dull subject.

But the next example, though it is still strange, does seem to achieve paragraphhood:

3   The albacore are beginning to run. However, in Montana it often snows in August. That is why Freud created a revolution in the way we view the human mind. Therefore, grammar seems to be a dull subject.

In the preceding passage, connectives—which you can easily pick out— have been supplied, and though we are puzzled by the paragraph (for we can't state exactly what it means), we sense a coherence—supplied, of course, by the connectives.

Chains of Meaning

In the following paragraph from *The Bern Book,* by Vincent O. Carter, coherence is maintained by chains of words and phrases that have the same referents. Those in rectangles refer to *the United States of America;* those in ovals refer to the *citizens* of the United States of America.

4   The United States of America may be described, among other things, as a land of great dynamic tensions. It is a land in which practically all of its citizens are emigrants. Most of the people who emigrated to America went as nobodies and their subsequent history, and therefore the history of America,

---

[1]Martin E. P. Seligman, "Fall Into Helplessness," *Psychology Today,* June 1973, pp. 43–44. Copyright © Ziff-Davis Publishing Company. Reprinted by permission.

is the history of (their) attempts to become (somebodies.) As to what ideas and culture (those criminals,)(prostitutes,)(fortune-hunters,)(speculators,) religiously oppressed and land-hungry (folk) possessed, (they) brought with (them) from England and France and Germany and Russia and Spain and Armenia and Ireland and Italy and anywhere else in the world one would wish to name. Are you surprised? Are you astonished to discover that (they) are (*your* relations,) only a few generations removed from the old country? You need not be surprised: (grandchildren,) look at (grandparents!) All of those (European no-bodies) trying hard to become (somebodies) in a land that belonged to the Indian and the Eskimo—that's America!

So transitional words—like ***however, therefore, thus,*** and ***then***—are part of the glue that keeps paragraphs together, and equivalence chains of words that have the same referents are another part.

Transitions and Equivalence Chains

To get a sense of how transitional words and chains of words having the same referents function to bring about paragraph coherence, let's look at two more interesting paragraphs. In these paragraphs, *transitional* words (such as ***however, but*** and ***thus***) are underlined; *adverbials* that give the reader the necessary time orientation are in rectangles; and words and phrases relating to *plows* and *plowing* are in ovals.

5   Until recently, agriculture has been the chief occupation even in "advanced" societies; hence, any change in methods of (tillage) has much importance. Early (plows,) drawn by two oxen, did not normally turn the sod but merely scratched it. Thus, (cross-plowing) was needed and fields tended to be squarish. In the fairly light soils and semi-arid climates of the Near East and Mediterranean, (this) worked well. But (such a plow) was inappropriate to the wet climate and often sticky soils of northern Europe. By the latter part of the seventh century after Christ, however, following obscure beginnings, certain northern peasants were using (an entirely new kind of plow,) equipped with a vertical knife to cut the line of the furrow, a horizontal share to slice under the sod, and a moldboard to turn it over. The friction of (this plow) with the soil was so great that (it) normally required not two but eight oxen. (It) attacked the land with such violence that (cross-plowing) was not needed, and fields tended to be shaped in long strips.

In the days of (the scratch-plow,) fields were distributed generally in units capable of supporting a single family. Subsistence farming was the presupposition. But no peasant owned eight oxen: to use (the new and more efficient plow,) peasants pooled their oxen to form (large plow-teams,) originally receiving (it would appear) plowed strips in proportion to their contribution. Thus, distribution of land was based no longer on the needs of a family but, rather on the capacity of a power machine to till the earth. Man's relation to the soil was profoundly changed. Formerly man had been part of nature; now he was the exploiter of nature. Nowhere else in the world did farmers develop any analogous agricultural implement. Is it coincidence that modern technology, with its ruthlessness toward nature, has so largely been produced by descendants of these peasants of northern Europe?[2]

Paragraphs hang together, then, because the words in them form chains of meaning, as in the series of words referring to plows and plowing; because time and space relationships are made clear ("Until recently," "By the latter part of the seventh century after Christ," and so on); and because transitional words establish logical relationships.

Sentence Relationships in Paragraphs

The relationships established by transitional words are interesting enough to warrant brief commentary. Consider these two sentences:

6 Early plows, drawn by two oxen, did not normally turn the sod but merely scratched it. Thus, cross-plowing was needed and fields tended to be squarish.

The *thus* establishes a cause-and-effect relationship between the two sentences. The next two sentences stand in what might be called an obversative relationship, established by the *but.*

7 In the fairly light soils and semi-arid climates of the Near East and Mediterranean, this worked well. But such a plow was inappropriate to the wet climate and often sticky soils of northern Europe.

In fact, if we see any paragraph as a coherent whole, we have obviously been able to establish relationships between the sentences that make it up. That is, our minds perceive automatically how one sentence relates to another. (If that were not the case, we would not feel that the paragraph was coherent, for incoherence is precisely the *lack* of relationships.) And here is a notion worth pondering: Obviously the relationships that we see among sentences must constitute a finite list. If there were an infinite number of possible relationships, then *any* sequence of sentences would constitute a stretch of coherent discourse; but, as we have seen, that is not the case. Sometimes the relationships that do exist are expressed by a word or a phrase; sometimes they are left unexpressed, for the reader to supply.

As an example of how one mind (mine) establishes relationships where none have been explicitly expressed, look at the following paragraph. In it, I have supplied the relationships that seem logical to me in my reading. These relationships are expressed by capitalized words in brackets.

[2]Lynn White, Jr., "The Historical Roots of Our Ecological Crisis," *Science,* 155 (March 1967), 1203–07. Copyright © 1967 by the American Association for the Advancement of Science. Reprinted by permission of the publisher and the author.

8   The working girl who marries, works for a period after her marriage and retires to breed, is hardly equipped for the isolation of the nuclear household. [FOR] Regardless of whether she enjoyed the menial work of typing or selling or waitressing or clerking, she at least had freedom of movement to a degree. [BUT] Her horizon shrinks to the house, the shopping center and the telly. [AND] Her child is too much cared for, too diligently regarded during the day and, when her husband returns from work, soon banished from the adult world to his bed, so that Daddy can relax. [SO] The Oedipal situation which is always duplicated in marriage is now intensified to a degree which Freud would have found appalling. [FOR] Father is very really a rival and a stranger. [FOR EVEN THOUGH] During the day the child may be bullied as often as petted: what is certain is that he has too much attention from one person who is entirely at his disposal. [AND] The intimacy between mother and child is not sustaining and healthy. [FOR] The child learns to exploit his mother's accessibility, badgering her with questions and demands which are not of any real consequence to him, embarrassing her in public, blackmailing her into buying sweets and carrying him. [BUT] Dependence does not mean love. [SO] The child's attitude toward school, which takes him away from his mother after five years of enforced intimacy, is an ambivalent as his feelings about his mother. [FOR] As long as it is an escape it is welcome but when it becomes demanding the child finds that he can play mother and school off against each other. [AND] The jealousy which mothers have of school and the attempt of the school to establish a source of control over the child in opposition to the mother can result in highly fraught situations. [SO] The antisocial nature of this mother-child relationship is very evident to school-teachers, especially when it is a question of discipline or treatment of emotional disturbance.[3]

If what I have done has made sense to you, you have achieved some insight into the way in which the mind—yours as well as mine—establishes the relationships that make for coherence.

The Sentence and the Paragraph

As we will see in Chapter 11, sentences tend to have a base, to which particular details are added. Thus:

9   The floor was filled with the poor white humans,
       running around,
       dodging,
       blinking their eyes,
       making a sound like a pen full of starlings or rats or something.   —Tom Wolfe, *The Pump House Gang*

Many paragraphs have exactly this same movement, beginning with a base (sometimes called the topic sentence) and then proceeding with details that make the idea in the base more and more specific. Thus:

10   Hope is *paradoxical.*
       It is neither passive waiting nor is it unrealistic forcing of circumstances that cannot occur.

[3]Germaine Greer, *The Female Eunuch* (New York: McGraw-Hill, 1971), pp. 221–22. Copyright © 1971 by Germaine Greer. Used with permission of McGraw-Hill Book Company.

It is like the crouched tiger, which will jump only when the moment for jumping has come.

Neither tired reformism nor pseudo-radical adventurism is an expression of hope.

To hope means to be ready at every moment for that which is not yet born, and yet not become desperate if there is no birth in our lifetime.

There is no sense in hoping for that which already exists or for that which cannot be.

Those whose hope is weak settle down for comfort or for violence; those whose hope is strong see and cherish all signs of new life and are ready every moment to help the birth of that which is ready to be born. —Erich Fromm, *The Revolution of Hope*

Of course, not all paragraphs work like this, even though a great many do. Some paragraphs, like some sentences, are "upside down," with the base at the conclusion. Thus:

11   By the middle of April,
for I made no haste in my work,
but rather made the most of it,
my house was framed and ready for the raising.
—Henry David Thoreau, *Walden*

12   Now, abruptly, [a certain man] sees a girl. *The* girl. He may have seen her before. Not necessarily. In either case, the symptoms of humanity's oldest malady begin popping out over him like a pox. He disolves into a stupor of manic ecstasy. In one moment he has symphonic dreams of the music he could make with this woman; in the next he is roweling himself with doubts as to whether or not she feels anything for him. He hangs around aching to have her look at him or say something that will make his day worthwhile, yet in terror that the glance or word might ruin it.

In between draughty, sentimental sighs, he is wont to behold himself as the luckiest of men, not seeming to care or realize that in the throes of this euphoria, which may last a few hours, days, or possibly years, his judgment is reduced to jelly and his liberty to slavery.[4]

There are other forms, but the important notion is this: *generally* the paragraph does have a base or topic sentence, to which the other sentences relate. The sentence and the paragraph are analogous in this respect.

An Anthology of Paragraphs

Enough of theory, then—even though we could go on at great length concerning the paragraph as a *real* form in discourse. The rest of the chapter will be devoted to the close analysis of a group of interesting and timely paragraphs, all of which can be read solely because they are engaging in themselves. The real purpose of the collection, however, is to take a fairly unsystematic, but penetrating, look at the anatomy of paragraphs so that you, almost unconsciously, will add to your own repertory of devices for making paragraphs work. A point is worth reiterating: you learn

[4]George Wiswell, "Why Men Fall in Love," *Esquire,* March 1955, p. 52.

to write by (usually) unconscious imitation of what you read. You adopt this technique from that writer and another technique from another writer, and so on—and the process of learning to write, of increasing one's versatility, never ends. The paragraphs and the analyses that follow are intended to help you increase your versatility as a writer.

Topic-Illustration-Restatement

The following paragraph is built on an interesting plan. The author states a topic, then he gives an illustration supporting that generality, and then he restates the topic.

13

Topic America is by far the most criminal nation in the world.
Illustration On a per capita basis, Americans commit about twice as many assaults as Frenchmen, triple the number of rapes as Italians, and five times as many murders as Englishmen.
Restatement From the price manipulations of Westinghouse-General Electric and the mass violence of Los Angeles down to the subway muggings and the petty thievery of juvenile gangs, it is apparent, in James Truslow Adam's words, that "lawlessness has been and is one of the most distinctive American traits."[5]

Examples and Illustrations

The following two paragraphs are interesting, both in their structure and in their subject matter. Look closely at how they work.

I

14

Example 1 Once another woman and I were talking about male resistance to Woman's Liberation, and she said that she didn't understand why men never worry about women taking their jobs away but worry only about the possibility that women may stop making love to them and bearing their children.
Example 2 And once I was arguing with a man I know about Woman's Liberation, and he said he wished he had a motorcycle gang with which to invade a Woman's Liberation meeting and rape everybody in it.
Conclusion based on examples There are times when I understand the reason for men's feelings.
Explanation of conclusion I have noticed that beyond the feminists' talk about the myth of the vaginal orgasm lies a radical resentment of their position in the sexual act. And I have noticed that when I feel most militantly feminist I am hardly at all interested in sex.

II

Actual topic sentence for both paragraphs Almost one could generalize from that: the feminist impulse is anti-sexual.

[5]William M. McCord, "We Ask the Wrong Questions About Crime," *New York Times Magazine*, 21 Nov. 1965, p. 27.

Restriction of the topic The very notion of women gathering in groups is some-how anti-sexual, anti-male, just as the purposely all-male group is anti-female.

Extended illustration There is often a sense of genuine cultural rebellion in the atmosphere of a Woman's Liberation meeting. Women sit with their legs apart, carelessly dressed, barely made-up, exhibiting their feelings or the holes at the knees of their jeans with an unprovocative candor which is hardly seen at all in the outside world. Of course, they are demon-strating by their postures that they are in effect off duty, absolved from the compulsion to make themselves at-tractive, and yet, as the world measures these things, such demonstrations could in themselves be seen as evidence of neurosis: we have all been brought up to believe that a woman who was "whole" would appear feminine even on the barricades.[6]

The second paragraph above is an example of a common and useful pattern: topic, one or more restrictions, and one or more illustrations.

Question-Answer

Another common pattern is question-answer.[7]

15   Psychotic experience goes beyond the horizons of our common, that is, our communal, sense.

Question What region of experience does this lead to?

Answers It entails a loss of the usual foundations of the "sense" of the world that we share with one another. Old pur-poses no longer seem viable; old meanings are senseless; the distinctions between imagination, dream, external perceptions often seem no longer to apply in the same old way. External events may seem magically conjured up. Dreams may seem to be direct communications from others; imagination may seem to be objective real-ity.   —R. D. Laing, *The Politics of Experience*

Development

Here is an exquisitely simple point about paragraphs: they need to be developed. And here is an exquisite paragraph to illustrate that point:

16   If we must have a slogan, let that slogan be the present. To move vigorously through chill water, and stretch like a snake in the sun—to do this actually, and to do the equivalent as regards the subtler pleasures of the mind—such is gratitude to makers. If I built a house, I should want the house to stand self-assertively, at peace with its placing. Let us then be as though builded. Let man take each brilliant day as one dropped from an eternity of silence. Let him enjoy the unique organization of his hulk. Let him be rained upon, wind

[6]Sally Kempton, "Cutting Loose," *Esquire*, July 1970, p. 53. Reprinted by permission of Esquire Magazine © 1970.

[7]For a full discussion of these paragraph patterns, see A. L. Becker, "A Tagmemic Approach to Paragraph Analysis," *The Sentence and the Paragraph* (Champaign, Ill.: National Council of Teachers of English, 1966).

driven, sunned, firm-footed—living first among the elements and shaping his other experiences by this immediacy. Surely no flower protests at withering in the autumn; even subsidence can be a purpose—and days of gentle ecstasy might bring us to welcoming our decline. Henceforth I will look upon no man with envy, since he is but repeating in his terms what I have discovered in my own. Nature has become the carpet of our sportiveness. Here is a skilful seller, repeating in the sound of birds what is suggested by stirrings of the air, maintaining by sunlight what is likewise proposed by the smell of damp soil, cradling the eye by the forms of a hill to make equivalence for the rushing of water. True, there are frogs, young and incautious, which land betimes in the belly of a heron. The heron's song is not their song. There are the sacrificed—there are those for whom the world was not created, but I am not one of them. For long I have hunted—and now I am feeding. Perhaps I am content.   —Kenneth Burke, *Towards a Better Life*

Kenneth Burke could have given us the gist of his thought by saying merely something like this:

17   Live for the present, enjoy life, and accept the world as it is.

In one sense, that is all he does say in the paragraph—but in quite another sense, he says a great deal more. By piling detail on detail, he conveys not only the raw idea but also its texture and nuances. The paragraph conveys not only bare thought but also a decidedly emotional overtone—one of robust joy in life: "To move vigorously through chill water, and stretch like a snake in the sun—to do this actually, and to do the equivalent as regards the subtler pleasures of the mind—such is gratitude to makers." The paragraph is highly imagistic; that is, Burke not only *tells* us what he is talking about but lets us *see* what is in his mind's eye. The catalogue of images in the paragraph is, in fact, amazing: a man swimming through chill water; a snake basking in the sun; a house standing self-assertively; a brilliant day; a man in the wind, rain, and sun; an autumn flower; singing birds, breezes, damp soil; a hill whose fluid shape is like that of water; herons that eat frogs.

Imagism

This same imagistic quality is found in the remarkable opening paragraph of "Holiday Memory," by Dylan Thomas, which was quoted in Chapter 2. Thomas speaks of the Bank Holiday that is celebrated in Great Britain in mid-August.

18   August Bank Holiday—a tune on an ice-cream cornet. A slap of sea and a tickle of sand. A fanfare of sunshades opening. A wince and whinny of bathers dancing into deceptive water. A tuck of dresses. A rolling of trousers. A compromise of paddlers. A sunburn of girls and a lark of boys. A silent hullabaloo of balloons.

This paragraph does not even contain sentences, just a series of vivid images conveyed by noun phrases.

Burke and Thomas pile image on image to convey the full sense of their meaning; that is, they add vivid details—and, in fact, Thomas's paragraph is nothing but vivid details. One way of viewing the Thomas paragraph is to say that "August Bank Holiday" is the base and the other noun phrases constitute the development.

Data

Not all detail used in development is imagistic, of course. Mere raw data—the facts of the case—can put life *and* vividness and meaning into a paragraph. For instance, the first paragraph of Mark Twain's *Life on the Mississippi* begins with these general statements:

19   The Mississippi is well worth reading about. It is not a commonplace river, but on the contrary is in all ways remarkable.

Twain goes on to support his generalities by citing data concerning the Mississippi:

20   Considering the Missouri its main branch, it is the longest river in the world—four thousand three hundred miles. It seems safe to say that it is the crookedest river in the world, since in one part of its journey it uses up one thousand three hundred miles to cover the same ground that the crow could fly over in six hundred and seventy-five. It discharges three times as much water as the St. Lawrence, twenty-five times as much as the Rhine, and three hundred and thirty-eight times as much as the Thames. No other river has so vast a drainage basin; it draws its water-supply from twenty-eight states and territories; from Delaware on the Atlantic seaboard, and from all the country between that and Idaho on the Pacific slope—a spread of forty-five degrees of longitude. The Mississippi receives and carries to the Gulf water from fifty-four subordinate rivers that are navigable by steamboats, and from some hundreds that are navigable by flats and keels. The area of its drainage basin is as great as the combined areas of England, Wales, Scotland, Ireland, France, Spain, Portugal, Germany, Austria, Italy, and Turkey; and almost all this wide region is fertile; the Mississippi valley, proper, is exceptionally so.

Data, then, need not mean mere grubbiness. In *Life on the Mississippi,* Mark Twain talks about the Mississippi River as the mythic central artery of America and about the time he spent on it as the most glorious period of his life; the book is largely prose poetry. But the facts and nothing but the facts contribute to the overall impression that our most American of American authors achieves in his magnificent book.

One more paragraph from *Life on the Mississippi* illustrates how Mark Twain uses the facts to delineate a picture of the river at its full:

21   From Cairo to Baton Rouge, when the river is over its banks, you have no particular trouble in the night; for the thousand-mile wall of dense forest that guards the two banks all the way is only gapped with a farm or wood-yard openings at intervals, and so you can't "get out of the river" much easier than you could get out of a fenced lane; but from Baton Rouge to New Orleans it is a different matter. The river is more than a mile wide, and very deep—as much as two hundred feet in places. Both banks, for a good deal over a hundred miles, are shorn of their timber and bordered by continuous sugar-plantations, with only here and there a scattering sapling or row of orna-

mental China trees. The timber is shorn off clear to the rear of the plantations, from two to four miles. When the first frost threatens to come, the planters snatch off their crops in a hurry. When they have finished grinding the cane, they form the refuse of the stalks (which they call *bagasse*) into great piles and set fire to them, though in other sugar countries the bagasse is used for fuel in the furnaces of the sugar mills. Now the piles of damp bagasse burn slowly, and smoke like Satan's own kitchen.

This paragraph is packed with details, giving the reader the sight and even the smell of the flooding Mississippi.

Analogy

Norman Mailer

Norman Mailer was exactly the right person to write the most complete journalistic report on the first flight to the moon. *Of a Fire on the Moon,* Mailer's account of the moon flight, is beyond doubt a classic in its own day, a consumately skillful interpretation of both the technical and mythic accomplishment of perching three men atop a giant firecracker (as Mailer termed the rocket) and propelling them out into space on a voyage that unbound humanity from earth. Below are two paragraphs from that book. In these paragraphs, Mailer uses analogy to explain the command module of Apollo 11 to the reader. *Analogy* is the process whereby the unfamiliar is made familiar through a description of the similarities between things or concepts that are in most respects dissimilar. It is a tremendously useful device for the writer.

22   To speak of a self-contained universe when one is dealing with a vehicle which is self-sustaining for a short period is to trespass on the meaning. A man is a universe by that measure, indeed he is more self-contained in his ability to adapt and survive than the ship of Apollo 11. In fact the Command Module is more like the sort of universe complete in itself one glimpses in a flower cut for a vase. Such an ornament receives food, breathes, exudes, molts, can even preside over a fresh development like the opening of a bud, and presumably this cut flower is capable of sending and receiving messages from other flowers and plants (if such communication is one of the functions of a flower) but still! we know the flower will live only a few days. It is a self-contained universe whose continuation is sealed off from itself.

The same was true of the Command Module. The men in it could live no longer than there were supplies of oxygen for them to breathe, and that was for two weeks. Nonetheless, Apollo 11 was more a cosmic expression than an ornament. Its vase was space, and through space it traveled, a ship, a species of man-made comet, a minuscule planet with an ability to steer. . . .

The comparison of the command module with a cut flower in a vase may at first seem outrageous, particularly when the comparison must be stretched to the breaking point by the assertion that flowers communicate, but in the second paragraph, Mailer redeems himself by saying, "Nonetheless, Apollo 11 was more a cosmic expression than an ornament." Finally, Mailer's outlandish comparison is more thought-provoking than, for instance, the following trite analogy:

23   To summarize the role of estrogen in the pituitary control center in the brain, I should like to quote a simile I once heard at a popular medical lecture. The speaker compared the pituitary to an irascible man who controls his entire family with strict discipline. But if something goes wrong, he is likely to fly into a rage and smash up the whole house. Estrogen, on the other hand, is like a calm, tactful woman who smoothes his irascible temper and keeps him from going to extremes. As long as estrogen is on hand, the temperamental pituitary keeps calm order in the endocrine family. But when estrogen is absent the overwrought pituitary makes a shambles of the entire household of the body.   —Robert A. Wilson, M.D., *Feminine Forever*

Certainly this analogy—the pituitary as the irascible father, estrogen as the serene mother, the endocrine system as the family—is not terribly imaginative, and is it not just a bit too cute, too cloying? Notice also that we gain very little new understanding from the author's analogy between the endocrine system and a family. In fact, the analogy is as farfetched as Mailer's equation of the Apollo 11 command module with a cut flower— except that Mailer's analogy is richly evocative and provocative.

Mark Twain

One more analogy, this one again from that glorious book, *Life on the Mississippi.*

24   But I am wandering from what I was intending to do; that is, make plainer than perhaps appears in the previous chapters some of the peculiar requirements of the science of piloting steamboats on the Mississippi. First of all, there is one faculty which a pilot must incessantly cultivate until he has brought it to absolute perfection. Nothing short of perfection will do. That faculty is memory. He cannot stop with merely thinking a thing is so and so; he must *know* it; for this is eminently one of the "exact" sciences. With what scorn a pilot was looked upon, in the old times, if he ever ventured to deal in that feeble phrase "I think," instead of the vigorous one, "I know!" One cannot easily realize what a tremendous thing it is to know every trivial detail of twelve hundred miles of river and know it with absolute exactness. If you will take the longest street in New York, and travel up and down it, conning its features patiently until you know every house and window and lamppost and big and little sign by heart, and know them so accurately that you can instantly name the one you are abreast of when you are set down at random in that street in the middle of an inky black night, you will then have a tolerable notion of the amount and exactness of a pilot's knowledge who carries the Mississippi River in his head. And then, if you will go on until you know every street-crossing, the character, size, and position of the crossing-stones, and the varying depth of mud in each of these numberless places, you will have some idea of what the pilot must know in order to keep a Mississippi steamer out of trouble. Next, if you will take half of the signs in that long street, and *change their places* once a month, and still manage to know their new positions accurately on dark nights, and keep up with these repeated changes without making any mistakes, you will understand what is required of a pilot's peerless memory by the fickle Mississippi.

Now that, it seems to me, is the perfect analogy, illuminating, imagistic in quality, completely worthy of the man who has been looked on as the father of American prose.

Definition

Often it is necessary to define, not in the technical sense of assigning a term to its genus and then stating the ways in which it differs from other members of that class, but in the sense of an *extended definition,* through which the author supplies details to present his particular meaning for a term. Here is a brief essay that defines "literature."

25 Literature is . . . but *literature* isn't; there is perhaps no such thing as *literature.* As far as general education is concerned there are poems, and plays, and stories, and cartoons, and jokes, but *literature? Literature* is an abstraction, a network. For different people, *literature* is different networks. For some it is all the information about the authors and publishers and audiences; just the way for some the Beatles were everything about Paul, Ringo, George, and John but their music. For some it is an elaborate code set forth to trap the unwary reader who must continually read between the lines. For some it is an infinite series of changes upon a few themes. For some it is a verbal manifestation of the totality of man's psyche—a model of man.

Perhaps the broadest definition is one that states: It is a vast assortment of verbal (usually) utterances, each of which in itself has some order. It includes *Mary Worth* and the *Divine Comedy.* Pieces of literature are such as to arouse a response—a sense of knowing, a sense of feeling, a sense of moving—in me. When these senses coalesce I have a kind of pleasure, a sense of the fitness of things. Out of having read what I've read, I construct a theory—a theory building upon the nature of language and upon the nature of the mind and upon the meeting of language and mind in what I would call response.[8]

The basic idea in these paragraphs is simple enough: literature is whatever you take it to be. However, that bald statement does not achieve the intention of the authors of the little essay, for they want you, the reader, not only to understand their premise but also to accept it; therefore, they have extended their definition, have included enough stipulations so that you are likely to say, "Well, that seems to make sense; at least there's something to think about"—a response that the bare definition can never bring.

A Final Specimen

What specific lessons can be learned from the following paragraph I really don't know. But the passage comes from one of the funniest put-ons ever published in America, *The Sensuous Woman,* by "J," a book that raises trashiness to the level of high art. This is from the chapter entitled "Sex—What to Wear":

26 Many men are swayed by the snow queen look—yards and yards of virginal white edged in lace or ruffles, with maybe a blue moire sash, the setting a canopy or elegant Empire bed covered with embroidered sheets, white satin coverlets and piles of pale silk pillows. The challenge of arousing and conquering icy, feminine, perfect *you* can become a fever to this kind of man. He will usually be an exceptionally ardent lover and buy you expensive trinkets.

[8]*How Porcupines Make Love,* ed. Alan C. Purves (Lexington, Mass.: Xerox, 1972), p. 25. Reprinted by permission of the publisher. © 1972 by Xerox Corporation, published by Xerox College Publishing.

This really isn't a bad paragraph. In fact, to be quite honest and unsnobbish, it's a very good paragraph. In the first place, think of the rich humor that emerges: the sensuous woman dressing herself in virginal white so that she can have a lusty tussle in an Empire bed; the ice-cold calculation with which the paragraph ends, the woman receiving expensive trinkets for the act she has put on. And the image is vivid, too: the Snow Queen, with her frills and lace, being attacked in elegant surroundings by a man who has been inflamed through sham. No, it's not a bad paragraph at all. And certainly "J" is not one of America's most enormously gifted writers; in fact, skills such as hers are by no means beyond the normally gifted college freshman.

The Paragraph and You

The discussion so far may well have implied that paragraphs are major structural components that are somehow external to the writer, like the structural components of prefabricated houses, which are shipped to the building site and then assembled. But, of course, nothing in language is external to the user, and an essay, for instance, is not assembled in the way that a prefabricated house is—the contractor sticking this part and that part together according to a set of instructions and a blueprint.

All this being the case, we should now attempt to delineate the close relationship among the methods of paragraph development that have been examined in this chapter, the notions about the composing process that were developed in Chapter 2, and the concepts of prewriting and invention (generating subject matter) that were discussed in Chapter 3.

Chapter 2 began with this quotation from Norman Mailer's *The Armies of the Night:*

27   Consider that a good half of writing consists of being sufficiently sensitive to the moment to reach for the next promise which is usually hidden in some word or phrase just a shift to the side of one's conscious intent.

Writing comes as if by chance, through the writer's ability to grasp the hope and the hint that every word and every sentence generates.

The Paragraph and the Composing Process

By way of a retrospective look at some important principles concerning the process of composition—and by way of a look forward at what remains to be said about paragraphs—let Bertrand Russell tell us about his method of composition.

28   Very gradually I have discovered ways of writing with a minimum of worry and anxiety. When I was young each fresh piece of serious work used to seem to me for a time—perhaps a long time—to be beyond my powers. I would fret myself into a nervous state from fear that it was never going to come right. I would make one unsatisfying attempt after another, and in the end have to discard them all. At last I found that such fumbling attempts were a waste of

time. It appeared that after first contemplating a book on some subject, and after giving serious preliminary attention to it, I needed a period of subconscious incubation which could not be hurried and was if anything impeded by deliberate thinking. Sometimes I would find, after a time, that I had made a mistake, and that I could not write the book I had had in mind. But often I was more fortunate. Having, by a time of very intense concentration, planted the problem in my subconscious, it would germinate underground until, suddenly, the solution emerged with blinding clarity, so that it only remained to write down what had appeared as if in a revelation.

The most curious example of this process, and the one which led me subsequently to rely upon it, occurred at the beginning of 1914. I had undertaken to give the Lowell Lectures at Boston, and had chosen as my subject "Our Knowledge of the External World." Throughout 1913 I thought about this topic. In term time in my rooms at Cambridge, in vacations in a quiet inn on the upper reaches of the Thames, I concentrated with such intensity that I sometimes forgot to breathe and emerged panting as from a trance. But all to no avail. To every theory that I could think of I could perceive fatal objections. At last, in despair, I went off to Rome for Christmas, hoping that a holiday would revive my flagging energy. I got back to Cambridge on the last day of 1913, and although my difficulties were still completely unresolved I arranged, because the remaining time was short, to dictate as best I could to a stenographer. Next morning, as she came in at the door, I suddenly saw exactly what I had to say, and proceeded to dictate the whole book without a moment's hesitation.[9]

The sentence by Mailer and the two paragraphs by Bertrand Russell could provide enough speculative material for a whole course on writing. But the intent here is more modest—simply to relate what Mailer and Russell say to the business of paragraph development.

The good writer knows how to follow the hints that his or her own writing generates. The mere act of writing will generate the possibility of more writing, provided that the writer is skilled enough to follow his or her leads. And the leads seldom present themselves at the conscious level; the mind generates in a mysterious way.

The Paragraph and Invention: Distances

A useful way to view the resources for paragraph development is to think of them as lying nearer to or further away from one's innermost concerns—from the intensely personal to the relatively impersonal.

Private Vision

The most intimate kind of subject matter is the mental event that has no analogue in the real world, the world outside one's mind. The most intensely personal sort of experience is the mystic vision, and, paradoxically, we can turn for an example to Bertrand Russell, who has come to stand for hardheaded rationality in the twentieth century.

[9]Bertrand Russell, "How I Write," *Portraits from Memory* (New York: Simon & Schuster, 1965), pp. 211–12. Copyright © 1951, 1952, 1953, 1956 by Bertrand Russell. Reprinted by permission of Simon & Schuster and George Allen & Unwin Ltd.

29   One day, Gilbert Murray came to Newnham to read part of his translation of the *Hippolytus,* then unpublished. Alys and I went to hear him, and I was profoundly stirred by the beauty of the poetry. When we came home, we found Mrs. [Alfred North] Whitehead undergoing an unusually severe bout of pain. She seemed cut off from everyone and everything by walls of agony, and the sense of the solitude of each human soul suddenly overwhelmed me. Ever since my marriage, my emotional life had been calm and superficial. I had forgotten all the deeper issues, and had been content with flippant cleverness. Suddenly the ground seemed to give way beneath me, and I found myself in quite another region. Within five minutes I went through some such reflections as the following: the loneliness of the human soul is unendurable; nothing can penetrate it except the highest intensity of the sort of love that religious teachers have preached; whatever does not spring from this motive is harmful, or at best useless; it follows that war is wrong, that a public school education is abominable, that the use of force is to be deprecated, and that in human relations one should penetrate to the core of loneliness in each person and speak to that. The Whiteheads' youngest boy, aged three, was in the room. I had previously taken no notice of him, nor he of me. He had to be prevented from troubling his mother in the middle of her paroxysms of pain. I took his hand and led him away. He came willingly, and felt at home with me. From that day to his death in the war in 1918, we were close friends.

At the end of those five minutes, I had become a completely different person. For a time, a sort of mystic illumination possessed me. I felt that I knew the inmost thoughts of everybody that I met in the street, and though this was, no doubt, a delusion, I did in actual fact find myself in far closer touch than previously with all my friends, and many of my acquaintances.[10]

This amazing passage gains its effect from at least two sources. As we read, we feel that we are indeed catching a glimpse of the most intimate part of Russell's being, for he is not reticent about recounting the depth of what he felt in as much detail as possible. Another source of the effect is the specificity of the passage—the wonderful concluding incident in the first paragraph, where Russell takes the child's hand and leads him away from his mother's agony.

After all, the mystic vision is hardly more wonderful than the ordinary "visions" that we experience second by second as we live: the peaceful euphoria of an evening in late summer, when the ocean breeze rattles the palm leaves; the rush of sensation on being suddenly awakened late at night; the utter cowardice before the plunge into a cold pool—these are the mental states that are just as mysteriously marvelous as anything that a mystic has experienced.

Personal Experience

Suppose that your mental life is a spectrum. The ultraviolet end is your visions, those thoughts, dreams, and reveries that have only the most tenuous and indirect connection with the exterior world, and the red end is your perception of something that is public, shared, unpersonal.

[10]Bertrand Russell, *The Autobiography of Bertrand Russell, 1872–1914* (Boston: Little, Brown, 1967), pp. 219–20. Copyright © 1951, 1952, 1953, 1956 by Bertrand Russell. Copyright © 1961 by George Allen & Unwin Ltd. Copyright © 1967 by George Allen & Unwin Ltd. Reprinted by permission of Little, Brown and Co. and George Allen & Unwin Ltd.

We have just seen how the private vision can be a source of ideas for writing. Next to the private vision on the spectrum—or, more properly, blending into the private vision—is what might be called personal experience. The following from *The Shadow That Scares Me,* by Dick Gregory, is a paragraph based on personal experience. When you read this paragraph, you should note that there is no topic sentence, no base, but if you supply the base or topic sentence, you'll have a flash of recognition that will make the paragraph seem profound to you.

30   I came from a family where I was expected to go to church on Sunday. I used to sit next to so many people who *loved* God—until the chips were down. My momma was like that. She was so busy loving God that it never occurred to her to respect Him. If she had respected God and the Bible, things would have been different in our house. Momma used to bring home food which she stole from the pantry of the white folks she was working for. She would cook it, serve it, and then *demand* that we pray over it. One day I took Momma down into the basement where I hid the things I had stolen. I said, "Here, Momma. You pray over what I have stolen and then I'll go back to the table and pray over what you have stolen." Momma didn't know that I was a better thief than she was. I just couldn't justify mine.

Personal experience? Yes. But on a different order from that of Russell. The inner vision is mystic in its intensely personal nature; there is only one observer for it—the person who is experiencing it. However, Gregory's experience could have had an outside observer, a friend of the family, for example.

Many lessons are to be learned from Gregory's paragraph, not the least of which is this: *Don't beat the reader over the head with your point.* Let me show you what I mean. The reader must become rather deeply involved in Gregory's paragraph, for the meaning is not stated outright; the reader must participate intensely enough to construct the meaning. And if Gregory had stated his point in a topic sentence, the paragraph would have lost much of its force. Suppose, for instance, that Gregory had begun with this sentence:

31   Religious people tend to be hypocritical.

Wouldn't this bare statement of the point have taken the real kick out of the paragraph?

Gregory's little narrative is, however, simple. It plainly tells about an experience from his life, an experience that had meaning for him and that conveys its meaning to the reader. Here is a rewrite of the paragraph:

32   Religious people tend to be hypocritical. They claim that they love God and use this love as their tacit excuse for not obeying His commandments. Some people use their religion to justify whatever acts they choose to perform, saying, in effect, "I'm religious, so whatever I do must be all right."

Certainly the rewrite does not have the vividness of the original, even though the rewrite probably conveys the message of the original more directly.

The Middle Distance

From the writer's inner mental resources and fund of personal experience as materials for developing paragraphs (that is, as sources of ideas to bring to bear upon topics under discussion in writing), we now move to the midpoint of the spectrum of the mental life, the area where the writer goes beyond private visions and personal experience.

In the paragraphs by Russell and Gregory, the writer's presence was overwhelming; the paragraphs were intensely personal. At the midpoint in the spectrum, the writer tends to disappear from view, hovering behind the subject matter itself. Here is such a relatively impersonal paragraph:

33   Why do readers want pornographic and obscene books, ask the moralists, expecting, as is their wont, that every decent and responsible person will agree that only perverse minds could harbor such a taste. The answer is plain: such books deal with one of the subjects, like war and religion, about which mankind can never hear enough. Taste governs our choice of such books, as it does in all literature; the man who likes *Mademoiselle de Maupin* is not usually the man who delights in *Eskimo Nell.* The public for *Lady Chatterley* is not the same as for Mark Twain's *Domestic Conversation,* though both use the same forbidden words; the one is the novel of a philosopher and the other is unmistakably the diversion of a river pilot. Nor does the outhouse humor of Eugene Field or James Whitcomb Riley appeal to readers whose interest is sexual rather than excremental; no Freudian needs to be told why. These works, of whichever category, supply an element which is lacking in the lives of most men and women. The demanding and inexorable tension of modern life, especially in North America, and the countless duties which are imposed by getting a living and maintaining the type of domesticity now fashionable, do not bring the satisfaction of some of the heart's deepest desires. These desires are not necessarily reprehensible, but they are at odds with much of our democratic slavery. Our modern way of life has not created the need for erotica, but it has perhaps increased it, and has made possible such a phenomenon as the publication, by a reputable house, of *A Treasury of Ribaldry,* edited by a respected man of letters, Louis Untermeyer, and sold freely in all bookshops. Ribaldry and erotica are safety valves for people who feel the weight of modern life heavily upon them; those whose ideal of civilized man approximates to the ox or the gelding, toiling to drag the plow, do not approve, and this is not the place to try to persuade them that their attitude is a dangerous one for the future of civilization.[11]

A number of things need to be said about this paragraph. In the first place, it does develop an interesting argument in favor of erotica and pornography, doesn't it? And notice that the argument is generalized. Where Russell and Gregory speak in very personal terms, Davies implies that his is the kind of thinking that any reasonable person might do. And what would have happened if Davies had reduced his argument to very personal terms? Something as unconvincing as this:

[11]Robertson Davies, *A Voice from the Attic* (New York: The Viking Press, 1972), pp. 282–83. Copyright © 1960, 1972 by Robertson Davies. Copyright © 1960 by The Curtis Publishing Co. Reprinted by permission of Collins-Knowlton-Wing, Inc. and McClelland & Stewart, Ltd.

34   During my lifetime, I've read a great deal of pornography and erotica, and it hasn't hurt me. In fact, after reading *Fanny Hill,* I felt considerably relieved; the tension of the modern world vanished. So on the basis of my strictly personal experience, I conclude that erotica and pornography are healthy for everyone.

An even more important point ought to be made. Where does Davies get the material for his paragraph? From intimately personal experience? From research? From a report by others? No. Davies calls merely—exclusively—upon his own general background of knowledge.

In fact, virtually everyone reading this book has sufficient background to write intelligently and interestingly about

35   the nature of the English language
the current economic situation in the United States
football
modern art
automobiles
health care
higher education
the identity crisis of the modern teen-ager
sexism
racism
and ten thousand other subjects

and to do so in such a way that the written result would fall at the midpoint of the spectrum from personal to impersonal—that is, to write a piece that conveys the sort of tone found in the Davies paragraph. The reason for this is that virtually everyone has a fund of general knowledge about, experience with, and opinions concerning these subjects (not that everyone, or anyone, is an expert on all or any of them).

This ability to call upon one's fund of knowledge and experience, to distance oneself, and to write in a relatively impersonal way is a skill that every writer needs to acquire.

This middle distance in using one's personal resources is important when one is writing about subjects that by their very nature are charged with emotion. Here is a paragraph by Edgar Smith, a man who lived under the sentence of death for several years:

36   At exactly 10 P.M., the cell door is opened and the man is led to the execution chamber behind the green door. Some men stop at each cell on the way, to shake hands with those they are leaving behind. There is not much you can say to a man who will be dead in three minutes. That is how long it takes. The man walks into the room, sits down, the straps are tightened, and three minutes later the doctor pronounces him dead. No hysterics, no noise, no dimming of lights when the switch is thrown. That dimming-of-lights business is another popular misconception fostered by a long line of Cagney movies. In real life—or is it real death?—the state is much more scientific. The electric chair draws current from a separate, outside power line, specially installed. So insulated is the process that anyone entering the Death House at the moment of an execution would never know it was happening.

—Edgar Smith, *Brief Against Death*

So both Davies and Smith use personal experience of one kind or another as material, but they achieve quite a different effect from that conveyed by Gregory, though Gregory uses the same general sort of material. Here is the real secret to this distancing: neither Davies nor Smith ever tell us anything that we don't feel another person could have told us—if that person had had the same experiences as Davies and Smith. Smith's paragraph is a clear-cut example. We get very little, if any, of Smith's own personal, private horror concerning electrocutions; he lets us see what presumably every other person in the death house might have seen; thus, his description of the process has a public quality. Now that public quality is, to be sure, an illusion, for the reader is seeing through Smith's eyes, is perceiving details through the filter of Smith's own sensibilities. And yet, in a strange way, Smith keeps the *strictly personal* out of the paragraph. We catch only glimpses of the author, in such statements as "There is not much you can say to a man who will be dead in three minutes" and "That dimming-of-lights business is another popular misconception fostered by a long line of Cagney movies."

The Impersonal

Moving toward the impersonal end of the spectrum, we find paragraphs that are developed on the basis of chains of logic. The effects of logical development are worth pondering for just a moment. Presumably, if an argument is perfectly logical, readers will be compelled to admit its validity, even though they might not accept its truth. To take a simple example: If you agree with the premise "All human beings have a soul," then you must accept the truth of the following argument, for it is internally consistent:

37   All human beings have a soul.
　　 George is a human being.
　　 Therefore, George has a soul.

If, however, you do not accept the truth of the major premise, you must nonetheless accept the validity of the argument. That is, you must say to yourself something like this: If it were true that all human beings do have souls, then the argument would prove that George has a soul. Later in this book, we will examine some of the conditions for logical argument, but at the moment we are merely exploring a writer's resources—and the ability to reason a premise through is one of those resources.

Read the following paragraph with the utmost care, for in it you will see how a tight chain of reasoning can lead to an inevitable conclusion—and in the process bring the reader inexorably to that conclusion.

38   Any crossing of two beings not at exactly the same level produces a medium between the level of the two parents. This means: the offspring will stand higher than the racially lower parent, but not as high as the higher one. Consequently, it will later succumb in the struggle against the higher level. Such mating is contrary to the will of Nature for a higher breeding of all life. The precondition for this does not lie in associating superior and inferior, but

in the total victory of the former. The stronger must dominate and not blend with the weaker, thus sacrificing his own greatness. Only the born weakling can view this as cruel, but he after all is only a weak and limited man; for if this law did not prevail, any conceivable higher development of organic living beings would be unthinkable.   —Adolf Hitler, *Mein Kampf*

In fact, this argument was powerful enough to sway millions of people to view themselves as members of a "Master Race" and to justify the subjugation and extermination of "inferior" races. If you accept Adolf Hitler's premises, you must also accept his conclusions. The premises are so outrageous, though, that they do not need to be refuted here.

The point is, when you are drawing upon your own powers of reasoning to develop an argument, *your premises mean everything.*

Another example of logical argumentation:

39   A proposition is not the same thing as the sentence which states it. The three sentences, "I think, therefore I am," *"Je pense, donc je suis," "Cogito, ergo sum,"* all state the same proposition. A sentence is a group of words, and words, like other symbols, are in themselves physical objects, distinct from that to which they refer or which they symbolize. Sentences when written are thus located on certain surfaces, and when spoken are sound waves passing from one organism to another. But the proposition of which the sentence is a verbal expression is distinct from the visual marks or sound waves of the expression. Sentences, therefore, have a physical existence. They may or may not conform to standards of usage or taste. But they are not true or false. Truth or falsity can be predicated only of the propositions they signify.   —Morris R. Cohen and Ernest Nagle, *An Introduction to Logic*

Finally

The purpose of this chapter has not been to give an exhaustive discussion of the concept "paragraph." But since the paragraph is a major structural unit of writing, it does provide a handy way of surveying the writer's resources for developing ideas, and it also gives us a way to begin talking about form (organization, structure) in writing.

Indeed, isolating a discussion of the paragraph into a chapter of its own has a certain falseness about it, for paragraphs are normally integral parts of larger units of writing. Nonetheless, discussing the paragraph as a unit has the strategic advantage of allowing sharp focus on concerns such as the types of material that the writer can bring to bear upon a subject and the writer's presence within what is written. We have seen that in some writing the writer's personality is in the foreground, never to be lost sight of. In other kinds of writing, the reader is barely aware of a writer behind the words. Of course, neither sort of writing is either better or worse than the other; one sort is useful for some purposes, and the other sort serves different functions.

Discussion and Activities

Paragraph Coherence

Analyze and explain the means whereby the following paragraphs achieve coherence.

a   The proper adjustment of a feed-back system is always a complex mechanical problem. For the original machine, say, the furnace, is adjusted by the feed-back system, but this system in turn needs adjustment. Therefore to make a mechanical system more and more automatic will require the use of a series of feed-back systems—a second to correct the first, a third to correct the second, and so on. But there are obvious limits to such a series, for beyond a certain point the mechanism will be "frustrated" by its own complexity. For example, it might take so long for the information to pass through the series of control systems that it would arrive at the original machine too late to be useful. Similarly, when human beings think too carefully and minutely about an action to be taken, they cannot make up their minds in time to act. In other words, one cannot correct one's means of self-correction indefinitely. There must soon be a source of information at the end of the line which is the final authority. Failure to trust its authority will make it impossible to act, and the system will be paralyzed.   —Alan Wilson Watts, *The Way of Zen*

b   The function of the critic and scholar is to make the past functional, for unless it can be used, it is deader than death itself. The only alternative is to adopt the view of Antoine Roquetin, Jean-Paul Sartre's non-hero, that the past has no existence, a thesis which does more than alienate him from bourgeois society—it negates all continuity, all history, all culture and renders scholarship and criticism impotent. Such an assault on animal wisdom, however, compels definition, or at least description. What is the past? Where does it begin and where does it end? Psychologists and philosophers enforce the presentness of the past by telling us that by the time our very inadequate perceptive apparatus reports an event it is already historic, and the very notion of the present is a conventional fiction. The past is time, or what we live in. The slippery present is that which has too much concerned the existentialists, certainly emotionally; but a paradoxical love of books shows how easy it would be to accept time or continuity. To emend Descartes, from whom they really take their being, "I think, therefore I exist *in time.*" With any sense of the all-enveloping past one cannot be a complete disaffiliate.   —Oscar Cargill, *Toward a Pluralistic Criticism*

c   Mammals, to which class the order of primates, including the species man, belongs, are distinguished by the facts that during the early stages of development the offspring is harboured inside the body of the female in an organ called the womb or uterus, and that after it is extruded from the mother's body, the mother nourishes it by elaborating a nutritious fluid, milk, in certain glands, the breasts or mammae. This general plan has been much praised and is supposed to represent a great improvement over methods of reproduction in the animal kingdom and a particular solicitation towards man and especially woman on the part of that force external to ourselves which makes for righteousness. I am not sure that such praise is entirely deserved.

The most sensible arrangement, I submit, is that developed in another branch of the tree of evolution—the birds, reptiles, and fishes. If I were picking out the animal mothers which seem to have had the advantage of the greatest amount of foresight on the part of that force external to ourselves which makes for righteousness, I should most unquestionably give my vote to an egg-laying order. The hen, it seems to me, has it all over the woman in this respect.   —Logan Clendening, *The Human Body*

Paragraph Development

1. Write a paragraph in which you state a *topic,* then *restrict* that topic, and then give two *illustrations.* Here is an example:

Topic	A traditional college education is a meaningless waste of time and money for some students, particularly those whose only interest is in acquiring some skill to make a living.
Restriction	However, if the curriculum were opened up, our institutions of higher learning could offer educational experiences for everyone.
Illustration	For instance, it seems futile to insist that an aspiring lab technician should take a course in literature if he or she is not so inclined. After all, there is no moral or civil law that compels all people to be cultured.
Illustration	Furthermore, students should be allowed to pick and choose more freely. It is tyranny of sorts to require that everyone fulfill the same kinds of general requirements.

2. Write a paragraph with a topic, two restrictions, and one example.
3. Write a paragraph in which you give three examples and then state the topic, which will be an explanation of the significance of the examples. Here is such a paragraph:

Example	Karen, who excelled in mathematics in her high school, decides not to go to college, but to begin her adult life by hitchhiking aimlessly about the country.
Example	Jeff is a gifted writer—editor of the high school literary magazine, author of a film script. Upon leaving high school, he becomes an apprentice bricklayer.
Example	Eric was fascinated by biological sciences and since his junior high school days had planned to enter college and become a marine biologist. In fact, for a year now he has been driving an ice cream truck.
Topic	All three of these young people have the talent and the financial means to gain a college degree, but they opted out; and they are far too typical. Obviously something is wrong, either with the students or with education.

4. Try various permutations of the topic-restriction-illustration formula for developing paragraphs. For example: $T\text{-}R_1\text{-}R_2\text{-}I_1\text{-}I_2$, $I_1\text{-}I_2\text{-}T\text{-}R$, and so on.
5. Example **16**, by Kenneth Burke, is a paragraph that uses imagery for its development; it makes its point by presenting visual images. Write an

imagistic paragraph, selecting "pictures" that demonstrate this proposition: Enjoy today, for tomorrow may never come.

6. Using the Mark Twain paragraph, example **20**, as a model, write a paragraph that gives the data about a trip that you frequently take—from home to school, from one class to another, or some such. Be as specific as Mark Twain is, and use as many of his devices (comparison, for instance) as you can.

7. Reread the paragraphs by Norman Mailer, example **22**, and example paragraph **24**, by Mark Twain. These paragraphs use analogy. Write a paragraph in which you use analogy to explain some concept or process.

8. After rereading the paragraphs in example **25** that define "literature," write a paragraph in which you develop an extended definition of some term.

Distances

1. Reread example paragraph **29**, by Bertrand Russell, and then write a paragraph that recounts one of your private visions: a dream, a reverie, an illusion.

2. Reread example paragraph **30**, by Dick Gregory. Choose an event from your personal experience that illustrates a point, and write a paragraph in which you briefly recount the event so that the point you are trying to make will be clear to the reader. But do not state the point directly.

3. Reread example paragraph **33**, by Robertson Davies. Now use your own general knowledge as the data you need to write a paragraph on a topic such as one of the following: pornography is not harmful; all guns should be registered; marriage is a form of slavery; everyone is entitled to death with dignity.

4. Develop a valid syllogism and use it as the skeleton for a paragraph. Here is an example.

> All human beings should have the right to marry whomever they choose.
> Homosexuals are human beings.
> Therefore, homosexuals should have the right to marry one another.
>
>   In a democratic society, every human being is entitled to equal rights and privileges under the law—including the right to enter into legally recognized marriages. Unfortunately, laws as well as public opinion seem to view homosexuals as something less than human, as beings with certain humanizing qualities missing. Therefore, gay marriages are illegal. Homosexuals are human beings, even though they are dehumanized by laws and public attitudes. Therefore, gays should have the right to marry one another.

The Uses of Writing: Exposition

5

Summary of the Chapter

Earlier in *The Contemporary Writer,* we explored one of the uses of writing: self-expression. After a long digression, this chapter returns to the concept of uses, this time to discuss writing that is used to explain ideas, events, things, and so on. This kind of writing is usually called exposition, and the main purpose of expository writing is to convey information.

Since expository writing conveys information, the reader must feel that the writer is reliable—honest and knowledgeable. The writer must gain the reader's confidence. But one need not be the world's foremost expert on a given subject in order to discuss it intelligently and informatively. However, one must be undogmatic and honest.

Much of the reader's estimate of the writer comes from the *tone* of the piece. Tone is the sense that the reader has of the writer's attitude toward the subject matter. Thus we speak of tone as serious, lighthearted, ironic, supercilious, somber, and so on.

Another way of viewing the writer and his tone is to say that the writer has a *rhetorical stance.* Rhetorical stance is the attitude that you take toward your readers, the way they perceive you as the author behind the piece, even though they might not know you personally. In speaking, we all adjust our rhetorical stance continually and automatically. In speaking to children, close friends, casual acquaintances, persons in authority, and so on, we vary our manner to suit the audience and the occasion. Rhetorical stance is not so obvious in written discourse as in spoken, but it is nonetheless important.

Sometimes—perhaps most of the time—you will not be writing for anyone in particular, but rather for what might be called the *universal audience.* When you have no particular, clearly defined audience in mind, you need to become your own universal audience by asking yourself, Does what I say make sense? Have I given enough information so that I would understand the point if I were the reader? Is there any specialized or personal information that I couldn't expect most people to be familiar with? Questions like these will allow you to adopt the proper rhetorical stance for an undefined audience.

Specialized audiences are in some ways easier to write for. If you are a member of a football team and are writing for the other members, you can assume that they will know your jargon, your in-jokes, the data concerning the team, and so on. If you are a physics major writing for other physics majors, you can assume a commonality of knowledge that you could not assume if you were writing for readers who are not physics majors.

For purposes of analysis and discussion, expository writing can be broken down into three types: *scientific, informative,* and *exploratory.* Scientific writing attempts to prove a hypothesis by presenting valid data; informative writing presents data concerning reality as the writer perceives it; and exploratory writing attempts to provide tentative answers to questions.

To Get Under Way

Back in Chapter 1, we explored one use of writing (perhaps the most important use): self-expression. Now, after a long digression in which we examined the composing process in general and explored some ways of generating subject matter, we return to the uses of writing, this time the use of writing for *explanation.*

The Reader's Purposes

A useful way of getting into a piece of writing, to see what makes it work, is to think of the various purposes the reader may have.

To Get to Know the Author

With self-expressive writing, as we have seen, the reader is interested in the writer. That is, when I read Mark Twain's autobiography or Allen Ginsberg's journals or Lenny Bruce's autobiography, my main interest is the personality that lies behind the pages. I want to get to know Twain or Ginsberg or Bruce. My focus is on the writer.

To Gain Imaginative Experience

In the case of most of the poetry that I read, my purpose is gaining pleasure from the poetry itself. Most of the time I am interested only slightly, if at all, in the poet; I take pleasure in the structure and the imaginative realization that I gain from the text. Often, my reading of poetry is much like my listening to music: I don't listen to *Mass of Life* in order to learn about Delius, the composer, or to gain a better understanding of early twentieth-century British history. The work is its own justification.

To Learn About the Medium

In rare instances, my purpose in reading is simply the method of publication. For instance, when I read Chaucer in the beautiful illuminated Ellesmere manuscript at the Huntington Library, I am more interested in the craftsmanship of the scribe than in the poetic artistry of Chaucer. To go beyond the bounds of written texts: often I am interested in TV programs simply because I'm fascinated by TV as a medium, by the limitations and opportunities that it confers on the transmission of messages.

To Enjoy the Style

Some readers read at times just to see how the author handles the English language. At times when I read Faulkner, for instance, I am fascinated simply by his sentence structures, regardless of what he is saying.

To Learn About the Audience

Finally, I sometimes speculate about the audience for a piece of writing. This is particularly true of advertising. I wonder what sort of people respond enthusiastically to some advertising messages. I wonder why the message is effective with these people.

In other words, my reading comes about because of these motives: (1) I am interested in the author as a human being; (2) I want the esthetic experience of reading well-written lines of poetry or prose; (3) I am interested in the art and craft of bookmaking; (4) I am interested in the way language functions; (5) I am interested in the audiences for various types of writing.

The Purpose for Reading Exposition

But there is another reason for reading: to find out about reality, including the reality of the human mind. Another way of putting this is to say that everyone reads in order to gain information. It is informative writing that this chapter will deal with.

Purpose: An Example

Before we go on, I should point out that the above catalogue of purposes for reading is an oversimplification. Let me give an example.

When I read *Of a Fire on the Moon,* I was primarily interested in the book simply because it was written by Norman Mailer, a fascinating person whose ego pervades the book. If the book had been written by George Zilch, the chances that I would have bought it and invested several hours in reading it would have been very low. However, I did want a complete account of the voyage of Apollo 11, and Mailer's book is the best source available for the layman. Too, the book is not merely reportage; it is an imaginative reconstruction of the whole adventure of going to the moon. And I could get the book in paperback and thus had to invest only a couple of dollars in it. Since I am fascinated by Mailer as a prose stylist, I enjoyed his use of language, regardless of what he said. And, finally, I was mildly interested in how a variety of audiences might respond to the book. In the back of my mind as I read was the question, Who else is reading this, and how are they reacting? In other words, in the case of Mailer's book, all the reader's purposes are involved in an intricate mix. The reader's motives might be listed as follows, in descending order of importance:

> Context
> Writer
> Message
> Code
> (Contact)
> Readers

Purpose: A Summary

Another way of putting this important point: We read to gain information *(context)*, to learn about or because we are interested in the author *(writer)*, to gain pleasure from the imaginative construct of the text *(message)*. We also read at times because we are interested in or gain pleasure from the writer's use of language *(code)*. If the language is badly handled, we react unfavorably, and sometimes, of course, we pay almost no attention to the author's style. Finally, we may well have at least marginal interest in the audience for a work *(readers)*. In fact, often a person reads a book in order to join the in-group of readers. This motive for reading is particularly obvious on college campuses, where certain books—like *The Catcher in the Rye, A Separate Peace,* and *Steppenwolf*—become "must" reading for the student who is with it. That is to say, sometimes, paradoxically enough, we read books so that we can join the group of people who have read those books.

In a sense, we can "walk around" a piece of writing and view it from different angles, thus:

 1

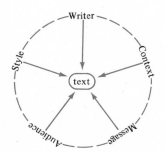

But all five positions are related, and each helps us understand the others.

When we view a text from the standpoint of *context,* we are interested in the information that it conveys, and writing that is intended primarily to convey information is called *exposition.*

An Expository Essay

Here is a brief expository essay:

2   *Serving Caviar*[1]

Craig Claiborne

All caviar, whether fresh or pasteurized, should be served thoroughly chilled. To keep it cold, the serving bowl is usually embedded in ice.

With fresh caviar, many gourmets declare, no embellishments are necessary. They heap it on fresh toast—either buttered or dry—and relish it as is. Others demand a dash of lemon juice. Caviar is also superb, and obviously more economical, when served with blini, melted butter and sour cream.

Chopped hard-cooked egg yolk, chopped hard-cooked egg white and raw onion rings or chopped raw onion often are offered with both fresh and pasteurized caviar. They are particularly recommended with the pasteurized product.

For a delicious spread for buttered bread fingers, mix pasteurized pressed caviar with cream cheese and enough sour cream to make it of spreading consistency.

Fresh caviar is highly perishable and must be kept refrigerated. Never put fresh caviar in a home freezer; freezing ruins it.

Two beverages are eminently suited for service with caviar. They are chilled vodka and chilled dry champagne.

As readers, what do we notice about this piece?

The Writer

Whereas in the self-expressive mode the personality of the writer is constantly with us, it almost seems as if the writer of "Serving Caviar" has disappeared behind his subject matter and his style. Notice, for instance, that the first person personal pronoun *I* is not used, and the writer does not insert his own opinions and preferences into the discussion. In fact, he scrupulously avoids slanting the discussion; we never know the way in which he prefers to have caviar served: "With fresh caviar, *many gourmets declare,* no embellishments are necessary" (emphasis added).

Another device that the author uses to achieve this impersonality is the passive voice. In the third paragraph, the author says **are offered** and **are particularly recommended.** Notice how the author suddenly appears when the paragraph is taken out of the passive voice:

3   I often offer chopped hard-cooked egg yolk, chopped hard-cooked egg white and raw onion rings or chopped raw onion with both fresh and pasteurized caviar. I particularly recommend them with the pasteurized product.

[1]"Serving Caviar," *The New York Times Cook Book,* ed. Craig Claiborne (New York: Harper & Row, 1961), p. 3. Copyright © 1961 by Craig Claiborne. Reprinted by permission of Harper & Row, Publishers, Inc.

Or look at this rewrite of the last paragraph:

4   I particularly like two beverages with caviar. They are chilled vodka and chilled dry champagne.

In this particular example of expository writing, then, the reader is hardly aware of a writer. *Which is not to say that all expository writing is or ought to be impersonal.* The purpose here is simply to look at an example that contrasts vividly with self-expressive writing.

The Context

Anyone who reads "Serving Caviar" has, it seems to me, one overriding purpose in mind: to gain information about how to serve caviar. That is, the reader is interested in what we have been calling context, and the demands of the context control the piece. The little essay contains only about 170 words, but note the fullness with which it covers its topic. At least, the piece seems to leave no questions unanswered, and that is the best test of completeness. If you want a quick check on the completeness of your own expository essays, ask yourself if the reader might have any questions that you have left unanswered. Ask yourself if you have given enough detail to explain all the points that you introduce in your essay.

The Structure

The structure of the caviar piece is so simple as to need little comment. You could easily make a simple outline like this:

5   Serving caviar chilled
    Serving fresh caviar
    Embellishments for caviar, particularly pasteurized caviar
    A caviar spread
    Keeping fresh caviar
    Beverages to serve with caviar

In most types of writing, organization is a major problem, one that is discussed in some detail throughout this book.

The Style

The style of the piece is simple and straightforward. There are no figures of speech. But notice how a few figures of speech would totally change the effect of the piece:

6   Caviar *is the tsar of hors d'oeuvres* and, whether fresh or pasteurized, should be served thoroughly chilled. To keep *the little black berries as fresh as dew,* the serving bowl is usually embedded in ice.

No improvement, I trust you'll agree. In fact, the figurative language is totally out of place in the piece.

The sentence structure is easy and lucid. After all, it makes sense to present simple concepts in uncomplicated sentences. Notice what happens to the tone of the second paragraph when the sentence structure is changed:

> 7   Many gourmets, heaping fresh caviar on fresh toast—either buttered or dry—and relishing it as it is, declare that no other embellishments are necessary, though it is also superb, and obviously more economical, when served with blini, melted butter and sour cream.

Again, no improvement. When the writing becomes ornate, with figures of speech and complicated sentences, the style and the subject clash. The successful writer learns to adjust style to subject.

The Audience

What about the audience for "Serving Caviar"? The very nature of the subject would indicate that the piece is aimed at a certain class; after all, only a small minority of the population wants to learn about serving caviar. But the author is not addressing anyone in particular. He is restrained and straightforward, aiming his message at those people who have the interest and the means to want to know about caviar.

Some Factors in Expository Writing

As with self-expressive writing, the vast majority of people do not need to be able to write expository essays in order to be successful in the real world. Observation and common sense tell us that much. Furthermore, I believe (and I think probably you believe) that one can be educated and cultured without possessing the skill of writing essays.

Then why spend time and energy improving your ability to write expository essays? There are several reasons. In the first place, you'll need that skill to get through college with maximum effectiveness and minimum nervous strain. Much of your grade in many of the courses will probably depend upon your ability to express yourself in writing. That is a simple fact, even though it does not hold true for all students.

More important: If you master the skills required in one sort of writing, you can transfer those skills to other kinds of writing. Therefore, improvement in one area brings about improvement in others.

Most important: Writing, in whatever mode, is an art, a means of self-expression that you can enjoy for its own sake, like playing the violin or making ceramics. In the universe, there is a lonely, isolated being called You. The only way to overcome your loneliness and isolation is to express yourself to others. All kinds of writing, including exposition, are means of self-expression.

The Writer: Establishing Credibility

As we have seen, when the reader turns to expository writing, the primary motive is usually to gain information. Therefore, establishing credibility is extremely important. That is, if the reader does not trust the writer, the writing has failed in its purpose. The reader must believe that the writer is honest and qualified—that the writer would not lie and knows what he or she is talking about.

The most direct way to establish one's credentials for writing on a subject is to state them:

> 8   When we at Boston University's Mental Health Clinic were first confronted, five years ago, with the new drug scene we knew very little about it and all pharmacology books were of little help beyond the chemical analysis which they offered. Although we were well-trained psychiatrists, drugs other than for therapeutic purposes were not part of our training. Drugs for the most part had been a ghetto problem and thus neglected and the very hard-core users were being treated in isolated government hospitals, and the results were worse than a dismal failure. But we were trained in the psychoanalytic model so we knew that we could learn, that we could see with sufficient experience how and in what ways drugs affected personality, if at all.[2]

This introduction helps prepare the reader to accept the information and conclusions in the essay, for it assures the reader that the writer has the proper background to discuss the subject.

In an essay on modern painting, Joseph Wood Krutch uses a more subtle method to introduce himself to the reader:

> 9   I am, I hope, not insensitive to any of the arts. I have spent happy hours in museums, and listen with pleasure to Bach, Mozart, and Beethoven. But I have more confidence in my ability to understand what is said in words than I have in my understanding of anything that dispenses with them. Such opinions as I hold concerning modern music or modern painting are as tentative as those I once expressed . . . about modern architecture.
>
>   Nevertheless . . . it is one of the privileges of the essayist to hold forth on subjects he doesn't know much about. Because he does not pretend to any expertness, those who know better than he what he is talking about need be no more than mildly exasperated. His misconceptions may give valuable hints to those who would set him right. If he didn't expose his obtuseness, his would-be mentors wouldn't know so well just what the misconceptions are and how they arose. An honest philistinism is easier to educate than the conscious or unconscious hypocrisy of those who admire whatever they are told that they should.[3]

Here Krutch gains our confidence by "coming clean"; he admits that he is not an expert on modern art, but, he tells us, he has opinions that are worth hearing and that he will set forth directly and undogmatically. Even if we had never heard of him before, Krutch would probably appear to us as an essayist that we could trust to tell the truth.

Though writers usually gain the reader's trust by less direct methods than are used in these two examples, the point is that you need not be the world's foremost expert to discuss a subject, provided that you are honest and undogmatic.

[2]Alan S. Katz, "The Use of Drugs in America: Toward a Better Understanding of Passivity," *Boston University Journal,* 19 (Spring 1971), 39.
[3]Joseph Wood Krutch, "Picasso versus Picasso," *And Even If You Do: Essays on Man, Manners & Machines* (New York: William Morrow, 1967), pp. 179–80.

The Writer's Tone

The concept of tone is hard to define but is nonetheless an extremely important aspect of writing. The word **tone** applies to the emotional shadings of a piece of writing. Therefore, we speak of tone as serious, lighthearted, ironic, supercilious, somber, and so on. Tone is the sense that the reader has of the writer's attitude toward the subject matter.

Modulations of Tone

For one example of tone, carefully read the following:

10 there is confusion in the kitchen!
we've got to develop kitchen consciousness or we may very well see the
end of kitchens as we now know them. kitchens are getting smaller. in
some apts the closet is bigger than the kitchen. something that i saw the
other day leads me to believe that there may well be a subversive plot to   5
take kitchens out of the home and put them in the street. i was sitting in
the park knitting my old man a pair of socks for next winter when a tall
well dressed man in his mid thirties sat next to me.
i didnt pay him no mind until he went into his act.
he pulled his irish linen hankie from his lapel, spread it on his lap, opened   10
his attache case, took out a box, popped a pill, drank from his thermos
jug, and turned and offered the box to me. thank you no said i. "i never eat
with strangers."
that would have been all except that i am curious black and i looked at the
label on the box, then i screamed. the box said INSTANT LUNCH PILL;   15
(imitation ham and cheese on rye, with diet cola, and apple pie flavor). i
sat frozen while he did his next act. he folded his hankie, put it back in his
lapel, packed his thermos jug away, and took out a piece of yellow plastic
and blew into it, in less than 3 minutes it had turned into a yellow plastic
castro convertible couch.   20
enough is enough i thought to myself. so i dropped the knitting and ran
like hell. last i saw of that dude he was stretched out on the couch reading
portnoys complaint.
the kitchens that are still left in the home are so instant they might as
well be out to lunch.   25
instant milk, instant coffee, instant tea, instant potatoes, instant old
fashioned oatmeal, everything is preprepared for the unprepared women
in the kitchen. the chicken is pre cut, the flour is pre measured, the rice is
minute, the salt is pre seasoned, and the peas are pre buttered. just goes
to show you white folks will do anything for their women. they had to   30
invent instant food because the servant problem got so bad that their
women had to get in the kitchen herself with her own two lily white
hands. it is no accident that in the old old south where they had slaves
that they was eating fried chicken, coated with batter, biscuits so light
they could have flown across the mason dixon line if they had wanted to.   35
they was eating pound cake that had to be beat 800 strokes. who do you
think was doing this beating?
it sure wasnt missy. missy was beating the upstairs house nigger for not
bringing her mint julep quick enough. massa was out beating the field
niggers for not hoeing the cotton fast enough. meanwhile up in the north   40

> country where they didnt have no slaves to speak of they was eating
> baked beans and so called new england boiled dinner.[4]

In this wonderful piece, there is a subtle shading of tone that is certainly as important as the overt content.

We know immediately that something is up, if for no other reason than that the author uses no capitals, but up to line 4, she is merely stating her thesis—literally, that kitchens are getting smaller and less important. Beginning with line 4, the tone changes, and soon we realize that we are dealing with some kind of satire, for we don't believe that kitchens will literally be moved out of the home.

Enter the tall, well-dressed man who sits next to the author as she knits her "old man" a pair of socks. Lines 9 through 13 begin a funny, almost burlesque, sequence, which ends with the prim statement, "i never eat with strangers"—even though the man had apparently not eaten, but merely popped a pill. The comedy grows even more delightfully slapstick in the paragraph that runs from line 14 to line 20. The climax of the wild humor comes with the statement (lines 22–23), "last i saw of that dude he was stretched out on the couch reading portnoys complaint."

Up to this point, then, the tone of the passage is simply humorous, slapstick, and it contains no trace of bitterness or ill humor. But an almost violent change takes place from line 24 on, and the piece concludes as a vitriolic condemnation of white society, which was built on a foundation of black servitude.

The modulations of tone in this passage are quite remarkable, and the author's skill in conveying them constitutes the real strength of the message.

The writer has conveyed her opinions, to be sure, but she has given them the tonal quality that imbues them with *affective* significance. That is, she manages to tell us not only what she thinks but her emotional attitude toward what she thinks.

Disinterested Tone

Tone at times can be *disinterested* in the old sense of "open-minded," "impartial." The tone of the passage by Verta Mae is not disinterested—and should not be. But at times neutrality serves the purpose.

Newspapers and news magazines, in their reportage of the events of the day, often attempt to maintain a strictly disinterested tone. And rightly so, for tone is an important factor in influencing opinion, as the piece by Verta Mae Smart-Grosvenor demonstrates.

On Sunday, September 30, 1973, this headline appeared on the front page of the Los Angeles *Times:*

11   POET W. H. AUDEN DIES IN VIENNA AT 66
      Struck by Apparent Heart Attack After a Lecture

[4]Verta Mae Smart-Grosvenor, "The Kitchen Revolution," *The Black Woman*, ed. Toni Cade (New York: Signet Books, 1970), pp. 119–20. Copyright © 1970 by Verta Mae Smart-Grosvenor. Reprinted by permission of Verta Mae Smart-Grosvenor and Ron Hobbs.

Anyone who likes poetry or admires creativity must have been moved by this news, for Auden certainly was one of the great poetic voices of this age. Here is how the article reads:

12   W. H. Auden, widely regarded as the greatest living English-language poet, died late Friday in a Vienna hotel of an apparent heart attack. He was 66.
    An official of the Vienna Municipal Undertaker's Department said Saturday that Auden died only a few hours after giving a Friday night lecture to the Austrian Society for Literature.[5]

That's disinterestedness—and we would want nothing else on the front page of the Los Angeles *Times,* or any other *Times* for that matter. But here is part of what Auden himself said when he received the news of the death of William Butler Yeats, that glorious poet who, with Eliot and Pound, ushered in the modern age in literature.

13   He disappeared in the dead of winter:
    The brooks were frozen, the airports almost deserted,
    And snow disfigured the public statues;
    The mercury sank in the mouth of the dying day.
    What instruments we have agree
    The day of his death was a dark cold day.[6]

And that's what tone is all about. There's no such thing as *good* tone or *bad* tone—just *effective* and *appropriate* or *ineffective* and *inappropriate* tone. It all depends—on the purpose, the audience, the subject matter, and . . . .

Tone: Rhetorical Stance

Rhetorical stance is a very fancy term for a very simple concept.

Most language transactions are verbal and face-to-face: we can see the people we are talking to. In these face-to-face transactions, we all make subtle shifts in our way of talking, depending upon the audience. It is these subtle shifts that constitute our rhetorical stance in spoken discourse.

As an illustration of this point, think of the many ways in which you adjust to different talk situations. When you're chatting about trifles with close friends on campus, you are probably totally at ease. Your diction is probably slangy, and you undoubtedly incorporate speech mannerisms that you would avoid in more formal situations—such features as repeatedly interjecting *ya know* into the stream of discourse. When you talk with your professors about official business, undoubtedly you shift your diction and try to exclude speech mannerisms. Probably even your physical bearing is more formal; you don't slump and sprawl quite as much.

In short, when you talk, you adjust your rhetorical stance continually. You talk in different ways to different people. Thus, the concept of rhetorical stance is meaningless without the concept of audience, for rhetorical stance is the way in which writing or speaking is adjusted for a particular audience.

[5]Los Angeles *Times,* 30 Sept. 1973, p. 1.
[6]W. H. Auden, "In Memory of W. B. Yeats," *Collected Shorter Poems 1927–1957,* p. 141. Copyright 1940 and renewed 1968 by W. H. Auden. Reprinted by permission of Random House, Inc. and Faber & Faber, Ltd.

The Universal Audience

In some discourse situations, special conditions prevail. For instance, when ophthalmologists talk to or write for professional colleagues, they can assume a shared body of knowledge that allows them to talk about certain subjects in certain ways—specialist to specialist. Often such discourse would be almost meaningless to a person who has not specialized in the field. Or consider the instance of a teacher speaking to a group of kindergarten children: very special conditions prevail.

There are times, however, when a piece of writing seems to be aimed not at any particular individual or group, but at what might be called the *universal audience.* This kind of writing entails some special problems that are well worth looking at.

Here is a paragraph that illustrates some important concepts concerning the general audience:

14   Man is nothing else but what he makes of himself. Such is the first principle of existentialism. It is also what is called subjectivity, the name we are labeled with when charges are brought against us. But what do we mean by this, if not that man has a greater dignity than a stone or table? For we mean that man first exists, that is, that man first of all is the being who hurls himself toward a future and who is conscious of imagining himself as being in the future. Man is at the start of a plan which is aware of itself, rather than a patch of moss, a piece of garbage, or a cauliflower; nothing exists prior to this plan; there is nothing in heaven; man will be what he will have planned to be. Not what he will want to be. Because by the word "will" we generally mean a conscious decision, which is subsequent to what we have already made of ourselves. I may want to belong to a political party, write a book, get married; but all that is only a manifestation of an earlier, more spontaneous choice that is called "will." But if existence really does precede essence, man is responsible for what he is. Thus existentialism's first move is to make every man aware of what he is and to make the full responsibility of his existence rest on him. And when we say that a man is responsible for himself, we do not only mean that he is responsible for his own individuality, but that he is responsible for all men.   —Jean-Paul Sartre, *Existentialism*

This paragraph is not easy to understand, but, on the other hand, the reader does not need specialized knowledge to comprehend it; that is, one does not need to be a dentist or an engineer or a philosopher to gain the meaning. What sort of audience is Sartre apparently aiming at, then? Certainly not at kindergarten children, and certainly not at ignoramuses. Might we not assume that the author is implying something like this: I am speaking seriously to all intelligent persons who might be interested in what I have to say?

Constructing a Universal Audience

But how does the writer construct such an audience? Here is the interesting—and useful—point: he or she must *imagine* it,[7] for no group in actual existence will hold precisely the same views as the writer.

[7]Chaim Perelman and L. Olbrechts-Tyteca, *The New Rhetoric: A Treatise on Argumentation,* trans. John Wilkinson and Purcell Weaver (Notre Dame, Ind.: Univ. of Notre Dame Press, 1969), pp. 31–35.

If all this sounds metaphysical and hazy, in practice it is nonetheless fairly concrete and easy. The writer must say at every turn; I am a reasonable person. Therefore, projecting my image, what can I expect other reasonable people, such as myself, to understand and agree with?

> Everyone constitutes the universal audience from what he knows of his fellow men, in such a way as to transcend the few oppositions he is aware of. Each individual, each culture, has thus its own conception of the universal audience.[8]

Now then, in constructing the universal audience for which you are writing, you must at every point also be the reader. The logic goes something like this: You say to yourself that you are writing for all reasonable people, and you base your image of "all reasonable people" on yourself. But, as a matter of fact, you are writing not merely for yourself but for the images of yourself that you have constructed as the universal audience. Therefore, you must ask yourself, if I were the reader would I understand this, would I believe this, would I agree with this?

Factors in Writing for the Universal Audience

There are some particular factors that might stand between you and the universal audience that you construct to address.

First is *culture*. Though you can assume that the audience shares much of your culture, you cannot assume that there will be a perfect agreement between your cultural background and that of the universal audience. Take as an example the Mormon culture of central Utah. In this culture, certain aspects of the general American culture have particular values. For instance, the drinking of coffee and tea is considered sinful (though not heinously so). Therefore, if I were discussing the concept of sin for the universal audience, I could not use as an example the drinking of coffee and tea unless I explained the background in great detail, for in the American culture at large, drinking coffee and tea is not considered sinful.

Another factor to be considered in writing for the universal audience is *the internal logic of the piece*. In Chapter 9 we will discuss logic in some detail, but for the moment it is interesting to note that we can virtually compel readers to arrive at a given conclusion. Suppose, for instance, that I convince you that drinking coffee and tea is sinful—which might call for a great deal of convincing. Suppose then that I demonstrate to you that all members of the local Elks lodge drink coffee and tea. You are then compelled to conclude that all members of the local Elks lodge are sinful. If you do not come to that conclusion, then discussion is pointless, for a gap has been created that all the arguing in the world will not bridge. This point is made clear if we reduce the argument to a syllogism, thus:

15   Drinking coffee and tea is sinful.
  All the members of the local Elks lodge drink coffee and tea.
  Therefore, all the members of the local Elks lodge are sinful.

If I can get you to accept the first premise and if I can demonstrate the second to you, you must accept the conclusion.

A third factor is *completeness.* An idea may exist as a coherent whole in your mind, but it must be transferred in its entirety to the mind of the reader if it is to be meaningful. The authors of the following sentence undoubtedly knew exactly what they meant when they presented their idea, but do you?

16 The most effective forms of oppression are those with which the victim covertly cooperates.

You perhaps have a vague notion of what the authors are getting at, but to say that you really understand, you must have more data; the vague outline must be filled in. Here is the way in which Ellen and Kenneth Keniston did fill in the details:

17 So long as coercion is exercised from without and experienced as such by the coerced, revolt is possible and ultimately probable. As the rulers of Chinese thought-reform centers know, coercion is truly effective only when its targets assent to its justice, and, more than that, accept their servitude as a part of their view of themselves. As long as American Negroes consciously or unconsciously saw themselves as an inferior race, they inevitably collaborated in their own exploitation; only the awareness of their unwitting connivance with oppression has released their energies toward relieving their second-class citizenship.[9]

So you must step out of yourself and ask, I know what I mean, but will my projected image of myself, my universal audience, know what I mean?

In general, the sorts of questions that one asks when writing for the universal audience are quite different from those that apply when readers are a specific group. If the audience is universal, one asks oneself, If I were reading this, would I agree with it, would I understand it, would it satisfy me?

Specialized Audiences

Every so often I go fishing with a group of physicians. On these trips, I am usually the only outsider, the only person in the group who does not really know the difference between the pancreas and the liver, between a sigmoidoscope and a sphygmomanometer. During the long drive to Baja California, when my fishing companions begin to talk about their specialty, I frequently must remind them that they'll have to talk in my terms if they want me to understand them. This experience of mine provides a good example of the interaction between a specialized audience and a universal audience: specialists talking to specialists versus specialists talking to a nonspecialist.

Specialization takes place along cultural, professional, and chronological lines. My wife and I can discuss the 1940s in great detail, but our sons are excluded from most of our specialized knowledge of that period. Members of subcultures gain knowledge that would qualify them as specialized audiences. And so on.

[9]Ellen Keniston and Kenneth Keniston, "An American Anachronism: The Image of Women and Work," *American Scholar,* 33 (Summer 1964), 355.

This raises the point once again that adjusting one's writing to an audience is of supreme importance.

Kinds of Expository Writing

Turning now from what is required of the writer and by the audiences for expository writing to the contents of expository writing, we can make a rough classification of types: scientific, informative, and exploratory. (But we must keep in mind that all the classifications in this book are somewhat artificial, though necessary, for we need a scheme of classification and a plan of attack.)

Scientific Writing

Scientific writing is not limited to lab reports and such; James L. Kinneavy characterizes it in this way:

> . . . Scientific discourse consists in a consideration of one facet of an object and the making of certain kinds of assertions (descriptive, narrative, classificatory, and evaluative) about this facet. These two characteristics, however, are certainly not enough to isolate scientific discourse from other discourse. First, the assertions must be referential. This means that the main concern of the discourse must be the reality under consideration. Therefore, the personal feelings and emotions of the writer are excluded (except as they intrude unconsciously or accidentally). Therefore, also, the reader as a target of persuasion, emotional or otherwise, intrudes only indirectly and implicitly. And finally, the discourse is not meant to call attention to itself as an object of delight; literary effect, therefore, is incidental and not usual in scientific discourse.[10]

Scientific discourse is more "thing-oriented" than exploratory or informative discourse. "Exploratory discourse fundamentally asks a question. Informative discourse answers it. Scientific discourse proves it."[11]

In the sense of this description, almost any subject can be approached from the point of view of science—particularly if one alters Kinneavy's statement so that it reads, "Scientific discourse *attempts to establish proofs.*" Thus, literary criticism and astrological treatises can be scientific, as well as lab reports or articles in the *Journal of the American Medical Association.* In talking about scientific writing, we are not using the word *scientific* in any exact or philosophical sense, but merely as a convenient label for the kind of writing that has the features that will be outlined and discussed below.

A Scientific Essay

Let's see how these abstract statements work in an actual piece of scientific writing:

[10]James L. Kinneavy, *A Theory of Discourse* (Englewood Cliffs, N.J.: Prentice-Hall, 1971), p. 88.
[11]*Ibid.,* p. 89.

Ain't *Again*[12]

Jean Malmstrom

18   The blanket statements in many textbooks that *ain't* is an "illiteracy,"
"barbarism," or "vulgarism" oversimplify the complex facts of its usage
as revealed by the Linguistic Atlas evidence collected in New England,
the Middle and South Atlantic States, the North Central States, and the
Upper Midwest.* *Ain't* has been investigated in its three different con-   5
texts: (1) as an alternate present negative form of *be* in sentences like "I
am not going to hurt him"; (2) as an alternate present negative form of
have in sentences like "I haven't done it"; and (3) as an alternate first
person singular present negative form of *be* in sentences like "I'm right,
am I not?"   10

In the first context, except in and around New York City, where all the
informants use *I'm not, ain't* is used in all areas by a few cultivated
speakers and many high school graduates. In Atlas terminology, therefore, *ain't* in the first context is "popular" usage; that is, it is characteristic of the speech of persons representing the middle level of education in   15
their respective communities. Further, *ain't* in this context is not "expanding"; that is, its use is not increasing through adoption by cultivated
speakers.

In the second context, "I haven't done it," approximately the same kind
of distribution is found, except that Eastern speakers who use *ain't* in   20
this context generally use *haven't* also. An old-fashioned form, *hain't,*
likewise occurs in this context. Apparently speakers who say both *ain't*
and *hain't* usually employ *ain't* to mean *am not* and *hain't* to mean *have
not.* In this context, as in the first context, *ain't* is popular usage, not
expanding.   25

In the third context, the Atlas shows that a large majority of the high
school graduates in all areas say *ain't I.* Of the cultivated informants,
about 20% in New England, about 35% in the Middle and South Atlantic
States, and about 73% in the North Central States use *ain't I,* although
no college graduate in the Upper Midwest does so. The cultivated   30
speakers who employ *ain't I,* however, almost always use another form
also. Generally this form is *am I not,* except in the North Central States
where no college graduate uses it. *Aren't I* occurs with some frequency in
New England and the Upper Midwest, but rarely elsewhere. *Amn't I* is
not used by any Atlas informant. In Atlas terminology, *ain't* in the third   35
context is standard in the North Central States, and strongly popular and
expanding elsewhere except in the Upper Midwest.

We must always remember that the Atlas investigates only speech and
offers no data on written English. However, since Fries reports no
instance of *ain't* in the more than three thousand letters he studied for his   40
American English Grammar, we may safely conclude that *ain't* occurs
predominantly in speech, not in writing. Therefore its usage may be
accurately judged in the light of the Atlas records. We may well remem-

[12]Jean Malmstrom, *"Ain't* Again," *English Journal,* 49 (March 1960), 204–05. Copyright © 1960
by the National Council of Teachers of English. Reprinted by permission of the publisher and
the author.

*The Atlas facts are presented in full by E. Bagby Atwood in *A Survey of Verb Forms in the
Eastern United States* (Ann Arbor: Univ. of Michigan Press, 1953) and by Virginia G. McDavid
in her Minnesota dissertation, *Verb Forms in the North Central States and the Upper
Midwest* (1956).

ber also that American usage is most adequately described in terms of five dimensions. Socio-educational, situational, methodological, tempo-ral, and regional dimensions all are vital to a comprehensive view.* Awareness of these five dimensions is especially enlightening in con-sidering a usage like *ain't I,* which shows regional as well as social and educational differences. Its absence from cultivated speech in the Upper Midwest, where a large proportion of the population is foreign-born and has learned English principally from textbooks, may be an interesting example of the conservative influence of the schools upon the normal patterns of change implicit in the development of any living language.

An exhaustive analysis of elementary, secondary, and college fresh-man textbooks reveals that only about one text in five discusses *ain't I* apart from the other uses of *ain't.* As a rule, textbooks forbid *ain't* in all its contexts, either stating or implying that it is a social shibboleth. The few texts which discuss *ain't I* separately recognize unanimously that English lacks and needs a first person singular present negative interrog-ative contraction parallel to *isn't he (she, it)* and *aren't we (you, they).* These texts usually discuss *am I not, amn't I, aren't I,* and *ain't I* as possible choices available to the speaker who has wandered unwarily into a syntactic trap like "I'm right . . ." and who wishes to end on an interrogative note. The textbooks' comments on these choices vary widely, perhaps because of regional differences in their authors' back-grounds. For instance, *am I not* is said to be "correct," "stilted," or "schoolmarmish." *Amn't I* is said to be "hard to pronounce," "nonexist-ent," or "Irish." *Aren't I* is called "ungrammatical," "affected," "liter-ary," "British usage gaining favor in the United States," or "British usage condemned by leading American authorities." *Ain't I* is said to be "wrong and usually avoided although accepted by some authorities," "histori-cally and logically justifiable but not standard," "an uncultivated collo-quial contraction," "universally condemned but needed in the language," or "the least objectionable use of *ain't.*"

Truly, English needs a form like the French *n'est-ce pas* or German *nicht wahr.* Historically, the language has always filled such needs. Today the schools are responsible for the teaching of the nationally standard form of written English and therefore inevitably retard the slow but incessant process of language change. However, as we teachers fulfill our professional duty to the standard written dialect, we may listen with interest to the linguistic grass grow.

This is an *almost* classical piece of scientific writing, in our sense of the term. Malmstrom begins with a hypothesis ("The blanket statements in many textbooks that *ain't* is an 'illiteracy,' 'barbarism,' or 'vulgarism' oversimplify the complex facts of its usage as revealed by the Linguistic Atals evidence . . . .") and then systematically sets out to prove that hypothesis. Proof in this case will be nothing so conclusive as a mathemati-cal or logical proof, but scientific writing need not establish its hypothesis in the rigorous ways defined by the exact sciences.

The paragraphs running from line 11 through line 74 present the evidence to verify the hypothesis.

Only in the last paragraph does the essay become nonscientific, for in this

*For a full discussion of these five dimensions of current American English, see Jean Malmstrom, "Linguistic Atlas Findings versus Textbook Pronouncements on Current American Usage," *The English Journal,* 48 (April 1959), pp. 191–198.

paragraph the author presents a plea, and a plea always goes beyond a proof. In fact, the nonscientific nature of the last paragraph underscores the scientific nature of the rest of the essay.

The Author. It so happens that I know Jean Malmstrom, an intelligent, lively woman with a vivid sense of humor and a deep commitment to her professional goals. But Jean Malmstrom as I know her does not appear in this essay. It could have been written by just about anyone who had formulated her hypothesis and who had assembled her supporting data. Jean Malmstrom the person does not appear until the last paragraph. And note how completely she succeeds in keeping herself out of the essay. She never says "I think" or "I have discovered" or "it seems to me." Lines 38 through 42 are typical. The *we* in "We must always remember" is really an impersonal use of the personal pronoun, meaning something very nearly like "all reasonable people." This passage ends with a sentence in the passive voice: "Therefore its usage may be accurately judged in the light of the Atlas records" (lines 42–43). If this had been written in the active voice, the author and her personal opinion would have emerged: "Therefore I can judge its usage accurately in the light of the Atlas records." Again, notice this sentence: "An exhaustive analysis of elementary, secondary, and college freshman textbooks reveals that only about one text in five discusses *ain't I* apart from the other uses of *ain't*" (lines 54–56). We assume, of course, that Malmstrom did this investigation, but if she had told us as much, she would have destroyed the impersonality that her scientific tone demands. If, for instance, she had said, "I did an exhaustive analysis of textbooks, and I found . . . ," she would have been injecting into the discussion an element of personal opinion (even though based on evidence) that is out of place in scientific writing.

Disinterestedness. In this essay, there is no overt attempt to make you believe, to persuade you that what Malmstrom says must be true or accurate. If the assertions are true and accurate, then you will perceive those qualities, and if they are not, you will respond accordingly. The author does not say, in effect, "I assure you that this is the straight stuff, and I really hope that you believe everything I say," for such persuasive techniques, though I have stated them crudely, would destroy the underlying assumption of the essay—namely, that the hypothesis is established solely on the basis of the data presented.

The Style. No one, I think, could say that this essay is unclear. No one could accuse Malmstrom of having written badly. However, conversely, no one would say that the essay is interesting *primarily* because it is so well-written.The style does not call attention to itself. As readers, we are not even aware of the "code" of the message, and the essay would be less scientific in its effect if we were interested in it because of its style. One might say that this style is "transparent"; it carries the message without obtruding itself. No one would claim that the essay is interesting because of its sentence structure or metaphoric language. Any interest that we have in the essay arises from our concern with the hypothesis and the data or reasoning that establishes it.

And this brings up an interesting point in regard to scientific writing. It is quite possible to read and enjoy a piece of writing that attempts to establish discredited hypotheses or hypotheses that we believe inaccurate. In such reading, we frequently are responding to the artistry of the text. In a broad sense, it wouldn't matter in particular what was said; we would enjoy the way it was said. In that case, the piece of writing would not be scientific for us at all. We would be responding to the text for esthetic reasons.

Faults. As a piece of scientific writing, the essay has its faults. For instance (starting with line 54), Malmstrom talks about an "exhaustive analysis" of textbooks, but the reader of her essay would like to know more than she tells. How many textbooks? What are they? What does **exhaustive** mean? The writer of scientific discourse must reveal as much data as possible.

Informative Writing

Whereas scientific writing sets out to prove or establish a hypothesis, the purpose of informative writing is merely to convey information. Therefore, it becomes necessary to understand what information is, to define **information.**

The Nature of Information

If I tell you that California is a state of the Union and that its westernmost extreme is on the Pacific Ocean, I have made a statement that everyone would accept as true and meaningful, but, as a matter of fact, I have probably not conveyed any information. Why not? Because information can be judged by its surprise value. Or to state the point another way, you can judge the information value of a statement by how much you might learn from it.

A *truism* is a statement that contains very little surprise value and hence almost no information: "One must study in order to learn a new and difficult subject"; "A successful marriage involves give-and-take"; "Children need nourishing food if they are to grow up strong and healthy"; "All people are equal in the eyes of the law"; and so on. The main reason such statements are so uninteresting is that they contain so little information. We may feel that they are indisputably true, but they tell us nothing.

The following statement is, I trust, novel enough, stating a proposition that no one would be likely to predict: "The one who solved the problem of overpopulation was an earthworm with a seventy-dollar electronic calculator for a brain." Even though that statement has a high degree of surprise value, its information value is extremely low, perhaps nonexistent. That is because it lacks content.

> To be informative, a statement must enable us to relate the factual basis to some explicit or implicit system about which information is desired. The content of the statement then comes to be equivalent to the logical implications about this system which may be inferred from the statement. In effect, the content of a statement consists in how much about a system is implied by the given statement. . . .
>
> By extrapolation the "content" of a discourse comes to be equivalent to the completeness or comprehensiveness of the discourse vis-à-vis the reality

being talked about. A discourse has more content if it has covered the reality being talked about in a more thorough way than say another discourse attempting to cover the same reality. If a substantial segment of the reality under consideration has not been covered, the content of a discourse is seriously deficient.[13]

The value of informative discourse depends, then, on both surprise and completeness. If I say, "I was born, and someday I'll die," there is content but almost no information, since you know that everyone who is now alive was born and will die. If I say, "I was never born, and someday I'll die," there is surprise value but almost no content, since the statement does not relate in a factual way to the implicit system (human life) that it is talking about. If a statement has both surprise value and content, then it is informative.

An Informative Essay

Here is a piece of informative discourse from *The Sea Around Us,* by Rachel Carson:

19 The events of which I write must have occurred somewhat more than 2 billion years ago. As nearly as science can tell that is the approximate age of the earth, and the ocean must be very nearly as old. It is possible now to discover the age of the rocks that compose the crust of the earth by measuring the rate of decay of the radioactive materials they contain. The oldest rocks found anywhere on earth—in Manitoba—are about 2.3 billion years old. Allowing 100 million years or so for the cooling of the earth's crust, we arrive at the supposition that the tempestuous and violent events connected with our planet's birth occurred nearly $2^{1}/_{2}$ billion years ago. But this is only a minimum estimate, for rocks indicating an even greater age may be found any time.

   The new earth, freshly torn from its parent sun, was a ball of whirling gases, intensely hot, rushing through the black spaces of the universe on a path and at a speed controlled by immense forces. Gradually the ball of flaming gases cooled. The gases began to liquefy, and Earth became a molten mass. The materials of this mass eventually became sorted out in a definite pattern: the heaviest in the center, the less heavy surrounding them, and the least heavy forming the outer rim. This is the pattern which persists today—a central sphere of molten iron, very nearly as hot as it was 2 billion years ago, an intermediate sphere of semiplastic basalt, and a hard outer shell, relatively thin and composed of solid basalt and granite.

   The outer shell of the young earth must have been a good many millions of years changing from the liquid to the solid state, and it is believed that, before this change was completed, an event of the greatest importance took place— the formation of the moon. The next time you stand on a beach at night, watching the moon's bright path across the water, and conscious of the moon-drawn tides, remember that the moon itself may have been born of a great tidal wave of earthly substance, torn off into space. And remember that if the moon was formed in this fashion, the event may have had much to do with shaping the ocean basins and the continents as we know them.[14]

[13]Kinneavy, p. 93.
[14]Rachel Carson, *The Sea Around Us* (New York: Oxford University Press, 1950), pp. 4–5. Copyright © 1950, 1951, 1961 by Rachel Carson. Reprinted by permission of Oxford University Press, Inc.

In these paragraphs, Carson is not attempting to prove anything; whether or not the hypotheses she speaks of have been established to everyone's satisfaction is beside the point. She merely reports what the scientific community believes. The reader has the sense that the paragraphs do have a great deal of content; that is, they fit the reality that they are discussing: theories concerning the formation of the earth.

As to their surprise value, these paragraphs will be a great deal more informative to some readers than to others. Presumably a geophysicist would gain little information from them; he or she would already know everything that they report. But for the average person they might be informative indeed, presenting information that he or she had never before encountered.

This brings us right back to the concept of audience. Informativeness (surprise value) depends upon the audience. If Carson had intended her book *The Sea Around Us* as a treatise to be read by oceanographers and marine biologists, she would have made a serious mistake, for they would have learned virtually nothing from it and would have been uninterested in it as informative discourse, though they might have enjoyed it as a work of art. On the other hand, when I first read the book, I found it highly informative; it was packed with information *for me.*

Exploratory Writing

As we have seen, the purpose of scientific writing is to prove a hypothesis, and the purpose of informative writing is to convey information. The purpose of exploratory writing is to solve a problem.

In Chapter 3 we investigated problem solving and invention in some detail. Now, in order to discuss exploratory writing, we must return to those concepts.

Exploring Problems[15]

How does the exploration of problems take place? Although everyone develops his or her own methodology, there are certain similarities among procedures, certain steps or facts in the process that seem to be common to a great many writers and thinkers. Understanding the process should be useful, and it is certainly interesting; therefore, let's take a look at what might happen when a person encounters a problem and goes about solving it.

In the first place, you must have *a preliminary knowledge of the field.* If you know almost nothing about writing insurance policies or planning the defense in a football game, then you cannot be aware of problems in those fields, at least not in a way that is specific enough to be useful. To define your problem as the need for health insurance or a desire to beat the Oklahoma team will be of little use, for these are general goals; they are not

[15]This discussion is adapted from Kinneavy, pp. 99–104.

penetrating enough to yield solutions, because in their very generality they give you nothing to work with.

The next step is known as *cognitive dissonance,* the awareness of a difficulty. Cognitive dissonance reveals itself in wonder (Why should such and such be the case?); in instability (There is a contradiction here that I cannot resolve); in anomaly (On the basis of my current knowledge I cannot explain this phenomenon).

Next comes *focus.* The problem becomes clear. It can be exactly defined and delimited.

Fourth is *the search for a new model* that can be tested.

Fifth, *the new model is imposed on the field* to see if it eliminates the cognitive dissonance.

Finally, *a new hypothesis is formed;* a tentative explanation is offered. Here is a thumbnail example:

20   Hanson's classic example of the whole exploration process vividly illustrates the use of the model. He uses Kepler's discovery of the elliptical orbit of Mars, for "Kepler typifies all reasoning in physical science" . . . [1. *Preliminary knowledge of field*] The dogma current from Aristotle to Galileo was that planetary orbits were necessarily circular. . . . He says, "Before Kepler, circular motion was to the concept of planet as 'tangibility' is to our concept of 'physical object' " . . . [2. *Cognitive dissonance*] But the circular model did not account for the anomalies in measurements of Mars's varied distances from the sun and of Mars's varied velocities at different points in its orbit. [3. *Focus of problem*] Even inaccuracies in measuring procedures should not have led to such notable departures from what the theory dictated. . . . [4. *Search for new model*] To explain these anomalies Kepler then repudiated the circular orbit model and cast about for another model. . . . He first tried an oval and then an ellipse as models, [5. *Imposition of new model*] settling eventually on the ellipse. . . . [6. *Hypothesis: tentative explanation*] The ellipse offered a plausible explanation of all the anomalies which had been bothering him and suggested other testable hypotheses. These he followed through and the results confirmed the validity of the new model. . . .[16]

This brief example is not meant to imply that problem solving takes place only in the exact sciences. Whenever a critic attempts to explain a poem, he or she is going through the same kind of procedure, and whenever you advance an opinion on any subject, you probably—consciously or not—go through at least some of these steps.

An Exploratory Essay

Jill Aeschbacher, the author of the following essay, has probably not heard of the model for exploration that has just been outlined, but in exploring her problems as a writer, she intuitively followed the steps that we have been discussing. Stated as a question, her problem is this: "Why do I want to write, and why can't I now?"

[16]*Ibid.,* pp. 103–04.

21   *It's Not Elves Exactly*[17]

                     Jill Aeschbacher

Something there is that doesn't love a wall,
That wants it down. I could say "Elves" to him,
But it's not elves exactly.
                          —Robert Frost, *"Mending Wall"*

[The essay begins with an outline of the author's *preliminary knowledge of the field*—her almost unconscious drift toward a certain way of life.]

(1) When I was a scrawny, copper-haired kid and someone asked me what I wanted to be when I grew up, I put my hand on my hip, imitating my mother's soup-stirring stance, and said, maintaining the imitation, that I wanted to be a mother because I liked children. Supposing that I didn't realize I was just a child myself, the interviewer would respond with odd warmth. It got to be a bore. Besides, when I was five, Elizabeth Taylor was much talked about around my house, and her life seemed far more glamorous than my mother's; so I started telling people I wanted to be an actress.

(2) I kept that attitude toward self-creation until I was eleven. We were writing papers on our chosen professions, and apparently something about my diction impressed my fifth-grade teacher. He said, "You write very well; you should be a writer instead of an actress." I liked him and valued his opinion, so from then on, when people asked what I wanted to be when I grew up, I told them "a writer."

[Now comes a detailed exploration of the *cognitive dissonance*—the puzzlement, the irritation, the knowledge that the "model" doesn't "fit."]

(3) Of course I had no idea what was involved in any of these careers, except that they seemed less boring than carrying mail and less demeaning than waiting on tables. But it didn't matter anyway, because I wasn't planning to grow up right away. It was all a matter of image; and I found in high school that could impress boys whose vocabularies and cynicism were larger than mine, by telling them I would be "great and rich, like J. D. Salinger and John Updike." They thought I was charmingly naive for thinking it was that simple. But after all, this was America; you could be whatever you wanted.

(4) Needless to say, I'm paying now for those green and essentialist attitudes with thousands of questions, rationalizations, and other pains. Having begun writing on these tenuous grounds, I'm going to tell you some things I've been thinking about writing since I quit doing it. But because how I got started weighs heavily on how I got stalled, I think you should know more about that first.

(5) I had early the notion that the writer wrote to give others pleasure, a noble occupation in my young estimation. That was my cheery social-working self coming out. And something else I think: my father kept my first story "Battle at Broken Branch Canyon" (age 10) his whole life. His pleasure over the story affected me considerably, even after I understood that the scaffold of his pleasure, like most fatherly love, was a little shaky. I wanted to say that Tough Bob kicked Mean Joe in the shin, but I figured "shin" was spelled like "chic." So Tough Bob ended up kicking Mean Joe in the chin. My father

[17]Jill Aeschbacher, "It's Not Elves Exactly," *College Composition and Communication,* 24 (Oct. 1973), 204–46. Copyright © 1973 by the National Council of Teachers of English. Reprinted by permission of the publisher and the author.

thought it was hilarious. I suppose now that his pleasure derived from my saying more about myself than I realized, something for which he had an obscure and personal appreciation; perhaps also he had just taught me the spelling of "chic."

(6) Saying more than one realizes can be something of a risk. At any rate, writing to please others seems now both frivolous and vain. *Intellectually* speaking, of course. For I seldom wrote anything without anticipating the thrill of charming my friends and family. Unfortunately, they were usually impressed by what I thought were the wrong things, particularly if they thought they saw themselves, and no two of them reacted similarly. They were like too many birds for a hungry cat, and sent me scurrying in six directions at once. I wrote a story about kites to impress one friend with how precisely I saw the real world, and ended up charming another with my keen sense of fantasy. My readers were also, perhaps, too easily pleased. Like my father, they were pleased by the whole if one little word struck some odd and unintended chord.

(7) Television, of course, can provide more people with more "pleasure" than any writer could hope to. And trying to make people love me for my writing proved to be a very risky and expensive enterprise. Thus my social and personal interests in writing for the pleasure of others disintegrated.

(8) A second more recently developed notion, I had insisted that writings told great and important truths. By playing "the game" I became quite proficient at picking out these truths and explaining them in blue books. Standing in this reference frame, I made the not illogical leap from awareness that this proficiency won good grades from learned professors to the assumption that the writer wrote in order to give these truths. By the time I got through with them, the writers of "great books" had in their hearts the desire to save the world by preaching love, brotherhood and peace. That seemed like a *very* noble occupation, and I invested in the image of the profession the whole meaning of life. Since God and immortality were out, the telling of these important truths was the only meaning life could have. But I didn't know any important truths; I had to get some. So I set about speculating on the meanings of freedom, morality, femininity, art, relativity, love, peace, joy, time, beauty, progress, space, history, Americanism, reality, education, friendship, death, religion, and of course, truth itself. I took philosophy classes and philosophized. Needless to say, I was known among some people as a "weird chick." A friend of mine whom I hadn't seen for a time told me he was working on a story he planned to send to *Evergreen Review*. "Are you writing the truth?" I asked intensely. He said, "I don't know, what difference does that make?" I considered him immoral for some time after. I'm not suggesting that it makes no difference what a writer writes, only that waiting for truth to fall on my head was rather fruitless for me.

(9) During this time, my stories were literally sets of class notes. One was anyway. It wasn't a bad set of class notes, but it wasn't a truth-telling story either. Another was a curious fugue about two kids searching for answers. The truth, skillessly told at the end, was, as I remember, that the teacher wasn't going to arrive. I didn't think that was a very important truth, and was disappointed again.

(10) So when meaninglessness first presented itself to me as a notion, I thought it lovely and easy, and talked drolly about it in conversations over coffee. That nothing *meant* anything was always well understood by my favorite fictional characters, and they accepted it with a casualness I envied. Meursault knew it didn't make any difference what he did with his life.

(11) Obviously, I had quite misunderstood Camus. So that, when meaning-lessness forced itself upon my life, became more than just an idea, I had some trouble. It got its claws into me in these ways: the war and the bomb and the population explosion began preying on my mind; I graduated from college; my father finally drowned himself in alcohol; someone I'd long been in love with informed me of his love affair with another man; communication with my oldest friends wore thin; I approached (one Christmas vacation) a nervous breakdown over my own failures, which was prevented only by my mother's iron insistence that I keep busy helping her with trivial preparations, and concluded in my purchase of $27 worth of books. I'd had enough of the real world.

(12) I had, however, to face the facts: the world would not be saved by important truths; no matter how well told they were, someone would have to come along tomorrow and tell them again in new words; and people simply weren't going to listen anyway. My life's ambition had lost its significance, for I had intended to create for myself and others the Meaning of Life. I didn't know that meaning is something one lives, not something one merely talks about.

(13) Still, like W. D. Snodgrass, "I had not learned how often I can win, can love, can choose to die." This ignorance is certainly nothing to brag about, but there was a time when I didn't even realize I was making choices. Perhaps one must find his world vision *before* he can learn how often he can win, can love, but chooses death. Or perhaps, like form and meaning, they come together.

(14) Fitzgerald and Hemingway taught me about a third reason a writer might have for writing. He might write down his life-difficulties in order to better understand them. I never did this consciously (as perhaps they did sometimes) because it seemed a little crazy to me. It's rather like talking to oneself. I also thought that this kind of writing usually failed to make very good reading. I found out how true that was: I had written a story called "Live People, Dead People, and Other People" about a young man who made lists. He was trying to create some order in his world. Unfortunately the story was pretty disorganized, as was my own mind at the time. It was I who was trying to create order, not my character. I wrote also a fictionalized set of letters which were an attempt to come to grips with what I've come to call "the mind-body problem" and learned that intellectualizing on paper was not the way to do that. Since then, I've been working in *other* ways toward ordering my world and maintaining a relationship between my mind and body.

(15) Toward order, I started buying my cigarettes by the carton and putting things where I can find them; I try to be the one to put fresh towels in the bathroom because the other members of the family invariably hang up two blue-and-green-plaids and one pink-and-white, or vice-versa ("A towel is a towel, for chrissake!"); I sprayed the dead weeds in my room with clear plastic so they wouldn't disintegrate all over the floor (which didn't work); and I try to wash the car every other Saturday, even if it's going to rain, because order is one thing and logic is something else.

(16) Toward a mind-body relationship, I stopped "thinking" about it and took up ice-skating.

[Now the problem starts to gain sharper *focus*.]

(17) Since I never seriously thought a writer wrote for money and my other notions about writing to please others, build a new world, maintain sanity,

and express love had crumbled, I found myself without a reason for doing it. But unfortunately, I have my brick wall, my ego-investment to contend with. I've given too much of my being over to the image of the profession, however vague and frightening that image has become. My brick wall has three dimensions; first, its width is the image I gave myself as "a writer"; second, it is long: my ego-oriented desire to express myself in words; and third, it is a tall fear of giving too much of myself. It keeps me from writing and from giving it up. What can I do about the wall, then? I can keep hitting my head against it. I can post sentries to guard it. I can dig under it, or bury it, or build another wall parallel to it. I can write my name on it or plant flowers on top. I could deny its existence; I could rent it for advertising space, or sell it to my neighbor at a profit. I could take it apart piece by piece, or desecrate it, or make a leap (of faith) over it. I can think about it; I could die for it. I can sit on it; I can write an article exposing it.

(18) But worrying about it has proved almost valueless. On the other hand, I can't exactly ignore it. "Something there is that doesn't love a wall, that wants it down." What I have been doing then is teaching school and taking classes and (an alternative I didn't mention) waiting for the seasons to destroy the bricks and leave either rubble from which I can build a new self-conception or free passage to the pasture on the other side. Writers say, "If you don't have to write, don't do it." Obviously I don't have to; I've survived long periods without it. But something in me (it's not elves exactly) roots for the destruction of the wall to leave free passage to write again; I can't imagine why, since there's no "reason" for writing and I hardly remember the pleasure of doing it.

[The *search for a new model* begins.]

(19) In studying my block, I've been forced to admit what it is not. I used to like to think that I could write if I only had more time. But I put that rationalization to the test last summer. I gave the summer to myself for writing, took few obligations and wasted my time wishing I were writing. Neither was "the man from Porlock" to blame, for I kept distractions at a distance (even emotionally) and insisted on being alone. I had no institutions to blame for making me into a research machine, a file clerk, or a hypocritical bureaucrat. My days were not unreasonably broken up by places to be and things to do, as they are at the other times of the year. I could order them as I wished; I could have been writing during any set of hours I chose. This home in suburbia has also taken the brunt of my blame at times. But last summer, it was, for hours on end, my place alone, a place I could have worked. It offers also, I've admitted, some protections I wouldn't have if I were on my own. Besides obvious financial worries I don't have, my friends visit me here almost seldom enough to suit me. That's right, I've even blamed my friends. But last summer I stayed away from them. I also avoided watching the news and thinking about the war.

(20) Thus you see, there was nothing in the external world to keep me from writing. That was how I discovered that my brick wall exists inside me, well protected from the rages of time and the weather. I also learned how difficult it is to write out of boredom, not, I think, a worthless lesson.

(21) These are hard things to admit, and existing consciously in bad faith is not painless. I promised myself that if I weren't writing at the end of the summer, I'd forget about it forever. I never did decide which took more courage, to give up the notion of writing, or stay (in conscious bad faith) with the absurd hope of someday doing it; but nevertheless, I couldn't give up.

(22) That waiting has sometimes seemed dishonest to me, has forced me to consider its alternatives. With this severe freedom we all face of choosing what we want to do and making what we want to make of ourselves, it seems sometimes more honest to me to force myself to write, to do whatever I have to do to get it going. Would you believe I've considered arranging for my family to bribe me to write; but there's no predicting what that would cost me in the end. I've even considered becoming a speed freak, for writing, I know, comes easier on amphetamines.

(23) But I suppose I am too much convinced that writing should come naturally or not at all, unless of course that is merely a convenient rationalization. At any rate, I have not been able to force myself to write.

(24) Thus, aside from trying to remain emotionally alive, to give some orderly arrangement to the events of my life, and to sharpen my appreciation for the technical skills involved in putting words together, I have spent the wait thinking about the brick wall inside me. I'm not sure this does any good at all, but it hardly seems that better mental attitudes could hurt. This has meant generally that I have been working to change my attitudes toward writing (1) to destroy my image of myself as a writer; (2) to stop looking at it as an ego-investment; and (3) to establish enough security so that I don't have to fear giving myself away.

(25) In trying not to think of myself as a writer, I've come to the rather obvious conclusion that writers are people who write. That excludes me. Joking about it has helped a little too, I think. "Oh no, I'm not a writer; I'm all talk." But I haven't thought it terribly funny.

(26) I have an acquaintance who is very worried about passing his Ph.D. orals. He feels that if he fails, the whole effort of his life for the last twenty years will be discolored. I said to him, "I thought you were a writer." "Yes," he said, "what does that have to do with it?" "If you are a writer, failing your exams wouldn't mean anything but a six-month delay." "Oh!" he said, "I see what you mean. No, I'm a scholar; if I thought of myself as a writer, I'd be so tense I wouldn't be able to do it." I was amazed at his casual knowledge of the fact.

(27) It's simple enough, I suppose, to think of myself as a student and a teacher.

(28) It was viewing writing as an ego-investment, and my attempt to change that view that started me thinking in the first place about the reasons I'd had for writing. That they were all pretty flimsy has been, I think, a good thing to face, though of course I don't deny the value of books I like to read. Toward reducing my ego-orientation for writing, I've tried in other areas of my life to listen to my inner self and do pretty much what I feel like doing. I've tried to avoid world-building, and "accomplishing" things *merely* because I "should." I've also thought a bit about stories I might write about other people, since I wrote too directly about myself, and thereby increased my ego-investment in writing.

(29) Of the changes I've been working to make in my attitude, developing an inner security has been most difficult. I've had some considerable paranoia to fight. My father's frustrated perfectionism, which I inherited, has also presented something of a battle. Admitting that I have no talent for cooking, for example, or for cool and sophisticated cocktail conversation, or for memorizing, admitting that I can't *be* everyone and be good at everything has been very difficult.

(30) Seeking solutions in a conscious way, I have learned, wrinkles the

brow. It is better to let the solutions find me. So, I don't know if changing my attitudes in these ways will allow me to write again, but if, when the bricks are down, they make of me a secure person who does what she likes doing, without attaching prefabricated labels to herself, that will be something.

[*The new model is imposed.*]

(31) Recently, I've been filling up the wait with fun. (I can't think of a less irreverent way to say it.) Why nearly everything seems fun to me lately, I can't imagine, for my activities are not so different. I have admitted that I'm in love, but I'm almost certain that's not all there is to it. Anyway: fun. Teaching composition has become so enjoyable that it hardly matters what specifically happens during a class—when it ends, I can't keep the grin down. Though I still sometimes lose track of what I'm doing, taking classes has become, since graduate school, more fun; it seems less often absurd. I love to follow the train tracks under one billion stars to the brickyard, where brick walls are merely stacks of bricks, thick but very temporary. And I like to go dancing, though drinking with my friends is something I still do occasionally, mainly because (they seem to think) I "should." I've come to believe that hardly anything is worth doing if it isn't fun. If that is true, writing also should be fun, or skipped. Perhaps that's the only real reason people have for doing it: they think it's fun. But what does that mean?

(32) If writing were merely fun as an activity, like swimming or skiing, there would be no need for others to read its results. But those activities too are more fun with other people. Part of the fun of writing, then, is sharing it with others (though one doesn't do it for the pleasure of others, any more than a skier skis for the pleasure of the people who wait in line at the lift and watch him). Like swimming, writing is more fun if you're good at it. So part of the fun is being good, and working continually to improve. Maybe also, the greatest swimmers feel within themselves the potential to be the BEST SWIMMER. They have a confidence that comes from thinking they know more about swimming than anyone, or that they know some secret no one else knows, or that they are absolutely in tune with the life of the water. Maybe writers have that kind of confidence. If they do, when and how did they get it? They weren't born with it. Perhaps it started out as a kind of game. The better they got, the more fun the game was. When they recognized the need for a new world, maybe they felt within themselves the power to create it. But they must also have feared failure, and some probably experienced it. Still perhaps, the passion and the fun of the activity kept them going until they found the secret and the confidence.

(33) Perhaps then, when they found the secret and the confidence, they knew that if their writing expressed or won love, or changed some small part of the world, or helped them understand themselves, or gave others pleasure, these were fortunate coincidences, but not their reasons or their motivations. Perhaps when they found the secret and the confidences their lives and their writing were passionately entwined, and that was their motivation. In fact, perhaps "reasons" for their writing were simply irrelevant, (their lives turned upside down) and they needed "reasons" for doing other things. But this is speculation.

(34) In addition to the fact that there are some things about writing that can't be learned by thinking about it, waiting has made me aware of a curious paradox. Life seems very short to me. Discounting the possibility of auto accident, nuclear war and earthquake, I have at best three-quarters of my life

left. What is three-quarters? Three-quarters of a quart of milk a shirtless boy in levis might come in from lawn mowing and drink in one gulp. People should do what they like with the last three-quarters of their lives, and waiting around has not been something I've really liked. It's a matter of making choices. The wait has chosen me; but when I'm done with waiting, if I can, I'll *choose* to write.

[*A new hypothesis is formed.*]

(35) On the other hand, all that has kept me sane, if I am, in the hard moments of the wait is this:

> There is here no measuring with time. No year matters and ten years are nothing. Being an artist means, not reckoning and counting, but ripening like the tree which does not force its sap but stands, confident in the storms of spring, without the fear that after them may come no summer. It does come, but only to the patient, who are there as though eternity lay before them, so unconcernedly still and wide. I learn it daily, learn it with pain to which I am grateful. Patience *is everything.*
> —Rilke, *Letters to a Young Poet*

It seems to me that fitting the essay into the schema does not do violence to the basic nature of what is said, and the analysis does, certainly, illuminate the nature of "It's Not Elves Exactly" as a piece of exploratory discourse.

Finally

Though it may not seem so, there has been a good deal of method in the madness of this chapter. In fact, the discussion has been tightly controlled by a method of approach that you can discover for yourself if you want to.

The chapter could be extended greatly, for we could explore style in expository writing, methods of discovering ideas, plans for developing those ideas, and so on. But all that is covered in other chapters.

Therefore, it is up to you to synthesize, to bring the various strands of your knowledge together, and to apply them when you think about and when you write expository prose.

Discussion and Activities

The Reader's Purposes

1. Find, and be prepared to discuss, examples of writing in which the author's purpose apparently is (a) to express himself or herself, (b) to inform, (c) to present an imaginative experience, (d) to persuade. What features in your examples lead you to believe that they have a given purpose? Do any of your examples seem to have just a single purpose, or do they represent ratios of purposes?
2. Using "Serving Caviar" (example 2) as a model, write a brief expository

essay on how to do something. For example, you might write a set of instructions for folding a paper airplane and then give the instructions to a classmate to follow. If, by following your instructions, your classmate completes a paper airplane that flies, obviously you have been successful in your writing.

Some Factors in Expository Writing

1. The editorial section of the Los Angeles *Times* for June 10, 1974, contains an article (urging President Nixon to resign) by Donald W. Riegle. In a box within the article is this note: "Elected in 1966 as a Republican, Rep. Donald W. Riegle of Michigan switched to the Democratic Party in February, 1973. An early opponent of the Vietnam war, he is a member of the Foreign Affairs Committee." Explain why the *Times* included this information about the author of the article.
2. In a relatively brief paragraph, describe one of your classes, keeping your tone as neutral as possible. Then rewrite the paragraph two or three times so that its tone changes, for example, to sarcasm, to humor, to self-pity. What adjustments did you make in order to change the tone?
3. Prepare a brief discussion (oral or written) of how you adjusted your rhetorical stance during one day. For instance, what were the characteristics of your stance when you talked to a friend, and how did your stance change when you had a conference with a professor that you do not know very well?

Scientific Writing

Choose a common subject about which you know a great deal (football, cooking, playing the clarinet, driving in heavy traffic, choosing stereo components) and write a scientific essay on it. The essay need not be long; one or two pages will do.

Keep in mind that scientific discourse makes assertions (descriptive, classificatory, evaluative) about one facet of a subject. The personal feelings of the writer are excluded as much as possible.

Informative Writing

Choose a subject about which everyone in your class will know quite a bit, and write a one- or two-page informative essay on that subject. (Some aspect of your college would be a good bet.) Remember that to be informative, your essay must have content and surprise value. In other words, you must tell your readers something that they do not already know, and they must believe that what you tell them squares with reality.

Exploratory Writing

1. Write an essay in which you explore the problems that you have with writing. This is a difficult assignment, but one that should be rewarding

for you and for your readers. Some problems that interfere with writing are obvious: lack of time, lack of interest in the subject, or even a broken typewriter. But others are difficult to discover and involve such matters as threats to one's ego, inability to achieve the breakthrough that will give one something to say, lack of experience in the "scribal mode."

You might want to use "It's Not Elves Exactly" (example **21**) as a model, dealing systematically with all the points that Jill Aeschbacher mentions, but from your own point of view.

2. Write an essay in which you explain a problem that you have solved. Use this formula for your essay: (a) explain what the problem was; (b) outline your preliminary knowledge of the field; (c) describe your cognitive disonance; (d) explain how the problem came into focus; (e) discuss your search for a new model and how you imposed that new model on the field; (f) explain your new hypothesis. (Some examples of problems: Which college should I attend? Why can't I stop smoking? How can I manage my finances? Is it ethical to cohabit prior to marriage?)

6

Special Uses of Writing: Literature

Summary of the Chapter

Readers do learn from literature, but the main purpose of literature is not to convey information. For instance, we would normally not read John Steinbeck's novel *The Grapes of Wrath* to gain information about migrant workers during the 1930s, but we would read the novel to gain the experience that it conveys—that is, to learn what it was like to be a migrant worker. Not only does literature convey experience; it also conveys values. The knowledge that we gain from literature, then, concerns experience and values, and the real use of literature is to provide an intense kind of pleasure that is difficult to explain, but that all readers experience.

When you write a literary essay, you are merely attempting to explain to your readers what a work of literature means to you and why it is meaningful. In other words, a literary essay is an attempt to share your experience with others.

A story (in either prose or verse) is told by someone, but it is a mistake to conclude that it is the author who is speaking. For instance, *Moby Dick* was written by Herman Melville, but the story is told by Ishmael, a character created by Melville. The storyteller or narrator can be omniscient (knowing everything that goes on everywhere, including the innermost thoughts of the characters), or the narrator can be like a motion picture camera, recording only that which can be seen and heard within its range. And there are variations on these two extremes.

Obviously, you can write about the narrator or the narrative *point of view*.

A work of literature must have a theme. Plot—the developing of the story itself—is different from theme; thus, the theme of humanity's basic sinfulness could be developed in an endless variety of plots. Theme can also serve as a subject for literary essays.

A work of fiction is an imaginative structure, involving characters, actions, scenes. In a story, characters perform various actions in various scenes, and it is this imaginative structure that carries the theme.

Some poetry is narrative (that is, tells a story), for example "The Rime of the Ancient Mariner." Most poetry, however, does not tell a story. It conveys its meaning in ways that are different from those found in prose fiction.

Poetry makes a statement, and the reader should be able to paraphrase that statement, realizing, of course, that the paraphrase is not the poem. Most poetry has a formal structure that differentiates it from prose, and the language of poetry is frequently more intense than that of prose. All these factors can serve as subject matter for essays about poetry.

The main problem in reading drama is this: the reader must serve as director and scene designer, staging the drama in his or her mind.

The chapter concludes with two examples of literary essays.

Some Preliminary Remarks on Literature as Knowledge

Imaginative writing is not informative in the same sense that expository writing is. That is, readers come to a poem or a story with different expectations than those they bring to an essay or a technical report. For instance, if I want to learn about conditions among migrant workers in California during the 1930s, I will not rely primarily upon John Steinbeck's novel *The Grapes of Wrath.* I will go to other sources for the facts—to sociological and economic studies, to government reports, and so on. Which is merely to say that *The Grapes of Wrath* is not a good source for *information* about the subject. However, if I want to know what it might have felt like to be a member of a migrant family, I can think of no better source than *The Grapes of Wrath.* Literature conveys knowledge, but of a different sort from that conveyed by expository writing. Essentially I agree with the critic Yvor Winters' statement concerning the value of poetry (and by "poetry" he means all imaginative literature):

> The poem is good in so far as it makes a defensible rational statement about a given human experience (the experience need not be real but must be in some sense possible) and at the same time communicates the emotion which ought to be motivated by that rational understanding of that experience.[1]

A work of literature, then, conveys knowledge of a certain kind—the knowledge of what it feels like to be in a given situation.

Andrew Marvell's poem "To His Coy Mistress," which we will encounter later in the chapter (page 196), gives us the experience of being hedonistic (living for pleasure) in a life that will end soon. From the poem, as from any work of literature, we have gained a particular kind of knowledge that—be it noted!—we could not gain from a paraphrase.

[1]Yvor Winters, *In Defense of Reason* (Denver: Alan Swallow, n.d.), p. 11.

Part of the experience of literature is the moral universe that it portrays. In coming to a work of literature, we bring our own moral values. Therefore, as readers, we respond to the moral universe of the work. I am *not* saying that we read and like only those pieces of literature that fit our own ethical and moral conceptions. It is possible to enjoy works such as those of the Marquis de Sade, and yet deplore his values. The point is this: part of our perception of the work of literature is the juxtaposition of value systems that it creates: the reader's values versus the values implicit in the work. And it is only dull readers who read only to have their own value system reinforced, for it is the nature of art to expand one's horizons of understanding.

Here, from *Philosophy in the Bedroom,* is an example of the Marquis de Sade's value system. One character, Dolmance, is talking to a young girl whom he has debauched:

1   *Dolmance*—There is crime in nothing, dear girl, regardless of what it be: the most monstrous of deeds has, does it not, an auspicious aspect?
Eugenie—Who's to gainsay it?
Dolmance—Well, as of this moment, it loses every aspect of crime; for, in order that what serves one by harming another to be a crime, one should first have to demonstrate that the injured person is more important, more precious to Nature than the person who performs the injury and serves her; now, all individuals being of uniform importance in her eyes, 'tis impossible that she have a predilection for some one among them; hence, the deed that serves one person by causing suffering to another is of perfect indifference to Nature.

The values expressed here are abhorrent; and yet, paradoxically, it is just this clash of values that could well be part of what makes a novel by de Sade fascinating (though I must confess that I find the Marquis largely boring). Or take another example: the value system that lies behind *Paradise Lost.* It is alien to me (and probably to most modern readers), but it is precisely the imaginative realization of the value system that gives Milton's work a great deal of its power.

We do learn things in a particular way from literature, then. We do not get very much information (as we defined "information" in Chapter 5, on expository writing), but we get something that might be called "knowledge." I think this is what Yvor Winters was speaking of.

The following poem contains a certain kind of knowledge. After the poem is the author's own explication of what he was getting at. This is particularly interesting because the poet, James Dickey, is standing back and acting as the interpreter of his own poem.

2   *The Night Pool*[2]

                              James Dickey

                There is this other element that shines
                At night near human dwellings, glows like wool
                From the sides of itself, far down:

[2]James Dickey, "The Night Pool," *Poems 1957–1967* (Middletown, Conn.: Wesleyan University Press, 1967). Copyright © 1960, 1965 by James Dickey. Reprinted by permission of Wesleyan University Press.

From the deep end of heated water
I am moving toward her, first swimming,
Then touching my light feet to the floor,

Rising like steam from the surface
To take her in my arms, beneath the one window
Still giving off unsleeping light.

There is this other element, it being late
Enough, and in it I lift her, and can carry
Her over any threshold in the world,

Into any of these houses, apartments,
Her shoulders streaming, or above them
Into the mythical palaces. Her body lies

In my arms like a child's, not drowned,
Not drowned, and I float with her off
My feet. We are here; we move differently,

Sustained, closer together, not weighing
On ourselves or on each other, not near fish
Or anything but light, the one human light

From above that we lie in, breathing
Its precious abandoned gold. We rise out
Into our frozen land-bodies, and her lips

Turn blue, sealed against me. What I can do
In the unforgivable cold, in the least
Sustaining of all brute worlds, is to say

Nothing, not ask forgiveness, but only
Give her all that in my condition
I own, wrap her in many towels.

"The Night Pool" is a poem that I have a great deal of affection for, because it says some of the things about love that I want to say. People generally think of love as a violent emotion, a situation where the lovers go from peak to peak of intensity. The most spectacular quality of love is this intensity, sexual as well as other kinds. But for me—I don't know how other people feel about it—the main thing I characterize as the emotion of love is the wish to protect the other person.

Swimming pools are very erotic places to me, especially at night when nothing is real. There's a frail, eerie light that comes up from the underwater lights at the sides of the pool. The situation in the poem is based on this feeling, and on a real incident. In October several years ago a girl and I went swimming in a pool at the apartment complex where she lived in Atlanta. The pool was going to be drained in a few days, and there was nobody in it because it was too cold. But it was a heated pool and the steam was rising from it when we went in at about two o'clock in the morning. Nobody else came. There were only one or two lights on in the apartments; everybody else was asleep. And it was just magical! All your earthly debts are canceled while you are in a heated pool in the middle of a cold night. Nothing that you have to contend with in day-to-day life is there. You don't even have your weight any more. You can perform prodigious feats: the man can lift the girl up in the water as if she were hardly there at all, and the girl can lift the man up. They can do court dances and water ballets around each other, and it's dream-like and lovely. You're in the warm, amniotic fluid of the pool, comfortable and protected, and the effect is superhuman. You never want to leave.

But then, as Jonathan Winters might say, there comes a time when "you gotta get out!" It's cold and the weight of the world hits you like a sledgehammer. You think the world has no right to do this to you after you've been so comfortable and erotic. It's the unsexiest possible situation: the girl is stringy-haired and freezing to death, and so are you. It's miserable. But that is the time when love is really love, when you wrap her up and protect her. You can stand it yourself, but you don't want her to have to stand it. So you "wrap her in many towels," and if you love her, you should.[3]

It is clear that the knowledge we get from a work of literature is another valid subject for writing.

The Real Use of Literature

There are two kinds of literature, one written with a capital letter—Literature—and one without—literature. The first kind—Literature—is to be studied in school, venerated, and analyzed by learned critics; the second kind—literature—is to be enjoyed, discussed with friends, and read to make life more tolerable and meaningful. We will be dealing only with the second kind. A good example of Literature is "To His Coy Mistress," by Andrew Marvell, and a good example of literature is "To His Coy Mistress," by Andrew Marvell—a paradox that will be resolved as this chapter proceeds. The only real use of *literature*—not *Literature*—is to give readers a certain kind of intense pleasure that is hard to explain but that everyone can experience. The only valid reason for writing about literature is to explain the basis of that pleasure, to clarify for *your* readers why you value the work. But, as we shall see, to write about literature is not merely to gush forth completely subjective impressions.

What Is a Literary Essay?

A literary essay is nothing more than an expository essay about literature. Since a great deal of this book concerns the writing of expository essays, much of what you have learned so far bears upon writing about literature. This chapter is intended primarily to help you understand literature, to give you some ways to systematize and explain your reactions to it and your perceptions of it, and thus to discover ideas to write about. It might be said that this whole chapter is intended to answer the question, What can I say about literature? But that question can be phrased in another way: How does literature work?

[3]James Dickey, *Self-Interviews,* with Barbara and James Reiss (New York: Doubleday, 1970). Copyright © 1970 by James Dickey. Reprinted by permission of Doubleday & Co., Inc.

Why Write About Literature?

There are a number of very good reasons for writing about literature. Professional scholars and critics make their livings, in part at least, by doing such writing—that is, by advancing knowledge about and understanding of literature. But these professionals, of course, constitute an extremely small portion of the total number of readers of literature. The odds are overwhelmingly against your ever writing about literature as a professional. The odds are very good, however, that you will need to write about literature in order to get through your composition course. However, learning a skill just to get through a course somehow doesn't make sense. If the course is an end in itself, with no application and no value in life, then it should be abolished.

In fact, it is undeniable that literature itself has great value. This being the case, readers of literature should have the urge to explain the literature itself and its values. To be specific: reading a good work of literature can be an intense and complex sort of pleasure. Explaining that work to others and describing the experience of reading it can also be rewarding, even pleasurable. In fact, at times we all feel the virtually insuperable urge to talk about works of art that we have experienced, to explain their meaning and their significance to us—whether those works be movies, novels, poems, plays, whatever.

Thus, explaining—writing about—literature and its pleasures can itself be a form of pleasure, and it can—it should!—increase our understanding of the work. Writing about literature is a way of sharing the experience of literature.

Prose Fiction

For reasons that are basically inexplicable, people have always thirsted for stories, and the great storytellers throughout history have taken their places among the most highly honored of the world's heroes: Homer, Chaucer, Dante, Cervantes, Goethe, Dickens, Tolstoy, Twain, Hemingway. The most basic response to the story is the eager question "And then what?" The great mystery about the story is that we know it is fiction, "untrue," and yet our thirst for this fictional experience drives us from story to story to story throughout our lives. (Even nonreaders almost without exception hunger for the imaginative experience of stories, and to satisfy the hunger, watch television or attend movies.) We feel that a person uninterested in stories would be slightly less than human, lacking some spark of playfulness and imagination that differentiates a human being from the less-than-human beings that populate science fiction.

In this chapter, we will explore the problems first of reading stories (any fictional prose narratives, including novels), and then of writing about them. Next we will turn to poetry, and finally we will address ourselves briefly to drama.

It makes no sense, of course, to talk about literature in a vacuum; we need a work to refer to. Therefore, we will begin by reprinting a classic American short story.

3

Young Goodman Brown
Nathaniel Hawthorne

Young Goodman Brown came forth at sunset into the street at Salem village; but put his head back, after crossing the threshold, to exchange a parting kiss with his young wife. And Faith, as the wife was aptly named, thrust her own pretty head into the street, letting the wind play with the pink ribbons of her cap while she called to Goodman Brown.

"Dearest heart," whispered she, softly and rather sadly, when her lips were close to his ear, "prithee put off your journey until sunrise and sleep in your own bed to-night. A lone woman is troubled with such dreams and such thoughts that she's afeard of herself sometimes. Pray tarry with me this night, dear husband, of all nights in the year." 10

"My love and my Faith," replied young Goodman Brown, "of all nights in the year, this one night must I tarry away from thee. My journey, as thou callest it, forth and back again, must needs be done 'twixt now and sunrise. What, my sweet, pretty wife, dost thou doubt me already, and we but three months married?"

"Then God bless you!" said Faith, with the pink ribbons; "and may you find all well when you come back."

"Amen!" cried Goodman Brown. "Say thy prayers, dear Faith, and go to bed at dusk, and no harm will come to thee."

So they parted; and the young man pursued his way until, being about 20 to turn the corner by the meeting-house, he looked back and saw the head of Faith still peeping after him with a melancholy air, in spite of her pink ribbons.

"Poor little Faith!" thought he, for his heart smote him. "What a wretch am I to leave her on such an errand! She talks of dreams, too. Methought as she spoke there was trouble in her face, as if a dream had warned her what work is to be done to-night. But no, no; 'twould kill her to think it. Well, she's a blessed angel on earth; and after this one night I'll cling to her skirts and follow her to heaven."

With this excellent resolve for the future, Goodman Brown felt himself 30 justified in making more haste on his present evil purpose. He had taken a dreary road, darkened by all the gloomiest trees of the forest, which barely stood aside to let the narrow path creep through, and closed immediately behind. It was all as lonely as could be; and there is this peculiarity in such a solitude, that the traveller knows not who may be concealed by the innumerable trunks and the thick boughs overhead; so that with lonely footsteps he may yet be passing through an unseen multitude.

"There may be a devilish Indian behind every tree," said Goodman Brown to himself; and he glanced fearfully behind him as he added, 40 "What if the devil himself should be at my very elbow!"

His head being turned back, he passed a crook of the road, and, looking forward again, beheld the figure of a man, in grave and decent attire, seated at the foot of an old tree. He arose at Goodman Brown's approach and walked onward side by side with him.

"You are late, Goodman Brown," said he. "The clock of the Old South was striking as I came through Boston, and that is full fifteen minutes agone."

"Faith kept me back a while," replied the young man, with a tremor in his voice, caused by the sudden appearance of his companion, though not wholly unexpected. 50

It was now deep dusk in the forest, and deepest in that part of it where these two were journeying. As nearly as could be discerned, the second traveller was about fifty years old, apparently in the same rank of life as Goodman Brown, and bearing a considerable resemblance to him, though perhaps more in expression than features. Still they might have been taken for father and son. And yet, though the elder person was as simply clad as the younger, and as simple in manner too, he had an indescribable air of one who knew the world, and who would not have felt abashed at the governor's dinner table or in King William's court, were it possible 60 that his affairs should call him thither. But the only thing about him that could be fixed upon as remarkable was his staff, which bore the likeness of a great black snake, so curiously wrought that it might almost be seen to twist and wriggle itself like a living serpent. This, of course, must have been an ocular deception, assisted by the uncertain light.

"Come, Goodman Brown," cried his fellow-traveller, "this is a dull pace for the beginning of a journey. Take my staff, if you are so soon weary."

"Friend," said the other, exchanging his slow pace for a full stop, "having kept covenant by meeting thee here, it is my purpose not to return whence I came. I have scruples touching the matter thou wot'st of." 70

"Sayest thou so?" replied he of the serpent, smiling apart. "Let us walk on, nevertheless, reasoning as we go; and if I convince thee not thou shalt turn back. We are but a little way in the forest yet."

"Too far! too far!" exclaimed the goodman, unconsciously resuming his walk. "My father never went into the woods on such an errand, nor his father before him. We have been a race of honest men and good Christians since the days of the martyrs; and shall I be the first of the name of Brown that ever took this path and kept"—

"Such company, thou wouldst say," observed the elder person, inter- preting his pause. "Well said, Goodman Brown! I have been as well 80 acquainted with your family as with ever a one among the Puritans; and that's no trifle to say. I helped your grandfather, the constable, when he lashed the Quaker woman so smartly through the streets of Salem; and it was I that brought your father a pitchpine knot, kindled at my own hearth, to set fire to an Indian village, in King Philip's war. They were my good friends, both; and many a pleasant walk have we had along this path, and returned merrily after midnight. I would fain be friends with you for their sake."

"If it be as thou sayest," replied Goodman Brown, "I marvel they never spoke of these matters; or, verily, I marvel not, seeing that the least 90 rumor of the sort would have driven them from New England. We are a people of prayer, and good works to boot, and abide no such wickedness."

"Wickedness or not," said the traveller with the twisted staff, "I have a very general acquaintance here in New England. The deacons of many a church have drunk the communion wine with me; the selectmen of divers towns make me their chairman; and a majority of the Great and

General Court are firm supporters of my interest. The governor and I, too—But these are state secrets."

"Can this be so?" cried Goodman Brown, with a stare of amazement at his undisturbed companion. "Howbeit, I have nothing to do with the governor and council; they have their own ways, and are no rule for a simple husbandman like me. But, were I to go on with thee, how should I meet the eye of that good old man, our minister, at Salem village? Oh, his voice would make me tremble both Sabbath day and lecture day."

Thus far the elder traveller had listened with due gravity; but now burst into a fit of irrepressible mirth, shaking himself so violently that his snake-life staff actually seemed to wriggle in sympathy.

"Ha! ha! ha!" shouted he again and again; then composing himself, "Well, go on, Goodman Brown, go on; but, prithee, don't kill me with laughing."

"Well, then, to end the matter at once," said Goodman Brown, considerably nettled, "there is my wife, Faith. It would break her dear little heart; and I'd rather break my own."

"Nay, if that be the case," answered the other, "e'en go thy ways, Goodman Brown. I would not for twenty old women like the one hobbling before us that Faith should come to any harm."

As he spoke he pointed his staff at a female figure on the path, in whom Goodman Brown recognized a very pious and exemplary dame, who had taught him his catechism in youth, and was still his moral and spiritual adviser, jointly with the minister and Deacon Gookin.

"A marvel, truly, that Goody Cloyse should be so far in the wilderness at nightfall," said he. "But with your leave, friend, I shall take a cut through the woods until we have left this Christian woman behind. Being a stranger to you, she might ask whom I was consorting with and whither I was going."

"Be it so," said his fellow-traveller. "Betake you to the woods, and let me keep the path."

Accordingly the young man turned aside, but took care to watch his companion, who advanced softly along the road until he had come within a staff's length of the old dame. She, meanwhile, was making the best of her way, with singular speed for so aged a woman, and mumbling some indistinct words—a prayer, doubtless—as she went. The traveller put forth his staff and touched her withered neck with what seemed the serpent's tail.

"The devil!" screamed the pious old lady.

"Then Goody Cloyse knows her old friend?" observed the traveller, confronting her and leaning on his writhing stick.

"Ah, forsooth, and is it your worship indeed?" cried the good dame. "Yea, truly is it, and in the very image of my old gossip, Goodman Brown, the grandfather of the silly fellow that now is. But—would your worship believe it?—my broomstick hath strangely disappeared, stolen, as I suspect, by that unhanged witch, Goody Cory, and that, too, when I was all anointed with juice of smallage, and cinquefoil, and wolf's bane"—

"Mingled with fine wheat and the fat of a new-born babe," said the shape of old Goodman Brown.

"Ah, your worship knows the recipe," cried the old lady, cackling aloud. "So, as I was saying, being all ready for the meeting, and no horse to ride on, I made up my mind to foot it; for they tell me there is a nice young man to be taken into communion tonight. But now your good worship will lend me your arm, and we shall be there in a twinkling." 150

"That can hardly be," answered her friend. "I may not spare you my arm, Goody Cloyse; but here is my staff, if you will."

So saying, he threw it down at her feet, where, perhaps, it assumed life, being one of the rods which its owner had formerly lent to the Egyptian magi. Of this fact, however, Goodman Brown could not take cognizance. He had cast up his eyes in astonishment, and, looking down again, beheld neither Goody Cloyse nor the serpentine staff, but his fellow-traveller alone, who waited for him as calmly as if nothing had happened.

"That old woman taught me my catechism," said the young man; and there was a world of meaning in this simple comment. 160

They continued to walk onward, while the elder traveller exhorted his companion to make good speed and persevere in the path, discoursing so aptly that his arguments seemed rather to spring up in the bosom of his auditor than to be suggested by himself. As they went, he plucked a branch of maple to serve for a walking stick, and began to strip it of the twigs and little boughs, which were wet with evening dew. The moment his fingers touched them they became strangely withered and dried up as with a week's sunshine. Thus the pair proceeded, at a good free pace, until suddenly, in a gloomy hollow of the road, Goodman Brown sat himself down on the stump of a tree and refused to go any farther. 170

"Friend," said he, stubbornly, "my mind is made up. Not another step will I budge on this errand. What if a wretched old woman do choose to go to the devil when I thought she was going to heaven: is that any reason why I should quit my dear Faith and go after her?"

"You will think better of this by and by," said his acquaintance, composedly. "Sit here and rest yourself a while; and when you feel like moving again, there is my staff to help you along."

Without more words, he threw his companion the maple stick, and was as speedily out of sight as if he had vanished into the deepening gloom. The young man sat a few moments by the roadside, applauding himself 180 greatly, and thinking with how clear a conscience he should meet the minister in his morning walk, nor shrink from the eye of good old Deacon Gookin. And what calm sleep would be his that very night, which was to have been spent so wickedly, but so purely and sweetly now, in the arms of Faith! Amidst these pleasant and praiseworthy meditations, Goodman Brown heard the tramp of horses along the road, and deemed it advisable to conceal himself within the verge of the forest, conscious of the guilty purpose that had brought him thither, though now so happily turned from it.

On came the hoof tramps and the voices of the riders, two grave old 190 voices, conversing soberly as they drew near. These mingled sounds appeared to pass along the road, within a few yards of the young man's hiding-place; but, owing doubtless to the depth of the gloom at that particular spot, neither the travellers nor their steeds were visible. Though their figures brushed the small boughs by the wayside, it could not be seen that they intercepted, even for a moment, the faint gleam from the strip of bright sky athwart which they must have passed. Goodman Brown alternately crouched and stood on tiptoe, pulling aside the branches and thrusting forth his head as far as he durst without

discerning so much as a shadow. It vexed him the more, because he could
have sworn, were such a thing possible, that he recognized the voices of
the minister and Deacon Gookin, jogging along quietly, as they were wont
to do, when bound to some ordination or ecclesiastical council. While yet
within hearing, one of the riders stopped to pluck a switch.

"Of the two, reverend sir," said the voice like the deacon's, "I had
rather miss an ordination dinner than to-night's meeting. They tell me
that some of our community are to be here from Falmouth and beyond,
and others from Connecticut and Rhode Island, besides several of Indian
powwows, who, after their fashion, know almost as much deviltry as the
best of us. Moreover, there is a goodly young woman to be taken into
communion."

"Mighty well, Deacon Gookin!" replied the solemn old tones of the
minister. "Spur up, or we shall be late. Nothing can be done you know
until I get on the ground."

The hoofs clattered again; and the voices, talking so strangely in the
empty air, passed on through the forest, where no church had ever been
gathered or solitary Christian prayed. Whither, then, could these holy
men be journeying so deep into the heathen wilderness? Young Goodman
Brown caught hold of a tree for support, being ready to sink down on the
ground, faint and overburdened with the heavy sickness of his heart. He
looked up to the sky, doubting whether there really was a heaven above
him. Yet there was the blue arch, and the stars brightening in it.

"With heaven above and Faith below, I will yet stand firm against the
devil!" cried Goodman Brown.

While he still gazed upward into the deep arch of the firmament and
had lifted his hands to pray, a cloud, though no wind was stirring, hurried
across the zenith and hid the brightening stars. The blue sky was still
visible, except directly overhead, where this black mass of cloud was
sweeping swiftly northward. Aloft in the air, as if from the depths of the
cloud, came a confused and doubtful sound of voices. Once the listener
fancied that he could distinguish the accents of towns-people of his own,
men, and women, both pious and ungodly, many of whom he had met at
the communion table, and had seen others rioting at the tavern. The next
moment, so indistinct were the sounds, he doubted whether he had heard
aught but the murmur of the old forest, whispering without a wind. Then
came a stronger swell of those familiar tones, heard daily in the sunshine
at Salem village, but never until now from a cloud of night. There was
one voice of a young woman, uttering lamentations, yet with an uncertain sorrow, and entreating for some favor, which, perhaps, it would
grieve her to obtain; and all the unseen multitude, both saints and
sinners, seemed to encourage her onward.

"Faith!" shouted Goodman Brown, in a voice of agony and desperation;
and the echoes of the forest mocked him, crying, "Faith! Faith!" as if
bewildered wretches were seeking her all through the wilderness.

The cry of grief, rage, and terror was yet piercing the night, when the
unhappy husband held his breath for a response. There was a scream,
drowned immediately in a louder murmur of voices, fading into far-off
laughter, as the dark cloud swept away, leaving the clear and silent sky
above Goodman Brown. But something fluttered lightly down through the
air and caught on the branch of a tree. The young man seized it, and
beheld a pink ribbon.

"My Faith is gone!" cried he, after one stupefied moment. "There is no good on earth; and sin is but a name. Come, devil; for to thee is this world given."

And, maddened with despair, so that he laughed loud and long, did Goodman Brown grasp his staff and set forth again, at such a rate that he seemed to fly along the forest path rather than to walk or run. The road grew wilder and drearier and more faintly traced, and vanished at length, leaving him in the heart of the dark wilderness, still rushing onward with the instinct that guides mortal man to evil. The whole forest was peopled 260 with frightful sounds—the creaking of the trees, the howling of wild beasts, and the yell of Indians; while sometimes the wind tolled like a distant church bell, and sometimes gave a broad roar around the travel-ler, as if all Nature were laughing him to scorn. But he was himself the chief horror of the scene, and shrank not from its other horrors.

"Ha! ha! ha!" roared Goodman Brown when the wind laughed at him. "Let us hear which will laugh loudest. Think not to frighten me with your deviltry. Come witch, come wizard, come Indian powwow, come devil himself, and here comes Goodman Brown. You may as well fear him as he fear you." 270

In truth, all through the haunted forest there could be nothing more frightful than the figure of Goodman Brown. On he flew among the black pines, brandishing his staff with frenzied gestures, now giving vent to an inspiration of horrid blasphemy, and now shouting forth such laughter as set all the echoes of the forest laughing like demons around him. The fiend in his own shape is less hideous than when he rages in the breast of man. Thus sped the demoniac on his course, until, quivering among the trees, he saw a red light before him, as when the felled trunks and branches of a clearing have been set on fire, and throw up their lurid blaze against the sky, at the hour of midnight. He paused, in a lull of the 280 tempest that had driven him onward, and heard the swell of what seemed a hymn, rolling solemnly from a distance with the weight of many voices. He knew the tune; it was a familiar one in the choir of the village meeting-house. The verse died heavily away, and was lengthened by a chorus, not of human voices, but of all the sounds of the benighted wilderness pealing in awful harmony together. Goodman Brown cried out, and his cry was lost to his own ear by its unison with the cry of the desert.

In the interval of silence he stole forward until the light glared full upon his eyes. At one extremity of an open space, hemmed in by the dark wall 290 of the forest, arose a rock, bearing some rude, natural resemblance either to an altar or a pulpit, and surrounded by four blazing pines, their tops aflame, their stems untouched, like candles at an evening meeting. The mass of foliage that had overgrown the summit of the rock was all on fire, blazing high into the night and fitfully illuminating the whole field. Each pendant twig and leafy festoon was in a blaze. As the red light arose and fell, a numerous congregation alternately shone forth, then disappeared in shadow, and again grew, as it were, out of the darkness, peopling the heart of the solitary woods at once.

"A grave and dark-clad company," quoth Goodman Brown. 300

In truth they were such. Among them, quivering to and fro between gloom and splendor, appeared faces that would be seen next day at the council board of the province, and others which, Sabbath after Sabbath, looked devoutly heavenward, and benignantly over the crowded pews, from the holiest pulpits in the land. Some affirm that the lady of the governor was there. At least there were high dames well known to her, and wives of honored husbands, and widows, a great multitude, and ancient maidens, all of excellent repute, and fair young girls, who trembled lest their mothers should espy them. Either the sudden gleams of light flashing over the obscure field bedazzled Goodman Brown, or he recognized a score of the church members of Salem village famous for their especial sanctity. Good old Deacon Gookin had arrived, and waited at the skirts of that venerable saint, his revered pastor. But, irreverently consorting with these grave, reputable, and pious people, these elders of the church, these chaste dames and dewy virgins, there were men of dissolute lives and women of spotted fame, wretches given over to all mean and filthy vice, and suspected even of horrid crimes. It was strange to see that the good shrank not from the wicked, nor were the sinners abashed by the saints. Scattered also among their pale-faced enemies were the Indian priests, or powwows, who had often scared their native forest with more hideous incantations than any known to English witch-craft.

"But where is Faith?" thought Goodman Brown; and, as hope came into his heart, he trembled.

Another verse of the hymn arose, a slow and mournful strain, such as the pious love, but joined to words which expressed all that our nature can conceive of sin, and darkly hinted at far more. Unfathomable to mere mortals is the lore of fiends. Verse after verse was sung; and still the chorus of the desert swelled between like the deepest tone of a mighty organ; and with the final peal of that dreadful anthem there came a sound, as if the roaring wind, the rushing streams, the howling beasts, and every other voice of the unconcerted wilderness were mingling and according with the voice of guilty man in homage to the prince of all. The four blazing pines threw up a loftier flame, and obscurely discovered shapes and visages of horror on the smoke wreaths above the impious assembly. At the same moment the fire on the rock shot redly forth and formed a glowing arch above its base, where now appeared a figure. With reverence be it spoken, the figure bore no slight similitude, both in garb and manner, to some grave divine of the New England churches.

"Bring forth the converts!" cried a voice that echoed through the field and rolled into the forest.

At the word, Goodman Brown stepped forth from the shadow of the trees and approached the congregation, with whom he felt a loathful brotherhood by the sympathy of all that was wicked in his heart. He could have well-nigh sworn that the shape of his own dead father beckoned him to advance, looking downward from a smoke wreath, while a woman, with dim features of despair, threw out her hand to warn him back. Was it his mother? But he had no power to retreat one step, nor to resist, even in thought, when the minister and good old Deacon Gookin seized his arms and led him to the blazing rock. Thither came also the slender form of a veiled female, led between Goody Cloyse, that pious teacher of the catechism, and Martha Carrier, who had received the devil's promise to be queen of hell. A rampant hag was she. And there stood the proselytes beneath the canopy of fire.

"Welcome, my children," said the dark figure, "to the communion of your race. Ye have found thus young your nature and your destiny. My children, look behind you!"

They turned; and flashing forth, as it were, in a sheet of flame, the fiend worshippers were seen; the smile of welcome gleamed darkly on every visage. 360

"There," resumed the sable form, "are all whom ye have reverenced from youth. Ye deemed them holier than yourselves, and shrank from your own sin, contrasting it with their lives of righteousness and prayerful aspirations heavenward. Yet here are they all in my worshipping assembly. This night it shall be granted you to know their secret deeds: how hoary-bearded elders of the church have whispered wanton words to the young maids of their households; how many a woman, eager for widows' weeds, has given her husband a drink at bedtime and let him sleep his last sleep in her bosom; how beardless youths have made haste to inherit their fathers' wealth; and how fair damsels—blush not, sweet ones—have dug little graves in the garden, and bidden me, the sole guest to an infant's funeral. By the sympathy of your human hearts for sin ye shall scent out all the places—whether in church, bed-chamber, street, field, or forest—where crime has been committed, and shall exult to behold the whole earth one stain of guilt, one mighty blood spot. Far more than this. It shall be yours to penetrate, in every bosom, the deep mystery of sin, the fountain of all wicked arts, and which inexhaustibly supplies more evil impulses than human power—than my power at its utmost—can make manifest in deeds. And now, my children, look upon each other." 380

They did so; and, by the blaze of the hell-kindled torches, the wretched man beheld his Faith, and the wife her husband, trembling before that unhallowed altar.

"Lo, there ye stand, my children," said the figure, in a deep and solemn tone, almost sad with its despairing awfulness, as if his once angelic nature could yet mourn for our miserable race. "Depending upon one another's hearts, ye had still hoped that virtue were not all a dream. Now are ye undeceived. Evil is the nature of mankind. Evil must be your only happiness. Welcome again, my children, to the communion of your race."

"Welcome," repeated the fiend worshippers, in one cry of despair and triumph. 390

And there they stood, the only pair, as it seemed, who were yet hesitating on the verge of wickedness in this dark world. A basin was hollowed, naturally, in the rock. Did it contain water, reddened by the lurid light? or was it blood? or, perchance, a liquid flame? Herein did the shape of evil dip his hand and prepare to lay the mark of baptism upon their foreheads, that they might be partakers of the mystery of sin, more conscious of the secret guilt of others, both in deed and thought, than they could now be of their own. The husband cast one look at his pale wife, and Faith at him. What polluted wretches would the next glance show them to each other, shuddering alike at what they disclosed and what they saw! 400

"Faith! Faith!" cried the husband, "look up to heaven, and resist the wicked one."

Whether Faith obeyed he knew not. Hardly had he spoken when he found himself amid calm night and solitude, listening to a roar of the wind which died heavily away through the forest. He staggered against the rock, and felt it chill and damp; while a hanging twig, that had been all on fire, besprinkled his cheek with the coldest dew.

The next morning young Goodman Brown came slowly into the street of Salem village, staring around him like a bewildered man. The good old 410 minister was taking a walk along the graveyard to get an appetite for breakfast and meditate his sermon, and bestowed a blessing, as he passed, on Goodman Brown. He shrank from the venerable saint as if to avoid an anathema. Old Deacon Gookin was at domestic worship, and the holy words of his prayer were heard through the open window. "What God doth the wizard pray to?" quoth Goodman Brown. Goody Cloyse, that excellent old Christian, stood in the early sunshine at her own lattice, catechizing a little girl who had brought her a pint of morning's milk. Goodman Brown snatched away the child as from the grasp of the fiend himself. Turning the corner by the meeting-house, he spied the head of   420 Faith, with the pink ribbons, gazing anxiously forth, and bursting into such joy at sight of him that she skipped along the street and almost kissed her husband before the whole village. But Goodman Brown looked sternly and sadly into her face, and passed on without a greeting.

Had Goodman Brown fallen asleep in the forest and only dreamed a wild dream of a witch-meeting?

Be it so if you will; but, alas! it was a dream of evil omen for young Goodman Brown. A stern, a sad, a darkly meditative, a distrustful, if not a desperate man did he become from the night of that fearful dream. On the Sabbath day, when the congregation were singing a holy psalm, he   430 could not listen because an anthem of sin rushed loudly upon his ear and drowned all the blessed strain. When the minister spoke from the pulpit with power and fervid eloquence, and, with his hand on the open Bible, of the sacred truths of our religion, and of saint-like lives and triumphant deaths, and of future bliss or misery unutterable, then did Goodman Brown turn pale, dreading lest the roof should thunder down upon the gray blasphemer and his hearers. Often, waking suddenly at midnight, he shrank from the bosom of Faith; and at morning or eventide, when the family knelt down at prayer, he scowled and muttered to himself, and gazed sternly at his wife, and turned away. And when he had lived long,   440 and was borne to his grave a hoary corpse, follwed by Faith, an aged woman, and children and grandchildren, a goodly procession, besides neighbors not a few, they carved no hopeful verse upon his tombstone, for his dying hour was gloom.

The Narrator

Who tells the story of "Young Goodman Brown"? The obvious, but misleading, answer would be, Nathaniel Hawthorne. Undeniably, Hawthorne *wrote* the tale, but we must separate the author from the character that he creates to do the telling. This is a simple but important point. Nathaniel Hawthorne the author is not omniscient; that is, he cannot know everything—just as you and I cannot know of two actions that are going on in different parts of the world simultaneously, and just as we cannot know all the secrets of the human heart.

However, the narrator in "Young Goodman Brown" knows *almost* everything. For example, in lines 30–31, the narrator says, "With this excellent resolve for the future, Goodman Brown felt himself justified in making more haste on his present evil purpose." Obviously, the narrator knows something that the mere observer could not possibly know, for how could you or I, as onlookers, determine what was going on in Goodman Brown's mind? We might speculate that he felt thus, but we could not know for certain. Yet, notice that we do not question the statement that the narrator gives us; we take it for granted that he knows and that he is telling us the truth.

In other words, the author is not the narrator, even though sometimes author and narrator may seem to be identical.

Author, Narrator, Storyteller

This point is extremely important. To illustrate what goes on in the telling of a story, think of a father who tells a scary story to his young child. His voice changes, perhaps he takes on unusual facial features, he gestures— he is no longer Daddy, but a teller of scary stories. When the tension becomes too great, the child might well clutch at Daddy, breaking the spell, signaling that the storyteller must once again become Daddy.

It turns out, then, that the imaginative experience of the story can involve a complex hierarchy of telling. We always, of course, have an author, and the author must always create a narrator, and the narrator might well create a storyteller to tell the story directly. This seemingly mystic concept is easily explained and illustrated. Joseph Conrad is the author of *Heart of Darkness.* He created an impersonal narrator to tell the tale, which begins like this:

4   The *Nellie,* a cruising yawl, swung to her anchor without a flutter of the sails, and was at rest. The flood had made, the wind was nearly calm, and being bound down the river, the only thing for it was to come to and wait for the turn of the tide.

The sea-reach of the Thames stretched before us like the beginning of an interminable waterway. In the offing the sea and the sky were welded together without a joint, and in the luminous space the tanned sails of the barges drifting up with the tide seemed to stand still in red clusters of canvas sharply peaked, with gleams of varnished sprits. A haze rested on the low shores that ran out to sea in vanishing flatness. The air was dark above Gravesend, and farther back still seemed condensed into a mournful gloom, brooding motionless over the biggest, and the greatest, town on earth. . . .

This impersonal narrator creates Marlow, a storyteller, to spin the yarn, to take the reader into the heart of darkness.

5   The sun set; the dusk fell on the stream, and lights began to appear along the shore. The Chapman lighthouse, a three-legged thing erect on a mud-flat, shone strongly. Lights of ships moved in the fairway—a great stir of lights going up and going down. And farther west on the upper reaches the place of the monstrous town was still marked ominously on the sky, a brooding gloom in sunshine, a lurid glare under the stars.

"And this also," said Marlow suddenly, "has been one of the dark places of the earth."

He was the only man of us who still "followed the sea." The worst that could be said of him was that he did not represent his class. He was a seaman, but he was a wanderer too, while most seamen lead, if one may so express it, a sedentary life. Their minds are of the stay-at-home order, and their home is always with them—the ship; and so is their country—the sea. One ship is very much like another, and the sea is always the same. In the inmutability of their surroundings the foreign shores, the foreign faces, the changing immensity of life, glide past, veiled not by a sense of mystery but by a slightly disdainful ignorance; for there is nothing mysterious to a seaman unless it be the sea itself, which is the mistress of his existence and as inscrutable as Destiny. For the rest, after his hours of work, a casual stroll or a casual spree on shore suffices to unfold for him the secret of a whole continent, and generally he finds the secret not worth knowing. The yarns of seamen have a direct simplicity, the whole meaning of which lies within the shell of a cracked nut. But Marlow was not typical (if his propensity to spin yarns be excepted), and to him the meaning of an episode was not inside like a kernel but outside, enveloping the tale which brought it out only as a glow brings out a haze, in the likeness of one of these misty halos that sometimes are made visible by the spectral illumination of moonshine.

His remark did not seem at all surprising. It was just like Marlow. It was accepted in silence. No one took the trouble to grunt even; and presently he said, very slow:

"I was thinking of very old times, when the Romans first came here, nineteen hundred years ago—the other day. . . . Light came out of this river since—you say Knights? Yes; but it is like a running blaze on a plain, like a flash of lightning in the clouds. We live in the flicker—may it last as long as the old earth keeps rolling! But darkness was here yesterday. Imagine the feelings of a commander of a fine—what d'ye call 'em?—trireme in the Mediterranean, ordered suddenly to the north; run overland across the Gauls in a hurry; put in charge of one of these craft the legionaries—a wonderful lot of handy men they must have been too—used to build, apparently by the hundred, in a month or two, if we may believe what we read. Imagine him here—the very end of the world, a sea the colour of lead, a sky the colour of smoke, a kind of ship about as rigid as a concertina—and going up this river with stores, or orders, or what you like. Sandbanks, marshes, forests, savages—precious little to eat fit for a civilised man, nothing but Thames water to drink. No Falernian wine here, no going ashore. Here and there a military camp lost in a wilderness, like a needle in a bundle of hay—cold, fog, tempests, disease, exile, and death—death skulking in the air, in the water, in the bush. They must have been dying like flies here. Oh yes—he did it. Did it very well, too, no doubt, and without thinking much about it either, except afterwards to brag of what he had gone through in his time, perhaps. They were men enough to face the darkness. And perhaps he was cheered by keeping his eye on a chance of promotion to the fleet at Ravenna by and by, if he had good friends in Rome and survived the awful climate. Or think of a decent young citizen in a toga—perhaps too much dice, you know—coming out here in the train of some prefect, or tax-gatherer, or trader, even, to mend his fortunes. Land in a swamp, march through the woods, and in some inland post feel the savagery, the utter savagery, had closed round him—all that mysterious life of the wilderness that stirs in the forest, in the jungles, in the hearts of wild men. There's no initiation either into such mysteries. He has to live in the midst of the incomprehensible, which is also detestable. And it has a fascination, too, that goes to work upon him. The fascination of the abomination—you know. Imagine the growing regrets, the longing to escape, the powerless disgust, the surrender, the hate."

He paused.

Thus, we have a hierarchy of tellers:
The Author, Joseph Conrad
The Impersonal Narrator, created by Conrad
The Storyteller Marlow, created by the Impersonal Narrator

First Person Narration

Grammatically, of course, the first person (singular) is represented by the pronoun *I.* Here is the first paragraph of Charles Dickens' novel *Great Expectations:*

6   My father' family name being Pirrip, and my christian name Philip, my infant tongue could make of both names nothing longer or more explicit than Pip. So I called myself Pip, and came to be called Pip.

In *Great Expectations,* Pip tells his own story; he is the chief character in the drama of the novel.

The narrator, then, can tell a story in which he or she is the chief character or a subsidiary character; in any case, the action involves him or her.

On the other hand, the first person narrator can be a mere onlooker, a reporter of events that did not involve him or her directly. Such is the case with the narrator in *Under Western Eyes,* another novel by Joseph Conrad, which begins thus:

7   To begin with I wish to disclaim the possession of those high gifts of imagination and expression which would have enabled my pen to create for the reader the personality of the man who called himself, after the Russian custom, Cyril son of Isidor—Kirylo Sidorovitch—Razumov.

 If I have ever had these gifts in any sort of living form they have been smothered out of existence a long time ago under a wilderness of words. Words, as is well known, are the great foes of reality. I have been for many years a teacher of languages. It is an occupation which at length becomes fatal to whatever share of imagination, observation, and insight an ordinary person may be heir to. To a teacher of languages there comes a time when the world is but a place of many words and man appears a mere talking animal not much more wonderful than a parrot.

 This being so, I could not have observed Mr. Razumov or guessed at his reality by the force of insight, much less have imagined him as he was. Even to invent the mere bald facts of his life would have been utterly beyond my powers. But I think that without this declaration the readers of these pages will be able to detect in the story the marks of documentary evidence. And that is perfectly correct. It is based on a document; all I have brought to it is my knowledge of the Russian language, which is sufficient for what is attempted here. The document, of course, is something in the nature of a journal, a diary, yet not exactly that in its actual form. For instance, most of it was not written up from day to day, though all the entries are dated. Some of these entries cover months of time and extend over dozens of pages. All the earlier part is a retrospect, in a narrative form, relating to an event which took place about a year before.

 I must mention that I have lived for a long time in Geneva. A whole quarter of that town, on account of many Russians residing there, is called La Petite

Russie—Little Russia. I had a rather extensive connexion in Little Russia at that time. Yet I confess that I have no comprehension of the Russian character. The illogicality of their attitude, the arbitrariness of their conclusions, the frequency of the exceptional, should present no difficulty to a student of many grammars; but there must be something else in the way, some special human trait—one of those subtle differences that are beyond the ken of mere professors. What must remain striking to a teacher of languages is the Russians' extraordinary love of words. They gather them up; they cherish them, but they don't hoard them in their breasts; on the contrary, they are always ready to pour them out by the hour or by the night with an enthusiasm, a sweeping abundance, with such an aptness of application sometimes that, as in the case of very accomplished parrots, one can't defend oneself from the suspicion that they really understand what they say. There is a generosity in their ardour of speech which removes it as far as possible from common loquacity; and it is ever too disconnected to be classed as eloquence. . . . But I must apologize for this digression.

Obviously, the possibilities for creating narrative effects are manifold. In Ken Kesey's *One Flew Over the Cuckoo's Nest,* the first person narrator is insane. In Thomas Mann's *Doctor Faustus,* the narrator is an obtuse, middle-aged man, telling the story of a great genius.

The author must create a narrator, and the narrator may create another narrator, a storyteller, such as Marlow in *Heart of Darkness.* In each instance, we "see" the story as it is filtered through the consciousness and sensibilities of the fictitious person who tells the tale.

Third Person Narration

The third person narrator can be either a camera, recording the sights and sounds within his or her range, or God, knowing all, seeing all—perceiving actions that take place simultaneously on opposite sides of the earth, knowing the innermost thoughts of the characters in the story. Or the third person narrator can take a position between the two extremes, knowing more than a mere mortal could know, but not having a godlike omniscience. The narrator in "Young Goodman Brown" seems to occupy this middle position. At times, he knows precisely what is going on in Goodman Brown's mind, but, nonetheless, must ask, "Had Goodman Brown fallen asleep in the forest and only dreamed a wild dream of a witch-meeting?" (lines 425–26). A totally omniscient narrator would not have to ask that question, for he or she would know the answer.

The following, the first paragraph of *The Portrait of a Lady,* by Henry James, is an example of the third person narrator as a camera:

8 Under certain circumstances there are few hours in life more agreeable than the hour dedicated to the ceremony known as afternoon tea. There are circumstances in which, whether you partake of the tea or not—some people of course never do—the situation is in itself delightful. Those that I have in mind in beginning to unfold this simple history offered an admirable setting to an innocent pastime. The implements of the little feast had been disposed upon the lawn of an old English country-house, in what I should call the perfect middle of a spendid summer afternoon. Part of the afternoon had

waned, but much of it was left, and what was left was of the finest and rarest quality. Real dusk would not arrive for many hours; but the flood of summer light had begun to ebb, the air had grown mellow, the shadows were long upon the smooth, dense turf. They lengthened slowly, however, and the scene expressed that sense of leisure still to come which is perhaps the chief source of one's enjoyment of such a scene at such an hour. From five o'clock to eight is on certain occasions a little eternity; but on such an occasion as this the interval could be only an eternity of pleasure. The persons concerned in it were taking their pleasure quietly, and they were not of the sex which is supposed to furnish the regular votaries of the ceremony I have mentioned. The shadows on the perfect lawn were straight and angular; they were the shadows of an old man sitting in a deep wicker-chair near the low table on which the tea had been served, and of two younger men strolling to and fro, in desultory talk, in front of him. The old man had his cup in his hand; it was an unusually large cup, of a different pattern from the rest of the set, and painted in brilliant colours. He disposed of its contents with much circumspection, holding it for a long time close to his chin, with his face turned to the house. His companions had either finished their tea or were indifferent to their privilege; they smoked cigarettes as they continued to stroll. One of them, from time to time, as he passed, looked with a certain attention at the elder man, who, unconscious of observation, rested his eyes upon the rich red front of his dwelling. The house that rose beyond the lawn was a structure to repay such consideration, and was the most characteristic object in the peculiarly English picture I have attempted to sketch.

In *The Plumed Serpent,* by D. H. Lawrence, the narrator functions as god, knowing all, even that which is hidden within the human breast:

9   Cipriano sat motionless as a statue. But from his breast came that dark, surging passion of tenderness the Indians are capable of. Perhaps it would pass, leaving him indifferent and fatalistic again. But at any rate for the moment he sat in a dark, fiery cloud of passionate male tenderness. He looked at her soft, wet white hands over her face, and at the one big emerald on her finger, in a sort of wonder. The wonder, the mystery, the magic that used to flood over him as a boy and a youth, when he kneeled before the babyish figure of the Santa Maria de la Soledad, flooded him again. He was in the presence of the goddess, white-handed, mysterious, gleaming with a moon-like power and the intense potency of grief.

Writing About the Narrator

It should now be obvious that narrative point of view is one of the major factors in creating the magic of a story. When we hear someone tell a story, face to face, we can easily sense the personality and skill of the teller and understand how these factors permeate and shape the narrative. Though the personality of the teller is not so obvious in stories that we read, nonetheless there is a fictional person who does the telling and who shapes our attitudes and expectations. Sometimes this teller is a hazy, impersonal figure whom we don't get to know very well, as in the case of the narrator of "Young Goodman Brown." Sometimes the teller is vividly realized: Huck Finn, Conrad's Marlow, Robinson Crusoe.

When we write about the narrator of a tale, we are basically answering two questions:

1. What sort of person is the narrator?
2. What effect does the person of the narrator have on the tale itself?

These two basic questions can be broken down into a sub-set of questions that will generate ideas for a discussion of narrative technique in a work of literature. We will apply these questions to the problem of narration in "Young Goodman Brown."

1. *What is the narrative point of view?* We have outlined some of the possibilities: (a) third person omniscient, in which the narrator knows all and sees all, even the secrets of the human heart; (b) third person limited, in which the narrator is like a camera, recording everything that might be seen and heard by an uninvolved onlooker; (c) first person as reporter, in which the narrator is not actively involved in the story, but nonetheless becomes a well-delineated character, (d) first person as character in the story, in which the narrator tells of a series of events in which he or she participates as a more or less important character.

Though these four points of view are the main ones, there are variations on them. For instance, the narrator who is in the main omniscient might withhold information that an omniscient narrator would normally be expected to know. In the previously quoted passage from *The Plumed Serpent,* a novel with an omniscient narrator, we read this:

> 10   Cipriano sat motionless as a statue. But from his breast came that dark, surging passion of tenderness the Indians are capable of. Perhaps it would pass, leaving him indifferent and fatalistic again.

If the narrator could know about the "dark, surging passion" in Cipriano's breast, we might ask, Why would he not know whether it would pass? The answer to this question is simple enough: Since he is omniscient, he could know if he chose to, but for the purposes of the tale he chooses not to know.

In short, when we explore narrative point of view, we determine what the narrator does tell us, what the narrator is capable of telling us, and what the narrator does not tell us.

Notice how narrative point of view functions in "Young Goodman Brown." In the first twenty-nine lines, we feel that the narrator is merely a camera, recording what transpires; but in lines 30–31 the viewpoint expands, for the narrator looks into Brown's mind and tells us what is found there: "With this excellent resolve for the future, Goodman Brown felt himself justified in making more haste on his present evil purpose."

It is extremely important to the story, of course, that the narrator be uncertain now and then, for the reader must be uncertain in reacting to the story: Was the experience real, or was it a dream? In describing Goodman's diabolical companion, the narrator tells us: "But the only thing about him that could be fixed upon as remarkable was his staff, which bore the likeness of a great black snake, so curiously wrought that it might almost be seen to twist and wriggle itself like a living serpent. This, of course, must have been an ocular deception, assisted by the uncertain light" (lines 61–65). The narrator, then, is not sure whether the wriggling of the staff was an ocular deception or not. If the narrator were sure, the whole effect of the story would be changed, perhaps damaged beyond repair.

2. *What values does the narrator hold, and what is the tone of the narration? Is it cynical, naive, or what?* There is a wonderful story of the Christian gentleman who could say nothing bad about anyone; even of the Devil, his only remark was this: "Well, it must be said that he's a hard worker." If "Young Goodman Brown" were narrated by this gentleman, it would be quite a different tale, for the narrator would be unwilling to believe that wickedness lies in the depths of every heart, even Faith's.

A narrator who is a sophisticated adult telling of marvelous experiences that a child encounters might sound like this:

11   Alice was beginning to get very tired of sitting by her sister on the bank, and of having nothing to do: once or twice she had peeped into the book her sister was reading, but it had no pictures or conversations in it, "and what is the use of a book," thought Alice, "without pictures or conversations?"

So she was considering in her own mind (as well as she could, for the hot day made her feel very sleepy and stupid), whether the pleasure of making a daisy-chain would be worth the trouble of getting up and picking the daisies, when suddenly a White Rabbit with pink eyes ran close by her.

There was nothing so very remarkable in that; nor did Alice think it so *very* much out of the way to hear the Rabbit say to itself "Oh dear! Oh dear! I shall be too late!" (when she thought it over afterwards, it occurred to her that she ought to have wondered at this, but at the time it all seemed quite natural); but when the Rabbit actually *took a watch out of its waistcoat-pocket,* and looked at it, Alice started to her feet, for it flashed across her mind that she had never before seen a rabbit with either a waistcoat-pocket, or a watch to take out of it, and, burning with curiosity, she ran across the field after it, and was just in time to see it pop down a large rabbit-hole under the hedge.   —Lewis Carroll, *Alice's Adventures in Wonderland*

Or suppose that an atheist narrates a tale concerning a devoutly religious person—or that the narrator of a story about a great love between a man and a woman is a homosexual. Obviously, the values, the stance, and the emotional tone of the narrator are of crucial importance in the story.

What seem to be the values of the narrator in "Young Goodman Brown"? In the first place, he implicitly believes in the Christian doctrine of sin, for the tale would be absurd if he did not. After all, why does the story end tragically? It is because Goodman Brown—whether he dreamed or actually participated in the witches' sabbath—discovers the reality of sin and begins to doubt his own beliefs about Good and Evil, and, therefore, "they carved no hopeful verse upon his tombstone, for his dying hour was gloom" (lines 443–44).

Nor is the narrator a cynic. He believes that the experience was agonizing for Goodman, and he conveys to the reader his deep pity for the character:

12   "Faith!" shouted Goodman Brown, in a voice of agony and desperation; and the echoes of the forest mocked him, crying, "Faith! Faith!" as if bewildered wretches were seeking her all through the wilderness.

> The cry of grief, rage, and terror was yet piercing the night, when the unhappy husband held his breath for a response. There was a scream, drowned immediately in a louder murmur of voices, fading into far-off laughter, as the dark cloud swept away, leaving the clear and silent sky above Goodman Brown. But something fluttered lightly down through the air and caught on the branch of a tree. The young man seized it, and beheld a pink ribbon. [lines 242–51]

The narrator, then, lets us know that he is Christian, and we perceive that he is deeply compassionate, not at all cynical or uncaring. If the narrator had implied that Goodman Brown was a fool to believe, we would have had quite a different story.

3. *What devices does the narrator use to establish contact with the reader?* The most obvious way for the narrator to establish contact is to address the reader directly, as happens in *Tristram Shandy,* by Laurence Sterne:

13 In the beginning of the last chapter, I informed you exactly when I was born; but I did not inform you how. No, that particular was reserved entirely for a chapter by itself;—besides, Sir, as you and I are in a manner perfect strangers to each other, it would not have been proper to have let you into too many circumstances relating to myself all at once.

Seldom, however, particularly in modern prose, is the narrator so direct.

In the *epistolary novel,* the narrative is carried on through letters that the characters write to one another. Thus, the epistolary novel is a novel consisting of letters. It would seem, then, that such a novel would have a number of narrators—or, to revert to our previous distinction, a number of storytellers, with no controlling narrator. That is indeed at least part of the case. But consider *Clarissa,* by Samuel Richardson, one of the most famous of all epistolary novels.

Richardson begins the novel with an "Author's Preface." In this preface is the author himself speaking? I think not. Rather he creates a narrator, who then creates the storytellers who write the letters. That is to say, the preface itself is part of the fiction. What sort of narrator emerges from the preface, the beginning of which is quoted here?

14 The following History is given in a Series of Letters written principally in a double yet separate correspondence.

Between two young Ladies of virtue and honour, bearing an inviolable friendship for each other, and writing not merely for amusement, but upon the most *interesting* subjects; in which every private family, more or less, may find itself concerned: And,

Between two Gentlemen of free lives; one of them glorying in his talents for Stratagem and Invention, and communicating to the other in confidence, all the secret purposes of an intriguing head and resolute heart.

But here it will be proper to observe, for the sake of such as may apprehend hurt to the morals of Youth, from the more freely written Letters, that the Gentlemen, tho' professed Libertines as to the Female Sex, and making it one of their wicked maxims, to keep no faith with any of the individuals of it, who are thrown into their power, are not, however, either Infidels or Scoffers; nor yet such as think themselves freed from the observance of those other moral duties which bind man to man.

Is this narrator not a prim, proper, sententiously correct person? Is he not so mincing in his conventionality that we find him comical?

And how does the narrator of "Young Goodman Brown" establish contact with the reader? That is, how does the reader get to know the narrator? How do we learn that he is a serious, even somber, person, deeply religious and with a tragic sense of life? As we saw earlier, a narrator tells us about the storyteller Marlow. In the case of *Tristram Shandy* the narrator addresses the reader directly. But in "Young Goodman Brown," the narrator establishes contact with the reader only through the way he tells the story.

In some tales, the devices that the narrator uses to establish contact are obvious; in others they are not. *Heart of Darkness* provides a complicated example of how a narrator establishes contact with readers. At the beginning of the tale, the narrator introduces us to Marlow, the storyteller, who is on a yawl with a group of his friends:

15   Marlow sat cross-legged right aft, leaning against the mizzen-mast. He had sunken cheeks, a yellow complexion, a straight back, an ascetic aspect, and, with his arms dropped, the palms of hands outwards, resembled an idol.

As one critic has pointed out, this is the lotus position typical of Zen meditation, and the position of the storyteller—his physical posture—shows the reader that Marlow is ready to indulge in "Yoga meditation, contemplation, and absorption."[4]

4. *What is the voice of the narrator?* This is essentially a matter of style and dialect. The narrator might be an illiterate boy speaking a Southern dialect, as in the case of Huck Finn:

16   You don't know about me without you have read a book by the name of *The Adventures of Tom Sawyer;* but that ain't no matter. That book was made by Mr. Mark Twain, and he told the truth, mainly. There was things which he stretched, but mainly he told the truth. That is nothing. I never seen anybody but lied one time or another, without it was Aunt Polly, or the Widow, or maybe Mary. Aunt Polly—Tom's Aunt Polly, she is—and Mary, and the Widow Douglas is all told about in that book, which is mostly a true book, with some stretchers, as I said before.
                            —Mark Twain, *The Adventures of Huckleberry Finn*

In contrast, the narrator's voice might be sophisticated, as in Henry James's *Portrait of a Lady,* or straightforward, as in Ernest Hemingway's "Soldier's Home":

17   Krebs went to the war from a Methodist college in Kansas. There is a picture which shows him among his fraternity brothers, all of them wearing exactly the same height and style collar. He enlisted in the Marines in 1917 and did not return to the United States until the second division returned from the Rhine in the summer of 1919.

      There is a picture which shows him on the Rhine with two German girls and another corporal. Krebs and the corporal look too big for their uniforms. The German girls are not beautiful. The Rhine does not show in the picture.

[4]William Bysshe Stein, "The Lotus Posture and *Heart of Darkness,*" *Heart of Darkness,* ed. Robert Kimbrough (New York: W. W. Norton, 1963), pp. 197–99.

The narrator here seems to be an uncomplicated guy, not looking for every nuance, getting on with the story in a matter-of-fact way.

The voice of the narrator in "Young Goodman Brown" is somber, to be sure, but also fairly straightforward, direct. The narrator gets the business of the telling done cleanly and efficiently, without worrying details to death. Perhaps the best way to illustrate the directness of narration in "Young Goodman Brown" is to compare the narrator's voice with that of the narrator in such a work as *The Golden Bowl,* by Henry James, about whose method as a storyteller this has been said: "[H. G.] Wells likened James's method in the later novels to that of a hippopotamus picking up a pea, and Edmund Wilson spoke for many anti-Jamesians when he said that the roundabout locutions and gratuitous verbiage of the later novels make them 'unassimilably exasperating and ridiculous'—in short, unreadable."[5] Here is the beginning of *The Golden Bowl,* in which the narrator is telling us, basically, that the Prince likes London and is walking in Bond Street:

18   The Prince had always liked his London, when it had come to him; he was one of the modern Romans who find by the Thames a more convincing image of the truth of the ancient state than any they have left by the Tiber. Brought up on the legend of the City to which the world paid tribute, he recognized in the present London much more than in contemporary Rome the real dimensions of such a case. If it was a question of an *Imperium,* he said to himself, and if one wished, as a Roman, to recover a little the sense of that, the place to do so was on London Bridge, or even, on a fine afternoon in May, at Hyde Park Corner. It was not indeed to either of those places that these grounds of his predilection, after all sufficiently vague, had, at the moment we are concerned with him, guided his steps; he had strayed, simply enough, into Bond Street. . . .

This is indeed ponderous narration, almost overwhelming in its attention to details. Compare it with the voice of the narrator of "Young Goodman Brown," who gets on with it, says what needs to be said and then turns to something else:

19   They continued to walk onward, while the elder traveller exhorted his companion to make good speed and persevere in the path, discoursing so aptly that his arguments seemed rather to spring up in the bosom of his auditor than to be suggested by himself. As they went, he plucked a branch of maple to serve for a walking stick, and began to strip it of the twigs and little boughs, which were wet with evening dew. The moment his fingers touched them they became strangely withered and dried up as with a week's sunshine. Thus the pair proceeded, at a good free pace, until suddenly, in a gloomy hollow of the road, Goodman Brown sat himself down on the stump of a tree and refused to go any farther. [lines 161–70]

To tell of this much action, James's narrator would have required ten or twenty pages.

To Sum Up

A story always has a narrator, and the character of the narrator and the method of narration have tremendous importance in the fictional universe

[5]John Halperin, "Afterword," *The Golden Bowl* (New York: World Publishing, 1972), pp. 549–50.

of the story. You might want to devote a whole essay to narrative technique in some story. In order to understand the narrative technique and hence to generate ideas for an essay, you can begin by asking these questions:

1. What is the narrative point of view?
2. What values does the narrator hold, and what is the tone of the narration?
3. What devices does the narrator use to establish contact with the reader?
4. What is the voice of the narrator?

As you conscientiously answer these questions, you will find that you have important things to say in an essay about the narrator in a work of fiction.

The Theme

A work of literature has a theme—is "about" something. The *plot* of a story is what happens. The *theme* of a story is the deeper meaning, the idea that underlies the narrative. The plot of "Young Goodman Brown" concerns a young man's experiences with the Devil. The theme of the story concerns the loss of innocence; it might be stated like this: The loss of innocence through the discovery of humanity's wickedness is one of the great tragedies of life.

Now, we must answer this important question: Do we read a story in order to learn the truth conveyed by the theme? The response, of course, is No! We read most often for experience, not for the discovery of an uplifting theme. The experience of reading is an immersion in the fictive universe of the story. However, a work of literature must have a theme, cannot avoid having one.

How Theme Is Conveyed

The theme of a famous poem—one that you have probably read—is this: Since life is very short, one should enjoy every moment of it. That theme in itself is almost totally uninteresting, but the poem that embodies it is so memorable as to be one of the most widely reprinted of English lyrics:

20
> Loveliest of trees, the cherry now
> Is hung with bloom along the bough,
> And stands about the woodland ride
> Wearing white for Eastertide.
>
> Now, of my threescore years and ten,
> Twenty will not come again,
> And take from seventy years a score,
> It only leaves me fifty more.
>
> And since to look at things in bloom
> Fifty springs are little room,
> About the woodlands I will go
> To see the cherry hung with snow.
>
> —A. E. Housman, *A Shropshire Lad*

It should be obvious that the theme of a work of literature is seldom stated directly, but is carried or revealed by the imaginative structure of the work. At no point in "Young Goodman Brown" does Hawthorne state his theme directly, but the theme is surely there, in the imaginative structure.

The Use of Theme in Literary Essays

When you write about literature, you need an organizational pivot for your essay—a thesis that will allow you to begin, a point of departure, something to work *from*. The theme of the work that you are discussing can well serve as the basis for your essay. For example, if you can state the theme of a work of literature, then you can ask how that theme was developed, and your answer to that question will be your essay.

This is a simple but important point. Which of the following two statements would better serve to get an essay under way?

21   "Young Goodman Brown" is about a young man's visit to a witches' sabbath.
"Young Goodman Brown" is about the tragedy of the loss of innocence.

To demonstrate the first statement, about all one could do would be to retell the story. To demonstrate the second statement, one would have to analyze and interpret the story. So the second statement is more generative, more productive of subject matter, than the first.

In one way or another, most writers of literary essays do use the theme of the work that they are discussing as their points of departure. Here is the beginning of Richard Harter Fogle's essay on "Young Goodman Brown." (The whole essay appears at the end of this chapter, on pages 204–15.)

22   "Young Goodman Brown" is generally felt to be one of Hawthorne's more difficult tales, from the ambiguity of the conclusions which may be drawn from it. Its hero, a naive young man who accepts both society in general and his fellowmen as individuals at their own valuation, is in one terrible night presented with the vision of human Evil, and is ever afterwards "A stern, a sad, a darkly meditative, a distrustful, if not a desperate man. . . ," whose "dying hour was gloom."

The Imaginative Structure

As we noted above, theme emerges from the imaginative structure of a work of literature; it is seldom stated directly. We read "Young Goodman Brown"—experience it imaginatively—and then we are able to say, "This story is 'about' the tragedy of the loss of innocence." That is to say, once Goodman Brown discovers the evil, the corruption, of all humanity—once he loses his innocence—he is no longer able to face life with optimism and cheer, and becomes a morbidly disillusioned man. We find this out through the imaginative structure of the work, and the imaginative structure of any work of literature consists of three elements: *characters, action* (including dialogue), and *scene.* In other words, our understanding of the theme of a work comes from our knowledge of the work's imaginative structure—its characters, its action, and its scene.

Characters

In "Young Goodman Brown," the three most important characters are Goodman Brown himself, Faith, and Goodman Brown's companion on the walk through the forest. It is interesting that these characters are both people and symbols. Goodman Brown symbolizes the innocent young man who, nonetheless, is curious about experience. (It must be noted that he went to the forest of his own volition, and he had arranged the journey earlier. Of course, every young person must make the journey into the symbolic forest of evil, for that is the way of the world.)

As to Faith—well, she is Goodman Brown's young wife, to be sure, but she is also, and somewhat heavy-handedly, his faith.

Doesn't Goodman Brown's companion on the walk turn out to be the Devil himself? And isn't he also the forebear of Goodman Brown? He is described as "bearing a considerable resemblance to him, though perhaps more in expression than features. Still they might have been taken for father and son" (lines 55–57).

A good deal more could be said about character, but the purpose here is not to write an essay; rather it is to show how an essay might be written, or, at the very least, to demonstrate how materials for an essay can be found in a work of literature.

Action

The actions in a story constitute the plot. In regard to plot, we ask not only What happened? but also Why? That is, we are concerned with motivation: Why did Goodman Brown go into the forest after all? Why did his companion want him to go? Why was his dying hour gloom? And so on.

Scene

In fiction, scene is frequently very important, as it is in "Young Goodman Brown." The forest that Goodman Brown enters is literally a gloomy and dangerous place, but it is also symbolically the "forest of evil":

23   He had taken a dreary road, darkened by all the gloomiest trees of the forest, which barely stood aside to let the narrow path creep through, and closed immediately behind. It was all as lonely as could be; and there is this peculiarity in such a solitude, that the traveller knows not who may be concealed by the innumerable trunks and the thick boughs overhead; so that with lonely footsteps he may yet be passing through an unseen multitude.

"There may be a devilish Indian behind every tree," said Goodman Brown to himself; and he glanced fearfully behind him as he added, "What if the devil himself should be at my very elbow!" [lines 31–41]

It is important to realize that characters, actions, and scenes may be taken either literally or symbolically. For instance, Faith is literally Goodman Brown's wife, but she is figuratively or symbolically the principle of faith. At the literal level, Goodman Brown's walk is merely a trip into a sinister forest, but at the symbolic level, Goodman Brown's journey is from innocence to the knowledge of humanity's wickedness. And the forest is on the one hand just a forest, but on the other hand the place deep in the human heart where wickedness lies.

Writing an Interpretative Essay on Prose Fiction

It is now time to pause to think about the uses of all this theory. The elements for a certain kind of essay—a literary essay—have already been implied. In summary, they are:

1. The theme of a work of literature as the topic for the essay.
2. How the characters contribute to the theme.
3. How the action (plot, dialogue) contributes to the theme.
4. How scene contributes to the theme.
5. The influence of narrative viewpoint and the narrator on character, action, and scene.

This list is not meant to imply an organization for an essay, but merely to point out the elements that can go into an interpretative essay, the organization of which will depend on what you are trying to do and the materials that you are working with.

And notice what these titles imply about the possibilities for interpretative essays:

24   "Theme and Character in 'Young Goodman Brown'"
"Theme and Plot in 'Young Goodman Brown'"
"Theme and Scene in 'Young Goodman Brown'"

That is, you can write about character or plot or scene in relation to theme. On the other hand, of course, you can explore how theme emerges from the whole imaginative universe of the work.

After all, an essay about literature is merely an expository essay, not some other, exotic genre; it is an essay about literature only because of its subject matter.

In Chapter 5—and at various other points in the book—we have discussed the problems of writing about prose nonfiction, and we will not re-cover that territory here.

The Problem of Poetry

Most poetry does not tell a story, is not *narrative.* It appeals to the reader for other reasons than curiosity concerning What happens next?

As the point of reference—the text—for what we will be saying about poetry, we will use "To His Coy Mistress," by Andrew Marvell (1621–1678). This is a sexy, ironic, moving poem—certainly one of the favorites in the English language. Because of the complexity of the moods that it conveys, it is extremely pleasurable to read and to discuss.

Here is the poem:

25   *To His Coy Mistress*
                               Andrew Marvell

Had we but world enough, and time,
This coyness, lady, were no crime.
We could sit down and think which way
To walk, and pass our long love's day;
Thou by the Indian Ganges' side   5
Shouldst rubies find; I by the tide
Of Humber would complain. I would
Love you ten years before the Flood;
And you should, if you please, refuse
Till the conversion of the Jews.   10

My vegetable love should grow
Vaster than empires, and more slow.
An hundred years should go to praise
Thine eyes, and on thy forehead gaze;
Two hundred to adore each breast,   15
But thirty thousand to the rest;
An age at least to every part,
And the last age should show your heart.
For, lady, you deserve this state,
Nor would I love at lower rate.   20

But at my back I always hear
Time's wingèd chariot hurrying near;
And yonder all before us lie
Deserts of vast eternity.
Thy beauty shall no more be found,   25
Nor in thy marble vault shall sound
My echoing song; then worms shall try
That long preserved virginity,
And your quaint honor turn to dust,
And into ashes all my lust.   30
The grave's a fine and private place,
But none, I think, do there embrace.

Now therefore, while the youthful hue
Sits on thy skin like morning dew,
And while thy willing soul transpires   35
At every pore with instant fires,
Now let us sport us while we may;
And now, like am'rous birds of prey,
Rather at once our time devour,
Than languish in his slow-chapped power.   40
Let us roll all our strength, and all
Our sweetness, up into one ball;
And tear our pleasure with rough strife
Thorough the iron gates of life.
Thus, though we cannot make our sun   45
Stand still, yet we will make him run.

When we begin to gather ideas for writing about this poem—or any other—our basic questions are simple: What does the poem mean? How does it convey that meaning? (But we must interpret the word *meaning* broadly, to include feelings, sensations, intuitions, and so on.)

"Footnoting"

First, we must make certain that we understand the individual words and phrases. Thus:

26 *Mistress* (in the title) does not mean "kept woman," but "sweetheart" or "beloved."

coyness (line 2) means "shyness, modesty."

Ganges (line 5) is a river in India, a distant and exotic place, at least from the standpoint of a seventeenth-century Englishman.

Humber (line 7) is a humble English stream, on the banks of which stood Marvell's family home.

the Flood (line 8) is the biblical deluge.

the conversion of the Jews (line 10) is not supposed to occur until the Last Judgment.

thy marble vault (line 26) means "your marble tomb."

quaint (line 29) means "possessing a strange, but charming oddness."

his slow-chapped power (line 40) means "slow-jawed," and we get the image of Time slowly but systematically chewing up the poet and his mistress.

thorough (line 44) is simply a version of *through*.

This glossing—"footnoting"—has perhaps taken us a fraction of an inch toward explaining the meaning and the power of the poem.

Literal Meaning (Paraphrase)

The next step is to see if we can translate the literal meaning, the surface meaning, into a code other than the one the poet uses and still keep the bare ideas that were in the original. Here is a paraphrase of the poem:

27 If we had enough time, Lady, I wouldn't be in any hurry. We could plan, and think, and travel, and wait. I would love you for the whole age of the earth. I'd be willing to spend hundreds of years on preliminaries, such as praising your beauty. For you're such a wonderful person that you deserve all the honor and dignity that I could bestow upon you, and, furthermore, I'm not a piker; I'm willing to give you everything that is your due.

However, I'm always aware of the brevity of life, and I know that before us lies the eternity of death. In the grave, we'll have no chance for love.

Therefore, while we're young and passionate, let's make love. We can't stop time, but we can give him a run for his money.

Now then, if all that we wanted from a work of literature were its literal meaning, we would like the paraphrase just as well as we do the poem. Obviously, a work of literature gives us something more than bare meaning, something more than information or opinion.

Character

As we saw when we were discussing prose fiction, one of the reasons for literature's meaningfulness is the people that we get to know through it. Ahab and Ishmael, Don Quixote, Huck Finn, Becky Sharp, Emma Bovary, King Lear, Dorothea Brooke, Walter Mitty—all these characters have entered into the imaginative life of civilized people.

In a poem such as "To His Coy Mistress," however, there seem to be no characters—at least in the sense that we can talk about the characters in a novel by Norman Mailer or Henry Fielding. But this absence of characters in the poem is illusory; if we take a close look, we will see that two very interesting people emerge from the poem, and furthermore we will see that if they did not emerge, our interest in the poem would wane.

The first character is the narrator of the poem—who is *not* Andrew Marvell. It is misleading to make a statement such as, "In 'To His Coy Mistress' Andrew Marvell says . . . ," for it is not Marvell who is speaking, but a character created by Marvell, the narrator of the poem. Marvell has created the narrator, but it is the narrator who is speaking, not Marvell, in the same sense that Shakespeare is not speaking in *Othello* when Iago says to Roderigo, over and over again, Forget about conscience and principle, and "Put money in thy purse." We can accuse Iago of being an unprincipled, venal villain, but not Shakespeare.

What sort of person is speaking in the poem, then? In the first place, we sense that the narrator is extremely complicated. There is good evidence that he is not quite sincere in what he says to the woman (who is the second character), but that he is profoundly sincere in his attitude about the brevity of life. After all, his elaborate argument boils down, quite simply, to this: "I want to go to bed with you." All his protestations about what he *would* do if he had infinite time, then, come off as mere ruses to convince the woman that she should yield to him. And the argument is unfair in several senses. In the first place, it does not follow that simply because life is short one should take every chance for pleasure. Notice how the argument fails logically when it is stated formally:

28   If we had forever, you could take all the time you wanted with your decision
      about letting me make love to you.
      But life is short.
      Therefore, let's make love immediately.

The conclusion simply does not follow. A valid conclusion would be something like this: Therefore, make up your mind. That conclusion, however, could be disastrous, for the woman might make an unfavorable decision, and the narrator does not want to present her with that chance.

This sophist then goes on to present the woman with a horrifying image of death: the cold tomb, and the worms. These images make us feel that the narrator is not deeply in love with the woman, for he is being more than a little cruel to her in his attempt to work his will.

Urbane, witty, intelligent, unprincipled—the narrator from this standpoint is something less than a sympathetic character for the reader; if he were nothing more than this, he would be too shallow to gain our interest. But underlying the wit, cool urbanity, and cynicism is the narrator's tragic sense of the brevity of life, the knowledge that all pleasure is momentary and that, indeed, "deserts of vast eternity" do lie before every person.

Toward the end, the whole tone of the poem changes and intensifies. When the narrator says, "Let us roll all our strength, and all/Our sweetness, up into one ball," the reader senses that the narrator views his union with the woman as a kind of forestalling of destiny. For the moment, in the intensity of union, even without deep love, two beings can forget the inevitable deserts of eternity that lie ahead.

The narrator is, then, a cynical and, in one sense, less then totally sincere character, but he is in the grip of the sense of his own mortality. What of the other character, the woman the narrator is addressing?

We would suppose that a clever person such as the narrator would develop the perfect argument to gain his will with the woman. But he does not. Therefore, we can construct an image of the woman from what the narrator says to her. Beautiful, to be sure, coy certainly, highborn and fastidious—and apparently very gullible. If the narrator thinks she will accept his sophistry and his scare tactics, she must be—or the narrator must think she is—less than highly perceptive.

In the second stanza, one can see a look of astonishment and fear come over her face as she hears about the tomb with its worms. The final couplet is devastating: "The grave's a fine and private place,/But none, I think, do there embrace."

Unless one can visualize these two characters, "To His Coy Mistress" does not come to life. But with the two characters present, the poem becomes a dramatic incident with conflict and a conclusion.

Characterization in literature can be more direct than it is in "To His Coy Mistress," of course. For instance, in *Hard Times,* Dickens introduces us to Josiah Bounderby:

> 29   . . . who was Mr. Bounderby?
>
> Why, Mr. Bounderby was as near to being Mr. Gradgrind's bosom friend, as a man perfectly devoid of sentiment can approach that spiritual relationship towards another man perfectly devoid of sentiment. So near was Mr. Bounderby—or, if the reader should prefer it, so far off.
>
> He was a rich man: banker, merchant, manufacturer, and what not. A big, loud man, with a stare, and a metallic laugh. A man made out of a coarse material, which seemed to have been stretched to make so much of him. A man with a great puffed head and forehead, swelled veins in his temples, and such a strained skin to his face that it seemed to hold his eyes open, and lift his eyebrows up. A man with a pervading appearance on him of being inflated like a balloon, and ready to start. A man who could never sufficiently vaunt himself a self-made man. A man who was always proclaiming, through that brassy speaking-trumpet of a voice of his, his old ignorance and his old poverty. A man who was the Bully of humility.

We get to know Mr. Bounderby through more direct ways than those that introduce us to the narrator of "To His Coy Mistress." Neither method of presenting character is superior to the other: each can be effective and satisfying.

The point is this: part of the experience of literature is getting to know fictive characters that are memorable and interesting. Indeed, much talk about literature revolves around interest in the characters that appear in the works under discussion. Perhaps most of the talk about *Paradise Lost* concerns Satan, as Milton constructed him in the poem.

An important point to remember when you write about literature is that one of the things you can discuss is the characters that you get to know, how you get to know them within the work, how they function in the text, and what they mean to you. This is exactly what this section has done.

Formal Structure

Works of literature have structure. For instance, plays are divided into acts, which break the movement into segments; novels are divided into chapters and sometimes sections; poems usually have clearly defined, formal patterns of stanzas. There is no need for you to be able to name these patterns, but you should be aware of them, for at least some of the enjoyment of poetry comes from the skill with which the poet embodies ideas in strictly defined patterns. For instance, the sonnet follows a pattern of just fourteen lines of ten syllables each (with some little room for variation in the number of syllables). As an example, here is Shakespeare's Sonnet 129, about another kind of "love": lust.

30   *Sonnet 129*

William Shakespeare

Th' expense of spirit in a waste of shame
Is lust in action; and, till action, lust
Is perjured, murd'rous, bloody, full of blame,
Savage, extreme, rude, cruel, not to trust;
Enjoyed no sooner but despisèd straight;
Past reason hunted, and no sooner had,
Past reason hated as a swallowed bait
On purpose laid to make the taker mad;
Mad in pursuit, and in possession so;
Had, having, and in quest to have, extreme;
A bliss in proof, and proved, a very woe,
Before, a joy proposed; behind, a dream.
    All this the world well knows, yet none knows well
    To shun the heaven that leads men to this hell.

The following is a poem with an extremely intricate form. It is presented without comment, but with this suggestion: after reading the poem, you should make a statement that will describe its form. In order to do this, you need no fancy terminology; you merely have to describe what you see on the page.

31   *Here in Katmandu*[6]

Donald Justice

We have climbed the mountain,
There's nothing more to do.

[6]Donald Justice, "Here in Katmandu," *The Summer Anniversaries* (Middletown, Conn.: Wesleyan University Press, 1956). Copyright © 1956 by Donald Justice. Reprinted by permission of Wesleyan University Press. "Here in Katmandu" first appeared in *Poetry*.

It is terrible to come down
To the valley
Where, amidst many flowers,
One thinks of snow.

As, formerly, amidst snow,
Climbing the mountain,
One thought of flowers,
Tremulous, ruddy with dew,
In the valley,
One caught their scent coming down.

It is difficult to adjust, once down,
To the absence of snow.
Clear days, from the valley,
One looks up at the mountain.
What else is there to do?
Prayerwheels, flowers!

Let the flowers
Fade, the prayerwheels run down.
What have these to do
With us who have stood atop the snow
Atop the mountain,
Flags seen from the valley?

It might be possible to live in the valley,
To bury oneself among flowers,
If one could forget the mountain,
How, setting out before dawn,
Blinded with snow,
One knew what to do.

Meanwhile it is not easy here in Katmandu,
Especially when to the valley
That wind which means snow
Elsewhere, but here means flowers,
Comes down,
As soon it must, from the mountain.

The section on Prosody in the Reference Guide at the back of this book contains a good deal more about form in poetry.

The Language of Poetry

The language of poetry often, but not always, contains features that are not found in prose—for instance, meter and rhyme (both of which are also discussed in the section on prosody in the Reference Guide). The language of poetry also is characterized by a greater intensity than that of prose. It is likely to be more *metaphorical* and *connotative*.

Here is a prose statement: Life is short; death is for eternity. In presenting those simple ideas, Marvell used two highly visual metaphors:

32   But at my back I always hear
        Time's wingèd chariot hurrying near;
        And yonder all before us lie
        Deserts of vast eternity.

The literal statement is thus translated into a form that is more characteristic of poetry than of prose.

Poetic language tends to be highly connotative. Think, for instance, of the connotations that the word *love* takes on in "To His Coy Mistress." It means, first of all, a tender emotion, but it soon comes to mean "sexual union," as in "to make love." By line 29, it has become mere lust:

33   And your quaint honor turn to dust,
     And into ashes all my lust.

In short, the language of poetry is usually everyday language—the same words in the same kinds of constructions—but made more intense, imbued with more meaning than is the case in prose.

Discovering Ideas for Writing About Poetry

All that we have said about poetry—and much of what we have said about prose fiction—can be used to construct a series of questions that will help you discover ideas to write about.

1. Concerning the Writer. What do I need to know about the author in order to understand the work? What sort of narrator does the author create to "tell" the work? (In the case of "To His Coy Mistress," this is, as we have seen, a crucial question.)

2. Concerning the Context. What is the meaning of the poem? What does it say when a prose paraphrase is written? What do I learn from the poem? (And how does this knowledge differ from the kind I'd get in a psychology or a chemistry class?)

3. Concerning the Structure. What happens in the poem? What kind of imaginative universe does the poem present? Are there characters in the poem? If so, what sort of people are they? How do I know? What about plot? Scene? (Not all poems have characters, plot, or scene in any direct sense.)

4. Concerning the Contact. What is the formal structure of the poem— the stanzaic pattern and the rhyme scheme? What effect does it have? (For example, the stanza divisions in "To His Coy Mistress" serve to mark clear-cut stages in the development of the meaning of the poem.)

5. Concerning the Style. What is the style of the work? What is its effect? Why?

6. Concerning the Audience. What is my personal, subjective reaction to the poem? Why do I react in this way? What effect is the poem likely to have on audiences in general? How do I know?

These questions apply to prose fiction and drama as well as poetry.

A Word About Drama

Most plays—but not all—are written to be seen and heard, not read. This means that scene, gesture, and movement are tremendously important in drama. When you read a play, you must construct the set and block the actors on the stage of your mind. You must know who is onstage at a given moment, and who is speaking to whom.

As a brief illustration of the reader's task with drama, here is the beginning of *Hamlet*:

34   [Elsinore. A guard platform of the castle.]
      Enter Barnardo and Francisco, two sentinels.

Bar.   Who's there?
Fran.   Nay, answer me. Stand and unfold yourself.
Bar.   Long live the king!
Fran.   Barnardo?
Bar.   He.
Fran.   You come most carefully upon your hour.
Bar.   'Tis now struck twelve. Get thee to bed, Francisco.
Fran.   For this relief much thanks. 'Tis bitter cold,
        And I am sick at heart.
Bar.   Have you had a quiet guard?
Fran.   Not a mouse stirring.
Bar.   Well, good night.
        If you do meet Horatio and Marcellus,
        The rivals of my watch, bid them make haste.

As you read, you must stage the play like a director. From the scanty evidence that this passage gives you, you must design a platform on the walls of a medieval castle in Denmark. You must light the scene dimly, for you have learned it is midnight. And somehow your scene must convey the notion that it is a cold winter night.

A Final Series of Questions

In Chapter 3, we mentioned *Rhetoric: Discovery and Change,* by Young, Becker, and Pike. In this work, the authors develop a complex theory concerning problem solving that is the basis for the following series of questions, which are extremely valuable for generating ideas in writing about works of literature:

1. How do you know the work is what it is? (In other words, if you say that the work is a poem, then you must be able to point to the features such as rhyme, meter, figurative language, typography, and so on, that you use as a basis for claiming that a work is a poem.) What are the distinctive features of a poem? A movie? A novel?
2. What is its meaning? Can you state its thesis? (In the case of "To His Coy Mistress": Life is very short, so let's enjoy every minute, for tomorrow we may be dead.) How does it convey its meaning? Plot? Scene? Character? Symbols? Direct statements?
3. What is its structure? Does it have parts? What are they?
4. How is it different from a range of other works of literature? How much can it be changed and still be the same kind of thing:? Why isn't a paraphrase a poem, a story, or a play?
5. How did you go about gaining your understanding of the work? (Understanding of a complex work does not come in a flash, but grows through analysis and thought.) How is your understanding of the work growing?

6. What are the different artistic devices in the various sections of the work?
7. How does the work relate to other statements concerning its theme? (Sociological, biological, psychological, and philosophic statements concerning lovemaking would differ in significant ways from the statement in "To His Coy Mistress.")
8. How does the work fit into or square with your understanding of life? Does it contradict or reinforce your value system?
9. How does the work relate to the whole range of possible kinds of utterances (emotive, informative, persuasive, and so on)?

Finally

Very few people need to learn to write literary criticism, but anyone who is unable to respond to literature coherently and intelligently is missing one of life's greatest pleasures. This chapter was an attempt to give you ways to "get into" literature with appreciation and understanding—and hence to have important things to say concerning the works of literature that you read.

Following are two literary essays, the first on "Young Goodman Brown" and the second on Shakespeare's Sonnet 129. Careful study of them will be useful in your own writing about literature.

35   *Ambiguity and Clarity in Hawthorne's*
                      "Young Goodman Brown" [7]

                      Richard Harter Fogle

"Young Goodman Brown" is generally felt to be one of Hawthorne's more difficult tales, from the ambiguity of the conclusions which may be drawn from it. Its hero, a naive young man who accepts both society in general and his fellowmen as individuals at their own valuation, is in one terrible night presented with the vision of human Evil, and is ever afterwards "A stern, a sad, a darkly meditative, a distrustful, if not a desperate man . . . ," whose "dying hour was gloom." So far we are clear enough, but there are confusing factors. In the first place, are the events of the night merely subjective, a dream; or do they actually occur? Again, at the crucial point in his ordeal Goodman Brown summons the strength to cry to his wife Faith, "look up to heaven, and resist the evil one." It would appear from this that he has successfully resisted the supreme temptation—but evidently he is not therefore saved. Henceforth, "On the Sabbath day, when the congregation were singing a holy psalm, he could not listen because an anthem of sin rushed loudly upon his ear and drowned all the blessed strain." On the other hand, he is not wholly lost, for in the sequel he is only at intervals estranged from "the bosom of Faith." Has Hawthorne himself failed to control the implications of his allegory?

[7]Richard Harter Fogle, "Ambiguity and Clarity in Hawthorne's 'Young Goodman Brown,'" *New England Quarterly,* 18 (Dec. 1943), 448–65. Reprinted by permission of *New England Quarterly* and the author.

I should say rather that these ambiguities of meaning are intentional, an integral part of his purpose. Hawthorne wishes to propose, not flatly that man is primarily evil, but instead the gnawing doubt lest this should indeed be true. "Come, devil; for to thee is this world given," exclaims Goodman Brown at the height of his agony, but he finds strength to resist the devil, and in the ambiguous conclusion he does not entirely reject his former faith. His trial, then, comes not from the certainty but the dread of Evil. Hawthorne poses the dangerous question of the relations of Good and Evil in man, but withholds his answer. Nor does he permit himself to settle whether the events of the night of trial are real or the mere figment of a dream.

These ambiguities he conveys and fortifies by what Yvor Winters has called "the formula of alternative possibilities,"* and F. O. Matthiesen "the device of multiple choice,"† in which are suggested two or more interpretations of a single action or event. Perhaps the most striking instance of the use of this device in "Young Goodman Brown" is the final word on the reality of the hero's night experience:

> Had Goodman Brown fallen asleep in the forest and only dreamed a wild dream of a witch-meeting?
> *Be it so if you will;*‡ but alas! it was a dream of evil omen for young Goodman Brown.

This device of multiple choice, or ambiguity, is the very essence of Hawthorne's tale. Nowhere does he permit us a simple meaning, a merely single interpretation. At the outset, young Goodman Brown leaves the arms of his wife Faith and the safe limits of Salem town to keep a mysterious appointment in the forest. Soon he encounters his conductor, a man "in grave and decent attire," commonplace enough save for an indefinable air of acquaintanceship with the great world. ". . . the only thing about him that could be fixed upon as remarkable was his staff, which bore the likeness of a great black snake, so curiously wrought that it might almost be seen to twist and wriggle itself like a living serpent.

> *This, of course, must have been an ocular deception, assisted by the uncertain light."*§

This man is, of course, the Devil, who seeks to lure the still-reluctant goodman to a witch-meeting. In the process he progressively undermines the young man's faith in the institutions and the men whom he has heretofore revered. First Goody Cloyse, "a very pious and exemplary dame, who had taught him his catechism in youth, and was still his moral and spiritual advisor," is shown to have more than casual acquaintance with the Devil—to

---

Maule's Curse (Norfolk, Connecticut, 1938), 18. Mr. Winters limits his discussion of the device to Hawthorne's novels.

†*American Renaissance* (New York, 1941), 276.

‡These and all subsequent italics are mine.

§Hawthorne may have taken this suggestion from the serpent-staff of Mercury. He later uses it for lighter purposes on at least two occasions in *A Wonder Book*. Mercury's staff is described by Epimetheus as "like two serpents twisting around a stick, and . . . carved so naturally that I, at first, thought the serpents were alive" ("The Paradise of Children"). Again, in "The Miraculous Pitcher," "Two snakes, carved in the wood, were represented as twining themselves about the staff, and were so very skillfully executed that old Philemon (whose eyes, you know, were getting rather dim) almost thought them alive, and that he could see them wriggling and twisting."

be, in fact, a witch. Goodman Brown is shaken, but still minded to turn back and save himself. He is then faced with a still harder test. Just as he is about to return home, filled with self-applause, he hears the tramp of horses along the road:

> On came the hoof tramps and the voices of the riders, two grave old voices, conversing soberly as they drew near. These mingled sounds appeared to pass along the road, within a few yards of the young man's hiding-place; *but, owing doubtless to the depth of the gloom at that particular spot, neither the travellers nor their steeds were visible. Though their figures brushed the small boughs by the wayside, it could not be seen that they intercepted, even for a moment, the faint gleam from the strip of bright sky athwart which they must have passed.* It vexed him the more, because he could have sworn, *were such a thing possible,* that he recognized the voices of the minister and Deacon Gookin, jogging along quietly, as they were wont to do, when bound to some ordination or ecclesiastical council.

The conversion of the minister and the deacon makes it only too clear that they also are in league with the evil one. Yet Goodman Brown, although now even more deeply dismayed, still resolves to stand firm, heartened by the blue arch of the sky and the stars brightening in it.* At that moment a cloud, "though no wind was stirring," hides the stars, and he hears a confused babble of voices. "*Once the listener fancied that he could distinguish* the accents of townspeople of his own . . . The next moment, so indistinct were the sounds, *he doubted whether he had heard aught* but the murmur of the old forest, whispering without a wind." But to his horror he believes that he hears the voice of his wife Faith, uttering only weak and insincere objections as she is borne through the air to the witch-meeting.

Now comes a circumstance which at first sight would appear to break the chain of ambiguities, for his suspicions seem concretely verified. A pink ribbon, which he remembers having seen in his wife's hair, comes fluttering down into his grasp. This ribbon, an apparently solid object like the fatal handkerchief in *Othello,* seems out of keeping with the atmosphere of doubt which has enveloped the preceding incidents.† Two considerations, however, make it possible to defend it. One is that if Goodman Brown is dreaming, the ribbon like the rest may be taken as part-and-parcel of his dream. It is to be noted that this pink ribbon appears in his wife's hair once more as she meets him at his return to Salem in the morning. The other is that for the moment the ribbon vanishes from the story, melting into its shadowy background. Its impact is merely temporary.

Be it as you will, as Hawthorne would say. At any rate the effect on Goodman Brown is instantaneous and devastating. Casting aside all further scruples, he rages through the wild forest to the meeting of witches, for the time at least fully accepting the domination of Evil. He soon comes upon a "numerous congregation," alternately shadowy and clear in the flickering red light of four blazing pines above a central rock.

---

*Cf. Bosola to the Duchess at a comparably tragic moment in Webster's *Duchess of Malfi:* "Look you, the stars shine still."

†"As long as what Brown saw is left wholly in the realm of hallucination, Hawthorne's created illusion is compelling. . . . Only the literal insistence on that damaging pink ribbon obtrudes the labels of a confining allegory, and short-circuits the range of association." Matthiessen, *American Renaissance,* 284.

Among them, *quivering to and fro between gloom and splendor,* appeared faces that would be seen next day at the council board of the province, and others which, Sabbath after Sabbath, looked devoutly heavenward, and benignantly over the crowded pews, from the holiest pulpits in the land. *Some affirm that* the lady of the governor was there. . . . *Either the sudden gleams of light flashing over the obscure field bedazzled Goodman Brown, or he recognized* a score of the church members of Salem village famous for their especial sanctity.

Before this company steps out a presiding figure who bears "With reverence be it spoken . . . *no slight similitude,* both in garb and manner, to some grave divine of the New England churches," and calls forth the "converts." At the word young Goodman Brown comes forward. *"He could have well-nigh sworn that* the shape of his own dead father beckoned him to advance, looking downward from a smoke wreath, while a woman, with dim features of despair, threw out her hand to warn him back. *Was it his mother?"* But he is quickly seized and led to the rock, along with a veiled woman whom he dimly discerns to be his wife Faith. The two are welcomed by the dark and ambiguous leader into the fraternity of Evil, and the final, irretrievable step is prepared.

A basin was hollowed, naturally, in the rock. *Did it contain water, reddened by the lurid light? or was it blood? or, perchance, a liquid flame?* Herein did the shape of evil dip his hand and prepare to lay the mark of baptism upon their foreheads, that they might be partakers of the mystery of sin, more conscious of the secret guilt of others, both in deed and thought, than they could now be of their own. The husband cast one look at his pale wife, and Faith at him. What polluted wretches would the next glance show them to each other, shuddering alike at what they disclosed and what they saw!

"Faith! Faith!" cried the husband, "look up to heaven, and resist the wicked one."

Whether Faith obeyed he knew not.

Hawthorne then concludes with the central ambiguity, which we have already noticed, whether the events of the night were actual or a dream? The uses of this device, if so it may be called, are multiple in consonance with its nature. Primarily it offers opportunity for freedom and richness of suggestion. By it Hawthorne is able to suggest something of the density and incalculability of life, the difficulties which clog the interpretation of even the simplest incidents, the impossibility of achieving a single and certain insight into the actions and motives of others. This ambiguity adds depth and tone to Hawthorne's thin and delicate fabric. It covers the bareness of allegory, imparting to its one-to-one equivalence of object and idea a wider range of allusiveness, a hint of rich meaning still untapped. By means of it the thesis of "Young Goodman Brown" is made to inhere firmly in the situation, whence the reader himself must extract it to interpret. Hawthorne the artist refuses to limit himself to a single and doctrinaire conclusion,* proceeding instead by

---

*"For Hawthorne its value consisted in the variety of explanations to which it gave rise." *American Renaissance,* 277. The extent of my indebtedness to Mr. Matthiessen is only inadequately indicated in my documentation.

indirection. Further, it permits him to make free with the two opposed worlds of actuality and of imagination without incongruity or the need to commit himself entirely to either; while avoiding a frontal attack upon the reader's feeling for everyday verisimilitude, it affords the author licence of fancy. It allows him to draw upon sources of legend and superstition which still strike a responsive chord in us, possessing something of the validity of universal symbols.* Hawthorne's own definition of Romance may very aptly be applied to his use of ambiguity: it gives him scope "so [to] manage his atmospherical medium as to bring out or mellow the lights and deepen and enrich the shadows of the picture."†

These scanty observations must suffice here for the general importance of Hawthorne's characteristic ambiguity. It remains to describe its immediate significance in "young Goodman Brown." Above all, the separate instances of this "multiple choice device" organically cohere to reproduce in the reader's mind the feel of the central ambiguity of theme, the horror of the hero's doubt. Goodman Brown, a simple and pious nature, is wrecked as a result of the disappearance of the fixed poles of his belief. His orderly cosmos dissolves into chaos as church and state, the twin pillars of his society, are hinted to be rotten, with their foundations undermined.‡ The yearning for certainty is basic to his spirit—and he is left without the comfort even of a firm reliance in the Devil.§ His better qualities avail him in his desperation little more than the inner evil which prompted him to court temptation, for they prevent him from seeking the only remaining refuge—the confraternity of Sin. Henceforth he is fated to a dubious battle with shadows, to struggle with limed feet toward a redemption which must forever elude him, since he has lost the vision of Good while rejecting the proffered opportunity to embrace Evil fully. Individual instances of ambiguity, then, merge and coalesce in the theme itself to produce an all-pervading atmosphere of uneasiness and anguished doubt.

Ambiguity alone, however, is not a satisfactory aesthetic principle. Flexibility, suggestiveness, allusiveness, variety—all these are without meaning if there is no pattern from which to vary, no center from which to flee outward. And, indeed, ambiguity of itself will not adequately account for the individual phenomenon of "Young Goodman Brown." The deliberate haziness and multiple implications of its meaning are counterbalanced by the firm clarity of its technique, in structure and in style.

This clarity is embodied in the lucid simplicity of the basic action; in the skilful foreshadowing by which the plot is bound together; in balance of episode and scene; in the continuous use of contrast; in the firmness and

---

*"It is only by . . . symbols that have numberless meanings beside the one or two the writer lays an emphasis upon, or the half-score he knows of, that any highly subjective art can escape from the barrenness and shallowness of a too conscious arrangement, into the abundance and depth of nature. . . ." W. B. Yeats, "The Philosophy of Shelley's Poetry," *Ideas of Good and Evil* (London, 1914), 90. Thus Hawthorne by drawing upon Puritan superstition and demonology is able to add another dimension to his story.

†Preface, *The House of the Seven Gables*.

‡Goodman Brown is disillusioned with the church in the persons of Goody Cloyse, the minister, and Deacon Gookin, and it will be recalled that the figure of Satan at the meeting "bore no slight similitude . . . to some grave divine of the New England churches." As to the secular power, the devil tells Brown that ". . . the selectmen of divers towns make me their chairman; and a majority of the Great and General Court are firm supporters of my interest. The governor and I, too—But these are state secrets."

§The story could conceivably be read as intellectual satire, showing the pitfalls that lie in wait for a too-shallow and unquestioning faith. Tone and emphasis clearly show, however, a more tragic intention.

selectivity of Hawthorne's pictorial composition; in the carefully arranged climactic order of incident and tone; in the detachment and irony of Hawthorne's attitude; and finally in the purity, the grave formality, and the rhetorical balance of the style. His amalgamation of these elements achieves an effect of totality, of exquisite craftsmanship, of consummate artistic economy in fitting the means to the attempted ends.

The general framework of the story has a large simplicity. Goodman Brown leaves his wife Faith and the safe confines of Salem town at sunset, spends the night in the forest, and at dawn returns a changed man. Within this simple pattern plot and allegory unfold symmetrically and simultaneously. The movement of "Young Goodman Brown" is the single revolution of a wheel, which turns full-circle upon itself. As by this basic structure, the action is likewise given form by the device of foreshadowing, through which the entire development of the plot is already implicit in the opening paragraph. Thus Faith is troubled by her husband's expedition, and begs him to put it off till sunrise. "A lone woman is troubled with such dreams and such thoughts that she's afeard of herself sometimes," says she, hinting the ominous sequel of her own baptism in sin. "'My love and my Faith,' replied young Goodman Brown, 'of all nights in the year, this one night must I tarry away from thee. My journey . . . forth and back again, must needs be done 'twixt now and sunrise.'" They part, but Brown looking back sees "the head of Faith still peeping after him with a melancholy air, in spite of her pink ribbons."

"Poor little Faith!" thought he, for his heart smote him. "What a wretch am I to leave her on such an errand! She talks of dreams, too. Methought as she spoke there was trouble in her face, as if a dream had warned her what work is to be done to-night. But no, no; 'twould kill her to think of it. Well, she's a blessed angel on earth; and after this one night I'll cling to her skirts and follow her to heaven."

This speech, it must be confessed, is in several respects clumsy, obvious, and melodramatic;* but beneath the surface lurks a deeper layer. The pervasive ambiguity of the story is foreshadowed in the subtle emphasizing of the dream-motif, which paves the way for the ultimate uncertainty whether the incidents of the night are dream or reality; and in his simple-minded aspiration to "cling to her skirts and follow her to heaven," Goodman Brown is laying an ironic foundation for his later horror of doubt. A broader irony is apparent, in the light of future events, in the general emphasis upon Faith's angelic goodness.

Hawthorne's seemingly casual references to Faith's pink ribbons, which are mentioned three times in the opening paragraphs, are likewise far from artless. These ribbons, as we have seen, are an important factor in the plot; and as an emblem of heavenly Faith their color gradually deepens into the liquid flame or blood of the baptism into sin.†

---

*It has the earmarks of the set dramatic soliloquy, serving in this case to provide both information about the plot and revelation of character. Mr. Matthiessen attributes Hawthorne's general use of theatrical devices to the influence of Scott, who leads in turn to Shakespeare. *American Renaissance*, 203.

†Further, in welcoming the two candidates to the communion of Evil, the Devil says, "By the sympathy of your human hearts for sin ye shall scent out all the places . . . where crime has been committed, and shall exult to behold the whole earth one stain of guilt, *one mighty blood spot*." For this discussion of the pink ribbons I am largely indebted to Leland Schubert, *Hawthorne, the Artist* (Chapel Hill, 1944), 79–80.

Another instance of Hawthorne's careful workmanship is his architectural balance of episodes or scenes. The encounter with Goody Cloyse, the female hypocrite and sinner, is set off against the conversation of the minister and Deacon Gookin immediately afterward. The exact correspondence of the two episodes is brought into high relief by two balancing speeches. Goody Cloyse has lost her broomstick, and must perforce walk to the witch-meeting—a sacrifice she is willing to make since "they tell me there is a nice young man to be taken into communion to-night." A few minutes later Deacon Gookin, in high anticipation, remarks that "there is a goodly young woman to be taken into communion." A still more significant example of this balance is contained in the full swing of the wheel—in the departure at sunset and the return at sunrise. At the beginning of the story Brown takes leave of "Faith with the pink ribbons," turns the corner by the meeting-house and leaves the town; in the conclusion

> . . . Young Goodman Brown came slowly into the street of Salem village, staring around him like a bewildered man. The good old minister was taking a walk along the graveyard to get an appetite for breakfast and meditate his sermon, and bestowed a blessing, as he passed, on Goodman Brown. He shrank from the venerable saint as if to avoid an anathema. Old Deacon Gookin was at domestic worship, and the holy words of his prayer were heard through the open window. "What God doth the wizard pray to?" quoth Goodman Brown. Goody Cloyse, that excellent old Christian, stood in the early sunshine at her own lattice, catechizing a little girl who had brought her a pint of morning's milk.* Goodman Brown snatched the child away as from the grasp of the fiend himself. Turning the corner by the meeting-house, he spied the head of Faith, with the pink ribbons, gazing anxiously forth, and bursting into such joy at the sight of him that she skipped along the street and almost kissed her husband before the whole village. But Goodman Brown looked sternly and sadly into her face, and passed on without a greeting.

The exact parallel between the earlier and the later situation serves to dramatize intensely the change which the real or fancied happenings of the night have brought about in Goodman Brown.†

Contrast, a form of balance, is still more prominent in "Young Goodman Brown" than the kind of analogy which I have mentioned. The broad antitheses of day against night, the town against the forest, which signify in general a sharp dualism of Good and Evil, are supplemented by a color-contrast of red-and-black at the witch-meeting, by the swift transition of the forest scene from leaping flame to damp and chill, and by the consistent cleavage between outward decorum and inner corruption in the characters.‡

---

*This touch takes on an ironic and ominous significance if it is noticed that Goody Cloyse has that night been Faith's sponsor, along with the "rampant hag" Martha Carrier, at the baptism into sin by blood and flame.

†Here we may anticipate a little in order to point out the steady and premeditated irony arising from the locutions "good old minister," "venerable saint," and "excellent old Christian"; and the climactic effect produced by the balance and repetition of the encounters, which are duplicated in the sentence-structure and the repetition of "Goodman Brown."

‡Epitomized by Brown's description of the assemblage at the meeting as "a grave and dark-clad company."

The symbols of Day and Night, of Town and Forest, are almost indistinguishable in meaning. Goodman Brown leaves the limits of Salem at dusk and reenters them at sunrise; the night he spends in the forest. Day and the Town are clearly emblematic of Good, of the seemly outward appearance of human convention and society. They stand for the safety of an unquestioning and unspeculative faith. Oddly enough, Goodman Brown in the daylight of the Salem streets is a young man too simple and straightforward to be interesting, and a little distasteful in his boundless reverence for such unspectacular worthies as the minister, the deacon, and Goody Cloyse. Night and the Forest are the domains of the Evil One, symbols of doubt and wandering, where the dark subterraneous forces of the human spirit riot unchecked.* By the dramatic necessities of the plot Brown is a larger figure in the Forest of Evil,† and as a chief actor at the witch-meeting, than within the safe bounds of the town.

The contrast of the red of fire and blood against the black of night and the forest at the witch-meeting has a different import. As the flames rise and fall, the faces of the worshippers of Evil are alternately seen in clear outline and deep shadow, and all the details of the scene are at one moment revealed, the next obscured. It seems, then, that the red is Sin or Evil, plain and unequivocal; the black is that doubt of the reality either of Evil or Good which tortures Goodman Brown and is the central ambiguity of Hawthorne's story.‡

A further contrast follows in the swift transformation of scene when young Goodman Brown finds himself "amid calm night and solitude.

. . . He staggered against the rock, and felt it chill and damp; while a hanging twig, that had been all on fire, besprinkled his cheek with the coldest dew.§

Most pervasive of the contrasts in "Young Goodman Brown" is the consistent discrepancy between appearance and reality,‖ which helps to produce its heavy atmosphere of doubt and shadow. The church is represented by the highly respectable figures of Goody Cloyse, the minister, and Deacon Gookin, who in the forest are witch and wizards. The devil appears to Brown in the guise of his grandfather, "in grave and decent attire." As the goodman approaches the meeting, his ears are greeted by "the swell of what seemed a

---

*"The conception of the dark and evil-haunted wilderness came to him [Hawthorne] from the days of Cotton Mather, who held that 'the New Englanders are a people of God settled in those which were once the devil's territories.'" Matthiessen, *American Renaissance,* 282–283. See also Matthiessen's remark of *The Scarlet Letter* that ". . . the forest itself, with its straggling path, images to Hester 'the moral wilderness in which she had so long been wandering'; and while describing it Hawthorne may have taken a glance back at Spenser's Wood of Errour." *American Renaissance,* 279–280. This reference to Spenser may as fitly be applied to the path of Young Goodman Brown, "darkened by all the gloomiest trees of the forest, which barely stood aside to let the narrow path creep through, and closed immediately behind."

†"But he was himself the chief horror of the scene, and shrank not from its other horrors."

‡Hawthorne not infrequently uses color for symbol. See such familiar instances as *The Scarlet Letter* and "The Minister's Black Veil."

§See Schubert, *Hawthorne, the Artist,* 63. One would presume this device to be traditional in the story of the supernatural, where a return to actuality must eventually be made. An obvious example is the vanishing at cockcrow of the Ghost in *Hamlet.* See also the conclusion of Hawthorne's own "Ethan Brand."

‖Evil must provisionally be taken for reality during the night in the forest, in spite of the ambiguity of the ending.

hymn, rolling solemnly from a distance with the weight of many voices. He knew the tune; it was a familiar one in the choir of the village meeting-house." The Communion of Sin is, in fact, the faithful counterpart of a grave and pious ceremony at a Puritan meeting-house. "At one extremity of an open space, hemmed in by the dark wall of the forest, arose a rock, bearing some rude, natural resemblance either to an altar or a pulpit, and surrounded by four blazing pines, their tops aflame, their stems untouched, like candles at an evening meeting." The worshippers are "a numerous congregation," Satan resembles some grave divine, and the initiation into sin takes the form of a baptism.*

Along with this steady use of contrast at the Sabbath should be noticed its firmly composed pictorial quality. The rock, the center of the picture, is lighted by the blazing pines. The chief actors are as it were spotlighted in turn as they advance to the rock, while the congregation is generalized in the dimmer light at the outer edges. The whole composition is simple and definite, in contrast with the ambiguity occasioned by the rise and fall of the flame, in which the mass of the worshippers alternately shines forth and disappears in shadow.†

The clarity and simple structural solidity of "Young Goodman Brown" evinces itself in its tight dramatic framework. Within the basic form of the turning wheel it further divides into four separate scenes, the first and last of which, of course, are the balancing departure from and return to Salem. The night in the forest falls naturally into two parts: the temptation by the Devil and the witch-meeting. These two scenes, particularly the first, make full and careful use of the dramatic devices of suspense and climactic arrangement; and Hawthorne so manipulates his materials as to divide them as sharply as by a dropped curtain.

The temptation at first has the stylized and abstract delicacy of Restoration Comedy, or of the formalized seductions of Molière's *Don Juan.* The simple goodman, half-eager and half-reluctant, is wholly at the mercy of Satan, who leads him step by step to the inevitable end. The tone of the earlier part of this scene is lightly ironic: an irony reinforced by the inherent irony of the situation, which elicits a double meaning at every turn.

> "Come, Goodman Brown," cried his fellow-traveller, "this is a dull pace for the beginning of a journey. Take my staff, if you are so soon weary."
>
> "Friend," said the other, exchanging his slow pace for a full stop, "having kept covenant by meeting thee here, it is my purpose now to return whence I came. I have scruples touching the matter thou wot'st of."
>
> "Sayest thou so?" replied he of the serpent, smiling apart. "Let us walk on, nevertheless, reasoning as we go; and if I convince thee not thou shalt turn back. We are but a little way in the forest yet."

Then begins a skilful and relentless attack upon all the values which Goodman Brown has lived by. His reverence for his Puritan ancestors, "a

---

*The hint of the perverse desecration of the Black Mass adds powerfully here to the connotative scope of the allegory.

†The general effect is very like that of the famous Balinese Monkey Dance, which is performed at night, usually in a clearing of the forest, by the light of a single torch. The chief figures, the Monkey King and the King of the Demons, advance in turn to this central torch, while the chorus of dancers remains in the semi-obscurity of the background. This dance is allegorical, the Monkeys, as helpers of the Balinese, representing Good against the Evil of the Demons.

people of prayer, and good works to boot," is speedily turned against him as the Devil claims them for tried and dear companions. Next comes the episode of Goody Cloyse, who taught the young man his catechism. Brown is sorely cast down, but at length sturdily concludes. "What if a wretched old woman do choose to go to the devil when I thought she was going to heaven: is that any reason why I should quit my dear Faith and go after her?" But no sooner has he rallied from this blow than he is beset by another, still more shrewdly placed: he hears the voices of the minister and Deacon Gookin, and from their conversation gathers that they are bound for the meeting, and eagerly anticipating it. This is nearly final, but he still holds out. "'With heaven above, and Faith below, I will yet stand firm against the devil!' cried Goodman Brown"; only to be utterly overthrown by the sound of his wife's voice in the air, and the crushing evidence of the fatal pink ribbon.

The style has gradually deepened and intensified along with the carefully graduated intensity of the action, and now Hawthorne calls upon all his resources to seize and represent the immense significance of the moment. Nature itself is made at once to sympathize with and to mock the anguished chaos of the young man's breast; in his rage he is both at once with and opposed to the forest and the wind.* The symphony of sound, which began with the confused babble of voices in the sky as Faith and her witch-attendants swept overhead, rises to a wild crescendo.†

> And, maddened with despair, so that he laughed loud and long, did Goodman Brown grasp his staff and set forth again, at such a rate that he seemed to fly along the forest path rather than to walk or run. The road grew wilder and drearier and more faintly traced, and vanished at length, leaving him in the heart of the dark wilderness, still rushing onward with the instinct that guides mortal man to evil. The whole forest was peopled with frightful sounds—the creaking of the trees, the howling of wild beasts, and the yell of Indians; while sometimes the wind tolled like a distant church bell, and sometimes gave a broad roar around the travel-ler, as if all Nature were laughing him to scorn. But he was himself the chief horror of the scene, and shrank not from its other horrors.

After ascending to this climax, Hawthorne disengages himself and sepa-rates his scenes with the definiteness of the dropping of a curtain—by the simple expedient of shifting his view from the hero to his surroundings. Goodman Brown coming upon the witch-meeting is a mere onlooker until the moment comes for him to step forward for his baptism into sin. Up to that moment Satan usurps the stage. The eye is first directed to the central rock-altar, then to the four blazing pines which light it. Next there is the sense of a numerous assembly, vaguely seen in the fitful firelight. Finally the figure of Satan appears at the base of the rock, framed in an arch of flame. Only when he is summoned are we once more fully aware of Goodman Brown, as he stands at the altar by his wife Faith. Then, a moment later, comes the

---

*"The intensity of the situation is sustained by all the devices Hawthorne had learned from the seventeenth century, for just as the heavens groaned in Milton's fall of the angels, the winds are made to whisper sadly at the loss of this man's faith." Matthiessen, *American Renaissance*, 284. The winds, however, roar rather than "whisper sadly."

†Cf. Schubert's account of the sound-effects in "Young Goodman Brown," *Hawthorne, the Artist*, 114–117. Mr. Schubert distorts the effect and purpose of Hawthorne's use of sound in the story by comparing it to "the last movement of Beethoven's Ninth Symphony"—description of sound is not the sound itself—but his perception is extremely valuable.

second crashing climax when Brown calls upon his wife to "look up to heaven, and resist the wicked one"—cut off abruptly by anticlimax as the meeting vanishes in a roaring wind, and Brown leaning against the rock finds it chill and damp to his touch.

The satisfaction one feels in the clean line of the structure of the story is enhanced by Hawthorne's steady detachment from his materials: an attitude which deepens the impression of classic balance, which in turn stands against the painful ambiguity of the theme. Even the full tone of the intensest scenes, as Goodman Brown rushing through the forest, is tempered by restraint. The participant is overweighted by the calm, impartial (though not unfeeling) spectator; Hawthorne does not permit himself to become identified with his hero. He displays young Goodman Brown not in and for himself, but always in relation to the whole situation and set of circumstances. This detachment of attitude is plainest in the almost continuous irony, unemphatic but nonetheless relentless: an irony organically related to the ever-present ambiguities of the situation, but most evident in sustained tone. Thus, after recording Goodman Brown's aspiration to "cling to Faith's skirts and follow her to heaven," the author adds with deadly calm, "With this excellent resolve for the future, Goodman Brown felt himself justified in making more haste on his present evil purpose."

This detachment is implicit in the quiet, the abstractness, and the exquisite gravity of Hawthorne's style, everywhere formal and exactly though subtly cadenced. It throws a light and idealizing veil over the action,* and as it were maintains an aesthetic distance from it, while hinting at the ugliness it mercifully covers. The difference between the saying and the thing said, at times provides dramatic tension and a kind of ironic fillip. Note, for example, the grave decorum and eighteenth-century stateliness, the perverted courtliness, of Satan's welcome to young Brown and Faith:

> This night it shall be granted you to know their secret deeds: how hoary-bearded elders of the church have whispered wanton words to the young maids of their households; how many a woman, eager for widows' weeds, has given her husband a drink at bedtime and let him sleep his last sleep in her bosom; how beardless youths have made haste to inherit their fathers' wealth; and how fair damsels—blush not, sweet ones—have dug little graves in the garden, and bidden me, the sole guest, to an infant's funeral.

The steady procession of measured, ceremonious generalizations—"hoary-bearded elders," "wanton words," "beardless youths," and "fair damsels," is in radical contrast with the implication of the meaning; and the grisly archness of "blush not, sweet ones" is deeply suggestive in its incongruity.†

---

*Hawthorne's notion of the ideality which art should lend to nature is apparent in his comment in the introductory essay to *Mosses from an Old Manse* upon the reflection of a natural scene in water: "Each tree and rock, and every blade of grass, is distinctly imaged, and however unsightly in reality, assumes ideal beauty in the reflection." And a few pages later—"Of all this scene, the slumbering river has a dream picture in its bosom. Which, after all was the most real—the picture, or the original? the objects palpable to our grosser senses, or their apotheosis in the stream beneath? Surely the disembodied images stand in closer relation to the soul."

†I would not be understood to affirm that this adaptation of the eighteenth-century mock-heroic is the sole effect of Hawthorne's style in "Young Goodman Brown." The seventeenth century plays its part too. The agony of the goodman in the forest, and the sympathy of the elements, is Miltonic. And in this same scene of the witch-meeting Hawthorne twice touches upon Miltonic

In "Young Goodman Brown," then, Hawthorne has achieved that reconciliation of opposites which Coleridge deemed the highest art. The combination of clarity of technique, embodied in simplicity and balance of structure, in firm pictorial composition, in contrast and climactic arrangement, in irony and detachment, with ambiguity of meaning as signalized by the "device of multiple choice," in its interrelationships produces the story's characteristic effect. By means of these two elements Hawthorne reconciles oneness of action with multiplicity of suggestion, and enriches the bareness of systematic allegory. Contrarily, by them he holds in check the danger of lapsing into mere speculation without substance or form. The phantasmagoric light-and-shadow of the rising and falling fire, obscuring and softening the clear, hard outline of the witch-meeting, is an image which will stand for the essential effect of the story itself, compact of ambiguity and clarity harmoniously interfused.

36   *Shakespeare's Sonnet 129*[8]

Karl F. Thompson

The opening and closing statements of the sonnet are generalizations, the first angry in tone, the last resigned. The intervening images shift as lust is imagined as a traitorous counselor, a hunted object and then a hunter. The ever-changing tenses of the verbs contribute a restless, distraught quality to which the resigned melancholy of the final couplet is sharp contrast.

The poet, after stating that "lust in action" (2) is a waste of mental and moral capabilities in an activity that is shameful, describes lust in its pre-operative state. "Till action" (2) must mean "until it becomes action." Lust in the mind or heart, before action, is "perjur'd, murderous, bloody, full of blame" (3). In other words, it is the betrayer within, employing blandishments, urgings, persuasion and compulsion to induce its victim to take action. "Not to trust" (4) sums up the nature of the traitor lust, the crooked counselor that presents the act of lust as unalloyed pleasure.

The act of lust is completed (5) and immediately becomes a source and object of loathing. Line 6, however, reverts to the situation before the completed act. The object of lust is "hunted" and pursued "past reason." The conflict is resumed in line 7 which begins with a repetition of "past reason," an emphasis of the irrationality of desire and ensuing disgust, the knowledge beforehand of the consequences, and the poet's sense of helplessness in the toils of the counselor lust that are for him the maddening aspects of the recurrent drama in which he is involved. He is at once the hunter (6) and the hunted (7) who has taken the poisoned bait, whereupon lust which had been the object of the hunt becomes the hunter, the ensnarer.

In line 12 the time element ("before" and "behind") is stressed to show the recurrence of the emotions connected with lust, a recurrence which has already been indicated in line 10 where the past tense "had" implies the act in the past, the present participle "having" brings it to the present, and the phrase "in quest to have" foretells recurrence. And every part of the cycle is termed "extreme" (10), a word repeated from line 4.

tenderness and sublimity: " 'Lo, there ye stand, my children,' said the figure, in a deep and solemn tone, almost sad with its despairing awfulness, as if his once angelic nature could yet mourn for our miserable race. . . . And there they stood, the only pair, as it seemed, who were yet hesitating on the verge of wickedness in this dark world."

[8]Karl F. Thompson, "Shakespeare's Sonnet 129," *The Explicator,* 7 (Feb. 1949), item 27. Copyright 1949 by *The Explicator.* Reprinted by permission of the publisher and the author.

The word "dream" is difficult here. Its normally pleasant associations must be discarded before the true connotation, unpleasant dream or nightmare, is sensed. Yet, the introduction here of the ordinarily pleasant connotations which accompany "dream" effects a subtle change in tone: that fretful self-loathing (3–10) is qualified by the melancholy realization (13–14) that experience is no guarantor of wisdom and that men will forever shuttle between this "heaven" and "hell."

The sonnet is, in a way, an answer to Donne's "Ah cannot we, As well as Cocks and Lyons jocund be, After such pleasures?" But Shakespeare's answer is a counsel of surrender, without Donne's ironic attitude toward human passion.

Special Uses of Writing: A Brief Guide to Research Writing 7

Summary of the Chapter

This chapter concerns the writing of papers that are based on library research. It surveys library resources and outlines procedures for gathering information and for documenting sources within the paper (that is, footnoting).

Sources available to researchers include general encyclopedias, unabridged dictionaries, general indexes of periodicals (including newspapers), collections of biographies, and a great variety of specialized sources.

The chapter outlines a systematic approach to research and research writing.

Some Preliminary Remarks

Much of this book has been a discussion of problem solving. (For instance, all of Chapter 3, on prewriting, concerned that.) And this chapter will not repeat what has been handled in detail elsewhere. Rather, it will attempt to give you some guidance with the kinds of problems that can be solved—or that apparently can be solved—through research.

Notice how common an occurrence it is to encounter a problematic situation and to do research to solve the problem. In your reading, you find a word that you don't know the meaning of. The problem is that you want to know the meaning. So you go to a dictionary. That's research. Your old car finally gives out, and you need a new one. Now you have a problem: what kind of car should you buy to replace the old one? You decide that you want a compact, not a subcompact, an intermediate, or a full-sized car: you have narrowed and focused the problem. You go to *Consumer Reports* to find out which compact is recommended: you have done research. You probably also visit dealers and take test drives in Hornets, Novas, and Valiants: you have done further research.

The first of these two problems would not provide the basis for a research paper. To solve it, you simply look up a discrete bit of data (the meaning of the word). But the second problem—what kind of new car to buy—could well provide the basis for an interesting paper. In outline, the paper might look like this:

> 1   I. Background of problem
>   A. My reason for needing a new car
>   B. Factors in my choice of a new car
>   1. Need for a car that will accommodate four passengers
>   2. Financial limitations, restricting the initial purchase price
>   3. Considerations of fuel economy
>   II. Formulation of problem [Taking passenger space, purchase price, and fuel economy into consideration, I decide to buy a compact. Thus, my problem is this: Which compact should I buy?]
>   III. Investigation of problem
>   A. *Consumer Reports*
>   B. Opinions of current owners of various brands of compacts
>   C. Test drives of various brands
>   IV. Conclusion based on investigation

The third section of the paper is the one that embodies the results of your research, and this is what your reader is most likely to be interested in. The reader will be asking: Where did the writer get this information? Are the sources reliable? Does the writer let me know what the sources are so that I can verify the accuracy of the paper? In other words, you would need some way of referring your reader to the issue of *Consumer Reports* that you used. You probably would also want to give some background information about the owners whose opinions you had solicited so that the reader could judge whether or not they were reliable. And you would want to report fully the results of your own test drives. All of this amounts to *documentation,* and we will be talking more about that subject as the chapter progresses.

A Brief Survey of Resources

Henceforth in this chapter, when we speak of "research" we will be talking about the kind that can be accomplished for the most part in the library, though of course this is only one among a large variety of methods of research (such as field work, laboratory experiments, and so on). Our question is simply this: once you have formulated a problem, how do you find printed material (articles, books, monographs, charts, tables, government reports, newspaper articles, and so on) that bear on it?

The basic assumption here is that you have a general familiarity with the card catalogue, that you know how to navigate in the library. If you do *not* have that knowledge, then you must obtain it immediately. Chances are, your college library conducts orientation tours or has prepared a free guide. In any case, you need to know how to use a library. What follows is a guide to the general categories of sources that you can find in a library.

General Encyclopedias

When you must do research in a field that is unfamiliar to you, you need some kind of introduction, or overview. The best source for this is a general encyclopedia. The five standard general encyclopedias are these:

The Encyclopaedia Britannica. Noted for the excellence of its articles concerning the humanities. Contains selected bibliographies that can be useful to a person who is just beginning to do research on a given topic.

The Encyclopedia Americana. Usually considered the best source for articles concerning the sciences. References will lead the researcher to other standard discussions of topics.

Chambers's Encyclopedia. Provides standard references on topics. A British publication.

Collier's Encyclopedia. The bibliography is centralized in the twenty-fourth volume.

Columbia Encyclopedia. Articles are not as extensive as those in the other encyclopedias. Useful for quick reference.

Unabridged Dictionaries

If the research in question involves the meanings of words, the un-abridged dictionaries are invaluable sources. The three that you ought to be aware of are these:

A Dictionary of American English on Historical Principles. This four-volume work, edited by Sir William A. Craigie and James R. Hulbert, gives the histories of meanings of words in American English.

A New English Dictionary on Historical Principles. Available as a thirteen-volume work or in a one-volume, reduced-print edition that must be read with a magnifying glass. Often called the *Oxford English Dictionary,* this work is the most complete source for the histories of word meanings in English.

Webster's Third New International Dictionary. This is the most widely respected unabridged dictionary of English, the huge book that you find in the reading rooms of most libraries. (When it first appeared in 1961, it caused an international uproar because of the alleged permissiveness in its treatment of usage.)

Other unabridged dictionaries are *Funk & Wagnall's New "Standard" Dictionary of the English Language, The Random House Dictionary of the English Language,* and *Webster's New Twentieth Century Dictionary.*

General Indexes

Suppose your research involved popular reaction to the comet Kohoutek, which approached Earth for the first time in the winter of 1973–74. Your library would contain books about comets in general, but none about Kohoutek specifically. Your primary source would be magazines and newspapers. Fortunately, a variety of general indexes direct you to specific newspaper and magazine articles. Most of these indexes are arranged like the card catalogue in your library; that is, each entry is listed by author, title, and subject.

Book Review Digest. Appears monthly (except February and July). As its name indicates, it is a guide to reviews of books.

International Index. Appears quarterly, with cumulative editions every year and every two years. It is an index to journals that publish articles in the humanities and social sciences.

New York Times Index. An author-subject-title listing of articles in the *New York Times.* Since newspapers all over the country deal with the same national and international news events, this index also serves as a rough index to other newspapers.

Nineteenth Century Reader's Guide to Periodical Literature, 1890–1899. An author-subject index covering some fifty periodicals that were published during the period concerned.

Poole's Index to Periodical Literature, 1802–1881. Index to British and American periodicals of the period covered.

Reader's Guide to Periodical Literature. An author-subject-title listing of articles in about 125 periodicals of general interest. Issued semimonthly, with annual and five-year cumulative editions.

Biographical Sources

Should your research involve biographical questions, you can go to

Biography Index: A Cumulative Index to Biographical Material in Books and Magazines.

Current Biography: Who's News and Why. Fairly extensive biographies of people in the news.

Who's Who. Brief biographies of notable people in the British Commonwealth.

Who's Who in America. American counterpart of *Who's Who.*

Dictionary of American Biography. Excellent and fairly extensive biographies of dead Americans.

Dictionary of National Biography. British counterpart of *Dictionary of American Biography.*

Specialized Sources

Our purpose in this chapter is to survey the kinds of sources available to the researcher, not to provide a complete bibliographical rundown of everything that a good library contains. Suffice it to say that there are specialized reference works (including indexes) for virtually every subject. For example, if your question involves mythology, you will find the *Larousse Encyclopedia of Mythology,* or if your question concerns physics, you may want to turn to *International Dictionary of Physics and Electronics.* To get some idea of the range of sources that are available, just glance through the following list: *Dictionary of Modern Ballet, Art Index, Cambridge Bibliography of English Literature, Encyclopedia of the Social Sciences, The New Schaff-Herzog Encyclopedia of Religious Knowledge, Van Nostrand's Scientific Encyclopedia, Education Index.* And the list could go on and on.

Your college or public library undoubtedly has trained people in its reference room who can guide you to exactly the sources that you need.

Research and Research Writing: A Systematic Approach

The following outline is a sort of recipe for cooking up a research paper. None of the steps are sacred, and you will undoubtedly develop your own modus operandi as you become a sophisticated researcher. Meanwhile, however, following the steps that are about to be explained will get you under way with a minimum of turmoil and wasted time.

Survey of Materials

Once your problem is formulated, you need to survey the materials that are available concerning it. Often, a good first step is to get an overview of the subject by reading pertinent articles in general and specialized encyclopedias. But the actual research will probably begin at the card catalogue. (What books, pamphlets, and other materials concerning the subject are in your college library?) Probably the next step will be to survey the periodical literature concerning the subject; therefore, you'll go to indexes, such as *The Reader's Guide* or *The International Index,* or others, depending on your subject.

Bibliography Cards

Obviously, you need some way of keeping track of the possible sources that you find. Therefore, you will want to make a bibliography card for each source. Listing each source separately on either a 3″ × 5″ or a 4″ × 5″ card will allow you to shuffle entries, alphabetize them, and locate them more quickly. Another tip: make absolutely certain that the information on your bibliography card is accurate and complete. You will be using this information to find the sources in the library, and later you will be using it as the basis for your footnotes.

For Books

The following is a useful and convenient form for a bibliography card for a book:

2

[a] *Merill, Thomas F.*

[b] *Allen Ginsberg*
[c] *New York:* [d] *Twayne*
Publishers, [e] *1969.*

[f] *PS*
3513
17428

Key: (a) author's name, last name first; (b) full title of the book; (c) place of publication; (d) publisher; (e) date of publication or copyright; (f) library call number for the book. You will need items (a) through (e) for your footnotes and for the bibliography that you append to your paper. You will need item (f) in order to find the book in your library.

For Journal or Magazine Articles

The following is a good form for a bibliography card for a journal or magazine article:

3

[a] *Dickstein, Morris*

[b] *"Allen Ginsberg and the*
60's," [c] *Commentary,* [d] *49*
[e] *(Jan. 1970),* [f] *64 - 70.*

Key: (a) name of the author of the article, last name first; (b) title of the article; (c) name of the magazine or journal in which the article appeared; (d) volume number of the issue in which the article appeared; (e) date of the issue; (f) pages on which the article appeared. (If the magazine is assigned a call number, it should be entered in the right-hand corner.)

These are the two basic forms, and they will cover about three-fourths of the sources that you normally encounter. If you encounter sources that pose special problems, you should speak to your instructor, or turn to *A Manual for Writers of Term Papers, Theses, and Dissertations,* by Kate L. Turabian. The thing to remember, however, is that you need full information on your bibliography card.

When we come to the discussion of footnotes, you will see forms for a variety of sources, and these will guide you to the information that you will need to include on your bibliography card. For example, you might read an article by one author that is included in a collection edited by another author. In that case, your card would look like this:

4

> [a] Jakobson, Roman
>
> [b] "Linguistics and Poetics,"
> [c] Style in Language.
> [d] Ed. Thomas A. Sebeok.
> [e] Cambridge, Mass.: [f] M.I.T. Press,
> [g] 1960.   [h] Pp. 379-386.
>
> [i] 808
> C748s

Key: (a) name of the author of the article; (b) title of the article; (c) title of the volume in which the article appears; (d) name of the editor—the abbreviation **ed.** means "edited by"; (e) place of publication; (f) publisher; (g) date of publication; (h) pages on which selection is found; (i) library call number.

Reading Notes

After your survey of the available materials is completed, you are ready to start your reading—though much of what you do will not be reading at all, but scanning. In other words, your initial survey has provided you with possible sources for information; now you must go to those sources to see if they contain materials that will be useful to you.

Once again, 3″ × 5″ or 4″ × 6″ cards are essential. When you find useful information, you need to record it; by recording it on cards, you can order the items according to the aspect of your subject that they deal with. Let's take a concrete example.

Your subject is the poetic development of Allen Ginsberg. You have done a complete survey of possible resources and have a large stack of bibliography cards that will guide you to those resources. Among the cards is this one:

5

> Roszak, Theodore
>
>
> *The Making of a Counter-Culture*
> Garden City, New York: Anchor
> Books, 1969.
>
>   HN
>   17.5
>   R6

In this book, on page 126, you find a passage claiming that Ginsberg's early poems are tighter and more formally satisfying than the later ones. The passage reads like this:

6   There is the willingness to be brief and to the point—and then to break off before the energy has been dissipated. By the early fifties, however, Ginsberg has abandoned these conventional literary virtues in favor of a spontaneous and unchecked flow of language. From this point on, everything he writes has the appearance of being served up raw, in the first draft, just as it must have come from his mind and mouth.[1]

You decide to incorporate this opinion into your paper, for it seems to be important. You have two choices: you can either transcribe it verbatim onto a note card, making sure that you do not miscopy, or you can paraphrase it.

[1]Theodore Roszak, *The Making of a Counter-Culture* (Garden City, N.Y.: Anchor Books, 1969), p. 126.

In most instances, you will want to paraphrase, for transcribing the exact words of your sources would be far too tedious a job and wouldn't be useful anyway, since you are looking for concepts and information, not quotes. Suppose, then, that you decide Roszak's opinion will be useful to you, but that you don't want to quote him exactly. In that case, you will make a note card that looks something like this:

7

> Roszak   poetic technique (crits.)
>
> 126. As G. progressed through the 1950's, he became more undisciplined, did not revise or tighten. R. says that by the early 50's, everything that G. writes has "The appearance of being served up raw, in the first draft."

At the top of your note card, in the left-hand corner, you have written the last name of the author of the book. Therefore, you can refer back to your bibliography card and find exactly where the material came from. (If in your bibliography you had more than one work by Roszak, you would include a key word of the title after his name, to indicate which of your sources this note had come from.) In the upper right-hand corner, you have put a key phrase, to indicate to yourself the general subject of the note. The **126** is the exact page on which the material was found. This information is extremely important for footnoting. Finally, you have paraphrased the material, but in so doing, you have used some of Roszak's phrases. Whenever you have quoted Roszak directly, you have put the material in quotation marks so that you will know which words are your own and which are Roszak's.

Let's pause to give an illustration that will clarify the process being discussed. You are writing your paper, and in one section of it you want to discuss the supposed artistic deterioration of Ginsberg. One passage in this section of your paper reads like this:

8   Ginsberg's work has changed through the years, but has it deteriorated? One critic claims that Ginsberg's earlier poems are tighter and more formally

satisfying than the later ones. As Ginsberg progressed through the 1950s, he became more undisciplined, did not revise or tighten. In fact, says this critic, by the early 1950s, everything that Ginsberg writes has "the appearance of being served up raw, in the first draft."[5]

Notice, first, that the information on your note card has been incorporated into this passage; then observe that the passage ends with superscript[5]. That number is the key to a footnote that will appear either at the bottom of the page or at the end of the paper, depending on the format that you choose to follow. In order to obtain the information for the footnote, you turn to the bibliography card for the Roszak source, and the footnote reads this way:

9   [5]Theodore Roszak, *The Making of a Counter-Culture* (Garden City, N.Y.: Anchor Books, 1969), p. 126.

Now the reader of the paper will know the exact origin of the opinion that you have taken from a source, including the page on which the material is found.

This example illustrates the interactive use of bibliography and note cards.

We have gotten a little ahead of ourselves; basically, we are discussing the gathering of material, not the actual writing of the paper. To recapitulate: we began our research task by making a list of sources available—that is, we compiled a working bibliography. Now we are looking at those sources, reading some in detail, scanning others, and rejecting those that do not suit our purpose. Every bit of data, information, or opinion that we take from a source appears on its own note card, with the name of the author, a subject key, and the page or pages from which the material was taken.

Organization

Now the reading for the paper is done. All the notes have been taken. It is time to organize. Suppose that your paper is titled "Ginsberg and the Critics"; its purpose is to find out and report what Ginsberg says he's been trying to do in his poetry and what the critics say he's actually done. It turns out that our note cards can be arranged into five groups, according to the key phrases in the upper right-hand corners. The five key phrases are these:

10   poetic technique (Gins.)
       poetic technique (crits.)
       content (Gins.)
       content (crits.)
       G's reputation

That is, we have cards that bear on five subject areas: Ginsberg's statements concerning his poetic technique; statements by critics concerning his poetic technique; Ginsberg's statements about his content; statements by critics concerning his content; and statements that bear on Ginsberg's general reputation as a poet. Here are note cards that give examples of each:

11

Writers at Work   poetic technique (Gins.)

282-3. G. says that his meters are "choriambic—Greek meters, dithyrambic meters." He says that he does not sit down to use a preconceived meter, but uses his own physiological movements to arrive at a pattern. The key is arriving at a pattern organically rather than synthetically.

12

Holmes   poetic technique (crits.)

56. Ginsberg and Holmes had long talks about the need for "a new literalness, and thus a new prosody." Studying Pound, Lanier, and W. C. Williams, Ginsberg became dissatisfied with the mechanical forms of most poetry.

13

Playboy interview   Content (Gins.)

88. G. comments on his anal erotic poetry. At first (and uncharacteristically), he was afraid to read it, but he did. "When I get to a barrier of shame like the one I felt when writing this poem, I know it's the sign of a good poem, because I'm entering new public territory. I write for private amusement and for the golden ears of friends who'll understand and forgive everything from the point of view _humani nihil a me alienum puto_—'Nothing human is foreign to me'—but it's fearsome to make a private reality public."

14

Fiedler   content (Crits.)

244. Fiedler puts Ginsberg in the Whitman tradition, but while Whitman viewed himself as a mystical healer, "Ginsberg celebrates himself as an angel of death and derangement. He is a prophet not of the beginnings of man, but of his end; and if, like Whitman, he tries to write first poems, they are the first poems of the next evolutionary stage beyond us, anticipating the verse of meta-humans."

15

> Trilling, Diana   G's reputation
>
> Trilling's essay was one of the first estimates of Ginsberg's value as a poet, and Trilling attacked him roundly. Her point is that Ginsberg is merely a barbarian who would like, in his secret soul, to be respectable and respected.

These are merely samples from a whole stack of note cards that have been gathered and organized under the five topics listed. Now the organization for your paper appears obvious. It will look something like this:

16
I. Ginsberg's place in modern poetry
II. The critics on Ginsberg
   A. His poetic technique
   B. His content
III. Ginsberg's own theories
   A. Poetic technique
   B. Content
IV. Conclusion

An alternate arrangement might be this:

17
I. Ginsberg's place in modern poetry
II. His poetic technique
   A. The critics
   B. Ginsberg
III. His content
   A. The critics
   B. Ginsberg
IV. Conclusion

Now the paper is ready to be written.

Footnote Form

Here is a list of commonly used footnote forms:
Book with One Author

18   [1]Truman Capote, *In Cold Blood* (New York: Random House, 1965), p. 65.

Book with Two Authors

19   [2]Alan C. Purves and Richard Beach, *Literature and the Reader* (Urbana, Ill.: National Council of Teachers of English, 1972), pp. 131–32.

Book with More Than Two Authors

20   [3]Albert C. Baugh et al., *A Literary History of England* (New York: Appleton-Century-Crofts, 1948), pp. 1021–22.

No Author Given

21   [4]*Psychology Today: An Introduction* (Del Mar, Cal.: CRM Books, 1970), p. 153.

Edited Collection

22   [5]Jack Davis, ed., *Discussions of William Wordsworth* (Boston: D. C. Heath, 1964), p. ix.

Second or Later Edition

23   [6]James M. McCrimmon, *Writing with a Purpose,* 5th ed. (Boston: Houghton Mifflin, 1972), p. 289.

Work of One Author Edited by Another

24   [7]Thomas Hardy, *Tess of the d'Urbervilles,* ed. Scott Elledge (New York: W. W. Norton, 1965), pp. 82–83.

Work of One Author in a Collection Edited by Another

25   [8]John W. Gardner, "Tyranny Without a Tyrant," in *A Preface to Our Times,* ed. William E. Buckler (New York: American Book Company, 1968), p. 87.

Magazine or Journal Article

26   [9]John Fraser, "Evaluation and English Studies," *College English,* 35 (Oct. 1973), 2.

Anonymous Article

27   [10]"L.B.J. and His Dollar," *Life,* 19 Jan. 1968, p. 4.
      [11]"Sitting Bull," *The Encyclopedia Americana,* 1962, XXV, p. 48.

Newspaper Article

28   [12]"Aussie, Russian Stars Compete in Times Games," Los Angeles *Times,* 21 Jan. 1968, Sec. D1, p. 1.

The following list of footnotes illustrates a couple of important principles:

29   [1]Leslie A. Fiedler, *Waiting for the End* (New York: Stein and Day, 1964), p. 109.
      [2]*Ibid.,* p. 112.
      [3]John Hollander, "Poetry Chronicle," *Partisan Review,* 24 (Spring 1957), 300.
      [4]*Ibid.,* p. 302.
      [5]Fiedler, p. 111.
      [6]Hollander, p. 303.

The principles that the above list illustrates are: (1) The first mention of a work in footnotes should be a full citation, as are 1 and 3. (2) The abbreviation ***Ibid.*** means "in the same place" and refers to the footnote directly above it. Thus, footnote 2 refers the reader back to footnote 1, and footnote 4 refers the reader back to footnote 3. (3) As footnotes 5 and 6 illustrate, full information concerning a source needs to be cited only once in the paper. After the first citation, shortened forms are in order.

Bibliography Form

Sometimes you will want to append to your paper a complete bibliography of all the works you have found concerning your subject. At other times, you will want simply to append a list of the works cited in footnotes. Here are some examples of the form that these lists should take:

Book

30 Abrams, M.H. *The Mirror and the Lamp.* New York: Oxford University Press, 1953.

Magazine or Journal Article

31 Chapman, Jewell A. "The Prose Portrait." *College Composition and Communication,* 18 (Dec. 1967), 252–54.

Edited Collection

32 Dean, Leonard F. and Kenneth G. Wilson, eds. *Essays on Language and Usage.* New York: Oxford University Press, 1963.

Magazine Article, No Author Given

33 "L.B.J. and His Dollar." *Life,* 19 Jan. 1968, p. 4.

Encyclopedia Article

34 "Sitting Bull." *The Encyclopedia Americana,* 1962, 48.

Finally

Two examples of research papers written by freshmen are included in the samples of student writing at the back of this book. You should take a close look at them.

This chapter has thrown a great many details at you, and you may feel overwhelmed. But the real problem of writing a research paper is not getting the forms of footnotes and bibliography entries just right. The real problem is to gather data and to make sure that the reader will know your source in every instance. Footnotes enable the reader to judge the validity of your materials and to separate your opinions from facts, data, and opinions that you have gathered elsewhere. They also allow the reader to check your accuracy or to read further concerning a topic, for your footnotes direct your reader to your sources.

Once you have put the paper together in a logical fashion, you can worry about the mechanical details. Guides such as Turabian's *Manual for Writers of Term Papers, Theses, and Dissertations* will help you, and you can always get advice from your instructor.

The main point is this: enjoy the adventure of research and enjoy the art of presenting your findings to a reader. If you do that, the mechanical details will pretty much take care of themselves.

Discussion and Activities

For some of the following exercises you will need specific answers, so you will have to go to the proper sources in the library to obtain them. Others involve only common sense or a bit of logic.

1. Give several reasons why footnotes are important in research writing.
2. George B. Griffenhagen of the American Pharmaceutical Association wrote a brief general discussion of cod-liver oil. Where did it appear?
3. Name a general reference source that deals with matters concerning Jews.
4. What is probably the best source for a relatively brief overview of the history of Greece?
5. Where would you find a list of magazine articles concerning Queen Victoria's accession to the throne of Great Britain?
6. Where would you find a reliable and relatively brief biography of Robert E. Lee?
7. Give the date of birth of George Cecil Winterowd, a well-known architect and a professor of architecture at the University of Minnesota. Where did you find this information?
8. Where would you find a complete list of all the periodicals that your library subscribes to?
9. What is the first recorded use of the word *screwy* meaning "tipsy"? Where did you find this information?
10. How would you go about locating the author and source of a magazine article entitled "Mother's Love"? Give the author, magazine, and date.
11. If your library has a microfilm collection, go to the microfilm room and become acquainted with these resources. For instance, the *New York Times* is available on microfilm, and you might want to run through some issues just to see how the equipment works.
12. Take a self-guided tour of the reference room in your library. List ten reference sources that you had not previously been aware of.
13. Find out whether your library catalogues its books according to the Dewey decimal system or the Library of Congress system. (Perhaps it uses both systems.) Explain these systems.
14. List three reviews of *Someday, Maybe,* by William Stafford (New York: Harper & Row, 1973). Where did you find this information?
15. A relatively brief biography of Henry A. Kissinger begins with the

words, "President Nixon's innovative approaches to international relations . . . ." Where does that biography appear?

16. Suppose that you want to find out how a local newspaper such as the *Salt Lake City Tribune* handled some national or international event from the 1940s. Where would you go to get a rough idea of the dates on which items concerning this event appeared in the *Tribune?*

17. Approximately how many volumes are in the library (or libraries) on your campus? On the basis of that figure, can you determine the approximate number of cards that must be in the card catalogue?

18. Explain the use and usefulness of bibliography cards. Why is it better to enter each bibliography item on a separate card than to list all of them sequentially on notebook paper?

19. Do you know what an *abstract* is? If not, find out. Name some of the abstracts in your college library. What is the usefulness of collections of abstracts?

20. If in a research paper you stated, "Richard Nixon was the first President of the United States to resign," would you need a footnote? Explain.

The Uses of Writing: Imagination

8

Summary of the Chapter

Imaginative writing does not convey information in the sense that expository writing does. Furthermore, imaginative writing normally does not make statements such as "Life is very short," but rather embodies those statements in an imaginative structure.

One resource for imaginative writing is your own experience, which you can transform in any way you see fit in order to construct your poem or story.

The elements of the imaginative universe that you create in fiction will be: a speaker, an imaginary character who will tell your story; a plot, the actions that transpire and the motives for these actions; characters; and a scene or scenes.

The characteristics of most poetry are imagery, metaphor, and intensity. Much bad poetry lacks these qualities.

The Reason for Writing Imaginatively

This chapter is unconditionally guaranteed not to make any of its readers into immortal writers of fiction, poetry, or drama. In fact, if any purchaser of *The Contemporary Writer* does become an immortal writer of imaginative literature, he or she may return the unused portion of the book to me, and I will gladly refund the purchase price.

What I'm trying to say is that this chapter is not to be taken as a deadly serious matter, but ought to be regarded as a form of play. (After all, isn't art the highest expression of the human need to play, of the desire to escape from the world of reality into the world of fantasy? Even realistic art is fantasy—or it wouldn't be art at all.)

Even for a person who thinks he or she has no writing talent there are good reasons for writing imaginatively—namely, to make life a more interesting affair, to express the creative part of one's being, to learn something about the making of literature. For instance, I am a poet who has never been published, and I don't suppose many of my works will ever be known by more than a handful of friends. I suspect that I'm not even a very good poet, though I'd like very much to be talented in that way. Nonetheless, I enjoy writing my poetry, in just the same way that my wife enjoys playing her piano—not because she will ever be a concert pianist, but because it is satisfying to make music.

So the use of writing for imaginative expression does have practical value.

Information and Imagination

At one point in his career, the poet Robert Herrick (1591–1674) wanted to say something like this:

1   I enjoy seeing Julia when she's all dressed up in silks, but I enjoy seeing her even more when she's naked.

Now that statement, though informative, is almost totally without interest. The inevitable response to it is, "So what?" But as a matter of fact, Herrick did not make the above statement; instead, he wrote,

2
Upon Julia's Clothes

Robert Herrick

Whenas in silks my Julia goes
Then, then (methinks) how sweetly flows
That liquefaction of her clothes.

Next, when I cast mine eyes and see
That brave vibration each way free;
O how that glittering taketh me!

Everyone would agree, I suppose, that the poem embodies the statement; in a sense—a very limited sense—they both mean the same. However, there is a very big difference. The statement *tells* us, but the poem *shows* us. In the first stanza of the poem, we gain an image of Julia in her silken gown and a fairly lukewarm comment. In the second stanza, we gain another image, that of Julia nude, and we get another comment, this one fervid. The poet does not make the statement directly; he makes it indirectly.

The eleventh verse of the ninth chapter of Ecclesiastes will serve as a kind of touchstone for much of the discussion in this chapter.

3   I returned, and saw under the sun, that the race is not to the swift, nor the
    battle to the strong, neither yet bread to the wise, nor yet riches to men of
    understanding, nor yet favour to men of skill; but time and chance happeneth
    to them all.

This passage embodies a tragic motif that has always fascinated artists; it
might be stated as the old saw, "There's no justice in this world." Again,
however, the Preacher (who is the speaker in Ecclesiastes) does not say as
much in so many words; he *shows* us what he means. He gives us the
possibility of visualizing his meaning—of living it—by presenting a group
of images that are rich with imaginative possibilities. As a visual experience, the passage is rich with possibilities. Under the sun, we see a broad
panorama: a race, a battle, an impoverished wise man, a foolish millionaire, and perhaps a great but neglected artist.

It is obvious that we are much more interested in the imaginative
statement of the message in Ecclesiastes than we are in the message itself,
and this is the case, I think, with all art.

Many variations on the Ecclesiastes theme have been written. Here are
some of them:

4   Perhaps in this neglected spot is laid
                        Some heart once pregnant with celestial fire;
                      Hands, that the rod of empire might have swayed,
                        Or waked to ecstasy the living lyre.

                      But knowledge to their eyes her ample page
                        Rich with the spoils of time, did ne'er unroll;
                      Chill penury repressed their noble rage,
                        And froze the genial currents of the soul.

                      Full many a gem of purest ray serene
                        The dark unfathomed caves of ocean bear;
                      Full many a flower is born to blush unseen,
                        And waste its sweetness on the desert air.

                      —Thomas Gray, "Elegy Written in a Country Churchyard"

5   *Hap*
                            Thomas Hardy

                  If but some vengeful god would call to me
                  From up the sky, and laugh: "Thou suffering thing,
                  Know that thy sorrow is my ecstasy,
                  That thy love's loss is my hate's profiting!"

                  Then would I bear it, clench myself, and die,
                  Steeled by the sense of ire unmerited;
                  Half-eased in that a Powerfuller than I
                  Had willed and meted me the tears I shed.

                  But not so. How arrives it joy lies slain,
                  And why unblooms the best hope ever sown?

—Crass Casualty obstructs the sun and rain,
And dicing Time for gladness casts a moan. . . .
These purblind Doomsters had as readily strown
Blisses about my pilgrimage as pain.

6

Thou art indeed just, Lord
Gerard Manley Hopkins

Thou are indeed just, Lord, if I contend
With thee; but, sir, so what I plead is just.
Why do sinners' ways prosper? and why must
Disappointment all I endeavour end?
　　Wert thou my enemy, O thou my friend,
How wouldst thou worse, I wonder, than thou dost
Defeat, thwart me? Oh, the sots and thralls of lust
Do in spare hours more thrive than I that spend,
Sir, life upon thy cause. See, banks and brakes
Now, leaved how thick! laced they are again
With pretty chervil, look, and fresh wind shakes
Them; birds build—but not I build; no, but strain,
Time's eunuch, and not breed one work that wakes.
Mine, O thou lord of life, send my roots rain.

We could find countless other variations on the theme—not just poems, but short stories, plays, and novels. (We use poems for our examples only because they are handiest in their relative brevity.)

Another way of looking at imaginative writing is to say that it conveys experience, not information. As was noted in Chapter 6, when we read *The Grapes of Wrath,* by John Steinbeck, we are not so much interested in what we learn about migrant workers during the 1930s as we are in the sense that we gain from the novel of having lived through the experiences of these workers. And the method used in imaginative writing to convey this immediacy is concreteness. In a novel, we don't follow ideas so much as we follow characters; and if it is a "novel of ideas," the ideas are developed through the actions of the characters.

Transforming Experience

Think of the difference between an incident in your autobiography and an autobiographical story that you might base on that incident. If you are writing your autobiography, you will ask yourself questions such as these: What actually happened? What are the literal details? How did I feel about what happened? How did the event influence me and my later life? But if you are writing a story based on that incident, your questions will be quite different: What are the imaginative possibilities of the event? How can I change it so that it will fit my artistic purpose better? What is the event's symbolic significance?

In other words, when you write your autobiography, you attempt to give an accurate representation of what you think actually happened; but when you are writing an autobiographical story, you use the event to stimulate you imaginatively, and in the process, the actual event might be so changed as to be almost unrecognizable, or it might even disappear into the imaginative construct.

Imaginative Transformation: An Example

A fascinating and instructive discussion of how experience is transformed for artistic purposes is the following analysis by James Dickey of one of his own poems:

7
The Performance[1]

James Dickey

The last time I saw Donald Armstrong
He was staggering oddly off into the sun,
Going down, of the Philippine Islands.
I let my shovel fall, and put that hand
Above my eyes, and moved some way to one side
That his body might pass through the sun,

And I saw how well he was not
Standing there on his hands,
On his spindle-shanked forearms balanced,
Unbalanced, with his big feet looming and waving
In the great, untrustworthy air
He flew in each night, when it darkened.

Dust fanned in scraped puffs from the earth
Between his arms, and blood turned his face inside out,
To demonstrate it suppleness
Of veins, as he perfected his role.
Next day, he toppled his head off
On an island beach to the south,

And the enemy's two-handed sword
Did not fall from anyone's hands
At that miraculous sight,
As the head rolled over upon
Its wide-eyed face, and fell
Into the inadequate grave

He had dug for himself, under pressure.
Yet I put my flat hand to my eyebrows
Months later, to see him again
In the sun, when I learned how he died,
And imagined him, there,
Come, judged, before his small captors,

---

[1]James Dickey, "The Performance," *Poems 1957–1967* (Middletown, Conn.: Wesleyan University Press, 1967). Copyright © 1960, 1965 by James Dickey. Reprinted by permission of Wesleyan University Press.

Doing all his lean tricks to amaze them—
The back somersault, the kip-up—
And at last, the stand on his hands,
Perfect, with his feet together,
His head down, evenly breathing,
As the sun poured up from the sea

And the headsman broke down
In a blaze of tears, in that light
Of the thin, long human frame
Upside down in its own strange joy,
And, if some other one had not told him,
Would have cut off the feet

Instead of the head,
And if Armstrong had not presently risen
In kingly, round-shouldered attendance,
And then knelt down in himself
Beside his hacked, glittering grave, having done
All things in this life that he could.

Almost every word of "The Performance" is literally true, except that the interpretation of the facts is my own. It's a poem about a boy named Donald Armstrong, who came from somewhere in the West. He was in my squadron, the 418th Night Fighter Squadron, during the Second World War. He was probably my best friend in the squadron, a very lovable, ugly fellow. You need somebody like him in a combat situation, someone who sees the humorous side of everything and is happy-go-lucky and daring. He was an awfully good pilot, but he took a lot of unnecessary chances, and the older air crews in the squadron were a bit chary of him. He was always doing crazy things like going to sleep with the airplane on Automatic Pilot. He and his observer—the P61 had a two-man crew—sometimes would both go to sleep and just drone along coming back from convoy cover or wherever they'd been.

Most of our missions were to the north of the island we were on, Mindoro, the island immediately south of Luzon. But we also had missions to the south, to Panay. As nearly as I can remember, some Japanese held the island and were using Filipino labor to build an airstrip. Armstrong and his observer, Jim Lalley, went down to Panay in a P61 one evening on a strafing run. Apparently it was just at dusk, when it's hard to judge distances, and the plane hit the ground. It was damaged and began to come apart, so Armstrong made a crash landing. They were both hurt, according to the reports we got from the Filipino guerillas, but they were alive. They were taken out of the aircraft by the Japanese, kept in an old schoolhouse, and beheaded the next day at dawn. We found out about this immediately from the guerrilla forces on Panay, but there was nothing we could have done about it.

Don Armstrong was always doing gymnastic tricks in the squadron area. He used to do flips and all kinds of such things, and would work on his handstands. He was a tall fellow, and because his center of gravity was high, it was hard from him to do handstands. I can remember him falling over on his head and back and getting up and trying again. For a long time I tried to write this poem, but the poems I wrote were all official tributes to my old buddy. They didn't have the distinctiveness that I thought the poem really ought to have. So I said to myself, "Goodness, Jim, what is the thing you remember *most* about Don? Do you remember how ugly he was, or how skinny he was, or something that he did?" There was a squadron movie area where we used to have movies when the Japanese weren't bombing us. Don and I saw a movie called *Laura* there, and he was wild about it. I remember sitting in the weeds watching that movie with him; so I put that into the poem, but it wasn't right. Then I remembered that he used to do all those flips and tricks in the squadron area. People would stand around watching him, but sometimes he'd just be out there by himself standing on his hands, or trying to. He never mastered it; I never saw him do a good handstand.

Finally I tried to bring together the unsuccessful handstand, the last trick he was trying to perfect, and the grotesque manner of his death, and I tried to describe the effect these would have on the beholders, the executioners, and on the poet who tells the poem. I thought, "Why not make it *really* crazy?" The poem isn't about the facts of Armstrong's death, because the narrator is trying to imagine them. I said to myself, "I'll bet that damned Armstrong would be crazy enough to throw off a dozen cartwheels before he got his head chopped off! And what would *that* do to the Japanese?"

Since you can make anything you like happen in a poem, I made it happen that way. I wrote the poem in a rather matter-of-fact way with no obvious rhetorical devices, like refrains. I did it straight because I didn't want to write amazingly about ordinary events, but matter-of-factly about extraordinary events. It seemed to be more effective that way, as well as much truer to the kind of experience that it might have been for the narrator. I suppose "The Performance" is the most anthologized of my poems. I've never taken an actual count, but I've come across it in more places than I have any other of my poems, maybe partly because it's been in circulation longer. I wrote it in the first part of 1958, also in an advertising office.

I'm always trying to synthesize, and I thought, "Boy, next week I'm going to try to get these two techniques together. (I had to drop poetry and do some radio commercials.) I'm going to use the crazy approach to subject matter I used in 'The Performance' and some other things, like refrains, and see what happens." As I said, experimentation is very, very important to me. That's what makes poetry so damned much fun! If you ask yourself the fundamental question, "What would happen if . . . ?" then the only one thing to do is to see what *would* happen if you did such-and-such a thing. That's always been very much a part of writing poetry for me, and that's the part I enjoy the most.[2]

The Elements of an Imaginative Universe

The Speaker

We encountered the notion of "speaker" or "narrator" in Chapter 6, on writing about literature; now we will turn back to that concept from a slightly different viewpoint.

Suppose that you want to use the passage from Ecclesiastes as the theme for a story. One method would be to tell the story from an impersonal point of view; you, the author, would in effect know all and see all, and you would select and present the details that you thought would fit your purpose. In this case, the reader might hardly be aware of a speaker.

[2]James Dickey, *Self-Interviews,* with Barbara and James Reiss (New York: Doubleday, 1970). Copyright © 1970 by James Dickey. Reprinted by permission of Doubleday & Co., Inc.

But suppose, on the other hand, you want your story to have a biblical ring, to be more like historical fiction. Then you might devise a speaker such as the following: a venerable wise man whose wisdom is ripe and who has learned to accept life's vicissitudes. He has a resonant voice, and, of course, he has flowing white hair and a long white beard—dresses in robes and wears sandals. He has no family and lives in beautiful simplicity in a little rock house that is always immaculately clean.

Suppose, however, that you want your tale to be absurd, that you want to say in effect, "Life is absurd, and my tale mirrors that absurdity." Then a speaker who believes that all human effort is ultimately futile might narrate the story of a great statesman who feels that his endeavors will change the course of history. The speaker's attitude would show that the efforts of his character would lead to nothing in the cosmic scheme of things. On the other hand, think of the irony that could be brought to the same story if the narrator were a wealthy and powerful, but stupid and greedy man.

In his book *The Rhetoric of Fiction,* Wayne C. Booth makes this telling statement:

> "There was a man in the land of Uz, whose name was Job; and that man was perfect and upright, one that feared God, and eschewed evil." With one stroke the unknown author has given us a kind of information never obtained about real people, even about our most intimate friends. Yet it is information that we must accept without question if we are to grasp the story that is to follow. In life if a friend confided his view that *his* friend was "perfect and upright," we would accept the information with qualifications imposed by our knowledge of the speaker's character or of the general fallibility of mankind. We could never trust even the most reliable of witnesses as completely as we trust the author of the opening statement about Job.[3]

Such is the power of the teller.

But you can play interesting games—with yourself and with your reader. What if my speaker is a liar? That is, what if I create a speaker that my reader does not trust? Then what is the effect on my story, and how do I tell it? Indeed, how do I bring my reader to distrust my speaker? (One obvious way would be to have your speaker trip himself or herself up in contradictions.) What if my speaker is an innocent little child, who cannot understand the evil motives of the characters that he or she is telling about?

Your speaker can know everything (as does the speaker in the Book of Job) or can be of severely limited insight.

The possibilities of narrative viewpoint are endless. Clearly, the narrative viewpoint that you choose as an author is one of the most important aspects of creating an imaginative universe.

The Speaker: An Example

Everyone, I suppose, has read *The Adventures of Huckleberry Finn.* Huck, an unlettered but infinitely good and loving person, tell his own story, and the depth of the book comes from the reactions of a boy who is naturally

[3]Wayne C. Booth, *The Rhetoric of Fiction* (Chicago: The University of Chicago Press, 1961), pp. 3–4.

good to a society in which slavery is an accepted social practice. At one point in the novel, Nigger Jim is drifting with Huck on a raft in the Mississippi. Huck is undergoing a real turnmoil of conscience, for he is helping Jim escape, and in the antebellum South this constitutes a social wrong, for Jim is someone else's property; therefore, Huck feels that he is involved in thievery as well as the violation of the norms of the society in which he grew up. So he takes a skiff and paddles away from the raft, determined to turn Jim in. Here is the scene as Huck narrates it.:

8   Right then along comes a skiff with two men in it with guns, and they stopped and I stopped. One of them says:
   "What's that yonder?"
   "A piece of raft," I says.
   "Do you belong on it?"
   "Yes, sir."
   "Any men on it?"
   "Only one, sir."
   "Well, there's five niggers run off to-night up yonder, above the head of the bend. Is your man white or black?"
   I didn't answer up prompt. I tried to, but the words wouldn't come. I tried for a second or two to brace up and out with it, but I warn't man enough—hadn't the spunk of a rabbit. I see I was weakening; so I just give up trying, and up and says:
   "He's white."
   "I reckon we'll go and see for ourselves."
   "I wish you would," says I, "because it's pap that's there, and maybe you'd help me tow the raft ashore where the light is. He's sick—and so is mam and Mary Ann."
   "Oh, the devil! we're in a hurry, boy. But I s'pose we've got to. Come, buckle to your paddle, and let's get along."
   I buckled to my paddle and they laid to their oars. When we had made a stroke or two, I says:
   "Pap'll be mighty much obleeged to you, I can tell you. Everybody goes away when I want them to help me tow the raft ashore, and I can't do it by myself."
   "Well, that's infernal mean. Odd, too. Say, boy, what's the matter with your father?"
   "It's the—a—the—well, it ain't anything much."
   They stopped pulling. It warn't but a mighty little ways to the raft now. One says:
   "Boy, that's a lie. What *is* the matter with your pap? Answer up square now, and it'll be the better for you."
   "I will, sir, I will, honest—but don't leave us, please. It's the—the— Gentlemen, if you'll only pull ahead, and let me heave you the headline, you won't have to come a-near the raft—please do."
   "Set her back, John, set her back!" says one. They backed the water. "Keep away, boy—keep to looard. Confound it, I just expect the wind has blowed it to us. Your pap's got the smallpox, and you know it precious well. Why didn't you come out and say so? Do you want to spread it all over?"
   "Well," says I, a-blubbering, "I've told everybody before, and they just went away and left us."
   "Poor devil, there's something in that. We are right down sorry for you, but we—well, hang it, we don't want the smallpox, you see. Look here, I'll tell you

what to do. Don't you try to land by yourself, or you'll smash everything to pieces. You float along down about twenty miles, and you'll come to a town on the left-hand side of the river. It will be long after sun-up then, and when you ask for help you tell them your folks are all down with chills and fever. Don't be a fool again, and let people guess what is the matter. Now we're trying to do you a kindness; so you just put twenty miles between us, that's a good boy. It wouldn't do any good to land yonder where the light is—it's only a wood-yard. Say, I reckon your father's poor, and I'm bound to say he's in pretty hard luck. Here, I'll put a twenty-dollar gold piece on this board, and you get it when it floats by. I feel mighty mean to leave you; but my kingdom! It won't do to fool with smallpox, don't you see?"

"Hold on, Parker," says the man, "here's a twenty to put on the board for me. Good-by, boy; you do as Mr. Parker told you, and you'll be all right."

"That's so, my boy—good-by, good-by. If you see any runaway niggers you get help and nab them, and you can make some money by it."

"Good-by, sir," says I; "I won't let no runaway niggers get by me if I can help it."

They went off and I got aboard the raft, feeling bad and low, because I knowed very well I had done wrong, and I see it warn't no use for me to try to learn to do right; a body that don't get *started* right when he's little ain't got no show—when the pinch comes there ain't nothing to back him up and keep him to his work, and so he gets beat. Then I thought a minute, and says to myself, hold on; s'pose you'd 'a' done right and give Jim up, would you felt better than what you do now? No, says I, I'd feel bad—I'd feel just the same way I do now. Well, then, says I, what's the use you learning to do right when it's troublesome to do right and ain't no trouble to do wrong, and the wages is just the same? I was stuck. I couldn't answer that. So I reckoned I wouldn't bother no more about it, but after this always do whichever comes handiest at the time.

I went into the wigwam; Jim warn't there. I looked all around; he warn't anywhere. I says: "Jim!"

"Here I is, Huck. Is dey out o' sight yit? Don't talk loud."

He was in the river under the stern oar, with just his nose out. I told him they were out of sight, so he come aboard. He says:

"I was a-listenin' to all de talk, en I slips into de river en was gwyne to shove for sho' if dey come aboard. Den I was gwyne to swim to de raf' agin when dey was gone. But lawsy, how you did fool 'em Huck! Dat *wuz* de smartes' dodge! I tell you, chile, I 'spec it save' ole Jim—ole Jim ain't going to forgit you for dat, honey."

Then we talked about the money. It was a pretty good raise—twenty dollars apiece. Jim said we could take deck passage on a steamboat now, and the money would last us as far as we wanted to go in the free states. He said twenty mile more warn't far for the raft to go, but he wished we was already there.

Towards daybreak we tied up, and Jim was mighty particular about hiding the raft good.

The whole effect of this passage—and of the novel—comes from the fact that Huck, who tells us the story, does not understand that his own natural morality is far superior and more humane than the standards that his society has imposed on him. In this sense, the reader knows more than Huck does, and the "wise" reader can thoroughly sympathize with the morally torn Huck.

This is just one example of the myriad effects that one can achieve in creating a speaker.

The Message

The speaker, whoever it may be, tells us something—conveys a message. In fiction, the message involves plot, characters, and scene. In other words, imaginary people perform imaginary actions in an imaginary place. Even in a historical novel, the people are imaginary, even though they may correspond more or less roughly to George Washington or Napoleon or Daniel Boone. And the action, the plot, is imaginary even though it may correspond more or less roughly to actual historical events. Scene is never a completely real place in fiction, for it is also a construct of the writer's imagination. In other words, sometimes it is difficult to draw a clear-cut line between history and fiction, but it is the element of imagination that separates the two genres.

Plot

To assume that every writer has a plot before beginning to develop a tale is like assuming that everyone outlines before beginning an essay. It just isn't so. For instance, in *Aspects of the Novel,* E. M. Forster talks about creating interesting characters, setting them in action, and letting plot develop almost as if by magic, on the basis of what these characters have the potential for doing. That is, plot can build itself—which is not to say that it can never be prefabricated.

In general, a plot involves *conflict, climax,* and *dénouement.* In the selection from *Huckleberry Finn,* the conflict is within Huck himself, between his sense of the norms of society and his own conscience, his own natural goodness. Of course, conflict need not be internal: in an adventure story, it can be between the good guy and the bad buy. The climax—the high point—comes when Huck says that the man on the raft is white; the tension brought about by the conflict dissipates: the decision is made. The dénouement is Huck's explanation of why he did what he did. (The dénouement is the "why" of a story as opposed to the "what.") In a murder mystery, for instance, the climax comes when we learn "who done it"; the dénouement comes when we understand the criminal's motives.

On the basis of these three elements, some easy questions for plot construction can be developed: What will be the nature of the conflict? What action will constitute the climax? How will the dénouement come about?

Characters

There are, in general, two kinds of characters: flat, and round. Flat characters are stylized, predictable; we generally recognize them on the basis of one or two controlling traits. Normally, we will not be surprised by anything that a flat character does: he or she is predictable. Round characters are like human beings, consistent in their inconsistency, unpredictable, complex in their motives and responses. Huck Finn is a good example of a round character.

This is not to say that round characters necessarily are artistically good and flat characters are artistically bad. Many of Dickens' most memorable characters are flat: Josiah Bounderby, Fagin, Harold Skimpole, Sarah Gamp, even Mr. Micawber.

Scene

In real life, tragedy can take place on a sunny spring morning, with the birds chirping and the cherry trees in bloom. But in fiction, scene is often symbolic, and place is matched to action. (Think of the movies: very seldom do the scene and the action clash in emotional content.) Here are the first two paragraphs of *The Return of the Native,* by Thomas Hardy. On the basis of this description of the scene, one can predict the emotional tone of the whole novel:

9   A Saturday afternoon in November was approaching the time of twilight, and the vast tract of unenclosed wild known as Egdon Heath embrowned itself moment by moment. Overhead the hollow stretch of whitish cloud shutting out the sky was as a tent which had the whole heath for its floor.

    The heaven being spread with this pallid screen and the earth with the darkest vegetation, their meeting-line at the horizon was clearly marked. In such contrast the heath wore the appearance of an instalment of night which had taken up its place before its astronomical hour was come: darkness had to a great extent arrived hereon, while day stood distinct in the sky. Looking upwards, a furze-cutter would have been inclined to continue work; looking down, he would have decided to finish his faggot and go home. The distant rims of the world and of the firmament seemed to be a division in time no less than a division in matter. The face of the heath by its mere complexion added half an hour to evening; it could in like manner retard the dawn, sadden noon, anticipate the frowing of storms scarcely generated, and intensify the opacity of a moonless midnight to a cause of shaking and dread.

Some Exercises in Creativity

You now might want to try your hand at imaginative writing. You certainly don't need the following exercises in order to do so. But you may find them challenging—and you may discover that they get you under way in the process of creating an imaginative universe. They will all be based on the passage from Ecclesiastes, which is repeated here for your convenience:

10   I returned, and saw under the sun, that the race is not to the swift, nor the battle to the strong, neither yet bread to the wise, nor yet riches to men of understanding, nor yet favour to men of skill; but time and chance happeneth to them all.

The theme of this passage will be your theme in all these exercises.

1. Choose an instance from your life that seems to illustrate the theme—an occasion when someone you considered undeserving gained success of some kind. The event should be one that was tremendously meaningful to you, that took on great importance in your own life, that caused you bitter disappointment. Briefly narrate that incident "like it was," making no attempt to tell anything but what actually happened as clearly as you can.

2. Choose a narrative viewpoint, and create a speaker for your story. For the purposes of this exercise, don't assume that you are the speaker. Imagine someone else who will tell the story. The speaker might be someone who was involved (excluding yourself) or an onlooker who knew what happened but didn't participate. It might be a psychiatrist to whom you told the story. You might have a very wise or a very foolish speaker, and the speaker could be young or old, male or female. In two or three paragraphs, characterize this speaker. Who is he or she? What sort of person? Relationship to you? Remember that your speaker can be based on some actual person or can be completely imaginary.

3. You have already told your story as it happened. Now make any changes that you feel will make it more dramatic. You have no obligation to stick to the facts of the case; what you want is a plot that will best convey your theme. The result may be almost identical with the actual event or almost completely different. As briefly as you can (without sacrificing pertinent details), write a plot outline. Remember that you can change the actual event as much as you like in order to construct a satisfactory plot.

4. Now sketch the characters who are to play roles in your story. Some of them may be flat, always reacting in exactly the same predictable way. You should be able to present each character in one paragraph. Concentrate on showing the reader those aspects of the character that will be useful to you in the story. For instance, one character may never say a word, but merely be a threatening presence in the story; in this case, we must know why he or she seems threatening. Another character may have a mannerism that is important. And so on.

5. Now sketch (in words) a scene in which your drama can take place. The scene should contribute to the total effect of your story.

6. You now have all the elements for a story. Write it.

Writing Poetry

In *The Medium Is the Massage,* Marshall McLuhan has said, "Art is anything you can get away with." Let's adopt that attitude concerning the art of poetry: it's anything you can get away with. Certainly it doesn't need to be in any given form. It can have rhyme and meter, or it can be free verse, without rhyme or meter. Its purpose can be to tell a story or simply to convey an emotion.

Imagery, Metaphor, Intensity

But most poetry does have certain characteristics: it is imagic, it is metaphoric, and it is intense. For instance, here's an anonymous medieval lyric:

11   *Western Wind*

> Western wind, when wilt thou blow?
> The small rain down can rain.
> Christ, that my love were in my arms,
> And I in my bed again.

Now, I'm not at all sure what this simple little poem means. But it is highly imagic; that is, it gives me visual experience: I see the rain, and I see two lovers snuggled close in a warm bed. I interpret "western wind" as a metaphor for autumn, simply because I have at the back of my mind Shelley's "Ode to the West Wind," the first line of which is "O wild West Wind, thou breath of Autumn's being." So "western wind" is imagic and metaphoric. What about its intensity? The intensity arises, I think, from these other two qualities.

Showing Versus Telling

Above all other literary artists, poets don't *tell;* they *show,* through their use of images and metaphors. Here is one more example of how poets show. The following is merely a statement. It tells:

12   Once I saw some beautiful daffodils. They still live in my memory. The beauty that we experience stays with us as an inner resource that we can call on for pleasure and solace.

Here is a familiar poem in which William Wordsworth *shows* us what that statement meant to him:

13   I wandered lonely as a cloud
>   That floats on high o'er vales and hills,
>   When all at once I saw a crowd,
>   A host, of golden daffodils;
>   Beside the lake, beneath the trees,
>   Fluttering and dancing in the breeze.
>
>   Continuous as the stars that shine
>   And twinkle on the milky way,
>   They stretched in never-ending line
>   Along the margin of a bay:
>   Ten thousand saw I at a glance,
>   Tossing their heads in sprightly dance.
>
>   The waves beside them danced; but they
>   Out-did the sparkling waves in glee:
>   A poet could not but be gay,
>   In such a jocund company:
>   I gazed—and gazed—but little thought
>   What wealth the show to me had brought:

> For oft, when on my couch I lie
> In vacant or in pensive mood,
> They flash upon that inward eye
> Which is the bliss of solitude;
> And then my heart with pleasure fills,
> And dances with the daffodils.

The poem is not really about the uses of beauty in life, but concerns an experience of beauty and conveys that experience to the reader. The poem is not a philosophical statement, but a small chunk of experience vividly conveyed.

Creating Images

It is easy enough to create images, for one merely needs to be observant and to report what one sees (either in actuality or in the imagination). Note the following image, which constitutes one of the most famous modern American poems.

14

The Red Wheelbarrow[4]

William Carlos Williams

> so much depends
> upon
>
> a red wheel
> barrow
>
> glazed with rain
> water
>
> beside the white
> chickens

Bad Poetry

To approach poetry negatively; we might ask: What constitutes a bad poem? Well, the following would certainly qualify as absolutely putrid:

15

A Garden of Love and Beauty

Silas Pennypacker

> There's a garden, as named above,
> A garden of beauty and love;
> Gardeners, toiling all the year round,
> Go there as if Paradise-bound!
>
> Clime without frost to fear, all year
> Plants from over the earth brought here;

---

[4]William Carlos Williams, "The Red Wheelbarrow," *The Collected Earlier Poems of William Carlos Williams* (New York: New Directions Publishing, 1938). Copyright 1938 by New Directions Publishing Corporation. Reprinted by permission of New Directions Publishing Corporation.

Folks over so much beauty gloat;
In the warm breeze, butterflies float!

Many paths here for lovers' feet.
Loves here walk and loves here meet.
My feet come here as of duty
To spend the day with love and beauty.

Of course, no one would take this poem seriously. But it's interesting to isolate the factors that make it a bad poem. In the first place, it is so general that it has no imagic quality. What does the garden look like? Anything and nothing. (The only real image—and that one seems accidental—is that of floating butterflies.) Furthermore, the thing is unfigurative; it does not work with metaphor. And anyway, what in the world is a garden of love and beauty? How does such a garden differ from, say, a vegetable garden? What are the lovers like? Why do they meet in this garden? And so on and so on and so on.

Specificity

One of the devices of writing poetry is to use the specific in order to evoke the general—which is what we've been saying all along. Notice how specific and imagic proverbs are:

16 Don't count your chickens before they're hatched.

A bird in the hand is worth two in the bush.

That's water under the bridge.

The squeaking wheel gets the grease.

Birds of a feather flock together.

When in Rome, do as the Romans do.

I suppose all this boils down to some basic advice about writing poetry: Choose images and metaphors so that your meaning will come alive for the reader. Don't *tell* the reader that you're in love; *show* the reader that you are.

Another piece of advice: Poetry usually arises from deep feeling. If you don't feel strongly about what you're trying to say, chances are your poem will lack intensity. But what does that advice add up to? Well, that you should speak poetically only about what really matters to you. If you do that, you'll be well on your way to writing a successful poem.

More Exercises in Creativity

1. Choose a group of abstract concepts such as "love," "sorrow," "fear," and "joy" and create images that illustrate each of them. For instance:

> Love: the young woman cradles her baby in her arms while it greedily nuzzles her breast.

Sorrow: On a golden autumn day, as the last leaves flutter from the trees, the old man stands with bowed head over the grave of his wife.

2. Each of the proverbs quoted in example **16** contains an image (for instance, of someone counting eggs—and assuming that all the eggs will become chickens), and each embodies a statement (for instance, "Don't make firm plans for the future before you see what actually happens in the present"). Write a one-sentence statement giving the meaning of each of the proverbs (or of any other that you can think of), and then construct a new image to illustrate that meaning (for instance, "A farmer in faded bib overalls and a tattered straw hat looks out over his recently planted wheat field; he mutters to himself, 'When this crop is harvested, I'll sell it and buy the new tractor'").

3. Choose five or six people that you know, and make statements concerning them in the following form: Name of person + is + adjective ("Norma is beautiful," "Tony is witty," "Jeff is sarcastic"). Now translate each of these statements into a metaphor (for instance, "Norma is a newly blown rose, fresh with dew, fragrant, and delicately hued"; "Tony's conversation is a pinball game, with lights flashing, bells ringing, and ideas ricocheting from one side to the other"; "Jeff's remarks are a mixture of vinegar and battery acid").

4. How about writing some imagist poems (such as "The Red Wheelbarrow," by William Carlos Williams, on page 248). The imagist poem, as the name implies, captures an image, and the poet is like an impressionist painter who depicts a verbal image of what he or she sees. For instance, from where I am sitting at the moment, I can see these images:

> On a tall white door,
> A brass knob gleams
> In the lamplight.
>
> A pipe smoulders in an ashtray,
> The smoke curling thinly upward.
>
> Fluttering in the evening breeze,
> The leaves of the calendar
> Rustle quietly.

5. One profitable kind of poetic exercise is imitation. Choose a part of your body, and write about it in imitation of the following poem by John Keats. Your poem might well be a humorous parody—for instance, if you choose to write on your toenail.

> This living hand, now warm and capable
> Of earnest grasping, would, if it were cold
> And in the icy silence of the tomb,
> So haunt thy days and chill thy dreaming nights
> That thou wouldst wish thine own heart dry of blood

So in my veins red life might stream again,
And thou be conscience-calm'd—see here it is—
I hold it towards you.

6. The limerick is a universally popular form of humorous verse. You might like to try your hand at writing some of them. In order to do so, simply make your verse fit the metrical pattern and rhyme scheme of the following:

There once was a fam'ly named Stein.
There was Gert, there was Ep, there was Ein.
Gert's poems were bunk,
Ep's statues were junk,
And nobody understood Ein.

The Uses of Writing: Persuasion

Summary of the Chapter

The sort of persuasion discussed here is not the trickery of some advertising, is not brainwashing (persuasion for its own sake), is not debate (argument for the sake of argument). Rather, the chapter discusses the kind of agreement that comes about when (to use a cliché) people achieve "a meeting of the minds." The goal of persuasion, as discussed in the chapter, is to achieve cooperation, not conflict; understanding, not hostility.

For an argument to be persuasive, the audience must believe that the persuader is reliable and ethical; that is, your audience must believe that you know what you're talking about and that you will not falsify.

The proposition for an argument must be fairly well defined, and it must not be truistic. Obviously, a proposition such as the following is not arguable: "Politicians should be honest." The following proposition is arguable: "Members of the city commission should not enter into business arrangements with the city government."

In any argument, there are two kinds of truth, *formal* and *material.* The following argument is true in the formal sense, but not in the material: "All men are rodents. George is a man. Therefore, George is a rodent." The following argument may be true in the material sense, but it is not so in the formal: "Some men are honest. George is a man. Therefore, George is honest." To be truly persuasive, arguments must be valid—must have both formal and material truth.

It is often said that reasoning (logic) can take two forms: *deduction* and *induction.* Deduction moves from general premises to a particular conclusion: "All men are mortal. George is a man. Therefore, George is mortal." Induction moves from particular examples to a general conclusion: "Socrates was mortal; Bacon was mortal; Kant was mortal; Dewey was mortal. Therefore I conclude that philosophers, like other men, are mortal." In fact, these two processes are not so different as simple examples make them seem. But the concepts of deduction and induction are useful when applied to organization.

Arguments are often flawed by informal fallacies, and these same informal fallacies can be used to trick the unwary. An example of an informal fallacy is *after this, therefore because of this:* "I got sick after eating at Jean's; therefore Jean's cooking made me sick."

Analogy—comparing the similarities between two essentially dissimilar things—is a useful but potentially dangerous tool of argumentation.

The persuader must be keenly aware of audience. There are *specialized audiences* (well-defined groups) and *universal audiences* (the persuader's notion of all reasonable people). The argument must, of course, be adjusted to the audience.

Traditionally, an argument has six parts: (1) introduction, (2) explanation of the case under discussion, (3) outline of the points, or steps, in the argument, (4) proof of the case, (5) refutation of opposing arguments, (6) conclusion. This classical structure can serve as an organizational framework for arguments, but its greatest use is to help the arguer make certain that no important elements of persuasion have been omitted.

The Goal of Persuasion

When one thinks of persuasion, the concept of "audience" becomes sharp and bright, for successful persuasion involves moving *someone or some group* to take a given action or adopt a certain idea or attitude. In self-expressive, expository, and imaginative writing, the writer can choose to adopt a take-it-or-leave-it stance, but not in persuasive writing.

The principle is clearly illustrated in advertising, where business firms spend millions of dollars to reach given audiences with their messages. The toy and breakfast cereal companies buy up virtually all the Saturday morning advertising time on TV; fashionable jewelry stores and expensive restaurants place their ads in the society section of the newspapers; beer companies pay premium prices for advertising time on telecasts of sporting events.

In fact, persuasion in the form of advertising is so pervasive that we might tend to think of it as the model for all persuasion and conclude that persuasion involves using every trick in the book to get an audience to act in the way that the persuader desires.

But that is not the kind of persuasion that this chapter will discuss, for there is another and more interesting model. The elements of this model for persuasion are these: a moral and candid persuader, an argument for or against some proposition, and an intelligent and aware audience that is willing to modify its viewpoint or adopt a new point of view. The action from persuader to audience is not debate, but rather dialectic, in which the goal is to arrive at "a meeting of the minds."

Notice that debate, paradoxically, seldom involves persuasion; rather, its goal is proving a point or advancing the best argument. The opposing sides in a debate seldom convince each other of anything, and one side loses and the other wins. In the model of persuasion that we will talk about in this chapter, both sides win, in that both sides learn, and the end result is mutual understanding, accommodation.

The text for the whole discussion is this sentence: *"You persuade a man only insofar as you can talk his language by speech, gesture, tonality, order, image, attitude, idea, identifying your ways with his."*[1] That is, you persuade a person only insofar as you understand that person sympathetically, only insofar as you can put yourself in his or her place. Therefore, we are not talking about the kind of persuasion that the advertising people use so successfully, even though we will discuss their devices so that we can protect ourselves against them.

Succinctly put, the goal of persuasion as discussed in this chapter is to achieve cooperation, not conflict; understanding, not hostility.

The Persuader

Of course, you must trust the persuader, or you will not accept the argument; conversely, when you are the persuader, your audience must trust you, or they will not accept your argument. In general, for an audience to trust you, they must believe that you are ethical and informed—that is, they must believe that you will not lie and that you know what you are talking about. The persuader must, then, have credibility.

If your audience knows you, knows that you are reliable and that you are an expert on your subject, then there is no problem of establishing credibility. But if your audience knows nothing about you, then your argument itself and the stance that you take toward your audience must establish your credibility. The substance of your persuasive argument and your use of language are the only means that you have of establishing credibility when your audience doesn't know you. (We will talk about the nature of audiences later in this chapter.)

The Substance of the Argument

The substance of your argument must be based on a proposition that is not truistic—that is, one that is open to question. Furthermore, the proposition must be clearly definable; the vaguer the proposition, the less chance there is of persuasion. To state this point another way: *An arguable proposition has definition and uncertainty.*

The proposition "Some changes in government might be beneficial to the nation" lacks definition and therefore is not really arguable. What changes?

[1]Kenneth Burke, *A Grammar of Motives and a Rhetoric of Motives* (Cleveland: World Publishing, 1962), p. 579.

Beneficial in what ways? This proposition is too unstable to serve as the base for the structure of an argument.

The proposition "Electing honest officials would improve government" is truistic; it does not contain the element of uncertainty. The response to this proposition is "So what else is new?" But the response we want to a proposition is "Why do you say that?"

The proposition "Government financing of presidential election campaigns would make America a more democratic nation" is arguable. It has definition, and it is not truistic.

The substance itself will be the proof of your case—your attempt to convince an audience that they should agree with you. You will undoubtedly use logic, and it must not be fallacious; your analogies must hold, must not be false; your examples must be truly representative; your data must be accurate. All these matters will be discussed in this chapter.

Tone

Your language—your tone—is the way you convey your attitude to the audience. A diatribe—heated language, ranting and raving—is seldom persuasive, for real persuasion results when persuader and audience achieve that mystic union known as "a meeting of the minds," which seldom results from browbeating.

It is a grave mistake to assume that the power of facts or logic or both inevitably results in persuasion. Both facts and logic convince me that smoking is harmful to the health, even fatal, and yet at this very moment as I type, I am puffing on a cigar. My wife tries in her sweet and subtle ways to convince me that I should stop smoking, but she does not give me the facts and nothing but the facts, for they, obviously, have no (or at best, little) persuasive force in my case.

Indeed, your attitude toward the audience is *the* crucial factor in persuasion, and attitude is not conveyed by the facts and nothing but the facts, nor by impeccable logic, nor by disinterest.

This is not to say that all successful persuaders are open, reliable, and ethical. All of us know enough about the world to realize that persuasion is often based on dissimulation and outright cheating. Again, this is not the kind of persuasion that we are concerned with in this chapter—except in that we want to learn to guard against it.

The persuader in ethical argumentation "woos" the audience (to use Kenneth Burke's term), first by identifying with them—talking their language—and second by making certain that the substance of the argument is as reliable as possible.

Formal Logic

At the very least, an argument for or against a proposition must not be inconsistent; that is, for an argument to have persuasive power, it must have the negative virtue of consistency. Why is consistency a negative virtue? For this reason: no one would praise an argument because it is consistent, whereas any reasonable audience would condemn an inconsistent argument. One expects consistency as the bare minimum of argumentation. For example, if I argue that all people are created equal, and therefore each is entitled to human dignity, no one will exclaim, "What a consistent argument!" However, if I argue that all people are created equal but nonetheless some should be deprived of dignity, my audience will be outraged or at least puzzled by my inconsistency.

Formal Truth and Material Truth

Another way of stating that an argument must be consistent is to say that it must be *formally true.*

The following brief argument is undoubtedly formally true:

1   The horoscope is infallible, based as it is on the exact science of astrology. My horoscope for today reads thus: "You are in the mood to make radical changes, but it is better to count your blessings instead." Since that is my reading for today, I must, indeed, be in the mood to make changes, but I won't do that; instead, I will count my blessings.

If the audience for this argument believes its premise—that the horoscope is infallible—then, *for that audience,* the argument has not only formal truth, but also *material,* or factual, truth. It will probably be convincing.

The following paragraph is a bit difficult to understand, but it is worth careful reading, for it sums up the whole problem of formal truth:

> In any given context it is relatively easy to distinguish between the categoric assertion that a given proposition is true and the formal truth, validity, correctness or adequacy of the proof or demonstration that it follows from certain other propositions. In any given case, also, it is rather easy to see that the material truth of premises or conclusion and the validity of the proof may be relatively independent of each other—a proposition known to be false may be correctly proved (from false premises), and the proof of a true proposition may be formally defective. But when we come to deal with the general nature of formal truth and its relation to material truth we begin to encounter difficulties. Many, however, of the traditional difficulties may be eliminated if we take the trouble to distinguish clearly between reasoning or inference as an operation or event which happens in an individual mind and the question of evidence or general conditions under which what is asserted can be true. When this is recognized it becomes clear that logical or formal truths are truths concerning the implication, consistency, or necessary connection between *objects* asserted in propositions, and the distinctive subject matter of logic may be said to be the relations generally expressed by *if–then necessarily.*[2]

In other words, strictly speaking, logic is concerned only with formal relationships. Thus, the logician's comment on the following would be that it is formally true:

2   *If* the moon is made of green cheese, *then necessarily* modern studies of the moon are misguided.

[2]Morris Raphael Cohen, *A Preface to Logic* (Cleveland: World Publishing, 1956), p. 18.

But, as Cohen points out, formal and material truth are never separated in fact.

> What we call the evidence for the material or factual truth of any proposition involves—excepting matters of immediate apprehension which are beyond argument—the question of the logical relation between the proposition in question and certain others which are taken for granted. Thus, we rule out the proposition that there is life on the planet Mercury, by the proposition that life cannot exist except at certain temperatures, etc.[3]

We will not go into the intricacies of formal logic in this book. One does not need to be a logician in order to construct formally true arguments (that is, arguments that are consistent), nor does one need a course in logic in order to recognize inconsistency. To repeat, the point (to remember) is that a persuasive argument is, at the very minimum, consistent.

The Syllogism and Argumentation

Here is a brief argument in the form of a syllogism:

3   If a professor is immoral, he or she should be discharged.
Professor X is immoral.
Therefore, Professor X should be discharged.

No one would question the formal truth of this argument, but in order for it to be persuasive, you as the arguer must accomplish a number of things. First, you must define satisfactorily what you mean by "immorality" and convince the audience to adhere to this definition. Next you must argue that morality is necessary for a professor to accomplish his or her job. Then you must establish to the audience's satisfaction that Professor X is indeed immoral. If you do all this, the audience is then likely to conclude that Professor X should be fired. The formal truth of the argument is self-evident. On the basis of how you fill out that formal structure, the audience may conclude that the argument is also materially—factually—true.

Deduction and Induction

Traditionally, arguments are classified as deductive or inductive. The deductive argument is best illustrated by the syllogism; if the premises are consistent, then the conclusion is inevitable. For instance,

4   All human beings are mortal. [major premise]
Jones is a human being. [minor premise]
Therefore, Jones is mortal. [conclusion]

We will not explore here the various forms that the classical syllogism can take, for they have little direct bearing on the way persuaders develop arguments in practice.

In the deductive argument, of course, persuasion depends on how completely the audience accepts the premises (provided that the argument itself is formally true).

[3]*Ibid.*

Obviously, the deductive argument moves from a general premise to a particular conclusion. The inductive argument moves from particular examples to a general conclusion:

5   Apple A is green, feels hard, and tastes sour.
Apple B is green, feels hard, and tastes sour.
Apple C is green, feels hard, and tastes sour.
Apple D is green, and it feels hard; therefore it will taste sour (that is, we conclude that hard, green apples are sour).

Now then, if you will take a close look at these two simple examples, you will come to the conclusion, I think, that even though they are radically different in organization, they are very similar in methodology. That is, the experimenter in the second example was probably trying to establish a certain major premise; otherwise, he or she would not have tested so many apples. Indeed, the inductive chain in the example could well be stated thus:

6   Apples that are green and hard are sour.
Apple D is green and hard.
Therefore, it is sour.

Induction and Persuasion

Drawing heavily on the work of Morris Raphael Cohen, let's discuss the concept of induction in some detail, for it throws light on the methods whereby persuasion is achieved.

It has often been said that the scientific method is inductive, but it is inconceivable that scientists would work with a set of data unless they felt that the data would illustrate some general principle that they had already formulated on the basis of past knowledge or intuition. In other words, before scientists begin their work, they have a premise that they hope to prove or disprove. Scientists do not examine a randomly selected set of data in the hopes that they will accidentally come up with a universal principle.

Many people have a mistaken view of the computer, believing that one can simply feed a mass of data into the computer and the machine will come up with something unexpectedly significant. Not at all. Ideally, the computer should be a perfect model of the inductive process, for it can handle such large masses of data with such lightning rapidity, but it turns out that you must tell the computer what you hope to derive before it can begin its work.

An Example of Induction

It has also been argued that induction is the sort of reasoning in which the conclusion is more general than the beginning, the assumption being that one begins with facts and ends with laws. But to counter that view, let's take a simple example from linguistics.

Here is a good deductive argument (though it is not stated in the form of a syllogism). We notice that all imperative sentences (like *Sit down!* or *Shut up!*) are addressed to the second person, the pronoun for which is *you*. We notice further that no second person pronouns ever appear as subjects of such sentences as they are written or spoken. We might conclude something like this: The pronoun *you* is not necessary to signal meaning in imperative sentences. However, such a conclusion would be quite trivial. Chances are, we would come to a much broader conclusion, like this perhaps: Sentences have two levels of structure, the one that is seen or heard (surface structure) and the one that represents the meaning (deep structure; see Chapter 10). And we would probably go on to find other facets of meaning that are not directly represented in sentences as we see or hear them. In other words, unless we were blind to the possibilities of our conclusion, it would be much broader than our premise—which does not sound like deduction at all, for deduction is a movement from the general rule to the specific case, whereas induction is the movement from specific cases to the general rule. So it seems that there is no sharp line to be drawn between deduction and induction.

Deductive and Inductive Organization

Our point of view, then, is that deduction and induction are not radically different processes, but, for purposes of persuasion, they represent radically different forms of organization. Let's go back to the argument concerning Professor X for an illustration. Here is that argument:

7   If a professor is immoral, he or she should be discharged.
    Professor X is immoral.
    Therefore, Professor X should be discharged.

An essay on this topic that moved deductively would look something like this in outline:

8   Thesis: If a professor is immoral, he or she should be discharged.
      I. Definition of professorial morality
         A. Professional honesty
         B. Fairness
         C. Sobriety
         D. Chastity
     II. Relationship of morality to professorial duties
         A. Need for integrity of scholarship
         B. Need for fairness
         C. Necessity of setting a good personal example for students
    III. Professor X's conduct
         A. Professional dishonesty
         B. Unfairness
         C. Drunkenness
         D. Promiscuity
     IV. Conclusion

That same topic handled inductively might look something like this:

9   I. Ideal professorial conduct [established inductively, on the basis of examples]
      A. PROFESSOR Y'S CONDUCT
      B. PROFESSOR Z'S CONDUCT
      C. PROFESSOR W'S CONDUCT

    II. Professor X's conduct
   III. Relationship of morality to professorial duties
   IV. Conclusion [including statement of thesis and recommendations]

The concepts "induction" and "deduction," then, have a great deal of meaning in regard to organization, but not much in regard to the way in which one establishes premises.

Fallacies

Fallacies are two-edged swords: they are traps into which an unwary arguer can fall, and they are traps into which an immoral persuader can lure an audience. The fallacies that we will be dealing with here are usually called *informal.* Most of them will be familiar to you, for you have encountered them again and again in advertising (which is not to say that all advertisers are unreliable).

Most of the fallacies that will be discussed fall into the general category of *non sequitur,* a Latin term meaning "it does not follow." A non sequitur is an argument in which the conclusion does not follow from the premises.

Ad Hominem (Against the Man)

Suppose that the thesis of your argument is that the President should not have vetoed a certain bill; as your argument progresses, you shift from an attack on that particular action by the President to an attack on the President as a person. You have committed the *ad hominem* fallacy.

The ad hominem trick is particularly shoddy, for it confuses issues with those who advocate them, and, needless to say, perfectly valid issues can be supported by reprehensible people. Even Hitler supported some causes that most of us would agree with, such as full employment.

Here is an example of an ad hominem argument: "The city council should not have voted to spend a million and a half dollars on a new library when there are other, more urgent needs and a shortage of funds. One wonders how much in kickbacks the members of the council will get from the contractors who build the library."

Bandwagon

This common fallacy goes something like this: "Everyone else is doing it, so you should too." In southern California, for instance, the Ford Motor Company advertises over and over again that more people in the area drive Fords than any other make of car. The implication is that you should join the crowd and purchase a Ford, but, of course, that argument ignores (or evades) the issues of price, quality, gas mileage, service—the very issues that a car buyer should take into consideration.

In politics, the bandwagon effect is of great concern. Voting places in the East close three hours earlier than those in the West; thus, the TV networks can broadcast voting trends before many western voters have gone to the polls. Some think that these broadcasts may create a bandwagon effect, influencing western voters to follow the patterns set by the easterners.

Begging the Question

This is sometimes called arguing in a circle, and it involves using one's premises as conclusions. A simple example: I argue that students at Golden West College are exceptionally intelligent, and you ask me why I think so. I reply, "Because only intelligent students go to Golden West College." I have begged the question by restating my premise in different terms.

Composition

In this fallacy, one assumes that what is valid for each member of a class will be valid for the class as a whole. For instance: "The gross national product of Thailand must be greater than that of Tibet, because individual incomes are higher in Thailand than in Tibet." This argument overlooks the possibility that the population of Tibet is greater than that of Thailand, so Tibet's smaller individual incomes may contribute to a greater gross national product than Thailand's.

Division

This is the opposite of composition. It is the assumption that what holds for the group will also hold for each member. For example, more beer is consumed in West Germany, per capita, than in any other nation. Therefore, it is accurate to say that West Germans drink more beer than, say, Japanese, but it would be inaccurate to conclude on this basis that German X drinks more beer than Japanese Y, for X might be a teetotaler, whereas Y might guzzle the stuff continually. An amusing argument that involves the fallacy of division is this one: "Blacksmiths are vanishing. Uncle George is a blacksmith. Therefore, Uncle George is vanishing."

Equivocation

In equivocation, the sense of a key word is shifted, thus invalidating the argument. For instance: "The dictionary defines **republican** as 'one who favors a republic,' and **republic** is defined as 'a state in which the supreme power rests in the body of citizens entitled to vote.'" Therefore, if you believe that the voters should control the government, vote Republican in the next election." The fallacy here lies in the shift of **republican** from its generic use, specifying one who favors a certain form of government, to its specific use as the designation for a political party.

Post Hoc, Ergo Propter Hoc (After This, Therefore Because of This)

This fallacy consists in attributing a cause-and-effect relationship to what is merely a time relationship. For example: "After Murgatroyd was elected, property taxes decreased; therefore, Murgatroyd must have lowered property taxes." (Murgatroyd may well have done so, but the mere time relationship does not establish that fact.)

Reification

In this fallacy, an abstraction is treated as if it had concrete reality. Here is the Puritan Thomas Hooker (1586–1647) talking about sin: "We must see it clearly in its own Nature, its Native color and proper hue . . . ." We cannot, of course, "see" sin as a concrete object. In discussing such abstractions as democracy, many arguers reify, talking as if the concept itself were somehow physically embodied by the United States, or as if Russia embodied the concept "communism."

Testimonial

Sports figures endorse breakfast cereals, movie stars speak on behalf of presidential candidates, Arthur Godfrey and Art Linkletter give pitches for just about everything. These are testimonials—famous people giving their endorsements. But there is no reason why a sports figure should know more about the nutritive qualities of breakfast cereals than you or I do. Nor does the fact that Sammy Davis, Jr., is a great entertainer give him any particular authority to speak knowledgeably about politics. The testimonial is a mendacious use of well-known people to push products and ideas.

There are other kinds of fallacies, but the point has undoubtedly been made: bad thinking can lead one into bad arguments, and bad thinking can also set one up as a pigeon for immoral arguers. Who, after all, wants to be either a huckster or a pigeon?

Analogy

To learn an important method of developing an argument, read the following passage carefully:

10   . . . the New Leftists are not Fifties Beats (and, by the way, I do not use the term Beat pejoratively). They are angry militants who see the poor as a new force in America, perhaps even as a substitute for the proletariat that failed. So Stokely Carmichael, one of the best of the breed, insists that the Mississippi and Alabama sharecroppers can choose for themselves. He understands that ultimately, to paraphrase an old labor song, no one can abolish poverty for you, you've got to abolish it yourself. And from this point of view, it does make quite a bit of difference whether the community organizing campaign works or not.

An analogy from the Thirties might illuminate the political hope that is here asserted by the young radicals. In 1932 or 1933, many polite Americans believed that if you gave a worker a bathtub, he would put coal in it. And the skilled AFL members thought it preposterous that mass production machine operators could form *their own* union. On paper, the right to organize was proclaimed by the Wagner Act. In fact, it took at least five tumultuous years of picketing, striking and sitting-in before the CIO turned the brave words into something of a reality. Similarly in 1964, America declared war on poverty; and most of the well-bred citizenry did not intend by that to have field hands and janitors speaking up for themselves; and the young radicals, who have this knack of taking America's promises seriously, sought a surge from below to give meaning to the phrasemaking on high. But, as I think the New Left realizes, this analogy is faulty in part. The mass production workers were, just as radical theory had said, forced by the conditions of their existence (thousands of men assembled at one miserable place with common problems and interests) into a solidarity which became the basis of union organization. The poor, as Tom Hayden noted in his *New Republic* contribution, are not grouped into incipient communities. A slum street fragments and atomizes people; the two largest groups of the poor, the young and the old, have little to do with one another; and even if they could get together, the poor are still a minority of the society. Therefore it is going to take even more creativity to help the outcasts into their own than it did to build industrial unionism.[4]

This passage is an excellent example of analogy. It compares the organization of the poor in the 1960s to the organization of industrial unions in the 1930s. Arguing by analogy is the process of pointing out similarities between two different concepts or things, X and Y, and saying that since such and such happened in the case of X, it will also happen in the case of Y. But note that the author of the passage points out where his analogy begins to fail him. Since X and Y are, by definition, not the same thing, they must have differences as well as similarities. Therefore, analogies cannot be pushed too far.

In Chapter 2 (page 37), I used an analogy to clarify a point:

11   No one can begin to understand at the conscious level the infinite number of factors that influence writing. Learning to write is largely the business of developing one's intuition. The writer is a computer with a soul, infinitely more complex than any that IBM will ever develop—working just as rapidly, making instantaneous choices, running well ahead of conscious knowledge of what is happening, drawing on a data bank that includes everything ever known or experienced or dreamed. The only service that a book about writing can perform is to help the writer put more options into the mental program.

This analogy helped me explain a point about learning to write, but note that it does contain areas of falseness. In the first place, the analogy between computers and the human brain simply can't be extended very far. In the second place, the techniques that a writer learns are more like the *programs* on the basis of which a computer runs than like the *data* that a computer stores or manipulates.

To the list of fallacies in this chapter we can add *false analogy.* Regarding false analogy, Abraham Kaplan has said:

. . . everything in the world resembles everything else, just as it differs from everything else. There is always an analogy to be drawn, and every analogy breaks down somewhere. The question is always whether just *that* likeness justifies an extension of what is known about one sort of case to the other.[5]

[4]Michael Harrington, "The Mystical Militants," *The New Republic,* 19 Feb. 1966, pp. 20–22. Reprinted by permission of *The New Republic,* Copyright © 1966 by The New Republic, Inc.
[5]Abraham Kaplan, *The Conduct of Inquiry* (Scranton, Pa.: Chandler Publishing, 1964), p. 107.

The Audience

The concept of audience has permeated *The Contemporary Writer*—so much so, in fact, that bringing it up again might seem redundant. Of course, the whole point of rhetoric is adjusting discourse to audience.

But most written arguments, as a matter of fact, are not addressed to one person, or even to a group that can be well defined. Most of the arguments that I have developed in writing are addressed to what I might call "all reasonable people." Paradoxically, then, I must construct my own audience by repeatedly asking the question, What can I expect all reasonable people to know and accept? In other words, my audience is a projection of my own feelings about reasonableness.

This means, of course, that I will avoid fallacies, for I would not expect a reasonable person to be taken in by them. And the concept "all reasonable people" (which, following Chaim Perelman, we will call the *universal audience*[6]) is useful when I check up on myself to ascertain that what I say is both credible and complete.

For instance, if I say that most residents of Orange County, California, are conservatives, I can expect my universal audience to want some kind of evidence to back up my statement. If, furthermore, I attempt to characterize the conservatism of residents of Orange County, I can expect my universal audience to want enough details to allow them to see what I mean.

The universal audience that you construct has great bearing on your premises. For instance, if the audience is Christian, then you do not need to argue that the injustices of this world will be righted in the next one, for Christians take that for granted. But many of your actual readers might well *not* be Christians, in which case they will not accept your premises. However, the universal audience is necessarily an ideal construct, a fiction, that gives you a basis for procedure. It goes without saying that your argument will fail with many individual readers because they fall outside the scope of your universal audience.

That there are specialized audiences is self-evident; the problem of adjusting discourse to specialized audiences is dealt with throughout Chapter 5.

Diatribe and the Audience

By now the nature of the argument as persuasion is probably fairly clear. It remains to set argument apart from *diatribe*. A diatribe is not an argument, but a harangue for or against some proposition. A diatribe may be effective in arousing emotions; it may even be delightful; but it is seldom convincing. Its purpose is to reaffirm convictions that the audience already holds. Here is Mark Twain in a diatribe against nineteenth-century capitalist morality:

[6]Chaim Perelman and L. Olbrechts-Tyteca, *The New Rhetoric: A Treatise on Argumentation*, trans. John Wilkinson and Purcell Weaver (Notre Dame, Ind.: University of Notre Dame Press, 1969), pp. 30–35.

12   The political and commercial morals of the United States are not merely food
for laughter, they are an entire banquet. The human being is a curious and
interesting invention. It takes a Cromwell and some thousands of preaching
and praying soldiers and parsons ten years to raise the standards of English
official and commercial morals to a respect-worthy altitude, but it takes only
one Charles II a couple of years to pull them down into the mud again. Our
standards were fairly high a generation ago, and they had been brought to
that grade by some generations of wholesome labor on the part of the nation's
multitudinous teachers; but Jay Gould [an American railroad tycoon], all by
himself, was able to undermine the structure in half a dozen years; and in
thirty years his little band of successors—the Senator Clarks [of Montana] and
their kind—have been able to sodden it with decay from roof to cellar and
render it shaky beyond repair, apparently.[7]

Delightful, yes. Persuasive, no—unless, of course, one happens to agree
with the viewpoint anyway.

Structure as Heuristic

The classical form of the persuasive speech or essay is a six-part
structure. This structure is useful as a basis for organization, but in this
discussion we will instead use it as a survey of the elements that we might
want to consider in constructing a persuasive essay. The classical persuasive oration had these six parts, arranged in this order: (1) introduction, (2)
explanation of the case under discussion, (3) outline of the points, or steps,
in the argument, (4) proof of the case, (5) refutation of opposing arguments, (6) conclusion.

These six parts of the classical persuasive speech form a heuristic,
generating useful questions concerning persuasion:

1. *Introduction.* How should I begin my essay? This focuses on the need
(a) to capture the audience's attention and (b) to establish yourself as a
reliable arguer.

2. *Explanation of the case under discussion.* Is my case clearly and fully
stated? The audience must know exactly what the persuader is getting at,
must be aware of all the facets of the case. This calls for you to make
certain that you know exactly what you are talking about.

3. *Outline of the argument.* What is the logical development of my case?
At times it will be useful for you to present your audience with an overview
of the argument so that they can follow more easily, particularly if the
argument is extremely complex. At times this procedure will be destructive, for it will raise anticipatory objections in the audience. It could well be
prudent *not* to raise issues before you are ready to deal with them in detail.

4. *Proof.* Is my proof adequate to convince either a specialized or a
universal audience? This question refers to the concepts of substance that
have been developed in this chapter.

5. *Refutation.* Does my argument sufficiently overcome opposing arguments? This is a productive question, for it forces you to think about the

---

[7]Quoted in Bernard De Voto, ed., *Mark Twain in Eruption* (New York: Grosset & Dunlap, 1940),
p. 81.

other side. What are the arguments in opposition to yours? Do they have merit? What are their weaknesses?

6. *Conclusion.* Is my argument really conclusive, or does it raise questions that it does not answer?

Of course, you might well choose to employ the classical structure as a formula for putting together a persuasive essay; after all, it has worked well for more than 2,000 years.

Persuasion: An Example

Now let's take a close look at a persuasive essay. It is an interesting piece of writing about a timely subject, but it is certainly not one of the world's great pieces of persuasive writing. As I think you'll agree, it is weighted toward refutation of counter-arguments and does very little to prove its own argument. It is interesting, however, to notice that the parts of the classical argument do, indeed, appear in this contemporary essay—certainly not because the author is a student of classical rhetoric, but because the classical framework identifies elements that are necessary to persuasion.

13   *American Prisons: Self-Defeating Concrete*[8]
                        Ronald L. Goldfarb

(1) Our prison system does not work. We waste over a billion dollars a year to continue a system that has not undergone fundamental reevaluation in 200 years. As a result, inmates, taxpayers and victims of crime all lose out. This is no news, of course. Liberals and conservatives alike criticize our correctional system. No one on either side of prison bars seriously doubts the overall negativism of the incarceration process. For one thing recidivism is very high. The best speculation suggests that between half and four fifths of the convicts now in prison will return.

(2) Presently in the U.S. there are about 5,000 city and county jails, 400 state and Federal prisons, plus innumerable local lockups, work houses, camps, farms, ranches, and detention centers. On an average day we confine about 1.3 million offenders in these places. Over the course of a year, about 2.5 million

Paragraphs 1–5 are the *introduction*. The author gets right to the point: "Our prison system does not work." But notice that he does not tip his hand by outlining his own proposal for reform. The audience wonders; So what does he have in mind? The first paragraph constructs a *universal audience:* "No one on either side of prison bars seriously doubts the overall negativism of the incarceration process." In effect, he is saying that all reasonable people agree with him, and he is, by implication, classing you, the reader, with other reasonable people. Paragraph 2 supports paragraph 1: *statistics* seem to indicate that the prison system is a failure. In paragraph 3, Goldfarb calls on the *testimony* of an expert witness, Tom Wicker, of the highly prestigious *New York Times.* Paragraph 4, talking about the design of prisons, is not sufficiently developed, it seems to me, and the reader wants

[8]Ronald L. Goldfarb, "American Prisons: Self-Defeating Concrete," *Psychology Today,* January 1974, pp. 20, 22, 24, 85, 88–89. Copyright © Ziff-Davis Publishing Company. Reprinted by permission of the publisher.

offenders see the inside of prison. And all these prisoners in all these prisons only breed more crime. If the city slum is the high school of crime, prison is the university and a colossally expensive one, at that.

(3) As Tom Wicker of *The New York Times* has pointed out, "Precisely at the point where the first offender has been apprehended, tried and placed in the custody of society, that crucial point at which—if it is ever to be possible—he ought to be treated, trained, redirected, and sent back to a useful place in society, he is instead cast into squalid and terrifying confinement among hardened criminals, homosexual brutes, and the dregs of society, trained (if at all) in the most menial or useless kind of work, in many cases treated little better than an animal, and effectively separated from any glimpse of decency or beauty or hope in life." In prison a man can learn anything, from safecracking to check-forging to murder, and from the nation's leading experts in each field.

(4) **Self-Defeating Concrete.** The design of our prisons, oppressive and life-hating, dictates what goes on inside them. Because our institutions are physically what they are, about 80 percent of the more than 50,000 prison workers and 90 percent of the budget go for security and housekeeping, not reform and correction. While two thirds of the correctional system theoretically operates outside prison (probation and parole, for instance), these programs get short rations on money and manpower. Since our prisons are built to last, they cast in concrete self-defeating correctional policies for decades to come.

(5) Ultimately, our prison system is absurd. It accomplishes the opposite of what it is designed to, increasing crime instead of decreasing it. No wonder, then, that the pressure for reform grows more in-

further discussion. Paragraph 5 contains a restatement of the thesis of paragraph 1: "Ultimately, our prison system is absurd." And again the author invites you to join the universal audience of reasonable people: "Few citizens want the status quo; the time seems right for a change." (Is this sentence a subtle use of the bandwagon fallacy?)

tense. Few citizens want the status quo; the time seems right for change. The key question today is what direction reform is going to take.

(6) **Getting Tougher.** The first possibility is more of the same, only in firmer and more potent doses: longer sentences, less probation and parole, less use of community-based programs like furloughs and halfway houses, no clemency, and renewal of capital punishment. Despite all the evidence that these techniques have failed in the past, this approach, the advocates of which are led by President Nixon, would call for more reliance on old ways, in the guise of toughness.

(7) This approach has simplistic appeal; if someone does something bad, lock him up and throw away the key. But the price we pay in money and public safety for our present correctional system is already high. Revving up this system will only increase the costs. As penologist Hans Mattick has put it, ". . . if men had deliberately set out to design institutions to maladjust their inmates, they would have planned the prisons and jails with which our penal administrators have to work."

(8) Reform could take the opposite direction. We could scrap the old correctional system and tear down most of the prison walls. We could condemn a system predicated on institutionalization. This would mean diverting offenders into varied and versatile community-based programs, and decriminalizing parts of the law relating to vice and victimless crimes. We could use other social welfare and health models to deal with such groups as alcoholics, addicts, young offenders, and sick people.

(9) We could compensate the victims of crimes, and employ offenders and former offenders in the correctional process, and rely as much as possible on contracts with

Paragraphs 6–11 are very much like the third division of the classical argument; the *outline of the case.* Three alternatives to the current penal system are offered. Paragraphs 6 and 7 suggest that one possibility for reform is getting tougher. But Goldfarb dismisses that possibility as simplistic, implying that reasonable people will not subscribe to such a simple-minded notion. Paragraphs 8 and 9 suggest that punishment in most instances should consist in forcing the criminal to compensate the victims of the crime. Paragraphs 10 and 11 outline the rehabilitative model, in which criminals are not punished, but treated as sick people who need therapy before they can re-enter society.

private groups to carry out many correctional functions. Institutions would be few, reserved for the relative minority of hopeless and dangerous cases. Most correctional experts say that only 10 to 20 percent of all prison inmates need to be locked up to protect society from personal harm. And the prisons we did not tear down could be redesigned, restaffed and reprogramed according to more civilized standards. This approach lacks political appeal, has few advocates, and may be considered radical. But it is the approach that I believe might significantly reduce crime in America, and would make much more sense.

(10) **"Sweet Joints."** A third direction for reform, less radical and more centrist than the first two possibilites, would call for keeping but improving the present system, making what the convicts call "sweet joints." Advocates of this approach want to improve the system but not change it. They would send guards to college, build new "model" prisons, and attempt to alter the custodial atmosphere of institutions to a more social services cast.

(11) This is the rehabilitative model. It would replace simple imprisonment with treatment techniques based on such theories as behavior modification. This approach impresses many reform-minded correctional officials, and demonstration projects are underway. The Government has loosened its purse strings to psychologists expressing an interest in penology.

(12) In my opinion, the rehabilitative model might well lead to disaster. It could lead to a second, well-intentioned but fundamental and centuries-long error in correctional policy.

(13) **Consider Our History.** In colonial America we had corporal and capital punishment, banishment, public ostracism, flogging, stocks

Paragraphs 12–30 are very much like the fifth part of the classical argument. They are a *refutation* of the rehabilitative model, which might, at first glance, seem extremely attractive. In paragraphs 13–16, Goldfarb outlines the history of penology in America and makes the point that it has always been rehabilitative in thrust. (Of course,

and branding. The crudeness and violence of these methods shocked sensitive citizens like the Quakers in Philadelphia. The Quakers sought a more humane, civilized form of punishment, one that would punish but at the same time reform offenders.

(14) At a gathering in the home of Benjamin Franklin on March 9, 1787, Benjamin Rush first suggested the notion of imprisoning offenders. His suggestion led to the founding of the Pennsylvania Prison Society, the construction of the Walnut Street Jail, housing the first prison cells in America, and eventually to the first organized prisons in Philadelphia and Pittsburgh. These penal institutions led to our present penitentiary systems, and it spread around the world.

(15) **Solitary Penitence.** The Quakers' idea was to replace punishment with rehabilitative treatment in the form of prolonged solitary confinement. Gradually, prison officials came to believe that confinement combined with labor would lead to rehabilitation. We followed that route with little fundamental reform for almost two centuries.

(16) In the mid-20th century, a few corrections officials began to experiment with new medical and psychiatric techniques. They tried to adapt the techniques developed at nonpenal therapeutic institutions, such as mental asylums, to the prison setting. In theory, their experiments made sense. In practice, the results have been imperfect and disturbing. For example, reformers pushed for indeterminate sentences so that punishment would fit the criminal as well as the crime. The idea was that if a man reformed, he should get out of prison earlier than the hardened criminal. In practice, because it was politically safer to keep everyone locked up for the maximum time to assure against

it has also been unsuccessful.) In paragraphs 17 and 18, he summarizes. But at the end of 18, for the first time, he directly states his argument: "A prison cannot punish and reform at the same time." In order to support that contention, he gives a detailed *example,* a long discussion (paragraphs 19–27) of the Patuxent Institution in Maryland. In the course of this discussion, Goldfarb also brings up the important question of the constitutionality of the Patuxent program (paragraphs 23–27). As a counter example (paragraphs 28–30), he briefly discusses the institution at Highfields, which seems to work "because it does not deprive the individual of his sense of worth and power. Highfields allows its inmates to participate in their own rehabilitation."

mistakes, sentences got longer and longer. The ideal did not fit reality.

(17) I have visited numerous new treatment-oriented institutions in the United States and abroad. I found these places disquieting and, if notably less violent than traditional prisons, little less futile. They present paradoxes of theory that leave treatment-oriented reformers in a classic correctional quandary.

(18) Franklin Roosevelt once pinpointed this dilemma in asking Sanford Bates, the first director of the Federal Bureau of Prisons, whether the goal of the prison system should be to reform the men incarcerated or to deter the general public from committing crimes. Bates answered, "Why not both?" It is this mentality that has plagued prison reform for two centuries, and is at the heart of the problem of treatment-oriented prisons. A prison cannot punish and reform at the same time.

(19) **Clockwork Orange.** Take the controversial Patuxent Institution in Maryland, created by special statute in 1951 to deal with persons considered emotionally or intellectually deficient, who have a history of antisocial behavior and have been convicted of serious crimes. A psychiatrist runs the place. The staff has an unusually high percentage of psychologists, psychiatrists (about one fifth of all the psychiatrists in the U.S. in full-time correctional work are at Patuxent) and social workers. Patuxent exemplifies the treatment-oriented prison.

(20) After an examination and special hearing, the court sends inmates to the maximum-security enclave of buildings at Patuxent for indeterminate sentences. The inmates must be "cured" to be released, and the keepers decide when the cure has been accomplished. The administrators' power is what makes Patuxent special: it is what upsets me the most, and causes crit-

ics to paint the institution Clockwork Orange.

(21) The prison administrators' decisions are subject to judicial review, but who will question an expert? The courts have shown great reluctance to second-guess penal psychologists. And who can say whether the inmates at Patuxent are conning their keepers? For that matter, the system encourages fabrication. If you were locked away in a prison and the only way out was to convince the staff that you were cured, what would you do? The alternative is to fight treatment, and stay incarcerated forever.

(22) On paper, Patuxent's program is impressive. Inmates earn their way up from one tier of cells to another by achieving set goals. They are rewarded for improved behavior with improved living conditions. Vocational training, for example, comes only after a man gets to the third tier. Families of fourth-tier men may visit and picnic on the lawn with the inmates. Individual and group therapy is available. After getting out of Patuxent, ex-cons can get follow-up therapy, a rare and critical part of the correctional process. For all the paper planning, however Patuxent is besieged with riots and lawsuits.

(23) The constitutionality of Patuxent's program has become snarled up in the courts. Two years ago a state court challenged Patuxent's administrators on pragmatic grounds. In *McCray v. Maryland* (November 1971), a two-judge state court ruled in favor of inmates with grievances against Patuxent's administrators. The inmates claimed that what happened to prisoners who refused to cooperate with the staff was illegal. They argued that recalcitrant prisoners' insulation from the outside world in the name of treatment was illegal.

(24) **Cruel and Unusual.** The court found that authorities at Patuxent

placed inmates in solitary confinement as "negative reinforcement"
for up to 30 days without adequate
light, ventilation, exercise or sanita-
tion, a punishment as bad as or
worse than what happened to trou-
blemakers in many old-fashioned
prisons. Such practices, the court
held, are "contrary to the rehabilitation of the inmates, and serve no
therapeutic value of any kind." In
fact, they are contrary to the Eighth
Amendment's ban on cruel and unusual punishment.

(25) The court went beyond the
issues raised by the inmates, and
dealt with some of Patuxent's basic
claims as a "total-treatment facili-
ty." It concluded that "the mainte-
nance of prisoners in cells in a pri-
sonlike setting with the offering of
group therapy and limited rehabilitative vocational training is not a
total rehabilitative effort." The case
was later reversed on jurisdictional
grounds, as well as on grounds of
the courts' reluctance to intervene
in administrative affairs.

(26) In another case *(McNeil v.
Director, Patuxent Institution),*
decided in June 1972, a Patuxent
inmate challenged his continued
confinement beyond the five-year
sentence levied against him for his
crime, assault. The administrators
had not released him because he
refused to submit to psychiatric examinations designed to assess the
appropriateness of his release.

(27) A unanimous Supreme Court
ruled that such confinement was an
unconstitutional denial of the inmate's 14th Amendment right to
due process of law. In an opinion by
Justice Thurgood Marshall, the
court found that the practical effect
of the Patuxent procedure was to
make confinement indefinite, possibly perpetual. Since the inmate
was ordered into that status without
a hearing, the detention to the extent that it exceeded his sentence,
was illegal. Justice William Douglas

added a concurring opinion stating that Patuxent's procedures also violated the inmate's Fifth Amendment right to remain silent.

(28) At Highfields, New Jersey, in contrast to Patuxent, there is an institution that has successfully applied treatment techniques to one class of criminal. Here young, male, repeat offenders are given one last chance. They live in an old country estate not unlike the English borstals that really are reform schools. They work all day at a nearby hospital. They run their own affairs under the guidance of a social scientist and his wife who live on the premises.

(29) The group itself handles nightly therapy sessions. The group thrashes out each others' day-to-day problems, and evaluates each others' development. And the group, not the administrators, decides when each boy is ready to return to freedom.

(30) Highfields is a therapeutic institution. But for all the behavior modification and group therapy, it works because it does not deprive the individual of his sense of worth and power. Highfields allows its inmates to participate in their own rehabilitation.

(31) **Science Replaces Religion.** The danger is that frequently, in moving from old-fashioned prisons to treatment-oriented prisons, all we really do is change our emphasis from physical punishment to enforced personality modification. The Quakers wanted to force prisoners to change through revelatory religious experiences. Today psychologists want the same thing, but they work with the criminals' heads instead of their hearts.

(32) In correction, as in much of our lives, we have substituted the auspices of science for the auspices of religion. The problem is that science, like religion, has proven inexact and frequently unpersuasive in

Paragraphs 31 and 32 provide further *refutation* of the rehabilitative model—even though Highfields admittedly does work. Goldfarb argues that in the rehabilitative model we might well "give the scientists more power than the religionists ever had and more than their theories warrant," substituting science for religion.

the correction business. And the scientists in correction, like the religionists, have not hesitated to lace their rehabilitative techniques with heavy doses of imprisonment and deprivation. The Quakers called it "penitence"; the psychologists call it "negative reinforcement." My concern is that we will give the scientists more power than the religionists every had and more than their theories warrant.

(33) **The Criminal Pays the Victim.** The theories of both these well-intended groups are fundamentally akin. Both make a man his own prison. The intention is to help the offender become happy and whole again, but in practice these theories put too much power over inmates in the hands of fallible prison administrators. I believe the only power society should have in forcing an individual to change his behavior is to require each criminal to pay for what he has done wrong. That is why I favor a program that would require a thief to pay back what he steals, to force a mugger to make adequate restitution to the person he assaults. In many cases this can be done outside prison; in most cases it cannot be done inside prison. Thus, prisons really are useful only for the small minority who need to be sequestered from society. Even treatment-oriented prisons create more behavior problems than they cure.

Paragraph 33 turns back to *proof* of Goldfarb's argument in favor of a compensatory model (outlined in paragraphs 8 and 9).

(34) A few years ago, when I visited the sprawling new Federal Institution for young offenders in Morgantown, West Virginia, I was impressed by the physical layout, the program and the staff. The institution's country setting adds to its air of informality and openness. The behavior-modification programs seemed sensible. There was lots of rapping, and some attempt to promote contacts with the local community. But I wondered what would happen when the inmates returned

Paragraphs 34–36 are further *refutation*. Goldfarb uses the *example* of the institution at Morgantown and again calls on expert *testimony,* in the form of a quotation from a psychiatrist at the institution. A further *example* is drawn from the prison system in Finland.

to the ghettos they came from, where a man often gets positive reinforcement for committing crimes.

(35) At dinner after my tour, I talked about this problem with Douglas Skelton, a psychiatrist there. I asked whether he thought psychiatrists made a big difference in prisons. He said, "No. We spend 99 percent of our time dealing with institution-induced anxieties, and never get to the problems that got the guy into prison in the first place." That is why I favor tearing down most prison walls.

(36) When I visited prisons in Finland, I met with criminologists who had recently completed a survey comparing recidivism rates of men in prisons with those of men in open labor camps. The rates were about the same for both groups. I asked the Finns if they felt their survey was a blow to the idea of camps instead of prisons, since they could not show that the open camps were more effective in reforming offenders. The Finns said they thought their results were proof that the camps should be used. "If the results are not worse," they argued, "and costs are less, and the technique is more humane, the camps must be better."

(37) **Reform Is Passé.** We should consider open prison camps, or their urban counterparts, the halfway houses. To the general public, however, the idea of tearing down prison walls is scary. It looses images of murderers and rapists wreaking havoc across the land. But those images often are irrational. And, in fact, these alternatives to prison are safe and economical.

(38) "The long history of 'prison reform' is over," writes penologist Robert Martinson. "On the whole, the prisons have played out their allotted role. They cannot be reformed and must gradually be torn down. But let us give up the comforting myth that the remaining fa-

Paragraphs 37–41 are the *conclusion.*

cilities (and they will be prisons) can be changed into hospitals.

(39) "Prisons will be small and humane; anything else is treason to the human spirit. We shall be cleansed of the foreign element of forced treatment with its totalitarian overtones. Officials will no longer be asked to do what they cannot do, and they will be relieved of the temptation to do what should not be done.

(40) "Crime arises from social causes and can be controlled and reduced (but not eliminated) through social action. The myth of correctional treatment is now the main obstacle to progress: it has become the last line of defense of the prison system; it prevents the sound use of resources to balance public protection and inmate rights; and it diverts energy away from defending democracy through widening opportunity. It is time to awake from the dream."

(41) Now, when the public seems ready for correctional reform, it is especially important to move carefully. Neither the get-tough approach nor the treatment-in-prison approach will make our correctional system work. For all the fear that it generates, for all the difficulties that it presents, I still believe we should seriously consider tearing down most prison walls, and deinstitutionalizing our whole correctional system.

Finally: A Critique

Use the model of the classical persuasive speech to generate a critique of Goldfarb's argument. Here is that model again:

1. Introduction. Does the beginning interest the reader? (Why or why not?) Does Goldfarb establish his reliability? (How?)

2. Explanation of the case. Does Goldfarb set forth his purpose adequately? (Explain.)

3. Outline of the argument. Is the argument well organized? (Explain.) Is it logically developed? (Explain.)

4. Proof. Does Goldfarb prove his case? Are you satisfied with his argument? What are its strengths and weaknesses?

5. Refutation. Does Goldfarb succeed in refuting counterarguments? (Explain.)

6. Conclusion. Are all the loose ends tied up? Is the argument conclusive? (Explain).)

Discussion and Activities

The Goal of Persuasion

Read the following paragraph; then, from your own experience, cite examples of the kinds of discord that the author outlines:

> We seek universal communication, but we know that discourse will not yet free us from discord. Customarily, two contrary arguments cannot exist in the same space at the same time. Typically, one will subside. Sometimes, both will persist, and he who holds both will be rendered inactive for his inability to choose and act. Less commonly, both will persist, and he who holds both will remain active, but at the cost of cynicism or sadness engendered by his pursuit of one option in the presence of an attractive or virtuous opposite. Less commonly still, both will persist, and he who holds both may yet act, marveling at the copiousness of creation.[9]

The Persuader

1. In Los Angeles, TV pitchmen who sell used cars are called "fender-benders." One of the greatest of the fender-benders always introduces himself this way: "Hi! I'm Cal Worthington, and this is my dog Spot." The dog always turns out to be a lion, a bear, an elephant, or some such. Why do you think that, as a persuader, Worthington uses this device?
2. Classical rhetoricians said that the arguer must demonstrate three characteristics in order to be convincing: good sense, good will, and good moral character. These characteristics might be called universals, for an audience will not be persuaded if it feels that the arguer is stupid, malicious, or immoral. The ads in magazines and newspapers use various means of establishing their apparent good sense, good will, and good moral character. Find examples of such attempts, bring them to class, and discuss whether or not they are successful and why.

The Substance of the Argument

Which of the following propositions are arguable, and which are not? Why? (Remember that an arguable proposition must have definition and uncertainty.)

(a) Drivers should not be forced by law to wear seat belts.
(b) The prices of many commodities are too high.

[9]Jim W. Corder, *Uses of Rhetoric* (New York: J. B. Lippincott, 1971), p. 207.

(c) The incidence of lung cancer would decline if no one smoked cigarettes.

(d) The United States should not increase its nuclear capability beyond the present level.

(e) All college and university students should be required to gain a knowledge of computer programming.

(f) King Henry VIII died in 1974.

Tone

Write a one-paragraph argument for or against requiring a course in freshman English of all college students, striving as you write to be objective and neutral in tone. Then rewrite the paragraph so that it is, first, humorous; second, bitter; third, raving and ranting.

Formal Logic

Analyze the validity or invalidity of the following logical chains (which are taken from *An Introduction to Logic,* by Morris R. Cohen and Ernest Nagel):

(a) A mother is said to have cautioned her son against entering politics, "For if you tell the truth, men will hate you; if you tell lies, God will hate you. But you must either tell the truth or tell lies. Therefore, either men or God will hate you." But the son replied: "If I tell the truth, God will love me; if I tell lies, men will love me. But I must either tell the truth or tell lies. Therefore, either men or God will love me."

(b) All musicians are proud.
All Scots are musicians.
Some Scots are not proud.

(c) All musicians are proud.
Some Scots are not proud.
Some Scots are not musicians.

(d) Some Orientals are polite.
All Orientals are shrewd.
Some shrewd people are polite.

(e) Some professors are not married.
All saints are married.
Some saints are not professors.

(f) All dictatorships are undemocratic.
All undemocratic governments are unstable.
All unstable governments are cruel.
All cruel governments are objects of hate.
All dictatorships are objects of hate.

(g) All sacred things are protected by the state.
All property is sacred.
All trade monopolies are property.
All steel industries are trade monopolies.
All steel industries are protected by the state.

(h) All Parisians are Frenchmen.
No Bostonians are Parisians.
No Bostonians are Frenchmen.

Deduction and Induction

In the form of a valid syllogism, state a deductive argument. On the basis of this syllogism, outline a theme that you might write in order to persuade an audience to accept your premises. (If the audience can be persuaded to accept your premises, then they must grant your conclusion.) Now rearrange your outline into inductive form.

Fallacies

Read the following essay, and discuss what you learn about logic from it.

Love Is a Fallacy[10]

Max Shulman

Charles Lamb, as merry and enterprising a fellow as you will meet in a month of Sundays, unfettered the informal essay with his memorable *Old China* and *Dream Children*. There follows an informal essay that ventures even beyond Lamb's frontier. Indeed, "informal" may not be quite the right word to describe this essay; "limp" or "flaccid" or possibly "spongy" are perhaps more appropriate.

Vague though its category, it is without doubt an essay. It develops an argument; it cites instances; it reaches a conclusion. Could Carlyle do more? Could Ruskin?

Read, then, the following essay which undertakes to demonstrate that logic, far from being a dry, pedantic discipline, is a living, breathing thing, full of beauty, passion, and trauma.

—Author's Note

Cool was I and logical. Keen, calculating, perspicacious, acute and astute—I was all of these. My brain was as powerful as a dynamo, as precise as a chemist's scales, as penetrating as a scalpel. And—think of it!—I was only eighteen.

It is not often that one so young has such a giant intellect. Take, for example, Petey Burch, my roommate at the University of Minnesota. Same age, same background, but dumb as an ox. A nice enough fellow, you understand, but nothing upstairs. Emotional type. Unstable. Impressionable. Worst of all, a faddist. Fads, I submit, are the very negation of reason. To be swept up in every new craze that comes along, to surrender yourself to idiocy just because everybody else is doing it—this, to me, is the acme of mindlessness. Not, however, to Petey.

One afternoon I found Petey lying on his bed with an expression of such distress on his face that I immediately diagnosed appendicitis. "Don't move," I said. "Don't take a laxative. I'll get a doctor."

"Raccoon," he mumbled thickly.

"Raccoon?" I said, pausing in my flight.

"I want a raccoon coat," he wailed.

I perceived that his trouble was not physical, but mental. "Why do you want a raccoon coat?"

[10]Max Shulman, "Love Is a Fallacy," *The Many Loves of Dobie Gillis* (Garden City, N.Y.: Doubleday, 1953). Copyright 1951 by Max Shulman. Reprinted by permission of Harold Matson Company, Inc.

"I should have known it," he cried, pounding his temples. "I should have known they'd come back when the Charleston came back. Like a fool I spent all my money for textbooks, and now I can't get a raccoon coat."

"Can you mean," I said incredulously, "that people are actually wearing racoon coats again?"

"All the Big Men on Campus are wearing them. Where've you been?"

"In the library," I said, naming a place not frequented by Big Men on Campus.

He leaped from the bed and paced the room. "I've got to have a raccoon coat," he said passionately. "I've got to!"

"Petey, why? Look at it rationally. Raccoon coats are unsanitary. They shed. They smell bad. They weigh too much. They're unsightly. They—"

"You don't understand." he interrupted impatiently. "It's the thing to do. Don't you want to be in the swim?"

"No," I said truthfully.

"Well, I do," he declared. "I'd give anything for a raccoon coat. Anything!"

My brain, that precision instrument, slipped into high gear. "Anything?" I asked, looking at him narrowly.

"Anything," he affirmed in ringing tones.

I stroked my chin thoughtfully. It so happened that I knew where to get my hands on a raccoon coat. My father had had one in his undergraduate days; it lay now in a trunk in the attic back home. It also happened that Petey had something I wanted. He didn't *have* it exactly, but at least he had first rights on it. I refer to this girl, Polly Espy.

I had long coveted Polly Espy. Let me emphasize that my desire for this young woman was not emotional in nature. She was, to be sure, a girl who excited the emotions, but I was not one to let my heart rule my head. I wanted Polly for a shrewdly calculated, entirely cerebral reason.

I was a freshman in law school. In a few years I would be out in practice. I was well aware of the importance of the right kind of wife in furthering a lawyer's career. The successful lawyers I had observed were, almost without exception, married to beautiful, gracious, intelligent women. With one omission, Polly fitted these specifications perfectly.

Beautiful she was. She was not yet of pin-up proportions, but I felt sure that time would supply the lack. She already had the makings.

Gracious she was. By gracious I mean full of graces. She had an erectness of carriage, an ease of bearing, a poise that clearly indicated the best of breeding. At table her manners were exquisite. I had seen her at the Kozy Kampus Korner eating the specialty of the house—a sandwich that contained scraps of pot roast, gravy, chopped nuts, and a dipper of sauerkraut—without even getting her fingers moist.

Intelligent she was not. In fact, she veered in the opposite direction. But I believed that under my guidance she would smarten up. At any rate, it was worth a try. It is, after all, easier to make a beautiful dumb girl smart than to make an ugly smart girl beautiful.

"Petey," I said, "are you in love with Polly Espy?"

"I think she's a keen kid," he replied, "but I don't know if you'd call it love. Why?"

"Do you," I asked, "have any kind of formal arrangement with her? I mean are you going steady or anything like that?"

"No. We see each other quite a bit, but we both have other dates. Why?"

"Is there," I asked, "any other man for whom she has a particular fondness?"

"Not that I know of. Why?"

I nodded with satisfaction. "In other words, if you were out of the picture, the field would be open. Is that right?"

"I guess so. What are you getting at?"

"Nothing, nothing," I said innocently, and took my suitcase out of the closet.

"Where are you going?" asked Petey.

"Home for the weekend." I threw a few things into the bag.

"Listen," he said, clutching my arm eagerly, "while you're home, you couldn't get some money from your old man, could you, and lend it to me so I can buy a raccoon coat?"

"I may do better than that," I said with a mysterious wink and closed my bag and left.

"Look," I said to Petey when I got back Monday morning. I threw open the suitcase and revealed the huge, hairy, gamy object that my father had worn in his Stutz Bearcat in 1925.

"Holy Toledo!" said Petey reverently. He plunged his hands into the raccoon coat and then his face. "Holy Toledo!" he repeated fifteen or twenty times.

"Would you like it?" I asked.

"Oh yes!" he cried, clutching the greasy pelt to him. Then a canny look came into his eyes. "What do you want for it?"

"Your girl," I said, mincing no words.

"Polly?" he said in a horrified whisper. "You want Polly?"

"That's right."

He flung the coat from him. "Never," he said stoutly.

I shrugged. "Okay. If you don't want to be in the swim, I guess it's your business."

I sat down in a chair and pretended to read a book, but out of the corner of my eye I kept watching Petey. He was a torn man. First he looked at the coat with the expression of a waif at a bakery window. Then he turned away and set his jaw resolutely. Then he looked back at the coat, with even more longing in his face. Then he turned away, but with not so much resolution this time. Back and forth his head swiveled, desire waxing, resolution waning. Finally he didn't turn away at all; he just stood and stared with mad lust at the coat.

"It isn't as though I was in love with Polly," he said thickly. "Or going steady or anything like that."

"That's right," I murmured.

"What's Polly to me, or me to Polly?"

"Not a thing," said I.

"It's just been a casual kick—just a few laughs, that's all."

"Try on the coat," said I.

He complied. The coat bunched high over his ears and dropped all the way down to his shoe tops. He looked like a mound of dead raccoons. "Fits fine," he said happily.

I rose from my chair. "Is it a deal?" I asked, extending my hand.

He swallowed. "It's a deal," he said and shook my hand.

I had my first date with Polly the following evening. This was in the nature of a survey; I wanted to find out just how much work I had to do to get her mind up to the standard I required. I took her first to dinner. "Gee, that was a delish dinner," she said as we left the restaurant. Then I took her to a movie. "Gee, that was a marvy movie," she said as we left the theater. And then I took her home. "Gee, I had a sensaysh time," she said as she bade me good night.

I went back to my room with a heavy heart. I had gravely underestimated the size of my task. This girl's lack of information was terrifying. Nor would it be enough merely to supply her with information. First she had to be taught to *think*. This loomed as a project of no small dimension, and at first I was tempted to give her back to Petey. But then I got to thinking about her abundant physical charms and about the way she entered a room and the way she handled a knife and fork, and I decided to make an effort.

I went about it, as in all things, systematically. I gave her a course in logic. It happened that I, as a law student, was taking a course in logic myself, so I had all the facts at my finger tips. "Polly," I said to her when I picked her up on our next date, "tonight we are going over to the Knoll and talk."

"Oo, terrif," she replied. One thing I will say for this girl: you would go far to find another so agreeable.

We went to the Knoll, the campus trysting place, and we sat down under an old oak, and she looked at me expectantly. "What are we going to talk about?" she asked.

"Logic."

She thought this over for a minute and decided she liked it. "Magnif," she said.

"Logic," I said, clearing my throat, "is the science of thinking. Before we can think correctly, we must first learn to recognize the common fallacies of logic. These we will take up tonight."

"Wow-dow!" she cried, clapping her hands delightedly.

I winced, but went bravely on. "First let us examine the fallacy called Dicto Simpliciter."

"By all means," she urged, batting her lashes eagerly.

"Dicto Simpliciter means an argument based on an unqualified generalization. For example: Exercise is good. Therefore everybody should exercise."

"I agree," said Polly earnestly. "I mean exercise is wonderful. I mean it builds the body and everything."

"Polly," I said gently, "the argument is a fallacy. *Exercise is good* is an unqualifed generalization. For instance, if you have heart disease, exercise is bad, not good. Many people are ordered by their doctors *not* to exercise. You must *qualify* the generalization. You must say exercise is *usually* good, or exercise is good for *most people.* Otherwise you have committed a Dicto Simpliciter. Do you see?"

"No," she confessed. "But this is marvy. Do more! Do more!"

"It will be better if you stop tugging at my sleeve," I told her, and when she desisted, I continued. "Next we take up a fallacy called Hasty Generalization. Listen carefully: You can't speak French. I can't speak French. Petey Burch can't speak French. I must therefore conclude that nobody at the University of Minnesota can speak French."

"Really?" said Polly, amazed. "Nobody?"

I hid my exasperation. "Polly, it's a fallacy. The generalization is reached too hastily. There are too few instances to support such a conclusion."

"Know any more fallacies?" she asked breathlessly. "This is more fun than dancing even."

I fought off a wave of despair. I was getting nowhere with this girl, absolutely nowhere. Still, I am nothing if not persistent. I continued, "Next comes Post Hoc. Listen to this: Let's not take Bill on our picnic. Every time we take him out with us, it rains."

"I know somebody just like that," she exclaimed. "A girl back home—Eula Becker, her name is. It never fails. Every single time we take her on a picnic—"

"Polly," I said sharply, "it's a fallacy. Eula Becker doesn't *cause* the rain. She has no connection with the rain. You are guilty of Post Hoc if you blame Eula Becker."

"I'll never do it again." she promised contritely. "Are you mad at me?"

I sighed deeply. "No, Polly, I'm not mad."

"Then tell me some more fallacies."

"All right. Let's try Contradictory Premises."

"Yes, let's," she chirped, blinking her eyes happily.

I frowned, but plunged ahead. "Here's an example of Contradictory Premises: If God can do anything, can He make a stone so heavy that He won't be able to lift it?"

"Of course," she replied promptly.

"But if He can do anything, He can lift the stone," I pointed out.

"Yeah," she said thoughtfully. "Well, then I guess He can't make the stone."

"But He can do anything," I reminded her.

She scratched her pretty, empty head. "I'm all confused," she admitted.

"Of course you are. Because when the premises of an argument contradict each other, there can be no argument. If there is an irresistible force, there can be no immovable object. If there is an immovable object, there can be no irresistible force. Get it?"

"Tell me more of this keen stuff," she said eagerly.

I consulted my watch. "I think we'd better call it a night. I'll take you home now, and you go over all the things you've learned. We'll have another session tomorrow night."

I deposited her at the girls' dormitory, where she assured me that she had had a perfectly terrif evening, and I went glumly home to my room. Petey lay snoring in his bed, the raccoon coat huddled like a great hairy beast at his feet. For a moment I considered waking him and telling him that he could have his girl back. It seemed clear that my project was doomed to failure. The girl simply had a logic-proof head.

But then I reconsidered. I had wasted one evening; I might as well waste another. Who knew? Maybe somewhere in the extinct crater of her mind, a few embers still smoldered. Maybe somehow I could fan them into flame. Admittedly, it was not a prospect fraught with hope, but I decided to give it one more try.

Seated under the oak the next evening I said, "Our first fallacy tonight is Ad Misericordiam."

She quivered with delight.

"Listen closely," I said. "A man applies for a job. When the boss asks him what his qualifications are, he replies that he has a wife and six children at home, the wife is a helpless cripple, the children have nothing to eat, no clothes to wear, no shoes on their feet, there are no beds in the house, no coal in the cellar, and winter is coming."

A tear rolled down each of Polly's pink cheeks. "Oh, this is awful, awful," she sobbed.

"Yes, it's awful," I agreed, "but it's no argument. The man never answered the boss's question about his qualifications. Instead he appealed to the boss's sympathy. He committed the fallacy of Ad Misericordiam. Do you understand?"

"Have you got a handkerchief?" she blubbered.

I handed her a handkerchief and tried to keep from screaming while she wiped her eyes. "Next," I said in a carefully controlled tone, "we will discuss False Analogy. Here is an example: Students should be allowed to look at their textbooks during examinations. After all, surgeons have X-rays to guide them during an operation, lawyers have briefs to guide them during a trial, carpenters have blueprints to guide them when they are building a house. Why, then, shouldn't students be allowed to look at their textbooks during an examination?"

"There now," she said enthusiastically, "is the most marvy idea I've heard in years."

"Polly," I said testily, "the argument is all wrong. Doctors, lawyers, and carpenters aren't taking a test to see how much they have learned, but students are. The situations are altogether different, and you can't make an analogy between them."

"I still think it's a good idea," said Polly.

"Nuts," I muttered. Doggedly I pressed on. "Next we'll try Hypothesis Contrary to Fact."

"Sounds yummy," was Polly's reaction.

"Listen: If Madame Curie had not happened to leave a photographic plate in a drawer with a chunk of pitchblende, the world today would not know about radium."

"True, true," said Polly, nodding her head. "Did you see the movie? Oh, it just knocked me out. That Walter Pidgeon is so dreamy. I mean he fractures me."

"If you can forget Mr. Pidgeon for a moment," I said coldly, "I would like to point out that the statement is a fallacy. Maybe Madame Curie would have discovered radium at some later date. Maybe somebody else would have discovered it. Maybe any number of things would have happened. You can't start with a hypothesis that is not true and then draw any supportable conclusions from it."

"They ought to put Walter Pidgeon in more pictures," said Polly. "I hardly ever see him any more."

One more chance, I decided. But just one more. There is a limit to what flesh and blood can bear. "The next fallacy is called Poisoning the Well."

"How cute." she gurgled.

"Two men are having a debate. The first one gets up and says, 'My opponent is a notorious liar. You can't believe a word that he is going to say.' . . . Now, Polly, think. Think hard. What's wrong?"

I watched her closely as she knit her creamy brow in concentration. Suddenly a glimmer of intelligence—the first I had seen—came into her eyes. "It's not fair," she said with indignation. "It's not a bit fair. What chance has the second man got if the first man calls him a liar before he even begins talking?"

"Right!" I cried exultantly. "One hundred per cent right. It's not fair. The first man has *poisoned the well* before anybody could drink from it. He has hamstrung his opponent before he could even start. . . . Polly, I'm proud of you."

"Pshaw," she murmured, blushing with pleasure.

"You see, my dear, these things aren't so hard. All you have to do is concentrate. Think—examine—evaluate. Come now, let's review everything we have learned."

"Fire away," she said with an airy wave of her hand.

Heartened by the knowledge that Polly was not altogether a cretin, I began a long, patient review of all I had told her. Over and over and over again I cited instances, pointed out flaws, kept hammering away without letup. It was like digging a tunnel. At first everything was work, sweat, and darkness. I had no idea when I would reach the light, or even *if* I would. But I persisted. I pounded and clawed and scraped, and finally I was rewarded. I saw a chink of light. And then the chink got bigger and the sun came pouring in and all was bright.

Five grueling nights this took, but it was worth it. I had made a logician out of Polly; I had taught her to think. My job was done. She was worthy of me at last. She was a fit wife for me, a proper hostess for my many mansions, a suitable mother for my well-heeled children.

It must not be thought that I was without love for this girl. Quite the contrary. Just as Pygmalion loved the perfect woman he had fashioned, so I loved mine. I determined to acquaint her with my feelings at our very next meeting. The time had come to change our relationship from academic to romantic.

"Polly," I said when next we sat beneath our oak, "tonight we will not discuss fallacies."

"Aw, gee," she said, disappointed.

"My dear," I said, favoring her with a smile, "we have now spent five evenings together. We have gotten along splendidly. It is clear that we are well matched."

"Hasty Generalization," said Polly brightly.

"I beg your pardon," said I.

"Hasty Generalization," she repeated. "How can you say that we are well matched on the basis of only five dates?"

I chuckled with amusement. The dear child had learned her lessons well. "My dear," I said, patting her hand in a tolerant manner, "five dates is plenty. After all, you don't have to eat a whole cake to know that it's good."

"False Analogy," said Polly promptly. "I'm not a cake. I'm a girl." I chuckled with somewhat less amusement. The dear child had learned her lessons perhaps too well. I decided to change tactics. Obviously the best approach was a simple, strong, direct declaration of love. I paused for a moment while my massive brain chose the proper words. Then I began:

"Polly, I love you. You are the whole world to me, and the moon and the stars and the constellations of outer space. Please, my darling, say that you will go steady with me, for if you will not, life will be meaningless. I will languish. I will refuse my meals. I will wander the face of the earth, a shambling, hollow-eyed hulk."

There I thought, folding my arms, that ought to do it.

"Ad Misericordiam," said Polly.

I ground my teeth. I was not Pygmalion; I was Frankenstein, and my monster had me by the throat. Frantically I fought back the tide of panic surging through me. At all costs I had to keep cool.

"Well, Polly," I said, forcing a smile, "you have certainly learned your fallacies."

"You're darn right," she said with a vigorous nod.

"And who taught them to you, Polly?"

"You did."

"That's right. So you do owe me something, don't you, my dear? If I hadn't come along you never would have learned about fallacies."

"Hypothesis Contrary to Fact," she said instantly.

I dashed perspiration from my brow. "Polly," I croaked, "you mustn't take all these things so literally. I mean this is just classroom stuff. You know that the things you learn in school don't have anything to do with life."

"Dicto Simpliciter," she said, wagging her finger at me playfully.

That did it. I leaped to my feet, bellowing like a bull. "Will you or will you not go steady with me?"

"I will not," she replied.

"Why not?" I demanded.

"Because this afternoon I promised Petey Burch I would go steady with him."

I reeled back, overcome with the infamy of it. After he promised, after he made a deal, after he shook my hand! "The rat!" I shrieked, kicking up great chunks of turf. "You can't go with him, Polly. He's a liar. He's a cheat. He's a rat."

"Poisoning the Well," said Polly, "and stop shouting. I think shouting must be a fallacy too."

With an immense effort of will, I modulated my voice. "All right," I said. "You're a logician. Let's look at this thing logically. How could you choose Petey Burch over me? Look at me—a brilliant student, a tremendous intellectual, a man with an assured future. Look at Petey—a knothead, a jitterbug, a guy who'll never know where his next meal is coming from. Can you give me one logical reason why you should go steady with Petey Burch?"

"I certainly can," declared Polly. "He's got a raccoon coat."

Analogy

1. In your own reading, look for examples of analogies, both valid and false. Bring several of them to class for discussion.
2. In one paragraph, draw an analogy between the novel as an art form and the motion picture. In a second paragraph, extend that analogy until it becomes invalid.

The Audience

1. Write two or three paragraphs characterizing the universal audience as you see it.
2. Find a few examples of brief pieces that were obviously written for specialized audiences. What are the "specialized" characteristics of these pieces?

Structure as Heuristic

Write a piece of persuasion that follows the six-part classical organization: (1) introduction, (2) explanation of the case under discussion, (3) outline of the points, or steps, in the argument, (4) proof of the case, (5) refutation of opposing arguments, (6) conclusion.

Be prepared to say whether the organizational scheme helped or hindered you and why.

PART TWO
Style

The Writer's Language

Part Two of *The Contemporary Writer* will deal in general with the concept of language and in particular with matters of style.

If you think about it, you'll realize a simple fact about the process of using language: it must somehow involve permeating structures with meaning. Unless the writer has mastery of a wide range of the structural resources of the language, he or she is severely handicapped.

In this section of *The Contemporary Writer,* then, we will be discussing a number of interesting theoretical matters concerning language, and these are worth knowing simply because humans are the talking (or language-using) animals. But the section will also be highly practical, in that its primary aim is to help you increase your ability to use all the structural resources of the language.

As will become obvious, no one ever has reached or ever will reach the ultimate in the ability to use language. Everyone can improve endlessly. Therefore, regardless of how well you write at present, you should find this section of the book useful.

Summary of the Chapter

Why study language? A great many students come into college writing classes with false notions about the nature of language and grammar. These notions stand in the way of learning to use the language with the utmost efficiency and effectiveness. Therefore, it is a good idea to begin a discussion of writing style by setting the record straight, by clearing away preconceptions and misconceptions that might stand in your way.

Furthermore, modern theories of language are fascinating in and of themselves, and the educated person ought to know something about them. Linguistics (the scientific study of language) has become one of the glamor sciences, along with physics and microbiology.

Finally, some of the concepts explained in this chapter are important for the understanding and appreciation of materials that you have already encountered in *The Contemporary Writer.*

What is the nature of language? Only human beings can talk. Other animals have languages of sorts, but these languages differ both qualitatively and quantitatively from human language.

Language behavior is intricately and rigidly patterned. It is not random. But the native speaker automatically and intuitively knows these patterns and can produce them without pondering.

Language is arbitrary. There is no inherent connection between a word and the thing it names. Language is not logical or illogical; it is alogical. Of course, the messages that it carries can be either logical or illogical.

What is grammar? A grammar of a language is a description of that language. It separates utterances that native speakers would be likely to produce from those that would be unlikely to occur. The more accurately a grammar describes what actually exists in the language, the better that grammar is.

It is impossible that language could be learned by imitation; the human brain must have within itself the latent potential of generating language.

The English sentence is propositional in nature. For instance, **Ducks like popcorn** is a proposition in which two nouns, **ducks** and **popcorn,** stand in relation to each other and to a predicate, **like.** The language provides the means of combining more than one proposition into a sentence: **Ducks like popcorn** and **Ducks swim on the lake** become **Ducks [that swim on the lake] like popcorn.** This combining capacity is one of the most powerful devices of language and one of the most important for the student of writing.

What is the difference between competence and performance? For a native speaker competence in the language is always greater than performance. Roughly, this means the following: all of us are able to understand speaking and writing that we ourselves would not be able to produce. This ability to understand is *competence.* The ability to produce language sequences in speaking or writing is *performance.* The goal of students of writing is to increase their performance.

Meaning and structure. Deep structure is the meaning that is conveyed by written or spoken sequences, which are the *surface structure.* The study of deep structure is, therefore, an inquiry into the way in which sentences carry meaning.

How does language mean? Individual sounds carry meaning, that is why there is a difference in meaning between **fat** and **vat.** Individual words and parts of words carry meaning, that is why there is a difference in meaning between **loyal** and **disloyal.** Structures carry meaning; that is why there is a difference in meaning between **Dog bites man** and **Man bites dog.** But meaning is also influenced by context, the larger language environment in which a sequence occurs. Finally, meaning comes about at the encounter between language and the human brain.

What is usage and how does it relate to grammar? Grammar describes language as it is and speculates about the way in which the brain generates sequences in the language. Therefore, the grammarian as a grammarian is just as interested in **Harry ain't got no car** as he is **Harry has no car** or **Harry doesn't have a car.** *Usage considers what is appropriate for a given subject at a given time and for a given audience. Usage and grammar should not be confused.*

What are the dynamics of language change? Languages continually change. They change their vocabulary, adding new words and dropping old ones. For example, English has almost completely eliminated inflections, whereby different meanings are signaled by different forms of the same word. Permissible structure also changes. But in the context of this book, the most interesting language changes are those that involve the word-stock, the addition of new words to the language.

Languages apparently do not become better or worse in any sense. They simply change. This is an important point.

What are dialects? Everyone speaks a dialect, either standard or some other. Standard is, generally speaking, the dialect that one hears national newscasters speak. Dialect differences arise primarily because of cultural or geographical isolation, but no dialect is in any fundamental sense better or worse than any other dialect. However, some dialects carry prestige while others do not. It is suggested that any normal speaker of the language is quite capable of mastering the niceties of any dialect, but it is also suggested that diversity of dialects is a cultural advantage for the nation and that perhaps we should attempt to change faulty attitudes toward dialects rather than the dialects themselves.

Why Study Language?

There are three very good reasons for including in a book about writing a nontechnical discussion of some facts and theories about language.

First, one of the great problems among users of language is attitude. Many students who have had problems with writing in the past think that mastering grammar will make them into superb writiers, but many of these same students also think that they will never be able to master grammar. This chapter, I hope, will convince you—if you need convincing—that (1) knowledge of the grammar of the language (in the traditional sense, at least) has nothing to do with anyone's ability to write, and (2) every speaker of the language has, essentially, mastered its complete grammar. In sum, studying grammar will not affect *your ability to write.* I won't attempt to prove that statement now, for the materials in the chapter will, I hope, make the truth of it self-evident.

So the first reason for studying language is to overcome some wrongheaded and destructive notions that prevent students from realizing their full potential as writers.

Second, modern linguistics (as the study of language is called) is simply a fascinating field, in many ways one of the most glamorous of the sciences. For instance, *Time* (February 16, 1968) has reported:

> Fashions in academe may be a bit more durable than those of Paris couturiers, but, like hemlines, the popularity of disciplines rises and falls. Much in vogue at the moment, right up there with particle physics and computer technology, is the study of linguistics. Its new popularity, contends Princeton Linguist William Moulton, stems from a growing recognition that it is "the most scientific of the humanities and the most humanistic of the sciences."

So gaining some familiarity with modern work in linguistics—with facts and theories concerning the nature of language—is justifiable, if on no other basis than that of one's obligation to general education: the educated person ought to know a little about linguistics. A general understanding of at least the assumptions of the field is useful, in that so many current social problems involve linguistic considerations—for instance, the reading crisis and the inequities that result from the varieties of dialects in the United States. (The problem of dialects will be explored later in this chapter.)

Finally, it will be useful for you to have a grasp of the linguistic principles that underlie much of this book. For instance, Chapter 11, on sentences, will be much easier for you if you understand what is meant by *deep structure* and *surface structure*.

What Is the Nature of Language?

In one sense, a great many species—bees, apes, dolphins, geese—have a language; that is, they communicate. But in another, stricter sense, only human beings have language. Bees execute dances to indicate distances to sources of honey to their hivemates; the fact that a hunter can call geese to within shooting range indicates that they have some system of communication; at the University of Nevada, the University of California at Santa Barbara, and elsewhere, studies are being made of the ability of chimpanzees to acquire human language. But in spite of the current excitement about dolphin language and "articulate apes," it is safe to say that (1) animal languages differ from human languages along two axes, that of quantity and that of quality, and (2) even if animals such as chimpanzees can learn to manipulate human languages, this manipulation will be so limited as to show a significant qualitative difference between the way the chimpanzee can "talk" and the way a five-year-old child can manipulate language. That is, language in the human sense is species-specific. It is meaningless to say that animals can talk, unless we use **talk** in a loose, metaphorical sense.

Current theory posits that the human brain contains speech mechanisms that are found in the brains of no other animals, even though the human "language centers" are but dimly understood at the present time.

But what really concerns us here is language—the instrument that all of us use with great fluency and ease—not highly theoretical questions about whether or not other animals have the capability of learning human language.

Before we get down to nuts and bolts, a word about your knowledge of language and an introduction to linguistics. In a real sense, you already "know" almost everything that will be discussed in this chapter. That is, you have a more or less complete mastery of the English language; if you did not have that mastery, you would have been unable to understand what you have been reading so far, and you would not be able to carry on conversations, answer questions, and so on. But your very closeness to the language has blinded you to some of its obvious characteristics. In one sense, linguistics can be characterized as a science that makes apparent what we already know intuitively.

Language Is Patterned Behavior

So, to the first principle: *Language behavior is intricately and rigidly patterned.*

These two sentences are exact opposites in meaning: **The man killed the king** and **The king killed the man.** The only difference between them is word order—patterning. But we would accept both of them as English sentences. However, we would not accept the following sequence as an English sentence:

1 *The killed man king the.

(Notice the asterisk. Whenever we put it before a series of words, we are indicating that we think that that series just isn't part of the normal English language.) In fact, ***The killed man king the** might puzzle us for a moment, might be almost meaningless until we arranged the words into one of their permissible sequences. The following is a slightly different situation:

2 *Over the fence to the cow some hay I threw.

No doubt about the meaning—and yet the sequence seems strange, un-English. We would demand

3 I threw some hay over the fence to the cow.

And notice that the following creates a different meaning from 3:

4 I threw some hay to the cow over the fence.

In **3**, it is the hay that *is going* over the fence; in **4**, the cow is over the fence. (Another way of putting this is to say that **over the fence** modifies **hay** in the one and **the cow** in the other.)

It is interesting to note that an explanation of our failure to accept **2** would take some little time and ingenuity, as well as grammatical sophistication. But we automatically, intuitively, immediately know what is English and what is un-English, without any reflection whatsoever. That is, *all of us have an extremely sophisticated knowledge of the language—* and that's an important point.

Take the following sequence:

5   *Swedish a girl young beautiful

If this sequence is to appear in an English sentence, it must be rearranged in one way and one way only:

6   **A beautiful young Swedish girl** milked a cow.

Another rearrangement is possible if a comma is added:

7   **A young, beautiful Swedish girl** milked a cow.

Again, describing the specific rules that dictated the arrangement of the series would be difficult, but somehow all of us must know those rules, else we could not arrange the series properly.

Questions

The interrogative counterpart of

8   Herbert can run twenty-six miles.

is

9   Can Herbert run twenty-six miles?

It is very easy to explain how **8** was made into a question: The word **can** was moved to the front of the sentence. Similarly, the interrogative counterpart of

10   George is smoking a cigar.

is

11   Is George smoking a cigar?

Another pair:

12   Norma has gone to the store.

13   Has Norma gone to the store?

It seems, then, that for declarative sentences with a single noun as the subject, we could state an easy rule for making the interrogative—that is, it seems that we could easily describe in specific terms an operation that we perform often, automatically and without thought. The rule might be something like this: *To form the interrogative counterpart of a declarative sentence in which the subject is a single noun, put the second element of that sentence in front of the noun subject.* That rule does indeed cover all the sentences that we have looked at so far. But what about these sentences?

14 Walter jogs.

15 Girls drink burgundy.

Following our rule, the interrogative counterparts would be

16 *Jogs Walter?

17 *Drink girls burgundy?

when, in fact, we know that the actual interrogative counterparts are

18 Does Walter jog?

19 Do girls drink burgundy?

Therefore, in order to account for sentences like **14** and **15**, we would need to expand our rule, thus: *To form the interrogative counterpart of a declarative sentence in which the subject is a single noun, put the second element of that sentence in front of the noun subject, but if the second element is a transitive or intransitive verb, leave the second element where it is, and put does or do before the noun subject.*

Our rule is obviously on the verge of becoming unmanageable. It is now so complicated that we have difficulty understanding it, and it is far from being complete if we want it to explain all kinds of interrogatives. Yet, to repeat an important concept, we apply just such a rule with no effort, unconsciously, all the time.

It is worthwhile and interesting to stand back from language and take a look at it, as if it were not an intrinsic part of our very being, obscured by the fact that we live so intimately with it. Questions are only one kind of language pattern, yet the following sentences give an idea of just how complicated forming interrogatives really is:

20 Herbert can run twenty-six miles.

21 How far can Herbert run?

22 Patty is a rollerskater.

23 What is Patty?

24 Peter gave the popcorn to Jeff.

25 To whom did Peter give the popcorn?

26 Who/Whom did Peter give the popcorn to?

27 Who gave the popcorn to Jeff?

28 What did Peter give to Jeff?

Substitution

While an asterisk means that I judge a string of words or a single word to be totally beyond the limits of the language, a question mark means that I think the string borders on being un-English. Can you see why I would put a question mark before the following?

29   ?Eldon likes to fish, and Beulah likes to fish.

It seems to me that the native speaker would never utter such a sequence, but would instead say either

30   Eldon likes to fish, and so does Beulah.

or

31   Eldon and Beulah like to fish.

The rigid patterning of language, then, virtually forces us to use *substitution* in a systematic and extremely intricate way. In **30**, *so does Beulah* substitutes for ***Beulah likes to fish,*** and in **31** *like to fish* serves as the predicate for both ***Eldon*** and ***Beulah.***

Language is, then, patterned bheavior, and its patterns are extremely intricate. We all use those patterns intuitively, but we would have great difficulty in explaining accurately what it is that we are doing. There is a central paradox of language: we know it, but we can't explain it. Furthermore, to repeat a point, there is no need for anyone except a professional linguist to be able to explain language operations specifically and accurately.

Let me repeat that idea in yet another form, and with emphasis: There is no reason in the world for anyone except a professional linguist to have a detailed understanding of the grammar of the language, for *grammar is simply an explicit statement of what we know already.* This idea may seem strange and contradictory at this point, but it will, I hope, become clearer and more readily acceptable as the discussion progresses.

Language Is Arbitrary

Meanings

A second characteristic of language—one that may seem almost too obvious to mention: *Language is arbitrary.* The account in Genesis of the naming of the animals nicely illustrates the arbitrary nature of language:

> And out of the ground the Lord God formed every beast of the field, and every fowl of the air; and brought them unto Adam to see what he would call them: and whatsoever Adam called every living creature, that was the name thereof.

There is nothing inherently bovine about the word *cow,* for example, but the language has arbitrarily assigned *cow* to describe that class of animals. Similarly, the arbitrariness of language is illustrated by the story of the little girl on her first visit to a farm, who said, "No wonder they call them pigs. They're so dirty!"

Structure

Language is arbitrary not only at the level of its word-stock (its *lexicon*), but also in its structure. The German sentence

32   Ich weiss, dass du hier bist.

translated word for word into English would be

33   *I know that you here are.

whereas the grammatical English word order is, of course,

34   I know that you are here.

In English, we are sometimes told that the double negative makes a positive. Thus, the argument runs,

35   I don't have no money.

must mean something like

36   I do have some money.

But such a dictum runs counter to common sense. If you ask a friend for a loan, and he says, "I don't have no money," you know perfectly well that you will have to seek financial aid elsewhere, because in spite of the "logic" of the statement, you know what it means. In fact, while standard English avoids the double negative, French demands it:

37   Je *n*'ai *pas* d'argent.

The point concerning the arbitrary nature of language is this: there is no need to seek some kind of internal logic in language operations. In English, the double negative is no more illogical than the single negative; there is no direct relationship between words and their meanings; English word order is no more and no less efficient and logical than German word order. Justifying rightness or wrongness on the basis of extra-linguistic considerations is like arguing that Car A is better than Car B because Car A more nearly looks like a horse.

Correctness

Now let me bring this discussion of the arbitrary nature of language down to earth by explaining why the concept is important in the context of *The Contemporary Writer*. This book has argued and will argue again and again that there is no such thing as absolute right or wrong in language *outside of context*. Rightness and wrongness are determined not by logic or by an abstract system of grammatical rules, but by the purpose for which the language is being used, by the audience at which it is directed, and by the situation in which the use is taking place. Therefore, it is silly to argue about whether the double negative or *ain't* or a split infinitive is right or wrong. It all depends. This book explores in great detail the question of appropriateness, and *a priori* rules are merely a hindrance in judging appropriateness.

What Is Grammar?

On Grammatical "Rules"

When the word **grammar** is mentioned, it is inevitable that we think of rules. But very seldom do we question the nature of the hundreds of rules that we associate with grammar. Here are a few of those rules:

38   The word **ain't** is not English.

39   A noun is the name of a person, place, or thing.

40   The third person singular present tense of **be** is **is.**

41   Never end a sentence with a preposition.

42   In context, every English noun has either the feature *definite* or the feature *nondefinite.*

Since student writers are often rule-ridden, uptight about their writing because they don't know the "rules," it will be useful, as therapy, to understand just what kinds of language rules there are and how they work. Therefore, we will deal with these five rules in sequence.

An Erroneous "Rule"

"The word **ain't** is not English" **(38).** No one with the slightest knowledge of the language would claim that **ain't** is not an English word. In fact, common sense tells us that it is. If one thousand people were told to underline the single English expression in the following list, chances are that all one thousand of them would underline **ain't: Mensch, caballero, ain't, tovarishch, giornale.**

The dictum that **ain't** is not an English word originates from a variety of misconceptions. The first is that if a word is not in the dictionary, it is not a word. In fact, **ain't** is now listed in virtually all dictionaries, although when it first appeared in *Webster's Third New International,* a tornado of indignation swept across the continent. Here is a typical reaction:

> A dictionary's embrace of the word "ain't" will comfort the ignorant, confer approval upon the mediocre, and subtly imply that proper English is the tool only of the snob; but it will not assist men to speak truly to other men. It may, however, prepare us for that future which it could help to hasten. In the caves, no doubt, a grunt will do.[1]

As if the dictionary had the mystical power to legislate what is in language and what isn't—when, in fact, the dictionary (at its best) records faithfully and fully what is there, not what someone would like to have there.

But a "rule" such as "The word **ain't** is not English" also comes from another, even deeper misconception about the nature of language: namely, that one dialect or one level of usage represents the "real" language and anything else is a corruption. This is a question that we will deal with later

[1]The Toronto *Globe and Mail,* 8 Sept. 1961. Quoted in *Dictionaries and* That *Dictionary,* ed. James Sledd and Wilma R. Ebbitt (Chicago: Scott, Foresman, 1962), p. 54.

in this chapter. Suffice it to say now that any rule that tries to falsify the language as we know it is simply misguided, even ignorant.

In this connection, notice the differences among the following three rules:

43 The word *ain't* is not English.

44 You should not use the word *ain't,* even though it is English.

45 In some situations, the word *aint'* is inappropriate and therefore ineffective.

Only the last rule corresponds to the actual facts of language.

A Confusing "Rule"

"A noun is the name of a person, place, or thing" **(39).** Almost every student that I have ever known in my nineteen years of teaching has memorized that rule, and for nineteen years I've been asking myself, Why? I suspect that the basic assumption is something like this: If students learn grammar, they will be able to use the language better. (That is an assumption—a false one, in my opinion—that we will deal with in great detail.) Suppose that the ability to define *noun* would indeed enhance one's ability to use language; we would, nonetheless, question the soundness of the definition advanced. If a noun is the name of a person, place, or thing, we can agree that the italicized words in **46** are nouns.

46 *Galileo* saw the *moon* through his *telescope.*

But we might well argue about whether *moon* in this context is a place or a thing. And what about:

47 Chris likes the *pinks* better than the *greens.*

It is easy to demonstrate that *pinks* and *greens* are nouns, for they take the definite article (*the*), they are plural, and only nouns are pluralized by the addition of *-s.* They could be modified by adjectives: *the <u>vivid</u> pinks, the <u>pale</u> greens,* and so on. But "pinks" and "greens" are not persons, places, or things, so perhaps we should expand our definition: "A noun is the name of a person, place, thing, or color." But then what about:

48 *Democracy* is the best form of government.

Should we expand our definition once again, to "A noun is the name of a person, place, thing, color, or political system"? What about:

49 My great *love* for you knows no bounds.

Now, it seems, we must add "emotion" to the definition of *noun.*

So the old, definition-centered grammar ("A sentence is the expression of a complete idea"; "A verb names an action or a state of being") was often frustrating, and certainly not always useful. For instance, in what ways is a sentence the expression of a complete idea? Indeed, can we define "complete idea"?

A Partially True "Rule"

"The third person singular present tense of *be* is *is*" *(40)*. For the majority of speakers of English, that rule is perfectly accurate: **Herbert *is* an astronaut.** But for a significant minority of speakers, the rule is not accurate—if by accuracy one means the rule's ability to describe what actually exists in language. Some black dialects use *be* to indicate usualness: **He *be* here**—meaning something like "He is usually here."

If rule **40** is an attempt to describe what exists in the language, then, it is faulty, and if it is an attempt to regulate what should exist in the language, it is futile; the language grows according to its own dynamics, and formulating rules to regulate that growth is like trying to divert the course of the Mississippi with a pick and shovel.

A Silly "Rule"

"Never end a sentence with a preposition" **(41)**. As someone (George Bernard Shaw, I think) put it, "A preposition is a bad word to end a sentence with." This rule is typical of a whole class of language regulations that we have somehow inherited, and such rules are interesting in that they never have reflected the actual facts of any dialect of English. Whereas the rule about the use of *is* at least makes an accurate statement concerning what is generally called standard English, rule **41** is a figment of someone's imagination, for users of the language frequently and typically end sentences with prepositions.

Of the same ilk are "Don't split infinitives" *(to quickly go/to go quickly)* and "Use **shall** in the first person to show futurity and **will** to show determination" *(I shall return/I will return)*. In fact, the only consistent use of **shall** in any variety of English is the interrogative: **Shall we go?**

So rules like **41** are downright weird in that one wonders (a) where they came from, (b) why they were dreamed up, and (c) why they have persisted.

A Valid Rule

"In context, every English noun has either the feature *definite* or the feature *nondefinite*" **(42)**. This is a useful and interesting rule, useful because it is accurate and interesting because it tells us something important about the way language operates. To illustrate briefly: you will notice that the italicized nouns all have, as part of their meaning, a quality of definiteness (signaled by +) or nondefiniteness (signaled by −):

50   The *dog* next door howls at night (+).

51   *Politicians* can't be trusted (−).

52   Any *port* in a storm (−).

53   Those *shoes* hurt my feet (+).

Useful Rules

In short, the only grammatical rules that interest us are those that make accurate statements about what language is and how it operates; we have no interest in grammatical rules that tell us how language ought to be according to someone's notions about the perfectability of language.

Notice the sharp contrast between the two statements that follow. Both are valuable, but the first is a grammatical statement, and the second is not; the second is a statement about usage.

54 Speakers of almost all dialects of English use **ain't** upon occasion as the negative copula, as in **George ain't here.**

55 Generally speaking, **ain't** should be avoided in scholarly writing, unless the word is used for some special effect such as humor.

Grammar Defined

We can now state one definition of **grammar:** *a grammar of a language is a description of that language, nothing more and nothing less.* The grammar of a language cannot tell you what locutions you should use or when you should use them; it can only describe the alternatives available to you in writing or speaking. (As we will see later, the above definition is not complete.)

Now then, the grammar of a language is intrinsic to it; the grammar of a language is simply the systematic, arbitrary structure that we have been talking about. But normally when we speak of a grammar of a language, we mean some more or less systematic attempt to *describe* that structure. There exists a great variety of descriptive methods: traditional grammar, structural linguistics, transformational generative grammar, tagmemics, stratificational grammar.

After brief remarks on two of these systems (traditional and structural), we will inquire into some interesting aspects of language.

Traditional Grammar

This is the grammar that most people think of when the word **grammar** is mentioned. As we saw earlier, it tends to classify language on the basis of definitions, such as "A noun is the name of a person, place, or thing" and "A sentence is the expression of a complete idea." It identifies nine parts of speech (noun, verb, adjective, adverb, pronoun, coordinating conjunction, subordinating conjunction, preposition, and interjection) and defines them largely on the basis of the kinds of meanings that they carry.

Traditional grammar is often identified with framework diagraming:

56 The man who came to dinner wore a flower in his buttonhole.

Most college freshmen have spent some time learning to diagram. But one should ask, What does one learn from diagraming? And the answer is simple: diagraming. In other words, diagraming can become an end in itself, with no application to any other area of language development.

However, one should not gain the impression that all of traditional grammar was useless. Indeed, the great scholarly traditional grammars of English—those by Poutsma, Kruisinga, Jespersen, and Curme—are insightful and tremendously useful. Criticizing traditional grammarians because they did not use the insights of modern linguistics would be like criticizing Newton for not using the concept of relativity. Ideas must await their times.

Structural Linguistics

The structural linguists set out to present a rigorous analysis of the structure of language, one that would not depend so exclusively on meanings for its categories as does traditional grammar. In general, structuralists would approach their categories in the following way. They would say that a noun is a word that will fit into the empty slots in these frames:

57   (The) _____ is/was good.
      _____ are/were good.

58   The _____ remembered the _____.

59   The _____ went there.

That is, only certain kinds of words from the complete English lexicon will fit into these slots: namely, nouns. Nouns also have certain *morphological* characteristics. For instance, the majority of them form their plurals by the addition of **-s.** Many are characterized by their nominal suffixes: democra*cy,* parent***hood,*** national***ity,*** substitu***tion,*** and so on.

These concepts are interesting because they give us some insight into our intuitive knowledge of language. The examples of the frames for nouns were taken from *The Structure of English,* by Charles C. Fries. In that book Fries makes an interesting point, which shows that we know what the parts of speech are whether or not we can define them and, even more important, that the definitions do not aid us in recognizing the parts of speech. This point is so important in regard to attitudes toward language that a bit of elaboration will be worthwhile.

To refresh your memory, here are the conventional definitions of the four principal parts of speech:

60   A noun is the name of a person, place, or thing.

61   A verb names an action or a state of being.

62   An adjective modifies a noun, a pronoun, or another adjective.

63   An adverb modifies a verb, an adjective, or another adverb.

Now, concerning these definitions, Fries says,

> The conventional definitions do not provide the necessary criteria [for determining parts of speech]. Our . . . problem is to discover just what the criteria are that the users of the language actually employ to identify the necessary various form-class units when they give and receive the signals of structural meaning.
>
> You will remember Alice's experience with the poem of the Jabberwocky:
> 'Twas brillig, and the slithy toves
>   Did gyre and gimble in the wabe;
> All mimsy were the borogoves,
>   And the mome raths outgrabe. . . .
> "Somehow [she said], it seems to fill my head with ideas—only I don't know exactly what they are!"
> What are the "ideas" she gets and how are they stimulated? All words that one expects to have clearly definable meaning content are nonsense, but any speaker of English will recognize at once the frames in which these words appear.
> 'Twas _____, and the _____y _____s
>   Did _____ and _____ in the _____;
> All _____y were the _____s,
>   And the _____ _____s _____.
> The "ideas" which the verse stimulates are without doubt the structural meanings for which the framework contains the signals. Most of these nonsense words have clearly marked functions in frames that constitute familiar structural patterns. These "ideas" seem vague to the ordinary speaker because in the practical use of language he is accustomed to dealing only with total meanings to which lexical content contributes the elements of which he is conscious.[2]

Fries goes on to point out that most of us can identify parts of speech even if we don't know the meanings of the words. For instance, look at the following:

64   The glippy diggles uggled the woggles motently.

Would not everyone agree that **glippy** is an adjective, **diggles** is a noun, **uggled** is a verb, **woggles** is a noun, and **motently** is an adverb? And yet, what in the world is a **diggle,** particularly a **glippy diggle?** And for the glippy diggles to uggle the woggles sounds almost sinister—particularly when it is done motently.

We can illustrate the same principle with a perfectly good English sentence, made up of words that you will find in any dictionary:

65   Idolatric philogyny is a philistinic cogency in oppugnancy to meliorism.

You do not know the meaning of that sentence (though you can discover what the meaning is), yet you know that it is an English sentence, and you probably identify the parts of speech: **idolatric,** adjective; **philogyny,** noun; **philistinic,** adjective; **cogency,** noun; **oppugnancy,** noun; **meliorism,** noun.

[2]Charles Carpenter Fries. *The Structure of English* (New York: Harcourt Brace Jovanovich, 1952), pp. 70–71. Reprinted by permission of the publisher.

Of course, as a language discipline, structural linguistics is much wider ranging and a great deal more penetrating than the discussion here might indicate; but in this book, we are interested in some general notions about language, and, more important, we are focusing on the linguistic principles that will be directly useful in some way to writers.

Language Acquisition

Let's think of the possible ways in which we learn our native language. Unless a child is severely retarded, it pretty much knows the basics of its language by the time it is, say, eight years old. That is, it can speak, and in so doing it can produce almost all the important structures that the language affords. This is truly a miracle. Without very much formal instruction—if any at all—the child pretty much masters the native language at a very early age.

One common-sense explanation of how the child does this is to assume that it hears sentences and then imitates them. For instance, the child hears its mother say, "I want some candy," imitates that sentence—repeats it—and thus adds it to its stock of sentences. This process is repeated thousands of times throughout the child's life until it has mastered all the possibilities of the language.

Such a theory does, at first glance, seem to have common sense going for it, but closer examination reveals that it is not common sense, but nonsense.

In the first place, think of the sentence that you are reading now. You understand it, but the chances that you have ever seen it before or will ever see it again are astronomically remote. The imitation theory of language acquisition does not explain our ability to produce unique sentences or to understand them, does it? The mathematics of the case are overwhelming:

> By a rough, but conservative calculation, there are at least 10^{20} sentences 20 words long, and if a child were to learn only these it would take him something on the order of 1,000 times the estimated age of the earth just to listen to them.[3]

Couple that astounding statement with the notion that the speaker has never before heard most of the sentences that he or she will utter in a lifetime, and the imitation theory begins to look dubious indeed.

There is also the fact that there is no *theoretical* limit to the length of English sentences (or sentences in any other natural language, for that matter). This principle is easily demonstrated; for instance:

66   This is the house that Jack built.
    This is the malt that lay in the house that Jack built.
    This is the rat that ate the malt that lay in the house that Jack built.
    This is the cat that chased the rat that ate the malt that lay in the house that Jack built.

[3]George A. Miller, "Some Preliminaries to Psycholinguistics," *Psycholinguistics and Reading,* ed. Frank Smith (New York: Holt, Rinehart and Winston, 1973), p. 18.

This is the dog that worried the cat that chased the rat that ate the malt that lay in the house that Jack built.

This is the cow with the crumpled horn that tossed the dog that worried the cat that chased the rat that ate the malt that lay in the house that Jack built.

This is the milkmaid all forlorn that milked the cow with the crumpled horn that tossed the dog that worried the cat that chased the rat that ate the malt that lay in the house that Jack built.

Not only is there no theoretical limit to the *length* of English sentences, but also the *number* of possible English sentences is infinite. That is another telling argument against the imitation theory.

Just as interesting is the way in which the child develops its language. Close observation will show you that the child does not begin by imitating other speakers, but that it constructs its own unique grammar, quite unlike any that it is likely to hear its family speak.

When the child begins to speak, it does so in single words: **mama, cookie, milk,** and so forth. But when it begins to put words together into sentences, it does so in a completely regular way that is quite unrelated to the structure of adult language. The child's first sentences rarely exceed three words, and its word-stock is divided into two classes: *Pivot* and *Open*. The Pivot class is limited, and the child makes relatively few additions to it. The Open class is larger, and the child quickly adds a great many new words to it. Typical Pivot class words are **allgone, see, my.** Typical Open class words are **milk, baby, big, truck.** By the age of about eighteen months, the child begins to construct little "sentences" from Pivot class and Open class words. In fact, it is very easy to describe the grammar of the sentences used by normal eighteen-month-old children:

67 A sentence consists of one Pivot class word followed by either one or two Open class words.

Thus the child will generate "sentences" of the following sort:

68 | Pivot | Open | Open |
    |---|---|---|
    | My | milk | |
    | Allgone | big | truck |
    | See | baby | |

The following quotation is worth pondering, not only for what it tells us about language development in children (for that is not our main concern here) but also for what it tells us about language learning in general:

> The words in each class vary of course from child to child, and a word that originates in one child's Pivot class may be in another child's Open. But all children appear to go through the same first-rule stage although no children are explicitly taught it. The development of the rule is one of the universals of language development in children.
>
> From the first coarse-grained Pivot–Open class distinction, children go on to make successive differentations within each class, progressively making their language more complex and gradually bringing it closer and closer to that spoken by adults. All the time a child is speaking a rule-governed language of his own; at no time does he just throw words together randomly, and at no time can he be said to be slavishly imitating an adult model. Those

rules which are productive in the construction and comprehension of sentences in adult language are retained, the others the child progressively modifies.[4]

Let's pause briefly in our headlong plunge into theory and consider the practical implications of what has been said so far.

First, it should be apparent that language is an endlessly creative individual faculty that grows according to its own inner dynamics and according to the needs of the user.

Second, it should also be apparent that a grammar of a language will be an infinitely complex mechanism that not only will explain what is—in either the spoken sentence or the written sentence—but that also will postulate how what is came to be.

Finally, and most important, some concept of the limitations of ordinary grammar—that kind that most of us have been drilled in—should be apparent.

The Propositional Nature of Language

You are bound to recognize that there is something drastically wrong with the following:

69   History in her page informs us. The page is solemn. The crusaders were but men. These men were ignorant. These men were savage. Their motives were those of bigotry. That bigotry was unmitigated. Their pathway was one of blood. Their pathway was one of tears.

This passage not only sounds simple-minded but also is difficult to read.

It turns out that **69** is a schematic breakdown of the following sentence from Kurt Vonnegut's *Slaughterhouse-Five.* The original runs thus:

70   History in her solemn page informs us that the crusaders were ignorant and savage men, that their motives were those of bigotry unmitigated, and that their pathway was one of blood and tears.

The diagnosis of the problem with **69** is that the individual ideas were not put together into a sentence as in **70** but were broken up into separate sentences.

As we shall see, a major problem in student writing is the tendency not to put separate ideas together via the syntactic devices of the language. Here is a beginning paragraph from a freshman essay:

71   My greatest love is the love of my possessions. I feel like a king when I am amongst my possessions. But my possessions are not material possessions such as a beautiful new automobile or an enormous new house. Rather, my possessions are the wonders of nature: the beautiful, snow-capped mountains and the deep, crystal-clear lakes.

I think most readers would say that **71** is either immature or awkward or both. One alternative to it is the following:

72   I feel like a king when I am amongst the wonders of nature, for they are my greatest love and my greatest possessions: snow-capped mountains and deep,

[4]Frank Smith, "The Learner and His Language," *Psycholinguistics and Reading*, p. 143.

crystal-clear lakes rather than material things such as a new automobile or an enormous house.

I would argue that **72** sounds more mature, perhaps even more intelligent, than **71,** and yet the idea content of both of them is essentially the same. The reason that most readers would prefer **72** over **71** is simply that in **72** the grammatical possibilities of the language have been used to put closely related ideas together in the neat syntactic package of a sentence. We will discuss this further in Chapter 11, on the sentence. For the moment, I simply wanted to indicate my reasons for demonstrating the propositional nature of language.

Sentences and Propositions

Every sentence in the language is made up of one or more propositions. If the sentence contains more than one proposition, the propositions are related syntactically through the grammatical devices that the language affords. All this probably sounds a good deal more complicated than it actually is. *If you understand a sentence, you intuitively recognize the propositions that it contains.* Let's take some examples. The following contains only one proposition.

73   The child sobs.

But the following contains two propositions.

74   The little child sobs.

Before reading on, see whether you can identify the two propositions—or, more accurately, see whether you can state them, for if you understood the sentence, you identified the propositions.

There's really no magic here, not even a great deal of mystery. The two propositions in **74** are **The child sobs** and **The child is little.** I can prove that both propositions are there, because if I ask you "Who is little?" you'll say, "The child is"—that is, "The child is little."

Notice how close in meaning **74** is to the following:

75   The child who is little sobs.

In **75** nearly the entirety of the embedded proposition is expressed—except that **who** has been substituted for **child,** but then we know that **who,** in fact, means "child" in this sentence.

A rough but perhaps useful way of showing the meaning that underlies both **74** and **75** is the following:

76   The child [the child is little] sobs.

This schematization shows both propositions in their full form.

So every sentence in the language is made up of one or more propositions, and each proposition can be expressed as a sentence. Another way of putting this idea is to say that some sentences are simple and other sentences are like Chinese boxes, with sentence within sentence within sentence within sentence. . . . For a good example of this, look at **66.** It must now also be obvious that there is no theoretical limit to the number of propositions that can be embedded within a sentence.

Propositions and Mature Style

Let's now take a look at some sentences written by people who are generally admired for their ability to use the language, with a view toward appreciating the way in which accomplished writers embed proposition within proposition. (Many of these examples were gathered by Francis Christensen and published in his book *Notes Toward a New Rhetoric*.) This brief excursion will have a couple of purposes. First, it will be our initial close look at the way sentences work. Second, it will contribute to your sentence-consciousness and sentence-sense—one of the main purposes of *The Contemporary Writer.*

77   The jockeys sat bowed and relaxed, moving a little at the waist with the
     movement of their horses.   —Katherine Anne Porter

There are two obvious propositions that can be expressed as sentences, thus: (1) The jockeys sat bowed and relaxed. (2) The jockeys moved (or were moving) a little at the waist with the movement of their horses. You might consider this tentative question: Do **bowed** and **relaxed** also represent embedded propositions?

78   She came among them behind the man, gaunt in the gray shapeless garment
     and the sunbonnet, wearing stained canvas gymnasium shoes.
                                                         —William Faulkner

How about this? (1) She came among them behind the man. (2) She was gaunt in the garment. (3) The garment was gray. (4) The garment was shapeless. (5) She was gaunt in the sunbonnet. (6) She was wearing gymnasium shoes. (7) The shoes were stained. (8) The shoes were canvas. That's a pretty good ratio, it seems to me: eight propositions for one sentence.

79   He [a hawk] could sail for hours, searching the blanched grasses below him
     with his telescopic eyes, gaining height against the wind, descending in
     mile-long, gently declining swoops when he curved and rode back, never
     beating a wing.   —Walter Van Tilburg Clark

In this wonderful sentence, which so vividly expresses what we all know about hawks, I find the following: (1) He could sail for hours. (2) He searched the grasses with his eyes. (3) The grasses were below him. (4) The grasses were blanched. (5) His eyes were telescopic. (6) He gained height against the wind. (7) He descended in swoops. (8) The swoops were mile-long. (9) The swoops were gently declining. (10) He curved. (11) He rode back. (12) He never beat a wing.

80   They regarded me silently, Brother Jack with a smile that went no deeper
     than his lips, his head cocked to one side, studying me with his penetrating
     eyes; the other blank-faced, looking out of eyes that were meant to reveal
     nothing and to stir profound uncertainty.   —Ralph Ellison

Notice how the intensity and effectiveness of this sentence simply disappear when the propositions are unembedded:

81   They regarded me silently. Brother Jack had a smile that went no deeper than
     his lips, and his head was cocked to one side. He was studying me with his

penetrating eyes. The other one was blank-faced. He was looking out of eyes that were meant to reveal nothing and to stir profound uncertainty.

It seems to me that the relaxation of syntactic intensity (the low level of embedding) in **81** has robbed the passage of its emotional intensity. Brother Jack and the other man are just not as sinister in **81** as they are in **80**.

An Example from Mark Twain

One more example before we turn our attention to other matters beside the embedding of propositions in this discussion of the nature of grammar. The following paragraphs from Mark Twain's *Roughing It* demonstrate that great prose need not consist of sentences that contain many embeddings. I think everyone who reads the following passage will agree that Mark Twain writes magnificently, and he does so by using a variety of simple devices that the language affords, including, of course, the device of embedding propositions:

82   In the afternoon I brought the creature [a horse, billed as a Genuine Mexican Plug, that Twain had bought in Virginia City, Nevada] into the plaza, and certain citizens held him by the head, and others by the tail, while I mounted him. As soon as they let go, he placed all his feet in a bunch together, lowered his back, and then suddenly arched it upward, and shot me straight into the air a matter of three or four feet! I came as straight down again, lit in the saddle, went instantly up again, came down almost on the high pommel, shot up again, and came down on the horse's neck—all in the space of three or four seconds. Then he rose and stood almost straight up on his hind feet, and I, clasping his lean neck desperately, slid back into the saddle, and held on. He came down, and immediately hoisted his heels into the air, delivering a vicious kick at the sky, and stood on his fore feet. And then down he came once more, and began the original exercise of shooting me straight up again.
    The third time I went up I heard a stranger say: "Oh *don't* he buck, though!"
    While I was up, somebody struck the horse a sounding thwack with a leathern strap, and when I arrived again the Genuine Mexican Plug was not there. A Californian youth chased him up and caught him, and asked if he might have a ride. I granted him that luxury. He mounted the Genuine, got lifted into the air once, but sent his spurs home as he descended, and the horse darted away like a telegram. He soared over three fences like a bird, and disappeared down the road toward the Washoe Valley.

Take a good look at that passage, both at its propositional nature and at its other features (such as Twain's choice of words), for the secret to becoming a good writer is to become aware of what others do so that you can learn from them.

Competence Versus Performance

Even if you are convinced that you know the grammar of English, some important questions must remain in your mind. For instance: If I really have mastered the grammar of the language, why can't I write like Mark

Twain or William Faulkner? The answer to that question is that there is a difference between *competence* and *performance.*

One way to define competence is to say that it is one's global knowledge of the language. Performance is the ability to activate that knowledge, to use it to produce speech or writing. Our performance always falls short of our competence. We can theorize that we all have roughly the same degree of competence; therefore, differences in ability stem from varying degrees of performance.

Undoubtedly much of the material in this chapter has been difficult to comprehend, but that difficulty does not arise because you have not mastered the English language; the concepts that have been developed in the language as I have used it in this chapter have been difficult.

The following chart explains an extremely important principle graphically:

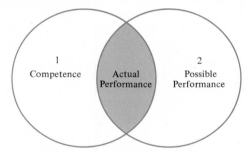

All normal adult speakers of the language have roughly the same competence (represented by circle 1). Therefore, every normal adult speaker of the language has the theoretical possibility of complete performance (represented by circle 2). But, in fact, complete performance is an unreachable ideal, for there are countless factors that block it. One of those factors is that our lives are so short as to preclude performance that begins to equal competence; the variety of uses to which language can be put is infinite, and our lives are finite. Standing in our way also are social factors, emotional sets, and physiological difficulties. In short, we are doomed to make only a limited use of our full potential as "languagers." The shaded area in the diagram represents what one is actually able to do, one's actual performance. Therefore, the goal of any teaching should be to move the circle of competence farther into the circle of performance to create a larger shaded area, thus:

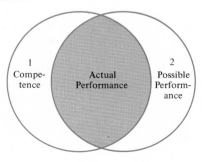

It is just at the level of the sentence that this area of actual performance can be dramatically increased. Or, to state the point more directly and accurately, you can, if you want to, become a great deal more versatile in your handling of sentences, and the sentence is so basic that any gain in this area is of tremendous value. But, analogically, there is no reason why you can't increase your performance generally: your ability to develop paragraphs, to argue logically, to use figurative language, to interest an audience, and so on.

Meaning and Structure

Suppose I asked you to tell me what was just said in the discussion of competence and performance. You might read the section to me. Or you might memorize the section and recite it to me. But more probably you would simply, explain what was said, in your own words. If you understood the section, you would not need to rely on your memory of the exact sentences, and in your explanation it is unlikely that you would use any of the sentences that appeared in the section. Meaning, then, is an elusive thing; it is conveyed by specific words and sentences, but seems not to be tied inseparably to them.

We can quickly dispel the notion that we gain meaning simply from knowing what a word, or a sentence, is referring to. For instance, **George Washington** and **the first president of the United States** have the same referent, but they do not have the same meaning. If they did, the following sentence would seem redundant:

83 George Washington was the first president of the United States.

There is a considerable difference between **83** and this:

84 ?The first president of the United States was the first president of the United States.

Would you agree that the following two sentences have very similar, if not identical, meanings?

85 The man bit the dog.

86 The dog was bitten by the man.

If they do have very similar, or identical, meanings, we have created a real problem for ourselves, because we must conclude that the meaning is not in one or the other, but somewhere else. We have trapped ourselves. If I ask you what **85** means and you answer with **86**, you have begged the question, for then I'll ask you what **86** means, and you'll have to respond with **85**. Of course, you could phrase another sentence, for instance:

87 The domestic canine was bitten by the human male.

But this would only compound the problem, for then I'd ask you what the three sentences mean, and you could only quote one or the other, or else make up a fourth sentence that you thought had nearly the same meaning as the other three. Each sentence that you made up, of course, would drift a bit further from the original, until finally both you and I would feel that we had gotten too far away from the original meaning that was intended.

Again, we are led almost mystically to believe that meaning is something separate from the sentences, even though they do indicate meaning. This elusive quality, this "pure" meaning, is what we call the *deep structure* of language. The *surface structure* is what you read (right now, for instance) and what you hear.

The concept of deep structure is fascinating; let's play around with it just a bit longer.

Take the following sentence. You know precisely what it means, and yet I can point out something about that meaning that you undoubtedly know but aren't aware of.

88   The log is ashes.

You know that if the log is ashes, it does not exist any more. However, there is nothing specific in the surface structure that gives you that important bit of information; you derive it from the deep structure. If we want to put the information explicitly in the surface structure, we will need to say something like this:

89   Something that **was** the log is ashes.

Can it be that nouns have tense in the deep structure? You've been told throughout your school career that only verbs have tense. What about this, then?

90   My wife was born in Fairview.

From reading that sentence, you know that the woman spoken of was not my wife when she was born. In other words, you know, without needing to have it stated explicitly, that

91   Someone who **is now** my wife was born in Fairview.

The following sentence is interesting because as it is written you can't tell exactly what it means, but when it is spoken the ambiguity disappears.

92   Napoleon doesn't drink brandy.

Now read the following aloud, putting the stress on the italicized words:

93   *Napoleon* doesn't drink brandy.

94   Napoleon doesn't *drink* brandy.

95   Napoleon doesn't drink *brandy.*

The meanings that the different emphases bring to the sentence can be explained something like this:

93a   Someone who is not Napoleon drinks brandy.

94a   Napoleon doesn't drink brandy. (He does something else with it—bathes in it, perhaps.)

95a   Napoleon drinks something that is not brandy.

So the one written sentence has three possible deep structures, but the spoken versions have only one deep structure each.

Now let's see how deep structure relates to the truth and falsehood of statements. Suppose that I have a dog and a cat, and suppose that last night the dog bit me. If I say

96   My feline bit me last night.

I have uttered a falsehood. Since truth is the opposite of falsehood, I should be able to utter a true statement simply by making **96** negative, thus:

97   My feline didn't bite me last night.

But, strangely, **97** is also a false report of what happened. We can explain this dilemma in terms of deep structure.

Sentence **96**, in its deep structure, means something like this:

98   Something that is my feline bit me last night.

Now we can see that the untruth of the sentence lies just in the proposition that the something that bit me was a feline, when, in fact, it was a dog. Therefore, negating the whole sentence will not correct the falsehood. If we are to correct the falsehood through negation, we must negate only the false proposition, thus:

99   Something that is **not** my feline bit me last night.

Sentence **99** is true.

Let's wrap this section up by exploring one more sentence.

100   Finish designing the airplane.

If you think about it, this is a strange sentence, for there can be no airplane if the design for it is not finished. So what does the sentence really mean? If you uttered that sentence in an actual context, you would know whom you were addressing, but no subject appears in the sentence. So there are two deep structure features that must be explained, and I think that **101** gives the explanations.

101   (You) Finish designing (something that will be) the airplane.

To conclude this section on deep and surface structure, I should answer a question that has probably occurred to you, namely, Of what value is this stuff?

I answer simply and directly: Knowing concepts such as those discussed in this section ought to convince you that the study of language is a potentially fascinating business, quite unlike the doleful exercises that so many people associate with grammar. And one thing that you need in order to be a good writer is a great interest in language. You must be alert to its nuances, and you must really care how it functions.

How Does Language Mean?

This is an interesting question that we will explore briefly here and in somewhat more detail when we get into the discussion of words in context in Chapter 12.

Phonemes

Individual sounds carry meaning, but not all sounds do. As you know, when you pronounce some consonants, your vocal chords vibrate, but when you pronounce others, you make no voice sound. For instance, the essential difference between /d/ and /t/ is that the vocal chords vibrate when one pronounces /d/. (The slashes indicate that we are talking about sounds.) Thus, in the case of these two consonants, voicing is meaningful. When a sound carries meaning we say that it is *phonemic.* We can show that this voicing is phonemic by contrasting /dam/ and /tam/. They are different in meaning simply because of the voicing factor. Are we to conclude, then, that sounds (and their written representations, namely letters) carry meaning?

Well, not all differences in sound make for a difference in meaning. A speaker of the legendary Brooklyn dialect pronounces **bird** in the same way that I would pronounce the sequence /boyd/, but my pronunciation of **bird** and that of the Brooklyn speaker both signify the same meaning. So not all sounds are phonemic. And we can demonstrate that point in another way. If a hundred people read the same sentence aloud, we will be able to tell that we are hearing different people, not just one person reading the sentence over and over again, but the meaning of the sentence won't change.

It is useful to realize, also, that not every letter in a word necessarily represents a phoneme. The word **thought** has seven letters, but only three phonemes: /th-ah-t/.

Morphemes and Syntax

So phonemes have something to do with meaning. And so do morphemes, the next largest chunk of language. That is, the phoneme is the smallest chunk, and the next point at which language can be segmented is the morpheme. I'll define *morpheme* by illustration. Sometimes a word and a morpheme are the same thing:

102   truth

Sometimes a word is made up or more than one morpheme:

103   truthful

In the case of **truthful,** one of the morphemes can appear alone; it is *free.* And one can appear only in conjunction with a free morpheme; it is *bound.* Free morpheme: **truth.** Bound morpheme: **-ful.** Some words are compounds of more than one free morpheme:

104   lighthouse, Watergate

Some words are compounded of more than one free morpheme and one or more bound morphemes:

105   lighthousekeeper: light house keep -er

Morphemes obviously affect meaning:

106   truthful, untruthful

But you'll never be able to explain the meaning of the sentence

107   George was not untruthful.

by looking only at phonemes and morphemes, for syntax—as was implied earlier—also contributes to meaning: ***The king killed the man/The man killed the king.***

It would seem that meaning comes from the interplay of a hierarchy of elements in the sentence itself. And yet the meaning of the sentence can depend on its context. For instance,

108   George is a hotshot historian.

109   George is a hotshot historian. He flunked History 101.

Again, we might assume that meaning lies in the complex of factors that one perceives on the printed page or in spoken discourse.

Mind

Enter the human mind. It is the mind that constructs meaning, and without mind, there is no meaning.

It would seem then that meaning comes into being neither down here on the printed page nor up there in the reader's brain, but somewhere in between. Meaning results from the interplay of mind and message.

This is an interesting and productive notion, for it implies that for writing to be meaningful, there must be a transaction between the writer and the reader. Nothing will happen if the writer does not compose in such a way that the reader will be interested in, and will understand, the message.

Word Classes: Content and Structure

To get back to words for a moment. We know somehow that they are basic "counters" in the meaning game, but most of us never stop to think that words fall into two distinct categories and that these categories are great clues in the puzzle of how language means.

Suppose we agree that ***huggle*** means "to dig, appreciate, or like." We can begin to construct meaningful sentences using the word:

110   I really ***huggle*** grammar.

111   Mary doesn't ***huggle*** grammar, but she's a good kid anyway.

Not only that, we can perform some magical, mystical, everyday operations on the word and construct meaningful sentences such as the following:

112   Herman's ***hugglification*** of grammar keeps him from going out on dates.

113   Beatrice has a really ***hugglific*** understanding of grammar.

114   ***Hugglifically*** speaking, grammar is a ball.

For those who are not initiated, we can translate as follows:

112a   Herman's digging of grammar keeps him from going out on dates.

113a   Beatrice has a really appreciative understanding of grammar.

114a   Appreciatively speaking, grammar is a ball.

It looks as if we can make up any words we want to and use them quite at will. Consider the following three sentences:

115   On top of the hill stands a bar and grill.

116   On dag of the hugel stets a rab and crilk.

117   *Ad top von der hill stands u bar i grill.

Even though we may not know what **116** means, we recognize that it is a *possible* sentence in English. If we had to know the meaning of a sentence before we knew that it was written in English, we would be in a terrible dilemma, particularly when reading materials about subjects we are unfamiliar with. Remember this one, quoted near the beginning of the chapter?

118   Idolatric philogyny is a philistinic cogency in oppugnancy to meliorism.

I assume that you didn't know what it meant, but you didn't question for a moment that it is English.

So some classes of words will freely accept new members, and some classes will not. Let me illustrate the point. During the height of the Vietnam war, I was teaching a beginning class in linguistics. Of course, one of the bastardized words often used during the war was *pacify,* which really meant "to wipe out," as in ***The patrol pacified the village.*** Now, there is a common operation in grammar that turns *active* sentences into *passives.* For instance, the following is active:

119   USC won the Rose Bowl.

and the following is the passive version:

120   The Rose Bowl was won by USC.

Using the *pacify* analogy, the class began to talk about *passifying* sentences. They simply coined the word on the basis of analogy. But that opened the way for coining a noun, an adjective, and an adverb. Therefore we had

121   The class *passifies* the sentence. [verb]

122   The *passification* of the sentence was easy. [noun]

123   Write a *passific* sentence. [adjective]

124   Writing *passifically* isn't hard. [adverb]

Nouns, verbs, adjectives, and *adverbs* are open classes and freely admit new members. The other parts of speech belong to closed classes and do not admit new members.

Sometimes we speak of *content words*—nouns, verbs, adjectives, and adverbs—and *structure words*—the other parts of speech. It is characteristic of content words that they carry *concepts,* and characteristic of structure words that they indicate *relationships:*

125   The wife *of* the king is the queen. [preposition]

126   The king *and* queen rule the land. [coordinating conjunction]

127   The king rules *because* he inherited the throne. [subordinating conjunction]

Structure words also characteristically indicate *features of meaning:*

128   *A* flower blooms in the garden. [nondefinite]

129   *The* flower blooms in the pot. [definite]

And structure words may also indicate *reference:*

130   Because the child was naughty, *he* was punished. [refers to *child*]

131   The child *who* was good was rewarded. [refers to *child*]

132   *Those* roses are healthier than *these.* [*Those* points to something relatively distant, and *these* points to something relatively near.]

Even in the lexicon (the word-stock of the language), then, meaning depends upon both concepts and relationships. And that constitutes much of the message of *The Contemporary Writer*—the development of concepts at all levels and the putting of those concepts into the most meaningful orders.

What Is Usage, and How Does It Relate to Grammar?

By pointing to the following list, I want to repeat a concept that has already been explored:

133   I shall not return.

134   I will not return.

135   I'm not going to come back.

136   I ain't never coming back.

137   Mary little brother, he name Alfie.

138   Alfie be in the bedroom.

139   *Tina no have a new dress.

140   *Hilmi comings.

The point is, only those sentences that would not be produced by a native speaker—**139** and **140**—are ungrammatical. Sentence **140**, as a matter of fact, is not a fabrication, but a typical locution of a Turkish friend of mine who had learned the "rule" that in standard English the third person singular present verb takes an *-s* ending, thus:

141   Hilmi come*s.*

but who had not learned how to handle the progressive, so that he characteristically produced sentences like **140**. Sentences **133** through **138** are, however, typical of those that native speakers of various dialects would produce and therefore are perfectly grammatical. (Which is not to say that all of them are appropriate in every situation.)

Usage, however, is quite a different matter. The student of usage investigates language to determine the sorts of language that various speakers use in different situations.

Usage focuses on *appropriateness to a situation,* and this is the all-important consideration in the manipulation of language: Is my usage appropriate to the situation and the audience? If usage is not appropriate, the effectiveness of language in the situation is diminished. A little story will make the point clear.

Traditional school grammar laid down the law that the subjective complement must be in the subjective case. Following that "law," we would say that

142   It is I.

is correct and that

143   It is me.

is incorrect. But suppose that some evening I were to come home and to respond to my wife's call, "Who is it?" with, *It is I.* She would laugh at me—and probably tell me to leave my professional snootiness behind when I come home. In other words, from the point of view of usage, in that situation *It is I* would be exactly the *wrong* thing to say, unless, of course, I wanted to be humorous.

It seems to me that the confusion of grammar and usage has done infinite harm to individual students and to the educational process in general.

If we are to point the finger of guilt at any culprit for starting the grammar-usage mess that has done such harm, we must refer to Bishop Robert Lowth, who in 1762 published *A Short Introduction to English Grammar.* In a way, he set the tone for what has been happening in English classes for two hundred years. A quote from Lowth will illustrate exactly the attitude that we all should try to avoid:

144   The Principal design of a Grammar of any Language is to teach us to express ourselves with propriety in that Language; and to enable us to judge of every phrase and form of construction, whether it is right or not. The plain way of doing this is to lay down rules, and to illustrate them by examples. But, besides showing what is right, the matter may be further explained by pointing out what is wrong.

Lowth used two bases to determine what is right: quotations from the "best" authors (Shakespeare, Milton, Dryden, Pope) and reference to the "universal," "logical" rules of language. The trouble is that he did not consider situation. A London bargeman who followed Lowth's rules would have been laughed off the Thames. Furthermore, in assuming that a language is governed by a set of universal, logical rules, he completely missed the point.

I don't want to be too hard on poor old Bishop Lowth; after all, his intentions were good, and we cannot expect that he would have held a twentieth-century view of language processes. But when Lowthian views are imposed on twentieth-century students, something is drastically wrong.

Of course, it is possible to cut the language pie in an infinite number of ways. The American linguist W. Nelson Francis[5] made a three-way division according to usage: *educated* or *standard English, vernacular English,* and *uneducated English.*

Educated or standard English is the language used by those who hold power in the society. It is best illustrated by the speech of network radio and television announcers. However, standard is not a uniform, monolithic entity. Among recent presidents of the United States, Ford, Nixon, and Eisenhower represent speakers of what we are calling standard, but Kennedy and Johnson differed markedly in their language from these three, Kennedy speaking with an identifiably northeastern accent and Johnson using a markedly southwestern form of the language. In spite of these differences, however, it can be said that all five represent users of standard.

Vernacular English differs from standard in the sorts of constructions that it allows, for instance:

145   *Vernacular*   Him and Joe went.
       Standard   He and Joe went.
       Vernacular   You and me can do it.
       Standard   You and I can do it.

Uneducated English diverges even more radically from standard. It is characterized by such locutions as **Them folks ain't got no money for to go to picture shows with.** It is usually associated with people who are virtually uneducated and who occupy the lowest positions in the socioeconomic hierarchy.

You should not, however, think that this division is clear-cut, for it isn't. Defining levels of usage precisely is extremely difficult. Nevertheless, any native speaker can sense differences in levels of usage. The important point is not to enumerate or clearly define levels, but simply to realize that they exist and that they are the result of social and economic circumstance.

We must also stress that identifying levels of usage and dialects does not imply making value judgments. So-called standard is no better and no worse than the various kinds of nonstandard. *Language is good or bad only in context.*

Developing a sensitivity to usage is, of course, one of your most important tasks if you are to become a successful writer. You always have an audience in mind, and you know that you must achieve just the right tone if you are to be effective with your chosen audience.

More about usage later, particularly in Chapter 11, on the sentence, and Chapter 12, on the word.

---

[5]W. Nelson Francis, *The English Language: An Introduction* (New York: W. W. Norton, 1965), pp. 246–53.

The Dynamics of Language Change

All the following quotations are in perfectly good English:

146   Tha ic tha this eall gemunde, tha wundrade ic swithe thara godena wiotana
the giu waeron giond Angelcynn. ("When I then this remembered, then
wondered I exceedingly of the good wise men who were formerly throughout
England."   —King Alfred's *Pastoral Care*, late ninth century

147   Thyn Astrolabie has a ring to putten on the thombe of thi right hond in taking
the height of thinges.
                    —Chaucer, *A Treatise on the Astrolabe*, late fourteenth century

148   When the right vertuous Edward Wotton, and I, were at the Emperors Court
together, wee gave our selves to learne horsemanship of John Pietro Puglia-
no: one that with great commendation had the place of an Esquire at his
stable.   —Sir Philip Sidney, *An Apologie for Poetry*, 1583

149   Norman, born sign of Aquarius, had been in Mexico when the news came
about Hemingway. He had gone through the *New York Times* to read the
well-turned remarks of notables who for the most part had never cared about
Papa, not that much! and had one full heart-clot of outraged vanity that the
Times had never thought to ask *his* opinion.
                    —Norman Mailer, *Of a Fire on the Moon*, 1969

150   Ain nothin in a long time lit up the English teaching profession like the
current hassle over Black English. One finds boucoup sociolinguistic research
studies and language projects for the "disadvantaged" on the scene in nearly
every sizable Black community in the country. —Geneva Smitherman,
" 'God Don't Never Change': Black English from a Black Perspective,"
College English, March, 1973

Obviously, the language has changed from the time of Alfred to the age
of Aquarius and Geneva Smitherman. Alfred is simply unintelligible to the
modern reader; most of Chaucer can be read, perhaps with some difficulty;
Sir Philip Sidney sounds archaic, but his language does not stand in the
way of our comprehension; Norman Mailer is recognizably mod; and
Smitherman is simply far out.

The following discussion will not trace the development of modern
English from its Anglo-Saxon beginnings, but will explore attitudes toward
change and the dynamics of change.

There is good evidence that nothing can stop language change; language
develops according to its own inner dynamics, and all the professors,
linguists, and academicians in the world are not going to have much
influence, if any at all.

In the eighteenth century, that wonderful old curmudgeon Samuel
Johnson compiled his famous dictionary, an avowed attempt to bring
regulation to the English language,

>   which, while it was employed in the cultivation of every species of literature,
>   has itself been hitherto neglected, suffered to spread, under the direction of
>   chance, into wild exuberance, resigned to the tyranny of time and fashion,
>   and exposed to the corruptions of ignorance, and caprices of innovation.
>   —Preface to the *Dictionary*

And Johnson's attitude is typical of opinions that are prevalent even today. A look at the dynamics of language will dispel some false ideas.

Does language decay? That is, does change ever make it worse in some way? There are two answers to that question. The language changed drastically between Chaucer's time and Shakespeare's, but I think no one would suggest that somehow Chaucer's language is better or more expressive than Shakespeare's or that Shakespeare's is more corrupt than Chaucer's.

So we can reverse the question and ask, Does language change bring about improvement? In the opinion of most students of language, the answer is an emphatic *No!* It is almost universally agreed that there is no such thing as a primitive, or incomplete, language; it is almost universally agreed that any language is capable of doing anything that its users want it to do. Therefore, Old English, for instance, was no less rich a source of expression than is modern English; the languages of primitive peoples today are not primitive, but are capable of doing anything that the languages spoken by the so-called civilized societies can do.

In some sense these questions must remain moot, however, for we have no way of really testing whether, for instance, Old English was a less viable instrument of communication than modern English. On the basis of the texts that survive, we would tend to say that English has changed drastically but that it has not developed in the sense of becoming better and better. And, by the way, we should not equate the lack of a vocabulary item with a basic deficiency in the language. Classical Latin had no word for **surfboard**, but that would not stop us from writing about surfing in Latin, for we would simply borrow or manufacture a word.

So, to the dynamics of language change.

Sound Change

The sounds of language change, apparently in a systematic way. You might be interested in seeing what happened to a series of vowels throughout the history of English. Old English (O.E.) **sae** and **claene** (with the vowel of modern **ran**) became Middle English (M.E.) **see** and **clene** (with the vowel of modern **see**) and then became modern English (Mod. E.) **sea** and **clean.** O.E. **grene, teth** (as in **pane**) → M.E. **grene, teeth** (**pane**) → Mod. E. **green, teeth.** O.E. **is, hydan** (as in **beet**)→M.E. **ise, hide** (**beet**)→Mod. E. **ice, hide.** O.E. **ban, bat** (roughly as in **drawn**)→M.E. **boon, bote** (roughly the open vowel in some pronunciations of **orange** as /ahrange/) → Mod. E. **bone, boat.** O.E. **toth, sona** (as in **both**) → M.E. **tooth, soone** (**both**)→ Mod. E. **tooth, soon.** O.E. **muth, hus** (as in **youth**) → M.E. **mouthe, hous** (**youth**)→ Mod. E. **mouth, house.**

Sound change in language is an extremely complex process, and the above is only a brief illustration of one sort of change.

There is no reason to believe that modern English is not undergoing gradual sound change at this very moment. In the span of a couple of hundred years, the pronunciation of **tea** has changed from /tay/ to the current form. My wife says /eekonomics/ rather than my /eckonomics/. A modern dictionary gives plenty of evidence of sound change in that it lists the various pronunciations of each of many words.

Differences in the pronunciations of words are matters of usage, and they are just as relative as are the surface differences in grammatical features. No one looked down on John F. Kennedy for pronouncing **Cuba** as /Cuber/, but some purists feel that a person who pronounces **police** with the stress on the first syllable—/pólice/—is inferior or stupid or both.

Loss of Inflections

In the case of English, one important change has been the loss of inflections.

The modern English noun **stone** has only three inflected forms:

151   Don't throw **stones.**

152   The **stone's** form was interesting.

153   The building was made of stones and glass; the **stones'** coloring was interesting.

But in Old English, the word for "stone" had six separate forms. To illustrate these, I will use the Old English **stan** in modern sentences:

154   A **stan** lay on the path. [nominative]

155   The **stanes** coloration is interesting. [genitive]

156   The girl walked to the **stane.** [dative]

157   Don't throw the **stan.** [accusative]

158   Many **stanas** went into the building. [nominative plural]

159   The five **stana** size was equal. [genitive plural]

160   The girl walked to the five **stanum.** [dative plural]

161   Don't lose the five **stanas.** [accusative plural]

Add to this the fact that every noun in Old English had an arbitrary gender. Thus **stan** is masculine, **hof** ("dwelling") is neuter, and **lar** ("learning") is feminine. And add to this the fact that the modern definite article **the** had eleven different forms, depending on gender and number (singular and plural), and one wonders how the Old English child ever managed to learn its language.

Or does one wonder? Was Old English in any fundamental sense more complicated than Modern English? We have been talking about language change, but is there any evidence that languages become simpler or less complicated in the sense that they are easier to master?

Certainly there is no such thing as a more or less complicated language in the modern world. Take German, for instance. It has kept many of its inflections, so that the phrase meaning "the man" undergoes the following changes, according to its use:

162	*Singular*	*Plural*
Nominative	der Mann	die Männer
Genitive	des Mannes	der Männer
Dative	dem Manne	den Männern
Accusative	den Mann	die Männer

But according to all the available evidence, German children master their language just as readily and just as quickly as American children master theirs. If one language were inherently more difficult than another, there would be differences in the rate of language development among the speakers of the various languages, but there are no such differences. It would appear, then, that all languages are either equally difficult or equally simple, depending on your point of view.

Since it is the human brain that constructs language, there is no reason to believe that that organ would generate communications systems that would put stumbling blocks in its own way. To be sure, German as a second language is much easier for a speaker of English to learn than is Chinese, but that is not because Chinese is more difficult than German; it is because German is more closely related to English than is Chinese.

So languages change in their phonology and in their morphology (their sound and their forms), but they apparently do not become either better or simpler.

Lexicon

Earlier in this chapter, we saw how easy it is to make up new nouns, verbs, adjectives, and adverbs—and it is precisely in the *lexicon* that language changes most radically and rapidly.

To put the English lexicon in perspective, a thumbnail sketch of the development of the language is in order.

In about the middle of the fifth century, three Germanic tribes—the Angles, the Saxons, and the Jutes—invaded the island of Britain. These tribes (whose native language was a branch of Germanic) drove out the native Celts. They isolated themselves from their native lands (now Germany), and one of the results of isolation (either geographical or social) is the development of new linguistic forms. The first English language, Old English, was Anglo-Saxon, a dialect of German.

Toward the end of the eighth century, Danes (the Vikings) began to attack England, conquering all of northern and most of eastern England. A century later, King Alfred expelled the Danes; therefore, Scandinavian did not become the language of the ruling classes in England.

The most famous date in English history is, perhaps, 1066; that is when the Norman French conquered England. The language of Normandy became the language of the power elite, and English changed drastically. The leveling of inflections (about which we have already spoken) took place, and English adjusted itself to the language of the conquerors. So it is fair to say that modern English is basically a Germanic language with a heavy overlay of French.

The point is this: our basic word-stock is Anglo-Saxon and French, with an admixture of Latin, Scandinavian, and other languages.

Before we go on, we ought to wring the moral from this brief historical sketch: All varieties of language aspire toward that of the power elite. If the president of the United States, his cabinet, and the members of Congress today spoke French, anyone who wanted to make it in the system would attempt to master that language. If the urban black dialect were the language of the power elite, everyone who wanted to enter the power structure would attempt to master the phonetic and grammatical characteristics of black English.

According to Edward L. Thorndike,[6] the English lexicon is composed of these elements:

163   Words of

Old English origin	61.7%
French	30.9
Latin	2.9
Scandinavian	1.7
Mixed	1.3
Uncertain	1.3
Low German and Dutch	.3

French has had a double influence, because English speakers first got vocabulary items from the Normans, and then picked up many French words when that language became an international means of communication among the elite.

Words Borrowed from French

By about 1154, Norman French words began to appear in English writing: *castel* ("castle"), *tur* ("tower"), *justice, pais* ("peace"). By the time Chaucer started writing, late in the fourteenth century, French had really taken hold, and it is estimated that about thirteen percent of his words are of French origin. Some of the words from French that ultimately established themselves in English: *contract, import, debt, felony, criminal, judge, ointment, medicine, surgeon, chamber, lodge, chapel, buttress, portal, vault.*

The following chart will give you some idea of the influence that French has had on English since about 1500. The words are categorized by general subject to which they apply, and the first date of their appearance in print is indicated in parentheses.

164   *Military and naval*   colonel (1548), dragoon (a doublet of dragon, 1622), reveille (1644), corps (1711 in the military sense; *corpse,* "body," is from 1325), sortie (1795), barrage (1859 "dam"; 1917 in the sense of "bombardment").

People   viceroy (1524), bourgeois (1564), coquette (1611), chaperon (1720, used earlier to mean "hood"), habitué (1818), chauffeur (1899).

[6]Edward L. Thorndike, "The Teacher's Word-Books," in Stuart G. Robertson, ed., *The Development of Modern English,* rev. Frederic G. Cassidy (Englewood Cliffs, N.J.: Prentice-Hall, 1954), p. 155.

Buildings and furniture scene (1540), parterre (1639), attic (1696), salon (1750), chiffonier (1806), hangar (1902).

Literature, art, music rondeau (1525), hautboy (1575; later spelled *oboe*), burlesque (1656), tableau (1699), connoisseur (1714), brochure (1756), carillon (1803), renaissance (1840), matinee (1880).

Dress, fashion, and materials grogram (1562; borrowed again as grosgrain, 1869), cravat (1656), denim (1695), chenille (1738), corduroy (1787), blouse (1840), cretonne (1870), suede (1884).

Food and cooking fricassee (1568), table d'hote (1617), soup (1653), croquette (1706), aspic (1789), restaurant 1827), chef (1842), mousse (1892).[7]

The Etymology Game

English has borrowed words from languages the world over. Seeing where your word-stock came from can be an interesting and informative game. Here are the rules. Printed below in the left-hand column are words from the English lexicon. In the right-hand column, the sources of those words are given. You are to cover the right-hand column and guess the language from which each word came. Only the language from which the word came into English is the right answer. For instance, suppose that a word came from Latin into French and then into English from French; French would be the right answer. Scoring: Give yourself two points for every right answer. 80–100: you are a linguistic genuis, and you should immediately apply to a publisher of dictionaries for a job as editor. 70–78: you have a real gift for words. 60–68: you're about average. 50–58: you aren't paying attention. Below 50: never mind; the game doesn't really tell anything about one's sense for language anyway. (The authority for the answers is *The American Heritage Dictionary of the English Language*, 1969.)

165

1. alcohol — New Latin. Latin got the word from the Arabic *al-kuhl* or *al-kohl.* In Medieval Latin, the word meant a fine powder of antimony used to tint the eyelids. By the way, we adopted the Arabic definite article along with the word, for *al* means "the."

2. assassin — French. The first source of the word was the Arabic *hashshashin,* meaning "hashish addicts." You might look up the fascinating story of this word in an encyclopedia.

3. basenji — Bantu, an African language.

4. Bible — Old French. The word was adopted during the Middle English period. The ultimate source was *Bublos,* the name of the Phoenician port from which papyrus, used for making paper, was shipped to Greece.

5. blitzkrieg — German. It means "lightning war."

6. booze — Dutch. It came into Middle English and originally meant "to carouse."

7. brougham — Scotch. From Henry Peter Brougham, Baron of Brougham and Vaux (1778–1868), a Scottish jurist. (Along the same lines, you might want to look up *sandwich.*)

[7]Francis, p. 144.

8. burlesque — French. From the Italian *burlesco.* The *-que* ending should have tipped you off.

9. cigar — Spanish *cigarro,* possibly taken from the Mayan word meaning "tobacco."

10. didactic — From Greek *didaktikos,* "skillful in teaching."

11. egg — Old Norse. It came into Middle English.

12. flak — German *Fl(ieger)a(bwehr)k(anone),* "aircraft defense gun." Thus, the word is an acronym, like *NASA, NATO,* and countless others that were compounded from the initial letters of their constituent words.

13. gin — From Dutch *jenever,* which came from the Latin word *juniperus,* "juniper."

14. goulash — Hungarian.

15. goy — Yiddish.

16. gumbo — Bantu. The Louisiana French adopted it.

17. hamburger — From the German city Hamburg; short for *hamburger steak.*

18. jazz — The origin is uncertain, so you can give yourself credit for this one.

19. junk (ship) — From Portuguese *junko* and Dutch *jonk.* The Portuguese and Dutch took the word from Malay *jong,* "sea-going ship." Give yourself credit if you said either Portuguese or Dutch.

20. khaki — From Urdu (a language of India), "dusty" or "dust-covered." Urdu borrowed it from Persian.

21. kimono — Japanese.

22. lariat — From Spanish *la reata.*

23. lemon — Old French. The French borrowed it from Arabic, and Arabic borrowed it from Persian.

24. marijuana — Mexican Spanish. If you said Spanish, give yourself credit.

25. moose — From Natick, an American Indian language.

26. mukluk — Eskimo.

27. obnoxious — Latin.

28. papoose — Algonquian. If you said American Indian, give yourself credit.

29. polka — French and German. Borrowed from Polish.

30. ranch — From the Mexican Spanish *rancho.*

31. robot — From Czech.

32. rodeo — Spanish.

33. safari — Arabic.

34. samovar — Russian.

35. sauerkraut — German, "sour cabbage."

36. sauna — Finnish.

37. schlemiel — Yiddish.

38. schmaltz — German.

39. smorgasbord — Swedish.

40. stucco — Italian, but the Italians got it from Old High German.

41. syphilis — Latin. Syphilis was the title character of a poem (1530) by Girolamo Fracastoro, a Veronese physician who supposedly had the disease.

42. tamale — Mexican Spanish.

43. tavern	Old French. The French took it from the Latin *taberna,* "hut." It is interesting to note that *tavern* and *tabernacle* come from the same source.
44. thug	From Hindi, a language of India.
45. tomato	Spanish. The Spanish borrowed it from Nahuatl, the language of the Aztecs and other related tribes.
46. totem	From Ojibwa, an American Indian language.
47. verandah	From Hindi.
48. vodka	Russian. It is the diminuitive of *voda,* "water," so *vodka* literally means "little water."
49. whiskey	From the Irish *usquebaugh.*
50. xenophobia	Made up of *xeno* from the New Latin meaning "stranger" and adopted from the Greek plus the Greek *phobos,* "fearing."

Other Sources for the English Lexicon.

It should now be obvious that borrowed words make up a great portion of the lexicon, but there are other interesting ways in which new words enter the language.

Many English words are *derived* from an existing word to which a prefix or suffix is added. That was the process used by my students to make the word *passive* into a verb by the addition of the suffix *-fy: passify.* The corresponding adjectival form would be *passific,* the noun would be *passification.* Once the word *telegraph* came into the language by the process of compounding the Greek root *tele,* meaning "far," with the Greek root *graph,* meaning "write," the words *telegraphy, telegrapher,* and *telegraphic* were easily derived.

Compounding is a common source of new words: *air-plane, free-loader, light-house-keeper.*

Words also undergo *functional shift;* that is, they move from one category to another. The noun *freak* is now used as a verb: *Gloria freaked Tony.* Or perhaps a better way of looking at this phenomenon is to say that the categories of English words are to some extent fluid. The noun *head,* for instance, is also used as

166   adjective: The *head* man is the president.

167   verb: Thompson *headed* the investigation.

An example of functional shift cited by W. Nelson Francis:

168   A secretary says, "I didn't back-file the letter; I waste-basketed it."[8]

In the process of *back-formation,* a new word is created by removing a suffix from an existing word: *editor/edit, burglar/burgle, lazy/laze,* and many more. *Clipping is much like back-formation, but does not limit itself to the deletion of suffixes: dormitory/dorm, omnibus/bus, examination/exam, laboratory/lab.*

In the etymology game, we saw a word that entered the language from a proper name: *brougham.* There are many more such words: *sandwich,*

[8]Francis, p. 157.

pasteurization, pander (from Chaucer's character Pandarus), *calico* (from Calcutta), and *bowdlerize* (from Thomas Bowdler, who produced a "cleaned-up" edition of Shakespeare).

Some words are simply *coined*. *Kodak* is one such word that was arbitrarily made up, and more recently Standard Oil coined *Exxon* as a trade name.

These are only some of the sources of words in the English lexicon. If this discussion has aroused your interest in words and their nature, it has served its purpose. To be a good writer, you should be interested in—even fascinated by—words and their ways, and in your writing you must make careful choices of words.

What Are Dialects?

The English language might be described as a collection of mutually intelligible dialects, from American standard to British Cockney to Australian to American Northeastern. In fact, even an untrained observer could recognize dozens—if not hundreds—of dialects of English. Therefore, we can conclude that from one point of view, at least, there is no such thing as the English language. It is a hypothetical construct that we speak about for the sake of convenience, not because it exists as a monolithic entity.

What, then, is a dialect? It is nothing more than a collection of idiolects that are related by certain phonological, morphological, and syntactic features. The *idiolect* is the language spoken by the individual, and no two idiolects are exactly alike; each person has his or her own idiolect. Therefore, to schematize:

A *language* is a collection of mutually intelligible dialects.

A *dialect* is a collection of idiolects with certain features in common.

An *idiolect* is the language used by the individual speaker.

It is possible, therefore, to say that *idiolect* is the speaker's personal identity; it is himself or herself. *Dialect* represents his or her social or geographical identification. *The English language* is two steps removed from the individual's most intense concerns. These are important distinctions that we will be considering as the discussion progresses.

Development of Dialects

Dialects develop, it seems, because of either *cultural* or *geographical isolation*. A little chart from W. Nelson Francis's book *The English Language: An Introduction* illustrates this point:

169

	Marked second person Plural Pronouns	
	Northern	Southern
Educated	you (men, etc.)	you all
Uneducated	youse	you all

The Northern *you* and *youse* mark a cultural distinction; the Southern *you all* is a regional usage. Therefore, when we consider dialect, we must always think of two axes of variation: the cultural and the geographical.

Prestige of Dialects

It is a fact that every speaker of every language speaks a dialect—that is, belongs to a dialect group. Some dialects have a good deal of prestige while some do not. The most common prestige dialect in America is what is generally called *standard,* and as we saw, it is the variety of English that most newscasters on the national radio and TV networks speak. John Chancellor, Walter Cronkite, Frank Blair, and Edwin Newman all speak standard.

Therefore, we can say that any dialect that varies from this standard is *nonstandard.* The word "nonstandard" does not imply "substandard." *Nonstandard* is descriptive, not normative.

Standard and Nonstandard

Dialects carry varying degrees of prestige. No doubt you recognize this fact on the basis of personal experience. But you should not assume that the only prestigious dialect is standard. For instance, there is considerable evidence that a certain kind of British accent confers an advantage in America—namely, the British accent used by announcers on the British Broadcasting Corporation. To a great many Americans, this dialect sounds refined, cultured, while the famous Brooklyn dialect sounds uncultured, even crude.

Dialect: An Example

The differences among dialects of a language are always superficial and unimportant. To give you some idea of how dialects differ, I would like to describe Sanpete, the dialect spoken by my wife's family in central Utah. Like other dialects, Sanpete differs from standard in certain *vocabulary* items, in a limited number of *phonetic ways,* and in a limited number of *structural ways.*

A *lexical* difference: The word **husband** is practically nonexistent in spoken Sanpete, so that my mother-in-law introduces me always as her daughter's **man,** not as her daughter's **husband.** In Sanpete, the noun **drink** means almost exclusively a carbonated beverage other than Coca-Cola. Therefore, if a Sanpeter asks you if you want a drink, he does not mean water, nor does he mean a martini, but rather root beer, orange soda, or something of the kind.

Sanpete has one pronounced *phonetic* variation from standard, and that is in the pronunciation of the sequence of letters **or** as in **horse.** The Sanpeter pronounces **horse** as a speaker of standard would pronounce **harse,** if there were such a word. Thus, my wife's name is pronounced /Narma/, not /Norma/.

The *structural* variations that differentiate Sanpete from standard are limited, but noticeable. The phrase **and them** means something like "and the others." Thus, when my mother-in-law wants to visit her son Ken and his family, she says, "Let's go visit Ken **and them.**" Also, the phrase **to home** is used for **at home:** "I wonder if Evelyn and them are **to home.**"

Let's go on briefly to discuss the Sanpete dialect, for we can learn some important lessons from it. My mother-in-law has lived in Sanpete all her life, and she has always been a respected member of her dialect community. Her dialect is extremely pronounced, because she has had no cultural reason for wanting to change it, and she has maintained her geographical isolation. My wife's speech, however, contains only barely perceptible traces of her native Sanpete. The reasons for this are that she moved into another dialect community and thus ended her geographical isolation, and, even more important, that she thus became a speaker of a nonstandard, nonprestige dialect in a community that spoke standard. Therefore, she had two choices: to change her dialect, or to suffer the sneers and snickers that her native dialect brought when she was dealing with members of the standard-speaking community. I don't suppose that she consciously made the decision to change her dialect, but change she did, as the easiest way to avoid the condescension and downright ridicule that her native dialect brought to her day after day.

Dialect and Social Mobility

The next point to be made is fairly complex, but it is interesting and important. Take a close look at the following chart from *The Study of Nonstandard English,* by William Labov (which is, by the way, the best short introduction to the study of dialect that I have ever found):

Class stratification of /r/ in *guard, car, beer, beard,* etc., for native New York City adults.

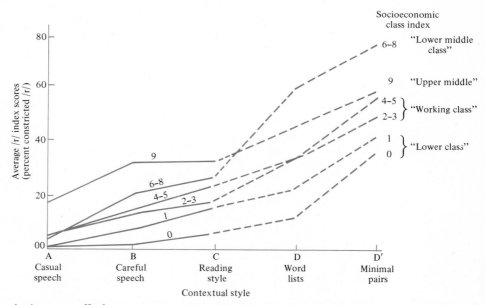

As is generally known, many New Yorkers tend to suppress the /r/ sound in such words as **guard, car,** and **beard,** pronouncing them something like this: /guahd/, /cah/, /behd/. From the point of view of standard English, this pronunciation is, of course, "improper." In casual speech, none of the groups of speakers pronounces the /r/ more than twenty percent of the time, but as the types of usage change from casual speech to careful speech to reading sentences to reading word lists and finally to reading minimal pairs (such as *car* and *far*), all groups increase the percentage of pronounced /r/'s. But notice which group increases most dramatically: the lower middle class, even more than the upper middle class in the socioeconomic spectrum.

The explanation for this fact is most interesting. As Labov says, "This 'hypercorrect' behavior, or 'going one better,' is quite characteristic of second-ranking groups in many communities." The more motivated a group is toward upward social mobility, the harder that group will try to speak the power dialect. Therefore, it would seem, change in dialect is intimately connected both with one's place in the socioeconomic hierarchy and with one's aspirations to move upward. No group will change its dialect as long as the members of the group feel that they have no chance to make it in the economic and social system that prevails.

> In highly stratified situations, where society is divided into two major groups, the values associated with the dominant group are assigned to the dominant language by all. Lambert and his colleagues at McGill University have shown how regular are such unconscious evaluations in the French-English situation in Quebec, in the Arabic-Hebrew confrontation in Israel, and in other areas as well. When English-Canadians heard the same person speaking Canadian French, on the one hand, and English, on the other, they unhesitatingly judged him to be more intelligent, more dependable, kinder, more ambitious, better looking and taller—when he spoke English. Common sense would tell us that French-Canadians would react in the opposite manner, but in fact they do not. Their judgments reflect almost the same set of unconscious values as the English-Canadians show. This overwhelmingly negative evaluation of Canadian French is a property of the society as a whole. It is an omnipresent stigma which has a strong effect on what happens in school as well as in other social contexts.[9]

In other words, the tragedy of the social stratification of dialects is twofold: the speakers of prestige dialects look down on the speakers of nonprestige dialects, and the speakers of nonprestige dialects *look down on themselves.*

It is hard to estimate the damage that this linguistic arrogance causes, but any American can look around and sense the devastation that whole classes and races have undergone because of attitudes toward dialect.

Two points are worth repeating. By definition, the dialects of a language are mutually comprehensible. When a dialect becomes incomprehensible to other speakers of a language, that dialect has become another language, as is the case with Dutch, which drifted so far away from High German as to become a separate language.

The second point is equally important. All the evidence indicates that no language or dialect is inferior to any other language or dialect. Every language and dialect will do everything that its speakers want it to do. The

[9]William Labov, *The Study of Nonstandard English* (Champaign, Ill.: National Council of Teachers of English, 1969), p. 31. Copyright © 1969 by the National Council of Teachers of English. Reprinted by permission of the publisher and the author.

idea that you can "think better" in one language or dialect than in another is simply a destructive myth.

Switching Dialects

Now a significant problem arises—one that you must solve for yourself: Should the individual learner make an effort to change his or her dialect? I am convinced that every normal speaker of English who wants to can master the niceties of standard spoken and standard written dialect. Let's take a representative structure from urban black dialect as an example of the insignificant differences between urban black and standard.

A typical urban black sentence is

170   Didn't nobody see it.

At first glance, this appears to be far removed from the standard

171   Nobody saw it.

But viewed from another vantage point, **170** is very near to the standard. Sentence **170** is merely a version of the double negative that appears in many dialects ("I haven't got **no** money"). Here is a simple explanation of how **170** relates to other double negatives. Take the following double negative:

172   Nobody didn't see it.

Now merely rearrange the sentence a bit to create the urban black version:

173   Didn't nobody see it.

Another characteristic of urban black is the omission of the genitive *-s,* so that a typical sentence would be

174   Fido is John dog.

rather than

175   Fido is John's dog.

Surely a child or young person who can master the complications of surviving in a modern city can, *if he or she wants to,* also master the negatives, genitives, and other features of standard English, for as the examples illustrate, differences among dialects are superficial and minor.

We have already mentioned the invariant **be** of the urban black dialect:

176   He **be** here now.

But we have not looked at the urban black tendency to prepose a noun before the pronoun, as in

177   John he going to the store.

But in standard, we prepose nouns all the time, as in

178   Chicago, that's where my aunt lives.

179   John, he's the one I called on.

Therefore, in this respect urban black and standard are very nearly alike.

In short, and to repeat a point, other dialects differ from standard in only unimportant and superficial ways.

In my own opinion, the best solution to the problem of dialect change is this: don't do it. We should change society's attitudes toward dialects and leave the dialects alone. America avowedly honors its cultural heritage and its cultural diversity, and certainly the most important aspect of a culture is its dialect. Why should people give up so important a part of themselves as the way in which they and the other members of their culture speak?

But, sadly, until society's attitudes do change, I honestly believe that the ability to speak and write standard proficiently can well mean money in your pockets and power in your hands.

Conclusion

To end this chapter, I would like to tell a true story and then raise some questions concerning it.

Not long ago, a major airline decided to increase its percentage of black stewardesses. In order to accomplish this goal, the airline ran an ad in the newspapers of a large city. The ad stated that black women of the proper age should appear at an office in the city at a given time. Some thirty women appeared, among them a friend of mine, whom we'll call Mary.

Of the thirty women, two were offered accelerated processing, and Mary was one of the two. As Mary herself pointed out, "The two of us were the only ones in the group who spoke standard English."

And here are some of the questions that that little tale raises in my mind:

1. What kind of a society would create a situation in which a giant firm would need to single out black women for recruitment?
2. Why did the airline officials think that black speakers of standard would make better stewardesses than speakers of urban black?
3. Why did the firm single out blacks when other minorities—such as speakers of the Chicano dialect—are not actively recruited?
4. Would the airline have lost customers if some of its stewardesses spoke urban black, or might it have gained new customers?
5. Why is it that, invariably, directors of passenger service on airplanes are male, while the positions for servants (stewardesses) are filled almost entirely by women?
6. When the captain of an airliner makes his announcements in a Southern drawl, why is it that no one pays any attention to his dialect? And what would passenger reaction be if the captain spoke urban black?
7. If the captain were a black who spoke standard English, would you be able to tell that he's black without seeing him?
8. Why do airlines recruit black stewardesses, but not black pilots?
9. What other questions does the story raise in your mind?

Discussion and Activities

Why Study Language?

If you are a typical student, you have probably studied the English language more or less systematically for as much as eight years during elementary and high school. Discuss this experience—particularly the study of grammar. What attitudes toward language study did you develop? Why? What most impressed you in your study of the language?

What Is the Nature of Language?

1. The chapter contains this statement: "It is meaningless to say that animals can talk, unless we use **talk** in a loose, metaphorical sense." How does that statement square with the following?

Chimpanzee Talks with Computer in Yerkish[10]

Bill Hendrick

Lana, a three-year-old chimpanzee, sits in a seven-foot cubed environment at the Yerkes Primate Research Center at Emory University and pushes keys on a computer console. By using Yerkish, a complex system of geometric symbols, each with a specific meaning, Lana can request food, candy, water, music, or motion pictures from the machine. Lana, who has learned to correlate the geometric symbols with words, now has a vocabulary of about 75 words and may one day have a vocabulary of 1,000 words, according to Duane M. Rumbaugh of Georgia State University, deviser of Yerkish.

In Lana's plastic environment, which measures seven feet in all directions, is a console with 75 different keys, each of which has on it a different geometric symbol; above the console are seven projectors on which Lana can see each sentence as she forms it. The console feeds into the computer, which is programmed to accept only properly phrased sentences, each of which must begin with the word "please" if the chimp is making a request or with the symbol for "question" if she is asking a question. And each sentence is ended when she depresses the key that means "period." For example, by depressing the correct symbols, Lana can ask, "Please machine give piece of banana." If the words were arranged in any other way, she would not receive a slice of banana. A teletype attached to the computer records every sentence Lana attempts. On an average night, she will wake up and ask the machine for water and then for music or a film. The film, which is on primate growth and development, stays on for 30 seconds. To see it in its entirety of about 17 minutes, Lana must write "Please machine make movie" every 30 seconds. Records reveal that she has watched the film to its conclusion a number of times.

In addition to making basic requests, the chimp can ask questions and make comments. Dr. Rumbaugh reports that she has learned that things have names. "We taught her names of M&M's and bananas by asking,

[10]Bill Hendrick (AP), Champaign-Urbana *Courier,* 29 Jan. 1974, as reprinted in NCTE *Council-Grams,* 35 (March 1974), 45–46. Reprinted by permission of the Associated Press.

'Question . . . What name of this . . . Period.' She would respond 'M&M's name of this' or 'Banana name of this.'" To make sure that Lana does not memorize the positions of the geometric symbols on her console, they are frequently moved about.

"This is the first time that there has been an open-ended language made available for use by chimps and humans with a computer as intermediary," Rumbaugh said. "It is also the first time a language project has entailed rudiments of sentence structure. We think she can master the rudimentary elements of grammar." Further, Rumbaugh and other scientists at the Yerkes center hope to converse with other apes, who, they believe, will show the same capacity for learning that Lana has shown.

2. Language is rigidly patterned behavior. Another way of putting this is to say that language is rule-governed. But there are two kinds of rules. For instance, without the rules there would be no such games as chess or baseball. In other words, the rules constitute the games. On the other hand, some rules are regulative: "Students may not drop classes after the eighth week." Language, too, has *regulative* and *constitutive* rules. Which of the following are regulative, and which are constitutive?

   a. A sentence must contain a subject and a predicate.
   b. Do not use slang in formal essays.
   c. In written English, the items in a coordinate series are separated by commas, thus: ***John, Jill, and Jack went up the hill.***
   d. The structural meaning of *spoken* sentences is signalled by tones, thus: *You are* ^go *ing. You are* ^go ^ing?
   e. Never end a sentence with a preposition.
   f. The article ***the*** signals definiteness, while the article ***a*** signals nondefiniteness.
   g. The word signifying the head of a school is spelled ***p-r-i-n-c-i-p-a-l.***
   h. In *spoken* English, both /orange/ and /ahrange/ have the same meaning.
   i. In written English, both ***aesthetic*** and ***esthetic*** mean the same thing.
   j. The spelling ***judgment*** is preferred over the spelling ***judgement.***

3. List as many more regulative and constitutive rules as you can think of.

What Is Grammar?

1. The chapter states one definition of "grammar": a description of a language, nothing more and nothing less. That is, a grammar of a language describes the language in the same way that an anatomy book describes the human body. In the light of this definition, discuss the grammatical rules and statements that you have learned throughout your schooling.
2. Why is the rule "The word ***ain't*** is not English" erroneous?
3. Why is the rule "A noun is the name of a person, place, or thing" confusing?
4. Why is the rule "The third person singular present tense of ***be*** is ***is***" a partially true rule, but only partially?

5. Why is "Never end a sentence with a preposition" a silly rule?
6. Why is "In context, every English noun has either the feature *definite* or the feature *nondefinite"* a valid rule?
7. Rules governing usage can be very helpful, even essential. An obvious example: It is essential to know that swear words are inappropriate, even disastrous, in certain situations. Discuss usage rules that apply to kinds of language that are appropriate or inappropriate in given situations.

Language Acquisition

You might like to do some linguistic field work. Record—either on tape or in writing—a number of the sentences produced by a child who is just learning to put words together into meaningful sequences. Do your findings square with the statements about language acquisition in the chapter? How do the sentences that you have recorded differ from adult sentences? (Be as specific as you can.)

The Propositional Nature of Language

1. Here are some sentences. Isolate the propositions that they contain. Remember, if you understand the sentences, you also understand the various propositions that make them up. For instance, *It is easy for George to milk goats* contains *It is easy* and *George to milk goats (George milks goats); The poet who read was Allen Ginsberg* contains *The poet was Allen Ginsberg* and *The poet read* (for, obviously, *who* is equivalent to *the poet).*

   a An apple that is rotten spoils the barrel.
   b A green peach can cause a stomachache.
   c The man who was sitting beside me was the dean.
   d The woman walking with me was a friend.
   e Playing catch with me, my son broke my glasses.
   f It is true that cats have nine lives.
   g That apes can talk seems strange.
   h The fact that dolphins are mammals amazes some people.
   i The book Jeff read was *The Secret Agent.*
   j We know which side our bread is buttered on.

2. Isolate all the propositions in example **82,** by Mark Twain.

What Is the Difference Between Competence and Performance?

1. In your own words, explain "competence" and "performance."
2. Discuss some of the factors that you think keep your performance in writing from being as fully developed as you would like it to be. Think of your education, your cultural background, your likes and dislikes.

What Are Dialects?

1. Explain some of the features that characterize your dialect or that set it apart from other dialects that you are familiar with. Think of words, pronunciations, and structures.
2. What are some of the unique features of your idiolect? Do you have any speech mannerisms that are typically your own?
3. Explain honestly how you react to some dialects that are not your own. For instance, if you speak standard, how do you react to urban black or Chicano? What are your feelings about the dialect spoken by the British upper classes?

The Sentence

Summary of the Chapter

The sentence conveys meaning, has esthetic value, and is a unique product of the human mind. Therefore, studying the sentence is fascinating: ultimately, one is studying the ways in which meanings get conveyed and is speculating about esthetic values and about the very nature of the human mind.

The sentence is propositional in nature, consisting of either one proposition or a combination of propositions. A proposition is a main word and the other elements that organize themselves around it. Thus, in the sentence **Mike whacked Mark, whacked** is the main word, and **Mike** and **Mark** stand in relation to that main word and thereby to each other. Most sentences contain more than one proposition—for example, **It is strange that George likes turnips,** in which the propositions are **It is strange** and **George likes turnips.**

In one sense, the native speaker of English already knows almost everything that can be said about English sentences, for the native speaker understands sentences and can produce them. The purpose of this chapter, then, is to make you aware of what you already know and to help you make use of this passive knowledge so that your syntactic versatility will increase—that is, so that you will have at your command a great variety of sentence structures for the expression of your ideas.

Out of context, there is no such thing as a "good" or a "bad" sentence. Sentences are good or bad only in relation to purpose and audience. Therefore, it makes no sense to talk about a sentence's "goodness" out of context.

Surely the most powerful operation in English grammar—or any grammar, for that matter—is the embedding of proposition within proposition. Language would be threadbare, and thought would be hindered, if a sentence could contain only one proposition. Prose would be like this: ***My car has 137,000 miles on it. It is a Plymouth. I intend to trade it in on a new one soon.*** Since the language does provide the capacity for embedding, prose can be like this: ***My car, a Plymouth, which I intend to trade in on a new one soon, has 137,000 miles on it.***

One of the most common and useful ways of embedding is through *relativization,* the use of relative clauses:

a   Cars ***that have bad brakes*** are dangerous.

b   Cars, ***which have bad brakes,*** are dangerous.

The relative clause in example **a** is *restrictive,* and the sentence means something like this: Some cars have bad brakes, and those that do are dangerous. The relative clause in example **b** is *nonrestrictive,* and the sentence means something like this: All cars have bad brakes, and all cars are dangerous.

Nominalization is another important facet of the process of embedding. Roughly speaking, this means that propositions can take the place of nouns. Thus we see sentences with nouns or whole propositions as subjects:

c   ***The case*** appeared strange to Inspector Cluff.

d   ***That the gem was missing*** seemed strange to Inspector Cluff.

Indeed, propositions can fill any sentence slot that a noun can: subject, object, indirect object, object of preposition, and so on.

Structures called *complements* are also an aspect of embedding. These sentences illustrate the kinds of complements discussed in the chapter:

e   ***Typing a manuscript*** is arduous work.

f   ***To type a manuscript*** is arduous work.

g   It is arduous work ***to type a manuscript.***

h   It pleases me ***that Friday is here.***

i   ***That Friday is here*** pleases me.

j   The fact ***that Friday is here*** pleases me.

An important modern concept is that of the *cumulative sentence.* As Francis Christensen has pointed out, the cumulative sentence consists of a base and a variety of modifiers that are attached to it:

k   *Prepositional phrase:*
      At the beginning of the book,
      you will find the preface.

l   *Noun cluster:*
      We boarded the boat,
      a beat-up old tub.

m   *Verb cluster:*
    Shaking himself vigorously,
    the dog sprayed ocean water over everyone.

n   Absolute:
    Our studies being done,
    we went to a concert.

o   *Adverb clause:*
    Allen went to California
    because he had a job there.

p   *Adjective cluster:*
    The ocean,
        calm as a lake,
    can suddenly become treacherous.

Certain traditional principles concerning the sentence are of use to the writer.

First, sentences can be classified according to their clause structure as *simple, compound, complex,* or *compound-complex.* A simple sentence contains only one clause:

q   Anthony brushes his teeth every morning.

A compound sentence contains two or more independent clauses:

r   Mary Margaret earns the living, and Paul maintains the house.

A complex sentence contains one independent clause and one or more dependent clauses:

s   While Tom cooks dinner, Grace reads the paper.

And a compound-complex sentence contains two or more independent clauses and one or more dependent clauses:

t   Raw spaghetti is brittle, but spaghetti that has been cooked is limp.

The second traditional principle is that of *periodic* and *loose* sentences. Roughly speaking, a periodic sentence is one in which the modifiers precede the base:

u   After having thoroughly sanded the table,
    Jeff began to paint it.

A loose sentence is one in which the modifiers follow the base:

v   Reading a poem is a challenge,
    demanding sensitivity and concentration.

The third traditional principle is that of *passive voice.* Transitive sentences like

w   Evelyn makes bread every week.

can be changed so that they are in the passive voice, like this:

x   Every week bread is made by Evelyn.

The fourth traditional principle has to do with *parallelism* and *balance*. Sentences such as the following seem strange because similar elements are not *parallel* in form:

y   Dave likes skiing, swimming, and to fish.

In **y**, ***skiing, swimming,*** and ***to fish*** fill the same grammatical slot as objects of the verb ***likes.*** Therefore, we would expect them all to be of the same grammatical order—to be parallel. A more normal version of **y** is the following:

z   Dave likes skiing, swimming, and fishing.

Sentence *balance*—closely related to parallelism—involves using identical or nearly identical structures. Here is a perfectly balanced sentence:

aa   To love learning   is   to question premises
     passionately   ardently.

And here is another:

bb   Astute patients know   which physicians devote their lives to healing people
                            and
                            which physicians give their efforts to making
                            money.

Finally, the grammar of the language affords various strategies for achieving different kinds of emphasis within sentences. For example, in the following sentence, ***the old ice-cream parlor*** receives strong emphasis:

cc   The old ice-cream parlor, that was my favorite place during my childhood.

But in the following, the emphasis shifts to ***During my childhood:***

dd   During my childhood, the old ice-cream parlor was my favorite place.

Studying Sentences

Can there be thought without language? Does language development bring about mental development, or does mental development bring about language development? Can we infer mental processes from the kinds of sentences that the language user produces? Does the language that we speak impose restrictions on our ability to think?

These questions—and a great many others—define some of the important theoretical considerations that linguists and psycholinguists hope to understand through unraveling the complexities of the sentences in a language.

The Mystery of Sentences

We touched on the mystery of sentences in Chapter 10, "The Writer's Language," in which we talked about deep and surface structures and explored the difficulty of explaining exactly why we understand even very simple sentences. For instance, everyone knows immediately what these two sentences mean:

1 John is easy to please.

2 John is eager to please.

But to explain our understanding in *specific* terms is rather difficult. We know that the deep structure (the meaning) of the first contains something like this: *(Someone) to please John.* That is, it is John who is going to be pleased. But the second sentence contains a meaning something like this: *John to please (someone).* That is, John will do the pleasing. Apparently our understanding depends on the way *easy* and *eager* act on the rest of the items in the sentences. However, it is difficult to specify just how or why *eager* and *easy* act as they do.

Students of writing need not be able to explain the mysteries of language. Linguists and psycholinguists can attempt to do that. It is important to sense, however, that the sentence is not a completely understood "given." From one point of view, the table that I am typing on is easily explicable. But from another point of view, explanation of it demands all the concepts of modern physics—and then some—for me to understand it, for it is not merely an assemblage of legs, top, hinges, screws, and so on. No, it is a collection of atoms.

What I am getting at is this: learning about the sentence involves just as much challenge, adventure, and mystery as learning about things (the amoeba) or processes (atomic fission) in the physical world.

Many discussions of sentences overlook or ignore the profundity and intrigue of the subject that they are dealing with. They describe the "hinges, joints, and screws," as if the sentence itself were not the best outward manifestation of the ultimate mystery that we must confront: the way a human being thinks.

The questions of how sentences are produced and how they function represent nothing less than a great intellectual adventure. That, in fact, is why modern linguistic studies have become so important to psychologists and estheticians.

Not that in this chapter we will unravel the mysteries of the human mind. That is not the point at all. But it is important to be continually aware that the questions dealt with in this chapter are not trivial—and to realize further that the sentence is one of the most accessible and explicable manifestations of the human thought process.

Sentences: The Esthetic Dimension

Another idea that runs throughout this chapter is this: there is an esthetic dimension to sentences. Some of them please us, and some of them, for reasons that we often don't understand, grate on our nerves or leave us dissatisfied, not because of what they say but because of the way they say it. For instance, the great American essayist E. B. White had this to say:

> If the student doubts that style is something of a mystery, let him try rewriting a familiar sentence and see what happens. Any much-quoted

sentence will do. Suppose we take "These are the times that try men's souls." Here we have eight short, easy words, forming a simple declarative sentence. The sentence contains no flashy ingredient, such as "Damn the torpedoes!" and the words, as you see, are ordinary. Yet in that arrangement they have shown great durability; the sentence is well along in its second century. Now compose a few variations:

    Times like these try men's souls.

    How trying it is to live in these times!

    These are trying times for men's souls.

    Soulwise, these are trying times.

It seems unlikely that Thomas Paine could have made his sentiment stick if he had couched it in any of these forms. But why not? No fault of grammar can be detected in them, and in every case the meaning is clear. Each version is correct, and each, for some reason that we can't readily put our finger on, is marked for oblivion. We could, of course, talk about "rhythm" and "cadence," but the talk would be vague and unconvincing. We could declare "soulwise" to be a silly word, inappropriate to the occasion; but even that won't do—it does not answer the main question. Are we even sure "soulwise" is silly? If "otherwise" is a serviceable word, what's the matter with "soulwise"?[1]

In this chapter on the sentence, then, we will have always at the backs of our minds two considerations: the sentence as a product of mind and the sentence as an art object. The chapter itself, however, will be mainly practical.

Propositions

To refer to part of the discussion in Chapter 10, every sentence is either one proposition or a combination of propositions.

What is meant by "proposition"?

Roughly speaking, a proposition is a main word or phrase, around which other words and phrases organize themselves into meanings. For instance, take the following two sentences:

3   The scooter and the skateboard collided.

4   The scooter collided with the skateboard.

Everyone would agree, I think, that these sentences mean the same or nearly the same thing. The main word (we will call it the *predicate*) is, of course, **collide.** Both **the scooter** and **the skateboard** are *noun phrases.* Notice that both have the same relationship with **collide.** In traditional terms, we might say that *both* of them receive the action of **collide.** We will call this relationship *neutral.* Therefore, we can represent the proposition of **3** and **4** thus:

5   collide: neutral neutral

Now look at the following sentences.

[1]William Strunk, Jr., and E. B. White, *The Elements of Style* (New York: Macmillan, 1959), pp. 53–54.

6   George gave Mary a hug.

7   George gave a hug to Mary.

8   A hug was given to Mary by George.

Again, we feel that the three sentences are either precisely or nearly synonymous, and we know that the elements organize themselves around the predicate **gave.** We might say that the relationship of **George** to **gave** is that of *agent,* the one doing the giving; the relationship of **Mary** is *goal,* the one receiving what was given; and the relationship of **hug** is *neutral,* what was given. Thus, all three sentences are based on the proposition

9   give: agent goal neutral

One more example. I assume that we take the following sentences to be synonymous or nearly synonymous:

10   Flies swarmed in the room.

11   The room swarmed with flies.

The predicate is clearly **swarmed.** We might say that the relationship of **flies** to the predicate is *X* (for it is difficult to think of an appropriate term, even though all of us understand the sentence perfectly well). The relationship of **room** with predicate might be termed *locative,* for it tells where the flies were swarming. Thus, underlying both **10** and **11** is the proposition

12   swarm: X locative

The point here is this: when we understand sentences, we organize their elements around a predicate. That is, elements other than the predicate have perceivable relationships with the predicate, and those relationships convey a good part of the meaning of sentences. We can infer also that when we produce sentences we are organizing noun phrases around a predicate.

Arrangements of Propositions

As the foregoing examples demonstrate, a proposition can have various surface forms (the forms that appear on the printed page or in the spoken language). For instance, sentences **13** and **14** have different surface arrangements, but they both are based on the same underlying proposition, **15**:

13   The baby made a fuss.

14   A fuss was made by the baby.

15   make: agent neutral

If we did not understand the relationships in the underlying propositions, we could not understand sentences. One rough way of stating this idea is that we need to know "who did what with which and to whom" if we are to understand a sentence.

Decoding Propositions

Now look at the following sentence, a command (an imperative sentence):

16   Shut up!

At first glance, it would seem that there is nothing but a predicate: ***shut up.*** But I think I can convince you that behind that simple verb and particle (***up,*** in grammatical jargon, is called a *particle*) there is a great deal more than appears on the surface.

In the first place, the sentence must be addressed to someone, and the pronoun of address is ***you.*** In other words, we interpret the meaning of ***Shut up!*** as something like ***(You) shut up!*** Notice that the following are *not* commands:

17   He shuts up.

18   I shut up.

19   They shut up.

Therefore, in ***Shut up!*** we seem to have the proposition

20   shut up: agent

But when we hear or read the sentence, we understand it to convey even more than ***(You) shut up!*** For we know that a command is always given in the first person, thus:

21   I command that you shut up!

or

22   I order that you shut up.

What I am saying is this: when we hear the sentence ***Shut up!*** we know that someone is being addressed, is receiving the command (and if we want to express this someone, we must resort to the pronoun ***you***); furthermore, we understand that someone is issuing a command; thus, underlying ***Shut up!*** is something like

23   (I command that you) Shut up!

Simply, if we did not know that much, we would not have understood the sentence.

Therefore, to understand the simple sentence ***Shut up!*** we must be able to sort out two propositions and understand their relationship to each other, something like this:

24   [I command (that you shut up)]

Another way of representing this is as follows:

25   [command: agent (shut up: agent)]

Of course, we do this all the time, and with no effort whatsoever; the ability to comprehend propositions is simply one facet of our *competence* in language. (Competence is discussed in Chapter 10.)

Propositions Within Propositions

Consider what happens in our understanding of sentences such as the following:

26   Bert knows that Mary thinks that Herb cheats.

27   That Mary thinks that Herb cheats is known by Bert.

When we interpret these sentences, we must do it somewhat as follows:

28   [know: agent (think: agent (cheats: agent))]

In other words, regardless of the surface form of the sentence, **knows** is the main predicate, and the subordinate predicates **think** and **cheat** (and the noun phrases that stand in relationships to them) organize themselves around **know.**

Sentences then, consist of either single propositions or of two or more propositions *embedded* within one another. This concept is important to you for two reasons.

First: You already *know* it thoroughly. I have merely pointed it out to you, made you aware of it. If you didn't already know it, you would not be able to understand the sentences that you read and hear, for your understanding depends in large measure on your ability to see the propositional relationships in sentences.

Second: Since you already know all this, increasing your ability to construct sentences is not really a matter of learning. It is simply a matter of activating in performance what you already know thoroughly.

Your Knowledge of Sentences

The purpose of this chapter is to help you bring into ready use what you already know about sentences. To illustrate with an analogy: you have an active and a passive vocabulary. Your passive vocabulary consists of words for which you know the meanings, but which you never use. You can move items from your passive vocabulary into your active vocabulary simply by willing to do so and by practicing a bit. But the analogy is not perfect, for while your active and passive vocabularies combined probably represent a fairly small portion of the 600,000 or so words in English, your passive knowledge of sentence structure is virtually global; that is, you probably know just about all there is to know, even though you may use only a small portion of the structural resources that the language makes available.

An Important Note on Terminology and Methodology

In the discussion that follows, I will be using the jargon of modern grammar. Now, that jargon has no particular value in itself, but I must have a vocabulary to name what I'm talking about. For instance, instead of talking about *nominals,* I might as well say *glips* or *589 Structures* or *X's.* But the fact is, I must have names to identify concepts, and I have chosen to use accepted terminology. But there is no reason for you to learn these terms. In context, what they are pointing to will be clear enough, so forget about the terminology; it has no importance here.

What is important is this: that you be made aware of what you already know. The purpose of this awareness is extremely practical: to trigger your ability to use a great variety of structures in your own writing.

The method will be to survey some principles of sentence structure in this chapter, and then in Chapter 14 to do a close analysis of "living" sentences in context.

What Constitutes a "Good" Sentence?

The purpose of this chapter is *not* to teach you how to write "good" sentences, for a sentence is "good" only in context. To judge the goodness of a sentence, one asks if it conveys the right tone and meaning to a given audience at a given time for a given purpose. Thus, to refer back to E. B. White's example, if one's purpose were to evoke humor, the sentence "Soulwise, these are trying times" might be infinitely better than "These are the times that try men's souls."

This chapter is intended to help you use what you know about sentences, to help you increase your *syntactic versatility* (that is, your ability to produce a variety of kinds of sentences), so that you will be able to make choices as to how you want to develop a sentence for a given audience at a given time and with a given purpose.

Relatives

In this discussion of relative clauses, the purpose is not to present grammatical explanations, but to make you *conscious* of the kind of embedding that relative clauses represent and of the sorts of structures that can be derived from relatives.

Restrictive and Nonrestrictive

A relative clause is nothing more than one sentence embedded within another. For instance, these two examples mean the same thing, or very nearly the same thing:

29 Cars, **which normally use gasoline as fuel,** are dangerous.

30 Cars are dangerous, and they normally use gasoline as fuel.

But these two do *not* have the same or nearly the same meaning:

31 Cars that have bad brakes are dangerous.

32 Cars are dangerous, and they have bad brakes.

Example **31** says that only those cars that have bad brakes are dangerous, and example **32** says that all cars are dangerous and that they all have bad brakes.

Schematically, we might represent the meaning that we gain from **29** thus:

33   [Cars are dangerous (and cars normally use gasoline as fuel)]

And we might represent the meaning that we gain from **31** thus:

34   [Cars (cars have bad brakes) are dangerous]

Example **29** contains a *nonrestrictive relative clause,* and example **31** contains a *restrictive relative clause.* (Remember, the terminology is not really important here.) Example **29** says something like this: All cars are dangerous, and all cars normally use gasoline as fuel. On the other hand, example **31** says something like this: Only those cars that have bad brakes are dangerous.

Here are two more examples, the first of a nonrestrictive clause and the second of a restrictive clause:

35   The much advertised Nordic race, **which centers in northern Europe,** has the general characteristics of the stock plus long heads, tall stature, and blond pigmentation.   —Ralph Linton

36   There are two other races **that are usually classed with the negroid stock** although their habitat lies far from the rest.   —Ralph Linton

Examples of Relatives

Here is a list of sentences containing various kinds of relative clauses. By studying the sentences and the analyses that follow them, you will learn a good deal about the sort of embedding of propositions that we call *relative.*

37   Fishermen who are patient and careful always triumph.
     [Fishermen (fishermen are patient and careful) always triumph]

38   Women, who have been subjugated since time immemorial, are now demanding their rights.
     [Women are now demanding their rights (*and* women have been subjugated since time immemorial)]

39   The books that the class read contained much poetry. The books the class read contained much poetry.
     [The books (the class read the books) contained much poetry]

40   Students, who as a general rule don't like poetry, often develop a taste for it.
     [Students often develop a taste for poetry (*and* students as a general rule don't like poetry)]

41   The games that people play are odd.
     The games people play are odd.
     [The games (people play the games) are odd]

42   At the time when the class started, I was not yet awake.
     [At the time (the class started at the time) I was not yet awake]

43   Joe returned to the place where he was born.
     [Joe returned to the place (Joe was born at the place)]

Relatives in "Living" Prose

Now let's consider some sentences by modern writers who are generally conceded to be skilled craftsmen in prose.

44   The tides of change *that move society on to new solutions or catastrophes* run deeper than the swirling events of the day.   —John W. Gardner

Gardner would have lost a good deal if he had not embedded the relative clause:

45   The tides of change run deeper than the swirling events of the day. These tides of change move society on to new solutions or catastrophes.

Notice that it is more difficult to gain a meaning from **45** than it is from **44**. The embedding of the clause in **44** establishes the relationship between propositions; in **45**, the reader must grope a bit in order to ascertain the relationship between the first sentence and the second one.

Here is an even more vivid example of that same principle:

46   Nothing much divides those *who are liberals by common political designation* from those *who are conservatives.*   —John Kenneth Galbraith

47   Nothing much divides a certain group of people from another group of people. The first group are liberals by common political designation, and the second are conservatives.

Of course, it is almost inconceivable that anyone would write **47**; it is simply too cumbersome, and it puts too many roadblocks in the way of the reader's understanding.

Yet another example:

48   Millions and tens of millions enjoy the highest standard of life *the world has ever known.*   —Michael Harrington

[Millions and tens of millions enjoy the highest standard of life (the world has ever known the standard of life)]

In this sentence, we can't even imagine disembedding the relative; without the relative, the idea is virtually impossible to express, except by some tortuous paraphrase such as the following:

49   Millions and tens of millions enjoy a high standard of life. In fact, there has never before been such a high standard of life.

Here is a slight variation from the kinds of relatives we have examined so far:

50   In the course of conquering America and so making Americans, habits were adopted out of urgent necessity *which may have survived that necessity.*
                    —Dennis Brogan

[In the course of conquering America and so making Americans, habits (habits may have survived that necessity) were adopted out of urgent necessity]

In other words, the relative is not placed exactly after the word that it modifies (*habits*), as has been the case with the other examples.

The following sentence contains two relative clauses:

51   The Freudian psychology is the only systematic account of the human mind *which, in point of subtlety and complexity, of interest and tragic power, deserves to stand beside the chaotic mass of psychological insights* <u>*which*</u> *literature has accumulated through the centuries.*   —Lionel Trilling
[The Freudian psychology is the only systematic account of the human mind (this systematic account of the human mind, in point of subtlety and complexity, of interest and tragic power, deserves to stand beside the chaotic mass of psychological insights [literature has accumulated the psychological insights through the centuries)]

These sentences contain other variations of the relative construction:

52   Let me say, first of all, in contrast to what some philosophers of history have proclaimed, that there is no iron law *according to which nations must decline.*   —Hans J. Morgenthau
[Let me say, first of all, in contrast to what some philosophers of history have proclaimed, that there is no iron law (nations must decline according to the iron law)]

53   In a nation of images without substances, in a politic of consensus *where platitude replaces belief or belief is fashioned by consensus,* genuine rhetoric, like authentic prose, must be rare.   —John Illo
[In a nation of images without substance, in a politic of consensus (platitude replaces belief or belief is fashioned by consensus in a politic of consensus), genuine rhetoric, like authentic prose, must be rare]

Here is an example of a nonrestrictive relative:

54   In most societies the unofficial attitude to sexual morality now is that at any rate among unmarried adults there is nothing inherently sinful or criminal about sexual experiences and adventures, whether or not they are accompanied by love, *which I will define as the desire to maintain a relationship irrespective of the sexual and, in the final analysis, any other enjoyment to be got from it.*   —John Fowles

So far, the relative clauses that we have seen have modified one word, as the nonrestrictive relative in **54** modifies *love.* But here is a sentence in which the nonrestrictive clause modifies the independent clause that it follows (that is, the proposition in the relative clause modifies the main proposition of the sentence):

55   I went to Sarah Lawrence and got to love it without ever taking it very seriously, *which I also suppose was the way the boys I loved in those days felt about me.*   —Sally Kempton

56   An extra acre or two gives a fine sense of possession to an adult; it does not compensate children for the give-and-take of our village *where there is always a contemporary to help swing the skipping rope or put on the catcher's mitt.*   —Phyllis McGinley

In this sentence, don't be fooled by the writer's failure to set the clause off with a comma; the meaning is nonrestrictive nonetheless.

Two more illustrations of professional authors' use of relative clauses, the first restrictive and the second nonrestrictive:

57   Here [in the suburb] domesticity could flourish, forgetful of the exploitation **on which so much of it was based.** Here individuality could prosper, oblivious of the pervasive regimentation beyond. This was not merely a child-centered environment; it was based on a childish view of the world, **in which reality was sacrificed to the pleasure principle.**   —Lewis Mumford

Finally, Thoreau and the relative (from *Walden*):

58   *Flint's Pond!* Such is the poverty of our nomenclature. What right had the unclean and stupid farmer, **whose farm abuted on this sky water, whose shores he has ruthlessly laid bare,** to give his name to it? Some skin-flint, **who loved better the reflecting surface of a dollar, or a bright cent, in which he could see his own brazen face; who regarded even the wild ducks which settled in it as trespassers;** his fingers grown into crooked and horny talons from the long habit of grasping harpy-like;—so it is not named for me. I go not there to see him nor to hear of him; **who never saw** it, **who never bathed in it, who never loved it, who never protected it, who never spoke a good word for it, nor thanked God that He had made it.** Rather let it be named from the fishes **that swim in it,** the wild fowl or quadrupeds **which frequent it,** the wild flowers **which grow by its shores,** or some wild man or child **the thread of whose history is interwoven with its own;** not from him **who could show no title to it but the deed which a like-minded neighbor or legislature gave him,**—him **who thought only of its money value; whose presence perchance cursed all the shores; who exhausted the land around it, and would fain have exhausted the waters within it; who regretted only that it was not English hay or cranberry meadow,—there was nothing to redeem it, forsooth, in his eyes,—and would have drained and sold it for the mud at its bottom.** It did not turn his mill, and it was no *privilege* to him to behold it. I respect not his labors, his farm **where everything has its price: who would carry the landscape, who would carry his God, to market, if he could get anything for Him; who goes to market** for **his god as it is; on whose farm nothing grows free, whose fields bear no crops, whose meadows no flowers, whose trees no fruits, but dollars; who loves not the beauty of his fruits, whose fruits are not ripe for him till they are turned to dollars.** Give me the poverty **that enjoys true wealth.**

Nominals

Nominals are words and phrases that can fill the sentence slots that can also be occupied by simple nouns. By way of showing you what this means, here is an inventory of nominal slots:

59   Subject:
Cities need rapid transit.
Cities that are overcrowded need rapid transit.

60   Direct object:
Students love *learning.*
Students love *to learn new facts about the world they live in.*

61   Indirect object:
The preacher gave *the sinners* hell.
The preacher gave *whoever sinned* hell.

62   Subjective complement:
Young people can become *millionaires.*
Young people can become *whatever they want to be.*

63   Objective complement:
The girl called her ex-boyfriend *a fink.*
The girl called her ex-boyfriend *whatever popped into her mind.*

64   Object of preposition:
Herman longed for *home.*
Herman longed for *the place where he was born.*

65   Vocative:
Students, shut up!
Whoever is chattering at the back of the room, shut up!

Nominalized Sentences

It is an interesting fact of grammar that sentences can be nominalized—
that is, can be made to serve as nominals within other sentences, like this:

66   Tony collects coins.

67   *That Tony collects coins* pleases me.

It is also an interesting fact of grammar that some nominals are very much
like sentences, for instance:

68   Jeff's interest in oceanography

69   Jeff is interested in oceanography.

Note that either of these can fill a nominal slot in another sentence:

70   *Jeff's interest in oceanography* may determine his major in college.

71   *That Jeff is interested in oceanography* may determine his major in college.

Now, in regard to nominals, let's look at some sentences.

72   *That any specific freedom can be deemed inviolable independently of its
consequences on other specific freedoms, as well as its consequences on the
health and welfare of the community,* seems on the face of it quite
unplausible.   —Sidney Hook

This sentence, I think you'll agree, is difficult to read, and the reason for
that difficulty is not difficult to explain. You'll recall that a sentence consists
of a proposition, with perhaps one or more additional propositions embedded in it. Each proposition contains a predicate, or a key word, around
which the rest of the proposition organizes itself. Thus:

73   Lillian paints landscapes. [paint: agent neutral]

In the case of a sentence with embedded propositions, there is always a
main predicate that serves as the organizational pivot for all the other
sentence elements. Thus, in the case of **74**, we organize our understanding

around the main predicate **proves,** not around the subordinate predicates *smell* or *cause:*

74   That cigars *smell* good *proves* that they must *cause* cancer.

One way of looking at **74** is to say that, since it contains three predicates, it is three sentences in one, perhaps like this:

75   (Something) proves (something).
Cigars smell good.
They must cause cancer.

In any case, **proves** is clearly the main predicate, the organizational pivot for the rest of the sentence.

Now go back to **72.** It contains thirty-seven words, but the main predicate (**seems**) is the thirtieth word in the sequence; that is, you must hold twenty-nine words in suspension in your mind before you reach the word that lets you know how to organize the meaning of the sentence. For this reason, **72** seems awkward and difficult to read. Interestingly, **72** can easily be revised so that it is easier to read and sounds much more natural:

76   It *seems* on the face of it quite unplausible that any specific freedom can be deemed inviolable independently of its consequences on other specific freedoms, as well as its consequences on the health and welfare of the community.

In **76,** the organizational pivot for the sentence (the predicate **seems**) appears immediately, and you have less to juggle in your mind than with **72.**

Example **77** is a sentence that can easily be improved:

77   *The nesting mallards pulling after them shadowy, long forgotten images* move in my memory, too.

Here is the way the author actually wrote it:

78   The nesting mallards move in my memory, too, pulling after them shadowy, long forgotten images.   —Wallace Stegner

In **78,** the complete nominal construction is broken up, so that the reader gets to the predicate early and can begin to organize the meaning of the sentence. And here is yet another example of how a skilled writer forms sentences so that the reader has minimum difficulty in decoding them. In this instance, it is a subordinate clause that we are concerned with:

79   My great moment came at six, when my father returned from work, his overalls smelling faintly of turpentine and shellac, white drops of silver paint still gleaming on his chin.   —Alfred Kazin

Note how easily this sentence can be ruined:

80   My great moment came at six, when *my father, his overalls smelling faintly of turpentine and shellac, white drops of silver paint still gleaming on his chin,* returned from work.

Nominals and Ease in Reading

The following is an example of a long nominal that ruins a sentence because its elements separate a prepositional phrase from the noun that it modifies:

81   There *is* a ***fading line, a very fading line, a goddamned, almost invisible line,*** between fantasy and reality.

As the author actually wrote the sentence, it looks like this:

82   There *is* a fading line between fantasy and reality, a very fading line, a goddamned, almost invisible line.   —Bruce Jay Friedman

The next sentence talks easily and lucidly about the process of manufacturing cars:

83   Automatic machines, linked by transfer equipment, move engine blocks through a complete manufacturing process, performing 530 precision cutting and drilling operations in $14\frac{1}{2}$ minutes as compared to 9 hours in a conventional plant.   —Ben B. Seligman

But what happens to that sentence when the predicate is deferred by an overpacked nominal slot?

84   ***Automatic machines performing 530 precision cutting and drilling operations in $14\frac{1}{2}$ minutes as compared to 9 hours in a conventional plant, linked by transfer equipment,*** move engine blocks through a complete manufacturing process.

Here is a sentence that is extremely difficult to read:

85   ***The fact that valuations are seldom overtly expressed except when they emerge in the course of a person's attempts to formulate his beliefs concerning the facts and their implications in relation to some section of social reality*** has already been hinted at.

As the sentence actually was written, it is much easier to read and understand:

86   We have already hinted at the fact that valuations are seldom overtly expressed except when they emerge in the course of a person's attempts to formulate his beliefs concerning the facts and their implications in relation to some section of social reality.   —Gunnar Myrdal

Why is **86** easier to read than **85**? Because in **86**, the predicate ***hinted at*** occurs early.

Two more examples:

87   As you know, I had ***two other interests, music and directing movies of my own authorship,*** just as strong a few years ago.

By breaking up the nominal, the original version achieves much more grace and readability:

88   As you know, I had two other interests just as strong a few years ago—music and directing movies of my own authorship.   —James Agee

The following lucid sentence

89   In science, Copernicus and Vesalius may be chosen as representative figures; they typify the new cosmology and the scientific emphasis on direct observation.   —Alfred North Whitehead

might have been put together in this way:

90   In science, ***Copernicus and Vesalius, who typify the new cosmology and the scientific emphasis on direct observation,*** may be chosen as representative figures.

Enough about nominal constructions and their effect within sentences. The writer needs to be aware of the strategies that the grammar of the language affords, and nominals are important elements in the way meanings get conveyed—either clearly or hazily, either gracefully or awkwardly—in English sentences.

Complements

Here is a series of sentences that are synonymous, or nearly so:

91   For George to milk goats is strange.

92   It is strange for George to milk goats.

93   That George milks goats is strange.

94   It is strange that George milks goats.

95   George's milking goats is strange.

96   It's strange, George's milking goats.

In these sentences, we have two propositions: ***It is strange*** and ***George milks goats.*** When we organize these sentences in our minds to derive their meanings, we arrive at something like this:

97   [It (George milks goats) is strange]

In other words, when we derive the meaning, we know that the sentence ***George milks goats*** is equivalent to, or embedded in, ***it.*** If, in the surface structure, the sentence ***George milks goats*** is the subject of the sentence, then ***it*** is no longer necessary and does not appear. But the following causes at least momentary puzzlement:

98   *George milks goats is strange.

The reason for this is easy to explain: the tendency in reading it is to organize the sentence around the first word that might be the main predicate, namely ***milks.*** But that is a false organization, for the main predicate in the sentence is really ***strange.*** Therefore, you can now explain the function of the word ***that*** as it appears in the following:

99   That George milks goats is strange.

That simply warns you that *milks* is not the main predicate, not the word around which you will organize the meaning of the sentence.

Embedding Again

It is well to keep in mind that one of the most powerful resources the language affords its users is the ability to embed propositions within one another. Relative clauses, as we have seen, are one of the ways in which propositions are embedded. *Complements* are another form of embedding, as important and prevalent as relatives. We will not attempt to define complements, but will look at and analyze a variety of them. For instance:

100   The trailer was attached by means of a trailer hitch, which I bought when *it* became clear *that the trailer could not be hitched up without one,* to the back of our new Rolls.   —Donald Barthelme

To make the point clear, let me rewrite that sentence:

101   The trailer was attached to the back of our new Rolls by means of a trailer hitch, which I bought when *that the trailer could not be hitched up without one became clear.*

Examples of Complements

In the rest of this section, we will play with a number of complements to illustrate some important concepts about how sentences work and how they can take a variety of surface forms.

Here's an easy enough sentence:

102   To produce necessary food and shelter is man's work.   —Paul Goodman

Goodman might well have written the sentence in any of these forms:

103   It is man's work to produce necessary food and shelter.

104   To produce necessary food and shelter—that is man's work.

105   Producing necessary food and shelter is man's work.

Whichever form the sentence takes, isn't the meaning something like this?

106   What is man's work is to produce necessary food and shelter.

107   [It (someone to produce necessary food and shelter) is man's work]

Here is a sentence with two complements, both of them objects of the verb *know:*

108   He knew also *that a man must endure his times* and *that his own times were undoubtedly evil.*   —Daniel Berrigan, S. J.

Now for some variations on the theme:

109   That a man must endure his times and that his own times were undoubtedly evil—this he knew.

110   That a man must endure his times and that his own times were undoubtedly evil was known by him.

111   It was known by him that a man must endure his times and that his own times
were undoubtedly evil.

Complements and Relatives

Closely compare the following two sentences. The first contains a complement, and the second contains a relative.

112   The most convincing proof *that the American high school has its heart in the
right place* is its leaders' continuing advocacy of a free press.

—Martin Mayer

113   The most convincing proof *that I can offer for the American high school
having its heart in the right place* is its leaders' continuing advocacy of a free
press.

Each of these sentences contains an embedded proposition, like this:

114   [The most convincing proof (that the American high school has its heart in the
right place) is its leaders' continuing advocacy of a free press]

115   [The most convincing proof (I can offer proof for the American high school
having its heart in the right place) is its leaders' continuing advocacy of a free
press]

This is an important concept. When you read *112,* you equate the whole
sentence *the American high school has its heart in the right place* with the
noun *proof.* If I were to ask what you mean by the word *proof,* you would
answer, "that the American high school has its heart in the right place." In
other words: *proof = the American high school has its heart in the right
place.*

But when you read *113* and understand it, you do something quite
different. You equate only the word *that* with *proof,* and as *115* indicates,
the *meaning* that you derive from the embedded sentence is *I can offer
proof for the American high school. . . .*

*However, you know all this intuitively, or else you would not have
understood the sentences.*

Complements and Sentence Variety

Here is another sentence that contains complements:

116   It is easy *to mistake the urgent technical difficulties of teaching a heterogeneous student group for the moral and development problems, less urgent and
far more serious, which it creates;* it is easy *to solve the former expediently
and evade the latter.*   —Edgar Z. Friedenberg

Isn't the meaning we derive something like this?

117   [It (*someone* to mistake the urgent technical difficulties of teaching a heterogeneous student group for the moral and development problems, less urgent
and far more serious, which it creates) is easy] [it (*someone* to solve the former
expediently and evade the latter) is easy]

If so, the sentence can take a variety of surface forms, all with the same, or very nearly the same, meaning:

118   To mistake the urgent technical difficulties of teaching a heterogeneous student group for the moral and development problems, less urgent and far more serious, which it creates is easy; to solve the former expediently and evade the latter is easy.

119   For someone to mistake the urgent technical difficulties of teaching a heterogeneous student group for the moral and development problems, less urgent and far more serious, which it creates is easy; for someone to solve the former expediently and evade the latter is easy.

120   Mistaking the urgent technical difficulties . . . for the moral and development problems . . . is easy; solving the former expediently and evading the latter is easy.

But none of these three variations is as satisfactory as the original, for the reader must wait too long to reach the predicate, the organizational pivot, which in this sentence happens to be the adjective ***easy.***

A Final Word About Complements

We have not exhausted the topic of complements, but completeness is not the purpose here. Again, the discussion is attempting to make you conscious of what you already know. And if you have understood the meanings of the example sentences, then you have intuitively understood what has been said in this section. The only difficulty is this: it is sometimes extremely difficult to express intuitive knowledge explicitly. Almost all of the discussion in this chapter is aimed at stating explicitly what you already know intuitively.

Embedding and Awareness

We will continue to talk about the meanings that one perceives in sentences that contain more than one proposition. Your conscious awareness of what goes on in sentences will pay dividends later as our discussion of style progresses, but the ultimate payoff will be in your own writing and in your appreciation of the writing of others.

Here is a two-proposition sentence:

121   Beautiful flowers bloom in the spring.

If you agree that **122** means the same or nearly the same as **121**, then you can see what the embedded proposition is.

122   Flowers ***that are beautiful*** bloom in the spring.

In the sentence ***Beautiful flowers bloom in the spring,*** we have something like this:

123   [Flowers (flowers are beautiful) bloom in the spring]

This is nothing more than our old friend the relative.

If you look closely, you'll realize that your understanding of this sentence

124   The battle was brief as always, lasting no more than two or three minutes, and disorderly.
                              —Paule Marshall

is based in large part on your ability to reconstruct the following propositions:

125   The battle was brief as always.
       The battle lasted no more than two or three minutes.
       The battle was disorderly.

In other words, you can't understand *lasting no more than two or three minutes* unless you understand what it was that lasted no more than two or three minutes, namely, the battle; therefore, in your understanding of the sentence, you supply a subject for the verb *lasting;* nor can you understand the sentence unless you know what was *disorderly,* and, of course, it was the battle that was disorderly.

Just a glance at **124** and **125** demonstrates the power of embedding. Example **124** is easy to read; it establishes the relationships that the reader needs to comprehend the individual propositions; it is economical: **124** contains sixteen words while **125** has twenty.

Even in an uncomplicated sentence like the following, embedding is important:

126   They thought I was kind, I think.
                              —Michele Wallace

Here we have something like this:

127   [I think (they thought [I was kind])]

which can be schematized in two other ways:

128   I think they thought I was kind.

129   I think (something).
       They thought (something).
       I was kind.

Analyses of Sentences

The following is a list of sentences with analyses of their propositional content. Study this list, and in each case ask yourself, Can I isolate the propositions for myself? Do I agree with the analysis?

130   I stepped into an oculist's shop to ask advice of a professional-looking older woman, wearing pince-nez, a hairnet, and white smock.
                              —Bernard Malamud

       I stepped into an oculist's shop.
       (I) to ask advice of a woman.
       (The woman was) professional-looking.
       (The woman was) older.
       (The woman was) wearing pince-nez.
       (The woman was wearing) a hairnet.
       (The woman was wearing) a smock.
       (The smock was) white.

131   To achieve economic stability, the president imposed a price freeze.
       The president imposed a price freeze.
       (The president) to achieve economic stability.

132   The class was apprehensive, wondering about the final.
       The class was apprehensive.
       (The class was) wondering about the final.

133   Concerned with his own problems, Harry ignored his neighbors.
       Harry ignored his neighbors.
       (Harry was) concerned with his own problems.

134   The dishes having been done, the family settled down in front of the TV.
       The family settled down in front of the TV.
       The dishes [had] been done (by someone). *Or* (Someone had) done the dishes.

A Final Word

You have now completed a fairly thorough survey of the ways in which one proposition can be embedded in another. I could summarize by giving a systematic overview of the various methods of embedding, but I do not want you to concentrate on the formal system, nor do I want you to memorize and classify. A heightened awareness of an important linguistic resource is all that has been attempted here. To state that point another way: the discussion has attempted to give explicit statement to some common knowledge that every native user of the language already possesses.

The Cumulative Sentence

We will shift focus a bit now, to view sentences from another perspective, one developed originally by Francis Christensen while he was Professor of English at the University of Southern California. Christensen stated his perspective this way:

> The typical sentence of modern English, the kind we can best spend our efforts trying to teach, is what we may call the *cumulative sentence.* The main clause, which may or may not have a sentence modifier before it, advances the discussion; but the additions move backward, as in this clause, to modify the statement of the main clause or more often to explicate or exemplify it, so that the sentence has a flowing and ebbing movement, advancing to a new position and then pausing to consolidate it, leaping and lingering as the popular ballad does.[2]

What Christensen meant is well exemplified by the following sentence, which I will break up into units so that its movement can be clearly seen:

135   I can see and hear Ransom and Jarrell now,
           seated on one sofa,
               as though on a love-seat,

---

[2]Francis Christensen, *Notes Toward a New Rhetoric* (New York: Harper & Row, 1967), pp. 5–6.

the sacred texts open on their laps,
one fifty,
the other just out of college,
and each expounding to the other's deaf ears his own inspired and
irreconcilable interpretation.   —Robert Lowell

This sentence consists of a base—***I can see and hear Ransom and Jarrell
now***—and quite a long string of modifiers. Christensen call such modifiers
free modifiers. I am going to call them *cumulative modifiers,* because it is
such modifiers that create the cumulative sentence.

Positions of Cumulative Modifiers

Cumulative modifiers can appear before the base, in the middle of the
base, or after the base:

136   Beyond this small point,
               raised only because of the film's stature,
         Man of Aran is unique for its quality of visual loveliness.   —Paul Rotha

137   The suit, a black job that dated from the days when he was fat and sassy,
       hung loosely about him as once it had upon a peg in the supermarket where
       the governor liked to buy his clothes.   —A. J. Liebling
       The suit, / , hung loosely about him. . . .
           / a black job
               that dated from the days
                   when he was fat and sassy

138   Thus he fought his last fight,
               thirsting savagely for blood.
                                                         —H. L. Mencken

A System of Diagraming

In order to make the notion of cumulative modifiers visual and easier to
grasp, most of the sentences that we will be discussing will be schematized
as shown above. Therefore, a brief explanation of this system of diagraming is necessary.

Indentations serve to show elements that the modifiers relate to. Thus, in
137, *a black job that dated from the days when he was fat and sassy* relates to
The suit. On the other hand, ***that dated from the days*** relates to ***a black job,***
and ***when he was fat and sassy*** relates to ***that dated from the days.*** The
principle is really very simple, and you will catch on to it with no trouble.
Notice also how we diagram modifiers that occur within their bases, as in
137: we put a slash in the place that they occupy in the sentence and then
drop them down to the proper level to show relationships of modification.

Here are some more examples, to make the point clear:

139   Walking through the fields,
         we learn quite a number of things about snails.   —Danilo Dolci

140   His mind, / , was a little boyish, disembodied, and brittle.
             /unearthly in its quickness   —Robert Lowell
       (His mind, unearthly in its quickness, was a little boyish, disembodied, and
       brittle.)

141 Harlan was the mastermind behind the "Gates Rebellion,"
    named for the unfortunate Amherst president
        against whom it was directed.   —Lewis S. Feuer

In the discussion of cumulative modifiers that follows, I will make certain adjustments in the Christensen model, but I will not take liberties with it.

Prepositional Phrases

In dealing with prepositional phrases as cumulative modifiers, we need to understand some technical (but not really difficult) points.

Prepositions and Particles

In the first place, we must distinguish between prepositions and what grammarians call *particles* (first mentioned on page 345). This is easily done. In the following sentence, the word **up** might appear at first to be a preposition:

142 The baby barfed up his breakfast.

This **up** seems to be of the same order as **up** in the following sentence:

143 The child skipped up the sidewalk.

However, carefully compare the following:

144 The baby barfed his breakfast **up**.

145 *The child skipped the sidewalk **up**.

In other words, a particle has a movability that a preposition does not:

146 Turn **off** the light.

147 Turn the light **off**.

148 Turn **off** the street at the corner.

149 *Turn the street **off** at the corner.

150 The speaker shouted **down** the crowd.

151 The speaker shouted the crowd **down**.

152 The speaker shouted **down** the corridor.

153 *The speaker shouted the corridor **down**.

Prepositional Phrases as Adverbials

It is also the case that some prepositional phrases are not freely movable, which is another way of saying that they are not *adverbial* in nature. Compare the following:

154 Jay sang *in the morning*.

155 *In the morning*, Jay sang.

156 Jay sang *of his love for Sandy.*

157 **Of his love for Sandy,* Jay sang.

158 Marty thought *of the good old days.*

159 **Of the good old days,* Marty thought.

We will class as cumulative modifiers only those prepositional phrases that are freely movable—that is, only those that are adverbials.

Placement of Prepositional Phrases

Prepositional phrases as cumulative modifiers can stand before the sentence base:

160 **At the end of a conference on human genetics last year,**
a biologist rose to summarize the proceedings. —Lucy Eisenberg

161 **To the lives of illustrious dead men**
we have glittering memorials,
 often more dazzling than the mortals
 they enshrine. —William L. Laurence

162 **In front,**
 on the broad summit,
reared the towers of Gavoi. —D. H. Lawrence

163 **On warm evenings,**
 with these windows open,
conversation was pleasant there,
for the wind rustled the interior
 like fan-breeze
 made by ancient ladies. —Truman Capote

Prepositional phrases as cumulative modifiers can also appear within the base:

164 Every man of normal strong emotion knows, / , the subjective phenomena
 / **from his own experience**
 that go hand in hand with the response of militant enthusiasm.
 —Konrad Lorenz
(Every man of normal strong emotion knows, **from his own experience,** the subjective phenomena that go hand in hand with the response of militant enthusiasm.)

165 Victorian standards, / , intensified the damage to those involved.
 / **besides perpetuating the white slave trade**

And prepositional phrases as cumulative modifiers can occur after the base:

166 Even the strongest critics of the government and its scientific policies . . . are surprisingly traditional
 in their approach to the political system. —Don K. Price

167 Eugenic proposals like this are commonplace
 at scientific meetings nowadays. —Lucy Eisenberg

And here, for good measure, are two more sentences containing prepositional phrases as cumulative modifiers:

168   ***Along the roads***
       laurel, viburnum and alder, great ferns and wild-flowers delighted the
       traveler's eye
              through much of the year.   —Rachel Carson

169   ***In this final relationship,***
       the Congress and the Administration have, / , cooperated well.
              / *on most issues*   —Dwight D. Eisenhower

Noun Clusters

Sentences like this one are common:

170   William Randolph Hearst was an only son, ***the only chick in the richly***
       feathered nest of George and Phoebe Hearst.   —John Dos Passos

We will call the italicized structure a *noun cluster.* Notice that the
important word, the *head word,* in the noun cluster is **chick,** and notice also
that the word **son** and the word **chick** have the same referent; in some
senses they are semantic equivalents. Notice also that the noun cluster is
closely related to the nonrestrictive relative clause, which we have already
discussed. Example **171**, therefore, is a close paraphrase of **170:**

171   William Randolph Hearst was an only son, ***who was the only chick in the***
       richly feathered nest of George and Phoebe Hearst. [William Randolph Hearst
       was an only son (*and* he was the only chick in the richly feathered nest of
       George and Phoebe Hearst)]

Noun clusters are obviously economical and easy ways of adding information to a sentence.

Here is another example of a noun cluster:

172   I am injected into this enormous silver monster,
              floating gently on a sea of barely audible Muzak,
                     the sweet Karo Syrup of Existence.   —Jean Shepherd

The noun cluster need not stand adjacent to the noun phrase that it is in
apposition with. For instance:

173   She reverses most of the values traditionally associated with the Virgin—
              poverty, humility, sacrifice.   —Harvey Cox
       [She reverses most of the values (poverty, humility, sacrifice) traditionally
       associated with the Virgin]

Placement of Noun Clusters

Like other cumulative modifiers, the noun cluster can occur before the
base, within the base, or after the base.

174   The Kennedy wit was so pronounced and so identifiable that it could be
       reproduced with near exactitude by Ted Sorensen,
              his speech writer.
              A deadly serious man,

Sorensen's few recorded public jokes include one perfect specimen of Kennedy-style wit.   —Tom Wicker

175   Neale Jones, 16, / , is standing nearby with a Band-aid on his upper lip,
          / *a boy with great lank perfect surfer's hair*
      where the sun has burnt it raw.   —Tom Wolfe
      (Neale Jones, 16, *a boy with great lank perfect surfer's hair,* is standing nearby with a Band-aid on his upper lip, where the sun has burnt it raw.)

Modifiers Within Modifiers

At this point, a slight complication regarding cumulative modifiers enters. Namely, *cumulative modifiers can be modified by (or contain) cumulative modifiers.* For instance, look at the noun clusters in **176.** (In the diagram, I will ignore modifiers other than noun clusters.)

176   It is difficult to imagine, at any other period in history, such a combination of varied qualities, so beautifully balanced—
          the profound scholar who was also a brilliant man of the world—
          the votary of cosmopolitan culture, who never for a moment ceased to be a supremely English "character."   —Lytton Strachey

The head nouns in these constructions are, of course, **scholar** and **votary,** but notice that these head nouns are modified by relative clauses:

177   [. . . scholar (scholar was also a brilliant man of the world)]
      [. . . votary (votary never for a moment ceased to be a supremely English "character")]

As a matter of fact, we can class all relative clauses as cumulative modifiers. Therefore, we can diagram **177** in this way, to show all the cumulative modifiers:

178   It is difficult to imagine, / , such a combination of varied qualities, so beautifully balanced—
          / at any other period in history
          the profound scholar
              who was also a brilliant man of the world—
          the votary of cosmopolitan culture,
              who never for a moment ceased to be a supremely English "character."

This principle of layering in sentences is, as Christensen pointed out, an important part of the way they work.

Back to Noun Clusters

More examples of noun clusters in sentences:

179   Our nearest neighbor, / , was Roland Thaxter;
          / dwelling / behind us
              / (at a decent distance)
          primarily the father of my loveliest playmate and ultimately professor of cryptogamic botany.   e. e. cummings
      (Our nearest neighbor, dwelling [at a decent distance] behind us, was Roland Thaxter; *primarily the father of my loveliest playmate and ultimately professor of cryptogamic botany.*)

180   Of course
        all life is a process of breaking down,
        but the blows that do the dramatic side of the work— / , don't show their effect
        all at once.
            / *the big sudden blows*
                that come, or seem to come, from outside—
                /*the ones*
                you remember and blame things on and, / , tell your friends about
                    / *in moments of weakness*   —F. Scott Fitzgerald
        (Of course all life is a process of breaking down, but the blows that do the
        dramatic side of the work—*the big sudden blows that come, or seem to come,*
        from outside—the ones you remember and blame things on and, in moments of
        weakness, tell your friends about, don't show their effect all at once.)

One last example of a noun cluster:

181   It was the darkness and emptiness of the streets I liked most about Friday
      evening, as if in preparation for that day of rest and worship which the Jews
      greet "as a bride"—*that day when the very touch of money is prohibited, all*
      work, all travel, all household duties, even to the turning on and off of a
      light. . . .   —Alfred Kazin

Diagramatically, that magnificent sentence looks like this:

182   It was the darkness and emptiness of the streets I liked most about Friday
      evening,
            as if in preparation for that day of rest and worship
                which the Jews geet "as a bride"—
            that day
                when the very touch of money is prohibited,
                    all work, all travel, all household duties,
                        even to the turning on and off of a light. . . .

Verb Clusters

Sentences like the following are very common:

183   *Trying to cling to something,* I liked doctors and girl children up to the age of
      about thirteen and well-brought-up boy children from about eight years old
      on.   —F. Scott Fitzgerald

The italicized structure is one of the kinds of *verb clusters.* Notice the
propositional nature of the verb cluster and its relationship to the main
proposition or base.

184   [I(I was trying to cling to something) liked doctors and girl children up to the
      age of about thirteen and well-brought-up boy children from about eight years
      old on]

That is, even though no subject is expressed in the modifier, we know *who*
is *trying;* in other words, we supply a subject. Example **185** is a close
paraphrase of **184:**

185   Because I was trying to cling to something, I liked doctors and girl children up
      to the age of about thirteen and well-brought-up boy children from about eight
      years old on.

The Grammar of Verb Clusters

Before we explore verb clusters thoroughly, a brief review of some grammatical principles is necessary. The head words in verb clusters are always *nonfinite verbs.* Nonfinite verbs are (1) *present participles,* always ending in *-ing:*

186   ***Wanting*** to go fishing, I rented a boat.

(2) past participles, the form of the verb that you normally use with **have, has,** or **had:**

187   [have, has, had] done
       Done with the yard work, the boys went off to play tennis.

188   [have, has, had] worried
       Worried by the assassination threats, the Secret Service took extra precautions.

(3) *infinitives,* the form of the verb that appears with the marker **to** (which is not a preposition here):

189   ***To report*** a fire, dial 801.

Not all constructions containing nonfinite verbs will be classed as cumulative modifiers. Some constructions containing nonfinite verbs seem to be paraphrasable as clauses of various types. For instance,

190   Hoping for a winner, the man bet all his money on the race.

seems to be paraphrasable as

191   ***Because he was hoping for a winner,*** the man bet all his money on the race.

That is, the verbal phrase in **190** seems to have nearly the same meaning as the adverb clause in **191**—and we will talk more about adverb clauses later.
    The verbal phrase in

192   ***Beaten to the draw,*** the sheriff was gunned down by the bad guy.

is paraphrasable as the adverb clause in

193   ***Because he was beaten to the draw,*** the sheriff was gunned down by the bad guy.

    The verbal phrase in

194   The man ***hoping for a winner*** bet all his money on the race.

is paraphrasable as the relative clause in

195   The man ***who was hoping for a winner*** bet all his money on the race.

    But the verbal phrase in

196   The desire ***to learn grammar*** is necessary.

is not easily paraphrasable as a clause, except in the following questionable way:

197   ?The desire, ***which is to learn grammar,*** is necessary.

In fact, as you will recognize, the verbal construction in **196** is embedded as a complement. Note:

198   The desire is necessary.

199   To learn grammar is necessary.

Another way of stating this is to say that the verbal phrase ***to learn grammar*** is not a modifier at all, but is the equivalent of ***The desire.***

We will class as cumulative modifiers only those verbal constructions that are modifiers (adjectivals and adverbials), not those that are complements in noun phrases. Thus, the following verbal constructions are *not* cumulative modifiers:

200   Davy didn't ever consider ***deserting the fort.***

201   The will ***to win the game*** is necessary for the team's success.

The nature of verbal constructions as cumulative modifiers will become obvious as we see a variety of examples of them.

Present Participles

The following sentences contain verb clusters with present participles as their head words:

202   ***Milling***
    and chatting,
we sat on the floor.   —H. L. Mountzoures

203   That night, / , at first reluctantly I read Levitansky's stories.
    sipping vodka from a drinking glass   —Bernard Malamud
(That night, ***sipping vodka from a drinking glass,*** at first reluctantly I read Levitansky's stories.)

204   So many of these white people are lost to history,
    waiting for the light to shine on them,
    waiting for some release from darkness.   —Elizabeth Hardwick

205   ***Standing there looking at the house***
        where our lives entangled themselves in one another,
I am infuriated that of that episode I remember less her love and protection
and anger than my father's inept contrition.   —Wallace Stegner

206   The house a quarter-mile beyond,
        just on the right of the road,
        standing with shade trees,
that is the Ricketts'.   —James Agee

207   ***Rubbing a dirty cloth on the counter—***
    formulating and reformulating a smear of grease before me—
he said, "If he was dying of a heart attack, what good would a Bromo do him?
And if he was not dying, what good is a Bromo?"   —Herbert Gold

Past Participles

The following sentences contain examples of verb clusters with past participles as head words:

208   *Concerned that the obstacles to voting be torn down*
       but concerned also that institutional progress go hand-in-hand with a
       quickening of the people's capacity for self-direction,
       SNCC could only experience Selma with mixed feelings and considerable
       frustration.
       —Staughton Lynd

209   The wife has the necessary appliances,
       often still being paid off,
       and the money / goes for your daughter's orthodontist, and later for her
       wedding.
       /you save
       —Peter Schrag

210   Since the market is assured, and virtually limitless,
       the production of schlock sociology for fun and profit is not particularly
       difficult,
       given a reasonable amount of imagination and a firm grasp of the major
       requirements.
       —Robert Claiborne

211   Behind our house
       there used to be a footbridge across the river,
       used by the Carpenters and others /, and by summer swimmers from the
       town.
       /who lived in the bottoms
       —Wallace Stegner

212   My own house faced the Cambridge world as a finely and solidly constructed
       mansion,
       preceded by a large oval lawn
       and ringed with an imposing white-pine hedge.
       —e. e. cummings

213   There, to everyone's astonishment, stood a collection of delegates from
       Hawaii,
       clad in gay shirts
       and talking happily among themselves.
       —Arthur Schlesinger, Jr.

Infinitives

The following sentences contain verb clusters in which the head words
are infinitives.

214   *To snare a sensibility in words,*
           especially one that is alive and powerful,
       one must be tentative and nimble.
       —Susan Sontag

215   *To find the square root of a hog's nose,*
       turn him into a garden patch.
       To enjoy a good reputation,
       give publicly, and steal privately.
       To remove grease from a man's character,
       let him strike some sudden oil.
       To get wrong things out of your child's head—comb it often.
       —Donald Day

Absolutes

An absolute is very much like a sentence with a nonfinite verb (a present
participle, a past participle, or an infinitive). This is easily illustrated:

216   Daniel arrived late. (sentence)

217   *Daniel arriving late,* we missed the first act. (absolute)

The absolute is also much like the verb cluster, except that the verb cluster does not have an expressed subject:

218   *Having finished the work,* we could relax. (verb cluster)

219   *Alison having finished the work,* we could relax. (absolute)

There is only one slight complication that you need to be aware of. If the verb in the absolute is a form of ***be,*** it is often deleted. This principle, too, is easily illustrated.

220   *Dinner (being) in the oven,* we chatted over drinks.

And that is about all there is to absolutes—simple, but extremely useful, constructions.

221   They ride around in their cars,
  their coats hanging primly in the back. . . . —Elizabeth Hardwick

222   Before being killed,
the turtles swim in dense kraals,
  bumping each other
   in the murky water,
  armor clashing,
  dully lurching against the high pens. —Herbert Gold

223   Crazy Louie [is] on the beach—
  a frantic grandfather with Latin records, maracas, castanets, silk Cuban shirts, feathers, straw skirt, rubber Halloween masks,
  a huge earring loosely hooked to his ear by a bent hairpin,
  thick glasses sliding down his nose,
  leathery withered legs, dancing and dancing,
  all sinews and grins and shakes to some inner song
   while the portable phonograph goes rattle-and-scrape, screech, rattle, and scrape. —Herbert Gold

224   ***Heads [being] up,***
  swinging with the music,
  their right arms swinging free,
they stepped out,
  crossing the sanded arena under the arclights,
  the cuadrillas opening out behind,
  the picadors riding after. —Ernest Hemingway

Adverb Clauses

In the discussion of the sentence so far, we have examined a variety of clauses. The sort that we will focus on as a cumulative modifier is the adverb clause. To recapitulate, here is a sentence that contains relative clauses:

225   Nothing, indeed, is more characteristic of the period ***in which Chaucer wrote*** than the strange, twisted mythology, transmogrified and confused, ***which emerged from the association of the planets and the gods.***
  —John Livingston Lowes

The meaning that we derive from the first relative clause in the sentence is something like this: ***Chaucer wrote in the period.*** And we see that the relative clause adds meaning to, or modifies, the noun ***period.*** The meaning that we derive from the second relative clause is something like this: ***The mythology emerged from the association of the planets and the gods.*** The clause modifies the noun ***mythology.*** In other words, relative clauses modify nouns and noun phrases—and in some rare instances whole clauses.

Noun clauses, of which we have seen many examples, stand in noun slots in sentences; they are subjects, objects, indirect objects, and so on.

226   The historian sometimes forgets ***that he has professional problems in common with all storytellers.***   —C. Vann Woodward

In this sentence, the noun clause is the object of the verb ***forgets.***

This is to say that the adjective clause functions like an adjective, modifying a nominal, and the noun clause functions like a noun, standing in a syntactic slot that typically could be filled by a noun. The adverb clause, not surprisingly, functions like a true adverb.

A true adverb is generally movable:

227   ***Unfortunately,*** we English teachers are ***easily*** hung up on this matter of understanding.   —John Holt
      We English teachers are, ***unfortunately,*** hung up ***easily*** on this matter of understanding.

Some words that are traditionally classed as adverbs are not movable:

228   The new dress was ***very*** pretty.

229   Larry's work was ***quite*** acceptable.

230   Sills' voice is ***pretty*** good.

Such words as these are called *intensifiers,* not adverbs.

Here is a typical adverb clause:

231   ***When the notion of man as machine was first advanced,*** the machine was a very simple collection of pulleys and billiard balls and levers.
                              —Wayne C. Booth

Notice what can be done with this clause:

232   The machine was a very simple collection of pulleys and billiard balls and levers ***when the notion of man as machine was first advanced.***

233   The machine, ***when the notion of man as machine was first advanced,*** was a very simple collection of pulleys and billiard balls and levers.

So an adverb clause, like an adverb, is movable.

Another characteristic of the adverb clause is that it is introduced by a *subordinating conjunction—****when, if, because, although,*** and so on.

234   During all his years of solitude,
      he was extraordinarily sociable
            WHENEVER he saw his family,
            AS IF the taciturnity he had assumed with his solitude was unnatural.
                              —Donald Hall

235   ***WHILE the Golden Rule in its classical versions prods man to strive consciously for a highest good and to avoid mutual harm with a sharpened awareness,***
our insights assume an unconscious substratum of ethical strength and, at the same time, unconscious arsenals of destructive rage.   —Erik H. Erikson

236   ***WHEN men begin to lie and steal,***
        in order to make the nation / great,
           /to which they belong
then comes not only disaster, but rational contradiction
    which / is worse than disaster,
       / in many respects
       BECAUSE it ruins the leadership of the divine machine, / ,
      / the human reason
        by which we chart and guide our actions.   —W. E. B. DuBois
(***When men begin to lie and steal,*** in order to make the nation to which they belong great, then comes not only disaster, but rational contradiction which in many respects is worse than disaster, ***because it ruins the leadership of the divine machine,*** the human reason, by which we chart and guide our actions.)

237   You hold till the last,
    EVEN IF it is only to a public seat in a railroad station. —Loren Eiseley

238   ***BEFORE we leave the topic of meaning,***
a final remark needs to be made about another subject: translation.
                          —William G. Moulton

Adjective Clusters

According to their syntax, adjectives in English sentences fall into three categories. Perhaps the most usual is the *attributive adjective.* It occurs before the noun (and after the determiner):

239
Determiner	*Adjective*	*Noun*
the	pretty	girl
that first	hard	question
several of the	tasty	meals

240   So Elvis Presley came, strumming a ***weird*** guitar and wagging his tail across the continent, ripping off fame and fortune as he scrunched his way, and, like a ***latter-day*** Johnny Appleseed, sowing seeds of a ***new*** rhythm and style in the ***white*** souls of the ***white*** youth of America, whose ***inner*** hunger and need was no longer satisfied with the ***antiseptic white*** shoes and ***whiter*** songs of Pat Boone.   —Eldridge Cleaver

The second use of the adjective is as *predicate.*

241   The girl is ***pretty.***
That first question seems ***hard.***
Several of the meals were ***tasty.***

But adjectives can also occur in *appositive* positions, and it is these adjectives (and adjective phrases), as cumulative modifiers, that we are concerned with. Here is a sentence with an adjective phrase in the predicate position:

242   We were **SERENE in the confidence that if we got the facts, all our problems would be solved.**

And here is a sentence with an adjective phrase used as a cumulative modifier:

243   Let us get the facts, we said,
      SERENE in the confidence that, / , all our problems would be solved.
       / if we did   —Robert Maynard Hutchins

Here is a sentence with less complicated adjectival cumulative modifiers in it:

244   Under the changes of weather,
  it may look like marble or like sea water,
     BLACK as slate
      in the fog,
     WHITE as tufa
      in the sunlight.   —Saul Bellow

Here is a variety of sentences with adjectivals as cumulative modifiers:

245   In one society
  technology is unbelievably slighted
    even in those aspects of life
      which seem necessary to insure survival:
  in another,
    equally SIMPLE,
  technological achievements are complex and fitted / to the situation.
    / with admirable nicety   —Ruth Benedict

246   The babies were all under one year old,
    very FUNNY and LOVABLE.
                      —Grace Paley

247   On we rush, / —and / see a large village,
    / through the morning
    / at length
    HIGH on the summit beyond,
    STONY on the high upland.   —D. H. Lawrence
(On we rush, through the morning—and at length see a large village, **high on the summit beyond, stony on the high upland.)**

248   **OBLIVIOUS to all else around me,**
  I reeled up the tangled yards of paper ribbon from the floor, draped them in coils about my arms and neck, and departed for home.
                      —Kurt Vonnegut, Jr.

249   When I first met Randall,
  he was twenty-three or four,
    and upsettingly BRILLIANT, PRECOCIOUS, KNOWING, NAIVE, and VEXING.   —Robert Lowell

Sentence Analysis

Our survey of cumulative modifiers is now complete. It doesn't matter if you don't understand the structures in great detail; your goal is to improve your own ability to write sentences, to become more competent, to develop syntactic versatility. If you paid fairly close attention to the structures that were illustrated in the preceding sections, you have probably taken a major step in the direction in which you want to go.

In this final section on the cumulative sentence, I am simply going to present some more analyses of cumulative modifiers, in an attempt to make the principles of the cumulative sentence vividly apparent. In these analyses, I will label the cumulative modifiers with the following abbreviations: prepositional phrase (PP), noun cluster (NC), verb cluster (VC), adjective cluster (AC), absolute (Abs), adverb clause (Adv), relative clause (Rel).

250   After the lions had returned to their cages, creeping angrily through the chutes, a little bunch of us drifted away and into an open doorway nearby, where we stood for a while in semi-darkness, watching a big brown circus horse go harumphing around the practice ring.   —E. B. White

   (Adv)   After the lions had returned to their cages,
   (VC)   creeping angrily through the chutes,
        a little bunch of us drifted away and into an open doorway nearby,
   (Rel)   where we stood for a while
   (PP)   in semi-darkness,
   (VC)   watching a big brown circus horse go harumphing around the practice ring.

251   There he [John F. Kennedy] soon will stand, perhaps in our lifetime—cold stone or heartless bronze, immortal as Jefferson, revered as Lincoln, bloodless as Washington.   —Tom Wicker

        There he soon will stand,
   (PP)   perhaps in our lifetime—
   (NC)   cold stone or heartless bronze,
   (AC)   immortal as Jefferson,
   (AC)   revered as Lincoln,
   (AC)   bloodless as Washington.

252   He felt no shock, no cold, he on one side of the swimming mule, grasping the pommel with one hand and holding his gun above the water with the other, Boone opposite him.   —William Faulkner

        He felt no shock, no cold,
   (Abs)   he [being] on one side of the swimming mule,
   (VC)   grasping the pommel with one hand and holding his gun above the water with the other,
   (Abs)   Boone [being] opposite him.

253   The savage, like ourselves, feels the oppression of his impotence before the powers of nature; but having in himself nothing that he respects more than power, he is willing to prostrate himself before his gods, without inquiring whether they are worthy of his worship.   —Bertrand Russell

        The savage, / , feels the oppression of his impotence
   (PP)   / like ourselves

(PP)   before the powers of nature;
(VC)   but having / nothing
(PP)   / in himself
(Rel)   that he respects more than power,
     he is willing to prostrate himself before his gods,
(PP)   without inquiring whether they are worthy of his worship.

254   Old men, smelling of Milford Haven in the rain, shuffled, badgering and cadging, round the edges of the swaggering crowd, their only wares a handful of damp confetti.   —Dylan Thomas
        Old men, / , shuffled, / , round the edges of the swaggering crowd,
(VC)   / smelling of Milford Haven in the rain
(VC)   / badgering and cadging
(Abs)   their only wares [being] a handful of damp confetti.

255   With this wisdom, dramatized in a tale that is a lucid model of his craft, few modern men will care to argue.   —Wright Morris
        With this wisdom, / few modern men will care to argue.
(VC)   dramatized in a tale
(Rel)   that is a lucid model of his craft,

256   One afternoon the previous May, a month when the fields blaze with the green-gold fire of half-grown wheat, Dewey had spent several hours at Valley View weeding his father's grave, an obligation he had too long neglected.   —Truman Capote
(NC)   One afternoon the previous May,
(NC)   a month
(Rel)   when the fields blaze with the green-gold fire of half-grown wheat,
        Dewey had spent several hours at Valley View
(VC)   weeding his father's grave,
(NC)   an obligation
(Rel)   he had too long neglected.

257   When Europe, after millennia of war, rapine, slavery, famine, intolerance, had sunk to the level of a sewer, America became the golden dream, the Eden where innocence could be recovered.   —Anthony Burgess
(Adv)   When Europe, / , had sunk to the level of a sewer,
(PP)   / after millennia of war, rapine, slavery, famine, intolerance
        America became the golden dream,
(NC)   the Eden
(Rel)   where innocence could be recovered.

And with this, we will conclude the discussion of the cumulative sentence. However, cumulative modifiers will be important in the analysis of sentences in context in Chapter 14.

Traditional Principles

So far, we have viewed sentences from the standpoints of their propositional nature and of their cumulative modifiers.

As you have undoubtedly noted, propositions and cumulative modifiers are not mutually exclusive categories, for cumulative modifiers—such as relative clauses, adverb clauses, verb clusters, noun clusters, adjective clusters, and absolutes—are either propositions in themselves or are derived from propositions that are easily recoverable. The propositions of relative and adverb clauses are fully expressed:

258   The man *who attended the meeting* was late.
[The man (the man attended the meeting) was late]

259   *Because the plane was late,* the man missed the meeting.

The propositions from which verb clusters, noun clusters, adjective clusters, and absolutes are derived are almost as apparent as those of adverb and relative clauses.

260   (VC)   *Panting heavily,*
the tubby man jogged around the track.
[the tubby man (the tubby man was panting heavily) jogged around the track]

261   The car, / , belched and stalled.
(NC)   / *an old Plymouth*
[The car (the car was an old Plymouth) belched and stalled]

262   (AC)   *Pretty as a picture,*
little Chris was dressed up for church.
[little Chris (little Chris was pretty as a picture) was dressed up for church]

263   The student stumbled down the stairs,
(Abs)   *books flying in all directions.*
[The student stumbled down the stairs (the books were flying in all directions)]

The prepositional phrase is the only cumulative modifier that does not represent a proposition. (Remember that a proposition is a predicate with one or more noun phrases relating to it.)

Clause Structure

Traditionally, sentences are classified according to their clause structure. Since this classification has some usefulness, we will take a brief look at sentences classified as *simple, compound, complex,* and *compound-complex* according to the clauses that make them up.

Simple Sentences

A simple sentence contains only one clause, an independent clause or one that is not embedded in some way.

264   Conspicuous production takes a great variety of forms.   —David Riesman

It is important to note that a simple sentence may contain more than one proposition, as does 264: *Production takes a variety of forms/production is conspicuous/variety is great.* However, as is obvious, much has been deleted from these embedded propositions, and in gaining the meaning, the reader supplies what has been deleted—which is to say that the complete propositions are recoverable. A clause, then, is a proposition in which all the elements (subject, object, indirect object, and so on) appear in the surface structure.

Here are more examples of simple sentences:

265 It takes time to acquire a usable command of any intellectual discipline.
—Arthur Bestor
[It (someone to acquire a command (command is usable) of any discipline (discipline is intellectual)) takes time]

266 A concentration camp is not a political seminar.   —Walter Lippmann
[A concentration camp is not a seminar (seminar is political)]

267 Earthworms are important among the various foods of the raccoon, and are eaten in the spring and fall by opossums.   —Rachel Carson

Example **267** might seem at first to contain two clauses, but it does not, for **Earthworms** is the subject of both **are important** and **are eaten.** (If the sentence contained two clauses, it would look like this: **Earthworms are important among the various foods of the raccoon, and they are eaten in the spring and fall by opossums.**)

Complex Sentences

Complex sentences contain one independent clause or base and one or more embedded (or dependent) clauses.

268 **If originality is what distinguishes art from craft,** tradition serves as the common meeting ground of the two.   —H.W. Janson

In **268,** the italicized clause is an adverb clause that modifies the main clause.

269 Again, nothing is more common than to attend a forum or a conference on social or artistic "problems" and to hear, after a few hours of guarded meandering, a growing majority declare **that a consensus is impossible.**   —Jacques Barzun

As object of the verb **declare, that a consensus is impossible** is a noun clause. Note that its slot could be filled by a simple noun phrase: **declare a moratorium.**

270 Jack Ruby shot Lee Oswald while tightly surrounded by guards **who were paralyzed by television cameras.**   —Marshall McLuhan

The italicized clause is a relative *clause* (actually an adjective, since it modifies the noun **guards**).

A clause, of course, contains a finite verb. Therefore, constructions that do not contain finite verbs are not clauses. For instance, the italicized string in **271** looks like a clause since it has a subject, a verb, and an object, but the verb is in the infinitive form, and therefore **271** is merely a simple sentence:

271 Norma asked **Jeff to do the dishes.**

Notice that the dependent clauses in **268, 269,** and **270** all contain finite verbs: *is, is,* and *were paralyzed,* respectively.

Here are some more complex sentences (with the dependent clauses italicized):

272   The anti-intellectual position must be repudiated *if a university is to achieve its ends.*   —Robert Maynard Hutchins

273   It has always been axiomatic *that the man of even a little education would foresake the hoe and the potter's wheel and would stop working with his hands.*   —Peter F. Drucker

274   It is, of course, part of the very genius of the human mind *that it can, as it were, stand aside from life and reflect upon it, that it can be aware of its own existence, and that it can criticize its own processes.*   —Alan Wilson Watts

Compound Sentences

Compound sentences are made up of two or more independent clauses— usually joined by a *coordinating conjunction*—but no dependent clauses.

275   The dump held very little wood, *for* in that country anything burnable got burned.   —Wallace Stegner

276   After all, next term was coming, *and* it never hurt a sixth grader to have a play sister in the eighth grade, or a tenth year student to call a twelfth grader Bubba.   —Maya Angelou

Example **276** contains two coordinating conjunctions, *and* and *or,* but only the *and* joins the clauses.

277   In my last years at school I had toyed with the idea of becoming a teacher for the gypsies, *and* later I thought of joining either the Ministry of Health and Social Services or the Ministry of Education, to work from within the citadel.   —Bernadette Devlin

278   I read heavily, *but* after three weeks I noticed a nervousness coming over me.   —Allan Seager

279   I became aware of a sharp burning in my eyes, *and* I jumped up in fright.   —Emma Goldman

Compound-Complex Sentences

Finally, compound-complex sentences contain two or more independent clauses and at least one dependent clause.

280   Born though I was in 1922, I am a child of the nineteenth century, *for* it was Anna Maria who raised me until I was four years old . . . .   —William Alfred

This sentence contains two independent clauses: *I am a child of the nineteenth century* and *for it was Anna Maria.* It also contains three dependent clauses: *Born though I was in 1922 (though I was born in 1922); who raised me;* and *until I was four years old.* Thus:

281   (Adv)   Born though I was in 1922, I am a child of the nineteenth century, for it was Anna Maria

(Rel)   who raised me
(Adv)   until I was four years old.

282   Finally things got worse *and* I was afraid that waiting longer would mean amputation.   —Bruno Bettelheim

Example **282** contains two independent clauses *(Finally things got worse* and *I was afraid)* and a noun clause *that waiting longer would mean amputation).*

283   My brother does not understand my husband's inability to perceive the advantage in the rather common real-estate transaction known as "sale-leaseback," *and* my husband in turn does not understand why so many of the people he hears about in my father's house have recently been committed to mental hospitals or booked on drunk-driving charges.   —Joan Didion

Independent clauses: *My brother does not understand my husband's inability to perceive the advantage in the rather common real-estate transaction known as "sale-leaseback"; my husband in turn does not understand.* Dependent clauses: *why so many of the people / have recently been committed to mental hospitals or booked on drunk-driving charges; / (that) he hears about in my father's house.*

Such is an outline of the types of English sentences, classed according to their clause structure: simple, compound, complex, and compound-complex. And if your head is swimming, remember that we are really dealing with the way propositions get put together in English sentences. Clauses are merely propositions with all their elements expressed in the surface structure, and either they are independent or they are subordinated, or embedded, in another clause.

The main thrust of this chapter has been to view the English sentence as a matrix for propositions, on the premise that recognizing the propositional nature of language will help you sort out the intricacies of sentence structure. Let it be said, however, that there is no reason for you to become an expert on the intricacies of English grammar. Your goal is to be able to produce sentences and, incidentally, to have some understanding of the structures produced and, ultimately, to appreciate the esthetic and rhetorical values of sentences in context.

We will now go on to discuss some other traditional principles concerning the sentence.

Periodic and Loose Sentences

We have seen that sentences consist of a base (or bases), to which clauses and modifiers are attached. Sometimes the modifiers come after the base;

284   Life disappears or modifies its appearances so fast that everything takes on an aspect of illusion—
   (NC)   a momentary fizzing and boiling with smoke rings,
   (PP)   like pouring dissident chemicals into a retort.   —Loren Eiseley

285   We caught two bass,
   (VC)   hauling them in briskly
   (Adv)   as though they were mackerel,

(VC)   pulling them over the side of the boat
(PP)   in a businesslike manner
(PP)   without any landing net,
(VC)   and   stunning   them   with   a   blow   on   the   back   of   the
         head.   —E. B. White

And sometimes the modifiers precede the base;

286   (Adv)   As the least drop of wine tinges the whole goblet,
                so the least particle of truth colors our whole life.   —Thoreau

287   (PP)   Instead of a squad of Nazi supermen in shiny boots, and packing
                Lugers,
                we were confronted by five of the most unkempt, stunted, scrubby
                specimens
      (Rel)   I have ever had the pleasure of capturing.   —Donald Pearce

In *loose* sentences, the modifiers follow the base, as in **284** and **285**, and in
periodic sentences, the modifiers precede the base, as in **286** and **287**. In **287**
a relative clause does follow the base, but notice that it is a restrictive
relative clause and cannot be placed at any other point in the sentence.
Therefore, **287** is a periodic sentence, because its movable modifiers
precede the base. And note also that it is simple to turn **287** into a loose
sentence:

288   We were confronted by five of the most unkempt, stunted, scrubby specimens
      I have ever had the pleasure of capturing, ***instead of a squad of Nazi supermen
      in shiny boots, and packing Lugers.***

There is much lore concerning periodic and loose sentences. For instance, in their influential little book *The Elements of Style,* William
Strunk, Jr., and E. B. White say,

> If the writer finds that he has written a series of loose sentences, he should
> recast enough of them to remove the monotony, replacing them by simple
> sentences, by sentences of two clauses, by sentences (loose or periodic) of
> three clauses—whichever best represent the real relations of the thought.[3]

Some handbooks state flatly: Loose sentences are not as effective as
periodic. But to all such advice and dicta, we must reply: it all depends—on
what the writer is trying to say, and to whom, and for what purpose.

Passive Voice

Perhaps the most common definition of *passive voice* is this: it is the
form of the sentence in which the subject receives the action. Thus,

289   Mary was punched by George.

is in the passive voice, and

290   George punched Mary.

is in the active voice. However, by that definition, we could argue that

291   Mary received the blow.

[3]Strunk and White, p. 20.

is in the passive voice, for **Mary** receives the action. Yet we know that **291** has another form, which is the passive:

292   The blow was received by Mary.

Let's examine the way in which **293** can be changed into the passive:

293   George saw Mary.

First, the subject and the object are flipflopped: **Mary saw George.** Second, the preposition **by** is inserted before the new object: **Mary saw by George.** Third, the appropriate form of **be** is inserted before the verb: **Mary was saw by George.** Fourth, the verb is changed into the past participial form: **Mary was seen by George.** And fifth, the prepositional phrase *can* be deleted: **Mary was seen.**

In other words, a passive sentence is one containing a **be** verb plus a past participle.

There is also a good deal of lore surrounding passive voice, most of it saying that active voice is more direct, vigorous, and effective than passive. Once again: it all depends! In the following paragraph, passive sentences are italicized:

294   I had a couple of close ones during this show. **On the way in, my platoon was evidently silhouetted against the night sky, and was fired on four times at a range of maybe 300 yards by an eighty-eight.** (This is a notorious and vicious gun. The velocity of the shell is so high that you hear it pass or explode near you almost at the same instant that you hear the sound of its being fired. You really can't duck it. Also, it's an open-sights affair—**you are aimed at particularly: not, as with mortars, aimed at only by approximation.**) Anyway, they went past me about an arm's length above or in front of me, I don't know which. We hit the ditches. **After pointing a few more, the gun was forced off by our return tank fire.**   —Donald Pearce, *Journal of a War*

Surely this passage would not be improved if all its sentences were in active voice.

When we discuss emphasis later in this chapter, we will return to the concepts of both periodic and loose sentences and passive voice.

Parallelism and Balance

Two traditional and related principles involving the sentence are *parallelism* and *balance.* Parallelism is a grammatical principle, and balance has to do with sentence effect.

Parallelism

Two or more items standing in the same grammatical slot in a sentence are usually grammatical equivalents. Thus, the sentence

295   Barbara likes *ice cream, candy,* and *soda water.*

is parallel, for the coordinate objects of the verb **likes** are all nouns.

296   Barbara likes ice cream
                    candy
                    soda water

But this sentence

297   Barbara likes *ice cream, candy,* and *to dance.*

is not parallel, for *ice cream* and *candy* are nouns, but *to dance* is an infinitive.

Here is another sentence that is faulty in parallelism:

298   Robert wants to learn algebra, play tennis, and he goes to college.

The best way to explain the faulty parallelism in **298** is to schematize;

299   Robert wants to learn algebra
　　　　　　　play tennis
　　　　　　　he goes to college

The faulty parallelism is easily corrected:

300   Robert wants to learn algebra and play tennis, and he goes to college.
　　　Robert wants to learn algebra
　　　　　　　play tennis
　　　he goes to college

As Virginia Tufte points out in her excellent book *Grammar as Style,*[4] some professional writers deliberately create sentences in which parallelism is faulty, to achieve specific effects. She cites these examples:

301   Here was himself,　　　　*young*　　　　　　*(adjective)*
　　　　　　　　　　　　　　good-looking　　　*(adjective)*
　　　　　　　　　　　　　　snappy dresser,　*(noun phrase)*
　　　　　　　　　　　　　　and making dough.　*(verbal phrase)*
　　　　　　　　　　　　　　　　　　　　　　—John Steinbeck

302   Is there any one period of English literature to which we can point as being
　　　fully mature,　　　　　*(adjective phrase)*
　　　comprehensive,　　　　*(adjective)*
　　　and in equilibrium?　*(prepositional phrase)*
　　　　　　　　　　　　　　　　　—T. S. Eliot

303   *Religiously,*　　　　　　　　　　　　　　*(adjective)*
　　　politically　　　　　　　　　　　　　　*(adjective)*
　　　and simply in terms of the characters'　*(prepositional*
　　　efforts to get along with one another,　*phrase)*
　　　this incongruity is pervasive.　　　　—Frederick C. Crews

Balance

Closely allied to parallelism, balance is a matter of the rhetoric of the sentence, not the grammar. As the name implies, it is a device in which structures are balanced, for emphasis or effect.

In the following sentence, coordinated noun phrases are balanced for effect:

304   There was a time also when in the first fine flush of
　　　laundries and bakeries,

[4]Virginia Tufte, *Grammar as Style* (New York: Holt, Rinehart and Winston, 1971), pp. 207–08.

> *milk deliveries and canned goods,*
> *ready-made clothes and dry-cleaning,*
it did look as if American life was being enormously simplified.
>   —Margaret Mead

In **305** the coordinate structures are exactly balanced:

305   There is no sense in hoping
> *for that which already exists*
or
> *for that which cannot be.*   —Erich Fromm

In **306** complex sentences are balanced against one another:

306   We go
> wherever the wind blows,
we take
> whatever we find.   —Danilo Dolci

Most balance is not quite that perfect, however. In the following sentence, we find phrases that nearly balance:

307   The view that neurosis is a severe reaction to human trouble is as
> *revolutionary in its implications for social practice*
as it is
> *daring in formulation.*   —Jerome S. Bruner

Sentence Strategies

The grammar of English affords the writer a great many devices for adjusting the effects of sentences. In this chapter, we have already explored three of them: the arrangements of modifiers that bring about *periodic and loose sentences, passive voice,* and *balance.*

Periodic and Loose Arrangements

For instance, compare the effect of this periodic sentence with its loose version:

308   Having entered the House of Commons in the customary manner for peers' sons, from a family-controlled borough in an uncontested election at the age of twenty-three, and, during his fifteen years in the House of Commons, having returned unopposed five times from the same borough, and having for the last twenty-seven years sat in the House of Lords, he had little personal experience of vote-getting.   —Barbara Tuchman

309   He had little personal experience of vote-getting, having entered the House of Commons in the customary manner for peers' sons, from a family-controlled borough in an uncontested election at the age of twenty-three, and, during his fifteen years in the House of Commons, having been returned unopposed five times from the same borough, and having for the last twenty-seven years sat in the House of Lords.

In **308** readers are held in suspense, waiting for the base to occur and thus for the sentence to resolve itself into a meaning. The main predicate **had** is the sixty-third word in the sentence, and, of course, readers cannot mentally organize the sentence until they reach the predicate. In **309** the predicate *had* is the second word, and the modifiers that follow the base fall into place immediately, not needing to be held in suspension.

In **308** there is a certain force and finality that one does not sense in **309**; **309** seems to go on and on. But this is not to say that **308** is inherently better than **309**; each of the two versions achieves a different effect, and the value of that effect can be judged only in context, in the light of purpose, audience, and subject. Being able to perceive the different effects—and to achieve them—is, however, important.

Here is another example of a sentence in periodic and loose forms:

310   In the autumn following Custer's expedition, the Sioux who had been hunting in the north began returning to the Red Cloud agency.   —Dee Brown

311   The Sioux who had been hunting in the north began returning to the Red Cloud agency in the autumn following Custer's expedition.

Again, we feel that **310** is crisper and sharper than **311**.

Passive Arrangements

The matter of passive is of some interest. In a language such as English that has few inflectional endings—an *analytic* language—relationships with the predicate must be shown by word order. That is, **The man killed the king** and **The king killed the man** are opposites in meaning. In synthetic languages such as Latin and Old English, word order is not so important, for changes in word form show relationships to the predicate. Thus, in Old English, both **Se man sloh thone kyning** and **Thone kyning sloh se man** mean "The man killed the king," for **se** is the subjective form of the definite article, and **thone** is the objective.

Therefore, synthetic languages had the advantage of being able to foreground words by putting them at either the beginning or the end of sentences without changing meaning. But such is not the case with modern English. Modern English does, however, have a number of devices that enable the writer to give words the desired stress in sentences. For instance, suppose that you want to stress the idea that the king was killed, not that the man killed him. In that case, you can use passive voice:

312   The king was killed by the man.

You can even delete the agent;

313   The king was killed.

The following illustrates the value of passive for foregrounding ideas:

314   In the winter of 1934, I spent several weeks in a federal transient camp in California. **These camps were originally established by Governor Rolph in the early days of the Depression to care for the single homeless unemployed of the state.**   —Eric Hoffer

Since the second sentence is in the passive voice, it is the camps that receive the stress, not who established them. Notice how the stress changes if the second sentence is put into the active voice:

315   Governor Rolph established these camps in the early days of the Depression to care for the single homeless unemployed of the state.

Balanced Arrangements

We have seen how balance works in the sentence. Balance also is a strategy for achieving emphasis. Structures that are balanced call attention to themselves. Here is a perfectly balanced sentence:

316   The difference
            between tragedy and comedy
        is
        the difference
            between experience and intuition.   —Christopher Fry

This balance emphasizes both halves of the equation. Here is another example of emphasis through balance:

317   There is often something beautiful,
        there is always something awful,
            in the spectacle of a person who has lost one of his faculties, a faculty he never questioned until it was gone, and who struggles to recover it.   —James Baldwin

Repetition

Another interesting and useful device in sentence strategies is *repetition:*

318   He had drunk a lot of *rezina* in his time: he said it was good for one, good for the kidneys, good for the liver, good for the lungs, good for the bowels and for the mind, good for everything.   —Henry Miller

This daring extensive repetition certainly underscores the opinion about the goodness of the Greek wine *rezina.*

In the following passage, the author uses repetition with great effect:

319   To be human, to be human, to be fully human. What does it mean? What is required?   —Wayne C. Booth

Not only does he repeat the infinitive phrase (with a variation in the last one), but he also repeats the question form twice. To illustrate the force of repetition, I will rewrite **319**, removing the repetition:

320   What is meant and required to be fully human?

Certainly **320** has a different effect from **319**.

Another example of repetition for emphasis:

321   Just as the prophets of the eighth century B.C. left their villages and carried their "thus saith the Lord" far beyond the boundaries of their home towns, and just as the Apostle Paul left his village of Tarsus and carried the Gospel of Jesus Christ to the far corners of the Greco-Roman world, so am I compelled to carry the gospel of freedom beyond my own home town.
                    —Martin Luther King, Jr.

Of course, in **321**, one sees not only repetition but also parallelism.

And a final example of the effectiveness of repetition:

322   Now what does this Let Him Be Poor mean? It means let him be weak. Let him be ignorant. Let him become a nucleus of disease. Let him be a standing exhibition and example of ugliness and dirt. Let him have rickety children.   —George Bernard Shaw

And, indeed, the passage goes on at great length, each repetition of **Let him** driving the point home more forcefully.

Varieties of Emphases

In order to explore how various sorts of emphases can be achieved, let's simply look at and comment on a collection of interesting sentences.

The following is simple enough:

323   Resistance was, I believe, his code.   —William Carlos Williams

By forming the sentence as he did, Williams placed emphasis on the word **Resistance.** Note how emphasis changes in the following rewrite of **323**:

324   I believe resistance was his code.

Now the stress is upon what the author believes, not upon resistance.

In the next example, Mark Twain apparently wanted his own attitude to dominate:

325   It was a heavenly place for a boy, that farm of my uncle John's.

                                                                                —Mark Twain

In Twain's version of the sentence, the heavenly nature of the farm is the dominant idea, as the following revised version will show:

326   That farm of my uncle John's was a heavenly place for a boy.

When an author wants to introduce a character dramatically, the following sort of sentence is obviously effective:

327   In the dawn light they saw a man at bay, crouching against the corral fence—Ishi.   —Theodora Kroeber

The reader is not likely to forget that name.

The demonstrative pronouns **this/these** and **that/those** "point": **that** man, **this** woman. Therefore, they can be used very effectively in achieving emphases in sentences.

328   Patience, horses or a fine carriage, a widow to wive, a sloping lawn with a river at the bottom, a thriving field, an adopted daughter—that was as far as his desire wandered.   —William Carlos Williams

The demonstrative **that** throws emphasis backward upon the nouns and noun phrases that precede it. Notice the emphasis in the following sentences:

329   Interesting work, enough money, plenty of exercise—that constitutes the good life.

330 This constitutes the good life: interesting work, enough money, plenty of exercise.

Examples **329** and **330** are quite different in their emphases from the following:

331 Interesting work, enough money, and plenty of exercise constitute the good life.

The grammar of the language allows writers a certain amount of latitude in arranging their sentences. We have seen that, for instance, in the case of the periodic and loose sentence. And we see it also in the syntax of complements, as in the following:

332 It is easy to sing "Yankee Doodle."

333 To sing "Yankee Doodle" is easy.

334 It was a pity that Mary missed the show.

335 That Mary missed the show was a pity.

Here are some other examples of ways in which sentences can achieve emphasis through arrangement:

336 Of all virtues, magnanimity is the rarest.   —William Hazlitt

The normal syntax of that sentence would be, of course,

337 Magnanimity is the rarest of all virtues.

The following is an even clearer illustration of an inversion:

338 Stress he could endure but peace and regularity pleased him better.
                                    —William Carlos Williams

The normal order for **338** is

339 He could endure stress but peace and regularity pleased him better.

This discussion could go on and on. The point has been to make you aware that there are a number of devices—easily mastered—by which you can achieve a variety of effects in your sentences. In Chapter 14, when we analyze various passages, we will return to the consideration of sentence effectiveness.

Finally

This chapter has been very detailed, even persnickety maybe, but I hope that the mystery of the sentence has not been lost in all the attention to modifiers and clauses, for the sentence is a thoroughly amazing product of a thoroughly amazing instrument, the human brain, and we are far from understanding the *what* that is produced, let alone the *how*.

So the sentence is fascinating as an outward manifestation of the inward process called thinking or the generation of language—if, indeed, the two concepts are separable.

But the sentence is also interesting as an esthetic object. In the symphony of a piece of writing, the sentence is a melody or phrase that has its value in relation to the whole. Granted, the discussion in this chapter has not viewed sentences in context. But in Chapter 14, all the principles that were covered in this chapter will be put to work.

Discussion and Activities

Propositions

Identify the propositions in the following sentences. Remember that if you understand the sentence, you intuitively understand the propositions that it contains; to state these propositions is merely to make explicit that which you know implicitly.

a   Brave men don't cry.

b   Typing the letter, Maude broke a fingernail.

c   The rose that blooms early often freezes.

d   Sometimes I wonder whether this is a true memory at all.
                                                    —Norman Podhoretz

e   It is self-interest to want to live in a society operating by the love of justice and the concept of law.   —Robert Penn Warren

f   The world is divided into *us* and *them*, a division made by psyches that have the geometric fragility of the designs children make with Indian beads.
                                                    —Leonard Kriegel

g   Graven tablets grace the scenes of long-past battles, births and deaths, that their fame might live on in perpetuity.   —William L. Laurence

h   Those who came too early, striving in vain to speed up the course of history, are also history's tragic heroes.   —Jan Kott

i   To understand the negative in experience we have then to go over to a radically different concept of Being.   —William Barrett

j   Since being a male necessitates some kind of relationship to females, *Playboy* fearlessly confronts this problem too, and solves it by the consistent application of the same formula.   —Harvey Cox

Relatives

Identify the relative clauses in the following sentences. State whether they are restrictive or nonrestrictive.

a   He took over the Dad's failing junk business rather than take jobs that would as a matter of course lead to moderate advancement.   —William Alfred

b   This is why the voices, real or unreal, which speak from the floating trumpets at spiritualist seances are so unnerving.   —Loren Eiseley

c   Surfboarding, which is a relatively dangerous sport, appeals to young people.

d   Let us take a mood in which you feel lost, deserted, where the world looks gray, a little frightening though not really dangerous.   —Erich Fromm

e   The logical use of language presupposes the meanings of the words it employs and presupposes them constant.   —Owen Barfield

f   Let us now take the opposite situation—that in which it is we ourselves who are being instructed.   —C. S. Lewis

g   In certain kinds of writing, particularly in art criticism and literary criticism, it is normal to come across long passages which are almost completely lacking in meaning.   —George Orwell

h   The dictum that style is the man is well known. It is one of those aphorisms that say too much to mean a great deal.   —W. Somerset Maugham

i   I told my students that every time they came upon a word in their book they did not understand, they were to look it up in the dictionary.   —John Holt

j   As you know, I began the semester in a way that departed from the manner in which I had taught composition classes in the past.   —Henry F. Ottinger

The Cumulative Sentence

Identify the cumulative modifiers in the following sentences. Perhaps the best way to do this is to diagram the sentences in the way explained in the chapter. Remember that the cumulative modifiers are absolutes (Abs), adjective clusters (AC), adverb clauses (Adv), noun clusters (NC), prepositional phrases (PP), relative clauses (RC), and verb clusters (VC).

a   The mail having arrived, we left for the city.

b   The students cheered, their team being seven points ahead.

c   The day, drizzingly damp, depressed Deborah.

d   The waitress smiled toothily, artificial in her unctuous friendliness.

e   If winter comes, can spring be far behind?

f   Computer programing, though it fascinates many students, takes a long time to master.

g   *Heart of Darkness,* a masterpiece of fiction, baffled LaWanda.

h   A spry octogenarian, my grandfather still plays golf.

i   In the morning, our whole family drinks tea.

j   Germans drink beer during the Oktoberfest.

k   Men never make passes at girls who wear glasses.

l   Girls, who are just as competent as boys, seldom become dentists.

m   Hoping for a strike, the fisherman cast his fly into the riffle.

n   A pelican dived for an anchovy, flopping ridiculously into the ocean.

o   Best went to Berlin and obtained a promise that all Jews from Denmark would be sent to Theresienstadt regardless of their category—a very important concession, from the Nazis' point of view.   —Hannah Arendt

p   Later, Ishi spoke with some diffidence of this, his first contact with white men.   —Theodora Kroeber

q   I stood open-mouthed, my mind racing.   —Konrad V. Lorenz

r   Appearing in public before an audience about whom he cared nothing, Salisbury was awkward . . . .   —Barbara Tuchman

s   Now a cotton merchant and banker, he had earlier run a factory, where he had experienced the decline of the Lancashire cotton industry . . . .
                                                   —Ian Watt

t   He smoked briefly, his eyes following a pattern of concrete blocks in the school building.   —J. D. Salinger

u   A learned man is an idler who kills time with study.   —George Bernard Shaw

v   All animals, both tame and wild, weaken in these circumstances, and the weakest go to the wall and die.   —John D. Stewart

w   We play out our days as we play out cards, taking them as they come, not knowing what they will be, hoping for a lucky card and sometimes getting one, often getting just the wrong one.   —Samuel Butler

x   Infuriated, Saville now ordered one of his workmen to ride to the Soldiers' Town (Fort Robinson) and request a company of cavalry to come to his aid.   —Dee Brown

y   Then only is freedom a reality, when men may voice their opinions because they must examine their opinions.   —Walter Lippmann

Traditional Principles

1. According to their clause structure, classify the following sentences as simple, complex, compound, or compound-complex.

    a   And Uriah departed out of the king's house, and there followed him a mess of meat from the king.   —The Book of Samuel

    b   When he reached the brook where he intended to fish, an angler found he had left his bait at home, but after considering matters, he thought he might be able to catch grasshoppers and use them instead.
                                                   —William March

    c   He who hesitates is sometimes saved.   —James Thurber

    d   One early group of theories, following seventeenth-century practice, regarded attraction and frictional generation as the fundamental electrical phenomena.   —Thomas S. Kuhn

e The habit is good or otherwise, according as it produces true conclusions from true premises or not; and an inference is regarded as valid or not, without reference to the truth or falsity of its conclusion specially, but according as the habit which determines it is such as to produce true conclusions in general or not. —Charles Sanders Peirce

f But we can study self-observation, and we must include it in any reasonably complete account of human behavior. —B. F. Skinner

g The kind of psychology which has addressed itself to these questions divides into two professional areas: academic personality research, and clinical psychology and psychiatry. —Naomi Weisstein

h The sexual assumption lies today in ruins. —Robert Ardrey

i Just as I was certain that desire has in itself an efficacy in the realm of spiritual goodness whatever its form, I thought it was also possible that it might not be effective in any other realm. —Simone Weil

j Myths of origin and eventual extinction vary according to the climate. —Robert Graves

2. Some of the following sentences are loose, and some are periodic. Rearrange the loose so that they become periodic and the periodic so that they become loose. What are the differences in effect? For example, here is a periodic sentence: ***And when it does happen, it is plain that our new understanding is bound up with the new metaphor.*** Here is a loose version of that sentence: ***And it is plain that our new understanding is bound up with the new metaphor when it does happen.***

a In certain kinds of writing, particularly in art criticism and literary criticism, it is normal to come across long passages which are almost completely lacking in meaning. —George Orwell

b The human species, according to the best theory I can form of it, is composed of two distinct races, *the men who borrow,* and *the men who lend.* —Charles Lamb

c The dog has long been bemused by the singular activities and the curious practices of men, cocking his head inquiringly to one side, intently watching and listening to the strangest goings-on in the world. —James Thurber

d The rolling period, the stately epithet, the noun rich in poetic associations, the subordinate clauses that give the sentence weight and magnificence, the grandeur like that of wave following wave in the open sea; there is no doubt that in all this there is something inspiring. —W. Somerset Maugham

e From the very beginning of school we make books and reading a constant source of possible failure and public humilitation. —John Holt

f I plodded on with the lesson, trying to get the class to locate Broad and Market streets, the site of Philadelphia's City Hall, on maps that had been passed out. —Peter Binzen

3. Some of the following sentences are in active voice, some in passive. Change the active to passive and the passive to active. Discuss the changes in emphasis that result.

  a   Rats and dogs are conditioned and are usually incapable of breaking that conditioning.

  —Henry F. Ottinger

  b   Classroom dynamics can be described in terms of teacher and student roles.

  c   The reader knows best how a productive wedding is arranged in his own field.

  —William G. Perry, Jr.

  d   I am using the word *image* in a wide meaning, which does not restrict it to the mind's eye as a visual organ.

  —Jacob Bronowski

  e   The presence of pleasure areas in the brain was discovered accidentally in 1954 by James Olds and Peter Milner in Canada.

  —H. J. Campbell

  f   The subject is told to administer a shock to the learner each time he gives a wrong response.

  —Stanley Milgram

Sentence Strategies

In the following sentences, various strategies are used to achieve various effects. Point these strategies out, and rearrange the sentences to achieve different effects.

  a   The good fortune of the physicist—and these matters are always relative, for the material monism of physics may have impeded nineteenth-century thinking and delayed insights into the nature of complementarity in modern physical theory—this early good fortune or happy insight has no counterpart in the sciences of man.

  —Jerome S. Bruner

  b   Since RKO-Radio Pictures first released *King Kong,* a quarter-century has gone by; yet year after year, from prints that grow more rain-beaten, from sound tracks that grow more tinny, ticket-buyers by thousands still pursue Kong's luckless fight against the forces of technology, tabloid journalism, and the DAR. They see him chloroformed to sleep, see him whisked from his jungle to New York, and placed on show, see him burst his chains to roam the city (lugging a frightened blonde), at last to plunge from the spire of the Empire State Building, machine-gunned by model airplanes.

  —X. J. Kennedy

  c   I went as far as the sixth grade in school. I'm 57 now. I was 16 and didn't want to be 16 in the seventh grade so I quit.

  —Linda Lane

  d   What is the function of sound in music? What is the function of sound in poetry? What is the function of sound in prose composition? What is the function of sound in drama?

  e   Just praise is only a debt, but flattery is a present.

  —Samuel Johnson

  f   And he took the pain of it, if not happily, like a martyr, at least willingly, like an heir.

  —Edward Lewis Wallant

g   *Mansions there are*—two or three of them—but the majority of the homes are large and inelegant.   —John Barth

h   I am sure of this, that by going much alone a man will get more of a noble courage in thought and word than from all the wisdom that is in books.
                                                        —Ralph Waldo Emerson

i   These times—they try men's souls.

j   A sudden idea of the relationship between "lovers." We are neither male nor female. We are a compound of both. I choose the male who will develop and expand the male in me; he chooses me to expand the female in him. Being made "whole."   —Katherine Mansfield

k   Now I think—I happen to think—that those three beliefs that I speak of, the self-belief, the love-belief, and the art-belief, are all closely related to the God-belief, that the belief in God is a relationship you enter into with Him to bring about the future.   —Robert Frost

l   are you ready for the demystification of diamondback terrapins???????? they ain't nothing but salt water turtles.   —Verta Mae Smart-Grosvenor

m   I was a caged panther. It was jungle. Survival was the law of the land. I watched so many partners fall along the way. I decided the modus operandi was bad. Unavailing, non-productive.   —Studs Terkel

n   Finally, one night they had Junior trapped on the road up toward the bridge around Millersville, there's no way out of there, they had the barricades up and they could hear this souped-up car roaring around the bend, and here it comes—but suddenly they can hear a siren and see a red light flashing in the grille, so they think it's another agent, and boy, they run out like ants and pull those barrels and boards and sawhorses out of the way, and then— Ggghhzzzzzzzhhhhhhhggggggzzzzzzzeeeeeong!—gawdam! there he goes again, it was him, Junior Johnson! with a gawdam agent's sireen and a red light in his grille.   —Tom Wolfe

Words 12

Summary of the Chapter

A word is a *symbol*, and symbols differ from *signs*. A sign merely announces the presence of something, but a word stimulates conceptualizing. Thus, a red light at an intersection is a sign that brings about stopping, but does not necessarily provoke thought about the concept "stopping."

Words convey meanings in a variety of ways. In the first place, they have *referents;* for instance, the word **cow** refers to a milk-giving ruminant. Words also have semantic features, built-in increments of meaning. For instance, **ewe** has the semantic feature "female," and **ram** has the semantic feature "male"; **love** has the semantic feature "abstract," and **candy** has the semantic feature "concrete." And words also come to life in *context.* Out of context, **man** means something like "male, human, adult," but in context, it can gain additional meaning, as in **Anthony Davis is a real man.**

Meanings of words are either *denotations* or *connotations.* Denotations are, roughly speaking, the core meanings, as in defining **stallion** as a "male equine." Connotations are the associations that a word carries; for instance, **stallion** has the connotation of fieriness and strength.

Dictionaries are, of course, a main source of our knowledge about words. It is important to understand that dictionaries only record what is in the language; they do not make value judgments on what should be. Thus, the compilers of a dictionary may deplore the use of **ain't,** but they must record that word and indicate that it is used by certain people in certain circumstances.

Words can be viewed from the standpoint of *levels of usage. Formal* usage excludes slang expressions such as **crazy** or **headshrinker,** and it observes niceties that *informal* usage does not. For instance, one is likely to find fewer contractions in formal usage than in informal. *Nonstandard* usage consists of those words and phrases that are generally avoided by the power elite in any society—the educators, the wealthy, the influential. A word such as **sody-pop,** common among many speakers, would generally not be allowed in standard usage. But the labels "standard" and "non-standard" should not be evaluative. Nonstandard is unacceptable only because it is not the language of the power elite, not because it is *sub*standard.

Slang is a rich and interesting part of every language. Terms in slang tend to pass out of the language rapidly, and nothing is staler than yesterday's slang. On the other hand, many slang terms have remained in the language for generations: *babe* (for girl), *chow, goofy, lousy.*

Jargon is a form of in-talk. It consists of special words and phrases used by various groups. There is a jargon of medicine, of the underworld, of the jazz world; there is a jargon of carnivals and of literary critics. Jargon serves a useful purpose only when one member of the in-group is addressing other members.

Gobbledygook is the use of polysyllables where shorter words would do, and of many words where few would do. A sentence like **Bring your locomotion to a cessation** is gobbledygook for **Stop.**

You should be aware of your options in word choice. For instance, you frequently can choose between a verbal and a nominal: **Franklin made THE INSCRIPTION in the book/Franklin INSCRIBED the book.** You also can often choose between a nominal and an adjectival expression: **We enjoyed the BEAUTY of the weather/We enjoyed the BEAUTIFUL weather.**

To Get Under Way

Words are symbols that convey concepts and, therefore, are basic to the thought process. In fact, the intricacies of words and their functions in sentences are topics that ought to intrigue the intellectually curious.

This chapter will work on two planes: the theoretical, because theories concerning words are inherently interesting, and the practical, because the ability to use words effectively is one of a writer's supremely important skills.

Sign and Symbol

Both *signs* and *symbols* convey meanings, but they are quite different in their nature. Signs stand in lieu of their objects or referents. A red light at an intersection can be either a sign or a symbol. Insofar as it brings about stopping by drivers of automobiles, it is merely a sign. But insofar as it triggers the concept "stopping" in the minds of drivers, it is a symbol.

Of course a word may be used as a sign, but that is not its primary role. Its signific character has to be indicated by some special modification—by a tone of voice, a gesture (such as pointing or staring), or the location of a placard bearing the word. In itself it is a symbol, associated with a conception, not directly with a public object or event. The fundamental difference between signs and symbols is this difference of association, and consequently of their *use* by the third party to the meaning function, the subject; signs *announce* their objects to him, whereas symbols *lead him to conceive their objects.* The fact that the same item—say, the little mouthy noise we call a "word"—may serve in either capacity, does not obliterate the cardinal distinction between the two functions it may assume.[1]

Nouns, verbs, adjectives, adverbs, and pronouns are signs. They are the "counters" wherewith we symbolize.

This much said, let us turn to a little tale composed by Jonathan Swift, who told of the marvelous adventures of Gulliver during his travels. Everyone knows about Gulliver's voyage to Lilliput, where he met the little people, but not everyone knows about his voyage to Balnibarbi, where he visited the great Academy of Lagado. In the academy, all sorts of learned and scientific projects were under way. One scientist, for instance, was attempting to distill sunbeams from cucumbers so that they could be used on gloomy days, and another was working at turning ice into gunpowder. Gulliver's tour of the academy progresses:

We next went to the School of Languages, where three Professors sat in Consultation upon improving that of their Country.

The first Project was to shorten Discourse by cutting Polysyllables into one, and leaving out Verbs and Participles; because in Reality all things imaginable are but Nouns.

The other, was a Scheme for entirely abolishing all Words whatsoever: And this was urged as a great Advantage in Point of Health as well as Brevity. For, it is plain, that every Word we speak is in some Degree a Diminution of our Lungs by Corrosion; and consequently contributes to the shortening of our Lives. An Expedient was therefore offered, that since Words are only Names for *Things,* it would be more convenient for all Men to carry about them, such *Things* as were necessary to express the particular Business they are to discourse on. And this Invention would certainly have taken place, to the great Ease as well as Health of the Subject, if the Women in Conjunction with the Vulgar and Illiterate had not threatened to raise a Rebellion, unless they might be allowed the Liberty to speak their Tongues, after the Manner of their Forefathers: Such constant and irreconcilable Enemies to Science are the common People. However, many of the most Learned and Wise adhere to the new Scheme of expressing themselves by *Things;* which hath only this Inconvenience attending it; that if a Man's Business be very great, and of various Kinds, he must be obliged in Proportion to carry a greater Bundle of *Things* upon his Back, unless he can afford one or two strong Servants to attend him. I have often beheld two of those Sages almost sinking under the Weight of their packs, like Pedlars among us, who when they met in the Streets, would lay down their Loads, open their Sacks, and hold Conversation for an Hour together; then put up their Implements, help each other to resume their Burthens, and take their Leave.

[1]Susanne K. Langer, *Philosophy in a New Key* (New York: New American Library, 1951), p. 61.

But, for short Conversations a Man can carry Implements in his Pockets and under his Arms, Enough to supply him, and in his House he cannot be at a Loss; therefore the Room where Company meet who practice this Art, is full of all *Things* ready at hand, requisite to furnish Matter for this kind of artificial Converse.

Another great Advantage proposed by this Invention, was, that it would serve as a universal Language to be understood in all civilized Nations, whose Goods and Utensils are generally of the same Kind, or nearly resembling, so that their uses might easily be comprehended. And thus, Embassadors would be qualified to treat with foreign Princes or Ministers of State, to whose Tongues they were utter Strangers.

Meaning Again

As was pointed out in Chapter 10, words do not take their meanings exclusively from their referents, the things or concepts that they refer to. If words gained their meanings exclusively from referents, the following two sentences would be identical in meaning:

1 Gerald Ford is the President of the United States.

2 Gerald Ford is America's chief executive.

Both **the President of the United States** and **America's chief executive** have the same referent (Gerald Ford); since the two sentences are not precisely synonymous, the noun phrases cannot gain their meaning solely from their reference, even though part of the meaning must come from reference.

Denotation

Words have built-in increments of meaning, denotations, which always come with the words. For instance, the word **stallion** has as one feature of its total meaning "male"; that is, it applies only to male referents. (We are talking here about words in isolation, *out of context*. In actual use, it is conceivable that the word **stallion** might be used to refer to a female.) **Stallion,** then, has the *semantic feature* "male." We can express this fact in this way:

3 **stallion**
   [+male]

Mare, on the other hand, has the feature "female," which we can express this way:

4 **mare**
   [−male]

Rock has the feature [+concrete], and **democracy,** an abstract noun, has the feature [−concrete]. **Professor** has the feature [+human], and **swine** has the feature [−human]. **Microbe** has the feature [+animate], and **molecule** has the feature [−animate].

Now let's look at the word **man.** It has the features

5   **man**
$$\begin{bmatrix} +\text{human} \\ +\text{concrete} \\ +\text{animate} \\ +\text{male} \\ +\text{adult} \end{bmatrix}$$

But this list of features is redundant, for anything that is human is also concrete and animate. We can express the features of **man** more economically:

6   **man**
$$\begin{bmatrix} +\text{human} \\ +\text{male} \\ +\text{adult} \end{bmatrix}$$

And we can express the features of **woman** thus:

7   **woman**
$$\begin{bmatrix} +\text{human} \\ -\text{male} \\ +\text{adult} \end{bmatrix}$$

It seems that our understanding of words is based in part at least on our automatic perception that they carry with them a variety of features that can be expressed in a binary (+ or −) way. Notice that, put into sentences, **6** and **7** constitute adequate definitions:

8   A man is a human who is an adult male.

9   A woman is a human who is an adult non-male.

What about a word such as **animal?** How about this:

10   **animal**
$$\begin{bmatrix} +\text{animate} \\ -\text{human} \end{bmatrix}$$

This would mean that **human** would be as follows:

11   **human**
$$\begin{bmatrix} +\text{animate} \\ +\text{human} \end{bmatrix}$$

Denotation in Action

Now think of nouns such as **steam, water, ice.** We can **inhale steam, drink water,** and **crush ice,** but we cannot *crush steam, *inhale water, or *drink ice.* The reason for this is interesting and easy to explain. **Steam, water,** and **ice** have semantic features that specify their degree of penetrability. Thus, **steam** [1 penetrable], **water** [2 penetrable], **ice** [3 penetrable]. The verb **inhale** demands as its object a noun with feature [1 penetrable], the verb **drink** demands as its object a noun with the feature [2 penetrable], and the verb **crush** demands as its object a noun with the feature [3 penetrable].

This can be expressed diagrammatically thus: *inhale* [_____ 1 penetrable], *drink* [_____ 2 penetrable], *crush* [_____ 3 penetrable]. Therefore, a sentence such as the following seems strange:

12   *Herman drank a carrot.

Nouns also have dimensional features. *Line* has the feature [1 dimension], *rectangle* has the feature [2 dimension], and *cube* has the feature [3 dimension]. The verb *build* has the feature [_____ 3 dimension]. Therefore, the following sentences seem odd:

13   *Margery built the line.

14   *Margery built the rectangle.

On the other hand, the verb *draw* has the feature [_____ 1 or 2 dimension]. Therefore,

15   Draw a line.

16   Draw a rectangle.

In other words, meaning is not just a matter of reference nor of the semantic features that individual words carry, but also of the interrelationships among words in sentences.

In this connection, let's speculate about a verb such as *draw*. We said that it has the feature [_____ 1 or 2 dimension]; that is, it will take as its objects only nouns that have one or two dimensions, such as *line* or *rectangle*. But, of course, we can *draw a man* or *draw a room*, and both *man* and *room* have the feature [3 dimension]. But doesn't *draw* impose its restrictions on both *man* and *room* in sentences?

17   Rembrandt drew a man.

18   Vermeer drew a room.

In these sentences, *man* and *room* lose their three-dimensional quality and become two-dimensional. Certainly in *a drawing of a room, room* is two-dimensional.

In fact, individual meanings from words and phrases permeate the sentence, so that, in a manner of speaking, the sentence, like a chemical compound, loses the individual distinctiveness of its components and becomes a meaning. Look at the following, for instance:

19   The boy chased the ball down the street.

We know that the boy and the ball are in motion because of the verb *chased,* and we know the direction of the motion because of the prepositional phrase *down the street.* In other words, we know that the boy and the ball are both moving in the same direction. Therefore, we can account for the strangeness of the following:

20   *The boy sitting on the porch chased the ball down the street.

21   *The boy running up the street chased the ball down the street.

Meaning and Metaphor

In connection with this discussion of how words mean, we can anticipate an important matter that will be dealt with in the next chapter: *metaphor*. A sentence such as the following is not literal, but metaphorical:

22   Hector was a lion in battle.

One explanation for the metaphorical nature of **22** is that **Hector** has the feature [+human] and **lion** has the feature [−human]. Thus, there is a disjunctiveness in meaning, and the sentence cannot be interpreted literally. Another metaphorical sentence:

23   All the Christmases roll down the hill towards the Welsh-speaking sea, like a snowball growing whiter and bigger and rounder, like a cold and headlong moon bundling down the sky that was our street. . . .   —Dylan Thomas

The verb **roll** normally takes a subject that has the feature [+concrete] or perhaps [3 dimension], but **Christmas** has the feature [−concrete]; therefore **Christmases roll** is interpreted metaphorically. As for **Welsh-speaking sea,** we can interpret this noun phrase something like this: "The sea speaks Welsh." But the verb **speak** demands a subject with the feature [+human], thus: **speak** [+human _____]. However, the noun **sea** has the feature [−human]; therefore, we must interpret **the Welsh-speaking sea** metaphorically.

Arbitrariness of Meaning

Another factor obviously enters into the meanings of words. So far, we have spoken as if words somehow, mystically, carried meanings with them, but that is true only metaphorically and from one point of view. From another point of view, we assign meanings to words. A word is merely a symbol, capable of evoking a concept.

It is perfectly possible for a group to endow a nonsense utterance such as **oompah** with a meaning, in which case **oompah** is a word for that group. Suppose that we arbitrarily decide it means "cavorting in the surf"; then we can talk meaningfully about **oompahing on a sunny summer day.** We have devised a word and assigned a meaning to it.

Since words are symbols that have their meanings assigned to them by the groups that use them, we can say that no word means *exactly* the same thing to any two people. Take the word **cat,** for instance. To my neighbors, who are cat fanciers, the word carries an aura of playfulness, cuddliness, and warmth. Since I am allergic to cats and don't like them at all, the word **cat** conveys to me a sense of sliminess, stealth, and coldness.

The situation becomes even more complicated with abstract words such as **democracy** or **honor.** A sentence such as the following is rife with the possibilities for misunderstanding that are inherent in various assignments of meaning:

24   A democracy always wants peace with honor.

We could spend lifetimes arguing about the meanings of **democracy, peace,** and **honor.**

Connotation

Consider the word **man** in the following two sentences:

25   A man is a male human.

26   Keith is a real man.

The first means something almost cut-and-dried, like this: **man** [+human, +male]. But the meaning of the second sentence is harder to specify and must be expressed by extensive paraphrase, perhaps like this: **Keith is strong and virile; he is courageous and trustworthy; there is nothing soft or effeminate about him.**

In these two kinds of meaning can be seen the difference between *denotation* and *connotation*. The core of meaning—the sort of thing that we can define with [+human, +male] or with the kind of statement found in a dictionary—is denotation. The secondary, largely affective associations that words carry with them, either in context or out of context, are called connotation.

The denotation of all these phrases is the same: **to die, to kick the bucket, to pass away.** But to illustrate the power of connotation, let's make up a little story.

A teen-age girl is deeply attached to her grandmother. The grandmother becomes ill and is hospitalized. One afternoon, the girl goes to the hospital and meets her grandmother's physician in the hall. "How's Grandma today?" she asks. The physician replies with *one* of the following:

27   Your grandmother died this morning.

28   Your grandmother kicked the bucket this morning.

29   Your grandmother passed away this morning.

If the physician replied with **27,** we might assume that he was a callous sort of guy, for **to die** is a bit harsh in its connotative value. If the physician replied with **28,** we would feel that he was utterly tactless, for **to kick the bucket** has humorous connotations, and the death of a beloved grandmother is not a humorous situation. Undoubtedly the physician—unless he was an insensitive slob—replied with **29,** for the connotation of **to pass away** is not as harsh as that of **to die.**

Some terms have unfavorable connotations: **garbage man, toilet, mortician, shit, dirty underwear, to lie, to fornicate, to vomit.** These can be replaced by terms with more favorable connotations: **sanitary engineer, water closet, funeral director, feces, soiled linen, to fib, to make love, to upchuck.**

The word **toilet** is interesting. Here is the *American Heritage Dictionary* definition of the word:

30   **1.** A disposal apparatus consisting of a hopper, fitted with a flushing device, used for urination and defecation. **2.** A room or booth containing such an apparatus and often a washbowl. **3.** The act or process of grooming and dressing oneself. **4.** A dressing table. **5.a.** Dress: attire. **b.** A costume or gown. **—make one's toilet.**

Thus, in *The Rape of the Lock,* Alexander Pope wrote,

31   And now, unveiled, the Toilet stands displayed,
Each silver Vase in mystic order laid.
First, robed in white, the Nymph intent adores,
With head uncovered, the Cosmetic powers.

But, of course, in modern English it is highly unlikely that one would hear, "Gloria is at her toilet, making herself beautiful." The word *toilet* simply has picked up too many unfavorable connotations. In the attempt to avoid these unfavorable connotations, *ladies' room* was substituted, and then when that term in turn picked up too many unfavorable connotations, *powder room* was substituted.

Here are some interesting sets of terms, each set having roughly the same denotations, but varying broadly in connotations:

32

Unfavorable	Neutral	Favorable
legal murder	euthanasia	mercy killing
birth control	contraception	family planning
spying	surveillance	
peddling	selling	marketing
farting	flatulation	breaking wind
crazy	psychotic	mentally unbalanced
cancer	carcinoma	lingering illness
	masculine	manly
soggy (day)	rainy (day)	
arid (climate)		dry (climate)

And, of course, to the residents of Los Angeles, *smog* is often *haze.*

Euphemism

The practice of substituting a word with favorable connotations for one with unfavorable connotations is known as *euphemism,* and the word so substituted is also known as a euphemism. Thus one might substitute *fibber* for *liar (Mike is a liar/Mike is a fibber)* because *fibber* has much less harsh connotations than *liar.* In **32** all the words in the "favorable" column might be viewed as euphemisms for the equivalents in the "unfavorable" column.

Another Word About Dictionaries

If you get hooked on words, nothing is more pleasant than thumbing through a dictionary, finding an unfamiliar word here and there, checking an occasional etymology, verifying a pronunciation. Of course, dictionaries are useful, but they are also pleasurable. And everyone—not just every student—ought to own a good desk dictionary: *Webster's Collegiate Dictionary, Webster's New World Dictionary of the English Language, The Standard College Dictionary,* or *The American Heritage Dictionary of the English Language,* for instance. (The most recent desk dictionary is the eighth edition of *Webster's Collegiate,* published in 1973.)

Most dictionaries provide a *usage label;* that is, they will tell you whether a word fits into formal or nonformal language situations and whether or not a word is archaic (out of date).

The American Heritage Dictionary is somewhat unusual in that its editors assembled a panel of respected writers to comment on word usage. The panel included such distinguished people as Morton W. Bloomfield, Professor of English at Harvard; George Gamow, Professor of Physics at University of Colorado; Katherine Anne Porter, the renowned American writer; and so on. The dictionary entries include comments on usage by these people.

Dictionary makers do not attempt to regulate what *should be* in language, but merely to record what *is.* Here is the entry for **ain't** from the *American Heritage:*

33   **ain't** (ānt). *Nonstandard.* Contraction of *am not.* Also extended in use to mean *are not, is not, has not,* and *have not.*

      Usage: *Ain't,* with few exceptions, is strongly condemned by the Usage Panel when it occurs in writing and speech that is not deliberately colloquial or that does not employ the contraction to provide humor, shock, or other special effect. The first person singular interrogative from *ain't I* (for *am I not* or *amn't I*), considered as a special case, has somewhat more acceptance than *ain't* employed with other pronouns or with nouns. (*Ain't I* has at least the virtue of agreement between *am* and *I*. With other pronouns, or nouns, *ain't* takes the place of *isn't* and *aren't* and sometimes of *hasn't* and *haven't*.) But *ain't I* is unacceptable in writing other than that which is deliberately colloquial, according to 99 per cent of the Panel, and unacceptable in speech to 84 per cent. The example *It ain't likely* is unacceptable to 99 per cent in both writing and speech. *Aren't I* (as a variant of the interrogative *ain't I*) is acceptable in writing to only 27 per cent of the Panel, but approved in speech by 60 per cent. Louis Kronenberger has this typical reaction: "A genteelism, and much worse than *ain't I*."

This discussion happens to be untypically extensive; most dictionary entries are much briefer.

So the usage label in this case is ***nonstandard.*** This usage label is not a value judgment, but an objective opinion concerning the usage of the word. The label says, in effect, that ***ain't*** is not normally a feature of standard English. Here is how the *American Heritage* explains ***nonstandard:***

34   This label implies, of course, the existence of standard American English. While it cannot be said that standard language is uniform throughout America, it is clear that there are forms that do not belong to any standard, educated speech. Such words and expressions are recognized as nonstandard not only by those whose speech is standard, but even by most of those who regularly use nonstandard expressions. One application of the label *nonstan-*

dard is for forms that have resulted from error. The label also covers forms such as **ain't** and **nowheres** that have never been admitted to standard language, though they have long existed alongside equivalent standard forms.[2]

In addition to the usage label, we get the *pronunciation* of the word (ānt). Each dictionary has a system of phonetic symbols for recording pronunciation, found typically either in the front material or at the bottom of each page.

A typical dictionary entry will also present a word's *etymology,* or derivational history. Here is the etymology of **hippopotamus** from the *American Heritage:*

35 Latin from Late Greek *hippopotamos,* from Greek *hippos ho potamios,* "horse of the river". . . .

Good dictionaries also contain biographical information on famous people, both living and dead:

36 **Sade** (säd), Comte **Donatien Alphonse Francois de.** Known as Marquis de Sade. 1740–1814. French man of letters, novelist, and libertine.

Of course, the best way to become familiar with the information in a dictionary—and to use and to enjoy it—is to buy one.

Levels of Usage

To the delight of most people who think about language, speakers and writers are gaining freedom from the strictures that society imposed so rigidly in the past. There was a time, for instance, when contractions (*isn't, haven't, don't,* and so on) were found only in extremely informal writing, and much fuss was made about the usage of **shall** and **will** (**shall** with the first person, as in *I shall return,* but **will** with the other persons, as in *you, he, they will return*). No sensible person nowadays would raise an eyebrow at finding an **isn't,** let alone an *I will,* even in publications, such as scholarly journals, that typically demand a great deal of formality.

On the other hand, as the discussion of **ain't** demonstrated, society does impose boundaries on usage, reacting against or proscribing certain features of so-called nonstandard.

Unwritten, tacitly accepted dress codes provide a good analogy with language usage. Not many years ago, the better restaurants in, say, Los Angeles demanded that male patrons wear ties and jackets, and not many years before that, suits were demanded. Now only the most exclusive restaurants expect men to wear ties and jackets, and one would have to search for a restaurant that demanded suits. In short, dress codes are becoming much more flexible.

But there are regional variations in this permissiveness. For instance, in San Francisco, dress tends to be a good deal more formal than in Los Angeles, while in Las Vegas anything goes.

From my point of view, in the best of all possible worlds, we would dress

---

[2]*The American Heritage Dictionary of the English Language* (Boston: Houghton Mifflin, 1969), p. xlvi.

just as we pleased, but we do not live in the best of all possible worlds. For this reason, I sometimes break down and put on a tie (the most nonsensical piece of attire ever conceived) and a suit, either because I could not gain admittance to a certain place without such dress or because I would feel conspicuous and uncomfortable if I did not conform to the expectations that the situation imposed.

Dress codes and language codes are analogous; they result from custom, and they are socially imposed. The individual is quite free (*most* of the time) to conform to them or to ignore them, but ignoring them has its consequences.

To divide language into levels of usage is to schematize, which must be, to a certain extent, artificial. Nonetheless, such a division is instructive in that it allows one to grasp very real differences in language use.

Formal and Informal Usage

At one end of the usage scale is what might be called *formal,* both written and spoken. As was pointed out in Chapter 10, formal written English might well contain fewer contractions than informal, and it avoids slang.

Here is an example of formal writing from a respected (and rather snooty, but very interesting) publication:

37   It is easy to grasp why stringed instruments make the sounds they do. When the strings are struck or plucked, they vibrate at different natural frequencies in accordance with their tension and diameter. The energy of the vibration is then transferred to the air by way of a vibrating plate of wood and a resonating air chamber, with the sound eventually dying away. The musician can vary the pitch, or frequency, of individual strings by changing their vibrating length with the pressure of his fingers on the frets or the finger-board.[3]

And here is an example of informal usage. A woman writes to Abigail Van Buren, "Dear Abby." The letter explains that the writer must pick her boyfriend up and drive him home because he doesn't have a car, and to add insult to injury, the woman must also pay a toll to cross a bridge to get to her boyfriend's house. Abby answers:

38   Thirty minutes in an automobile beats two and a half hours in a subway, no matter who does the driving. If he hasn't offered to pay for the toll, suggest it. If he can't or won't pay for it, you will have to decide whether dating him is worth the portal to portal service you're providing.[4]

The characteristics of this informal usage, as opposed to the formal, are obvious. First is the contractions: ***hasn't, can't, won't, you're.*** In fact, Abby's failure to contract ***you will*** is almost jarring. The slang is also a feature of informality: "Thirty minutes in an automobile ***beats*** two and a half hours in a subway. . . ."

Here is an example of formal spoken English:

39   I don't look at aggression in such traditional terms as Reich or Lowen. I don't make the assumption that there is any one right way to reach out to the world,

[3]Arthur H. Benade, "The Physics of Brasses," *Scientific American,* July 1973. p. 24.
[4]Los Angeles *Times,* 30 Aug. 1973, Sec. IV, p. 26.

nor any single correct pattern for sexual expression. In a primitive culture if a man couldn't be aggressive, kill and rape a little, he wouldn't survive. But that has all changed. Civilization has allowed some of us to become artists and poets, to assert our existence in soft ways.[5]

The contractions, the double negative ("I don't make the assumption . . . *nor* any single correct pattern"), the relative brevity of the sentences—all these features mark the passage as spoken. Indeed, **39** demonstrates that the line between formal written and formal spoken is thin.

Informal written and spoken English differ from formal largely on the basis of the words that they allow. For instance, in formal English, one might speak of being very **fond** of sherry; in informal English, one might be **crazy about** sherry. In informal English, one might **get a job,** but in extremely formal English, one would probably **obtain a position.**

Nonstandard Usage

As we have seen, *nonstandard* usage has nothing to do with good or bad, and nonstandard usage is *not sub*standard. In fact, as Chapter 10 pointed out, every society contains a power elite—the group of people who control the economy, who set educational policy, who determine the program content of the media, who edit the newspapers—and the concept of standard is derived from the usage that this power group finds acceptable.

It would be wrong to assume that there is a monolithic, well-defined entity called standard English. But standard can be defined by the usages that it proscribes, if not by a complete description of what it allows. For instance, standard allows midwesterners to sit on the **stoop** while western-ers sit on the **front porch**. It doesn't matter whether you carry a **bucket** or a **pail** in standard, but you can't **tote** either one. In standard, you are perfectly free to say either **I know WHO you gave it to** or **I know WHOM you gave it to,** but you can't say **HIM and ME went.**

The concept of levels of usage is no great mystery. The importance of usage is a social condition that we might deplore, but that we nonetheless must recognize. Both **Sandy ain't been here for an hour** and **Sandy hasn't been here for an hour** convey the same meaning, so from one point of view it's silly to prefer one form over the other. On the other hand, however, one of those sentences is the more negotiable in terms of the expectations set up by the power elite in society.

A Word About Slang

Slang terms can be characterized as follows. They are used to produce an effect, such as humor, hipness, or cynicism. They are markedly excluded from formal usage. And they frequently are *nonce words* or terms, appear-

[5]Stanley Keleman, in "A conversation with Stanley Keleman about bioenergetics and the language of the body ("We do not have bodies, we are our bodies")," by Sam Keen, *Psychology Today*, Sept. 1973, p. 69.

ing in the language briefly and then fading away, even though some slang persists for decades or even centuries. As an illustration of how short-lived most slang is, think about the following terms: **twenty-three skiddoo, bundling, petting, necking, hubbahubbahubba, skirt** (for "woman"), **frail.** On the other hand, some slang terms stick around forever, it seems: **bones** (for "dice"); **shake a leg; nuts, screwy; rod** (for "pistol").

Sometimes, interestingly, a slang term appears to have no nonslang equivalent. When a child runs with a sled and then slams it down and jumps on it face down to ride downhill, he is doing a **belly-flop.** In his *Linguistic Atlas of the Upper Midwest,* Harold B. Allen lists these synonyms for **belly-flop,** all of them slang: **belly-bump, belly-gut, belly-buster, belly-bust, belly-booster, belly-bunt, belly-wopper, bellity-bumper, belly-butting, belly-coaster, belly-down, belly-slam, belly-slide.**[6] Allen also lists **slamming,** which is unfamiliar to me.

The big problem with slang in writing, of course, is that it is so rapidly dated, and nothing sounds more cornball than yesteryear's or yesterday's slang. Another problem with slang is its typically vivid connotativeness. Writing that uses slang is likely to sound as if the author is straining for effect.

Jargon

Jargon refers to those words and expressions that are used by members of an occupation, profession, or social set. Thus, physicians speak of a **sphygmomanometer,** not of a **blood pressure machine.** A patient has **phlebitis,** never inflammation of a vein. Every physician would much prefer to mention **iatrogenic** disease than to talk about diseases that are caused by the treatments that physicians administer.

As you have discovered in this book, modern linguistics has its own, virtually impenetrable jargon: **suprasegmental phonemes** for intonation patterns in speech; **deep structure** for meaning; and a whole array of such exotics as **phoneme, morpheme, complementation,** and **deletion transformation.**

Subcultures also develop their own jargons. One example is the vernacular of jazz, as described by Robert S. Gold in an extremely interesting article.[7] Gold calls the language of the jazz world *jive.* Like jazz, it was developed by black Americans as a unique form of expression, creating a social identity. It has been said that the word **jive** itself was derived from the standard English word **jibe,** "to scoff at, to sneer at, to ridicule." A brief jazz glossary lists these items: **apple:** the earth, the universe, New York City; **balling:** having a good time (but in current slang this term means something quite different); **beat:** tired (this bit of jive has been adopted as slang in general usage); **benny:** overcoat; **capped:** excelled; **cat:** a musician,

[6]Harold B. Allen, *Linguistic Atlas of the Upper Midwest,* I (Minneapolis: Univ. of Minnesota Press, 1973), pp. 390–92.
[7]Robert S. Gold, "The Vernacular of the Jazz World," *American Speech,* 32 (Dec. 1957), 271–82.

a man; **chick:** a girl; **conk:** the head; **dicty:** snobbish; **dig:** understand; **dims and brights:** days and nights; **drape:** a suit; **groovy:** great; **hep, hip:** aware of; **juice:** liquor; **kick:** a pocket; **kill:** thrill, fascinate; **mad:** fine, capable, able, talented; **nod:** sleep; **ofay:** white person; **pad:** house, apartment, room; **scoff:** food; **sky:** hat; **stroll:** street, avenue; **trey:** three; **twister:** key.

There is nothing inherently wrong with jargon. One physician talking to another would be deemed naive if he spoke of **the blood pressure machine,** rather than **the sphygmomanometer;** one plumber speaking to another is quite justified in talking about **P-traps, U-joints,** and **nipples;** literary critic to literary critic, there's nothing at all wrong with **affective fallacy** and **objective correlative.**

It's all a matter of audience. When one specialist is addressing another, the jargon of the group is useful and informative, but when a specialist (a jazz musician or a plumber or a linguist) is addressing a layman, jargon simply obfuscates—it doesn't convey meaning.

Gobbledygook

Stuart Chase had this to say about gobbledygook:

40   Said Franklin Roosevelt, in one of his early presidential speeches: "I see one-third of a nation ill-housed, ill-clad, ill-nourished." Translated into standard bureaucratic prose this statement would read:

It is evident that a substantial number of persons within the Continental boundaries of the United States have inadequate financial resources with which to purchase the products of agricultural communities and industrial establishments. It would appear that for a considerable segment of the population, possibly as much as 33.3333 of the total, there are inadequate housing facilities, and an equally significant proportion is deprived of the proper types of clothing and nutriment.

This rousing satire on gobbledygook—or talk among the bureaucrats—is adapted from a report prepared by the Federal Security Agency in an attempt to break out of the verbal squirrel cage. "Gobbledygook" was coined by an exasperated Congressman, Maury Maverick of Texas, and means using two, or three, or ten words in the place of one, or using a five-syllable word where a single syllable would suffice. Maverick was censuring the forbidding prose of executive departments in Washington, but the term has now spread to windy and pretentious language in general.[8]

Here is another example of gobbledygook:

41   Due to the fact that hydro-electric generation of electrical current now involves costly materials and operations, it is respectfully requested that personnel be assiduous in ascertaining that all electrical appliances, particularly those used for illumination, are turned off if not in use.

That sloggy sentence means nothing more than this: Since electricity is expensive, please turn off the lights.

[8]Stuart Chase, *Power of Words* (New York: Harcourt Brace Jovanovich, 1954), p. 249.

Abstractness

Closely related to the disease called gobbledygook is another, just as frustrating: *abstractness*. Here is an example:

42   Objective consideration of contemporary phenomena compels the conclusion that success or failure in competitive activities exhibits no tendency to be commensurate with innate capacity, but that a considerable element of the unpredictable must invariably be taken into account.

Example **42** is George Orwell's rewrite of a glorious passage from the Bible:

43   I returned and saw under the sun, that the race is not to the swift, nor the battle to the strong, neither yet bread to the wise, nor yet riches to men of understanding, nor yet favour to men of skill; but time and chance happeneth to them all.

Orwell wrote his parody in order to illustrate what happens to prose when it becomes totally abstract. In the Bible passage, concrete images not only convey but also reinforce the idea; the reader has specific examples of what the passage means. In the Orwell parody, the reader has nothing specific to grasp, nothing to peg ideas on.

The best prose is concrete and imagistic, even when it is dealing with abstruse subject matter. Here is a brilliant example. The American psychologist William James is discussing habit, certainly an abstract subject, but notice how he handles it concretely:

44   Habit is thus the enormous fly-wheel of society, its most precious conservative agent. It alone is what keeps us all within the bounds of ordinance, and saves the children of fortune from the envious uprisings of the poor. It alone prevents the hardest and most repulsive walks of life from being deserted by those brought up to tread therein. It keeps the fisherman and the deck-hand at sea through the winter; it holds the miner in his darkness, and nails the countryman to his log-cabin and his lonely farm through all the months of snow; it protects us from invasion by the natives of the desert and the frozen zone. It dooms us all to fight out the battle of life upon the lines of our nurture or our early choice, and to make the best of a pursuit that disagrees, because there is no other for which we are fitted, and it is too late to begin again. It keeps different social strata from mixing. Already at the age of twenty-five you see the professional mannerism settling down on the young commercial traveler, on the young doctor, and the young minister, on the young counselor-at-law. You see the little lines of cleavage running through the character, the tricks of thought, the prejudices, the ways of the "shop," in a word, from which the man can by-and-by no more escape than his coat-sleeve can suddenly fall into a new set of folds. On the whole, it is best he should not escape. It is well for the world that in most of us, by the age of thirty, the character has set like plaster, and will never soften again.[9]

James starts off with a metaphor: habit is the flywheel of society, the force that keeps all the other parts moving. He then gives a number of examples of how habit keeps people in their appointed places. Next, he points out that

[9]William James, *The Principles of Psychology*, I (New York: Henry Holt and Company, 1890), p. 121.

members of given professions adopt the habits of those professions. Finally, he ends with two wonderful figures of speech: it is as unlikely that people will change their habits as that a coat will suddenly change its folds, and the character sets like plaster.

Verbs

As they contribute to the effects of prose, verbs are interesting and important. Strunk and White cite these two sentences:

45   There were dead leaves all over the ground.

46   Dead leaves covered the ground.[10]

Example **46** has certain advantages over **45**. Most obviously, **46** is shorter. But even more important, most readers would agree that **46** is more vigorous and vivid. The verb ***covered*** carries more semantic impact, more vigor, than ***were all over.***

When I look for examples of writing that I admire, I frequently turn to Mark Twain, who succeeded so brilliantly as a stylist in virtually everything that he undertook. One of the reasons that I like Mark Twain so intensely is his use of verbs. In *Roughing It,* for example, he tells of a stagecoach trip. Here is one paragraph from that narrative, with his verbs in italics:

47   Every time we ***avalanched*** from one end of the stage to the other, the Unabridged Dictionary would ***come*** too; and every time it ***came*** it ***damaged*** somebody. One trip it ***"barked"*** the Secretary's elbow; the next trip it ***hurt*** me in the stomach, and the third it ***tilted*** Bemis's nose up till he could ***look*** down his nostrils—he ***said.*** The pistols and coin soon ***settled*** to the bottom, but the pipes, pipe-stems, tobacco and canteens ***clattered*** and ***floundered*** after the Dictionary every time it ***made*** an assault on us, and ***aided*** and ***abetted*** the book by spilling tobacco in our eyes, and water down our backs.

It will be instructive to take the passage apart piece by piece, to see what happens when we tamper with Twain's selection of verbs.

Twain might have said, ***we slid from one end of the stage to the other,*** but then he would have sacrificed the imagistic force of ***avalanched,*** which implies all the power and tumult of a rockslide or snowslide. He might have said that the dictionary ***struck*** someone every time it avalanched, but that would not have implied the potentially lethal impact that ***damaged*** does. "The pistols and coin soon settled to the bottom," wrote Twain; if he had written, ***The pistols and coin soon were on the bottom,*** he would have lost all the imagistic power of the verb ***settled,*** which implies that smaller objects have sifted their way through larger objects. The pipes, pipe-stems, tobacco, and canteens ***clattered*** and ***floundered;*** if they had simply ***rolled around,*** there would not have been the sound implied by ***clattered,*** and the uncontrolled awkwardness implied by ***floundered*** would have been lost. The verbs ***aided*** and ***abetted*** tell us that what was going on was an absolute "crime," for those words normally apply to criminal activities.

[10]William Strunk, Jr., *The Elements of Style,* rev. E. B. White (New York: Macmillan, 1972), p. 14.

Nominals

The discussion of verbs as devices of style takes us back to the concept of nominals. Nominal constructions have a different effect from verbal constructions. Here are two sentences that are very nearly, if not completely, synonymous:

48   The audience heard Olivier's narration of the tale.

49   The audience heard Olivier narrating the tale.

Since **narration** is a noun and **narrating** is a verbal form, **narrating** carries with it verbal force, which is traditionally described as the transfer of action. With verbals, something more does happen than with nouns.

The following passage is highly nominalized:

50   Obedience is as basic an element in the structure of social life as one can point to. ***Some system of authority is a requirement of all communal living,*** and ***it is only man dwelling in isolation who is not forced to respond, through defiance or submission, to the commands of others. Obedience as a determinant of behavior is of particular relevance to our time.*** It has been reliably established that from 1933–45 millions of innocent persons were systematically slaughtered on command. Gas chambers were built, death camps were guarded, daily quotas of corpses were produced ***with the same efficiency as the manufacture of appliances.*** These inhumane policies may have originated in the mind of a single person, but they could only be carried out on a massive scale if a very large number of persons obeyed orders.[11]

The passage achieves a different—and I think more forceful—effect when the nominals are eliminated:

51   Obedience is as basic an element in the structure of social life as one can point to. ***All communal living requires some system of social authority, and only man dwelling in isolation is not forced to respond, through defiance or submission, to the commands of others. Obedience as a determinant of behavior is particularly relevant to our time.*** It has been reliably established that from 1933–45 millions of innocent persons were systematically slaughtered on command. Gas chambers were built, death camps were guarded, daily quotas of corpses were produced ***as efficiently as manufacturing appliances.***

In English, countless verbs have noun equivalents, for example:

52   avow/avowal (Sutton **avowed** his innocence/Sutton's **avowal** of his innocence)
bequeath/bequest (Grandpa **bequeathed** his cufflinks to me/Grandpa's **bequest** of his cufflinks to me)
campaign/campaign (The senator **campaigned** for re-election/the senator's **campaign** for re-election)
damn/damnation (The Lord **damned** Faust/the Lord's **damnation** of Faust)
elect/election (**Electing** Smithers was a mistake/The **election** of Smithers was a mistake)
fail/failure (That Mervin **failed** is a shame/Mervin's **failure** is a shame)
grow/growth (Nelly is an expert on **growing** petunias/Nelly is an expert on the **growth** of petunias)

[11]Stanley Milgram, "A Behavioral Study of Obedience," *Journal of Abnormal and Social Psychology*, 67 (1963), 371–78.

narrate/narration (***narrating*** the tale/the ***narration*** of the tale)

publish/publication (***Publishing*** the story was disastrous/***publication*** of the story was disastrous)

stink/stench (The garbage ***stinks*** horribly/The ***stench*** of the garbage is horrible)

think/thought (It is terrifying ***to think*** of nuclear war/the ***thought*** of nuclear war is terrifying)

The point here is not that verbal constructions per se are better than nominal constructions, but that you should be aware of your options and of the different effects brought about by the two kinds of constructions.

You have similar options with adjective/noun pairs, such as the following:

53   beautiful/beauty (The ***beautiful*** sunset inspired me/The ***beauty*** of the sunset inspired me. In this pair, the shift of emphasis is obvious. In the first, the *sunset* is stressed; in the second, the *beauty* is stressed.)

dramatic/drama (The ***dramatic*** nature of the event enthralled me/I was enthralled by the ***drama*** of the event)

glorious/glory (Who would not enjoy this ***glorious*** meal?/Who would not enjoy the ***glory*** of this meal?)

kingly/king (The lion is ***kingly***/The lion is ***king*** of the beasts)

morbid/morbidity (Karl is a ***morbid*** person, and I don't like him because of that/Because of his ***morbidity,*** I don't like Karl)

trivial/triviality (A ***trivial*** matter/the ***triviality*** of the matter)

Finally

Chapter 10, "The Writer's Language," contains a good deal more about words. You might want to review that material at this point.

A fascination with words (and with sentences) is, it seems to me, a characteristic of most good writers. They are not necessarily interested in theories, but they do pay close attention to the effects that they achieve with various arrangements of different words.

In Chapter 11 we examined sentences, in this chapter we examined words, and in Chapter 13 we will take a close look at figurative language.

Discussion and Activities

Sign and Symbol

1. In what sense is the ***STOP*** that appears on street signs a sign, and in what sense is it a symbol?

2. In 1667, Richard Sprat published a history of the British Royal Society in which he said that one goal of the Society would be to "reject all amplifications, digressions, and swellings of style: to return back to the primitive purity, and shortness, when men deliver'd so many *things,* in almost an equal number of words." In what way does this statement show Sprat's failure to differentiate between sign and symbol?

3. In what ways is the passage from *Gulliver's Travels* (pages 398–99) a commentary on Sprat's statement?

Meaning Again

1. Explain why the following two sentences demonstrate that reference is only one factor in the meaning of a term:

    a   George Washington was the first president of the United States.

    b   *The first president of the United States was the first president of the United States.

2. In terms of denotation, explain why the following sentences seem strange.

    a   *Mervin drank a brick.

    b   *The boy climbing the tree chased the ball sitting in the box down the street.

    c   *Marilyn built a line.

    d   *Gertrude is a retarded microbe.

3. On the basis of binary features, invent definitions for these words: **water, molasses, rabbit, petunia, anger, pottery, spider, cigar.** (You need not attempt great accuracy. As a hint, here is a possible definition of **molasses:** [+ liquid + viscous + sweet].)

4. On the basis of binary features, explain the following metaphors:

    a   Hector was a lion in battle.

    b   This City now doth . . . wear/The beauty of the morning. . . . —Wordsworth

    c   After great pain a formal feeling comes. . . .   —Emily Dickinson

    d   Lay your sleeping head, my love,/Human on my faithless arm. . . .
    —W. H. Auden

    e   My vegetable love should grow/Vaster than empires, and more slow.   —Andrew Marvell

    f   Do not go gentle into that good night,
    Old age should burn and rave at close of day;
    Rage, rage against the dying of the light.   —Dylan Thomas

5. Explain arbitrariness of meaning. If possible, give an example of a word to which you have assigned an arbitrary meaning.

6. Explain the connotations of the italicized words in the following passage:

> It seemed like hours had passed before the ambulance finally arrived. **Mama** wanted to go to the hospital with me, but the **ambulance attendant** said she was too excited. On the way to **Harlem** Hospital, the **cop** who was riding with us asked **Dad** what he had to say. His answer was **typical:** "I told him about

hanging out with those **bad-ass** boys." The cop was a little surprised. This must be a **rookie,** I thought.   —Claude Brown

7. For each of the following words, supply, wherever you can, both a synonymous term that is less favorable and one that is more favorable in connotation. For example: **doctor, sawbones** (less favorable), **man of medicine** (more favorable).

> **stomach, plumber, stew, sour, liquor, old** (as furniture), **cop, steal, curiosity, student, girl, spit**

Another Word About Dictionaries

Examine your own (current) desk dictionary. What kinds of information does it contain?

Levels of Usage

Characterize the following passages as nonstandard, informal, or formal. Indicate the features that led you to make your characterization.

a   *What about the young dissenters?*
If you gave 'em a push, they'd turn into homosexual. When the German hordes fifty years ago surrounded Paris, Marshall Petain brought out the pimps, whores, thieves, underground operators, he says: Our playground is jeopardized by the German Hun. Well, all Paris, every thief, burglar, pimp, he come out and picked up a musket. Stopped the German hordes. —Quoted in Studs Terkel, from *Hard Times: An Oral History of the Great Depression*

b   My recall is nearly perfect, time has faded nothing. I recall the very first kidnap. I've lived through the passage, died on the passage, lain in the unmarked, shallow graves of the millions who fertilized the Amerikan soil with their corpses; cotton and corn growing out of my chest, "unto the third and fourth generation," the tenth, the hundredth. My mind ranges back and forth through the uncounted generations, and I feel all that they ever felt, but double. I can't help it; there are too many things to remind me of the $23\frac{1}{2}$ hours that I'm in this cell. Not ten minutes pass without a reminder. In between, I'm left to speculate on what form the reminder will take.   —George Jackson

c   Now about Yolanda is a good friend to me all my friend is very nice to me, but Yolanda is the most good friend to me. In my class Yolanda and me we are alway talking about people especially about boy and a teacher the teacher is a nice teacher he teach me and Yolanda in a school called _____ Junior High School it is located in Los Angeles, California. Yolanda has a brother name Orlando she has two more brother but I do not know their name but if Yolanda is a good friend to me well I guess her brothers are nice but one of them had got kick out of school. —A junior high school student

d   An abundant and increasing supply of highly educated people has become the absolute prerequisite of social and economic development in our world. It is rapidly becoming a condition of national survival. What matters is not that there are so many more individuals around who have been exposed to long years of formal schooling—though this is quite recent. The essential new fact is that a developed society and economy are less than fully effective if anyone is educated to less than the limit of his potential. The uneducated man is fast becoming an economic liability and unproductive. Society must be an "educated society" today—to progress, to grow, even to survive.   —Peter F. Drucker

A Word About Slang

Make an inventory of the slang that is current on your campus right now. Define the words and terms now in use. Do any of them seem to have been around for some time? (For example, *flunk* is a slang term that has had great staying power.)

Jargon

Are you familiar with the jargon of any particular field or group? If so, list and explain the words and terms that appear.

Gobbledygook

Revise the following sentences to eliminate the gobbledygook:

a   Return with the utmost haste.

b   Before he retires for the night, Paul scrupulously observes a regimen of oral hygiene.

c   Do not enumerate your domestic fowls before they emerge from the ovarian state.

d   Feathered vertebrates of the same genus show a decided tendency to congregate.

e   George always set aside a portion of his earnings so that he would be prepared in the event that inclement weather should precipitate unforeseen circumstances which would necessitate his having extra coin of the realm.

f   The domestic canine is frequently homo sapien's most devoted ally.

Verbs

At points in the following passages, you are given the choice of two verbs. Which is more effective? Why? (The first verb in each pair is the one used by the author of the passage.)

a   Since the Negro revolt (ignited/set) the fire that had been smoldering for generations and (shook/roused) America out of its complacency about the racial problem, a key phrase, uttered by many of its leaders as well as rank and file shock troops, (has echoed/has been heard) around the land: the White Power Structure.   —Allan Morrison

b   Every so often I (run across/encounter) the statement that *Webster's Unabridged Dictionary* contains five hundred Yiddish words.

—Leo Rosten

c   The old truth—"we must all come from someplace"—(is amended/is changed). We can (create/make) ourselves in our own image.

—Herbert Gold

d   Nineteen-eighteen did not (usher in/bring in) the millennium; it (ushered in/brought in) a half century of conflict—turbulence, war, revolution, desolation, and ruin on a scale never before seen or even imagined. It was a half century that (leveled/ruined) more cities, (ravaged/laid waste) more countries, (subverted/destroyed) more societies, (obliterated/did away with) more of the past, (endangered/threatened) more of the future, (cost/took) more lives, and (uncovered/revealed) more savagery than any time since the barbarians swarmed over Western Europe.

—Henry Steele Commager

e   No one, except perhaps a few college administrators, (mourns/regrets) the passing of "the silent generation." But it must be said in its favor that at least one knew what the American university students of the 1950s were silent about, and why. They were conformists for plain, indeed, obvious and traditional, conformist reasons. We may have been (distressed/made unhappy) and (vexed/irritated) by this conformism; we were not (mystified/puzzled) by it . . . .   —Irving Kristol

Figurative Language 13

Summary of the Chapter

Language can be either figurative or literal. The figurative expression **night's candles** means literally "stars." It might seem, at first glance, that figurative language is nothing but poetic, unnecessary decoration that is stuck onto language by people who really don't want to say what they mean. It turns out, however, that figurativeness is an indispensable property of language; without figures, many ideas would be difficult or even impossible to express, and it is doubtful that some kinds of thought can proceed at all without figurativeness.

The most important kind of figurative language is *metaphor.* Basically, a metaphor consists in a comparison between two essentially unlike things. Thus, **George is a bull** is a metaphor meaning that George is strong and virile. But most metaphors are a good deal more complex and provocative than this one.

A *simile* is a kind of metaphor that makes a comparison through the use of **like** or **as:** Hercules fought **like** a lion in the battle.

Another important figure of speech is *irony.* The ironic effect comes about when the reader realizes that the author intends something other than what he or she actually says. If George is the worst student in the class, and the professor says, "George is certainly gifted in this subject," the professor is undoubtedly being ironic. *Dramatic irony* comes about when the reader knows something that a character in fiction or drama does not. For instance, in a play, the hero is planning to marry a beautiful, wealthy woman, but, as the audience knows, the woman is already married. Such a situation gives rise to dramatic irony.

There are other figures of speech, hundreds of them in fact, such as *overstatement* and *understatement.* But the purpose of the chapter is not to survey all possible figures of speech; it is, rather, to point out how figurative language helps convey meanings and to aid you in using figures effectively.

Why Figurative Language?

Meanings can be expressed either *literally* or *figuratively.* For instance, here is an idea expressed literally:

1   Nature is holy and mysterious, and can be understood only dimly by man.

The French poet Charles Baudelaire (as translated by R. G. Stern) expressed that idea figuratively in this way:

2   Nature is a temple from whose living pillars
     Confusing words are now and then released.

Comparison of **1** and **2** raises a significant question: Why express ideas figuratively when they can be stated literally? The answer to that question is complex and will take up much of this chapter. But, just as a gambit for getting our discussion of figurative language under way, two extremely tentative answers might be advanced.

Imagism

First, the figurative statement is more imagistic in quality; it presents something for the reader's mind to "see." As has been pointed out again and again in this book, imagistic language has a vividness that language without images does not. And the mind seems, for some reason, to take more pleasure in that which it can visualize.

Compression of Meaning

Second, as if by magic, a great deal more meaning can usually be compressed into a figurative statement than into a literal one. Everyone would agree, I think, that **2** is a good deal more suggestive than **1**. This is simply another way of saying that figurative language compresses meaning, and is thus economical. The figure **Nature is a temple** is a good example. The noun **temple** implies the whole history of humanity's veneration of something higher than itself: a magnificent structure (for a temple is not a mere church), a holy place, the concept of worship, the notion of the universality of that worship (for all religions have temples, though not all have cathedrals or synagogues), the smallness of the individual in relation to the structure (for a temple is not the Little Brown Church in the Vale), the concept of Deity, an aura of quietness and wonder, a sense of mystery and awe—and my explication of what **temple** means to me could go on and on.

So, everyone would grant, figurative language has its power. But not everyone—in fact, almost no one—wants to write poetry.

The Need for Figurativeness

It turns out, however, that figurative language—and thought—is not only vivid and useful, but unavoidable. Quite literally, we live by *metaphors*.

An Example: Skinner

In his controversial book *Beyond Freedom and Dignity*, B. F. Skinner asked "What Is Man?" Here is part of his answer:

> 3   The picture that emerges from a scientific analysis is not of a body with a person inside but of a body that *is* a person in the sense that it displays a complex repertoire of behavior. The picture is, of course, unfamiliar. The man we thus portray is a stranger, and from the traditional point of view he may not seem to be a man at all.
>
> C. S. Lewis put it bluntly: "Man is being abolished."
>
> There is clearly some difficulty in identifying the man to whom Lewis referred. He cannot have meant the human species; far from being abolished, it is filling the earth. Nor are individual men growing less effective or productive. What is being abolished is autonomous man—the inner man, the homunculus, the possessing demon, the man defended by the literatures of freedom and dignity.
>
> His abolition is long overdue. Autonomous man is a device we use to explain what we cannot explain in any other way. We constructed him from our ignorance, and as our understanding increases, the very stuff of which he is composed vanishes. Science does not dehumanize man, it dehomunculizes him, and it must do so if it is to prevent the abolition of the human species.
>
> To man *qua* man we readily say good riddance. Only by dispossessing autonomous man can we turn to the real causes of human behavior—from the inferred to the observed, from the miraculous to the natural, from the inaccessible to the manipulable.[1]

Skinner, of course, is a behavioral psychologist who views human behavior as merely the reactions of an organism to environmental stimuli; it is not unfair to say that Skinner denies such traditional concepts as soul and mind. In short, Skinner takes the *least* poetic view of man of any modern theorist.

Yet it is difficult to see how he might have expressed his ideas without figurative thought and language, particularly metaphor.

Skinner begins with a root metaphor: human being as animal, subject to the same laws as other animals, explicable only in terms of observed behavior; like other animals, humans react inexorably to stimuli. (Though it is terribly unfair to Skinner, the image of the Pavlovian dog is unavoidable here, because the Pavlovian dog has become a metaphor for behavioral psychology.)

Skinner's first sentence is highly metaphorical: scientific analysis creates a **picture** of the human being, and it turns out (in the third sentence) that the **human** thus portrayed is a **stranger** to us, a sort of person that we have not known in the Western tradition. Then Skinner quotes a metaphorical statement by C. S. Lewis: "Man is being abolished." Lewis, of course, does not mean that those physical entities we identify as humans are disappearing, but that the conception we traditionally held of the human being is being displaced by something new and strange. (In the Western tradition, humanity, with its unique soul, has stood halfway between animals and angels, touched by a spark of the divine.)

Skinner says that "Autonomous man is a device we use to explain what we cannot explain in any other way. We constructed him from our ignorance, and as our understanding increases, the very stuff of which he is composed vanishes." In this figurative sentence, Skinner might have used **metaphor** for **device,** thus: "Autonomous man is a metaphor . . . ."

In short, the whole passage is based on metaphor and is *metaphorical.*

A Second Example: Bruner

Jerome S. Bruner is a psychologist from the camp opposed to behaviorism. Here he outlines the Freudian view of mind:

4   Freud's is a theory or a proto-theory peopled with actors. The characters are from life: the blind, energic, pleasure-seeking id; the priggish and punitive super-ego; the ego, battling for its being by diverting the energy of the others to its own use. The drama has an economy and a terseness. The ego develops canny mechanisms for dealing with the threat of id impulses: denial, projection, and the rest. Balances are struck between the actors, and in the balance is character and neurosis. Freud was using the dramatic technique of decomposition, the play whose actors are parts of a single life. It is a technique that he himself had recognized in fantasies and dreams, one he honored in "The Poet and the Daydream."[2]

Tellingly, Bruner asks this question: "Can Freud's contribution to the common understanding of man in the twentieth century be likened to the impact of such great physical and biological theories as Newtonian physics and Darwin's conception of evolution?" And he answers: "The question is an empty one. Freud's mode of thought is not a theory in the conventional sense; it is a metaphor, an analogy, a way of conceiving man, a drama."

The point of all this? Figurativeness is not just decoration, added to language to make it pretty, but the very stuff of thought. We cannot conceive of handling complex ideas without metaphor and other figures.

A Third Example: Einstein

Just one more example of figurative language. Here is no less a thinker than Albert Einstein, explaining atomic fission:

5   What takes place can be illustrated with the help of our rich man. The atom M is a rich miser who, during his life, gives away no money *(energy).* But in his will he bequeaths his fortune to his sons M′ and M″, on condition that they

[2]Jerome S. Bruner, "Freud and the Image of Man," *Partisan Review,* 23 (Summer 1956).

give to the community a small amount, less than one thousandth of the whole estate *(energy or mass)*. The sons together have somewhat less than the father had *(the mass sum M' + M'' is somewhat smaller than the mass M of the radioactive atom)*. But the part given to the community, though relatively small, is still so enormously large *(considered as kinetic energy)* that it brings with it a great threat of evil. Averting that threat has become the most urgent problem of our time.   —Albert Einstein, *Out of My Later Years*

This passage is a great example of *analogy*.

In a real sense, we can view metaphors as instruments by which we generate and organize our knowledge of the world. If we view humans as animals, our conclusions about them will be quite different from those that are based on a view of humanity as a divine image of God.

The Anatomy of Metaphor

Any of the four major parts of speech can be used metaphorically—nominals, verbals, adjectivals, and adverbials.

Nouns

The following is metaphorical because of the interpretation that the passage forces on the noun **nightmare:**

6   Nodding, its great head rattling like a gourd,
      And locks like seaweed strung on the stinking stone,
      The **nightmare** stumbles past, and you have heard
      It fumble your door before it whimpers and is gone:
      It acts like the old hound that used to snuffle your door and moan.[3]

To refer to a concept from the last chapter, nouns have semantic features—increments of meaning. For instance, the noun **boy** has at least these features: [+common], for it is a common as opposed to a proper noun (such as **Tom**); [+human]; [+male]; and [−adult]. In other words, **boy** is a common noun referring to a human male who is not an adult. Now, in **6**, the noun **nightmare** has, among others, the feature [−concrete]; that is to say, it is an abstract noun (as opposed to a concrete noun such as **rock** or **bird**). That is the first fact that we automatically recognize when we understand the metaphorical nature of **6**.

We recognize further that the verb **nod** demands as its subject in literal usage a noun that has at least the feature [+animate], for only something animate can nod. (Can horses nod *literally?* Can snakes? Can microbes? Perhaps we need a more discriminating feature than [+animate], something like [+humanoid], on the theory that we attribute human characteristics to anything that nods. For me, the verb **nod** implies assent, and assent implies rational thought, and only humans think rationally. But we are getting into unnecessary depths here.) The point is that the passage contains an embedded proposition, **The nightmare is nodding,** and since **nightmare** has the feature [−concrete], it cannot literally nod.

[3]Robert Penn Warren, "Original Sin: A Short Story," *Selected Poems: New and Old, 1923–1966* (New York: Random House, 1966). Copyright © 1942 by Robert Penn Warren. Reprinted by permission of Random House, Inc.

Note also that the nightmare *stumbles* and *whimpers.* Animals can stumble and whimper as well as humans, but nightmares can't. Again, these verbs demand animate subjects. (As we saw in Chapter 12, an easy way of stating this idea is with the following: [+animate_____].)

The last line of the passage compares the nightmare to an old hound that *snuffles.* And by the time we have read the five lines, we have an eerie impression of *nightmare* as something almost, but not quite, human: the adjective *humanoid* is particularly appropriate here. The very fact that the nightmare has a head makes it more than literal. Warren might have said something like this: *the nightmare's head.* Just that coupling of *nightmare* with *head* would have made *nightmare* figurative.

Verbs

Verbs also frequently carry the metaphorical sense of a passage.

7   Headstones *stagger* under great draughts of time. . . .   —John Berryman

Literally, this line would read something like this:

8   The headstones stand at odd angles. . . .

The metaphorical force of the line is in the verb *stagger.* Here, too, it is a case of the verb demanding a humanoid subject. Drunks stagger, and dogs can stagger *as if* they are drunk. But *gravestones* have the feature [–animate], and only that which is animate can stagger: *stagger* [+animate_____].

Adjectives

Adjectives also can carry the metaphorical burden:

9   After great pain a *formal* feeling comes—
           The nerves sit *ceremonious* like tombs;
           The *stiff* Heart questions—was it He that bore?
           And yesterday—or centuries before?   —Emily Dickinson

In what sense is a feeling formal? We know of formal statements, dress, dinners. But feelings? The adjective *formal* seems to apply only to nouns that are in some way tangible; we can hear the formality of speech and see the formality of a dinner, but there is no direct way for us to experience someone else's feelings. The adjective *ceremonious* seems to have the same quality; it will not apply literally to that which cannot be experienced directly in some way. And, of course, the adjective *stiff* applies only to substances, like rubber, that have varying degrees of flexibility. (Notice that *tough heart* has two meanings: a heart that is not easily broken or a heart that is not easily chewed or cut.)

Adverbs

Finally, adverbials can create metaphorical sense.

10   When men were all asleep the snow came flying,
           In large white flakes falling on the city brown,
           Stealthily and perpetually settling and loosely lying. . . .   —Robert Bridges

The point here is that **stealth** is an act of volition; a cat or a burglar can be stealthy. Snow, rain, and soot can merely fall.

Charting Metaphors

Metaphor comes into being, then, when semantic features of one word or phrase clash with or contradict semantic features of another word or phrase in an expression.

The chart below gives a visual explanation of metaphor. Rosemarie Gläser, who devised the chart, also provided the explanation that follows.

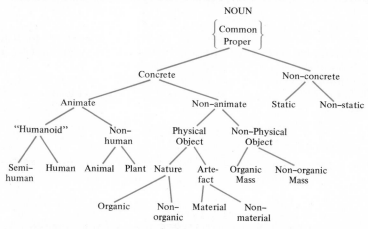

(As an auxiliary node, the marker "humanoid" had to be included because in poetic diction there occurs the vocabulary of mythology, such as proper names of ancient gods; in everyday usage we find figures from fairytales and allusions to them quite often in advertising texts.)

Comment on the tree diagram:

[Non-Human] comprises the markers [animal] and [plant]

[Nature] covers [organic] and [non-organic] matter:

    organic: parts of body, parts of a plant, e.g., trunk, finger, root, organs, secretions, e.g., tear.

    non-organic: ores, topographic formations such as mountain, hill, river, island; elementary forces like rain, thunderstorm, etc.

[Artefact] is understood as the result of intentional production of man, the result of work:

    physical objects: table, bread, fibre, book; non-material: song, poem, word.

[Organic mass]: substance not having contours:

    blood, sweat; organic substance and mixtures: flour, dough.

[Non-organic mass]: metals, gravel, sand, lava, raw material like Orlon.

[Non-concrete] (= abstract)

    static: moods like happiness, frustration; system; non-static (= dynamic): revolution, war, upheaval, development.[4]

For instance, referring to the chart, the statement

[4]Rosemarie Gläser, "The Application of Transformational Generative Grammar to the Analysis of Similes and Metaphors in Modern English," *Style,* 5 (Fall 1971), 265–83. Reprinted by permission.

11   Herman is a young Greek god.

is metaphorical because **Herman** has the feature [human], while **Greek god** has the feature [semihuman], and the statement

12   Happiness is a warm blanket.

is metaphorical because of the disjunction between **happiness** [noncon-crete] and **blanket** [concrete].

However, not every instance of nouns in semantic disjunction can be taken as metaphorical. For instance, if I encountered the following, I would be puzzled by it, and interpret it as nonsense, not as metaphor:

13   *A carrot is a revolution.

Carrot, with its features [concrete, animate, nonhuman, plant], is simply too far removed from **revolution,** with its features [nonconcrete, nonstatic], for me to make any kind of interpretation.

Metaphor depends, then, on some kind of interpretability, the exact nature of which is especially hard to explain. This is why the famous sentence

14   *Colorless green ideas sleep furiously.

is taken to be not metaphorical, but surrealistic.

The "poems" that computers write have this enigmatic, surreal quality:

15   *Poem No. 078*

> THOUGH STARS DRAINED SICKLY UPON IDLE HOVELS
> FOR LIFE BLAZED FAST UPON EMPTY FACES
> WHILE BLOOD LOOMED BITTER ON IDLE FIELDS
> NO MARTIAN SMILED[5]

Even the most sophisticated computers are unable to make the intricate decisions necessary to create metaphors. For, as should now be apparent, metaphors are extremely delicate mixes of meaning.

Four Types of Metaphors

In an extremely interesting discussion, Laurence Perrine sheds further light on the nature of metaphor. Here is his definition:

> A metaphor . . . consists of a comparison between essentially unlike things.
> There are two components in every metaphor: the concept actually discussed,
> and the thing to which it is compared. I shall refer to these, ordinarily, as the
> literal term and the figurative term. The two terms together compose the
> metaphor.[6]

Keeping in mind that a metaphor always consists of a literal term and a figurative term, we can identify four classes of metaphors: (1) those in which both terms are named; (2) those in which only the literal term is named, the figurative term being supplied by the reader; (3) those in which only the figurative term is named, the literal term being supplied by the

[5]"Poem No. 078," RCA 301, RCA *Electronic Age.* Reprinted with permission of RCA *Electronic Age.*
[6]Laurence Perrine, "Four Forms of Metaphor," *College English,* 33 (Nov. 1971), 125–38.

reader; (4) those in which neither the literal nor the figurative term is named, both being supplied by the reader. Let's see how this works, using mostly examples supplied by Perrine.

Type 1

Shakespeare provides an example of the first type, in which both literal and figurative terms are named:

16   All the world's a stage,
And all the men and women merely players.

This metaphor is "equational": *world* (literal term) = *stage* (figurative term). But the linking need not take place with the copula ("literal term *is* figurative term"). Prepositions can establish the link:

17   Too long a sacrifice
Can make a stone *of* the heart.   —William Butler Yeats

Here the literal term is *heart* and the figurative term is *stone.* The link can be established through a variety of other grammatical relationships.

18   Come into the garden, Maud,
For the black bat, night, has flown.   —Alfred, Lord Tennyson

In **18** the metaphorical link between the literal term *night* and the figurative term *bat* is established through grammatical apposition. In **19** the demonstrative *that* establishes the link between *beauty,* the literal term, and *lamp,* the figurative term:

19   Be watchful of your beauty, Lady dear!
How much hangs on that lamp, you cannot tell.   —George Meredith

Type 2

In metaphors that state only the literal term, the reader must supply the figurative term.

20   Sheathe thy impatience; throw cold water on thy choler.
                                                    —William Shakespeare

To understand these two metaphors the reader must supply the figurative terms *sword* and *fire,* for one *sheathes* a sword and *throws cold water on* a fire. Indeed, the metaphorical equation comes out something like this: *impatience = sword* and *choler = fire.*

21   The tawny-hided desert crouches watching her.   —William Butler Yeats

Here, the reader makes the equation *desert = lion,* because the adjective *tawny-hided* and the verb *crouches* suggest that animal.

Type 3

Here is an example of a metaphor in which the figurative term is given and the literal term must be supplied by the reader:

22   Night's candles are burnt out.   —William Shakespeare

The reader makes the inevitable equation **night's candles** = **stars.** Riddles often take this form:

23   In spring I look gay
        Decked in comely array,
    In summer more clothing I wear;
        When colder it grows,
        I fling off my clothes,
    And in winter quite naked appear.

The child might ask, "What am **I?**" And the answer is the equation **I** = **tree.**

Type 4

The most difficult type of metaphor to interpret is that in which neither the literal term nor the figurative term is expressed.

24   Let us eat and drink, for tomorrow we shall die.   —Isaiah 22:13

The literal meaning of this is **Life is very short.** But the word **tomorrow** gives the clue to the proper figurative term: **day.** Example 24 means this: **Life is only a day. Life** is the literal term, and **day** is the figurative.

Metaphors in Prose: Two Examples

As a demonstration that metaphor is not just ornamentation stuck onto the outside of writing to make it pretty, like the gingerbread on a Victorian house, here are two prose passages.

Isaac Asimov

In speculating on the origin of the universe, Isaac Asimov discusses the "big bang" theory, which holds that the universe began with a titanic explosion, and the "continuous creation" theory, which contends that galaxies are continually forming and breaking down. In Asimov's view, the evidence points toward the "big bang."

25   The elimination of "continuous creation" does not necessarily mean the establishment of the "big bang." Suppose there is some third possibility that is as yet unsuggested. To strengthen the "big bang" theory it would be useful to consider some phenomenon that the "big bang" theory could predict, some phenomenon that could then actually be observed.

Suppose, for instance, that the universe *did* begin as an incredibly dense cosmic egg that exploded. At the moment of exploding, it must have been tremendously hot—possibly as hot as 10 billion degrees Centigrade (which is equivalent to 18 billion degrees Fahrenheit). Then if our instruments could penetrate far enough, to nearly the very edge of the observable universe, they might reach far enough back in time to catch a whiff of the radiation that accompanied the "big bang." At temperatures of billions of degrees, the radiation would be in the form of very energetic X-rays. However, the expanding universe would be carrying that source of X-rays away from us at nearly the speed of light. This incredible speed of recession would have the effect of vastly weakening the energy of the radiation; weakening it to the point where it would reach us in the form of radio waves with a certain group of properties. Through the 1960s, estimates of what those properties might be were advanced.

Then, early in 1966, a weak background of radio-wave radiation was detected in the skies; radiation that would just fit the type to be expected of the "big bang." This has been verified and it looks very much as though we have not only eliminated "continuous creation" but have actually detected the "big bang." If so, then we have lost something. In facing our own individual deaths, it was possible after all, even for those who lacked faith in an afterlife, to find consolation. Life itself would still go on. In a "continuous creation" universe, it was even possible to conceive of mankind as moving, when necessary, from an old galaxy to a young one and existing eventually through all infinity and for all eternity. It is a colossal, godlike vision, that might almost make individual death a matter of no consequence.

In the "big bang" scheme of things, however, our particular universe has a beginning—and an ending, too. Either it spreads out ever more thinly while *all* the galaxies grow old and the individual stars die, one by one. Or it reaches some maximum extent and then begins to collapse once more, returning after many eons to a momentary existence as a cosmic egg.

In either case, mankind, as we know it, must cease to exist and the dream of godhood must end. Death has now been rediscovered and Homo sapiens, as a species, like men as individuals, must learn to face the inevitable end.

—Or, if the universe oscillates, and if the cosmic egg is re-formed every hundred billion years or so, to explode once more; then, perhaps, in each of an infinite number of successive universes, a man-like intelligence (or a vast number of them) arises to wonder about the beginning and end of it all.[7]

Stripped of its metaphor, the passage probably could not convey its ideas. *Big bang* itself is a perfect metaphor for one theory of the creation of the universe, a great deal more meaningful than something like *the sudden creation theory.* In the second paragraph, the metaphor *universe = incredibly dense cosmic egg* is particularly apt, for an egg generates life; this metaphor is more packed with meaning than the unmetaphorical *universe = incredibly dense cosmic ball.* Instruments sensitive enough might catch a *whiff* of the radiation from the "big bang," Asimov tells us, and *whiff,* too, is metaphorical; it is particularly descriptive, for it creates the image of a person smelling the barest trace of an odor. Even *background of radio wave radiation* is metaphorical, for the word *background* literally applies to that which is visible to the eye, and radio waves are not. The notion of *old* and *young* galaxies is metaphorical, so vast is the time involved in the formation and decay of galaxies and so brief is the span between youth and old age in creatures. And isn't the final paragraph a powerful metaphor?

Alfred North Whitehead

Another example, without comment:

26   The thesis which these lectures will illustrate is that this quiet growth of science has practically recoloured our mentality so that modes of thought which in former times were exceptional are now broadly spread through the educated world. This new colouring of ways of thought had been proceeding slowly for many ages in the European peoples. At last it issued in the rapid development of science; and has thereby strengthened itself by its most

[7]Isaac Asimov, "Over the Edge of the Universe," *Harper's Magazine,* March 1967, pp. 97–98. Copyright © 1967 by Harper's Magazine Incorporated. Reprinted by permission of the author.

obvious application. The new mentality is more important even than the new science and the new technology. It has altered the metaphysical presuppositions and the imaginative contents of our minds; so that now the old stimuli provoke a new response. Perhaps my metaphor of a new colour is too strong. What I mean is just that slightest change of tone which yet makes all the difference. This is exactly illustrated by a sentence from a published letter of that adorable genius, William James. When he was finishing his great treatise on the *Principles of Psychology*, he wrote to his brother Henry James, "I have to forge every sentence in the teeth of irreducible and stubborn facts."   —Alfred North Whitehead, *Science and the Modern World*

Simile

Simile is really a variety of metaphor, but one in which the equation between the figurative and literal is expressed, usually by *like* or *as.* Here is Shakespeare's Sonnet 29:

27   When, in disgrace with Fortune and men's eyes,
            I all alone beweep my outcast state,
            And trouble deaf heaven with my bootless cries,
            And look upon myself and curse my fate,
            Wishing me like to one more rich in hope,
            Featured like him, like him with friends possessed,
            Desiring this man's art, and that man's scope,
            With what I most enjoy contented least;
            Yet in these thoughts myself almost despising,
            Haply I think on thee, and then my state,
            Like to the lark at break of day arising
            From sullen earth, sings hymns at heaven's gate;
                 For thy sweet love rememb'red such wealth brings
                 That then I scorn to change my state with kings.

The figure here is ***my state*** = ***the lark at break of day arising from sullen earth.***

Here is a simile from John Donne's "A Valediction: Forbidding Mourning":

28   Our two souls therefore which are one,
                     Though I must go, endure not yet
                 A breach, but an expansion,
                     Like gold to airy thinness beat.

And similes in Andrew Marvell's magnificent "To His Coy Mistress":

29   Now therefore, while the youthful hew
                 Sits on thy skin *like morning dew,*
                 And while thy willing soul transpires
                 At every pore with instant fires,
                 Now let us sport us while we may,
                 And now, *like amorous birds of prey,*
                 Rather at once our time devour
                 Than languish in his slow-chapped power.

Irony, Verbal and Dramatic

The tapestry of language is richly woven with figurativeness, not only metaphor and simile, but a variety of other nonliteral ways of conveying meaning.

Suppose I want to convey the notion that I disapprove of cheating on tests. I can state this idea literally:

30   Cheating on tests is bad.

I can also convey my attitude through a metaphor or a simile:

31   Cheating on tests is assassination of academic integrity.

32   Cheating on tests is like playing cards with a marked deck.

I might also use irony:

33   Cheating on tests is obviously an extremely noble thing for students to do.

For **33** to have an ironic effect, the reader must somehow see that I intend something quite different from what I say literally.

Metaphor comes about because of a mix of semantic features. Another way of saying this is that metaphor is a function of the denotations of words. Irony can result from a mix of *connotations*.

For example, the connotative value of ***emperor*** is one of glory, magnificence, and power. ***Ice cream*** has none of these connotative values. Therefore, when Wallace Stevens titled a poem "The Emperor of Ice-Cream," he created verbal irony. The irony is reinforced by the opening of the poem:

34   Call the roller of big cigars,
      The muscular one. . . .

What does an emperor have to do with ice cream or rollers of big cigars?
   Another example of this sort of irony:

35   Rod McKuen is the poet laureate of the pimpled generation.

The phrase ***poet laureate*** is elevated in connotation, but ***pimpled generation*** is just the opposite. The clash of connotations between these two terms conveys irony, which reveals a highly unfavorable attitude toward Rod McKuen.

Irony: An Example

The following is a richly ironic passage, and the irony stems largely from the word ***momma*** applied to America, for ***momma*** has a richly (perhaps overly) sentimental connotation, and the writer's attitude toward America is hardly sentimental:

36   *America Was Momma's Momma*
                  Dick Gregory

      Now that I am a man, I have "given up childish ways." I realize that
      America is my momma and America was Momma's momma. And I am going
      to place the blame for injustice and wrong on the right momma. Even today,

when I leave my country to appear on television and make other public appearances in foreign countries, I find it difficult to speak of the injustices I experience in this country. Because America is my momma. Even if Momma is a whore, she is still Momma. Many times I am asked if I would go to war if drafted. I always answer, "Yes, under one condition; that I be allowed to go to the front line without a gun. Momma is worth dying for, but there is nothing worth killing for. And if I ever change my opinion about killing, I will go to Mississippi and kill that Sheriff who spit in my wife's face."

America is my momma. One fourth of July, I want to go to the New York harbor and talk to Momma—the Statue of Liberty. I want to snatch that torch out of her hand and take her with me to the ghetto and sit her down on the street corner. I want to show her the "tired, the poor, the huddled masses yearning to breathe free." I want to show Momma what she has been doing to her children. And Momma would weep. For the grief of the ghetto is the grief of the entire American family.

—Dick Gregory, *The Shadow That Scares Me*

The passage is not, of course, unrelieved irony. It is a mixture of the ironic and the straightforward. In particular, the last sentence in each paragraph is completely straight.

Irony: A Second Example

In this passage, Lenny Bruce attacks Americans' homogenized version of themselves and their country:

37 I credit the motion picture industry as the strongest environmental factor in molding the children of my day.

Andy Hardy: whistling; a brown pompadour; a green lawn; a father whose severest punishment was taking your car away for the weekend.

Warner Baxter was a doctor. All priests looked like Pat O'Brien.

The superintendent of my school looked like Spencer Tracy, and the principal looked like Vincent Price. I was surprised years later to discover they *were* Spencer Tracy and Vincent Price. I went to Hollywood High, folks. Lana Turner sat at the next desk. Roland Young was the English teacher and Joan Crawford taught general science. "She's got a fabulous body, but she never takes that shop apron off."

Actually, I went to public school in North Bellmore, Long Island, for eight years, up until the fifth grade. I remember the routine of milk at 10:15 and napping on the desk—I hated the smell of that desk—I always used to dribble on the initials. And how enigmatic those well-preserved carvings were to me: BOOK YOU."   —Lenny Bruce, *How to Talk Dirty and Influence People*

The irony in this passage comes from the fact that the reader knows what Bruce's attitude is, even though he does not specify it. He is saying something like this: Americans' vision of themselves is false and callow and unthinking. The last paragraph, where Bruce begins to tell it like it really was, is the tip-off to the irony of what goes before.

The effect of irony is powerful, for it makes the reader a conspirator with the writer. The reader says unconsciously, "I know what this guy is getting at; I'm in on the secret of his meaning—even though he doesn't give that meaning directly, in so many words."

Dramatic Irony

Dramatic irony is a powerful literary device that adds richness to imaginative literature. The effect of dramatic irony comes about because the reader of a play, novel, or story understands aspects of the situation that the characters themselves don't. Sometimes the reader knows that certain decisions or actions will bring the characters into circumstances that they themselves are unaware of, and sometimes the reader understands the motives and psychology of the characters better than other characters in the work do. Here is a richly ironic scene from Joseph Heller's *Catch-22* in which the chaplain completely misunderstands the intentions of Colonel Cathcart, but the reader knows all:

38   Colonel Cathcart wanted to be a general so desperately he was willing to try anything, even religion, and he summoned the chaplain to his office late one morning the week after he had raised the number of [bombing] missions to sixty and pointed abruptly down toward his desk to his copy of *The Saturday Evening Post.* The colonel wore his khaki shirt collar wide open, exposing a shadow of tough black bristles of beard on his egg-white neck, and had a spongy hanging underlip. He was a person who never tanned, and he kept out of the sun as much as possible to avoid burning. The colonel was more than a head taller than the chaplain and over twice as broad, and his swollen, overbearing authority made the chaplain feel frail and sickly by contrast.

"Take a look, Chaplain," Colonel Catchcart directed, screwing a cigarette into his holder and seating himself affluently in the swivel chair behind his desk. "Let me know what you think."

The chaplain looked down at the open magazine compliantly and saw an editorial spread dealing with an American bomber group in England whose chaplain said prayers in the briefing room before each mission. The chaplain almost wept with happiness when he realized the colonel was not going to holler at him. The two had hardly spoken since the tumultuous evening Colonel Cathcart had thrown him out of the officers' club at General Dreedle's bidding after Chief White Halfoat had punched Colonel Moodus in the nose. The chaplain's initial fear had been that the colonel intended reprimanding him for having gone back into the officers' club without permission the evening before. He had gone there with Yossarian and Dunbar after the two had come unexpectedly to his tent in the clearing in the woods to ask him to join them. Intimidated as he was by Colonel Cathcart, he nevertheless found it easier to brave his displeasure than to decline the thoughtful invitation of his two new friends, whom he had met on one of his hospital visits just a few weeks before and who had worked so effectively to insulate him against the myriad social vicissitudes involved in his official duty to live on closest terms of familiarity with more than nine hundred unfamiliar officers and enlisted men who thought him an odd duck.

The chaplain glued his eyes to the pages of the magazine. He studied each photograph twice and read the captions intently as he organized his response to the colonel's question into a grammatically complete sentence that he rehearsed and reorganized in his mind a considerable number of times before he was able finally to muster the courage to reply.

"I think that saying prayers before each mission is a very moral and highly laudatory procedure, sir," he offered timidly, and waited.

"Yeah," said the colonel. "But I want to know if you think they'll work here."

"Yes, sir," answered the chaplain after a few moments. "I should think they would."

"Then I'd like to give it a try." The colonel's ponderous, farinaceous cheeks were tinted suddenly with glowing patches of enthusiasm. He rose to his feet and began walking around excitedly. "Look how much good they've done for these people in England. Here's a picture of a colonel in *The Saturday Evening Post* whose chaplain conducts prayers before each mission. If the prayers work for him, they should work for us. Maybe if we say prayers, they'll put *my* picture in *The Saturday Evening Post*."[8]

The effect of this passage is rich and complex. The reader, who knows Colonel Cathcart, understands that he would not be interested in prayer for altruistic reasons, but the reader also knows that the chaplain is completely naive and does not have an inkling of the colonel's self-serving motives. The reader, then, knows a good deal that the chaplain doesn't, and that brings about the effect of dramatic irony. But there is more irony. The reader doesn't know exactly *why* the colonel is interested in prayers; therefore, when the whole truth is revealed, the reader has a flash of insight that heightens the irony, for the reader suspects that the chaplain still does not understand the colonel, even though the reader's understanding is now complete.

Other Figures

Literally hundreds of kinds of figures of speech have been identified and have been given such tongue-twisting names as *aposiopesis, diacope, epitimesis, hypozeuxis, poiciologia,* and so on. We will let most of these rest in peace. But a few of them are useful enough to most writers to deserve a brief mention.

Metonymy

Metonymy is actually a form of metaphor in which a term that is closely associated with the literal term is substituted for the literal term. Thus

39   He lived by the sword and died by the sword.

substitutes the noun **sword** for **force** or **violence,** the sword being closely associated with force and violence.

Oxymoron

Oxymoron conjoins two contradictory terms to create its effect. Some examples:

40   holy devil, Hell's Angels, darkness visible (Milton), palpable fear

---

[8]Joseph Heller, *Catch-22* (New York: Dell Publishing, 1962), pp. 194–95. Copyright © 1955, 1961, by Joseph Heller. Reprinted by permission of Simon & Schuster.

Overstatement and Understatement

Overstatement and *understatement* (*hyperbole* and *litotes* in the jargon) also are figurative devices. The figurative effect arises when the reader understands that the writer is overstressing or understressing a statement. In other words, there is a disjunction between the importance that the writer *seems* to put on a statement and its actual importance. Here is an example of overstatement:

41   He [a lion] roared so loud, and looked so wonderous grim,
     His very shadow durst not follow him.
                       —Alexander Pope

And here is an example of understatement:

42   God loves his children not a little.

This means, of course, that God loves his children a very great deal.

Finally

Figurative language is a device that no writer can avoid using, for only completely literal statements are without figurative value, and it is impossible to communicate in totally literal terms.

This chapter was intended to help you learn to use figurative language more skillfully to convey meanings. The chapter was also intended to bring about a deeper and more appreciative understanding of how language functions—to help unravel the mystery of how you, in the isolation of your selfhood, explain yourself to others.

Discussion and Activities

The following passages use a variety of kinds of figurative language. Underline the figurative elements, and name them if you can. Try to restate the ideas, eliminating the figures. What is lost? What is gained, if anything? Why?

a   Madison Avenue frequently exaggerates the importance of new features and encourages consumers to dispose of partially worn-out goods to make way for the new.
                       —Alvin Toffler

b   Nobody knows how many people in America moonlight . . . . —Peter Schrag

c   In the magazines and newspapers, top management, formerly so autocratic (think of Henry Luce), now casts itself at the feet of the publicity intellectuals, seeking their intercession with the youth-worshiping public. One picks up *The New York Times* and reads on the front page that the posthumous homosexual novel of E. M. Forster is about to appear in England. Why not simply Forster's posthumous novel, on page 40? No, the word is HOMOSEXUAL and it is on the front page. The *Times* still keeps up its statesmanlike and grave appearance, but its journalism is yellower than ever. It has surrendered without a fight to the new class.
                       —Saul Bellow

d   The bridge by which we cross from tragedy to comedy and back again is precarious and narrow.
                       —Christopher Fry

e   Miss Nims, take a letter to Henry David Thoreau. Dear Henry: I thought of you the other afternoon as I was approaching Concord doing fifty on Route 62. That is a high speed at which to hold a philosopher in one's mind, but in this century, we are a nimble bunch.   —E. B. White

f   Sex is dead. Nobody seems to have noticed its passing, what with the distraction caused by recent reports of the death of God, the death of Self, the death of the City, the death of Tragedy, and all the other cultural obituaries of the past few years. Yet it is a fact: sex is dead and we must begin to learn how to live in a world in which that is an incontrovertible fact.   —Earl H. Brill

g   I have been told to "look down from a high place over the whole extensive landscape of modern art." We all know how tempting high places can be, and how dangerous. I usually avoid them myself. But if I must do as I am told, I shall try to find out why modern art has taken its peculiar form, and to guess how long that form will continue.   —Kenneth Clark

h
>
> I am the daughter of earth and water,
> And the nursling of the sky:
> I pass thro' the pores of the ocean and shores;
> I change, but I cannot die.
> For after the rain when with never a strain,
> The pavilion of heaven is bare,
> And the winds and sunbeams with their convex gleams,
> Build up the blue dome of air,
> I silently laugh at my own cenotaph,
> And out of the caverns of rain,
> Like a child from the womb, like a ghost from the tomb,
> I arise and unbuild it again.
>
> —Percy Bysshe Shelley, *"The Cloud"*

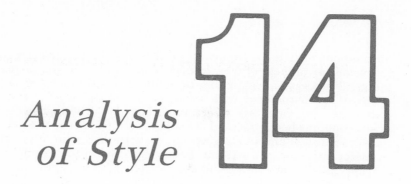

Analysis of Style

Summary of the Chapter

This chapter systematically analyzes the style of a variety of writers, applying the principles that were developed in the last three chapters. Thus, the analyses focus on sentence devices (such as clause structures, cumulative modifiers, and structural arrangements like passive voice); the words that the author chooses; and figurative language.

The purpose of the chapter is to bring stylistic devices into your conscious awareness so that you can use them in your own writing. There is also a secondary purpose: to explore the ways in which writers express themselves so that you can develop an appreciative awareness of prose as an art form.

To Get Under Way

In this chapter, we will gather up the notions concerning style that have been developed in the last three chapters—put it all together, wind it up, and see if it works. We will systematically apply concepts of style to passages of modern prose to see how they achieve some of their effects.

In the process, you should pick up techniques for use in your own writing, and this is the real goal of the chapter. In fact, the main purpose of the discussion of style in Chapters 11, 12, and 13 has been to give you a conscious awareness of what you are doing and what you might do in that magical process called writing or composing. Of course, the concepts of style—those associated with sentence structure, words, and figurative language—are rich and interesting, but the driving force behind the discussion has been practical. This final chapter will be the most practical of all, for it will analyze "living" prose, with the intent of enabling you to transfer into your own writing the devices used in the examples.

This transfer, of course, will not take place without practice. Therefore, you should attempt some imitations of the passages that are analyzed, for such imitations will bring abilities from the area of your passive competence into the area of your performance as a writer.

The T-Unit

Before we begin, it is important that you grasp one fairly simple concept. Our analysis will not use the sentence as its basis; rather, we will focus on the *transformational unit,* or *T-unit.* A T-unit is simply any stretch of discouse that can legitimately be punctuated as a sentence. Another way of stating this point: to isolate the T-units in a passage, ignore the author's punctuation, and put either a period or a question mark wherever one *could* appear in conventional American punctuation. This is important because writers frequently use erratic punctuation in order to achieve various effects. To illustrate what I mean, I will concoct a passage with deviant punctuation, and then I will isolate the T-units.

> 1   Circling and gliding. Swooping lower and then riding a current upward. The hawk never moved its wings. A magnificent bird. I watched it for several minutes, and then it disappeared behind the hill.

This passage contains three T-units, thus:

> 2   [1] Circling and gliding. Swooping lower and then riding a current upward. The hawk never moved its wings. A magnificent bird. [2] I watched it for several minutes, [3] and then it disappeared behind the hill.

The first T-unit is merely a sentence that conventionally would have been punctuated thus:

> 3   Circling and gliding, swooping lower and then riding a current upward, the hawk never moved its wings—a magnificent bird.

The second and third T-units constitute a compound sentence, which might have been punctuated thus:

> 4   I watched it for several minutes. And then it disappeared behind the hill.

To repeat, each point at which a period or question mark might have been placed constitutes the end of a T-unit. As we analyze various passages, this principle will be repeatedly illustrated.

Analytic Procedure

The analysis of style is a complex and demanding task, and we will not attempt in this chapter to do extensive analyses, even though many of the things that we find will represent penetrating insights.

The analysis might proceed at random, jumping from this feature to that and to another. But as Chapter 3, on prewriting, made clear, systematic procedure is almost always more productive than random procedure; therefore, we will follow the analytic procedure that is outlined below. The advantages of the procedure are its economy and its value as a heuristic; following the procedure will allow us to save time, to avoid "wandering around" with no purpose, and the procedure itself will aid us in discovering features that we might well have overlooked if we had worked at random.

Following the order of the discussion of style in Chapters 11, 12, and 13, we will first deal with *sentence structure.* We will look at sentence arrangements: loose and periodic, passive, and others. Then we will find the types of sentences used: simple, compound, complex, and compound-complex. Next we will isolate the cumulative modifiers, and finally we will focus on miscellaneous kinds of embeddings that seem important in the passage. After analyzing the sentences in the passage, we will turn to the *words* the author uses: nouns, verbs, adjectives, adverbs. Finally we will take a close look at the author's *figurative language*—metaphors and other types.

All of this can be succinctly expressed in outline form.

Stylistic Analysis

Sentences
    Arrangements
        Loose and periodic
        Passive
        Other arrangements
    Types (simple, compound, complex, compound-complex)
    Cumulative modifiers
    Miscellaneous embeddings
Words (nouns, verbs, adjectives, adverbs)
Figures
    Metaphors
    Other figurative language

A Passage by Mark Twain

5   ## From *Roughing It*

[T-unit 1] It was the end of August, [2] and the skies were cloudless and the weather superb. [3] In two or three weeks I had grown wonderfully fascinated with the curious new country [the Nevada Territory], and concluded to put off my return to "the States" awhile. [4] I had grown well accustomed to wearing a damaged slouch hat, blue woolen shirt, and pants crammed into boot-tops, and gloried in the absence of coat, vest, and braces. [5] I felt rowdyish and "bully" (as the historian Josephus phrases it, in his fine chapter upon the destruction of the Temple). [6] It seemed to me that nothing could be so fine and so romantic. [7] I had become an officer of the government, [8] but that was for mere sublimity. [9] The office was an unique sinecure. [10] I had nothing to do and no salary. [11] I was private secretary to his majesty the Secretary, [12] and there was not yet writing enough for two of us. [13] So Johnny K——— and I devoted our time to amusement. [14] He was the young son of an Ohio nabob and was out there for recreation. [15] He got it. [16] We had heard a world of talk about the marvelous beauty of Lake Tahoe, [17] and finally curiosity drove us thither to see it. [18] Three or four members of the Brigade had been there and located some timber lands on its shores and stored up a quantity of provisions in their camp. [19] We strapped a couple of blankets on our shoulders and took an ax apiece and started—[20] for we intended to take up a wood ranch or so ourselves and become wealthy. [21] We were on foot. [22] The reader will find it advantageous to go horseback. [23] We were told that the distance was eleven miles. [24] We tramped a long time on level ground, and then toiled laboriously up a mountain about a thousand miles high and looked over. [25] No lake there. [26] We descended on the other side, crossed the valley and toiled up another mountain three or four thousand miles high, apparently, and looked over again. [27] No lake yet. [28] We sat down tired and perspiring, and hired a couple of Chinamen to curse those people who had beguiled us. [29] Thus refreshed, we presently resumed the march with renewed vigor and determination. [30] We plodded on, two or three hours longer, [31] and at last the lake burst upon us—a noble sheet of blue water lifted six thousand three hundred feet above the level of the sea, and walled in by a rim of snow-clad mountain peaks that towered aloft full three thousand feet higher still! [32] It was a vast oval, [33] and one would have to use up eighty or a hundred good miles in traveling around it. [34] As it lay there with the shadows of the mountains brilliantly photographed upon its surface I thought it must surely be the fairest picture the whole earth affords.

[35] We found the small skiff belonging to the Brigade boys, and without loss of time set out across a deep bend of the lake toward the landmarks that signified the locality of the camp. [36] I got Johnny to row—not because I mind exertion myself, but because it makes me sick to ride backward when I am at work. [37] But I steered. [38] A three-mile pull brought us to the camp just as the night fell, [39] and we stepped ashore very tired and wolfishly hungry. [40] In a "cache" among the rocks we found the provisions and the cooking-utensils, [41] and then, all fatigued as I was, I sat down on a boulder and superintended while Johnny gathered wood and cooked supper. [42] Many a man who had gone through what I had, would have wanted to rest.

[43] It was a delicious supper—hot bread, fried bacon, and black coffee. [44] It was a delicious solitude we were in, too. [45] Three miles away was a sawmill and some workmen, [46] but there were not fifteen other human beings throughout the wide circumference of the lake. [47] As the darkness closed down and the stars came out and spangled the great mirror with jewels, we smoked meditatively in the solemn hush and forgot our troubles and our pains. [48] In due time we spread out blankets in the warm sand between two large boulders and soon fell asleep, careless of the procession of ants that passed in through rents in our clothing and explored our persons. [49] Nothing could disturb the sleep that fettered us, [50] for it had been fairly earned, [51] and if our consciences had any sins on them they had to adjourn

court for that night, anyway. [52] The wind rose just as we were losing consciousness, [53] and we were lulled to sleep by the beating of the surf upon the shore.

[54] It is always very cold on that lake-shore in the night, [55] but we had plenty of blankets and were warm enough. [56] We never moved a muscle all night, but waked at early dawn in the original positions, and got up at once, thoroughly refreshed, free from soreness, and brim full of friskiness. [57] There is no end of wholesome medicine in such an experience. [58] That morning we could have whipped ten such people as we were the day before—sick ones at any rate. [59] But the world is slow, [60] and people will go to "water cures" and "movement cures" and to foreign lands for health. [61] Three months of camp life on Lake Tahoe would restore an Egyptian mummy to his pristine vigor, and give him an appetite like an alligator. [62] I do not mean the oldest and driest mummies, of course, but the fresher ones. [63] The air up there in the clouds is very pure and fine, bracing and delicious. [64] And why shouldn't it be?—[65] it is the same the angels breathe. [66] I think that hardly any amount of fatigue can be gathered together that a man cannot sleep off in one night on the sand by its side. Not under a roof, but under the sky: [67] it seldom or never rains there in the summer-time. [68] I know a man who went there to die. [69] But he made a failure of it. [70] He was a skeleton when he came, and could barely stand. [71] He had no appetite, and did nothing but read tracts and reflect on the future. [72] Three months later he was sleeping out-of-doors regularly, eating all he could hold, three times a day, and chasing game over mountains three thousand feet high for recreation. [73] And he was a skeleton no longer, but weighed part of a ton. [74] This is no fancy sketch, but the truth. [75] His disease was consumption. [76] I confidently commend his experience to other skeletons.

[77] I superintended again, [78] and as soon as we had eaten breakfast we got in the boat and skirted along the lake shore about three miles and disembarked. [79] We like the appearance of the place, [80] and so we claimed some three hundred acres of it and stuck our "notices" on a tree. [81] It was a yellow-pine timber-land—a dense forest of trees a hundred feet high and from one to five feet through at the butt. [82] It was necessary to fence our property [83] or we could not hold it. [84] That is to say, it was necessary to cut down trees here and there and make them fall in such a way as to form a sort of inclosure (with pretty wide gaps in it). [85] We cut down three trees apiece, and found it such heartbreaking work that we decided to "rest our case" on those; [86] if they held the property, well and good; [87] if they didn't, let the property spill out through the gaps and go; [88] it was no use to work ourselves to death merely to save a few acres of land. [89] Next day we came back to build a house—[90] for a house was also necessary, in order to hold the property. [91] We decided to build a substantial log house and excite the envy of the Brigade boys; [92] but by the time we had cut and trimmed the first log it seemed unnecessary to be so elaborate, [93] and so we decided to build it of saplings. [94] However, two saplings, duly cut and trimmed, compelled recognition of the fact that a still modester architecture would satisfy the law, [95] and so we concluded to build a "brush" house. [96] We devoted the next day to this work, [97] but we did so much "sitting around" and discussing, that by the middle of the afternoon we had achieved only a half-way sort of affair which one of us had to watch while the other cut the brush, [98] lest if both turned our backs we migh not be able to find it again, it had such a strong family resemblance to the surrounding vegetation. [99] But we were satisfied with it.

[100] We were landowners now, duly seized and possessed, and within the protection of the law. [101] Therefore we decided to take up our residence on our own domain and enjoy that large sense of independence which only such an experience can bring. [102] Late the next afternoon, after a good long rest, we sailed away from the Brigade camp with all the provisions and cooking-utensils we could carry off—borrow is the more accurate word—[103] and just as the night was falling we beached the boat at our own landing.

The first order of business is to enjoy this marvelous narrative: its wry humor, its vividness, its ease. The second order of business—less heady, but also interesting—is to see "what's there" in Mark Twain's sentences and, even more important, to see what we can learn from them.

Sentences

You will recall that in Chapter 11 we differentiated between loose and periodic constructions. A loose sentence is one in which modification follows the base, like this:

6   The robins sing early in the morning.

A periodic sentence is one in which the modification precedes the base, like this:

7   Early in the morning, the robins sing.

In the passage by Mark Twain, the periodic/loose principle applies to only fifteen of the T-units: periodic, 3, 34, 40, 47, 51, 58, 102; loose, 31, 33, 35, 36, 41, 46, 48, 90. T-unit 47 is a typical periodic construction:

8   ***As the darkness closed down and the stars came out and spangled the great mirror with jewels,*** we smoked meditatively in the solemn hush and forgot our troubles and our pains.

It is perhaps significant that, of the sentences to which the principle applies, seven are periodic and eight are loose; in other words, Twain varied the structure.

Balance

Balance is not one of Twain's major devices. In T-unit 6, one finds a trace of balance:

9   It seemed to me that nothing could be ***so fine***
                                    and
                                    so romantic.

But this is really more like parallelism than like balance, for the structures are merely coordinate adjectives with intensifiers. The only marked use of balance is in T-unit 63:

10   The air up there in the clouds is very
       pure and fine,
       bracing and delicious.

Variation of Length

One sentence device that Twain uses with great effectiveness is variation of length. For example, note the blunt, mildly humorous effect of the short sentence that follows the relatively long one in the passage below:

11   [14] He was the young son of an Ohio nabob and was out there for recreation. [15] He got it.

And notice the wonderful effect of varying sentence length in the following:

12   [24] We tramped a long time on level ground, and then toiled laboriously up a mountain about a thousand miles high and looked over. [25] **No lake there.** [26] We descended on the other side, crossed the valley and toiled up another mountain three or four thousand miles high, apparently, and looked over again. [27] **No lake yet.**

These, of course, are elliptical sentences: **(There was) no lake there/ (There was) no lake yet.** In their brevity and abruptness, they perfectly convey the mood of disappointment, even disgust, that they are intended to convey.

Repetition

In one instance Twain uses repetition of structure, with marvelous effectiveness:

13   [43] **It was a delicious** supper—hot bread, fried bacon, and black coffee. [44] **It was a delicious** solitude we were in, too.

Notice that the first use of **delicious** is literal, for bread, bacon, and coffee can be literally delicious, but the second use is metaphorical, for solitude cannot be tasted.

Passive Voice

In only three instances does Twain choose passive voice over active:

14   [23] We **were told** that the distance was eleven miles.
15   [50] . . . . for it **had been fairly earned.**
16   [53] . . . and we **were lulled to sleep** by the beating of the surf upon the shore.

In the first one, **14**, who did the telling is unimportant. Twain wants to stress *who* and *what* were told. (Notice how active voice changes the emphasis of the sentence: **Someone told us that the distance was eleven miles.** In this version, the "someone" gains emphasis.) Only in the last instance, **16**, would the T-unit be just as effective in active voice: **and the beating of the surf upon the shore lulled us to sleep.**

This completes the survey of sentence-arrangement devices. We can say in summary that Twain does not use conspicuous devices, such as inverted order and heavy balance, in order to achieve his effects. In fact, such devices would take away from his prose its easy naturalness.

Sentence Types

As to sentence type according to clause structure, here is a chart that tells the story:

T-units	Sentence types	T-units	Sentence types
1–2	Compound	48	Complex
3	Simple	49–51	Compound-Complex
4	Simple	52–53	Compound-Complex
5	Complex	54–55	Compound
6	Complex	56	Simple
7–8	Compound	57	Simple
9	Simple	58	Complex
10	Simple	59–60	Compound
11–12	Compound	61	Simple
13	Simple	62	Simple
14	Simple	63	Simple
15	Simple	64–65	Compound-Complex
16–17	Compound	66	Complex
18	Simple	67	Simple
19–20	Compound	68	Complex
21	Simple	69	Simple
22	Simple	70	Complex
23	Complex	71	Simple
24	Simple	72	Complex
25	Elliptical (Simple)	73	Simple
26	Simple	74	Simple
27	Elliptical (Simple)	75	Simple
28	Complex	76	Simple
29	Simple	77–78	Compound-Complex
30–31	Compound-Complex	79–80	Compound
32–33	Compound	81	Simple
34	Complex	82–83	Compound
35	Complex	84	Complex
36	Complex	85–88	Compound-Complex
37	Simple	89–90	Compound
38–39	Compound-Complex	91–93	Compound-Complex
40–41	Compound-Complex	94–95	Compound-Complex
42	Complex	96–98	Compound-Complex
43	Simple	99	Simple
44	Complex	100	Simple
45–46	Compound	101	Complex
47	Complex	102–103	Compound-Complex

Totals: simple, 30; compound, 12; complex, 18; compound-complex, 12; elliptical (simple), 2.

This passage averages about 1.4 T-units per sentence, an average that is typical for Mark Twain, but would be low for some other writers.

The chart indicates a minor point about Mark Twain's prose: he varies his sentence structure. More interesting are the various effects that Twain achieves with different kinds of sentences. Notice the brisk, even choppy, effect of the sentences that comprise T-units 7 through 15:

17   [7] I had become an officer of the government, [8] but that was for mere sublimity. [9] The office was an unique sinecure. [10] I had nothing to do and no salary. [11] I was private secretary to his majesty the Secretary, [12] and there was not yet writing enough for two of us. [13] So Johnny K____ and I devoted our time to amusement. [14] He was the young son of an Ohio nabob and was out there for recreation. [15] He got it.

Compare this with the fluid, leisurely effect brought about by the more "massive" sentence structure that runs from T-unit 45 through T-unit 53.

In other words, the very clause structure of sentences has its consequences, not only in the conveying of meaning but also in the effect of prose movement.

Punctuation

It is interesting to note how Twain handles T-unit 66. Here are 66 and 67:

18   [66] I think that hardly any amount of fatigue can be gathered together that a man cannot sleep off by its side. Not under a roof, but under the sky; [67] it seldom or never rains there in the summer-time.

He has obviously used deviant punctuation to achieve an effect, for **Not under a roof, but under the sky** would normally be joined with T-unit 66 to make a sentence, not with T-unit 67:

19   I think that hardly any amount of fatigue can be gathered together that a man cannot sleep off by its side, not under a roof, but under the sky. It seldom or never rains there in the summer-time.

The punctuation that Twain chose to use stresses that the sleeping was outdoors, not indoors: the unusual punctuation of the two structures (they are prepositional phrases) as if they were a part of the next sentence calls the reader's attention to them, isolates them, and thus stresses them.

Cumulative Modifiers

The following chart shows the cumulative modifiers in each T-unit. Once again, the abbreviations used are: Abs (absolute), AC (adjective cluster), Adv (adverb clause), NC (noun cluster), PP (prepositional phrase), RC (relative clause), VC (verb cluster).

T-unit	Cumulative modifiers	T-unit	Cumulative modifiers
1	none	6	none
2	none	7	none
3	PP	8	none
4	VC	9	none
5	Adv, PP	10	none

T-unit	Cumulative modifiers	T-unit	Cumulative modifiers
11	none	57	PP
12	none	58	RC, NC, PP
13	none	59	none
14	none	60	PP
15	none	61	none
16	none	62	PP
17	none	63	none
18	PP, PP	64	none
19	PP	65	RC
20	none	66	RC, PP, PP, PP, PP
21	none	67	PP
22	none	68	RC
23	none	69	none
24	none	70	Adv
25	none	71	none
26	none	72	PP
27	none	73	none
28	RC	74	none
29	VC, PP	75	none
30	none	76	none
31	PP, NC, VC, RC	77	none
32	none	78	Adv
33	PP	79	none
34	Adv, RC	80	none
35	VC, PP, RC	81	NC, PP
36	Adv, Adv, Adv	82	none
37	none	83	none
38	Adv	84	none
39	AC, AC	85	none
40	PP	86	Adv
41	Adv, Adv	87	Adv
42	RC	88	VC
43	NC	89	none
44	none	90	PP
45	none	91	none
46	PP	92	pp, RC
47	Adv, PP	93	none
48	PP, AC, RC	94	VC
49	RC	95	none
50	none	96	PP
51	Adv, PP	97	RC, Adv
52	Adv	98	Adv, Adv
53	none	99	none
54	PP, PP	100	VC, PP
55	none	101	RC
56	PP, PP, PP, VC, AC, AC	102	PP, PP, RC
		103	Adv, PP

Totals: absolutes, none; adjective clusters, 5; adverb clauses, 18; noun clusters, 4; prepositional phrases, 36; relative clauses, 15; verb clusters, 7.

This constitutes a total of 85 cumulative modifiers, or about .82 per T-unit. Compared with writers that we have already seen (and with writers that we will soon be looking at), Mark Twain used very few cumulative modifiers to convey his meanings and to achieve his effects. However, some of the T-units and sentences in which he did use cumulative modifiers are worth looking at.

20   [5] I felt rowdyish and "bully" (as the historian Josephus phrases it, in his fine chapter upon the destruction of the Temple).

We can diagram this T-unit thus:

21   I felt rowdyish and "bully"
            (Adv)   (as the historian Josephus phrases it,
            (PP)   in his fine chapter upon the destruction of the Temple).

Much of the delight of this sentence comes from Twain's use of the adjectives **rowdyish** and **bully** coupled with the allusion to Josephus (A.D. 37–100?), who was a Jewish general and historian. The position of the cumulative modifiers, after the base, creates a good part of the humor of the sentence, for the reader is surprised to learn that, according to Twain, so august a writer as Josephus used such slangy terms.

Here are some more instances of Twain's use of cumulative modifiers:

22   [29] (VC)   Thus refreshed,
                   we presently resumed the march
            (PP)   with renewed vigor and determination.

23   [31] and at last the lake burst upon us—
            (NC)   a noble sheet of blue water
            (VC)   lifted six thousand three hundred feet above the level of the
                          sea,
            (VC)   and walled in by a rim of snow-clad mountain peaks
            (RC)   that towered aloft full three thousand feet higher still!

24   [36] I got Johnny to row—
            (Adv)   not because I mind exertion myself,
            (Adv)   but because it makes me sick to ride backward
            (Adv)   when I am at work.

25   [56] We never moved a muscle all night, but waked / , and got up
            (PP)   / at early dawn
            (PP)   / in the original positions
            (PP)   at once,
            (VC)   thoroughly refreshed,
            (AC)   free from soreness,
            (AC)   and brim full of friskiness.

In regard to cumulative modifiers, then, Mark Twain relies heavily upon adverb clauses and prepositional phrases (in this passage, at least). It is interesting that he does not use the absolute at all.

Coordination

The single device that is most typical of how Twain has put ideas together in sentences is coordination.

The great majority of the seventy-four sentences in the passage contain some kind of coordination; every time a coordinating conjunction *(and, but, for, so, yet, or, nor)* appears, coordination has taken place. Yet of the seventy-four sentences, only twelve are compound (sentences in which whole clauses are coordinated); the coordination tends to be between elements within clauses, not between clauses.

Twain coordinates verb with verb:

26   [3] In two or three weeks I *had grown* wonderfully fascinated with the curious new country, AND *concluded* to put off my return to "the States" awhile. [4] I *had grown* well accustomed to wearing a damaged slouch hat, blue woolen shirt, and pants crammed into boot-tops, AND *gloried* in the absence of coat, vest, and braces.

At times, he coordinates three verbs:

27   [18] Three or four members of the Brigade *had been* there AND *located* some timber lands on its shores AND *stored up* a quantity of provisions in their camp. [19] We *strapped* a couple of blankets on our shoulders AND *took* an ax apiece AND *started*—[20] for we intended to take up a wood ranch or so ourselves and become wealthy.

In connection with coordination, note that Twain establishes the link between T-units 19 and 20 with coordination rather than subordination. That is, he might have written

28   We strapped a couple of blankets on our shoulders and took an ax apiece and started—BECAUSE we intended to take up a wood ranch or so ourselves and become wealthy.

In T-unit 20 we also see coordination between infinitives:

29   [20] for we intended *to take up* a wood ranch or so ourselves AND [to] *become* wealthy.

In the first sentence (T-units 1 and 2), Twain uses coordination in an intricate manner. He coordinates full clauses (the T-units), and within the second T-unit, he coordinates a full clause with an elliptical clause:

30   [1] It was the end of August, [2] AND *the skies were cloudless* AND *the weather* [was] *superb.*

In short, Twain refined the art of coordination until it served him as one of his main stylistic devices. Be it noted, however, that if he had merely coordinated main clauses, his prose would have been monotonous and would, indeed, have sounded childish.

Words

We now turn to an analysis of Twain's use of words.

Nouns

I think you would agree that the prose, in general, is low-key, understated. It is not "flashy" or terribly complex. Any deviation from this simple, easygoing tone stands out almost glaringly. For instance, look at the use of *sublimity* in the following:

31   [7] I had become an officer of the government, [8] but that was for mere *sublimity.*

The noun *sublimity* means "grandness, almost supernatural elevation, nobility"; therefore, Twain's use of the term in connection with his lowly position as secretary to the Secretary brings about some gentle humor—aimed, of course, at himself.

Twain had a remarkable talent for choosing just the right word. For instance, in T-unit 38, he talks about a "three-mile *pull*," not a *row* or a *journey.* In T-unit 47, he tells us he was in a "solemn *hush*," not a *silence,* and *hush,* with its verbal connotations, makes the silence more profound and almost an active, visible presence.

Here is another noun that is unexpected, but, nonetheless, just right:

32   [56] We never moved a muscle all night, but waked at early dawn in the original positions, and got up at once, thoroughly refreshed, free from soreness, and brim full of *friskiness.*

Try replacing *friskiness* with other nouns such as *vigor, energy,* or *enthusiasm,* and see what happens to the effect of the sentence.

Verbs

In Chapter 12 (page 412), we discussed Twain's masterful use of verbs; a second brief look here will be profitable.

33   [31] and at last the lake *burst* upon us. . . .

34   [41] and then, all fatigued as I was, I sat down on a boulder and *superintended* while Johnny gathered wood and cooked supper.

35   [48] . . . careless of the procession of ants that passed in through rents in our clothing and *explored* our persons.

36   [51] and if our consciences had any sins on them they had to *adjourn* court for that night, anyway.

One final example of Twain's imaginative use of the verb:

37   [85] We cut down three trees apiece, and found it such heartbreaking work that we decided to "rest our case" on those; [86] if they held the property, well and good; [87] if they didn't, let the property *spill out* through the gaps and go. . . .

Adjectives

In his novel *Pudd'nhead Wilson,* Twain wrote this adage:

38   *As to the Adjective: when in doubt, strike it out.*

Twain knew that dull prose is not made vivid by inserting adjectives—like sprinkling garlic salt over an undistinguished stew. When he did elect to use an adjective, he invariably achieved just the right effect with it. The two italicized adjectives in the following are prime examples of his skill:

> **39**   [5] I felt ***rowdyish*** and ***"bully"*** (as the historian Josephus phrases it, in his fine chapter upon the destruction of the Temple).

It is the connotative clash between these adjectives and ***Josephus*** that brings about the humor in the sentence—the idea of the classical Jewish historian using American slang.

Other examples of Twain's adjectives:

> **40**   [43] It was a ***delicious*** supper—hot bread, fried bacon, and black coffee. [44] It was a ***delicious*** solitude we were in, too.

It is the metaphorical repetition of ***delicious*** that brings about the effect here.

> **41**   [56] We never moved a muscle all night, but waked at early dawn in the original positions, and got up at once, thoroughly ***refreshed, free*** from soreness, and brim ***full*** of friskiness.

These adjectives are in the appositive position: therefore, they are classed as cumulative modifiers.

Twain often achieves his humor through an afterthought:

> **42**   [61] Three months of camp life on Lake Tahoe would restore an Egyptian mummy to his pristine vigor, and give him an appetite like an alligator. [62] I do not mean the ***oldest*** and ***driest*** mummies, of course, but the ***fresher*** ones.

Adverbs

Twain uses adverbs only when they will highlight his meaning, and then he tends to use words that are somewhat unusual and hence unexpected:

> **43**   [39] and we stepped ashore very tired and ***wolfishly*** hungry.

> **44**   [47] As the darkness closed down and the stars came out and spangled the great mirror with jewels, we smoked ***meditatively*** in the solemn hush. . . .

Figurative Language

As to figurative language: Twain relies on metaphor, overstatement, and irony.

Metaphor

His metaphors are interesting and apt. The first example is of a metaphor that is created by a verb:

> **45**   [34] As it lay there with the shadows of the mountains brilliantly ***photographed*** upon its surface. . . .

The literal version of this might be ***the shadows of the mountains brilliantly reflected up on its surface.***

In **45** the verb ***photographed*** makes the view of the lake into a photograph. In the next example, the metaphor centers in a noun, and the lake becomes a mirror:

46 [47] As the darkness closed down and the stars came out and spangled the great ***mirror*** with jewels. . . .

Of course, in **46** there is a double metaphor, both ***mirror*** and ***stars spangling the mirror with jewels.***

Example **47** is a somewhat more complicated metaphor:

47 [63] The air up there in the clouds is very pure and fine, bracing and delicious. [64] And why shouldn't it be—[65] it is the same the angels breathe.

If we turn into a simple equation, we get something like this: ***air at Lake Tahoe = air that the angels breathe.***

One final example of metaphor:

48 [85] We cut down three trees apiece, and found it such heartbreaking work that we decided to "rest our case" on those; [86] if they held the property, well and good; [87] if they didn't, let the property spill out through the gaps and go. . . .

This example contains two metaphors. The first centers in ***rest our case,*** which in this context literally means "stop working." But Twain has made it clear that there were certain legal requirements for people who wanted to establish timber claims; therefore, the term ***rest our case,*** with its legal connotations, is a particularly appropriate metaphor. The second metaphor is ***let the property spill out through the gaps and go.*** Its meaning, which involves ambiguity, is complex and interesting. Think of the word ***property:*** in one sense, it is an abstract noun (that is, it has the feature [−concrete]); and, of course, anything that is not concrete cannot spill. But ***property*** can also be a concrete noun, meaning the physical stuff that is owned (that is, it can also have the feature [+concrete]). But in any case, the verb ***spill out*** demands a subject with the feature [2 penetrable], thus: [2 penetrable _____]. Another way of putting this is to say that ***spill out*** demands a liquid subject, and whether one construes ***property*** as abstract or concrete, it cannot have the semantic feature that the verb requires. Hence the metaphorical nature of the expression.

Overstatement

Overstatement (or hyperbole) is a figurative device that Mark Twain used frequently throughout his work, and it is prominent in the passage that we are analyzing. Some examples:

49 [24] We tramped a long time on level ground, and then toiled laboriously up *a mountain about a thousand miles high* and looked over. [25] No lake there. [26] We descended on the other side, crossed the valley and toiled up *another mountain three or four thousand miles high*. . . .

50 [61] Three months of camp life on Lake Tahoe would restore an Egyptian mummy to his pristine vigor, and give him an appetite like an alligator.

51 [68] I know a man who went there to die. [69] But he made a failure of it. [70] He was a skeleton when he came, and could barely stand. [71] He had no

appetite, and did nothing but read tracts and reflect on the future. [72] Three months later he was sleeping out-of-doors regularly, eating all he could hold, three times a day, and chasing game all over mountains three thousand feet high for recreation.

It should be noted that Twain's hyperbole is in the great American tradition of the "tall tale."

Irony

Finally, two examples of Twain's use of irony.

52   [36] I got Johnny to row—not because I mind exertion myself, but because it makes me sick to ride backward when I am at work.

53   [41] and then, all fatigued as I was, I sat down on a boulder and superintended while Johnny gathered wood and cooked supper. [42] Many a man who had gone through what I had, would have wanted to rest.

The reader knows that Twain means he was too lazy to do his share, and it is the reader's knowledge of what Twain really means as opposed to what he says that creates the ironic (and humorous) effect (but bear in mind that not all irony is humorous). Note, too, that Twain heightens the irony by repetition. In T-unit 41 we learn that he **superintended** the preparation of supper, and then in T-unit 77 he blandly lets us know that the next morning he **superintended** the preparation of breakfast as well.

This completes a fairly thorough inventory of the elements of style used in the passage by Mark Twain. A great deal more could be said, but our analysis has been extensive enough to teach us something about how Twain put his ideas into memorable prose.

A Passage by Tom Wolfe

The T-units are numbered in the following passage from Tom Wolfe's *The Electric Kool-Aid Acid Test,* as in the Mark Twain selection. The reason for relying on T-units, rather than the author's punctuation, will become obvious in this passage.

54   [1] That's good thinking there, Cool Breeze. [2] Cool Breeze is a kid with three or four days' beard sitting next to me on the stamped metal bottom of the open back part of a pickup truck. Bouncing along. Dipping and rising and rolling on these rotten springs like a boat. [3] Out of the back of the truck the city of San Francisco is bouncing down the hill, all those endless staggers of bay windows, slums with a view, bouncing and streaming down the hill. One after another, electric signs with neon martini glasses lit up on them, the San Francisco symbol of "bar"—thousands of neon-magenta martini glasses bouncing and streaming down the hill, and beneath them, hundreds, thousands of people wheeling around to look at this freaking, crazy truck we're in, their white faces erupting from their lapels like marshmallows—streaming and bouncing down the hill—[4] and God knows they've got plenty to look at.

[5] That's why it strikes me as funny when Cool Breeze says very seriously over the whole roar of the thing, "I don't know—when Kesey gets out I don't know if I can come around the Warehouse."

[6] "Why not?"

[7] "Well, like the cops are going to be coming around like all feisty, [8] and I'm on probation, [9] so I don't know."

[10] Well, that's good thinking there, Cool Breeze. [11] Don't rouse the bastids. [12] Lie low—like right now. [13] Right now Cool Breeze is so terrified of the law he is sitting up in plain view of thousands of already startled citizens wearing some kind of Seven Dwarfs Black Forest gnome's hat covered in feathers and fluorescent colors. [14] Kneeling in the truck, facing us, also in plain view, is a half-Ottawa Indian girl named Lois Jennings, with her head thrown back and a radiant look on her face. Also a blazing silver disk in the middle of her forehead alternately exploding with light when the sun hits it or sending off rainbows from the defraction of lines in it. [15] And, oh yeah, there's a long-barreled Colt .45 revolver in her hand, only nobody in the street can tell it's a cap pistol as she pegs away, kheew, kheew, at the erupting marshmallow faces like Debra Paget in . . . in . . .

[16]—Kesey's coming out of jail!

[17] Two more things they are looking at out there are a sign on the rear bumper reading "Custer Died for Your Sins" and, at the wheel, Lois's enamorado Stewart Brand, a thin blond guy with a blazing disk on his forehead too, and a whole necktie made of Indian beads. No shirt, however, just an Indian bead necktie on bare skin and a white butcher's coat with medals from the King of Sweden on it.

[18] Here comes a beautiful one, attaché case and all, the day-is-done resentful look [19] and the . . . shoes—how they shine!—[20] and what the hell are those beatnik ninnies—[21] and Lois plugs him in the old marshmallow [22] and he goes streaming and bouncing down the hill . . .

[23] And the truck heaves and billows, blazing silver red and Day-Glo, [24] and I doubt seriously, Cool Breeze, that there is a single cop in all of San Francisco today who does not know that this crazed vehicle is a guerrilla patrol from the dread LSD.[1]

Tone and Point of View

Wolfe's prose is syncopated, hip, and brash; the sentences are characterized by an almost obtrusive idiosyncrasy. Therefore, a question inevitably arises: Is the style annoyingly mannered, or is it appropriate and effective? My answer is that Wolfe's method serves as a proper instrument for a book on the psychedelic generation.

This passage is a good example of the whole spectrum of Wolfe's prose. In it the author takes his readers on a psychedelic joyride in the back of a pickup truck. We see everything from the author's point of view. For example, as the truck careens along, we see the city as he does:

55   [3] Out of the back of the truck the city of San Francisco is bouncing down the hill, all those endless staggers of bay windows, slums with a view, bouncing and streaming down the hill.

[1]Tom Wolfe, *The Electric Kool-Aid Acid Test* (New York: Farrar, Straus, & Giroux, 1968), pp. 1–2. Copyright © 1967 by the World Journal Tribune Corporation. Copyright © 1968 by Tom Wolfe. Reprinted with the permission of Farrar, Straus & Giroux, Inc.

This point of view never varies; we observe the world through Wolfe's eyes. If the author had for one moment let his grip on point of view relax, I think we would not buy his bizarre style, but as it is, we see with his eyes and sense with his brain and therefore are quite willing to accept his prose.

Sentences

Wolfe uses deceptively simple devices to achieve his effects. With the exception of the ellipsis at the end of T-unit 15, the T-units are complete and well within the idiom of standard written English—except for *punctuation.* For instance, T-unit 3 runs from ***Out of the back*** to ***down the hill,*** in spite of the nonstandard punctuation. The author's method in this T-unit is characteristic of the shock devices that he uses in his prose.

Cumulative Modifiers

Analysis of the cumulative modifiers in relation to the punctuation reveals that Wolfe fragments his T-units for emphasis.

56   [3] (PP)   Out of the back of the truck
                     the city of San Francisco is bouncing down the hill,
      (NC)   All those endless staggers of bay windows,
      (NC)   slums with a view,
      (VC)   bouncing and streaming down the hill.
      (NC)   One after another,
      (NC)   electric signs with neon martini glasses lit up on them, / ,
      (NC)   / the San Francisco symbol of "bar"—
      (Abs)   thousands of neon-magenta martini glasses bouncing and streaming down the hill
      (Abs)   and / , hundreds, thousands of people wheeling around to look at this freaking, crazy truck
      (PP)   /beneath them
      (RC)   we're in,
      (Abs)   their white faces erupting from their lapels like marshmallows—
      (VC)   streaming and bouncing down the hill—
      [4]   and God knows they've got plenty to look at.

Granted, number 3 is quite a T-unit! Its most unusual characteristic is the period stop before ***One after another.*** The other characteristic is, of course, the piling up of cumulative modifiers. (Of the ninety-five words in T-unit 3, eighty-six are in cumulative modifiers.) This sort of sentence is obviously unusual in modern prose.

T-unit 14 is similar:

57   Kneeling in the truck, facing us, / , is a half-Ottawa Indian girl named Lois Jennings,
      (PP)   / also in plain view
      (PP)   with her head thrown back and a radiant look on her face.
      (Abs)   Also a blazing silver disk in the middle of her forehead

(VC)	alternately exploding with light / or sending off rainbows
	. . . .
(Adv)	/ when the sun hits it

Here again is the device of breaking the T-unit with a period.

Elliptical Sentences

Another way of viewing this method of emphasis is to state that the author uses fragments or elliptical sentences for effect: ***Bouncing along*** (in T-unit 2); ***Dipping and rising and rolling on these rotten springs like a boat*** (in T-unit 3); ***Also a blazing silver disk . . . .*** (in T-unit 14); ***No shirt, however . . . ."*** (in T-unit 17).

Sentence Types

From the point of view of sentence type (simple, compound, complex, compound-complex), there is little variety in the prose; *clausal* structure is notably uncomplicated. Nor does balance play an important part in achieving the overall effect.

Repetition

One of the most obvious devices is repetition, particularly of ***bouncing*** and ***bouncing and streaming.*** Note also the beginnings of the first paragraph ***(That's good thinking there, Cool Breeze)*** and of the fourth ***(Well, that's good thinking there, Cool Breeze).***

Coordination

One further important syntactic device is Wolfe's use of simple coordination, for instance in the following:

58   [18] Here comes a beautiful one, attaché case and all, the day-is-done resentful look [19] AND the . . . shoes—how they shine!—[20] AND what the hell are those beatnik ninnies—[21] AND Lois plugs him in the old marshmallow [22] AND he goes streaming and bouncing down the hill . . .

In summary, then, Wolfe uses a few quite unextraordinary devices to give his sentence structure its decidedly mod, hip feeling.

Figurative Language

Wolfe's figurative language consists largely of similes: ***like a boat*** (T-unit 2), ***like marshmallows*** (T-unit 3). The only obvious metaphor is in T-unit 21, where the equation ***face = marshmallow*** is established:

59   [21] and Lois plugs him in the old marshmallow . . . .

Words

The diction in the piece is not extraordinary. ***Bastids, oh yeah,*** and ***pegs away*** are typical of the breeziness of the vocabulary.

Wolfe's use of unusual verbs and vivid sense-words should be mentioned. The pickup truck ***dips*** and ***rises*** and ***rolls.*** White faces ***erupt*** from lapels. Neon martini glasses ***bounce*** and ***stream*** down the hill. People ***wheel*** around to look at the crazy truck. The signs are ***neon-magenta.*** Lois wears a ***blazing silver*** disk, alternately ***exploding*** with light or sending off ***rainbows.***

Certainly Wolfe does not write clam, conventional prose. But as the passage illustrates, this chronicler of the modern scene can make a prose instrument that very aptly plays the music of the latter half of the twentieth-century counterculture.

A Passage by Norman Mailer

Here is Norman Mailer's account of the first step on the moon, from his superb account of the flight of Apollo 11, *Of a Fire on the Moon:*

60   [1] Armstrong was connected at last to his PLSS [portable life support system]. [2] He was drawing oxygen from the pack he carried on his back. [3] But the hatch door would not open. [4] The pressure would not go low enough in the Lem. [5] Down near a level of one pound per square inch, the last bit of man-created atmosphere in Eagle seemed to cling to its constituency, reluctant to enter the vacuums of the moon. [6] But they did not know if they could get the hatch door open with a vacuum on one side and even a small pressure on the other. [7] It was taking longer than they thought. [8] While it was not a large concern since there would be other means to open it—redundancies pervaded throughout—nonetheless, a concern must have intruded: [9] how intolerably comic they would appear if they came all the way and then were blocked before a door they could not crack. [10] That thought had to put one drop of perspiration on the back of the neck. [11] Besides, it must have been embarrassing to begin so late. [12] The world of television was watching, [13] and the astronauts had exhibited as much sensitivity to an audience as any bride on her way down the aisle.

[14] It was not until nine-forty at night, Houston time, that they got the hatch open at last. [15] In the heat of running almost two hours late, ensconced in the armor of a man-sized spaceship, could they still have felt an instant of awe as they looked out that open hatch at a panorama of theater: [16] the sky is black, [17] but the ground is brightly lit, bright as footlights on the floor of a dark theater. [18] A black and midnight sky, yet on the moon ground, "you could almost go out in your shirt-sleeves and get a suntan," Aldrin would say. [19] "I remember thinking, 'Gee, if I didn't know where I was, I could believe that somebody had created this environment somewhere out in the West and given us another simulation to work in.' " [20] Everywhere on the pitted flat were shadows dark as the sky above, shadows dark as mine shafts.

[21] What a struggle to push out from that congested cabin, now twice congested in their bulky-wham suits, no feeling of obstacle against their flesh, their sense of touch dead and numb, spaceman body manipulated out

into the moon like an upright piano turned by movers on the corner of the stairs.

[22] "You're lined up on the platform. [23] Put your left foot to the right a little bit. [24] Okay, that's good. [25] Roll left."

[26] Armstrong was finally on the porch. [27] Could it be with any sense of an alien atmosphere receiving the fifteen-layer encapsulations of the pack and suit on his back? [28] Slowly, he climbed down the ladder. [29] Archetypal, he must have felt, a boy descending the rungs in the wall of an abandoned well, [30] or was it Jack down the stalk? [31] And there he was on the bottom, on the footpad of the leg of the Lem, a metal plate perhaps three feet across. [32] Inches away was the soil of the moon. [33] But first he jumped up again to the lowest rung of the ladder. [34] A couple of hours later, at the end of the EVA [extravehicular activity], conceivably exhausted, the jump from the ground to the rung, three feet up, might be difficult in that stiff and heavy space suit, [35] so he tested it now. [36] "It takes," said Armstrong, "a pretty good little jump."

[37] Now, with television working, and some fraction of the world peering at the murky image of this instant, poised between the end of one history and the beginning of another, he said quietly, "I'm at the foot of the ladder. [38] The Lem footpads are only depressed in the surface about one or two inches, although the surface appears to be very fine-grained as you get close to it. [39] It's almost like a powder." [40] One of Armstrong's rare confessions of uneasiness is focused later on this moment. [41] "I don't recall any particular emotion or feeling other than a little caution, a desire to be sure it was safe to put my weight on that surface outside Eagle's footpad."

[42] Did his foot tingle in the heavy lunar overshoe? [43] "I'm going to step off the Lem now."

[44] Did something in him shudder at the touch of the new ground? [45] Or did he draw a sweet strength from the balls of his feet? [46] Nobody was necessarily going ever to know.

[47] "That's one small step for man," said Armstrong, "one giant leap for mankind." [48] He had joined the ranks of the forever quoted. [49] Patrick Henry, Henry Stanley and Admiral Dewey moved over for him.[2]

Sentences

Here are some raw data about Mailer's prose in this selection:

Type	T-units	Cumulative modifiers
simple	1	PP
complex	2	RC
simple	3	
simple	4	PP
simple	5	AC AC
complex	6	PP
simple	7	
compound-complex	8–9	Adv Adv Adv
simple	10	

Type	T-units	Cumulative modifiers
simple	11	
compound	12–13	
complex	14	PP
compound-complex	15–17	PP VC Adv PP AC
simple	18	NC PP
complex	19	Adv
simple	20	PP NC
simple	21	VC PP Abs PP Abs Abs PP VC
simple	22	
simple	23	
simple	24	
simple	25	
simple	26	
simple	27	
simple	28	
compound	29–30	Abs
simple	31	NC
simple	32	
simple	33	
compound	34–35	PP VC NC PP
simple	36	
simple	37	PP VC
complex	38	Adv Adv
simple	39	
simple	40	
simple	41	NC
simple	42	PP
simple	43	
simple	44	
simple	45	
simple	46	
simple	47	NC
simple	48	
simple	49	

Totals: simple, 33; compound, 3; complex, 5; compound-complex, 2; absolutes, 4; adjective clusters, 3; adverb clauses, 7; noun clusters, 6; prepositional phrases, 15; relative clauses, 1; verb clusters, 5. Averages: cumulative modifiers per sentence, .88; cumulative modifiers per T-unit, .77; T-units per sentence, 1.13.

Sentence Types

These data reveal some interesting aspects of Mailer's style. First, he relies heavily on simple sentences; there are three times as many of them as there are of the others combined. Apparently, then, frequent use of simple sentences does not in itself "destroy" prose or make it sound immature.

Cumulative Modifiers

Next, Mailer uses the full range of cumulative modifiers, but interestingly and strangely includes only one relative clause, perhaps the most common sort of cumulative modifier after the prepositional phrase.

The following diagrams give a sense of Mailer's use of cumulative modifiers:

61

[21] What a struggle to push out from that congested cabin,
- (VC)   now twice congested in their bulky-wham suits,
- (Abs)   no feeling of obstacle against their flesh,
- (Abs)   their sense of touch dead and numb,
- (Abs)   spaceman body manipulated out into the moon
- (PP)   like an upright piano
- (VC)   turned by movers on the corner of the stairs.

62

[15] (PP)   In the heat of running almost two hours late,
- (VC)   ensconced in the armor of a man-sized spaceship,
    could they still have felt an instant of awe
- (Adv)   as they looked out that open hatch at a panorama of theater:

[16]   the sky is black,

[17]   but the ground is brightly lit,
- (AC)   bright as footlights on the floor of a dark theater.

63

[31]   And there he was on the bottom, on the footpad of the leg of the Lem,
- (NC)   a metal plate perhaps three feet across.

64

[2]   He was drawing oxygen from the pack
- (RC)   he carried on his back.

65

[5] (AC)   Down near a level of one pound per square inch, the last bit of man-created atmosphere in Eagle seemed to cling to its constituency,
- (AC)   reluctant to enter the vacuums of the moon.

Repetition

As to other sentence devices: Mailer uses repetition effectively.

66   [16] the sky is black . . . . [18] A black and midnight sky . . . .

67   [20] Everywhere on the pitted flat were ***shadows dark*** as the sky above, ***shadows dark*** as mine shafts.

Example **67,** by the way, is one of the few hints of *balance* in the passage.

Inversion

In one instance, Mailer uses inversion to stress an idea:

68   [29] Archetypal, he must have felt . . . .

This ordering stresses the adjective **archetypal** in a way not achieved by the normal ordering **He must have felt archetypal.**

Passive

Mailer uses the passive voice only four times (once to quote Armstrong):

69   [1] Armstrong **was connected** at last to his PLSS.

Obviously, it is not important who did the connecting, but the fact that the connection was accomplished is.

70   [9] how intolerably comic they would appear if they came all the way and then **were blocked** before a door they could not crack.

71   [38] "The Lem footpads **are** only **depressed** in the surface about one or two inches . . . ."

72   [40] One of Armstrong's rare confessions of uneasiness **is focused** later on this moment.

Figurative Language

We will not examine Mailer's vocabulary, but will turn directly to his figurative language.

Similes

He uses a number of effective similes:

73   [13] and the astronauts had exhibited as much sensitivity to an audience as any bride on her way down the aisle.

The picture created by this simile is delightfully humorous, comparing the mincing, coy, self-conscious awareness that a bride might display with the astronauts' concern for a worldwide audience that was witnessing one of humanity's most heroic feats.

74   [20] Everywhere on the pitted flat were shadows dark as the sky above, shadows dark as mine shafts.

75   [21] . . . spaceman body manipulated out into the moon like an upright piano turned by movers on the corner of the stairs.

This simile gives a vivid sense of how awkward it was for the astronauts to maneuver in their bulky suits.

Rhetorical Questions

A rhetorical question is a question asked for effect, with no expectation that it will be answered; frequently it is a question to which only one answer can be made. Mailer asks four rhetorical questions:

76   [27] Could it be with any sense of an alien atmosphere receiving the fifteen-layer encapsulations of the pack and suit on his back?

77   [42] Did his foot tingle in the heavy lunar overshoe?

78   [44] Did something in him shudder at the touch of the new ground?

79   [45] Or did he draw a sweet strength from the balls of his feet?

In fact, Mailer tells us that these questions are probably unanswerable: "[46] Nobody was necessarily going ever to know."

Metaphors

The metaphors in the passage are essential and brilliant, well worth looking at. In T-unit 5 the atmosphere in the capsule is *personified* (given human attributes), as Mailer says that it **clung** to its constituency and was **reluctant** to enter the vacuum of the moon.

T-unit 10 is a simple but highly effective metaphor:

80   [10] That thought [that the hatch might not open] had to put one drop of perspiration on the back of the neck.

Mailer might have said literally **That thought must have worried them a bit,** but then he would have lost the concrete vividness of the metaphorical expression. This metaphor is also an instance of *understatement.* Indeed, the thought that the hatch might not open must have been a nightmare for the astronauts, for if it did not open, their mission would be meaningless.

In T-units 15–17 is an extended metaphor, that of the theater.

81   [15] . . . could they still have felt an instant of awe as they looked out that open hatch at a panorama of theater: [16] the sky is black, [17] but the ground is brightly lit, bright as footlights on the floor of a dark theater.

The metaphors in T-units 29–30 need no comment. The equations they present are **Armstrong = boy descending the rungs in the wall of an abandoned well** and **Armstrong = Jack of beanstalk fame.**

The metaphor with which the passage ends is rich and important. It constitutes Mailer's judgment of Armstrong's famous words:

82   [49] Patrick Henry, Henry Stanley and Admiral Dewey moved over for him.

Patrick Henry ("Give me liberty or give me death!"), Sir Henry Stanley ("Dr. Livingston, I presume?"), and Admiral George Dewey ("You may fire when you are ready, Gridley") have all been immortalized by pithy statements. Therefore, Mailer is saying that Armstrong's remark put him among these immortals. But he is also saying a good deal more than that, for he is being ironic. Consider the literal meaning of the metaphor: Armstrong added another memorable quotation to the collection—or something of the kind. But the irony of the metaphor comes from the image of such august persons as Henry, Stanley, and Dewey **moving over** to make room for one more coiner of unforgettable sentences. In the context of the whole book, this final bit of irony is crucial, for Mailer cannot quite reconcile the typical astronaut—team player, engineer, WASP—with his vision of the true hero—and yet he admires the astronauts tremendously.

Passages by Eiseley and Capote

We will now glance at brief passages from two other notable prose craftsmen: Loren Eiseley and Truman Capote.

Eiseley and Metaphor

From *The Firmament of Time,* by Loren Eiseley:

83   [1] Over a hundred years ago a Scandinavian philosopher, Soren Kierkegaard, made a profound observation about the future. [2] Kierkegaard's remark is of such great, though hidden, importance to our subject that I shall begin by quoting his words. [3] "He who fights the future," remarked the philosopher, "has a dangerous enemy. [4] The future is not, [5] it borrows its strength from the man himself, [6] and when it has tricked him out of this, then it appears outside of him as the enemy he must meet."

[7] We in the western world have rushed eagerly to embrace the future—[8] and in so doing we have provided that future with a strength it has derived from us and our endeavors. [9] Now, stunned, puzzled, and dismayed, we try to withdraw from the embrace, not of a necessary tomorrow but of that future which we have invited and of which, at last, we have grown perceptibly afraid. [10] In a sudden horror we discover that the years now rushing upon us have drained our moral resources and have taken shape out of our own impotence. [11] At this moment, if we possess even a modicum of reflective insight, we will give heed to Kierkegaard's concluding wisdom: [12] "Through the eternal," he enjoins us, "we can conquer the future."

[13] The advice is cryptic; the hour late. [14] Moreover, what have we to do with the eternal? [15] Our age, we know, is littered with the wrecks of war, of outworn philosophies, of broken faiths. [16] We profess little but the new and study only change.

[17] Three hundred years have passed since Galileo, with the telescope, opened the enormous vista of the night. [18] In those three centuries the phenomenal world, previously explored with the unaided senses, has undergone tremendous alterations in our minds. [19] A misty light so remote as to be scarcely sensed by the unaided eye has become a galaxy. [20] Under the microscope the previously unseen has become a cosmos of both beautiful and repugnant life, while the tissues of the body have been resolved into a cellular hierarchy whose constituents mysteriously produce the human personality.

[21] Similarly, the time dimension, by the use of other sensory extensions, and the close calculations made possible by our improved knowledge of the elements, has been plumbed as never before, [22] and even its dead, forgotten life has been made to yield remarkable secrets. [23] The great stage, in other words, the world stage where the Elizabethans saw us strutting and mouthing our parts, has the skeletons of dead actors under the floor boards, [24] and the dusty scenery of forgotten dramas lies abandoned in the wings. [25] The idea necessarily comes home to us then with a sudden chill: What if we are not playing on center stage? [26] What if the Great Spectacle has no terminus and no meaning? [27] What if there is no audience beyond the footlights, and the play, in spite of bold villains and posturing heroes, is a shabby repeat performance in an echoing vacuity? [28] Man is a perceptive animal. [29] He hates above all else to appear ridiculous. [30] His explorations of reality in the course of just three hundred years have so enlarged his vision and reduced his ego that his tongue sometimes fumbles for the proper lines to speak, [31] and

he plays his part uncertainly, with one dubious eye cast upon the dark beyond the stage lights. [32] He is beginning to feel alone and to hear nothing but echoes reverberating back.[3]

What we immediately notice about this passage is its metaphorical nature. And we ask ourselves, Could Eiseley have successfully presented his ideas without metaphor?

In the second paragraph (T-units 7–9), Eisely *personifies* the future—gives it human attributes—saying that we rush to embrace it, and our embrace gives it strength; thus, it becomes something sentient, a malevolent enemy with which we must contend.

Unless we pay attention, we might not notice the metaphorical nature of the third paragraph (T-units 17–19). But observe that Galileo used the telescope to **open** "the enormous vista of the night," as if the telescope rolled back the darkness and allowed humanity to peer into space. T-unit 18 is literal, quite unmetaphorical, but 19 is metaphorical because of the verb **become;** the misty light was always a galaxy, but humanity did not know that.

The last paragraph, T-units 21–32, is an extended metaphor. The equation is exactly the same one that we saw in Shakespeare: **world** = **stage** (Chapter 13, page 427). The metaphor is particularly rich, for in it Eiseley alludes to Elizabethan drama, and we are led to think of the great tragic heroes of that stage: Hamlet, King Lear, Othello. Such tragedy, of course, is impossible in our age, for as Eiseley points out in his metaphor, we doubt the meaningfulness of the drama we are acting in. What if there is nothing "out there"? What if we are playing to an empty house? We are "beginning to feel alone and to hear nothing but echoes reverberating back." Such was not the case with the Elizabethans; they had no doubt about the final meaning of the human experience.

The metaphor, then, carries a tremendous freight of meaning, but it is also imagistic in its effect. We both *hear* and *see* what the author is saying. To strip the passage of its metaphor and give the literal "sense" would be to rob these paragraphs of their overtones, their suggestiveness, their allusiveness. Modern humanity posturing and declaiming upon the world stage, with no audience to view the drama—that is a perfect statement of one attitude toward the human condition.

Capote and Images

In 1959, the Clutter family—mother, father, son, and daughter—were slaughtered by two psychopaths in Holcomb, Kansas. This mass killing, senseless and apparently inexplicable, fascinated the American author Truman Capote, and he became an expert on its circumstances. The result was the book *In Cold Blood,* his account of the murder, the apprehension, trial, and execution of the murderers, and the reasons why two young men became killers.

[3]Loren Eiseley, "How Human Is Man?" *The Firmament of Time* (New York: Atheneum, 1960). Copyright © 1960 by Loren Eiseley. Copyright © 1960 by The Trustees of the University of Pennsylvania. Reprinted by permission of Atheneum Publishers.

The book marked the beginning of a new art form, the nonfiction novel. In this genre, the writer uses the imaginative techniques of the novelist to interpret factual occurrences, such as the Clutter murders. Norman Mailer's *Of a Fire on the Moon* and *The Armies of the Night* are in this new tradition, and even the TV series *An American Family* is related.

Capote begins *In Cold Blood* by setting the scene for the killing:

84   [1] The village of Holcomb stands on the high wheat plains of western Kansas, a lonesome area that other Kansans call "out there." [2] Some seventy miles east of the Colorado border, the countryside, with its hard blue skies and desert-clear air, has an atmosphere that is rather more Far West than Middle West. [3] The local accent is barbed with a prairie twang, a ranch-hand nasalness, [4] and the men, many of them, wear narrow frontier trousers, Stetsons, and high-heeled boots with pointed toes. [5] The land is flat, [6] and the views are awesomely extensive: [7] horses, herds of cattle, a white cluster of grain elevators rising as gracefully as Greek temples are visible long before a traveler reaches them.

[8] Holcomb, too, can be seen from great distances. [9] Not that there is much to see—simply an aimless congregation of buildings divided in the center by the mainline tracks of the Santa Fe Railroad, a haphazard hamlet bounded on the south by a brown stretch of the Arkansas (pronounced "Ar-kan-sas") River, on the north by a highway, Route 50, and on the east and west by prairie lands and wheat fields. [10] After rain, or when snowfalls thaw, the streets, unnamed, unshaded, unpaved, turn from the thickest dust into the direst mud. [11] At one end of the town stands a stark old stucco structure, the roof of which supports an electric sign—*Dance*—[12] but the dancing has ceased [13] and the advertisement has been dark for several years. [14] Nearby is another building with an irrelevant sign, this one in flaking gold on a dirty window—*Holcomb Bank*. [15] The bank closed in 1933, [16] and its former counting rooms have been converted into apartments. [17] It is one of the town's two "apartment houses," the second being a ramshackle mansion known, because a good part of the local school's faculty lives there, as the Teacherage. [18] But the majority of Holcomb's homes are one-story affairs, with front porches. [4]

The effectiveness of this descriptive passage arises largely from Capote's selection of concrete details for the reader. Capote has obviously looked carefully at Holcomb, and he gives us his view. We learn about the accent of the townspeople; it is *"barbed* with a prairie twang, a ranch-hand nasalness." We see the dress of the men, the view of the town from afar. Capote does not merely tell us that the town is run down; he shows us, by portraying the buildings.

Finally

In more or less detail, we have now examined passages from five memorable prose stylists: Mark Twain, Tom Wolfe, Norman Mailer, Loren Eiseley, and Truman Capote. There are many lessons to be learned from

[4]Truman Capote, *In Cold Blood* (New York: Random House, 1965), pp. 3–4. Copyright © 1965 by Truman Capote. Reprinted by permission of Random House, Inc. Originally appeared in *The New Yorker* in slightly different form.

each of them. Most of those lessons are subtle, involving modulations of structures, tone, figures, and diction. Other lessons are obvious and even quantifiable. For instance, here are some comparative statistics concerning the five passages that we have looked at.

Average Number of T-Units per Sentence

Twain	1.4
Wolfe	1.5
Mailer	1.13
Eiseley	1.28
Capote	1.5

Average Number of Cumulative Modifiers per T-Unit

Twain	.73
Wolfe	2.8
Mailer	.77
Eiseley	1.03
Capote	1.5

Percentages of Kinds of Cumulative Modifiers Used

	Abs	AC	Adv	NC	PP	RC	VC
Twain	0	4	20	5	44	16	6
Wolfe	8	0	8	22	24	4	31
Mailer	10	7	18	18	26	2	15
Eiseley	0	3	9	6	42	21	12
Capote	7	0	7	29	18	11	25

These data, while they do not by any means tell all about the passages, nonetheless begin to create a profile of the styles that the authors use. Twain, Wolfe, and Capote use significantly more T-units per sentence than do Mailer and Eiseley, and Twain and Mailer use fewer cumulative modifiers than Eiseley and Capote, while Wolfe uses significantly more.

Twain and Eiseley use no absolutes, while the other three authors do. Wolfe and Capote use no adjective clusters, and Twain and Mailer use more adverb clauses than do the other three. Twain and Eiseley tend not to use noun clusters, but rely heavily on prepositional phrases, as they do on relative clauses. Wolfe uses twice as many verb clusters as any of the others, and Twain uses the fewest.

The first general lesson that we can learn from these data is that the authors we have looked at tend not to use long compound or compound-complex sentences, for all of them average fewer than two T-units per sentence.

The second lesson is that, on the average, each T-unit will contain a cumulative modifier: however, Wolfe uses more cumulative modifiers than the other four authors, with an average of 2.8 per T-unit, as opposed to .77 for Mailer and .73 for Twain. The effects of this piling up of cumulative modifiers are evident in Wolfe's prose, for it is heavily textured, to the point that it is idiosyncratic.

One more chart:

An Overview of the Cumulative Modifiers Used

	Twain	Wolfe	Mailer	Eiseley	Capote	Total	Percentage
Abs	0	4	4	0	2	10	4.3
AC	5	0	3	0	0	8	3.4
Adv	18	4	7	4	2	35	15.2
NC	4	10	6	1	8	29	12.6
PP	36	11	15	14	5	81	35.3
RC	15	2	1	7	3	28	12.2
VC	7	14	5	5	7	38	16.5
						229	

These data show, for one thing, that the authors that we have examined tend not to use a great many absolutes or adjective clusters. Also, they rely heavily on adverb clauses, which is not surprising because adverb clauses make such important connections as cause-and-effect: ***BECAUSE IT WAS GETTING LATE, we left the party.*** The frequent use of prepositional phrases as cumulative modifiers is also understandable, for these constructions are usually adverbials of time ***(AT NINE O'CLOCK, the chimes started),*** place ***(We saw a camel AT THE ZOO),*** and manner ***(WITH NO TROUBLE AT ALL, we waded across the creek).***

Noun clusters, verb clusters, and relative clauses are, as we have seen, closely related. For instance, the following relative clause can be reduced to a verb cluster:

85   The children ***who were playing in the street*** dodged the cars.

86   The children ***playing in the street*** dodged the cars.

Noun clusters are also reduced relative clauses:

87   The old man, ***who was a great friend of mine,*** told me tales about the early days in California.

88   The old man, ***a great friend of mine,*** told me tales about the early days in California.

The authors whose passages we have examined obviously tend to reduce a great many of their relative clauses in the manner illustrated above.

A conclusion to this chapter can serve as the conclusion to the whole book. The chapter and the book have had a double focus, dealing with both theory and practice. Theoretically, the problems of written composition are fascinating; they range from the concepts of meanings in individual words to the real miracle of an extended piece of writing that conveys the meaning of the writer to his or her audience. If a discussion lacks theoretical grounding, it will not engage the intellectually curious reader.

On the other hand, both the chapter and the whole book have the practical purpose of increasing your competence as a writer. Therefore, what you have read in these pages might be called theories for application.

Discussion and Activities

1. Discuss in detail the style in the two passages that follow. Use the analytical schema that is outlined on page 439, and make detailed notes concerning the features that you discover.

a

From *Once More to the Lake*[5]
E. B. White

[1] One afternoon while we were there at the lake a thunderstorm came up. [2] It was like the revival of an old melodrama that I had seen long ago with childish awe. [3] The second-act climax of the drama of the electrical disturbance over a lake in America had not changed in any important respect. [4] This was the big scene, still the big scene. [5] The whole thing was so familiar, the first feeling of oppression and heat and a general air around camp of not wanting to go very far away. In midafternoon (it was all the same) a curious blackening of the sky, and a lull in everything that had made life tick; and then the way the boats suddenly swung the other way at their moorings with the coming of the breeze out of the new quarter, and the premonitory rumble. Then the kettle drum, then the snare, then the bass drum and cymbals, then crackling light against the dark, and the gods grinning and licking their chops in the hills. Afterward the calm, the rain steadily rustling the calm lake, the return of light and hope and spirits, and the campers running out in joy and relief to go swimming in the rain, their bright cries perpetuating the deathless joke about how they were getting simply drenched, and the children screaming with delight at the new sensation of bathing in the rain, and the joke about getting drenched linking the generations in a strong indestructible chain. And the comedian who waded in carrying an umbrella.

[6] When the others went swimming my son said he was going in too. [7] He pulled his dripping trunks from the line where they had hung all through the shower, and wrung them out. [8] Languidly, and with no thought of going in, I watched him, his hard little body, skinny and bare, saw him wince slightly as he pulled up around his vitals the small, soggy, icy garment. [9] As he buckled the swollen belt, suddenly my groin felt the chill of death.

b

From *Shooting an Elephant*[6]
George Orwell

[1] It was perfectly clear to me what I ought to do. [2] I ought to walk up to within, say, twenty-five yards of the elephant and test his behavior. [3] If he charged, I could shoot; [4] if he took no notice of me, it would be safe to leave him until the mahout came back. [5] But also I knew that I was going to do no such thing. [6] I was a poor shot with a rifle [7] and the ground was soft mud into which one would sink at every step. [8] If the elephant charged and I missed him, I should have about as much chance as a toad under a

[5]E. B. White, "Once More to the Lake," *One Man's Meat* (New York: Harper & Row, 1944), pp. 252–53. Copyright 1941 by E. B. White. Reprinted by permission of Harper & Row Publishers, Inc.

[6]George Orwell, "Shooting an Elephant," *Shooting an Elephant and Other Essays* (New York: Harcourt Brace Jovanovich, 1950), pp. 9–10. Copyright 1945, 1946, 1949, 1950, 1973, 1974, by Sonia Brownell Orwell. Reprinted by permission of Harcourt Brace Jovanovich, Inc., Mrs. Sonia Brownell Orwell, and Secker & Warburg.

steam-roller. [9] But even then I was not thinking particularly of my own skin, only of the watchful yellow faces behind. [10] For at that moment, with the crowd watching me, I was not afraid in the ordinary sense, as I would have been if I had been alone. [11] A white man mustn't be frightened in front of "natives"; [12] and so, in general, he isn't frightened. [13] The sole thought in my mind was that if anything went wrong those two thousand Burmans would see me pursued, caught, trampled on and reduced to a grinning corpse like that Indian up the hill. [14] And if that happened it was quite probable that some of them would laugh. [15] That would never do. [16] There was only one alternative. [17] I shoved the cartridges into the magazine and lay down on the road to get a better aim.

[18] The crowd grew very still, [19] and a deep, low, happy sigh, as of people who see the theatre curtain go up at last, breathed from innumerable throats. [20] They were going to have their bit of fun after all. [21] The rifle was a beautiful German thing with cross-hair sights. [22] I did not then know that in shooting an elephant one should shoot to cut an imaginary bar running from ear-hole to ear-hole. [23] I ought, therefore, as the elephant was sideways on, to have aimed straight at his ear-hole; [24] actually I aimed several inches in front of this, thinking the brain would be further forward.

[25] When I pulled the trigger I did not hear the bang or feel the kick—[26] one never does when a shot goes home—[27] but I heard the devilish roar of glee that went up from the crowd. [28] In that instant, in too short a time, one would have thought, even for the bullet to get there, a mysterious, terrible change had come over the elephant. [29] He neither stirred nor fell, [30] but every line of his body had altered. [31] He looked suddenly stricken, shrunken, immensely old, as though the frightful impact of the bullet had paralysed him without knocking him down. [32] At last, after what seemed a long time—it might have been five seconds, I dare say—he sagged flabbily to his knees. [33] His mouth slobbered. [34] An enormous senility seemed to have settled upon him. [35] One could have imagined him thousands of years old. [36] I fired again into the same spot. [37] At the second shot he did not collapse but climbed with desperate slowness to his feet and stood weakly upright, with legs sagging and head drooping. [38] I fired a third time. [39] That was the shot that did for him. [40] You could see the agony of it jolt his whole body and knock the last remnant of strength from his legs. [41] But in falling he seemed for a moment to rise, [42] for as his hind legs collapsed beneath him he seemed to tower upward like a huge rock toppling, his trunk reaching skywards like a tree. [43] He trumpeted, for the first and only time. [44] And then down he came, his belly toward me, with a crash that seemed to shake the ground even where I lay.

2. An extremely good way to develop your own style is to imitate other writers, attempting to catch their sentence structure, diction, use of figures, tone, and rhythms. Using your own subject matter, do relatively brief imitations of Mark Twain, Norman Mailer, Loren Eiseley, Tom Wolfe, and Truman Capote.

PART THREE

A Spectrum of
Student Essays

The essays in this section were all written by people in the freshman English program at the University of Southern California, and all of them were assigned better-than-average grades. After you have read them, you will probably agree that they range in quality from competent to exceptionally fine.

As you read these essays, you should ask yourself a number of questions: How much do mechanical errors such as misspellings detract from the total effect, if at all? Do awkward or unclear sentences slow the reading down? Does the writer develop his or her point sufficiently? Is the essay well organized? Is it logical? Why do I like or dislike it?

The essays in the section are

1. "One Moment," by Joe Shum—an introspective piece of writing, almost a meditation.
2. An extremely personal autobiographical narrative by Melvin Higa.
3. "A Personal Search for Ancestors," by Mark Landstrom—a documented expository essay about genealogy as a hobby.
4. "Breeders Breed Trouble," by Wesley Mizutani—an extremely effective piece of argumentative (persuasive) writing.
5. "The Idea of Guilt Transference in *The Crucible*," by Steve Franceschi—a critical paper that was written during a fifty-minute class period.
6. "What Is Style?" by Sarah Pelham—a research or library paper.

One Moment
Joe Shum

I sat alone on the park bench overlooking the parlor, 31 Flavors, which I had just left behind, holding my tangy cherry-lime erect, clenching it firmly yet gently so as not to crush its shell-like patchwork grill. My fingers, not yet numbed by the chill, wrapped completely around the funnel, fragile as a corn chip, yet with the texture blatant, dry, rough, not unlike the feel of a peanut shell. A shimmering ball of frozen sugar crystals stuck to the base of this graham cracker-like funnel. It was a mound of fresh churned cream: some slowly oozing its way into a hollow center towards that crunchy tip; some forming bubbles, lucent red, draping the sides, obscuring the base, making the image appear uneven, jagged. Still my red-on-green, balanced on a tinge of caramel, fit snuggly in my grasp.

That was my tower—silent, magical, the symbol of a total memory, the eagerness and freshness of my youth. That was the memory, still vivid with experiences to be relived even after a decade—the shimmering ball, a frozen snowball thrown right on Kathy's cheek; the crunch, the feel from chewing iced-cold hay; the taste, glyceride, the sweet syrup seeping from papa's maple grove; the cone, an inverted pyramid, the snow castle I built Johnny. Life was a wonderland then. I had conquered my kingdom.

Those first few licks were moist, stinging-sharp. It was the same shivering, the instant burn, the cold-bitten toes I had received at seven when I challenged Freddy-boy to a barefoot sprint one frozen morning. How I yearn for that winter, the weather-torn face, chapped-dry lips, a pair of almost frost bitten ears, numbed by the snow. More delight I had on a pile of iced haymow with two or the gang and Bear, a big dog—a delight which brought me near intoxication—than I experienced in many following holidays of my life. I bit the words "NO CONE" out of the rim and swallowed that memory.

I took larger bites. For the ball, much lighter, was creamy soft now, melting, dribbling down one side of the cone. Gummy, no longer stiff, the wafer part became sogged, nearly tasteless cardboard. A milky streak of red-green, fused chocolate brown, flowed to the tip. Two drops. I curled two fingers, sticky as plastic, over, around the rim, and forced the mush down. Now there was cream till the bottom.

Then there were other years. The time I joined the Sunday cricket contest, or slept all afternoon in the treehouse, the adventures of those childhood pleasures, my companions—all my youth, it seemed, melted away. It just couldn't last. When boyhood went, much went with it. When manhood came, much came with it—much too many tasks, burdens, responsibilities. Why the need to exchange a world of delightful sensations and stirring impressions for one of duties, studies, or meditations?

I crunched the last point pensively, licked my fingers, then sloshed my tongue to savor the last bit. Just 10¢—just 10¢ more was all it took to relive my tower, to take again into my hand, to crunch once more its one final tip. But, oh, how insatiable. With lips cherry red, teeth chattering, tongue frozen, I burst into tears. "My tower, my wonderland, come back. Ice cream, ice cream." It was a silent scream.

[Untitled]
Melvin Higa

It is a fairy tale, really. It would have been no different had this one been the beggar-boy who cunningly outwitted the evil king to win the hand of the beautiful princess, the kingdom, and the happy ending. Satisfaction is simple. All one has to do is to find the pieces of the broken magic jug, to be the prince who quietly carries off the princess while the troll dozes off on the bowl of magic mushrooms you cleverly left for him, or at most, to endure the hardship of another cold winter while effortlessly turning into a beautiful swan. That my own success would come in such a fairy tale is an expectation I learned early in life.

Sometimes, very infrequently and when depressed, I suspect that the beggar-boy knew that the princess and the kingdom awaited him at the end of the story. All the while the little tugboat in the next story of the mildewed *Red Fairy Tale Book* itched to show me how easy it was to rescue the magnificent ocean liner from disaster, thereby gaining the respectful toots of the big tugboats and never again having to suffer the humiliation of being called "little." I do my best to follow the path of the beggar-boy and the little tugboat, and I have, lately, led my life down that path with enthusiastic over-confidence. The beggar-boy's path leads through a treacherous dark forest in which dwell a band of mischievous and un-sympathetic elves who find gratication in frustrating and thwarting the journeys of passing beggar-boys. I am well acquainted with the frustrations which sometimes serve to make the vision of the princess at path's end hazier and more enticing. Occasionally, if you follow this path you will see a toothy beggar-boy with hairy knuckles walking in the opposite direction. Laughing, he will catch your passing shoulder solidly with his cold hand to tell you that the princess is a false vision. He is a disguised elf, you might say, and if you shake violently enough he will let go, but the coldness of his hairy grip remains and the memory of the toothy grin obscures the secure vision at the path's end. This is the fear and the frustration that motivates me to ramble on while I rest at the side of this well-travelled pathway.

When I was younger, and love, security, and a little coddling could always be depended upon, I had different concerns. Life was simple and needed no artificial simplifications and securities of the adult world. The *Red Fairy Tale Book* was on the third shelf in the dark hallway, still out of my reach. It had been some time before I grew up above the second shelf but I was able to observe the fairy tale concepttion of success, which I eventually came to accept, even before that.

My grandfather at one time, I am told, was once a beggar boy. He found the path in his early teens and was led across the ocean to America with thousands of other eager beggar-boys like himself. His motivations are still unclear to me for motivations are never part of fairy tales. Or perhaps, at times, it seems, he needed none, since he secretely knew of the castles, the jewels, and the cow-like contentedness that waited at the end of his own story.

Like the other immigrants my grandfather worked hard in the fields, but never worked harder or suffered more than the fairy tale demanded. Money was something to be collected not out of prudence or for its future benefits but because it felt good in the palms. It kept the story line moving. It reassured him that he had not wandered off the path. His sense of certainty was hardened long before the vision came into full focus.

My grandfather was never an evil man, but a weak one. Certainty, when realized by a person of strength, is a freedom and further strengthens his goodness. Weak men like my grandfather find themselves unable to handle the power that comes with certainty and become capricious men. The power they hold causes them to stand out where their capriciousness only emphasizes their weakness.

The vision was to become a successful farmer and to this end he bought a parcel of farmland and taught himself to become an efficient farmer. Yet, he did not develop an attatchment to his land as did other farmers. There was no sense of rejuvenation when the seedlings were set into the wet spring soil and no regretful hesitation as the harrow plowed the plants under the ground after the last harvest. To have such feelings would have been to stray from the path. Everything had to be done just right or the rewards would not be granted.

And the fairy tale came true. He hit upon the idea of a plantation system for flower growing and became known as the state's "Flower King", acquired a substantial amount of money, became fat, and insulting, and lapsed into a state of contentedness. He raised ten children who among themselves fought for his favor and worshipped his riches and power as peasants do kings. To close his story the one time beggar-boy left the farm to his first son, my father, and found a home to his liking on a mountain high above his sons and daughters and the farmlands where he could look back through the path of the fairy tale.

My father, too, was a firm believer in the fairy tale. He was another beggar-boy that my grandfather intentionally produced in his own image. My father feared and worshipped his own, but before long, he had accepted as fact that no fairy tale was written for him.

As a young man my father showed a romantic kind of restlessness. He quit a promising college career and traveled through the country unconsciously looking for the starting point of the path to success or the elf who spoke in rhymes who would show him the way to the hidden pot of gold. The search was troubled and fruitless and my father turned to follow the path of my grandfather. With his father's image in mind he sought to become the state's "strawberry king". No one before had tried to grow them in a tropical climate and the idea was even more appealing and novel than flowers and made success even more promising. My father, as was his father, was confident that this was the action that would lead to the happy ending.

But there was none. The berries rotted before they ripened, worms fed off their roots, and other farmers succeeded where he failed. For twenty years he struggled. Each year was a constant defeat and a denial of the certainty he longed for. He, too, was a weak man, and was unable to counter uncertainty with deliberate action. It took years to convince him that there was no certainty and as he grew older he made plans and dreamt of goals which were more and more unattainable. The fact of his failure to find fairy tale success could never be shaken off and he found security in accepting his discontentment and final defeat.

The fairy tale path was laid before me by my father. "Will you be an engineer or a scientist?" he asked me as a child. Find that simple pathway for it is essential for the attainment of the simple and satisfying fairy tale success. I, too, might follow in my grandfather's image.

There is something appealing about this approach to life beyond its simplicity. If one trusts the approach then life is no struggle, the story carries the beggar-boy to the end. And final contentment is quite acceptable. This is the nature of the fairy tale path I am now following. At the end is th promise of a medical career. And the trick here is to be accepted into medical school. And everything must be done correctly, the application, the recommendations, the grades, and the molding of the personality. If these are carried out correctly then simplicity and security, as I and others like me believe, necessarily follow.

But the path is becoming too narrow, too confining for this one's own feet. The forest surrounding the path is dark and mysterious and has become more enticing than the princess and the castle at the end of the path. There are the mischievous elves to contend with, of course, but if the journey can be directed with a sense of deliberate action the defeat is meaningless since deliberacy itself is success. The fairy tale path is a one-dimensional line, offering little chance for a growing desire to attempt a little creativity in this beggar-boy's life.

A Personal Search for Ancestors
Mark Landstrom

Genealogy, though a science, is rarely studied. The reasons for searching out one's family history are quite few, and indeed for most people are non-motivating. The only physical gains made might be a membership into the Daughters of the American Revolution, a legal right to inherited property, or, more symbolicly, the right to a family crest or coat of arms. If one would take a poll of the various reasons for searching for ancestors, he would find the the most common inducements to do so would be to feel part of history, sentimentality and more frequently: curiosity. Europeans have been known to search for royalty in their blood while "Americans get as much kick out of finding a highwayman as a royal highness on the Ancestral Tree."[1] In my first attempt to search out my ancestors I found an interesting story. My great-great-great grandfather, through a direct paternal line, was a German army officer fighting the Danish. According to my grandfather, he was held responsible for the loss of a certain battle and would be court martialed. In order to avoid this he deserted and fled to Sweden. On top of my having an actual pride in this story, I find myself considering the possiblility that someone in my family set a precident which is being followed today.

The search for ancestors is almost always a long hard one; one can never complete his family tree. If the completed tree for merely three and one half centuries is to be found (ten generations) then 1023 direct grandparents must be located. A search to the 20th generation back would include over one million names. The most common problem for genealogists is now apparent: spelling changes in names. With so many people to locate one misspelled or legally changed name can cause havoc. Individual researchers have reported 65 variations on the surname "Merford" and 123 way of spelling "Zabriskie".[2] When one faces this problem it is a matter of trial and error and luck. "Although most genealogists are realistic, practical persons who pursue their hobby in a businesslike way, there are few who cannot tell you of some experience that has involved a compelling hunch, extrasensory perception or just plain coincidence."[3] Talking with older family members may bring out stories which have been exaggerated to get a certain effect. For example, the story of my great great great grandfather might not be anywheres near the truth. He might have been a poor foot-soldier who was left behind because he was scared to fight, but the story was injected, through the generations, to create some redeeming value. Other family scandals and smears on the family record may be played down. One genealogist found in his old family Bible the phrase: "Sylvester died suddenly today of a neck injury." This caught his curiosity so he investigated it. Some time later he found the tombstone of Sylvester and was amased to find out that the last line of the epitaph read: "He was hung for robbing banks."[4] "L. G. Pines, [a prominent English professional genealogist] finds that one out of six family trees he traces springs from an illegitimate root. On some branches there may be found a highway robber—hanging by the neck."[5]

Since most of our relatives are dead the researcher must do the walking; they will not come to him. The first clues are of course taken from the remaining relatives, but few are satisfied with the memories of others. The three sourses that promise any chance of success are the family Bible, church records and legal records. Although "letters mentioning births and funerals, diaries, even business ledgers yield many details"[6] they often will be only half complete. A letter will rarely mention a surname or the year of a date. A trip to the family church will reveal a plentitude of dates (births, deaths, baptisms, etc.) while legal records will supply property ownership, tax status, family census and locations of where the family came from and where it moved to. The grave stone is just one example of the hiden clues which can be found. Stones of dark slate were present in the 1780–1820 period; grayish-blue slate from 1800–1850; hard marble with roman letters began around 1840; granite with raised letters—1890; and sand blasting was instituted in the 1930's.[7] These dates are enough to narrow a lost date down to within a reasonable time.

Loyal genealogists get much more out of their search than names and dates. To them it is "the study of family pattern",[8] early manners, customs, and economic and social conditions. I gain a deep satisfaction everytime I uncover a new name because to me my ancestors have the right of being remembered. Genealogy will never be a course of required study because it is a hobby; something that one get's out as much as he puts in.

FOOTNOTES

[1]"Life Guide," *Life, 54* (January 18, 1963), 13.
[2]John J. Stewert, "Try Climbing Your Family Tree," *Reader's Digest,* 41 (September 1960), 104.
[3]*Ibid.,* p. 103.

[4]*Ibid.*
[5]"Want a Coat of Arms? Trace Your Family Tree," *Life,* 54 (May 3, 1963), 103.
[6]"Life Guide," *Life,* 54 (January 18, 1963), 13.
[7]Gilbert H. Doane, *Searching for Your Ancestors* (St. Paul: 1937), pp. 57–61.
[8]J[oseph] C[harles] Wo[lf], "Genealogy," *World Book Encyclopedia,* VIII (Chicago: 1956), 2902.

BIBLIOGRAPHY

Doane, Gilbert H. *Searching for Your Ancestors.* St. Paul: North Central Publishing Co., 1937.
"Life Guide," *Life,* 54 (January 18, 1963), 13.
Pine, L. G. *Your Family Tree.* London: Herbert Jenkins Ltd., 1962.
Stewert, John J. "Try Climbing Your Family Tree," *Reader's Digest,* 41 (September 1967), 103–107.
"Want a Coat of Arms? Trace Your Family Tree," *Life,* 54 (May 3, 1963), 103–108.
Wo[lf], J[oseph] C[harles]. "Genealogy," *World Book Encyclopedia.* Chicago: Field Enterprises Inc., 1956.
Wright, Norman E. and Pratt, David H. *Genealogical Research Essentials.* Salt Lake City: Bookcraft Inc., 1967.

Breeders Breed Trouble
Wesley Mizutani

The Atomic Energy Commission claims that the nuclear breeder reactors are the best source of energy for mankind. They are now in the process of developing the nuclear reactor at a 1,364 acre site in Tennessee. The AEC (Atomic Energy Commission) anticipates building several of these reactors throughout the United States. These reactors should not be built, for they will endanger the lives of all humanity.

Before presenting my arguments, it would be of advantage to the reader if I explained the basics of the nuclear reactors. There are three basic types of nuclear reactors. The type of reactors used today are the pressure water reactor (PWR) and the boiling water reactor. The third type is the breeder reactor. The boiling water reactor (BWR) and the (PWR) are quite similar. They utilize uranium 235 (which is available in limited supply on the earth) as a fuel which produces heat. The uranium is contained in long tubes or rods of an alloy. One reactor contains about 100 tons of uranium. The atom of uranium 235 splits, a process termed fission, and releases heat. As the heat from the rods is given off, pressurized water is run over them. This water vaporizes into steam. In the BWR this steam turns the generator which generates power. In the PWR, the heat from this steam is used to vaporize water in another tube. Then the vaporized water turns the generator. The steam is condensed and recycled in both processes. These two processes present a problem in that they rely on U-235 which is contained in uranium ores. Uranium ore contains about three per cent U-235 and is relatively scarce. Thus, the AEC conceived the breeder reactor. The breeder reactor utilizes more common uranium 238 as a fuel. This reactor differs from the others in that the U-238 is converted into plutonium. The plutonium undergoes fission and gives off heat. The rest of the process is the same as the BWR except the coolant used is liquid sodium. An advantage of the breeder reactor is that the remaining plutonium after fission can produce more plutonium. This means that the amount of fuel will double every ten years. Thus, the breeder reactor is more efficient than the old reactors. Then why am I against its development?

The liquid sodium in a nuclear breeder reactor serves two purposes. To transfer heat to the generator and also to cool the fuel rods. One of the dangers of the nuclear reactors is the loss of coolant. This occurs when the largest pipe containing liquid sodium snaps due to excessive pressure. The pressurized liquid sodium in these pipes is then released and no longer cools down the rods. Then the emergency backup system, known as ECCS, would flood the core (where the fuel rods are located) with coolant. If the coolant never reaches the core the temperature would immediately rise to 2700 degrees fahrenheit. After a few minutes, the temperature will be over 4000 degrees fahrenheit and the core melts. In a half an hour the radioactive plutonium will melt through the six to eight inch thick carbon steel wall encasing. In a day the molten core will break through the three and one half foot concrete and steel outer encasing. An explosion will occur when the plutonium mixes with oxygen in the air. The result will be the extinction of mankind because the plutonium is so toxic that more than .6 micrograms of it in a human is fatal. In addition, the contamination of the environment with plutonium will last for 24,000 years. In the preceeding description, to avoid confusion I neglected to mention that liquid sodium also reacts explosively in contact with air. Therefore, there will be two explosions when the concrete wall is shattered.

The AEC claims a failure in the ECCS is virtually imposible. However, in the Enrico Fermi reactor in Detroit a partial meltdown of the fuel rods occured in 1966. The Aerojet Nuclear Company, a major safety contractor, ran a series of tests on the aspects of coolant loss. It reported "essentially no emergency core coolant reached the core. The coolant ran out the break in the coolant pipe." These indicate that a failure is quite feasable.

A nuclear explosion in a reactor can be caused by a simple flaw in the construction of the reactor. In 1971, in the Ginna reactor in New York, deformed fuel rods were found. The great pressures inside the reactor, with no escape of fuels, caused this to occur. Fortunately, the flaw was found and remedied. In 1972, the Dresden 2 plant had a malfunction that damaged the core, but stopped short of disaster. Although these two reactors are BWRs they reveal how likely a disaster could occur when one is dealing with atomic power.

Another problem which involves todays reactors, as well as future breeder reactors, is where to put the radioactive waste materials. At present, they are stored in concrete vaults, but what happens when the waste materials begin to accumulate?

The most formidable argument of proponents of the breeder reactor is that it is the best way to solve our energy crisis. The proponents insist that breeders are the only plausible source of vast amounts of energy. They seem to shun solar power as impractical. However, it is a fact that if the sunlight that falls on a square mile of desert could be harnessed at forty per cent efficiency, it would be equal to the power generated by one of the big new million kilowatt nuclear power plants. Proponents of the breeder reject the proposal as being to costly, but in fact, if one examines the vast amount of money being spent on the development of the breeders (1 billion dollars) it would be astounding.

Geothermal Energy is another alternative. This is the obtaining of energy from the center of the earth. Dr. J. Hilbu Anderson, a consulting engineer, has developed a process which utilizes the natural hot springs to drive turbines.

The most promising source of energy is nuclear fusion. This process involves the combining of hydrogen isotopes to form helium. As a result, a large amount of energy is released. Fusion eliminates the problem of storing radioactive wastes for there aren't any. Helium gas is the only product. Most importantly, however, is the fact that since there aren't any radioactive elements involved in the reaction, there is no chance of a nuclear disaster. I believe that we should explore fusion before we begin building the breeder reactors.

The major question I ask you is, are we willing to sacrifice the lives of people so that we may have energy?

The Idea of Guilt Transference in The Crucible
Steve Franceschi

In reading Arthur Miller's *The Crucible,* it is essential that the reader understand the motivations of the characters. Perhaps the most important of these motivations—for it is the direct cause of the tragedy—is transference of guilt. Miller makes it quite clear that the Salem society was a natural place for guilt transfer to occur. In an extremely strict society with rigorous religious and sexual habits, any act which a person living in that society commits he must question, to be sure that he did not do anything anti-social. The guilt which Abigail and the other girls must have felt when they were found dancing in the woods—dancing was not approved by the Salemites—coupled with their rigid religious background would make them unable to admit that it was *their* fault that they had done something wrong. Instead, the girls blame supernatural forces for their dancing in the woods. To the stoic Salemites, the angelic girls must have been bewitched, for surely, they reasonably assume, these upright young women would not succumb to the devil's temptations otherwise.

The young girls, unable to admit to themselves and to the community that they did wrong, strike out at others as being witches. The girls transfer their own guilt by accusing those who will be most readily thought of as witches (Sarah Good, and Tituba) and, it is even more revealing that the girls also accuse the most devout, respected members of the community (Rebecca Nurse). By accusing the respected people the girls hope to taint them with sin—the girls' own sin. If the girls can make the most religious members of the community seem bad, the girls will appear good in comparison to the others. The Freudian nature of the guilt transference syndrome makes the accusations spiral—as the girls become more involved in accusations which they know are untrue, they feel more and more guilty—hence, they have more guilt to transfer and they accuse more people. The girls are too young and cowardly to face up to what they did, so they put one lie on top of another until the whole thing is out of control, but by then it is too late.

Other characters besides the girls are motivated by guilt transfer, but of the girls themselves, Abigail is a particularly fascinating example. A young girl, feeling the flush of womanhood, indulges her newfound sensual nature by dancing (naked?) in the woods. But the girl is still a child—she gets childish thrills from practicing witchcraft with Tituba. And this girl has also had illicit sexual relations with a married man. All three of these things which Abigail has done would make her a harlot, a witch, a hedonist in the eyes of her society. Her presence in the community would be intolerable if her true personality were known. Abigail feels the pressure and guilt which comes from her social background. She must rationalize her actions—she cannot accept what she has done. The immediate answer: she is not a bad person, she has been bewitched.

Mrs. Putnam is another example of guilt transference. Mrs. Putnam had lost seven of eight babies—they died so rapidly after birth that the reader must believe Mrs. Putnam's previous babies to have been premature or miscarriages of some sort. However, a woman in Salem society was supposed to have many babies. Mrs. Putnam could not, and she felt guilty because of her failure. Nor could she blame her husband, for, as he says, "I am one of nine sons; the Putnam seed peopled this province." (Nor could her husband blame himself for the sickly babies.) Mrs. Putnam is jealous of women like Rebecca Nurse who have many children and grandchildren. To relieve herself of her own guilt, Mrs. Putnam has to believe that witchcraft caused the deaths of her babies. She and her husband, unable to blame themselves, are quick to accuse their former midwives of sorcery. As Mrs. Putnam says, "There are wheels within wheels in this village and fires within fires."

Reverend Parris is also anxious to believe that witchcraft is afoot in the village. He cannot understand why his congregation is bewitched. Parris also must—to salve his own conscience—believe that Abigail was bewitched, for he is her guardian, and if she did anything wrong, Parris would be held partly responsible by the community. Parris' own anxiety and the fervor with which he derides all those who attempt to stop the trials and expose the true nature of Abigail are proof of his own feelings of guilt.

Miller's central theme of guilt transference is counterbalanced by John Proctor—Proctor accepts his own guilt and makes no excuses. He realizes he cannot blame others for his own mistakes and inadequacies. Obviously, Proctor is one of Miller's most admirable creations. He is not a perfect man, but he is strong, realistic man with a great deal of character. Proctor's characterization underlines the essential nature of the other characters like Abigail and Parris.

Miller's plea is to all human beings. He wants man to accept himself for what he is—man. A man has errors and shortcomings, but he is still a man if he accepts his errors and shortcomings. As Rebecca Nurse says, "There is prodigious danger in the seeking of loose spirits [to blame for our sins]. I fear, I fear it. Let us rather blame ourselves. . . ."

What Is Style?
Sarah Pelham

"Style" has many meanings, as the following usages illustrate: "He has an interesting life style." "I don't like the style of her dress." "The American style is hard work and honesty." In this paper, however, I will deal only with style as "the manner of expression in writing."

At the very least, style is nothing more than black squiggles against a white background, as in this paper, but those squiggles form patterns that convey meanings and effects to readers. For instance, I think that everyone would agree that the following sentences are different in effect:

> The baby threw down the ball that her mother picked up.
> The baby threw the ball that her mother picked up down.

The second one seems clumsier and harder to read than the first one. Now we must ask if they mean the same thing. In other words, can we separate the *what* from the *how?*

> This simple distinction between the *what* and the *how* is a thumbnail definition of style and it is one that every user of language acts on in practice. It is not, however, altogether satisfactory and it has more than once been challenged by aestheticians. Their argument is based on the claim that every form has its own particular meaning. This implies that there cannot be two ways of saying the same thing because each way says something different.[1]

If every different form—like the two example sentences—conveys a different meaning, then there is no such thing as style, just meaning.

But most people would take the common sense position that there is something called style. I think that the two example sentences say the same thing, but in different ways. Here is a simple test of the claim that *how* and *what* can be separated. Which two of the following sentences are most nearly synonymous?

> (1) My favorite flavor is strawberry.
> (2) The moon will shine brightly tonight.
> (3) The little boy gave the kitten some milk.
> (4) Kansas City is humid in August.
> (5) Some milk was given to the kitten by the little boy.

If you agree that three and five are the most nearly synonymous of these sentences, then you must conclude that they share meaning even though they differ in form.

Another way to look at the form versus meaning puzzle is the following:

> One basic meaning may be expressed in a number of different forms. But also one form may stand for more than one basic meaning. All languages have sentences which have more than one meaning. Ambiguity is a universal property of language. Ambiguity, schematically described here,

and synonymy,

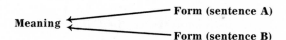

> are two universal characteristics of language that show meaning to be related to form in an indirect way.[2]

We will take it for granted, then, that there is a *how* as well as *what,* but this leads us to a question that seems easy to answer, but is really quite difficult: "What is the *how?*" In other words, how is "style" defined?

Nils Erik Enkvist explains the different kinds of definitions that are possible for the word "style." Some definitions relate style to the writer; in this view, style is the expression of the writer's personality. Others are more objective, pointing to features of the text itself, such as word choice, sentence structure, and so on. Finally, some definitions rely upon the impressions of the reader.[3]

I would like to discuss each of these views of style.

If style is the expression of the author's personality, then we will be led to say that Jones's style is outgoing and happy, Smith's style is morose and introverted; Black's style is moral, and White's style is immoral. Most intelligent people would think that statements like these are strange.

If style is the impression that the reader gets, then we must conclude that it is almost impossible to discuss style because different readers at different times get different impressions. One experiment was performed which proved that a group of readers will get different impressions about style. Forty-four English teachers read a passage from *In Cold Blood,* by Truman Capote, and here are some of the ways that they described the style: plain, formal, matter-of-fact, pedestrian, literary, moving, ominous, sensitive. And this is only a sample of 222 different adjectives that these English teachers used.[4]

So it appears that defining "style" as the author's expression of his personality or as the impression that the reader gets are not very useful. "Most talk about style, by professional critics as well as amateurs, leaves much to be desired: it is often subjective, impressionistic, unhelpful, sometimes misleading."[5]

We are left with style as features of the text, and what I mean is words and how they get used in sentences. We can point to them. We can classify them. We can talk about sentence structure. But when we have done all of this, what do we have left? One critic has made a statement that bears directly on this question:

> Now the number of five-syllable words in a novel is a partial description of the novel; it is not a description of the experience of the novel, and it does not prove or form partial proof of the value or meaning of the novel. It is a fact, but the critical act rests less upon fact than upon the organization of impression and apprehension. Criticism is a description more of a state of consciousness of the critic than a description of the object being described: words may "objectively" describe that state of consciousness; numerical descriptions of the phenomenon do not.[6]

In other words, once we have "pointed out" and counted all of the features of the text, what are we left with? The answer seems to be: Nothing! In other words, all of the data in the world will not explain the experience we go through when we read.

The title of this paper is a question: What Is Style? When a paper begins by asking a question, the reader expects an answer. So far, the question has not been answered.

We are left with style as a physical phenomenon. It is not our experience of reading, for by pointing to what we see on the page we cannot explain our reaction. ("I am sad because the poem contained so many prepositions.") We cannot point to the page to prove that we know the author. ("I am sad because the author must be sad because he told such a sad story.") We are really left up in the air.

We can get down to the ground by saying that style has nothing to do with effect. If we say that style is the quantifiable aspects of a piece of writing, then we can point and count. " . . . we can . . . assert that a work of literature is usefully considered as a verbal structure, whatever else it may be. This verbal structure may be described."[7]

Take for example the sentence "Pass the peas, please." If this sentence were uttered at the dinner table, the result would be the passing of peas, from someone to someone. If the line occurred in a poem, the result probably would be an awareness of the alliteration (the repetition of the *p* sound) and of the rhyme, *please* and *peas*.[8] In other words, depending on the context, the effect would vary, but the sentence would remain the same, and it could be described in the same terms, regardless of whether it was a request at the dinner table or a line spoken during the reading of a poem.

The study of style is a branch of information theory.

> To begin with, in information theory . . . the meaning of a message is inconsequential. A message is simply an arrangment of symbols which differs from every other possible arrangement. Thus a code of maximal efficiency would contain the number of messages which represented the largest possible variety of arrangements of its constituent symbols. Assume a set of two symbols (A,B) arranged in groups of three. The number of possible messages in this code would be eight ($2\times2\times2$): AAA, AAB, ABA, ABB, BAA, BAB, BBA, BBB. It is immaterial whether a message represents a numeral, a name, a word, a phrase, a sentence, or a paragraph. The potential message content of the code is eight.[9]

Style is nothing more than information and code. Information is not meaning. Code is structure. In other words, the structured information DOT DOT DOT DASH can be translated into another code, the alphabet, in which it means V. Beethoven's Fifth Symphony begins with four notes, and during the Second World War, these were interpreted as DOT DOT DOT DASH, standing for V, which stood for VICTORY. Whether DOT DOT DOT DASH "means" only DOT DOT DOT DASH or V or VICTORY is beside the point of its style. It is the same phenomenon in any case. It can be described as THREE DOTS followed by ONE DASH.

The theories of style that I have surveyed come down to this point. Enkvist wonders whether we can separate style from meaning in *It is pouring* and *It is raining cats and dogs.*[10] If style is information, then such a separation can be made, for though the sentences might mean roughly the same, the information that they convey through their code is different. We can conclude with Enkvist that "Deciding whether they mean more or less the same is hardly a satisfactory basic operation in investigations of style."[11]

FOOTNOTES

[1]Louis T. Milic, *Stylists on Style* (New York: Charles Scribner's Sons, 1969), pp. 1–2.
[2]Roderick A. Jacobs and Peter S. Rosenbaum, *Transformations, Style, and Meaning* (Waltham, Mass.: Xerox College Publishing, 1971), pp. 3–4.
[3]Nils Erik Enkvist and others, *Linguistics and Style* (London: Oxford University Press, 1964), pp. 10–11.
[4]Virginia Tufte, *Grammar as Style* (New York: Holt, Rinehart and Winston, Inc., 1971), pp. 2–3.
[5]*Ibid.,* p. 2.
[6]A. C. Purves, "Impressionism, Statistics, and the Experience of Literature," *Style,* 5 (Spring 1971), 176–168.
[7]Roger Fowler, *The Language of Literature* (New York: Barnes & Noble, Inc., 1971), p. 101.
[8]John T. Grinder and Suzette Haden Elgin, *Guide to Transformational Grammar* (New York: Holt, Rinehart and Winston, 1971), p. 101.
[9]Milic, p. 3.
[10]Enkvist, p. 20.
[11]*Ibid.*

LITERATURE CITED

Enkvist, Nils Erik and others. *Linguistics and Style.* London: Oxford University Press, 1964.
Fowler, Roger. *The Language of Literature.* New York: Barnes & Noble, Inc., 1971.
Grinder, John T. and Suzette Haden Elgin. *Guide to Transformational Grammar.* New York: Holt, Rinehart and Winston, 1971.
Jacobs, Roderick A. and Peter S. Rosenbaum. *Transformations, Style, and Meaning.* Waltham, Mass.: Xerox College Publishing, 1971.
Milic, Louis T. *Stylists on Style.* New York: Charles Scribner's Sons, 1969.
Purves, A. C. "Impressionism, Statistics, and the Experience of Literature." *Style,* 5 (Spring 1971), 164–169.
Tufte, Virginia. *Grammar as Style.* New York: Holt, Rinehart and Winston, Inc., 1971.

PART FOUR
Reference Guide

The Reference Guide provides discussions of matters that are not dealt with directly in the body of the text. The guide should be used in conjunction with the index to the book, for topics that are dealt with in detail in the text are not repeated in the guide.

The entries in the guide are intended to answer your questions about such matters as grammar, usage, and punctuation, but the entries also frequently go beyond merely providing information and encourage you to speculate about the nature of language. The general aim is to be as informative as possible, but always to convey the sense that almost nothing concerning language and its use is cut-and-dried.

In the guide, as in the text, an asterisk (*) means that a word, phrase, or sentence is a violation of the principle being explained. For instance, in standard English the second person present tense form of *be* is *are.* Therefore, **You is a student* violates that "rule" and is preceded by an asterisk. In some dialects, however, the sentence would be perfectly acceptable, and if the discussion concerned one of those dialects, the sentence would not be preceded by an asterisk.

Here is an alphabetical list of the entries in the Reference Guide:

Adjectives	Dash	Parentheses
Adverbs	Demonstratives	Plagiarism
Agreement	Diction	Prepositions
Ambiguity	Double Negative	Pronouns
Antecedent	Edited Standard English	Prosody
Apostrophe	Fragmentary Sentences	Quotation Marks
Auxiliary	Gender	Reference
Brackets	Gerunds	Relatives
Capitalization	Hyphen	Semicolon
Case	Interjections	Shifted Constructions
Clauses	Italics	Spelling
Colon	Malapropism	Split Infinitive
Comma	Mood	Tense
Comma Fault	Nominals	Verbs
Conjunctions	Nouns	Voice
Dangling Modifiers	Parallelism	Wordiness

Adjectives

Adjectives are descriptive words like **beautiful, nasty, intelligent, good, bad**—all of which have some common characteristics. They all modify substantives. They can all be compared, as the following list illustrates:

Positive degree	*Comparative degree*	*Superlative degree*
beautiful	more beautiful	most beautiful
nasty	nastier	nastiest
intelligent	more intelligent	most intelligent
good	better	best
bad	worse	worst

The comparison is brought about through the addition of intensifiers (**more beautiful, most beautiful**), through the addition of suffixes to the word (**nastier, nastiest**), or through morphological changes (**good, better, best; bad, worse, worst**).

Some adjectives have suffixes that are typical of their class: **pretty, nasty, gushy, flowery; beautiful, thoughtful, painful; sensible, remarkable, chewable; warmish, pinkish, longish; retentive, pensive, expensive.**

As the following sentences illustrate, adjectives typically can appear in three structural slots in a sentence:

Attributive
> The **pretty** girl was a cheerleader.
> Informing David was a **painful** duty.
> Flunking an exam is **bad** karma.

Appositive
> **Gloomy** and **overcast**, the day depressed me.
> The ocean surged, **mighty** in its power.
> The boat, **graceful** and **trim**, cut through the waves.

Predicate
> The meal was **glorious**.
> The story became **funnier** as it developed
> Something smells **fishy** to me.

In the attributive position, the adjective stands between the determiner and the noun that it modifies:

Determiner	*Adjective*	*Noun*
the	funny	shows
several of the	funny	shows
several of just the	funny	shows
several of just the first	funny	shows
several of just the first ten	funny	shows

In the appositive position—as the examples illustrate—the adjective may stand before the determiner and noun (**TRAGIC, the death of Ivan Ilyitch**) or in various slots after the noun.

A predicate adjective is the main word in the predicate of a sentence, and it always follows a linking verb (**IS costly; BECOMES difficult; SEEMS strange; TASTES good; SMELLS sweet**).

Such is an outline of the most obvious characteristics of adjectives. But there are other interesting things to say about this part of speech, concepts that, while not essential to the writer, are worth noting.

Verbs and adjectives are, strangely enough, much alike. (In fact, linguists claim that they are identical in the deep structure—the basic meaning.) For one thing, adjectives, like verbs, can be either transitive or intransitive; that is, adjectives can take objects. Here is a sentence containing a verb with an infinitive as its object:

> Herman **wants TO DRIVE A TRACTOR.**

And here is a sentence with an adjective that takes the same object as the verb in the preceding:

> Herman thinks it is **easy TO DRIVE A TRACTOR.**

Other examples:

> Norma **likes TO KNIT.**
> Norma is **able TO KNIT.**
> Jeff **hates TO WASH DISHES.**
> Jeff seems **unwilling TO WASH DISHES.**

Furthermore, some verbs have *oblique objects;* that is to say, a preposition intervenes between the verb and its object, as in the following:

> Tony always **thinks OF** football.

And adjectives may occur in similar constructions:

> Tony is **fond OF** football.

All these phrases mean the same, or very nearly the same:

> to die
> to become dead
> to become not alive

If we want to capture the meaning of all three, then we must conclude that the most general of the three most nearly approximates the deep structure. Therefore, we must conclude that **to become not alive** underlies **to become dead** and that **to become dead** underlies **to die.** Another way of putting this is to say that the best definition of **to die** and **to become dead** is **to become not alive.** The adjectivals **not alive** and **dead** seem to underlie the verbal **to die.**

The same principle seems to hold with other verbs, such as **to kill** and **to heat.**

> Brutus killed Caesar.
> Brutus caused Caesar to die.
> Brutus caused Caesar to become **dead.**
> Brutus caused Caesar to become **not alive.**
>
> Sandy heats the soup.
> Sandy causes the soup to become **hot.**
>
> The soup heats.
> The soup becomes **hot.**

These interesting semantic games indicate that grammar entails more than meets the eye. The following example contains another hint about adjectives:

> The soprano was magnificent as Isolde. The soprano was *fat.*
> The soprano—the soprano was *fat*—was magnificent as Isolde.
> The soprano—who was *fat*—was magnificent as Isolde.
> The soprano—*fat*—was magnificent as Isolde.
> The *fat* soprano was magnificent as Isolde.

Adjectives do not necessarily make for vividness in writing; in fact, they can easily be overused. Compare the following:

> a *big* car/a limousine, a *good* person/a saint, a *fancy* house/a mansion

The exactly right noun often is better than a vaguer noun modified by an adjective.

See also *Clauses, Reference, Relatives, Verbs.*

Adverbs

An adverb is a word or phrase that modifies a verb, an adjective, or another adverb. Paradoxically, the grammar of adverbs is extremely complex—even though they are extremely simple to use. After all, any five-year-old can plug an adverb into almost any sentence: *Jimmy ate dinner/Jimmy ate dinner QUICKLY, Sally complained/Sally complained SADLY.* However, linguists have not yet developed an adequate account of how adverbs are generated—and that does indeed seem strange, even though it is true.

Adverbs have certain syntactic, morphological, and semantic characteristics.

Syntactically, *most* adverbs are movable modifiers:

> Henrietta *quickly* typed the manuscript.
> *Quickly* Henrietta typed the manuscript.
> Henrietta typed the manuscript *quickly.*

However, some adverbs in some sentences are not movable:

> Chris ran *fast.*
> *Chris *fast* ran.
> **Fast* Chris ran.

Morphologically, adverbs are like adjectives in that they can be compared:

Positive degree	Comparative degree	Superlative degree
fast	faster	fastest
quickly	more quickly	most quickly
well	better (more well)	best (most well)

Also, a great many adverbs have the characteristic *-ly* suffix: *quickly, sadly, hurriedly, badly, quietly, noisily.* Of course, some adjectives also take the

-ly suffix: **George was a sick*ly* boy.** But notice the difference between adverbs that end in *-ly* and adjectives with the same ending. We can say,

> George was a sick*ly* boy.
> George was a sick*lier* boy than Bill.
> George was the sick*liest* boy I knew.

In other words, the adjective can take the comparative and superlative suffixes. But note the adverb:

> George ran quick*ly.*
> *George ran quick*lier* than Jim.
> *George ran quick*liest* of anyone in the class.

The two ungrammatical sentences must be changed to

> George ran *more* quick*ly* than Jim.
> George ran *most* quick*ly* of anyone in the class.

Semantically, adverbs can be classified within a fairly narrow range. The following is an incomplete but representative spectrum of the kinds of meanings that adverbs carry:

> *Time*
>   **In the morning,** we drink tea.
>   The professor arrived **early.**
> *Place*
>   Sissy was going **to London.**
>   **In Los Angeles,** smog is a considerable problem.
> *Manner*
>   Jay heaved at the rock **with all his might.**
>   Bob mowed the lawn **quickly.**
> *Frequency*
>   **Every night,** Tommy says his prayers.
>   Jean drinks wine **with each meal.**

The examples so far have indicated that adverbs can be either single words or phrases. But, in fact, traditional grammar places more sorts of things under the classification "adverb" than logical analysis would allow. For instance, traditional grammar would classify the italicized words in the following sentences as adverbs:

> Poor Mike was **very** sick.
> That's a **pretty** dirty thing to do.
> The machine functioned **quite** efficiently.

In the first two examples, **very** and **pretty** modify the adjectives **sick** and **dirty.** In the third example, **quite** modifies the adverb **efficiently.** Notice first that they are not movable *(*Poor Mike was sick VERY, *PRETTY that's a dirty thing to do, *QUITE the machine functioned efficiently);* second that they cannot be compared *(*VERIER sick, *a PRETTIEST dirty thing, QUITER efficiently);* and third that they can be classified in a relatively short list of words like them (**AWFULLY ugly, FAIRLY rich, TERRIBLY poor,** and so on). Modern grammarians call such words *intensifiers,* not adverbs.

One anomalous and interesting adverbial is the word **home** used in certain constructions, such as **I'm going HOME.** One way to look at it is to say that it is merely an adverb of destination with the usual preposition omitted: **I'm going TO the movies, Grace is going TO bed.**

Words like **however, moreover,** and **thus** are frequently called *transitional adverbs.* The following examples will illustrate how they function:

Roy wanted to play; **however,** his mother wouldn't let him, for it was dark.
his mother, **however,** wouldn't let him, for it was dark.
his mother wouldn't let him, **however,** for it was dark.

The transitional adverb is movable within its own clause. Note the punctuation—a semicolon between the two clauses. The transitional adverb is not a conjunction; therefore, standard usage demands the semicolon, which is a symbolic conjunction.

Many vacuous disputes arise over the usage of adverbs. For instance, many speakers of standard would object to **The painter did the job GOOD,** for, they would contend, **good** is an adjective, not an adverb; therefore, the sentence should be **The painter did the job WELL.** This kind of argument misses the whole point about dialect and levels of usage. **Good** can be an adverb just as certainly as **well** can—in fact, it *is* one in **do the job GOOD.** And in many instances, that use of **good** is perfectly acceptable. However, speakers of standard English are likely to react against the use of **good** as an adverb, not because its use blocks meaning, but because language norms are deep-seated (and basically irrational) parts of cultures. Thus, speakers of power dialects, such as American standard, tend to look down on usages that are not a usual part of their language.

Some adverbs seem to be in a state of transition. For instance, both **drive SLOW** and **drive SLOWLY** are perfectly acceptable, as are **dive DEEP** and **dive DEEPLY.**

With regard to the nature of adverbs in the deep structure of sentences, is it possible that in the deep structure (the meaning) of sentences all adverbs are prepositional phrases? The following examples illustrate what I mean:

Surface structure	*Deep structure*
Go **home.**	Go **to some place that is home.**
Turn **left.**	Turn **in some direction that is left.**
Work **fast.**	Work **in some manner that is fast.**
Come **every day.**	Come **with a frequency that is every day.**

At least that seems like a productive line of reasoning to me. (Of course, as we have seen, many adverbs are prepositional phrases in the *surface* structure. **Go TO THE STORE, Turn TO THE LEFT, Work WITH SPEED, Come ON EACH TUESDAY**).

See also *Clauses, Split Infinitive.*

Agreement

Agreement has to do with the forms that verbs and pronouns take in context. The rules for agreement are numerous and a bit confusing.

Therefore, rather than begin by enumerating a list of rules, we will concentrate on the principles underlying agreement.

In general, verb agreement concerns using singular verbs with singular subjects, and plural verbs with plural subjects:

> **Boys LIKE** girls. (***Boys LIKES** girls.)
> **This girl LIKES** that boy. (***This girl LIKE** that boy.)

Pronoun agreement concerns the influence of antecedents upon the forms that pronouns must take. For instance, a singular antecedent demands a singular pronoun:

> **The little girl** chose the toy that **SHE** liked.

If all instances of agreement were as simple as the ones in these examples, there would be no problem, but complications do occur, as we will see.

The rules concerning agreement are not the same in all dialects. For instance, in dialect X, **is** might well be a universal form: **I is, you is, he is, we is, they is.** In most dialects, however, the present tense of **be** is *conjugated* as follows: **I am, you are, he is, we are, they are.** We all know that much. But, of course, in effect there is only one *written* dialect, Edited Standard English (see that entry), and in ESE the rules for agreement are quite rigid. As we discuss agreement, we will be talking only about ESE.

Agreement can be either *formal* or *notional.* For instance, the noun **man** is singular in form (the plural is **men**), and the verb **sleeps** is also singular in form (the plural is **sleep**); therefore, in the sentence **The man sleeps,** the verb agrees with its subject formally. The word **all** has no plural form, the normal sign of the plural in English being the suffix **-s;** but the sentence **All are here,** with the verb **be** taking the plural form **are,** is perfectly acceptable, because **all** is a notional plural (it has a plural meaning), and therefore the verb agrees with it notionally, if not formally. If you keep this idea of notional and formal agreement in mind, you will be able to solve many of your agreement problems.

Take a compound subject like **Dick and Jane;** it would demand a plural verb: **Dick and Jane CLIMB the hill** (***Dick and Jane CLIMBS the hill).** But **ham and eggs** can be either singular or plural, depending on whether *it* is regarded as one dish or *they* are regarded as two separate items. Thus, both of these are correct: **Ham and eggs IS good for breakfast, Ham and eggs ARE good for breakfast.** Indeed, sometimes what appears to be a compound subject demands a singular verb: **The Stars and Stripes FLIES over the White House,** not ***The Stars and Stripes FLY over the White House.**

In ESE, however, one encounters some strange problems. For instance, consider the following sentence:

> Neither **my brothers** nor **my father IS** home.

Since **neither my brothers nor my father** is a compound subject, one would think that the verb would be plural, particularly since **brothers** is plural. Not so. In ESE, the verb takes the number of the nearest noun when the subjects are joined by alternative conjunctions **(neither . . . nor, either . . . or).**

There are other such hairsplitting points concerning verb agreement, and you can look them up in a good grammar of English. (The easiest procedure in really doubtful cases is to check with your instructor.) The important point to remember is that *the verb must agree with its subject.* Don't be thrown off by sentence elements that come between subject and verb. For instance, each of the following sentences contains a singular subject, and hence the verb is singular:

> *The conduct IS* being investigated.
> *The conduct* of students when they are on other campuses *IS* being investigated.

Pronoun agreement in ESE causes problems only in a few instances. The formal rule states that pronouns must agree with their antecedents in person, gender, and number. So a third person antecedent takes a third person pronoun: *The boys played hockey; THEY enjoyed the game.* A feminine antecedent takes a feminine pronoun: *The woman knitted a sweater; SHE was very skillful.* A plural antecedent takes a plural pronoun: *Bob and I talked while WE fished.* Easy enough.

The stumbling blocks come when notional plurals demand singular pronouns. Look at the following sentence, for instance:

> The mother gave *each child* a cookie, so *THEY* all had *THEIRS.*

The noun phrase *each child* is a formal singular (the plural of *child* is *children*) but a notional plural, meaning "all the children." ESE would probably demand

> The mother gave *each child* a cookie, so *EACH* had *HIS.*

But this is not really a big point, is it? One wonders why some people would make a fuss over a sentence such as

> *Every worker* was given a bonus, and *THEY* were all happy.

Even though the pronoun *they,* a plural, does not agree with its singular antecedent *every worker,* the meaning of the sentence is perfectly clear. It is, however, a fact of life that many people who use the power dialects do indeed make a fuss over such minor points. Therefore, errors in agreement sometimes, for some audiences, ruin the effect of a piece of writing.

Verb and pronoun agreement is not important in itself; it is important because of the value that many readers assign to it.

See also *Antecedent, Case, Demonstratives, Gender, Pronouns, Reference, Relatives, Verbs.*

Ambiguity

An ambiguous statement is one from which more than one meaning can be derived. To express this idea in terms of modern linguistic theory: an ambiguous sentence has more than one deep structure. For instance, consider the following:

> Flying airplanes can be dangerous.

Out of context, this sentence definitely has at least two meanings (or deep structures), which can be represented as follows:

Airplanes that are flying can be dangerous (but those on the ground are not).
It can be dangerous to fly airplanes.

Here is the propositional nature of the two deep structures:

Airplanes [airplanes are flying] can be dangerous.
([Someone flies airplanes] can be dangerous.)

Ambiguity can spring from at least three sources: the word, the structure,
and the context.

Here is an example of ambiguity caused by one word:

The old man sat by the bank.

Does **bank** here mean "the edge of a body of water" or "an institution that
deals with money"?

Here is an example of ambiguity caused by structure:

The lamb was too hot to eat.

Does the sentence mean that the roast lamb had just come out of the oven
or that the woolly little lamb was sweltering in August? Propositionally:

(The lamb was too hot [for someone to eat the lamb].)
(The lamb was too hot [for the lamb to eat something].)

Context would clear up the ambiguity of both examples. If one encountered **The old man sat by the bank** and **The lamb was too hot to eat** in
context, undoubtedly there would be no ambiguity. For instance, if the
context tells us that the old man is sitting somewhere on Wall Street, it will
never occur to us that he is sitting by the bank of a stream.

Is ambiguity good or bad? The answer should be obvious. It all depends
on purpose. Ambiguity can serve a valid function, can be a device to show
the reader that some situations in life cannot be exactly defined. Many
great works of literature have survived at least partly because of their
ambiguity: *Hamlet, Heart of Darkness, Paradise Lost.* Generally, though,
ambiguity results from carelessness. For instance:

Don said that the earth is flat. That interested me a great deal.

What interested me? Was I interested in the statement itself, or that Don
made it? I might well have been totally uninterested in the statement, but
fascinated that Don would make it. This kind of ambiguity serves no
purpose but to confuse the reader. The problem here is one of *pronoun
reference:* what exactly does **that** refer to?

What seems clear and straightforward to the writer may be ambiguous to
the reader. So once again we are back to the concept of audience. If you
always remember that you are writing for someone, you will be able to
eliminate careless ambiguities.

See also *Antecedent, Reference.*

Antecedent

Pronouns—*this, that, she, they,* and so on—are words that point either
backward toward something that preceded them or forward toward some-

thing that follows them. What pronouns point to are called *antecedents* (even though the etymology of **antecedent** indicates only something that comes before). This principle is made clear through examples. In the following sentences, antecedents are underlined and pronouns are capitalized:

> <u>The little girl</u> **THAT** knocked on my door asked for a stick of gum. **SHE** lives down the street.
> **THIS** is what we need: <u>more tolerance</u>.
> <u>More tolerance</u>—**THAT** is what we need.

Obviously the pronoun gains its semantic content, its "meaning," from its antecedent.

It is commonly said that the antecedent can be substituted for the pronoun in a sentence, thus: *I like <u>cigars</u>; THEY calm my nerves/I like <u>cigars</u>; cigars calm my nerves.* Enter an interesting paradox (called the Bach-Peters Paradox). Look at the following sentence:

> **The man who was mixing IT** fell into **the cement HE was making.**

In other words, the antecedent of **IT** is **the cement HE was making,** and the antecedent of **HE** is **the man who was mixing IT.** Notice what happens if we try to substitute the antecedents for the pronouns in this sentence (remember: **IT** = **the cement HE was making,** and **HE** = **the man who was mixing IT**):

> The man who was mixing the cement the man who was mixing the cement the man who was mixing the cement. . . .

In other words, if in this sentence you try to substitute the complete antecedent for the pronoun, you catch yourself in what computer programers call a "tight loop" and merely perform the same operation over and over again for all eternity.

In regard to antecedents, two common problems arise—the first having to do with *reference* and the second, *agreement.*

Since a pronoun takes its semantic content from an antecedent, the reader should not have to grope, even momentarily, to find the antecedent. Look at the following sentence:

> Boys like adventure stories because they are lively.

The pronoun, of course, is **they.** But what is the antecedent? It might be either **boys** or **adventure stories.**

In formal usage, pronouns must agree with their antecedents. Therefore, a sentence such as the following is questionable:

> Will **everyone** please take off **THEIR** hat.

Since **everyone** is singular and **their** is plural, the two do not agree in number. This sentence also illustrates that *possessive adjectives* (**THEIR shoes, HER gloves, YOUR trousers,** and so on) also have antecedents.

See also *Agreement, Ambiguity, Case, Clauses, Demonstratives, Gender, Pronouns, Reference, Relatives.*

Apostrophe

Most English nouns have only four forms: singular, genitive singular, plural, and genitive plural. This is illustrated by the following:

Singular:	**Smith** is a tenor.
Genitive singular:	**Smith's** voice is exceptionally fine.
Plural:	The **Smiths** are all fine singers.
Genitive plural:	The **Smiths'** voices are all exceptionally fine.

In other words, the apostrophe is used to mark the genitive case of nouns.

If a singular noun ends in *s,* its genitive form may be either a mere apostrophe or an apostrophe plus an *s:*

Ross' typewriter
Ross's typewriter

The latter is probably the more common.

In compound names, the genitive sign is attached only to the last one:

Keith and **Lil's** house
Merrill, Lynch, Pierce, Fenner, and **Smith's** quotation

Some dialects of English have what might be called the *unmarked genitive.* Thus, in at least one dialect, **Mary house** is the equivalent of **Mary's house.** It is a natural tendency for speakers of a dialect that has the unmarked genitive to write exactly what they would say—that is, to delete the genitive marker in their writing. And when they attempt to correct this deviation from Edited Standard English, they tend not to use the apostrophe before the *s,* so that **Mary house** becomes **Marys house.** Notice that both **Mary house** and **Marys house** convey exactly the same meaning as **Mary's house.** Therefore, failure to include the genitive marker in either writing or speaking does not affect meaning. Including the genitive marker *s* without the apostrophe is also insignificant in terms of meaning. However, Edited Standard English (see that entry) is fairly rigid in its requirements concerning punctuation. Another way to put this is to say that those who write Edited Standard English—and they are the people who have economic and social power—expect all writers to observe the niceties of that written dialect. Therefore, the apostrophe, which is insignificant so far as meaning is concerned, takes on great significance in the context of the written language that will be accepted by the power elite.

The apostrophe has other conventional uses. It shows deletions, as in

the class of **'74**
the Spirit of **'76**

It is used to indicate the plurals of letters and figures:

George is in his **40's**
Barbara's s**'s** look like e**'s.**

It is also used in contractions:

cannot—**can't**
should not—**shouldn't**

Auxiliary

Auxiliary verbs are usually defined as "helping verbs."

> The sun *has* set. The children *have* gone indoors. The family *had* eaten. The evening *may/might* be boring. Time *can/could* hang heavy. Herbie *shall/ should* study. Mary *will/would* knit. Father *must* read.

These are the auxiliary verbs. But this brief list does not tell the whole story of the auxiliary in English—and the story is worth telling, for it provides a fascinating exercise in thinking about the English language. If you follow closely, you will learn something about the language and will, possibly, be entertained in the process.

It turns out that every sentence has an auxiliary, though not necessarily an auxiliary verb, for we will define "auxiliary" (Aux) in the following way:

Aux = Tense (Modal) (Aspect)

That is, Aux is made up of Tense, Modal, and Aspect. (Modal and Aspect will be explained in a minute.) The parentheses around *Modal* and *Aspect* mean that a given sentence may or may not have one or both. Therfore, in a given sentence, Aux will equal at least Tense, and may include *either* Modal *or* Aspect *or* both. Though it may at first seem strange, we will say that Tense = *either* Present *or* Past—and *only* those two. We will symbolize this in the following way:

$$\text{Tense} \;=\; \begin{Bmatrix} \text{Present} \\ \text{Past} \end{Bmatrix}$$

That is, in any given sentence, you will find either Present or Past Tense.

Furthermore, in any given sentence, you may find one, but only one, of the so-called modal auxiliaries:

Modal = *can, may, shall, will, must*

Moreover (and this gets a bit tricky), you may find *either* a form of *Have* + a Past Participle (Past P) *or* a form of *Be* + a Present Participle (*-ing,* since all Present Participles end in *-ing*) *or* both. Thus:

Aspect = (*Have* + Past P) (*Be* + *-ing*)

Now let's put this list of rules together:

Aux = Tense (Modal) (Aspect)

> (Auxiliary consists of at least Tense, and may contain Modal and Aspect.)

$$\text{Tense} = \begin{Bmatrix} \text{Present} \\ \text{Past} \end{Bmatrix}$$

> (Tense consists of either Present or Past.)

Modal = *can, may, shall, will, must*

Aspect = (*Have* + Past P) (*Be* + *-ing*)

> (Aspect consists of a form of *Have* + a Past Participle and *Be* + a Present Participle. A given sentence may contain one, both, or neither.)

Interestingly, with this brief set of rules, you can describe and analyze all the forms that the complete verb in the English sentence takes. Let's put that statement to the test.

A sentence in which Aux is only Present:

> *Ingrid eats grapefruit.*
> *Ingrid* + Present + *eat* + *grapefruit.* (Read this as "*Ingrid* plus the Present Tense of *eat* plus *grapefruit.*" Since the Present Tense of *eat* with a third person singular subject such as *Ingrid* is *eats,* this way of reading the sentence describes it perfectly.)

A sentence in which Aux = Past:

> *Ingrid ate grapefruit.*
> *Ingrid* + Past + *eat* + *grapefruit.* (Read this as "*Ingrid* plus the Past Tense of *eat* plus *grapefruit*"—a perfect description of the complete verb.)

A sentence in which Aux = Present + Modal:

> *Ingrid can eat grapefruit.*
> *Ingrid* + Present + *can* + *eat* + *grapefruit. ("Ingrid* plus the Present Tense of *can* plus *eat* plus *grapefruit.")*

A sentence in which Aux = Past + Modal:

> *Ingrid could eat grapefruit.*
> *Ingrid* + Past + *can* + *eat* + *grapefruit.* (The Past Tense of *can* is *could; may/might, shall/should, will/would. Must* is the only modal auxiliary with no past tense.)

A sentence in which Aux = Present + Modal + *have* + Past P:

> *Ingrid may have eaten grapefruit.*
> Ingrid + Present + *may* + *have* + Past P + *eat* + *grapefruit. ("Ingrid* plus the Present Tense of *may* plus *have* + the Past Participle of *eat* plus *grapefruit.")*

A sentence in which Aux = Past + Modal + *have* + Past P + *be* + *-ing:*

> *Ingrid would have been eating grapefruit.*
> *Ingrid* + Past + *will* + *have* + Past P + *be* + *-ing* + *eat* + *grapefruit. ("Ingrid* plus Past Tense of *will* plus *have* plus Past Participle of *be* plus Present Participle of *eat* plus *grapefruit.")*

Notice that this neat and logical descriptive method allows us to analyze all the tenses of English:

> *Present*
> > *Ingrid eats grapefruit.*
> > *Ingrid* + Present + *eat* +*grapefruit*
> *Past*
> > *Ingrid ate grapefruit.*
> > *Ingrid* + Past + *eat* + *grapefruit*
> *Future*
> > *Ingrid will eat grapefruit.*
> > *Ingrid* + Present + *will* + *eat* + *grapefruit*

Present perfect
   Ingrid has eaten grapefruit.
   Ingrid + Present + **have** + Past P + **eat** + **grapefruit**
Past Perfect
   Ingrid had eaten grapefruit.
   Ingrid + Past + **have** + Past P + **eat** + **grapefruit**
Future perfect
   Ingrid will have eaten grapefruit.
   Ingrid + Present + **will** + **have** + Past P + **eat** + **grapefruit**
Present progressive
   Ingrid is eating grapefruit.
   Ingrid + Present + **be** + **-ing** + **eat** + **grapefruit**
Past progressive
   Ingrid was eating grapefruit.
   Ingrid + Past + **be** + **-ing** + **eat** + **grapefruit**
Future progressive
   Ingrid will be eating grapefruit.
   Ingrid + Present + **will** + **be** + **-ing** + **eat** + **grapefruit**
Present perfect progressive
   Ingrid has been eating grapefruit.
   Ingrid + Present + **have** + Past P + **be** + **-ing** + **eat** + **grapefruit**
Past perfect progressive
   Ingrid had been eating grapefruit.
   Ingrid + Past + **have** + Past P + **be** + **-ing** + **eat** + **grapefruit**
Future perfect progressive
   Ingrid will have been eating grapefruit.
   Ingrid + Present + **will** + **have** + Past P + **be** + **-ing** + **eat** + **grapefruit**

All this may at first seem terribly complicated, but, really, the explanation just given is an economical and accurate way to state some important facts about the way sentences work.

To summarize: We have said that every sentence must have an absolute tense, which will be either *present* or *past.* That is to say, one auxiliary verb (the modals, **have,** and **be**) or the main verb of the sentence will carry either present or past tense. The other tenses in English are formed by the addition of other elements of the auxiliary, as has been outlined above.

It is interesting to note that in some dialects tense is sometimes unmarked. Thus, **I go today** is in present tense, but **I go yesterday** is in past tense, though the standard past tense form of **go** is **went.** Even in Edited Standard English, the *historical present* does not mark past tense:

> Yesterday I **go** down to the beach, and the wind **starts** to blow, so I **come** home without taking my swim.

See also *Fragmentary Sentences, Gerunds, Tense, Verbs.*

Brackets

Brackets [ ] are useful marks of punctuation. Here is an outline of how they function.

They are used as parentheses within parentheses. For instance:

> A satire (either Horatian [gentle and good-natured] or Juvenalian [biting and pointed]) is generally intended to reform humanity.

They are also used to set off material that is interpolated within a quotation. For instance, suppose that you found the following in a source that you wanted to quote:

Grammer is an interesting subject.

Obviously the word **grammar** is misspelled, but if you are going to make a direct quote, you cannot alter the spelling; you must reproduce the sentence exactly as you found it. Therefore, you can indicate that the misspelling is in the original and is not your own error by interpolating the Latin word *sic* (meaning "thus") into the quotation, in the following way:

"Grammer [*sic*] is an interesting subject."

You can use brackets for any material that you need to insert into direct quotations. For example, suppose that you want to quote the following sentence, which you have found in a source:

He said recently that the economic problems of private colleges and universities will become more severe in the decades ahead.

Your reader will want to know whom the pronoun **he** refers to, and you can supply that information by using brackets, thus:

"He [George McMahon, president of Kingsley College in Baker, Nevada] said recently that the economic problems of private colleges and universities will become more severe in the decades ahead."

Capitalization

In Edited Standard English (see that entry), the conventions of capitalization are fairly rigid and are generally known. For instance, proper nouns are capitalized: **Mary Smith, Los Angeles, Exxon.**

In some instances, writers use capitals for emphasis. See, for instance, the entry for Auxiliary, in which I have capitalized such common nouns as **Tense** and **Modal.**

On the other hand, it is currently fashionable to avoid capitals altogether in some poetry and other writing. See, for instance, the selection by Verta Mae Smart-Grosvenor on pages 144–45. Needless to say, merely to avoid capitals is not to create a poem. Nor is the avoidance of capitals a particularly imaginative device in any writing.

The point, however, is this: in formal writing that uses Edited Standard English, conventional rules of capitalization must be followed. Those rules are easily summarized: (1) The first letter of a sentence is capitalized. (2) Proper nouns—the names of persons (**George Smith**), cities (**Dallas**), states (**Texas**), firms (**Shell Oil Company**), and so on—are capitalized.

Case

Case is the relationship that nominals (nouns, noun phrases, noun clauses) have with the verb in a sentence. Traditionally it has been said that English has four cases:

Nominative, or *subjective* (in which the nominal is the subject of the verb)
Bert sees Lena.

Genitive, or *possessive*
   Bert's sister is Lena.
Dative (in which the nominal is the so-called indirect object of the verb)
   Lena gives **Bert** a kiss *or* Lena gives a kiss to **Bert.**
Accusative (in which the nominal is the direct object of the verb)
   Lena sees **Bert.**

If we view case only as the form that nouns take, then we can say that there is a *common case* and a *genitive case,* for nouns have only two forms in regard to case: **Bert/Bert's, the child/the child's, horses/horses'.**

Pronouns, on the other hand, have the following forms:

Nominative	*Accusative*	*Genitive*
I	me	mine
you	you	yours
he	him	his
she	her	hers
it	it	its
we	us	ours
they	them	theirs

The genitive pronouns are not to be confused with possessive adjectives, as the following will make clear:

Adjectives: The Cranes like **their** house better than **our** house.
         Grace pets **her** cat, and Tom pets **his** dog.
Pronouns: The Cranes like **theirs** better than **ours.**
         Grace pets **hers,** and Tom pets **his.**

Usage of pronouns is strictly regulated in standard English, so that it is considered a gross error to use, for instance, a nominative form in an accusative slot, or vice versa:

*The teacher gave **he and I** a C. (Standard English would demand "The teacher gave **him and me** a C.")
***Him and me** attended the movies together. (Standard would demand "**He and I** attended the movies together.")

But these rules do not apply in all dialects, only in standard.

The interrogative **who** has the following forms:

Nominative: **Who** knocked on the door?
Genitive: **Whose** did Mary pick?
Accusative: **Whom** did Mary pick? (In the deep structure, **whom** is the object of the verb **pick.**)

And the relative **who** has exactly the same forms.

Nominative: Kirby knows **who** knocked on the door.
Genitive: Kirby knows **whose** it was.
Accusative: Kirby knows **whom** he saw.

If, as we have seen, case is the relationship that a nominal has to the verb (or, more properly, the predicate), then we might ask whether English does indeed have only four cases. Consider the following sentences. In each, we would traditionally say that the italicized nominal is in the nominative, or subjective, case:

> ***Kirby*** collided with Hortense.
> ***The room*** swarmed with flies.
> ***The dam*** withstood the force of the flood.

But does it really make sense to say that ***Kirby, the room,*** and ***the dam*** have the same relationship with their predicates that ***George*** does with ***see*** in ***George sees Mary***? Hardly. To say that all of them are in the same case is to cover up important relational meanings. Note, for instance, what can be done with two of them:

> Kirby and Hortense collided.
> Flies swarmed in the room.

Note also that we can change the surface forms of sentences without changing the relational meanings. (That is, we always know who did what and with which and to whom.)

> George gave Gertie a whack with a bat.
> George gave a whack to Gertie with a bat.
> A whack was given by George to Gertie with a bat.

I would say that the nouns in the above do not shift their case relationships from one version to another. In fact, if we know the meaning of all three versions, don't we have something like the following?

Predicate	*Agent*	*Goal*	*Neutral*	*Instrument*
gave	George	Gertie	a whack	a bat

That is, I would claim that the sentences contain four cases. (What I call these cases is unimportant.) Just how many cases are there in English? I can only answer, "I don't know, but there are obviously quite a few." For instance, I have labeled the subjects of the following sentences either with case names that are generally used in modern grammar or with arbitrary names that I have devised (indicated by question marks):

> The room [location] swarmed with flies.
> The dam [antik?] withstood the flood.
> Gravel [contentive?] filled the wheelbarrow.
> The hammer [instrument] broke the window.
> The boy [agent] broke the window with a hammer.
> The window [neutral] broke.

It should be stressed that the concept of case has to do both with the surface forms of nouns and pronouns and with the meanings that sentences convey. For instance, both these sentences convey the same meaning:

> Me and her played basketball.
> She and I played basketball.

In no absolute sense is one superior to the other, for both convey the same intended meaning. However, in Spoken Standard English and Edited Standard English, ***She and I played basketball*** is preferable. In other words, if the audience for the sentence consists of speakers of standard, they may well react unfavorably to ***Me and her played basketball.***

One sticky point concerning case involves the choice between the relatives ***who*** and ***whom***—a problem more easily illustrated than explained:

> The police know who robbed the bank.

In this sentence, **who** is the subject of the verb **robbed,** and thus is in the subjective case. But since **who** immediately follows the verb **know,** you might tend to use the objective case **whom** instead of the subjective **who.** To choose the proper form of the relative, ask yourself what sentence the relative clause represents. The following will illustrate this principle:

> The teacher asks whom we should elect. (The relative is the object of **elect: we should elect whom.**)
> Everyone likes the person who was elected. (The relative is the subject of the verb phrase **was elected: who was elected.**)
> Tell me whom you gave it to. (The relative is the object of the proposition **to: you gave it to whom.**)

See also *Agreement, Nominals, Nouns, Pronouns, Relatives.*

Clauses

Clauses can be *independent* or *dependent.* The familiar explanation is that independent clauses can stand alone, but dependent clauses cannot. Sometimes an independent clause is merely a sentence:

> The sun shines every day in Huntington Beach.

Sometimes independent clauses are coordinated:

> The wind blows every afteroon, and the air is fresh.

Dependent clauses come in three varieties: noun, adjective, and adverb. A noun clause is merely a nominal. It fills the slot of a noun:

> **Fish** interest me.
> **That I am interested in fish** interests me.

> Jackson knows **the information.**
> Jackson knows **that enrollment will rise.**

> Dave sees **the visitor.**
> Dave sees **who is knocking on his door.**

An adjective clause, it is traditionally said, modifies a nominal, just as adjectives do:

> The sentence **that I am writing** illustrates clauses.
> The clauses **which it illustrates** are adjectives.
> The person **who understands adjective clauses** is smart.

Adverb clauses are, like true adverbs, movable; they begin with subordinating conjunctions:

> **Because the noise was loud,** Debbie could not hear the music.
> Debbie could not hear the music **because the noise was loud.**

> **Although the music was loud,** the noise was louder.
> The noise was louder, **although the music was loud.**

> **If you want to go,** make reservations.
> Make reservations **if you want to go.**

That, in brief outline, constitutes the clause structure of English.

See also *Adjectives, Adverbs, Antecedent, Comma, Comma Fault, Conjunctions, Fragmentary Sentences, Nominals, Relatives, Semicolon.*

Colon

The colon (:) is a mark of punctuation that directs attention forward to what follows it.

> This is Tom's goal in life: to become a concert violinist.
> These are the items that we need: sugar, tea, and salt.
> There is only one word to describe him: jerk.

The colon also has certain conventional uses:

> 3:41 P.M.
> Dear Sir:

A colon is *always* placed outside closing quotation marks in Edited Standard English:

> We know this about "Ode on a Grecian Urn": it was inspired by the Elgin marbles.

Comma

Commas are used both to separate sentence elements and to enclose them.

Separating commas are used

to separate items in a coordinated series:

> George, Bill, and Tom joined the fraternity.
> The President, the Secretary of State, and the general conferred.

to separate coordinate clauses:

> Snapper lost the first race, but he tried again.
> Kurtz went up the Congo, and he died there.

to separate initial adverbial modifiers from the rest of the sentence:

> Early in the morning, the fleet leaves Ensenada.
> In the afternoon, the fleet returns.

after other introductory elements:

> That being the case, we will reconsider.
> Nonetheless, we are skeptical.
> Yes, I know that.

after a vocative noun of address:

> Miss Plaichinger, will you dance?
> Lupikhin, you're a liar.

after a transitional adverb:

> Marlow was a good storyteller; however, he bored us.
> Werle was selfish; nevertheless, he helped Hjalmar.

after the introduction to a direct quotation:

> Heyst said, "Come with me."
> Lena replied, "With great pleasure."

in certain conventional ways:

> March 5, 1974
> Salt Lake City, Utah

A comma is *always* placed inside closing quotation marks in Edited Standard English.

Enclosing commas are used

to set off nonrestrictive relative clauses:

> The task, which I really hated to start, is now almost done.
> The captain saw the enemy, who also saw him.

to set off interpolations:

> The job, in spite of everything, will be done.
> The job, nevertheless, will be done.

Comma Fault

In Edited Standard English, independent clauses are conventionally linked by either a conjunction or a semicolon:

> The sun sank in the west, and the evening breeze began to blow.
> The sun sank in the west; the evening breeze began to blow.

The comma fault occurs when such independent clauses are linked with a comma, rather than with a conjunction or a semicolon:

> The sun sank in the west, the evening breeze began to blow.

This comma linkage is probably inappropriate in the most formal kinds of writing, but it is becoming more and more common in other kinds of writing. But as the following passage will make clear, overuse of comma linkage becomes obtrusive and hence ineffective:

> The sun sank in the west, the evening breeze began to blow, we had decided to barbecue chicken for supper, so I started the coals, in the meantime, I poured myself a glass of mellow sherry and drank in the delicious smell of the ocean mingled with the aroma of charcoal, when the coals were glowing, we put the chicken on. . . .

See also *Clauses, Comma, Conjunctions, Fragmentary Sentences, Semicolon.*

Conjunctions

Think about the following ordinary sentence:

> Jim **and** Larry play basketball.

What it really means is something like this:

> Jim plays basketball/Larry plays basketball.

The simple *coordinating conjunction and,* then, allows both economy of expression and the statement of a relationship. All the coordinating conjunctions do the same. The relationships that they establish might be labeled as follows:

> *Coordinate:*   Jim *and* Larry play basketball.
> *Obversative:* Jim plays basketball, *but* Tony doesn't.
> *Alternative:* Stop, *or* I'll shoot!
> *Causative:*   The thief stopped, *for* he didn't want to get shot.
> *Conclusive:*   The police caught him in the act, *so* they knew they had their man.

The coordinating conjunctions are: *and, but, for, so, or, nor, yet.* They always stand between the elements joined—words, phrases, or clauses:

> Sandy *and* Jay have two daughters.
> The man on the corner *or* the woman in the house called out.
> The team rallied in the last quarter, *but* it was too late.

Correlative conjunctions always come in pairs: *both . . . and, not . . . but, either . . . or, neither . . . nor.*

> *Both* coffee *and* tea contain caffeine.
> The supper was *not* just good, *but* absolutely delicious.
> If *either* Sir William *or* Lady Henrietta stole the diamond, Sherlock will solve the case.
> *Neither* Sir William *nor* Lady Henrietta stole the diamond; therefore the case remains unsolved.

Correlative constructions must balance. In other words, if, for instance, *either* is followed by a clause, then *or* must be followed by a clause. In that case, the following would be unacceptable:

> I wonder if *either* you would do it, *or* if she would.

The sentence should be revised in one of these two ways:

> I wonder *either* if you would do it, *or* if she would.
> I wonder if *either* you would do it, *or* she would.

Another example of the breakdown of parallelism in correlative constructions:

> The child wanted *either* ice cream *or* to go to the park.

Here we have correlative + noun and correlative + infinitve. The most formal usage would demand a rewrite such as the following:

> *Either* the child wanted ice cream, *or* he wanted to go to the park.

Of course, sometimes the breakdown in parallelism becomes more obvious and annoying, as in the following:

> If *either* you want an *A or* a *B,* you must study.

This awkward collocation probably ought to be revised so that it reads as follows:

> If you want *either* an *A or* a *B,* you must study.

Subordinating conjunctions (*because*, *if*, *although*, *as*, *when*, *where* . . .) join adverb clauses to main clauses. They establish a variety of adverbial relationships, for instance:

Cause:	The family cancelled its vacation plans *because* gasoline was in short supply.
Concession:	*Although* the President claimed that there would be ample fuel by June, many people were afraid to set out on journeys.
Time:	*When* September comes, the petunias freeze in Missoula.
Place:	*Where* the river flows into the sea, one finds brackish water.
Frequency:	The pelican dives *whenever* it sees an anchovy.

Of course, there are other relationships.

Coordinating conjunctions, as we noted, always stand between the elements joined. Subordinating conjunctions always join clauses and always stand at the beginning of the subordinate clause. The subordinate clause may precede or follow the main clause:

Because it was raining, the game was canceled.
The game was cancelled *because* it was raining.

Therefore, it is easy to distinguish between coordinating and subordinating conjunctions.

All conjunctions form finite lists. New nouns, adjectives, adverbs, and verbs are continually entering the language, and old ones are dropping out, but the lists of all other parts of speech—including conjunctions—are stable.

See also *Adverbs, Clauses.*

Dangling Modifiers

The following sentence creates a strange and humorous image:

Standing on one leg in the swamp, Joe saw the blue heron.

The reason for this grotesqueness is that the verbal modifier *Standing on one leg in the swamp* dangles, or is misrelated. The momentary impression is that Joe, rather than the heron, is standing on one leg in the swamp.

To process the sentence for meaning, the reader must find out who or what is doing the standing, and the tendency is to take the first nominal as the subject of the verbal, so that the reader at first comes out with something like this:

[Joe was] Standing on one leg in the swamp.

The sentence can easily be revised in order to eliminate the problem:

Joe saw the blue heron standing on one leg in the swamp.

In terms of propositions, this sentence contains the following:

(Joe saw the blue heron [the blue heron was standing on one leg in the swamp])

The problem with ***Standing on one leg in the swamp, Joe saw the blue heron*** is not really one of meaning, for any reader will know what is intended in the sentence. The reason for avoiding dangling modifiers is that they say to the reader that you, the writer, are not in control, that you don't handle the language precisely and with ease. Therefore, this error, like many others, diminishes the value of what you write.

Here is another example of a dangling modifier:

> To start a business venture, money must be raised.

Again, the sentence begins with a verbal that does not have a surface subject, and before the sentence can be understood the reader must supply a subject for the verbal ***to start***. The first nominal that will work as the subject is ***money,*** and momentary confusion ensues, for the first meaning that the reader processes is "money to start a business venture." The following correction is very nearly identical with the original version.

> For someone to start a business venture, money must be raised.

And so is the following:

> To start a business venture, one must raise money.

In general, a modifier dangles when the possibility exists that it will be misrelated when the sentence is processed for meaning.

Dash

The dash directs the reader's attention back toward what precedes it. In this sense, it is just the opposite of the colon.

> Lloyds and Elwood's Dry Wit—this is my favorite sherry.

The dash also shows unexpectedness, as when a surprise element is added to a sentence:

> Marian was pleasingly plump—really fat as a hog.

The dash also is frequently used before the name of the author of a quote:

> All during the reading for a biography, subjects for future books suggest themselves, stepping from the records with a brave refusal to rest quietly in their past.   —Catherine Drinker Bowen

Paired dashes, like paired commas, are used to enclose material. They carry a stronger effect of setting off the material they enclose than do commas:

> Joseph Conrad—one of the world's greatest writers of adventure stories—was born in Poland.

When the interpolated material contains comma punctuation within itself, dashes are used to avoid confusion:

The subjects Jess was taking—physics, calculus, Spanish, and cinema—kept him busy on weekends.

Demonstratives

The most common demonstratives are *this, these, that, those,* and *such.* They can be either pronouns (functioning in nominal slots) or adjectives.

> *Pronouns:*   ***This*** is the car Dave bought.
> ***Those*** are the winners.
> ***Such*** is foolish.
> *Adjectives:* ***This*** Oldsmobile is the car Dave bought.
> ***Those*** boys are the winners.
> ***Such*** talk is foolish.

Obviously, demonstratives are "pointing" words; that is, they refer the reader to something outside of the clause in which they occur. (In the examples, the "something outside" is presumably something in the world of reality. That is, the demonstratives "point" to a car, some boys, and something that was said somewhere.)

When demonstratives refer to a word or a concept in another clause or sentence, problems sometimes arise. For instance, look at the following:

> The fact that demonstratives are "pointing" words makes them very useful. ***This*** seems strange.

What seems strange? The fact that demonstratives are pointing words or the fact that they are useful? In other words, the reader cannot determine the exact antecedent of the demonstrative *this* in the example passage.

Here is another, and more egregious, example of unclear reference:

> Ideas have consequences that men claim influence the histories of nations. ***These*** are the subject of my essay.

The first sentence contains five plural nouns *(ideas, consequences, men, histories, nations),* each of which could conceivably be the antecedent of the plural demonstrative *these.*

A careful writer makes certain the reference of all demonstratives is clear.

See also *Agreement, Antecedent, Nominals, Pronouns, Reference.*

Diction

Diction concerns one's choice of words in speaking or writing. Formal occasions demand formal diction, and informal occasions allow less formal diction. The concept is easily illustrated.

> I went to the eye doctor yesterday.
> The ophthalmologist tested my eyes.

The term *eye doctor* is definitely less formal than is *opthalmologist,* though both mean the same.

Notice the different effects of the following:

> The preacher hitched us.
> The minister united us in the bonds of holy matrimony.

These two sentences mean the same, but are at quite different levels of diction.

Mixing levels of diction can create humor:

> We regret to announce that on the ninth day of May, nineteen hundred and seventy-three, Grandpa kicked the bucket.

For **Grandpa kicked the bucket,** substitute **Grandfather passed away,** and note the change in effect.

If you are in doubt concerning a word's level of usage, consult your dictionary.

See also *Adjectives, Adverbs, Edited Standard English, Interjections, Malapropism, Nouns, Verbs.*

Double Negative

In Spoken Standard English and Edited Standard English, though not in some other dialects, the double negative is considered an error. Forming a double negative, as its name implies, consists in negating a sentence or sentence element more than once, thus:

> The bank has**n't** got **no** more money.

Standard English would demand,

> The bank has no more money.

Sometimes double negation is not quite so obvious as in the above example. For instance:

> I do**n't hardly** have the time.

Standard English would demand either **I don't have the time** or **I hardly have the time.**

See also *Edited Standard English.*

Edited Standard English

This might well be viewed as the prestige *written* dialect. In general, it is the sort of writing that one finds in the weekly news magazines, in learned journals, in newspapers, and in textbooks—this one, for instance.

Its most obvious characteristics are its conventions of punctuation and spelling. The ESE conventions of punctuation are the ones that are outlined under various entries (Comma, Dash, Colon, Semicolon, and so on) in this Reference Guide. ESE spelling is that which is listed as preferred in modern dictionaries.

In ESE, the writer has some leeway with punctuation. For instance, it is becoming more and more common to splice independent clauses with commas rather than semicolons:

> The article was written, the paper went to press.

However, a survey of national magazines, newspapers, scholarly books, most fiction, learned journals, and so on, will reveal that the system of punctuation in English is clearly defined and is pretty generally adhered to.

The standards of spelling in ESE allow the writer very little leeway. In a few limited cases, one has options: ***traveled*** or ***travelled.*** But, in general, spelling is fixed.

ESE has power just because it is accepted and written by those who have power in society. Power classes tend to endow their own dialects with a great deal of prestige and to react (perhaps irrationally) against dialects, either written or spoken, that diverge from their own. Therefore, learning to write ESE, like learning to speak standard, is tactically desirable.

Fragmentary Sentences

Basically, a fragmentary sentence, or "sentence fragment," is characterized by the absence of tense, for a complete sentence always has a tense.

The following is an example of the sort of construction that is termed a fragment:

> The school erupted into confusion. Classes being over.

Even though ***Classes being over*** is punctuated as though it were a sentence, it is not one in the conventional sense. Notice that its verb, ***being,*** does not have tense. If the sequence contained tense, it would read, ***Classes are/ were over.*** Since ***Classes being over*** is not a sentence, but really a modifier of the sentence ***The school erupted into confusion,*** normally it would appear as follows:

> The school erupted into confusion, classes being over.

Most fragmentary sentences involve nonfinite (tenseless) verbs.

> In the evening, Stanley engages in his favorite pastime. Reading murder mysteries.
> (In the evening, Stanley engages in his favorite pastime, reading murder mysteries.)
>
> Every good American has an objective in life. To make money.
> (Every good American has an objective in life, to make money.)

Another common type of fragment is the subordinate clause that is set off as though it were an independent clause:

> The economy is in a state of crisis. Because investors are uncertain about the future of energy sources.
>
> (The economy is in a state of crisis because investors are uncertain about the future of energy sources.)

Is the fragmentary sentence an absolute "wrong" in language? Not at all. (Notice that **Not at all** is not a complete sentence in the usual sense.) Answers to questions are most frequently not complete sentences:

"What's your name?" "George."

Furthermore, it is often effective to set a phrase or a dependent clause apart with sentence punctuation in order to achieve emphasis.

The little child uttered a shocking word. "Darn."
The sport fishery on the California coast is declining. Because commercial fishermen are harvesting too many anchovies.

It should be apparent that the concept of sentence fragments is intimately linked with the standard system of punctuation. In this system, sequences such as **Sitting on the lawn** do not receive sentence punctuation.

See also *Auxiliary, Clauses, Comma, Comma Fault, Conjunctions, Tense.*

Gender

In some languages, every noun has a marked gender. In German, for instance, gender is marked by the definite article, the form of which is **das** for neuter, **die** for feminine, and **der** for masculine.

Gender	Article	Noun	Meaning
Neuter	das	Messer	"the knife"
Feminine	die	Gabel	"the fork"
Masculine	der	Loeffel	"the spoon"

The gender of nouns in German is quite aribtrary; there is nothing particularly "neuter" about a knife, "feminine" about a fork, or "masculine" about a spoon. Furthermore, the German equivalent of **the girl** is **das Maedchen,** a neuter.

In English, very few nouns are marked for gender, but some of them have gender as part of their meaning. Masculine: **man, boy, stallion, rooster.** Feminine: **woman, girl, mare, hen.** Other nouns might be said to have a common gender, neither masculine, feminine, nor neuter.

However, the third person singular pronouns are marked for gender: **he** (masc.), **she** (fem.), **it** (neut.). Through our use of these pronouns, we can assign gender to nouns that otherwise would not have it.

The ship tacked through the chop. **She** was a beauty.
The horse reared. **He** was full of spirit.

In the last few years, gender has become a political and social problem. (Strangely, grammar has actually become a worldwide issue.) Women's liberationists point out that a sentence such as **Will everyone please take off his hat** (with the masculine adjective) is one more sign of the male chauvinism that pervades Western society. That is, we customarily use masculine forms to refer to both males and females.

And what about such common nouns as **mankind, chairman,** and **congressman?** One alternative is to speak of **personkind, chairperson,** and **congressperson.** But somehow those terms rub—at least me—the wrong way.

Furthermore, what about a sentence such as **Will everyone please take off his hat?** No doubt about it. It smacks of male chauvinism. Should we then say, **Will everyone please take off their hats?** That would be a logical solution to the problem, but grammatical purists would argue that **everyone** is singular, **their** is plural, and therefore the solution runs counter to the grammatical rules of standard English and is a debasement of the language.

To solve the problem of sexism in writing, you can easily adopt some new habits. For instance, **humanity,** which has no sexist connotations, is a good substitute for **mankind.** You can speak of a **congressman,** a **congresswoman,** or **members of Congress,** whichever is appropriate. When a construction such as **Will everyone please take off his hat** occurs, you can readily substitute **Will you please take off your hats.** And notice how easy it is to remove sexist overtones from the following:

> Will every student please be sure to sign his paper.
> Will every student please be sure to sign his or her paper.

> The American voter casts his ballot in November.
> American voters cast their ballots in November.

> All congressmen have free mailing privileges.
> All members of Congress have free mailing privileges.

> Every member of the Faculty Club must pay five dollars a month; this fee gives him the privilege of using the facilities.
> All members of the Faculty Club must pay five dollars a month; this fee gives them the privilege of using the facilities.

The writer needs to be aware of these problems; in other words, the writer—whether he or she—needs to be sensitive to audience.

See also *Agreement, Antecedent, Nouns, Pronouns.*

Gerunds

A gerund is a present participle used as a nominal. A present participle is a verb ending in **-ing: fishing, sleeping, reading, drinking.** Any verb ending in **-ing** can be used as a nominal.

> Sport is fun.
> **Fishing** is fun.

> I enjoy a firm mattress.
> I enjoy **sleeping.**

> Moe is devoted to literature.
> Moe is devoted to **reading.**

> The report stated that alcohol is a national problem.
> The report stated that **drinking** is a national problem.

So far, so good. But there are complications. A verb can have modifiers, direct objects, and indirect objects, and so can gerunds. The following will illustrate the point:

Paul *jogs steadily for thirty minutes* every day.
Jogging steadily for thirty minutes is good for the heart.

Norman *gives the devil his due.*
Philosophers recommend *giving the devil his due.*

In other words, a gerund is simply a verb ending in *-ing,* and a gerund phrase is that verb plus anything that can work with a verb in a sentence.
Let's take a complete sentence and turn it into a gerund phrase:

Mary Jo knits socks for orphans.
Mary Jo's knitting socks for orphans keeps her busy.
or
Mary Jo's knitting of socks for orphans keeps her busy.

The subject of the gerund is normally in the possessive case, as the above examples illustrate.
Here are various gerunds in nominal slots:

Subject: Milking cows on a winter morning chaps one's hands.
Direct object: Grace resented *Tom's yelling at her.*
Indirect object: The audience gave *the soprano's singing of the aria* warm applause.
Subjective complement: The purpose of armies is *winning wars.*
Objective complement: Christians call faith *winning the battle of belief.*
Object of preposition: An honest man never thinks of *falsifying his tax returns.*
Appositive: The objective of Scrabble, *constructing as many words as possible,* demands a good vocabulary.

See also *Nominals, Nouns, Verbs.*

Hyphen

The hyphen is used to link words and parts of words:

brother-in-law
a devil-may-care attitude

The hyphen is also used to link a part of a word that comes at the end of one line with the rest of the word, which appears at the beginning of the following line. Conventionally, words are broken in this way only between syllables. (There are many examples in this book.)
The hyphen links numbers from twenty-one to ninety-nine:

seventy-six trombones
twenty-one years

The hyphen also links fractions:

one-half
two-thirds

However, numbers above ninety-nine are not linked:

> one hundred
> three million
> four billion

Interjections

Interjections, or exclamations, can be regarded as adverbials that are used to express emotion:

> **Egad!** I'm late.
> **My golly,** you missed your plane!
> I'll try until I succeed, **by darn!**

The more colorful interjections need not be reproduced here. We have all heard them, and most of us use at least some of them upon occasion.

Different cultures and dialects accept different kinds of interjections. In German, **Mein Gott!** is an extremely mild interjection that could be used in almost any circumstance, but the English equivalent, **My God!** carries more weight and would be offensive in some situations. In short, the values assigned to interjections arise from the cultures in which they are used.

See also *Diction*.

Italics

In print, italics are indicated by type such as the kind that you are now reading. In handwriting or typewriting, italics are indicated by underlining, like this:

> Colorless green ideas sleep furiously.

Italics are used
to call attention to a word or phrase:

> A *noun* is not necessarily the name of a person, place, or thing.

to show emphasis:

> I vow that I *will not* resign.

to indicate titles of books, plays, movies, long poems:

> *Moby Dick,* by Herman Melville
> *A Streetcar Named Desire* (play)
> *The Bank Dick* (movie)
> *The Odyssey* (epic poem)

to set off foreign words and phrases:

> The *point d'appui* of the discussion is theme.
> The view of art as *das Ding an sich* is solipsistic.

Malapropism

This is the unintentionally humorous misuse of a word. The word comes from the name Mrs. Malaprop, a character in the eighteenth-century comedy *The Rivals,* by Richard Brinsley Sheridan. Here is one of Mrs. Malaprop's speeches:

> I would by no means wish a daughter of mine to be a ***progeny*** of learning. . . . she should have a ***supercilious*** knowledge of accounts:—and as she grew up, I would have her instructed in ***geometry,*** that she might know something of the ***contagious*** countries.

What Mrs. Malaprop probably meant to say was this:

> I would by no means wish a daughter of mine to be a ***prodigy*** of learning. . . . she should have a ***superficial*** knowledge of accounts:—and as she grew up, I would have her instructed in ***geography,*** that she might know something of the ***contiguous*** countries.

The humorous inappropriateness of Mrs. Malaprop's statement becomes obvious when you think about the meanings of the malapropistic words she has used: ***progeny*** = "offspring"; ***supercilious*** = "patronizingly haughty or proud"; and you already know the meanings of ***geometry*** and ***contagious***.

The best way to avoid malapropisms is to use only those words that are in your *active* vocabulary—and to shun the thesaurus like the plague.

Mood

The mood of a verb has to do with the way in which a reader or hearer regards a sentence: as a statement; as a wish, condition contrary to fact, or doubt; or as a command. The moods are

> *Indicative:* George is a pleasant chap.
> *Subjunctive:* If only George were a pleasant chap.
> *Imperative:* George, be a pleasant chap!

Mood is seldom a problem for writers of Edited Standard English. Purists would demand ***I wish he were here*** rather than ***I wish he was here***—the subjunctive form of the verb rather than the indicative. Notice the difference between these two sentences:

> If he ***was*** here, he probably saw the streaker. (But I don't know whether or not he was here.)
> If he ***were*** here, he could explain the problem. (But he is not here.)

The second example expresses a condition contrary to fact and, therefore, is in the subjunctive mood.

Nominals

Nominals are nouns, noun phrases, or noun clauses that serve as

> *Subjects of Verbs:*
>   ***Marty*** likes basketball.
>   ***The majority of Americans*** like basketball.
>   ***Whoever is an American*** likes basketball.
> *Direct objects of verbs:*
>   Everyone ignores ***a burp.***
>   Everyone ignores ***a discreet burp after a meal***.
>   Everyone ignores ***what could be offensive.***
> *Indirect objects of verbs:*
>   Sinners must give ***the devil*** his due.

Sinners must give *the man with horns and cloven hooves* his due.
Sinners must give *whoever tempts them* his due.
Subjective complements:
Children soon become *adults.*
Children soon become *men and women with problems.*
Children soon become *whatever their parents want them to be.*
Objective complements:
The wife called her husband *a fool.*
The wife called her husband *a fool of the first degree.*
The wife called her husband *whatever popped into her mind.*
Object of preposition:
The hungry man thought of *food.*
The hungry man thought of *baked beans with wieners.*
The hungry man thought of *what would satisfy his appetite.*
Appositives:
The symphony, *the "Pastorale,"* was well performed.
The symphony, *the sixth of Beethoven's nine,* was well performed.
The symphony, *whatever you want to call it,* was well performed.
Vocatives:
Herbert, be quiet.
That man over there, be quiet.
Whoever made the noise, be quiet.

All languages, it seems, have ways of turning sentences or sentence-like structures into nominals; this is the process of nominalization, and it warrants a bit of exploration. For instance, consider this series:

Someone tamed the shrew.
The shrew was tamed.
The taming of the shrew is the theme of *The Taming of the Shrew.*
Petruchio enjoyed *taming the shrew.*
We all know that *someone tamed the shrew.*

We can create a whole string of nominals and put them together into a fairly horrendous sentence, like this:

Jane says something.
George knows something.
Bill told him something.
Mary thinks something.
This sentence is getting too long.
Jane says that George knows that Bill told him that Mary thinks that this sentence is getting too long.

An interesting kind of nominalization is the absolute:

Mark having arrived, the party began.

The absolute is merely a sentence *(Mark has arrived)* with a simple change in verb form.

See also *Clauses, Demonstratives, Nouns, Pronouns, Relatives.*

Nouns

Nouns are words that function in nominal slots in sentences. They can be pluralized: *boy/boys, man/men, child/children, alumnus/alumni, cherub/*

cherubim. They frequently have nominal suffixes: ***childhood, freedom, beauty, realization, statesmanship, actuality,*** and so on. They are modified by adjectives: ***good food, fair play, honest opinion.***

Proper nouns are names of particular people, places, works of art, and so on: ***George Washington, San Francisco, Hamlet.*** Common nouns are all other nouns—all nouns that are not proper.

Specifying the meanings of nouns is a fairly interesting inquiry. Part of this specification can be accomplished through listing a noun's features. For instance, the noun ***man*** has the features "human, male, adult," and the noun ***woman*** has the features "human, female, adult." The noun ***automobile*** has the feature "concrete," and the noun ***democracy*** has the feature "abstract." The noun ***microbe*** has the feature "animate," and the noun ***oxygen*** has the feature "inanimate." The noun ***line*** has the feature "one-dimensional," the noun ***rectangle*** has the feature "two-dimensional," and the noun ***cube*** has the feature "three-dimensional."

As we saw in Chapter 12 (page 400), *penetrability* can also be a feature of meaning, thus: ***air*** [1 penetrable], ***water*** [2 penetrable], ***ice*** [3 penetrable]—which explains the strangeness of **Bert drank the air* and **Bert drank the ice,* for the verb ***drink*** normally takes as its object only a noun that has the feature [2 penetrable], like ***milk, booze,*** and ***orange juice.***

In context, nouns always have the meaning either Definite or Nondefinite:

> ***The book*** was interesting. (Def)
> ***A book*** can be interesting. (Nondef)
> ***This book*** is interesting. (Def)
> ***Books*** are interesting. (Nondef)
> ***Some books*** are interesting. (Nondef)
> ***Any book*** is interesting. (Nondef)

Nouns always have determiners, structures that precede them and that contribute information or semantic value to them. The minimal determiner is the article, either definite or nondefinite. The definite article is ***the.*** There are a variety of nondefinite articles, including the *null* [∅]. In other words, all of the following have "nondefinite" as part of their meaning:

> ***a*** child
> ***some*** children
> ∅ children

Of course, the null does not appear in writing or speaking, and that's just the point: a noun that has no determiner is automatically nondefinite.

The following diagram will give you some idea of how complex determiner structure can be in English:

Predeterminer	Prearticle	Article Demonstrative Genitive	Ordinal	Cardinal	Noun
several of	just	the those his	first	hundred	days

See also *Capitalization, Clauses, Gender, Nominals.*

Parallelism

Parallelism is the principle that constructions that stand in identical grammatical slots must have the same grammatical value. This is easily illustrated.

> Ken liked reading and martinis.

Both **reading** and **martinis** are objects of the verb **liked**, but **reading** is a gerund and **martinis** is a common noun (though they are both nominals). Therefore the sentence is not parallel. The following sentences are parallel:

> Ken liked books and martinis.
> Ken liked reading and drinking.

Here is another unparallel sentence:

> Dilligan asked **for a raise** [prepositional phrase] and **that he be promoted** [clause].

Another example:

> Wolfe studied Chinese, **for he was interested in the Orient** [coordinate clause] and **because he had spare time** [subordinate clause].

Some readers demand parallelism, and some don't seem to care. In its most "pure" form, Edited Standard English does observe the strictures of parallelism.

See also *Shifted Constructions.*

Parentheses

Parentheses are used to include material that is loosely related to the main topic of a sentence or that is inserted in order to clarify:

> Josh Billings (a nineteenth-century American humorist) was overshadowed by Mark Twain.

Often the choice between paired commas and parentheses is only a matter of style, parentheses tending, perhaps, to isolate and highlight more than commas.

See also *Brackets, Comma.*

Plagiarism

Plagiarism is the use of someone else's ideas or exact words without giving credit.

If you quote the exact words of a source, you must put those words in quotation marks and indicate, either by a reference in the text or through footnotes, what your source was. If you paraphrase an idea from a source, you must also indicate what that source was.

Here is a direct quotation, with the source indicated:

> As Jonathan Kozol says in *Death at an Early Age,* "Many people in Boston are surprised, even to this day, to be told that children are beaten with thin bamboo whips within the cellars of our public schools and that they are whipped at times for no greater offense than for failing to show respect to the very same teachers who have been describing them as niggers."

Here is a paraphrase of that quotation, with the source indicated:

> In *Death at an Early Age,* Jonathan Kozol points out that children in the Boston public schools are still being beaten with bamboo whips. The reason for the beatings, he says, is often that students have failed to show respect to the same teachers who have been calling them niggers.

It is not necessary to indicate the source for common knowledge. For instance, if I were to look up the exact date of George Washington's death and then use that information in a piece of writing, I would not name my source, for anyone can find the information readily in a desk dictionary, among other places.

Prepositions

Prepositions *(on, in, to, over, through, under, at, by, for . . .)* are words that relate nominals to other sentence elements:

> the Wife *of* Bath
> the flowers *under* the tree
> The ball sailed *over* the fence.

Prepositions differ from *particles,* as these examples demonstrate:

> Turn *off* the light. Turn the light *off.* (particle)
> Turn *up* the street. *Turn the street *up.* (preposition)
> Choke *down* your medicine. Choke your medicine *down.* (particle)
> Look *down* the hallway. *Look the hallway *down.* (preposition)
> Think *over* this idea. Think this idea *over.* (particle)
> Jump *over* the log. *Jump the log *over.* (preposition)

In regard to prepositions, let's do a bit of language logic. Insofar as we understand a sentence, we understand the relationship of all its nominals to their predicates. In other words, we can't understand.

> George gave Mary a whack with a bat.

unless we know who performed the action, who received the action, what action was done, and what the instrument of the action was. When we process this sentence for meaning, then, we come up with something like the following:

> *Predicate:* gave *Agent:* George *Goal:* Mary *Object:* a whack *Instrument:* a bat

In other words, we must know the relationships that all the nominals have in the sentence, or we can't understand the sentence.

Now, decide whether you think this makes sense: Since prepositions are the relation markers in the language, every nominal in a sentence must be the object of a preposition. The sentence analyzed above contains only one preposition, **with;** but I can demonstrate that other prepositions are lurking in the sentence and that we can easily bring them out of hiding:

A whack was given **to** Mary **by** George **with** a bat.

In other words, we have demonstrated that **Mary, George,** and **bat** all have prepositions associated with them. What about **whack?** No rearrangement of the sentence will make that word the object of a preposition—and yet we know the relationship that **whack** holds in both versions of the sentence. Might we say that the preposition associated with objects of the verb **give** is *null* [Ø]? In that case, our sentence looks something like this:

[by] George gave [to] Mary [Ø] a whack **with** a bat.

But why, you might ask, introduce such complications into the grammar? My answer is that I have just simplified the grammar immeasurably. Which is the simpler of the following two rules?

In sentences, some nominals in some slots with some verbs are objects of prepositions and some are not. For instance, with a cognate object, the verb **think** does not demand a preposition, as in **think a thought,** but if the object is not cognate, as in **think of home,** the preposition appears . . . (and the rule must go on and on and on and on in order to be anywhere near complete).

In sentences, nominals are marked by prepositions that specify their cases or roles. Sometimes the preposition is null [Ø].

I think you'll agree that the second rule is extremely simple. It also has the virtue of being airtight.

To summarize: Prepositions are nothing more than role markers that allow us to perceive relational meanings in sentences.

See also *Case.*

Pronouns

The *personal pronouns* of English, in their various forms, are

	First Person	*Second Person*	*Third Person*
Singular			
Nominative	I	you	he/she/it
Genitive	mine	yours	his/hers/its
Accusative	me	you	him/her/it
Plural			
Nominative	we	you	they
Genitive	ours	yours	theirs
Accusative	us	you	them

The *demonstrative pronouns* are

	Singular	*Plural*
Proximal	this	these
Distal	that	those

The word **such** is sometimes considered to be a demonstrative: **Such is humanity's fate.**

Relative pronouns are used in the following sentences:

> The man *who* came to dinner wore a beard.
> The man *whom* we invited to dinner wore a beard.
> The man *that* came to dinner wore a beard.
> The dinner *which* we served him was elegant.
> We enjoy such guests *as* relish their chow.
> *Whoever* came to dinner ate well.
> *Whomever* we invited ate well.
> *Whatever* we served was delicious.

It is characteristic of pronouns that they gain their full semantic value only when they have an antecedent. Thus, in the following sentence we know what *who* means only because of *the boy,* its antecedent:

> The *boy* *WHO* mowed the lawn earned fifty cents.

In illustration of this principle, antecedents are underlined once and their pronouns are underlined twice in the following examples:

> My wife is named *Norma. SHE* was born in Utah.
> We wanted to see *Cabo San Lucas.* And *THIS* is where we went.
> *THAT* is when we went—*in June.*
> *Larry was fascinated by chemistry. THAT* is why he went to college.

Indefinite relative pronouns, which introduce noun clauses, do not have antecedents and thus are partially "hollow" semantically:

> Tommy does *whatever* he wants.
> *Whoever* eats spinach is strong.

See also *Agreement, Antecedent, Case, Demonstratives, Gender, Nominals, Reference, Relatives.*

Prosody

Prosody is the theory of versification, particularly as it applies to meter and rhythm.

Meter in poetry is an arrangement of syllables in a line such that a more or less clear-cut pattern of more heavily stressed and less heavily stressed syllables occurs. A reading of this line will reveal the following stress pattern:

> Come LIVE with ME and BE my LOVE

The ear catches the natural alternation of less heavily and more heavily stressed syllables, just as the ear naturally catches stress patterns in individual words:

> unDRESS
> TELegraph
> teleGRAPHic
> teLEGrapher

It is meter—along with such other sound features as rhyme, assonance, and alliteration—that creates the "music" of poetry and that constitutes one of the many ways in which we differentiate poetry from prose.

The four most common verse feet (patterns of stressed and unstressed syllables) are the *iamb,* the *trochee,* the *anapest,* and the *dactyl.* The *iamb* is a less heavily stressed syllable followed by a more heavily stressed syllable, as in the line

> Come LIVE with ME and BE my LOVE

The *trochee* is the reverse of the iamb, taking the pattern strong-weak instead of weak-strong:

> DOUble, DOUble, TOIL and TROUble

The *anapest* is a three-syllable foot with a weak-weak-strong pattern:

> Like a CHILD from the WOMB, like a GHOST from the TOMB

And the *dactyl* is the opposite of the anapest, being strong-weak-weak. The words **TENderly** and **MANnikin** are dactylic in meter.

A line containing one metrical foot is *monometer;* two, *dimeter;* three, *trimeter;* four, *tetrameter;* five, *pentameter;* six, *hexameter;* seven, *heptameter;* eight, *octameter.*

All this is simple and regular enough, but fortunately meter in most poetry is not so simple and regular, for the reader would soon grow tired of reading lines that did not vary their rhythm. According to the formulas that were outlined above, the "perfect" iambic pentameter line would fit this pattern: W-S-W-S-W-S-W-S-W-S. However, it is extremely difficult to find actual lines that exactly fit that pattern. For instance, here is my reading of the first four lines of Shakespeare's Sonnet 18:

> Shall I comPARE THEE to a SUMmer's DAY?
> THOU art more LOVELy and more TEMperate.
> Rough WINDS do SHAKE the DARling BUDS of MAY,
> and SUMmer's LEASE HATH all TOO short a DATE.

In the first place—and this is an important point—I do not read the lines to make them fit a metrical pattern; I read the poem for the sense, letting the stresses fall where they naturally would if I were reading prose. In the second place, this natural reading (which we assume Shakespeare intended) creates only one "perfect" line of iambic pentameter, the third. The other three deviate from the "perfect" form in obvious ways. Nevertheless, all four lines are perfectly acceptable iambic pentameter.

The limits within which lines can vary from their "perfect" form are rather narrowly restricted and can be precisely defined. In other words, a line of iambic pentameter (or any other metrical pattern) can take a variety of forms, but not just any form. Yet very few lines that poets and readers accept as iambic pentameter fit the matrix W-S-W-S-W-S-W-S-W-S. (If you are interested in this concept and like the notion of applying precise, scientifically accurate descriptions to matters that have always seemed to be vague and not amenable to precise formulation, read "A Theory of Meter," in *English Stress: Its Form, Its Growth, and Its Role in Verse,* by Morris Halle and Samuel Jay Keyser [New York: Harper & Row, 1971].)

To return to an important point: When you read a poem, you ignore meter and read for meaning, following the natural stress patterns that are part of the grammar of English. If you do this, meter in poems written by skillful artists will take care of itself, and you will come to enjoy the varied sound patterns that emerge within the strictures of iambic pentameter or anapestic trimeter or whatever. You will have an intuitive sense of the "rightness" of the metrical patterning.

Another of the sound effects in some poetry is *rhyme,* the repetition of sounds according to more or less regular patterns, usually at the ends of lines.

> Of Heaven or Hell I have no power to sing;
> I cannot ease the burden of your fears,
> Or make quick-coming death a little thing,
> Or bring again the pleasure of past years,
> Nor for my words shall ye forget your tears,
> Or hope again for aught that I can say—
> The idle singer of an empty day.   —William Morris

The rhyme scheme here is *ababbcc.* This stanza happens to be in *rhyme royal,* supposedly named after the Scottish King James I. It illustrates the principle that stanzas in poetry can take their form from the rhyme scheme that they employ. In a poem written in rhyme royal, each stanza would repeat the pattern illustrated above. There are a great many other stanzaic patterns in the tradition of English verse.

When a poem rhymes *aabbccdd . . . ,* it is said to be written in couplets. Compare these two passages, both written in couplets:

> But a meek humble man, of modest sense,
> Who preaching peace, does practice continence;
> Whose pious life's a proof he does believe
> Mysterious truths which no man can conceive.
> If upon Earth there dwell such God-like men,
> I'll here recant my paradox to them.
> Adore those shrines of virtue, homage pay,
> And with the rabble world their laws obey.
> If such there are, yet grant me this at least,
> Man differs more from man than man from beast.
>   —John Wilmot, *Earl of Rochester*

> That's my last Duchess painted on the wall,
> Looking as if she were alive. I call
> That piece a wonder, now. Fra Pandolf's hands
> Worked busily a day, and there she stands.   —Robert Browning

The first passage is written in *closed couplets,* two-line units rhyming *aabbcc,* which are grammatical entities and complete in meaning. Another way of putting this is to say that the reader makes a full pause at the end of each couplet. Such is not the case with the *open couplets* of Robert Browning; the full stops are within lines, after **alive** and **now.** As you can immediately see, the musical effect of closed couplets is quite different from that of open couplets.

Two further kinds of sound effects in poetry are alliteration and assonance. *Alliteration* is the repetition of letters or sounds in words that are
closely associated:

> When *f*ortitude has lost its *f*ire,
> And *f*reezes into *f*ear—   —Edward Young

> The *m*oan of doves in i*mm*emorial el*m*s,
> And *m*ur*m*uring of innu*m*erable bees.   —Alfred, Lord Tennyson

Assonance is the effect that is brought about by similarity in sounds
(whereas rhyme is the effect that is brought about when sounds are
identical). The words **moon** and **June** rhyme; the pairs **fate/lake, catch/
wretch, breeze/whiz** are assonant.

A full discussion of prosody would require a good-sized book. This brief
survey is merely an attempt to make you aware of the musical possibilities
of poetry so that your enjoyment will be increased.

Quotation Marks

Quotation marks are used to set off direct quotations:

> Harry Truman said, "If you can't stand the heat, get out of the kitchen."

They are also used to enclose words and phrases that are being referred to:

> The word "phthisic" is frequently misspelled.
> The term that is normally applied to the study of language history is
> "philology."

There are a few intricacies in the use of quotation marks with other
marks of punctuation. When a question is posed within a quotation, the
question mark is placed within the quotation marks:

> Luther said, "When are we going fishing?"

When a question is posed in the introductory statement, the question mark
is placed outside the quotation marks:

> Did Luther say, "Let's go fishing"?

When both the introductory statement and the quotation are in the form of
questions, the question mark is placed within the quotation marks:

> Did Luther say, "When are we going fishing?"

To set off quotes within quotes, double marks are alternated with single
marks:

> Luther said, "Bob vowed, 'We are going fishing soon.'"

In modern American punctuation, commas and periods are *always*
placed within quotation marks, and colons and semicolons are always
placed outside:

> Bob said, "We are going fishing," but I didn't hear him.

> Luther's favorite word is "fishing," and it's mine too.
> The technical name for spelling is "orthography."
> I seldom use the word "orthography"; it is too formal.
> This is the meaning of "orthography": correct spelling.

Quotation marks are also used to enclose the names of poems, short stories, magazine articles, movies, plays.

> "Byzantium," a poem by Yeats
> "The Country Husband," a story by John Cheever
> "The Gasification of Coal," an article by Harry Perry
> "The Graduate," a movie
> "The Wild Duck," a play by Ibsen

However, the titles of movies, plays, and long poems are frequently set in italics without quotation marks.

See also *Brackets, Italics, Plagiarism.*

Reference

Reference has to do with pronouns and possessive adjectives, which (unless they are indefinite relatives) take part of their meaning from their antecedents. Thus, in this sentence

> **The barber** shaved me. In the process, **he** drew blood.

we don't know who **he** is unless we can relate that pronoun to the antecedent **the barber.**

When reference is unclear, as in the following sentence, the reader is slowed down and annoyed.

> The man told my brother he should practice the piano if he wanted to achieve his goal of playing at the Music Center.

In the sentence are two antecedents, **man** and **brother,** two uses of the pronoun **he,** and one use of the possessive adjective **his.** The reader must pause to make the proper connections.

Here is an example of unclear reference in connection with a demonstrative:

> The teacher told a funny story. **This** made the class laugh.

What made the class laugh? The fact that the teacher told the story? Or the story itself?

See also *Adjectives, Agreement, Antecedent, Demonstratives, Pronouns, Relatives.*

Relatives

The language affords us an easy way to make clauses modify nominals: relative pronouns, adjectives, and adverbs provide links between the nominals and the clauses. As an elementary example of how this works, look at the following two sentences:

> The man told me to practice. The man taught me to play the piano.

Most readers would expect these to be joined in some way such as the following:

> The man *who taught me to play the piano* told me to practice.
> The man *who told me to practice* taught me to play the piano.

The italicized structures are relative clauses, introduced by the relative pronoun *who.*

Definite relative pronouns always have clearly identifiable antecedents:

> *The class* **WHICH** Eric enjoyed most was political science.
> There was no *place* at **WHICH** Junior felt more at home.
> *The class* **THAT** Eric took was political science.
>
> *The man* **WHOSE** daughter I married was a schoolteacher.
> *The place* **WHERE** we must begin is at the beginning.

Relative pronouns may be deleted if they are objects in their own clauses.

> The doctor (whom) *we saw* was a veterinarian.
> The house (that) ***Bob bought*** is in Torrance.

See also *Antecedents, Case, Clauses, Pronouns, Reference.*

Semicolon

The semicolon *(;)* is a symbolic conjunction that is used to link clauses:

> Fads come and go; truth remains forever.

Notice that the above might have appeared as coordinate clauses or as separate sentences:

> Fads come and go, but truth remains forever.
> Fads come and go. Truth remains forever.

Semicolons are also used to separate seriated items that have internal comma punctuation of their own:

> The members of the committee are Joel Parks, Santa Monica; Paul Knoll, Pasadena; Walter Fisher, West Covina; and Ed Finegan, San Pedro.

Shifted Constructions

Shifted constructions are sentence elements that are not parallel, but should be. The following examples illustrate a variety of shifted constructions, each followed by a revision that eliminates the shift.

> *Shift in subject:*
> ***The violin*** is difficult, demanding, and ***Mary*** is learning to play it.
> Mary is learning to play the violin, a difficult, demanding instrument.
> *Shift from the personal to the impersonal:*
> When ***you*** begin to learn to play the French horn, ***you*** soon find out that ***a person*** needs to practice at least two hours a day.
> When you begin to learn to play the French horn, you soon find out that you need to practice at least two hours a day.

Shift from adjective to noun:

    The trip to Mazatlan was **educational** and a relaxing **vacation.**

    The trip to Mazatlan was educational and relaxing.

Shift from noun to verbal:

    To play chess, you must learn **the rules** and **to plan ahead.**

    To play chess, you must master the rules and learn to plan ahead.

Shift from noun to clause:

    Two requirements for long-distance running are **stamina** and **you must have patience.**

    Two requirements for long-distance running are stamina and patience.

Shift from phrase to clause:

    The captain knew **about navigation** and **that the passengers might get seasick.**

    The captain knew about navigation, and he was aware that the passengers might get seasick.

See also *Parallelism.*

Spelling

The concept of spelling as a rigid set of rules to which all writers must conform is a fairly late development in the language. It came about, first, because of the development of the printing press and, second, because of the stress that, in about the eighteenth century, the rising middle classes began to put on linguistic propriety—one aspect of which, they seemed to think, was consistency in spelling. If consistency is the sign of a small mind, Chaucer certainly wasn't small-minded, in his spelling at least. Here is just a sample of variant spellings from Chaucer's works: **adama(u)nt, atthamaunt** ("adamant"); **biwreyen, bewrayen, biwryen** ("reveal, make known"); **eschewen, eschu(w)en** ("escape, avoid"); **qwher, qwghwhere** ("anywhere").

It is an undeniable fact, however, that society now places a high (though haps irrational) value on orthography—consistent spelling. In fact, orthodox spelling is one of the main features of Edited Standard English, and Edited Standard English is, of course, the only power "dialect" in writing. Readers who will either allow or fail to notice other deviations from the norms of Edited Standard English frequently react violently against misspellings, often assuming that a person who fails to spell properly is uneducated or unintelligent or both. Orthography, then, is of great importance if a writer's message is to be accepted.

If your spelling is erratic, you should not, I think, turn to spelling lists, but should conscientiously use the dictionary, looking up every word about which there is the slightest doubt. In this way, as you write more and more, you will become progressively more certain about spelling.

The writer can become consciously aware of certain spelling problems. For instance, in English, unstressed vowels often become "neutrals." Thus the vowel sounds in **sav_or_, driv_er_,** and **fak_ir_** are all the same, even though they are represented by different letters. Such is the case with **_u_pon, _a_bout,** and (in some pronunciations) **_e_rect.** Therefore, you should make sure that your neutral vowels are the proper letters. (The technical term for a neutral vowel is *schwa.*)

Doubling of consonants is also a problem. For example, either **travelled** or **traveled** is acceptable, but the consonant must be doubled for the past of **infer, inferred.**

Obviously it is wrong to assume that there is some kind of one-to-one correspondence between sound and spelling, as the following will illustrate if you will pronounce the words: **though, tough, trough, through.** And, as George Bernard Shaw said, in English **fish** might well be spelled **ghoti:** Take the **gh** of **tough,** the **o** of women, and the **ti** of **nation,** and the result is **ghoti, fish.**

See also *Edited Standard English.*

Split Infinitive

The infinitive is the form of a verb that appears with the marker **to:**

> Margie and I like **to jog.**

The infinitive can be, and often is, split, as the following illustrates:

> Margie and I like **to** frequently **jog.**

In extremely formal usage, one seldom finds split infinitives. Thus, the above sentence would be rewritten in one of these two ways:

> Margie and I like to jog frequently.
> Margie and I like frequently to jog.

However, the split infinitive is becoming less and less a concern in any kind of writing or speech. Very few listeners or readers would now react against the split infinitive.

See also *Verbs.*

Tense

Tense is not to be confused with time. For instance, in English the simple present tense is seldom used to indicate an action that is going on at the present moment. Thus, **I eat grapefruit** does not mean that I am currently eating grapefruit, but that I habitually or characteristically do. In order to indicate that I am eating a grapefruit at the present moment, I must use the *progressive* (or *durative*) form of the present tense: **I am eating grape-fruit.**

The tenses in English are

Present:	Getty **makes** billions.
Past:	Getty **made** billions.
Future:	Getty **will make** billions.
Present perfect:	Getty **has made** billions.
Past perfect:	Getty **had made** billions.
Future perfect:	Getty **will have made** billions.

Errors in tense almost never occur in writing or speaking (of native users of the language, at least), but "errors" in verb form—deviations from Spoken Standard or Edited Standard English—are fairly common. A speaker who says, **Wanda go to the store yesterday** has not made an error in the use of tense, but has used a form of the verb **go** that would not be used to indicate past in standard English, which would demand **went.**

A matter of tense that frequently bothers writers is the historical present, in which the present tense is used to narrate past events or to summarize plots of fictional works:

> Marlow **arrives** at the first station in Africa and **gets** his first experience of colonialism. The Company **has** exploited the natives, and Marlow **is** disgusted.

Thus a segment of the plot of *Heart of Darkness* is summarized in historical present. When you use the historical present, you should be careful not to shift tenses, as happens in the following narrative:

> In April, the family **decides** to vacation in Sun Valley. We **make** our plans and **save** our money, eagerly awaiting the trip. And then along **came** the gas shortage, and we **wondered** if we **would** be forced to cancel our plans.

See also *Auxiliary, Verbs.*

Verbs

The common definition of verbs is that they are words that convey "action or state of being." We would all agree that **sense** in the following is a verb:

> The teacher **sensed** the class's hostile attitude.

However, from my point of view at least, it does not name an action or a state of being. It's probably a good idea to forget the old definition. It is not very helpful; in fact, it can be downright confusing.

Formally speaking, verbs are words that undergo morphological changes to show tense:

> walk/walked
> run/ran

take the agreement morpheme **-s** in the third person singular present indicative:

> He/she/it seem**s** interesting.

and are modified by adverbs:

> **slowly** walk
> **quickly** run

Like all other parts of speech, verbs have characteristic distributional patterns within the sentence. These are so obvious and commonly understood that they will not be summarized here.

Verbs are traditionally divided into three classes:

> *Intransitive:*
>   Babies *cry.*
>   Seagulls *squawk.*
> *Transitive:*
>   Misers *hoard* money.
>   Gourmets *eat* snails.
> Linking:
>   Max *is* a gourmet.
>   He *feels* good.
>   He *becomes* plump.

This simple tripartite division, however, doesn't begin to indicate the complexity of the verb system in English. For example, both *become* and *seem* are classed as linking verbs, and yet they are very different in character, as the following demonstrates:

> The child becomes quiet [adjective].
> The child becomes a man [noun].
> The child seems quiet.
> *The child seems a man.
> The child seems to be a man.

Some transitive verbs, like *give,* will take two objects:

> Give Jill a kiss.

And some transitive verbs demand an oblique object (an object introduced by a preposition):

> think *of* something

Modern grammarians do not consider *be* (and its various forms: *am, was, is, are, were, have/had been*) a verb at all, but set it aside and call it "the copula" or simply *be.* If you'll think about *be,* you'll realize that its only function is to carry tense, as Tarzan-talk proves:

> Me Tarzan. You Jane. (I *am* Tarzan. You *are* Jane.)

Some languages simply omit the *be* when tense is present. Thus, for *Ivan is a boy,* Russians say *Ivan malcheek,* which translated word for word means "Ivan boy."

The so-called principal parts of verbs are

> *Infinitive:*
>   to walk, to sing, to think
> *Present participle:*
>   walking, singing, thinking
> *Past participle:*
>   Helen has *walked.*
>   Dietrich has *sung.*
>   All of us have *thought.*
> *Past tense form:*
>   Helen *walked.*
>   Dietrich *sang.*
>   All of us *thought.*

It makes sense to pay careful attention to the verbs that you choose. The following sentence pairs illustrate the different effects that verbs can bring about:

> The girl **talked** on and on.
> The girl **babbled** on and on.

> The dictator **asked** for complete allegiance.
> The dictator **demanded** complete allegiance.

> There **was** trash all over the beach.
> Trash **covered** the beach.

See also *Adjectives, Agreement, Auxiliary, Gerunds, Mood, Split Infinitive, Tense, Voice.*

Voice

Some transitive verbs can be in either *active* or *passive* voice. The following sentences illustrate the difference:

> Man bites dog. (active)
> Dog is bitten by man. (passive)

The traditional definition of a passive sentence is "a sentence in which the subject receives the action of the verb"; but in the following sentence, the subject appears to receive the action even though the verb is not in passive:

> The boxer caught a right to the chin.

And in the following passive sentence, the subject seems not to receive the action:

> A right to the chin was caught by the boxer.

In other words, the traditional definition doesn't tell us much.

The change from active to passive can be precisely (but somewhat cumbersomely) described as follows:
The positions of subject and object are interchanged:

> Man bites dog *becomes* Dog bites man.

The appropriate form of **be** is inserted:

> Dog bites man *becomes* Dog is bites man.

The verb is changed to the past participal form:

> Dog is bites man *becomes* Dog is bitten man.

The preposition **by** is inserted before the original subject:

> Dog is bitten man *becomes* Dog is bitten by man.

Finally, the prepositional phrase *may be* deleted:

> Dog is bitten by man *becomes* Dog is bitten.

That, then, is a description of the technicalities of passive voice and constitutes a good definition.

The passive is an extremely useful stylistic feature of the language. It allows us to achieve varying emphases in sentences. For example, in

> The scientist put the chemicals in the test tube.

the noun **scientist** achieves at least equal emphasis with **chemicals,** but suppose we want to emphasize what happened to the chemicals; then we can use passive:

> The chemicals were put in the test tube.

It should be apparent that one should not unconsciously and habitually use passive voice.

See also *Auxiliary, Verbs.*

Wordiness

Wordy writing—writing that contains unnecessary verbiage—is usually annoying. Sentences ought to get to the point without a pileup of useless words.

Some causes of wordiness are
circumlocutions in which one or two words will substitute for several:

> The barn **was destroyed by fire.**
> The barn **burned down.**
>
> Hand me **the thing you use to tighten nuts.**
> Hand me **the wrench.**
>
> George has **the equipment which is necessary for cycling.**
> George has **a bicycle.**

introductory phrases that can be replaced by one or two words:

> **During the time that** the craft is **in motion,** passengers must remain seated.
> **While** the craft is **moving** . . . .

deadwood, or words that add no meaning and can be deleted:

> The girl **who was** standing on the corner was pretty.
> **The town of** Huntington Beach is in **the state of** California.

Index

This Index supplements and expands on the Reference Guide. The entries in green refer to matters that are dealt with in the Reference Guide as well as in the body of the text, or to matters that might have been included in the Reference Guide but were not because they are fully discussed in the text. In any case, the Index and the Reference Guide should be used together.

Index of Writers and Writings Analyzed

A　5
B　6
C　7
D　8
E　9
F　0
G　1
H　2
I
J　3

Alternate Sequences for <u>The Contemporary Writer</u>

Alternate Sequence I

1. To encourage students to begin writing in the least technical and most available mode, the self-expressive.

> Chapter 1   The Uses of Writing: Self-Expression

2. To make students aware of language and to help them overcome misconceptions concerning language matters, including grammar.

> Chapter 10   The Writer's Language

3. To explore the composing process as it actually takes place; to help students solve the problems of finding and developing ideas.

> Chapter 2   Survey of the Composing Process
> Chapter 3   Prewriting: Generating Subject Matter
> Chapter 4   Developing Ideas: The Paragraph

4. To introduce the concepts of style and to activate scribal fluency.

> Chapter 11   The Sentence
> Chapter 12   Words
> Chapter 13   Figurative Language
> Chapter 14   Analysis of Style

5. To explore and give practice in the various modes of "public" writing.

> Chapter 5   The Uses of Writing: Exposition
> Chapter 6   Special Uses of Writing: Writing About Literature
> Chapter 7   Special Uses of Writing: A Brief Guide to Research Writing
> Chapter 8   The Uses of Writing: Imagination
> Chapter 9   The Uses of Writing: Persuasion

Alternate Sequence II

1. To make students aware of language and to help them overcome misconceptions concerning language matters, including grammar.

> Chapter 10   The Writer's Language

2. To encourage students to begin writing in the least technical and most available mode, the self-expressive.

> Chapter 1   The Uses of Writing: Self-Expression

3. To explore the composing process as it actually takes place; to help students solve the problems of finding and developing ideas.

> Chapter 2   Survey of the Composing Process
> Chapter 3   Prewriting: Generating Subject Matter
> Chapter 4   Developing Ideas: The Paragraph

4. To explore and give practice in the various modes of "public" writing.

> Chapter 5   The Uses of Writing: Exposition
> Chapter 6   Special Uses of Writing: Writing About Literature
> Chapter 7   Special Uses of Writing: A Brief Guide to Research Writing
> Chapter 8   The Uses of Writing: Imagination
> Chapter 9   The Uses of Writing: Persuasion

5. To introduce the concepts of style and to activate scribal fluency.

> Chapter 11   The Sentence
> Chapter 12   Words
> Chapter 13   Figurative Language
> Chapter 14   Analysis of Style